# The Police in the Community
## Strategies for the 21st Century

Second Edition

thomson com

changing the way the world learns℠

To get extra value from this book for no additional cost, go to:

## http://www.thomson.com/wadsworth.html

*thomson.com* is the World Wide Web site for Wadsworth/ITP and is your direct source to dozens of on-line resources. *thomson.com* helps you find out about supplements, experiment with demonstration software, search for a job, and send e-mail to many of our authors. You can even preview new publications and exciting new technologies.

**thomson.com:** *It's where you'll find us in the future.*

# The Police in the Community
## Strategies for the 21st Century

Second Edition

**Linda S. Miller**
*Director of the Minnesota Community
Policing Institute
Bloomington Police Department
Bloomington, Minnesota*

**Kären M. Hess**
*Normandale Community College
Bloomington, Minnesota*

West/Wadsworth
I⟨T⟩P® An International Thomson Publishing Company

Belmont, CA • Albany, NY • Bonn • Boston • Cincinnati • Detroit • Johannesburg • London
Madrid • Melbourne • Mexico City • New York • Paris • Singapore • Tokyo • Toronto • Washington

Criminal Justice Editor: Sabra Horne
Editorial Assistant: Jeff Kellner
Marketing Manager: Mike Dew
Project Editor: Dianne Jensis
Print Buyer: Karen Hunt
Permissions Editor: Veronica Oliva
Production: Shepherd, Inc., Cindy Hass
Photo Researcher: Roberta Spieckerman
Copy Editor: Joan Lyon
Indexer: Christine Orthmann
Cover Design: Seventeenth Street Studios
Cover Image: © Mary Kate Denney/Tony Stone Images
Compositor: Shepherd, Inc.
Printer: Courier-Westford Plant

Printed in the United States of America
1 2 3 4 5 6 7 8 9 10

For more information, contact Wadsworth Publishing Company, 10 Davis Drive, Belmont, CA 94002, or electronically at
http://www.thomson.com/wadsworth.html

International Thomson Publishing Europe
Berkshire House 168-173
High Holborn
London, WC1V 7AA, England

Thomas Nelson Australia
102 Dodds Street
South Melbourne 3205
Victoria, Australia

Nelson Canada
1120 Birchmount Road
Scarborough, Ontario
Canada M1K 5G4

International Thomson Publishing GmbH
Königswinterer Strasse 418
53227 Bonn, Germany

International Thomson Editores
Campos Eliseos 385, Piso 7
Col. Polanco
11560 México D. F. México

International Thomson Publishing Asia
221 Henderson Road
#05-10 Henderson Building
Singapore 0315

International Thomson Publishing Japan
Hirakawacho Kyowa Building, 3F
2-2-1 Hirakawacho
Chiyoda-ku, Tokyo 102, Japan

International Thomson Publishing Southern Africa
Building 18, Constantia Park
240 Old Pretoria Road
Halfway House, 1685 South Africa

**Library of Congress Cataloging-in-Publication Data**

Miller, Linda S.
    The police in the community: strategies for the 21st century/
Linda S. Miller, Kären M. Hess. — 2nd ed.
        p.   cm.
        Rev. ed. of: Community policing. c1994.
        Includes bibliographical references and index.
        ISBN 0-534-53789-8 (alk. paper)
        1. Community policing. 2. Public relations—Police. 3. Community
policing—United States—Case studies. 4. Public relations—Police-
-United States—Case studies.   I. Hess, Kären M.
II. Miller, Linda S. Community policing. III. Title.
    HV7936.C83M58   1997
    363.2'3—dc21                                          97-37745
                                                              CIP

*This book is printed on acid-free recycled paper.*

# Contents in Brief

# Contents

# Section 3    Projects and Programs: Coordinated Efforts    445

## Chapter 14    Early Experiments in Crime Prevention and Community Policing Strategies    447

# List of Figures

# List of Tables

**xix**

# List of Acronyms

**AARP**—American Association of Retired Persons

**ACW**—Around the Corner to the World

**AD**—Alzheimer's disease

**ADA**—Americans with Disabilities Act

**AIM**—American Indian Movement

**BIA**—Bureau of Indian Affairs

**CAT**—Combat AutoTheft

**CCPP**—Citywide Crime Prevention Program

**CCRP**—citizen crime reporting program

**CHANGE**—Citizens Helping Austin Neighborhood Gang Environment

**CIT**—crisis intervention team

**COP**—Community-Oriented Policing

**COPE**—Community/Citizen-Oriented Police Enforcement

**CPTED**—crime prevention through environmental design

**CRB**—civilian review board

**CRT**—crisis response team

**CSO**—community service officer

**DARE**—Drug Abuse Resistance Education

**DFZ**—drug-free zone

**DSO**—deinstitutionalization of status offenders

**EBD**—emotionally/behaviorally disturbed

**ESL**—English as a second language

**FCC**—Federal Communications Commission

**HIV**—human immunodeficiency virus

**HOPE**—Homes on Portland Enterprise

**HUD**—Housing and Urban Development

**IACP**—International Association of Chiefs of Police

**ICD**—International Center for the Disabled

**IHS**—Indian Health Service

**LD**—learning disabled; learning disabilities

**LEAA**—Law Enforcement Administration Assistance

**LULAC**—League of United Latin American Citizens

**MADD**—Mothers Against Drunk Driving

**MALDEF**—Mexican American Legal Defense and Education Fund

**NAACP**—National Association for the Advancement of Colored People

**NABCJ**—National Association of Blacks in Criminal Justice

**NAD**—National Association of the Deaf

**NCH**—National Council on the Handicapped

**NCTI**—National Corrective Training Institute

**NFPP**—National Foot Patrol Program

**NHIF**—National Head Injury Foundation

**NIJ**—National Institute of Justice

**NOBLE**—National Organization of Black Law Enforcement Executives

**NOP**—neighborhood-oriented policing

**NOVA**—National Organization for Victim Assistance

**NSA**—National Sheriffs' Association

**OJJDP**—Office of Juvenile Justice and Delinquency Prevention

**OJP**—Office of Justice Programs

**PAL**—police athletic league

**PCR**—police-community relations

**PEP KIDS**—Parents, Educators, Police and Kids

**PIN**—Pager Information Network

**PIO**—press information officer

**PIP**—Positive Interaction Program

**POMC**—Parents of Murdered Children

**POP**—problem-oriented policing

**POST**—Peace Officer Standards and Training

**PTSD**—post traumatic stress disorder

**RID**—report incidents directly

**SAT**—Stanford Achievement Test

**SODAA**—Stop Our Drug and Alcohol Abuse

**SWRL**—South West Regional Laboratory

**TAB**—temporarily able-bodied

**TDD**—telecommunication device for the deaf

**TOP**—Teens on Patrol

**VCAN**—Victims Constitutional Amendment Network

**VIP**—Volunteers in Parole

**VIP**—Volunteers in Policing

**VIS**—victim impact statement

**VOCA**—Victims of Crime Act

**VSO**—victim statement of opinion

**VWPA**—Victim/Witness Protection Act

**WIN**—Women in Need

**YGSP**—Youth Gang Services Project

# Preface

Community policing offers one avenue for making neighborhoods safer. Community policing is not a program or a series of programs. It is a philosophy, a belief that working together, the police and the community can accomplish what neither can accomplish alone. The *synergy* that results from community policing can be powerful. It is like the power of a finely tuned athletic team, with each member contributing to the total effort. Occasionally heroes may emerge, but victory depends on a team effort.

Community policing differs from earlier efforts such as team policing, community relations, crime prevention programs or neighborhood watch programs. Community policing involves a rethinking of the role of the police and a restructuring of the police organization. Its two core concepts are community/police collaboration and a problem-solving approach to policing. These dual themes are present throughout the text. This text discusses in Section 1 the evolution of community policing and the changes in our communities and our law enforcement agencies which have occurred. The section then examines the problem-solving approach to policing and how community policing might be implemented.

The text emphasizes developing the interpersonal skills needed to build good relationships with all those the police have sworn "to serve and protect." This includes those who are culturally, racially or socioeconomically different from the mainstream, those who are physically or mentally disabled and those who are elderly. It also includes youth, both as victims and as offenders, gangs and gang members, and victims of crime. In addition, interacting effectively with members of the media is vital to the success of community policing. Developing these relationships is the focus of Section 2.

Section 3 looks at individual projects and programs, including those that involve coordinated efforts of the police, the entire criminal justice system and the community. It discusses past successes and failures.

## How to Use This Text

The text is structured to enhance understanding and remembering the main concepts. To get the most from this text, first look through the listing of Contents to give yourself a framework. Think about the specific subjects included in the topic of community policing as a whole. Then read the section openers for a closer look at the three broad divisions of the text. Finally, complete the following steps for each chapter:

1. Read the "Do You Know" questions at the beginning of the chapter. These present the chapter objectives in a way that should make you think about your current level of knowledge. For example:

   Do You Know . . . When modern policing began?

2. Read the chapter, highlighting, underlining or taking notes. Watch for answers to the "Do You Know" questions. Pay special attention to information between the diamonds. For example:

◆

Modern policing began with the formation of the London Metropolitan Police.

◆

Also pay attention to words in bold type. These are key terms which you should be able to define. The definitions should be clear from the text.

3. Read the chapter summary. You will find that you have now read key points three times. This triple-strength approach should take the information from your short-term memory into your long-term memory.

4. To solidify the information, return to the "Do You Know" questions at the beginning of the chapter and answer each question. Write down any questions you have about the information in the chapter. Look at the list of key terms and make certain you understand and can define each term. If you do not remember what a specific term means, look it up in the glossary to refresh your memory.

5. Read the discussion questions at the end of the chapter and think about what you can contribute to a class discussion.

If you follow these steps, and if you periodically review the "Do You Know" questions, you should master the content of this text.

# *Acknowledgments*

We would like to thank the following individuals for their careful review of the manuscript for this text and for their numerous suggestions for improvement: Michael B. Blankenship, Department of Criminology & Criminal Justice, Memphis State University; W.D. Braddock, Department of Criminal Justice, Boise State University; Vincent Del Castillo, Department of Law and Police Science, John Jay College of Criminal Justice; Burt C. Hagerman, Oakland Community College; Robert Ives, Rock Valley College; James E. Newman, Department of Public Services, Rio Hondo Community College; Carroll S. Price, Social Science Division, Penn Valley Community College; Charles L. Quarles, Criminal Justice Program, Department of Political Science, University of Mississippi; B. Grant Stitt, Department of Criminal Justice, University of Nevada-Reno; and Gary T. Tucker, Department of Criminal Justice, Sinclair Community College.

A sincere thank you, also, to the reviewers of the first edition for their invaluable suggestions for improving the text.

James S. Albritton
*Marquette University*

William Castleberry
*The University of Tennessee at Martin*

Burt C. Hagerman
*Oakland Community College*

Robert Ives
*Rockford Community College*

Deborah Wilkins Newman
*Middle Tennessee State University*

James E. Newman
*California State University, Fullerton*

Willard M. Oliver
*Glenville State College*

Charles Quarles
*University of Mississippi*

Mittie D. Southerland
*Murray State University*

Gregory B. Talley
*Broome Community College*

Gary T. Tucker
*Sinclair Community College*

Thanks also to Penny Parrish for her review of and substantial contribution to the chapter on police-media relations and to Paul Bailey for his review of and contributions to the chapter on communication. An additional thank you goes to Christine Orthmann for her comprehensive indexes and for her review of and data entry for the Instructor's Manual that accompanies this text. Finally, a sincere thank you to our editors at Wadsworth, Sabra Horne, Dianne Jensis, Claire Masson and Dan Alpert, and to Cindy Hass, Senior Project Editor at Shepherd, Inc. Any errors in content or expression are the sole responsibility of the authors.

# *Foreword*

A democratic society has to be the most difficult environment within which to police. Police in many countries operate for the benefit of the government. The police of America operate for the benefit of the people policed. Because of that environment, we are compelled to pursue ways to advance our policing approach, involve people who are part of our environment and enhance our effectiveness. Our policing methodology is changed or molded by trial and error, the daring of some policing leaders, the research and writing of academicians and the response of our communities to the way we do business.

Over the past thirty years, we have tried a variety of approaches to doing our job better. Some have remained. Many have been abandoned, thought to be failures. They may, however, have been building blocks to our current policing practices and for what is yet to come. For instance, the community relations and crime prevention programs of the 1960s and the experiments with team policing in the 1970s are quite visible in the business of community policing. So should be the knowledge gained from research such as that conducted in the 1970s and 1980s associated with random patrol, directed patrol, foot patrol, one-officer/two-officer cars and the effectiveness (or lack thereof) of rapid response to all calls for service.

If we look at our past, we should not be surprised at the development and support of community policing as the desired policing philosophy in our country today. It merely responds to the customers' needs and their demand for our policing agencies to be more effective. And therein lies the most important outcome of community policing—effectiveness. Yes, we have responded to millions of calls for service, made millions of arrests and added thousands to our policing ranks. If we're honest about it, however, we may be hard-pressed to see the imprint of our efforts in our communities. Community policing, involving problem solving, community engagement and organizational transformation, can contribute significantly to the satisfaction of the community policed and to those policing.

This text provides insight into the meaning of community policing and presents many dimensions necessary to consider when developing a community policing strategy. Its content should help readers to understand the practical side of community policing, recognize the community considerations that need to exist and develop methods applicable to their unique environments.

Donald J. Burnett
General Partner
Law Enforcement Assistance Network

**Linda S. Miller** is director of the Minnesota Community Policing Institute (MCPI) and a sergeant with the Bloomington (Minnesota) Police Department. She has been with the department 20 years. She has been a patrol supervisor, a crime prevention officer, a patrol officer and a police dispatcher. Sgt. Miller is a member of the Minnesota Peace and Police Officers Association, the International Police Association, the Midwest Gang Investigator's Association, the International Association of Women Police and the Minnesota Association of Women in Police. She was a member of the People-to-People's Women in Law Enforcement delegation to the Soviet Union in 1990. Sgt. Miller is a frequent presenter to community groups and is also an instructor.

**Kären M. Hess,** PhD, has written extensively in the field of law enforcement and criminal justice. Dr. Hess is a frequent instructor for report writing workshops and seminars for law enforcement agencies. She is a member of the English department at Normandale Community College and president of the Institute for Professional Development. Dr. Hess belongs to the National Criminal Justice Association and the National Council of Teachers of English. She is also a member of the Bloomington Crime Prevention Association board of directors.

# Section

# An Overview

The community and the police depend on each other. The common police motto—"To serve and protect"—suggests a target population, individuals requiring service and protection. Most police departments stress the importance of community relations, and many have taken community relations beyond image enhancement and crime prevention programs and have started involving the community in policing itself.

The section looks first at the evolution of police-community relations. Since people first came together in groups, they have had some responsibility for seeing to it that those within the group did as was expected. The United States' method of "preserving the peace," modeled after that used in England, has gone through several stages. The relationship between the community and its police has been severely strained at times, and attempts to improve it have taken several forms. Recently, emphasis on improved public relations and crime prevention has expanded to a more encompassing philosophy of community policing, including problem-solving policing in many jurisdictions (Chapter 1).

The focus in Chapter 2 is on the people and agencies involved in community-police relations. Who are the members of a community? How do communities differ? How have they changed over the years? What future changes might be anticipated? What aspects of a community must be understood by those working within it? What is expected of community members? What do community members expect?

Next an in-depth look at the police is presented (Chapter 3). Who are the individuals behind the badges? How have they changed over the years? How might they change in the future? How does the public generally view the police? What aspects of the police role contribute to this view?

This is followed by an examination of problem-solving policing, a key component of the community policing philosophy (Chapter 4). The section concludes with a discussion on implementing community policing—guidelines and cautions (Chapter 5).

## Chapter 1

# The Evolution of Community Policing

*The police are the public and the public are the police.*

—Sir Robert Peel

 ### Do you know

- When "modern" policing began?
- What Sir Robert Peel's principles emphasized?
- What the three strategic eras of policing are?
- What the police relationship with the community was in each era?
- What the professional model of policing emphasized?
- What some common types of crime prevention programs are?
- What community policing is?
- What the focus of problem-solving policing is?

## Definitions

Can you define these terms: community policing, community relations, community wellness, frankpledge system, hue and cry, human relations, incident, paradigm, paradigm shift, patronage system, proactive, problem-solving policing, professional model, progressive era, public relations, reactive, spoils system, "thin blue line," tithing, tithing system.

# Introduction

Community policing did not just magically appear as a panacea for society's ills. It has been centuries in its evolution, and may, indeed, be merely a stepping stone to yet another form of policing in the future. As society's needs change so do the methods it uses to "keep the peace."

This chapter begins with a brief history of policing and its evolution in the United States. This is followed by an examination of three strategic eras of policing and the paradigm shifts that occurred. Next the influence of public relations, community relations and crime prevention programs is explored. The chapter concludes with an in-depth look at community policing, including definitions, major features, potential problems and the incorporation of a problem-solving approach.

## A BRIEF HISTORY OF POLICING

Throughout history, societies have established rules to govern the conduct of individuals and have devised punishments for those who broke the rules. The earliest record of an ancient society's need for rules to control human behavior dates back to approximately 2300 B.C. when the Sumerian rulers set forth standards for what was an offense against society. For thousands of years such rules were modified and adapted. According to Wrobleski and Hess (1997, p. 6):

> The early beginnings of just laws and social control were destroyed during the Dark Ages as the Roman Empire disintegrated. Hordes of Germanic invaders swept into the old Roman territory of Britain, bringing with them their own laws and customs. These German invaders intermarried with the conquered English, the result being the hardy Anglo-Saxon.

The Anglo-Saxons grouped their farms around small, self-governing villages that policed themselves. This informal arrangement became more structured under King Alfred the Great (A.D. 849–899), who required that every male enroll for police purposes in a group of ten families, known as a **tithing.** The **tithing system** established the principle of collective responsibility for maintaining local law and order.

The tithing system worked well until 1066 when William the Conqueror, a Norman, invaded and conquered England. William, concerned about national security, replaced the tithing system of "home rule" with fifty-five military districts, each headed by a Norman shire-reeve. William also established the **frankpledge system** which required all freemen to swear loyalty to the king's law and to take responsibility for maintaining the local peace.

By the seventeenth century, law enforcement duties were divided into two separate units, a day watch and a night watch. The day watch consisted of constables who served as jailers and fulfilled other government duties. Citizens worked on the night watch. Each citizen was expected to take a turn watching for fires, bad weather and disorderly individuals. Some towns also expected the night watchman to call out the time.

If a watchman or any other citizen saw a crime in progress, they were expected to give the **hue and cry,** summoning all citizens within earshot to join in pursuing and capturing the wrongdoer. Preserving the peace was the duty of *all* citizens.

By the end of the eighteenth century, most people with sufficient means paid others to stand their assigned watch for them, marking the beginning of a paid police force and, in effect, the original neighborhood watch.

The system of day and night watchmen was very ineffective. Because wealthy citizens could avoid the watch duty by hiring someone to take their place, those they hired were hesitant to invoke their authority against the well-to-do. According to Richardson (1970, p. 10), by the mid-1700s New York City's night watch was: "A parcel of idle, drinking, vigilant snorers, who never quelled any nocturnal tumult in their lives . . . but would, perhaps, be as ready to join in a burglary as any thief in Christendom."

London, suffering from the impact of the Industrial Revolution, was experiencing massive unemployment and poverty. It had become a disorderly city, with enormous, crime-ridden slums and a significant juvenile delinquency problem. Some citizens had even begun to carry weapons for self-protection. Parliament was concerned and in their attempt to address the problems, convened five parliamentary commissions of inquiry between 1780 and 1820. When Sir Robert (Bobbie) Peel was appointed Home Secretary, he proposed that London appoint civilians, paid by the community, to serve as police officers. The Metropolitan Police Act was passed in 1829 and modern policing began.

## THE BEGINNING OF "MODERN" POLICE FORCES

◆

"Modern" policing began with the formation of the London Metropolitan Police, founded by Sir Robert Peel in 1829.

◆

Peel set forth the following principles on which the police force was to be based:

- The duty of the police is to prevent crime and disorder.
- The power of the police to fulfill their duties is dependent on public approval and on their ability to secure and maintain public respect.

*London Metropolitan Police uniforms have a distinctive look that sets them apart from police departments in other parts of the world.*

- Public respect and approval also mean the willing cooperation of the public in the task of securing observance of the law.
- The police must seek and preserve public favor not by pandering to public opinion, but by constantly demonstrating absolutely impartial service to law.
- The police should strive to maintain a relationship with the public that gives reality to the tradition that the police are the public and the public are the police.
- The test of police efficiency is the absence of crime and disorder, not the visible evidence of police action in dealing with these problems (Inkster, 1992, p. 30).

◆

Peel's principles emphasized the interdependency of the police and the public as well as the prevention of crime and disorder.

◆

Peel envisioned a close relationship between the police and the citizens they served which helped the police maintain order in London.

As originally envisioned by the architects of London's Metropolitan Police— acknowledged to be the first modern police department, a police officer's job was primarily crime prevention and social maintenance, not crime detection. Police were to serve as local marshals who actively maintained order by interacting with the neighborhoods they served (Taft, 1986, p. 21).

## POLICING IN THE UNITED STATES

Harr and Hess (1998, p. 21) note: "Those who came to America in 1620 and their descendants, through the American Revolution, ultimately rejected rule under the British Crown and what it had come to symbolize." British soldiers took over homes and had complete authority over the colonists. Our founding fathers wanted to assure that no such power would exist in the newly created nation. As former Chief Justice of the United States Supreme Court, Warren E. Burger (1991, p. 26), stated: "The Founders, conscious of the risks of abuse of power, created a system of liberty with order and placed the Bill of Rights as a harness on government to protect people from misuse of the powers." Nonetheless, the system of policing and maintaining order in the United States is modeled on the police system developed in England.

At the time the Metropolitan Police Force was established in London, the United States was still operating under a day and night watch system similar to that which had been used in England. In the 1830s several large cities established separate paid day watches. In 1833 Philadelphia became the first city to pay both the day and night watches. Boston followed in 1838 with a six-officer police force. In 1844 New York City took the first step toward organizing a big city police department similar to what exists today across the country when it consolidated its day and night watches under the control of a police chief. The police department was modeled on the London Metropolitan Police and Peel's principles. Other cities followed the example set by New York. By 1857 Boston, Chicago, New Orleans, Newark, Cincinnati, Philadelphia and Baltimore had consolidated police departments, modeled on the Metropolitan Police of London. The new police chiefs of these departments faced the beginning of tremendous personnel problems among their officers. Early professionals found security services in disarray.

> What those first chiefs of police found in their newly consolidated forces was a motley, undisciplined crew composed, as one commentator on the era described it, principally of "the shiftless, the incompetent, and the ignorant." Tales abounded of police officers in the 1850s who assaulted their superior officers, who released prisoners from the custody of other officers, who were found sleeping or drunk on duty, or who could be bribed for almost anything (Garmire, 1989, p. 17).

Despite these problems, and because there were also many honest, dedicated police officers, the citizens considered the police a source of assistance. Early police officers' duties included more community assistance and service than often imagined. Even at the beginning of this century, law enforcement was one of the only government-sanctioned services to help citizens twenty-four hours a day, seven days a week. Welfare, parole, probation and unemployment offices did not exist. Police in New York, for example, distributed coal to the poor, monitored the well-being of vulnerable citizens, served as probation and parole officers and helped establish playgrounds in the city.

It was more than a decade after the formation of the first police forces in the United States that attempts were made to require police officers to wear uniforms. The well-known resistance to change by police officers was apparent even then. The rank-and-file reaction against uniforms was immediate. Police officers claimed that uniforms were "un-American" and "a badge of degradation and servitude." In Philadelphia, police officers even objected to wearing badges on their coats. It was a bitter four-year struggle before they were finally persuaded to wear a complete uniform.

In 1856 New York City required its officers to be uniformed, but each local ward* could determine the style of dress. The results were that in some sections of the city police officers wore straw hats while in others they wore felt. In some wards summer uniforms were white duck suits. In other wards they were multicolored outfits.

Thus began the challenge of modern policing to provide for the needs of an ever-changing and more complex society while shaping and maintaining a well-trained, competent workforce to accomplish that mission.

The task has not been easy. The United States grew and changed rapidly. Cities developed and a very diverse population grew at breakneck speed as cultures met and clashed. Government officials had to decide how to maintain order in such a society, how much authority to give the police and how to hold them accountable.

## THE STRATEGIC ERAS OF POLICING

Three major paradigm shifts have occurred in the evolution of policing in the United States. A **paradigm** is a model or a way of viewing a specific aspect of life such as politics, medicine, education and, yes, the criminal justice system. A **paradigm shift** is simply a new way of thinking about a specific subject. Kelling and Moore (1991, p. 6) describe these paradigm shifts as specific "eras" of policing in the United States.

◆

The three eras of policing are political, reform and community.

◆

*A *ward* is a division of a city or town for administrative purposes.

## The Political Era

The political era extended into the first quarter of the twentieth century and was the time when police departments were formed. During this era police were closely tied to politics. This was very dissimilar to the situation in England. In England the police were centralized under the King, and the police chief had the authority to fire officers. In the United States the police were decentralized, under the authority of the municipality in which they worked. The chief had no authority to fire officers; therefore, the police were often undisciplined. "The image of 'Keystone Cops'—police as clumsy bunglers—was widespread and often descriptive of realities in U.S. policing" (Kelling and Moore, 1991, p. 9).

Police officers usually lived in their community and were members of the majority group. Since foot patrol was the most common policing strategy used, officers became close to the public.

♦

During the political era the police sought an intimate relationship with the community.

♦

During this era, chiefs of police were politically appointed and had a vested interest in keeping those who appointed them in power. Politicians rewarded those who voted for them with jobs or special privileges. This was referred to as the **patronage system,** or the **spoils system,** from the adage "To the victor go the spoils." Under the patronage system, corruption flourished. The effects of this system, according to Pace (1991, p. 132), are still present: "The spoils system extends from street level appointments to the Supreme Court. This includes privileges for the party in power in jobs, prime assignments, and special favors in a police agency, court, or correctional installation."

The inefficiency and corruption of the police led to the second era of policing, the reform era.

## The Reform Era

August Vollmer and O. W. Wilson are usually attributed with spearheading the reform movement that called for a drastic change in the way police departments were organized and functioned. This era was often referred to as the **progressive era.**

One basic change during this era was to disassociate policing from politics. Disassociation was accomplished in a variety of ways. In Los Angeles, for example, the chief of police position became a civil service job requiring applicants to pass a civil service test. In Milwaukee the chief of police was appointed for life by a citizen commission.

With the disassociation of policing from politics came a change in emphasis on the role of the police. Citizens began to equate policing with fighting crime. The police considered social service type functions less desirable and avoided them whenever possible.

The relationship between the police and the public also changed during the reform era. As noted by Kelling and Moore (1991, p. 12): "Police leaders in the reform era redefined the nature of a proper relationship between police officers and both politicians and citizens. Police would be impartial law enforcers who related to citizens in professionally neutral and distant terms."

*Dragnet,* one of the first and most popular police shows ever televised, depicted this era perfectly. The main character, Sgt. Joe Friday, typified the impartial and distant reform era officer with his often repeated line, "Just the facts, ma'am." The public viewed the police as professionals who were to remain detached from the citizens they served.

◆

During the reform era the police relationship with the community they served was professionally remote.

◆

During this era the concept of the **"thin blue line"** developed. This phrase refers to the line that separates law-abiding, peaceful citizens from the murderous, plundering villains who prey upon them. The phrase also suggests a distance between the police and the public they serve. The "thin blue line," as noted by Kelling and Moore (pp. 12–13), "connotes the existence of dangerous external threats to communities, portrays police as standing between that danger and good citizens, and implies both police heroism and loneliness."

Adding to the distancing of police from the public during the reform era was the replacement of foot patrol with motorized patrol. O. W. Wilson's preventive patrol by squad car coupled with an emphasis on rapid response to calls for service became the dual focus of policing during this era. The police image became one of officers roaring through city streets in high-powered squad cars, lights flashing and sirens wailing. The police were viewed as professional crime fighters. Consequently, policing during the reform era is often referred to as the *professional model.*

◆

The **professional model** emphasized crime control by preventive automobile patrol coupled with rapid response to calls.

◆

The problems faced by the first police administrators did not change much, but under the professional model their answers did. Many police methods were challenged during the 1960s when social change exploded in the United States as the result of several significant events which occurred almost simultaneously.

*Antiwar riots and flag burnings in the 1960s pitted police against protesters.*

The civil rights movement began in the late fifties as a grassroots movement to change the blatantly unequal social, political and economic systems in the United States. Confrontations between blacks and the police, who were almost completely male and white, increased during this time. Representing the *status quo* and defending it, the manner in which the police handled protest marches and civil disobedience often aggravated each situation.

Punctuated by the assassinations of President Kennedy, Malcolm X, Martin Luther King, Medgar Evers and Robert Kennedy, the events of the decade were, for the first time in history, documented in detail and viewed by millions of Americans on television. The antiwar movement, based on college campuses, was also televised. When demonstrators at the 1968 Democratic Convention in Chicago were beaten by the Chicago police, the demonstrators chanted, "The whole world is watching." Americans watched what was later termed a police riot, and they were shocked.

Plagued by lack of training and confronted by a confusing array of social movements as well as an emerging drug culture, the police became the "enemy." Officers heard themselves referred to as "pigs" by everyone from students to well-known entertainers. They represented the *status quo*, the establishment and everything standing in the way of peace, equality and justice. Police in the sixties were at war with the society they served. Never had the relationship between the law enforcement community and the people it served been so strained.

In addition to the questionable way police handled race riots and antiwar demonstrations in the sixties, several big city police departments were charged with being corrupt at that time. The sixties changed the face of America, and law enforcement was no exception. Studies in the seventies on corruption and criminal behavior among police agencies brought great pressure on the entire criminal justice system to change its methods, attitudes and image. Media coverage of law enforcement practices educated the public who ultimately demanded change.

*Understanding Community Policing* (1994, pp. 6–7) describes the social and professional "awakening" that occurred during the 1960s and 1970s:

> Antiwar protestors, civil rights activists, and other groups began to demonstrate in order to be heard. Overburdened and poorly prepared police came to symbolize what these groups sought to change in their government and society. Focusing attention on police policies and practices became an effective way to draw attention to the need for wider change. Police became the targets of hostility, which ultimately led police leaders to concerned reflection and analysis. . . .
>
> Between 1968 and 1973 three Presidential Commissions made numerous recommendations for changes in policing. . . .
>
> A number of organizations within the policing field also became committed to improving policing methods in the 1970s. Among those on the forefront of this movement for constructive change were the Police Foundation, the Police Executive Research Forum, the National Organization of Black Law Enforcement Executives, the Urban Sheriff's Group of the National Sheriffs' Association and the International Association of Chiefs of Police. These organizations conducted much of the basic research that led police to reevaluate traditional policing methods.

In response to the negative police image that emerged during the 1960s, several departments across the country established programs to enhance relationships. These programs included public relations programs, community relations programs and crime prevention programs.

**Efforts to Enhance Relations between the Police and the Community.**  To avoid confusion, it is helpful to distinguish *public relations, community relations* and *human relations* as these terms are used frequently throughout this text and in other literature on policing.

- **Public relations:** Efforts to enhance the police image—"We'll tell you what we're doing, but leave us alone to fight crime."
- **Community relations:** Efforts to interact and communicate with the community—team policing, community resource officers, school liaison officers.

- **Human relations:** Efforts to relate to and understand other individuals or groups of individuals—the focus of Section 2.

Public relations efforts are usually one-way efforts directed at raising the image of the police. These efforts by police departments include hosting department open houses and providing speakers for school and community events. Many police departments have established a public relations office or division and assign specific officers to the public relations effort. Such efforts reflect the growing recognition by police administrators that they need public support.

During the past several decades, especially in the late 1970s and also as a result of the widening gap between the police and the public, many police departments began community relations programs. According to Senna and Siegel (1996, p. 275): "For the past 20 years, police agencies have been making an effort to gain the cooperation and respect of the community they serve, or, in other words, to improve police-community relations."

Unlike public relations efforts, which were primarily one-to-one communications, often media generated, community relations programs sought to bring the police and community closer through isolated police tactics such as team policing and community resource officers. Efforts to enhance community relations also frequently involved citizens through crime prevention programs.

## Crime Prevention Programs.

◆

Crime prevention programs that enlist the aid of citizens include operation identification programs, neighborhood or block watch programs and home and automobile security programs.

◆

Such programs continue to be strategies used in many community policing efforts and will be discussed in detail in Section 3.

**The Law Enforcement Assistance Administration (LEAA).** Another response to the negative image of the police was the establishment of the Law Enforcement Assistance Administration in 1968. Over the next several years LEAA provided billions of dollars to the "war on crime," funding studies and programs for law enforcement.

LEAA awarded more than $9 billion to state and local governments to improve police, courts and correctional systems, to combat juvenile delinquency, and to finance innovative crime-fighting projects.

Every state and locality felt the impact of LEAA's nationwide anticrime program. Tens of thousands of programs and projects were supported with

LEAA funds, and millions of hours were applied to identify effective, efficient, economical ways to reduce crime and improve criminal justice. Projects were developed to reduce crime, improve the management and administration of courts, deploy police officers more effectively, find jobs for ex-offenders, sharpen the skills of criminal justice personnel, give prosecutors better tools to fight crime, and break the jail-street-crime-jail cycle of the drug addict (Wrobleski and Hess, 1997, p. 50).

Although the consensus among law enforcement officials today is that LEAA was mostly mismanaged, there was a very positive aspect of LEAA. This was the Law Enforcement Education Program (LEEP) which provided thousands of officers with funding for higher education.

**The Courts.**  The courts also had a major impact on criminal justice during the 1960s. Several legal decisions limited police powers and clarified the rights of the accused. The 1965 *Miranda v. Arizona* decision had a significant impact on police methods. *Miranda* was not the first or the last Supreme Court decision to limit police discretion, but it is perhaps the best known. This landmark decision requires police officers to inform suspects of their right to remain silent, to have counsel present and to have court-appointed counsel if they cannot afford to pay for counsel. Also, suspects must be warned that anything they say may be used against them in a court of law.

**Other Problems and Challenges During the Progressive Era.**  Despite these efforts, reported crime increased and the public's fear of crime intensified. An influx of immigrants added to the problems of major cities. The deinstitutionalizing of mental patients in the 1970s caused thousands of mentally disabled individuals to enter the mainstream of America, often without means to support themselves. This, coupled with the return of many Vietnam veterans who found it difficult to reenter society, resulted in a large homeless population.

Another challenge to the effectiveness of the professional model was the Kansas City Preventive Patrol Study. This classic study found that increasing or decreasing preventive patrol efforts had no significant effect on crime, citizen fear of crime, community attitudes toward the police, police response time or traffic accidents. As noted by Klockars (1983, p. 130): "It makes about as much sense to have police patrol routinely in cars to fight crime as it does to have firemen patrol routinely in fire trucks to fight fire."

Many law enforcement officials view the Kansas City Preventive Patrol Study as the beginning of a new era in policing. It was considered by police as the first experimental design used in policing and, as such, was a landmark. It set the stage for further research in policing and is viewed as the first true movement in the *professionalization* of policing. Its findings are also controversial. There were real problems with the research design and implementation of this study; however, it caused us to begin to question the assumptions we had made in policing. It concluded what many police officials already knew but did not want publicized for fear of the impact on police budgets.

Other research conducted in the 1970s also questioned police effectiveness.

> Research about preventive patrol, rapid response to calls for service, and investigative work—the three mainstays of police tactics—was uniformly discouraging.

> Research demonstrated that preventive patrol in automobiles had little effect on crime, citizen levels of fear, or citizen satisfaction with police. Rapid response to calls for service likewise had little impact on arrests, citizen satisfaction with police, or levels of citizen fear. Also, research into criminal investigation effectiveness suggested that detective units were so poorly administered that they had little chance of being effective (Kelling, 1988, p. 4).

However, as noted by Walker (1993, p. 35): "By the mid-1970s that movement [general period of reform in American policing] had run its course. Many of the promising reforms, such as team policing, had not effected any major changes." (Team policing and its demise are discussed in Chapter 5.) The reform movement was revived, according to Walker, by the publication of two "provocative" articles: Herman Goldstein's "Problem-Oriented Policing" article in 1979 and James Q. Wilson and George L. Kelling's "Broken Windows" article in 1982. Says Walker: "They are the seminal articles in the current community policing/problem-oriented policing movement."

Other reasons for reevaluating police methods were the changing nature of the individuals who became police and their frustration with the traditional role of the patrol officer. As noted by Kelling (1988, p. 4): "Despite pieties that patrol has been the backbone of policing, every police executive has known that, at best, patrol has been what officers do until they become detectives or are promoted. At worst, patrol has been the dumping ground for officers who are incompetent, suffering from alcoholism or other problems, or simply burned out." A change was needed at the patrol level to attract more highly educated and less militaristic recruits. The patrol officer had to become important to the department in accomplishing its mission.

Finally, many businesses and individuals began to hire private security officers to assure their safety. The public assumed that the police alone were unable to "preserve the peace." While some called for greater cooperation between public and private policing, others argued that the public should collaborate with all policing efforts.

A combination of the dissatisfaction with criminal justice and the role of patrol officers, research results, the trend toward private policing and the writings of Goldstein and Wilson and Kelling led to the third era of policing—the community era.

## The Community Era

In the 1980s many police departments began experimenting with more community involvement in the "war on crime." Also during this decade several cities tested Herman Goldstein's problem-oriented approach to policing. The emphasis in many departments began to shift from crime fighting to crime prevention.

Gradually law enforcement has become more responsive to the public's desire for a different kind of policing. Today there is considerable citizen-police interaction and problem solving. While still resistant to change, police agencies are now more likely to respond to the needs and wishes of the communities they serve. The significant changes in the way police address sexual assault, domestic violence, sexual abuse of children, drunk driving and missing children attest to this new responsiveness. The public wants the police to be proactive; citizens want police to try to prevent crime in addition to apprehending criminals after a crime has been committed.

◆

During the community era the police sought to reestablish a close relationship with the community.

◆

Highlights of the three eras of policing are summarized in Table 1.1. The community era is referred to by many names: community policing, community-oriented policing, neighborhood policing and the like. Currently the term *community policing* is most commonly used.

At the heart of most "new" approaches to policing is a return to the ancient idea of community responsibility for the welfare of society. As noted by former New York City Police Commissioner Brown (1990, p. 8): "At the heart of policing is a requirement for understanding between the police and the citizens they are sworn to protect. Put simply, police officers must be *a part* of the community, not *apart* from it." Brown (1991, p. 6) further contends:

Permanent interaction between officers and neighborhood residents and merchants is the first step toward identifying the community's problems. When the people of the community get involved and realize they have a voice in improving their quality of life, it creates good will and makes it easier for the police to fulfill their mission. . . .

We need to *solve* chronic community problems rather than just react to them. It is time to adopt new strategies to address the dramatic increases in crime and the fear of crime. I view community policing as a better, smarter and more cost-effective way of using police resources.

A need for community involvement is also stressed by VanBlaricom (1989, p. 7):

The traditional police department is an insular organization that responds to citizens' wishes from behind the blue curtain when a crisis of sufficient magnitude erupts to demand political damage control. Community policing changes that approach by bringing the police officers back into the neighborhoods to talk with residents about what they want and how they can lawfully accomplish their goals together.

*Table 1.1* **The Three Eras of Policing**

| | *Political Era*<br>*1840s to 1930s* | *Reform Era*<br>*1930s to 1980s* | *Com*<br>*1980* |
|---|---|---|---|
| **Authorization** | politics and law | law and professionalism | community support (political), law and professionalism |
| **Function** | broad social services | crime control | broad provision of services |
| **Organizational Design** | decentralized | centralized, classical | decentralized, task forces, matrices |
| **Relationship to Community** | intimate | professional, remote | intimate |
| **Tactics and Technology** | foot patrol | preventive patrol and rapid response to calls | foot patrol, problem solving, public relations |
| **Outcome** | citizen, political satisfaction | crime control | quality of life and citizen satisfaction |

SOURCE: Summarized from George L. Kelling and Mark H. Moore, "From Political to Reform to Community: The Evolving Strategy of Police." In *Community Policing: Rhetoric or Reality.* Edited by Jack R. Greene and Stephen D. Mastrofski 6, 14–15, 22–23. New York: Praeger Publishers, 1991.

A comparison of traditional policing and community policing is made in Table 1.2.

> Viewed from one perspective, it is not a new concept; the principles can be traced back to some of policing's oldest traditions. . . .

> What is new is the idea that community policing is not a particular program within a department, but instead should become the dominant philosophy throughout the department (Brown, 1989, p. 1).

While community policing is considered innovative, one of its central tenets of involvement with and responsiveness to the community is similar to the principles set forth by Sir Robert Peel in 1829 when he established the London Metropolitan Police. Policing has strayed so far from these principles in the past century that the concepts central to community policing seem fresh and sensible today.

## COMMUNITY POLICING DEFINITIONS

According to Seagrave (1996, p. 1): "Although the issue of community policing has been a subject of academic interest for almost 10 years, there is debate and confusion over what exactly community policing is. Both academics and

*Table 1.2*  **Comparison of Traditional Policing and Community Policing**

| Question | Traditional Policing | Community Policing |
|---|---|---|
| *Who are the police?* | A government agency principally responsible for law enforcement. | Police are the public and the public are the police: the police officers are those who are paid to give full-time attention to the duties of every citizen. |
| *What is the relationship of the police force to other public service departments?* | Priorities often conflict. | The police are one department among many responsible for improving the quality of life. |
| *What is the role of the police?* | Focusing on solving crimes. | A broader problem-solving approach. |
| *How is police efficiency measured?* | By detection and arrest rates. | By the absence of crime and disorder. |
| *What are the highest priorities?* | Crimes that are high value (e.g., bank robberies) and those involving violence. | Whatever problems disturb the community most. |
| *What, specifically, do police deal with?* | Incidents. | Citizens' problems and concerns. |
| *What determines the effectiveness of police?* | Response times. | Public cooperation. |
| *What view do police take of service calls?* | Deal with them only if there is no real police work to do. | Vital function and great opportunity. |
| *What is police professionalism?* | Swift effective response to serious crime. | Keeping close to the community. |
| *What kind of intelligence is most important?* | Crime intelligence (study of particular crimes or series of crimes). | Criminal intelligence (information about the activities of individuals or groups). |
| *What is the essential nature of police accountability?* | Highly centralized; governed by rules, regulations and policy directives; accountable to the law. | Emphasis on local accountability to community needs. |
| *What is the role of headquarters?* | To provide the necessary rules and policy directives. | To preach organizational values. |
| *What is the role of the press liaison department?* | To keep the "heat" off operational officers so they can get on with the job. | To coordinate an essential channel of communication with the community. |
| *How do the police regard prosecutions?* | As an important goal. | As one tool among many. |

SOURCE: Malcolm K. Sparrow. *Implementing Community Policing.* U.S. Department of Justice, National Institute of Justice. (November 1988): 8–9.

*New Orleans police officers keep the peace during a Second Line Funeral procession through the Florida and Desire public housing projects. The parade was in honor of the last man to die in the projects before the police department opened police sub-stations in both Florida and Desire. The officers are part of a special volunteer unit to work out of the sub-stations. Since the sub-stations opened, the murder rate in these projects has gone from almost 10 percent of the record 1994 total of 421 to almost nothing.*

practitioners have been content to treat it as an intangible, fluid and nebulous concept, and consequently have failed to devise a common definition."

Oliver (1992, p. 46) also notes that the term *community policing* is an intangible term, based on intangible ideas.

> The phrase "community policing" is an all-encompassing idea that focuses on a single goal: reducing crime and public fear. . . .
>
> Community policing is an imperceptible term that has no concrete definition or limits (Oliver, 1992, p. 46).
>
> Indeed, community policing is many different things to many different people.
>
> Community oriented policing is a philosophy, a style, and a method of providing police service and managing the police organization. It is value based and involves long term institutional change (Vaughn, 1991, p. 35).
>
> Community policing is about developing partnerships that bring together the necessary resources to solve problems and reduce crime (Brann, 1996, p. 1).

> I take it [community policing] in the broadest sense to mean any concerted endeavor to bring together the police of a jurisdiction and those in that jurisdiction who are not the police (the short-hand for which is the "community"). This togetherness can take many forms, but it requires a shared understanding of problems that require attention, as well as some degree of joint responsibility in undertakings to deal with those problems (Mastrofski, 1993, p. 65).
>
> This philosophy, called community policing, gives officers the necessary time to connect with the communities they serve, and to work with those communities to actually solve problems instead of just offering quick and momentary fixes (Miller, 1996, p. 6).
>
> Community policing is the only legitimate kind in a free society. Any significant deviation from it suggests a police state (Murphy, 1995, p. 4).
>
> Community policing is most broadly regarded as a philosophy requiring significant and fundamental organizational change. It has been defined as a recognition and acceptance of the community in influencing the philosophy, management and delivery of police services (Seagrave, 1996, p. 5).
>
> As it is generally conceptualized, community-oriented policing (COP) is a set of values relating to the proper role that the police play in a contemporary democratic society, one that embodies the principles of COP as shared empowerment of both the agency and the community in controlling crime and reducing disorder (Thurman and Bogen, 1996, p. 97).

Running through these definitions are two basic themes: police/community collaboration and a problem-solving approach to the police function. These two themes are also incorporated throughout this text.

As Kelling (1994, p. 3) cautions: "Whether one calls community policing a philosophy, a strategy, a model, or a paradigm, it is a complex set of ideas that simply cannot be put into a simple one-sentence definition that will encompass all the elements to everyone's satisfaction."

This may be partially due to the various "levels" police departments may consider "community policing" as described by Weatheritt (1991, pp. 153–154):

> Community policing is talked about at a number of levels and it is important to distinguish between them. At one level community policing is about developing a set of programs or activities for police: foot patrol, community-based crime prevention, ways of consulting communities about the kinds of problems they have and the kind of policing they want. The emphasis tends to be on the pragmatic and small-scale. . . . [On a second level] community policing is about promoting better police-public relations and a better police image. . . . It is undertaken because community policing activities are seen as good in themselves. . . .
>
> Community policing is also about changing the ethos of policing to emphasize notions of service, flexibility, consumer responsiveness, conciliation, consultation, and negotiation.

Weatheritt (1991, p. 172) suggests: "Community policing is an elastic term that is often used to give a superficial coherence to a wide and disparate set of policing activities and various forms of police community dialogue."

According to the Police Executive Research Forum: "Community policing should be seen as part of an on-going reform movement that includes various foundations, educational institutions, urban politicians in non-machine cities, and criminal justice educators" (Manning, 1991, p. 45).

Defining community policing is not without its problems. Trojanowicz and Bucqueroux (1990, p. 5) have a page-long definition that begins like this:

> Community policing is a new philosophy of policing, based on the concept that police officers and private citizens working together in creative ways can help solve contemporary community problems related to crime, fear of crime, social and physical disorder and neighborhood decay. The philosophy is predicated on the belief that achieving these goals requires that police departments develop a new relationship with the law-abiding people in the community, allowing them a greater voice in setting local police priorities and involving them in efforts to improve the overall quality of life in their neighborhoods. It shifts the focus of police work from handling random calls to solving community problems.

In other words, where traditionally policing has been **reactive,** responding to calls for service, the trend is for policing to be **proactive,** anticipating problems and seeking solutions to these problems. The term *proactive* is beginning to take on an expanded definition. Not only is it taking on the meaning of anticipating problems, but it is taking on the Steven Covey slant, that of accountability and choosing a response rather than reacting the same way each time a similar situation occurs. Police are learning that you do not obtain different results by applying the same methods. In other words, to get different results you need to apply different tactics. This is the focus of Chapter 4.

◆

**Community policing** is a philosophy that emphasizes working proactively with citizens to reduce fear, solve crime-related problems and prevent crime.

◆

## FEATURES OF COMMUNITY POLICING

Trojanowicz and Bucqueroux (1994, pp. 131–132) state what they perceive to be the goal of community policing and several major features associated with it:

### Community Policing

**Goal:** Solve problems—improved relations with citizens is a welcome by-product.

A department-wide philosophy and department-wide acceptance.

**Line Function:** Regular contact between officers and citizens.

Internal and external influence and respect for officers.

Well defined role—does both proactive and reactive policing—a full-service officer.

Direct service—same officer takes complaints and gives crime prevention tips.

Citizens identify problems and cooperate in setting up the police agenda.

Police accountability is ensured by the citizens receiving the service in addition to administrative mechanisms.

Officer is the leader and catalyst for change in the neighborhood to reduce fear, disorder, decay and crime.

Chief of police is an advocate and sets the tone for the delivery of both law enforcement and social services in the jurisdictions.

Officers educate public about issues (like response time or preventive patrol) and the need to prioritize services.

Increased trust between the police officer and citizens because of long-term, regular contact results in an enhanced flow of information to the police.

Officer is continually accessible in person, by telephone or in a decentralized office.

Regular visibility in the neighborhood.

Officer is viewed as having a "stake in the community."

Officer is a role model because of regular contact with citizens (especially youth role model).

Influence is from "the bottom up"—citizens receiving service help set priorities and influence police policy.

Meaningful organizational change and departmental restructuring—ranging from officer selection to training, evaluation and promotion.

When intervention is necessary, informal social control is the first choice.

Officer encourages citizens to solve many of their own problems and volunteer to assist neighbors.

Officer encourages other service providers like animal control, firefighters and mail carriers to become involved in community problem solving.

Officer mobilizes all community resources, including citizens, private and public agencies and private businesses.

Success is determined by the reduction in citizen fear, neighborhood disorder and crime.

All officers are sworn personnel.

## POTENTIAL PITFALLS ASSOCIATED WITH COMMUNITY POLICING

Bayley (1991, pp. 226–36) cites several potential problems associated with community policing. First, public safety might decline because the public is not that interested in participating in crime prevention efforts. Second, he suggests that the police may become too soft on crime and lose the ability to control violence in the community. "Can the police put on a velvet glove and keep their iron hand in shape?" asks Bayley (p. 228).

Another potential problem with community policing is that the rationale for having police is diminished. As crime fighters, they were extremely important to communities. If, however, the police prove to be ineffective crime fighters, there is no reason to believe they will be effective crime preventers. Further, the public may become a special interest group for the police. According to Bayley (p. 229): "Community policing seeks to transform the police from what has been described as 'an army of occupation' into an accepted, unremarkable, and individually responsive part of the community."

Community policing may also adversely increase the power of the police in comparison to that of other governmental agencies. Community policing seeks to build strong ties between the police and the community. Such ties may cause problems, however, when other government officials realize and resent the power police departments and individual officers may have to lobby citizens for financial resources and officer assignments or transfers. Police chiefs nationwide have found themselves in conflict with mayors and city councils as individual police officers lobby for needed resources. A closer relationship between the police and the public may also result in the citizens' increased ability to influence internal department matters.

Another potential problem with community policing is that its emphasis on crime prevention gives police the authority to keep careful watch on individuals in the community. Closely related to this problem is a fear that community policing will increase government surveillance of private citizens. To date, the problems cited by Bayley (p. 18) have not come to pass. In addition, the old guard police, who have been very apprehensive about COP, are beginning to see that COP is not soft on crime.

In addition, community policing, because it promotes adapting policing to local circumstances, may lead to the unequal application of justice. "Local commanders may begin to think it is more important not to alienate loud voices than to protect quiet ones" (Bayley, p. 232). Closely related to this is the potential that community policing may lessen the protection given to unpopular individuals such as the homeless. It may even lead to vigilantism.

Finally, community policing may worsen a growing dualism in policing; affluent neighborhoods embrace the community-oriented mode while poorer urban areas and ghettos return to an emphasis on law enforcement and crime fighting.

Despite these potential problems, Bayley does not advocate abandoning community policing. Rather, he suggests that if a department adopts community policing as a philosophy, it should be aware of the potential hazards and avoid them. He cautions (p. 236): "Community policing does not represent a small, technical shift in policing; it is a paradigmatic change in the way police operate. It is the most fundamental change in policing since the rise of police professionalism early in this century. Because community policing is serious and fateful, we must be open minded about its potential infirmities as well as its promise." In other words, community policing cannot be considered a cure-all for the problems of crime and fear of crime in our communities.

Similar possible problems associated with community policing are discussed by Wycoff (1991, p. 116):

1. *Illegal Policing.* Community-based officers may become more responsive to local norms than to legal constraints.

2. *Inequitable Policing.* Some groups may benefit more than others from police service.

3. *Politicization of the Police.* Officers might use their community organizing skills and good relationships with the neighborhood to mount a campaign to accomplish political objectives, e.g., salary increases or ouster of an unappreciated judge or chief.

4. *Corruption.* Close contact between police and business people or residents creates possibilities of unacceptable behavior.

5. *Police Intrusion into Private Arenas.* In a democratic society, how effective do we really want our police to be?

Despite these potential problems, Wycoff is also an advocate of community policing. She cites Peel's 1829 statement that the police are the "only members of the public that are paid to give full-time attention to duties incumbent on every citizen in the interest of community welfare and existence. What we may be seeing is not a new concept under the sun but rather a new sunrise on a fine old concept" (Wycoff, p. 120).

Perhaps the single biggest problem with community policing is gaining acceptance of the first-line supervisor, whose authority may appear to be weakened by allowing the patrol officer a great deal of discretion. In addition, patrol officers may not accept community policing as an effective method to reduce crime, and without their genuine support, it will not work. Another problem touched on by Wycoff is the tremendous community support that patrol officers may garner, giving the officers tremendous power. A positive twist to this potential problem, however, is that some police agencies are finding there is no longer a need for police boards since the police are in such close and constant contact with the citizens of the community.

Although none of these potential pitfalls and problems have been documented to date, they remain a consideration. Also of critical importance to community policing efforts is use of a problem-solving approach. As noted, the writings of Herman Goldstein served as one catalyst for the community policing movement. Goldstein is credited with introducing a proactive, problem-solving approach to policing. This approach has become an integral part of most successful community policing efforts and, like community policing, is rooted in police and citizen interaction.

# PROBLEM-SOLVING POLICING

Goldstein (1990, p. 20) criticizes the professional model of policing as being incident driven: "In the vast majority of police departments, the telephone, more than any policy decision by the community or by management, continues to dictate how police resources will be used." The primary work unit in the professional model is the **incident,** that is, an isolated event that requires a police response. The institution of 911 has greatly increased the demand for police services and the public's expectation that the police will respond quickly.

Goldstein (p. 33) suggests: "Most policing is limited to ameliorating the overt, offensive symptoms of a problem." He suggests that police are more productive if they respond to incidents as symptoms of underlying community problems. Goldstein (p. 66) defines a problem as "a cluster of similar, related, or recurring incidents rather than a single incident, a substantive community concern, and a unit of police business." Once the problems in a community are identified, police efforts can focus on addressing the possible causes of such problems.

◆

**Problem-solving policing** requires police to group incidents and, thereby, identify underlying causes of problems in the community.

◆

While problem-solving policing may be ideal, law enforcement cannot ignore specific incidents. When calls come in, most police departments respond. Problem-solving policing has a dual focus. First, it requires that incidents be linked to problems. Second, time devoted to "preventive" patrol must be spent proactively, determining community problems and their underlying causes. As noted by Wilson and Kelling (1989, p. 46):

> The police know from experience what research by Glenn Pierce, in Boston, and Lawrence Sherman, in Minneapolis, has established: fewer than 10 percent of the addresses from which the police receive calls account for more than 60 percent of those calls. If each call is treated as a separate incident with neither a history nor a future, then each dispute will be handled by police officers anxious to pacify the complaints and get back on patrol as quickly as possible. . . .
>
> A study of domestic homicides in Kansas City showed that in eight out of ten cases the police had been called to the incident address at least once before; in half the cases they had been called *five times* or more.

A problem-solving approach relies heavily upon citizen involvement. According to Goldstein (1990, p. 21): "The police must do more than they have done in the past to engage the citizenry in the overall task of policing. . . . A community must police itself. The police can, at best, only assist in that task."

An illustrative analogy can be drawn between a physician and a patient. The physician can examine the patient, take his history and based on the patient's symptoms, prescribe a treatment. For the patient to recover he must, however, be

*Members of the diverse San Fernando Valley, Calif. community, march through downtown Los Angeles Thursday, April 4, 1996, condemning the videotaped beating of illegal immigrants by Riverside County Sheriff's deputies in South El Monte, Calif., on Monday. At right, Los Angeles police officers assist demonstrators to avoid oncoming traffic at a stop light.*

honest and thorough in describing the symptoms and must follow the prescribed treatment. Further, in medicine as in policing, the best approach is to prevent the illness in the first place. As noted by Wadman and Olson (1990, p. 37): "In order to understand current trends in policing, we should compare the problem of crime with the problem of disease. For centuries, scientists have searched for cures to the various ailments that afflict mankind. It wasn't until the twentieth century that medical science discovered that the best cure was not to have the disease at all." Just as physicians cannot be blamed for the existence of disease, police cannot be blamed for the existence of crime.

> The police can no longer accept total responsibility for our crime problems. Success will be achieved only when the police and the community join forces to develop solutions.
>
> Community wellness is the result of a sharing of responsibility and authority for the causes of crime and for crime itself. . . . Unless the community actively involves itself with its police department and the department's attempt to solve community problems, we will forever be mired in reactive, rather than proactive, policing (Nila, 1990, p. 47).

Wadman and Olson (1990, p. 92) make this analogy: "Much like fighting a forest fire, the wellness concept demands that personnel and equipment be diverted to create the 'firebreaks' that reduce the opportunities for crimes to be committed. This is where the real risks come in." The **community wellness** approach to policing also recognizes that police must fulfill their "crime fighter" role. In that role, too, however, the relationship between the police and community can be critical.

Regardless of whether police officers respond to incidents, seek symptoms of problems, or both, the public can help or hinder their efforts. Police and community members must discuss and agree to any community involvement program before it is adopted. At times well-meaning individuals and community groups, acting unilaterally, can actually interfere with a police effort and cause unnecessary destruction, injury and even death.

The dual themes of this book are the manner in which police can engage the community in the problems of crime and disorder and the necessity of a problem-solving approach to such crime.

## SUMMARY

"Modern" policing began with the formation of the London Metropolitan Police, based on principles set forth by Sir Robert Peel. Peel's principles emphasized the interdependence of the police and the public as well as the prevention of crime and disorder.

Policing in the United States has had three distinct paradigm shifts or eras: political, reform and community. During the political era the police sought an intimate relationship with the community. During the reform era the relationship was professionally remote. During the community era the relationship was again perceived to be intimate.

During the 1960s and 1970s relations between the police and the public were extremely strained. In an effort to improve relations, many police departments instituted public relations programs. The goal of these programs was to improve the image of the police. Many departments also began crime prevention programs that enlisted the aid of citizens, including such programs as operation identification, neighborhood or block watches and home and automobile security programs.

Community policing is a philosophy that emphasizes working with citizens to reduce fear, solve crime-related problems and prevent crime. Problem-solving policing, an integral part of community policing, requires the police to group incidents so as to identify and solve community problems.

### *Discussion Questions*

1. From the perspective of law enforcement, what are the strengths and weaknesses of each of the three eras of policing?
2. From the perspective of a citizen, what are the strengths and weaknesses of each era?
3. Is any community policing strategy being used in your community? If so, which?
4. What advantages does community policing offer? Disadvantages?

5. How is the relationship between the police and the public typically portrayed in popular television programs and movies?
6. How is the relationship between the police and the public typically portrayed in the news media?
7. Can you see any evidence of the patronage or spoils system of policing in the 1990s?
8. What is the relationship of community policing and problem-solving policing?
9. Which form of policing do you believe has the most potential for your community? Why?
10. Have you witnessed any examples of the "thin blue line"?

## *References*

Bayley, David H. "Community Policing: A Report from the Devil's Advocate." In *Community Policing: Rhetoric or Reality,* edited by Jack R. Greene and Stephen D. Mastrofski, 126–237. New York: Praeger Publishers, 1991.

Brann, Joe. "COPS Director Joe Brann Welcomes New Community Policing Publication for Sheriffs." *Sheriff Times.* (Spring 1996): 1.

Brown, Lee P. "Community Policing: Its Time Has Come." *The Police Chief.* (September 1991): 6.

Brown, Lee P. "The Police-Community Partnership." *The Police Chief.* (December 1990): 8.

Burger, Warren E. "Introduction." *The Bench & Bar of Minnesota.* (May/June 1991): 26.

Garmire, Bernard L., ed. *Local Government Police Management.* Mimeographed. Published by the International City Management Association, *Law and Order.* (August 1989).

Goldstein, Herman. *Problem-Oriented Policing.* New York: McGraw-Hill Publishing Company, 1990.

Harr, J. Scott and Hess, Kären M. *Constitutional Law for the Criminal Justice Professional.* Belmont, Calif.: West/Wadsworth Publishing Company, 1998.

Inkster, Norman D. "The Essence of Community Policing." *The Police Chief.* (March 1992): 28–31.

Kelling, George. "Defining Community Policing." *Subject to Debate.* (April 1994): 3, 6.

Kelling, George L. "Police and Communities: The Quiet Revolution." *Perspectives on Policing.* (June 1988).

Kelling, George L. and Moore, Mark H. "From Political to Reform to Community: The Evolving Strategy of Police." In *Community Policing: Rhetoric or Reality,* edited by Jack R. Greene and Stephen D. Mastrofski, 3–25. New York: Praeger Publishers, 1991.

Klockars, Carl B. *Thinking about Police: Contemporary Readings.* New York: McGraw-Hill, 1983.

Manning, Peter K. "Community Policing as a Drama of Control." In *Community Policing: Rhetoric or Reality,* edited by Jack R. Greene and Stephen D. Mastrofski, 27–45. New York: Praeger Publishers, 1991.

Mastrofski, Stephen D. "Varieties of Community Policing." *American Journal of Police.* (Vol. XII, No. 3, 1993): 65–77.

Miller, Linda. "Community Policing as a Viable Alternative to Traditional Crime Fighting Methods." *Minnesota Cities.* (August 1996): 6–9.

Murphy, Patrick. "Community Policing Works When Officers Connect with People." *Subject to Debate.* (December 1994/January 1995): 4.

Nila, Michael J. "Defining the Police Mission: A Community/Police Perspective." *The Police Chief.* (October 1990): 43–47.

Oliver, Willard M. "Community Policing Defined." *Law and Order.* (August 1992): 46, 56–58.

Pace, Denny F. *Community Relations Concepts.* Placerville, Calif.: Custom Publishing Company, 1991.

Richardson, J. F. *The New York Police.* New York: Oxford University Press, 1970.

Seagrave, Jayne. "Defining Community Policing." *American Journal of Police.* (Vol. XV, No. 1, 1996): 1–22.

Senna, Joseph J. and Siegel, Larry J. *Introduction to Criminal Justice.* 7th rev. ed. St. Paul: West Publishing Company, 1996.

Taft, Philip B., Jr. *Fighting Fear: The Baltimore County COPE Project.* Washington, D.C.: Police Executive Research Forum, 1986.

Thurman, Qunit C. and Bogen, Phil. "Research Note: Spokane Community Policing Revisited." *American Journal of Police.* (Vol. XV, No. 1, 1996): 97–116.

Trojanowicz, Robert and Bucqueroux, Bonnie. *Community Policing.* Cincinnati: Anderson, 1994.

Trojanowicz, Robert and Bucqueroux, Bonnie. *Community Policing: A Contemporary Perspective.* Cincinnati: Anderson, 1990.

*Understanding Community Policing: A Framework for Action.* Washington, D.C.: Bureau of Justice Assistance, August 1994.

VanBlaricom, D. P. "Shaking the Pillars of Police Tradition." *Law Enforcement News.* (October 31, 1989): 7.

Vaughn, Jerald R. "Community Oriented Policing . . . You Can Make It Happen." *Law and Order.* (June 1991): 35–39.

Wadman, Robert C. and Olson, Robert K. *Community Wellness: A New Theory of Policing.* Washington, D.C.: Police Executive Research Forum, 1990.

Walker, Samuel. "Does Anyone Remember Team Policing? Lessons of the Team Policing Experience for Community Policing." *American Journal of Police.* (Vol. XII, No. 1, 1993): 33–55.

Weatheritt, Mollie. "Community Policing: Rhetoric or Reality." In *Community Policing: Rhetoric or Reality,* edited by Jack R. Greene and Stephen D. Mastrofski, 153–75. New York: Praeger Publishers, 1991.

Wilson, James Q. and Kelling, George L. "Making Neighborhoods Safe." *The Atlantic Monthly.* (February 1989): 46–49.

Wrobleski, Henry M. and Hess, Kären M. *Introduction to Law Enforcement and Criminal Justice.* 5th ed. St. Paul: West Publishing Company, 1997.

Wycoff, Mary Ann. "The Benefits of Community Policing: Evidence and Conjecture." In *Community Policing: Rhetoric or Reality,* edited by Jack R. Greene and Stephen D. Mastrofski, 103–20. New York: Praeger Publishers, 1991.

# Chapter 2

# The Community

*I believe in the United States of America as a Government of the people, by the people, for the people . . .*
—American Creed

## Do you know

- How U.S. citizens established the "public peace"?
- What a social contract is?
- How to define community?
- What the broken window phenomenon refers to?
- What demographics includes?
- What role organizations and institutions play within a community?
- How private policing compares to public policing in terms of personnel and budget?
- What power structures exist within a community?
- What the three components of the criminal justice system are?
- What issues in the criminal justice system affect police-community relations?
- How the medical model and the justice model view criminals?
- What restorative justice is?
- How citizens/communities have been involved in community policing?

## Definitions

Can you define these terms: broken window phenomenon, community, demographics, diversion, formal power structure, ghetto, heterogeneous, homogeneous, informal power structure, justice model, medical model, NIMBY syndrome, plea bargaining, privatization, recidivism, restorative justice, social contract, syndrome of crime.

# *Introduction*

The opening sentence of the American Creed, adopted by the House of Representatives on April 3, 1918, uses language attributed to Abraham Lincoln in his *Address at Gettysburg,* November 19, 1863: "We here highly resolve that these dead shall not have died in vain; that this nation, under God, shall have a new birth of freedom; and that government of the people, by the people, and for the people, shall not perish from the earth." The philosophy implicit in the American Creed is central to the concept of "community" in the United States. Each community is part of a larger social order.

◆

The U.S. Constitution and Bill of Rights, as well as federal and state statutes and local ordinances, establish the "public peace" in the United States.

◆

In the United States individual freedom and rights are balanced with the need to establish and maintain order. The United States was born out of desire for freedom. In fact, Former President Jimmy Carter noted: "America did not invent human rights. In a very real sense, it is the other way around. Human rights invented America."

The importance of individual rights to all citizens is a theme that is central to the following discussion of community. Citizens have established a criminal justice system in an effort to live in "peace," free from crime and violence. The influence of the criminal justice system on police-community relations is discussed later in the chapter. To ensure the peace, citizens of the United States have also entered into an unwritten *social contract.*

◆

The **social contract** provides that for everyone to receive justice, each person must relinquish some freedom.

◆

In civilized society, people cannot simply do as they please. They are expected to conform to federal and state laws, as well as local rules and regulations established by and for the community in which they live. Increased mobility and economic factors have weakened the informal social contract which once helped to keep the peace in our society. As a result the police, as agents of social control, have had to fill the breach, increasing the need for law-abiding citizens to join with the police in making their communities free from drugs and crime.

This chapter begins with definitions of *community* and an explanation of community demographics and how our population is changing. This is followed by a discussion of crime and violence in our communities. Next the organizations and institutions within a community, the public-private policing interaction and the power structure within a community are described. Then the role of the criminal justice system in community policing is discussed. The chapter concludes with an explanation of citizen/community involvement in community policing.

## COMMUNITY DEFINED

What does the word *community* bring to mind? To many people it conjures up images of their hometown. To others it may bring images of a specific block, a neighborhood or an idyllic small town where everyone knows everyone and they all get along.

Community has also been defined as a group of people living in an area under the same government. In addition, community can refer to a social group or class having common interests. Community may even refer to society as a whole—the public. This text uses a specific meaning for *community*.

◆

**Community** refers to the specific geographic area served by a police department or law enforcement agency and the individuals, organizations and agencies within that area.

◆

Police officers must understand and be a part of this defined community if they are to fulfill their mission. The community may cover a very small area and have a very limited number of individuals, organizations and agencies; it may, perhaps, be policed by a single officer. Or the community may cover a vast area and have thousands of individuals and hundreds of organizations and agencies and be policed by several hundred officers. According to Goldstein (1990, p. 25), the police tend to use the word *community* to "describe those affected in any way by the specific problems they are attempting to address, or the program being launched in response to the problem." *Understanding Community Policing* (1994, p. 14) stresses:

Although the delivery of police services is organized by geographic area, a community may encompass widely diverse cultures, values, and concerns, particularly in urban settings. A community consists of more than just the local government and neighborhood residents. Churches, schools, hospitals, social groups, private and public agencies, and those who work in the area are also vital members of the community. In addition, those who visit for cultural or recreational purposes or provide services to the area are also concerned with the safety and security of the neighborhood. Including these "communities of interest" in efforts to address problems of crime and disorder can expand the resource base of the community.

In addition, police are recognizing more and more that community is more than a bond created by geography, but includes people with common interests across a wide geographic area and are also directing efforts toward these groups.

In a more philosophical sense, according to Manning (1991, p. 33): "'Community' represents a sense of integration that people wish, hope, and envision as being a central part of their collective lives." Where such integrated communities exist, people share a sense of ownership and pride in their environment. They also have a sense of what is acceptable behavior, which makes policing in such a community much easier. As noted by Mastrofski (1991, p. 49):

> A basis for police action requires that a group of people—say a neighborhood—shares a definition of what constitutes right order, threats to it, and appropriate methods for maintaining it. To the extent that community implies a basis for citizens to work collectively with police to restore and preserve order, it also requires a sense of group identity or attachment— a "we-ness" derived from shared experience and integration.

◆

Community also refers to a sense of integration, a sense of shared values and a sense of "we-ness."

◆

According to Seagrave (1996, p. 3): "Community is associated with warm, positive ideas."

Klockars (1991, pp. 247–48) suggests: "Sociologically, the concept of community implies a group of people with a common history, common beliefs and understandings, a sense of themselves as 'us' and outsiders as 'them,' and often, but not always, a shared territory."

Unfortunately, many communities lack this "we-ness." In such areas, the police and public served have a "them v. us" relationship. As noted by Goldstein (1990, p. 25): "Areas of cities requiring the most police attention are usually those with few shared values and little sense of community."

Skogan (1996, p. 31) cautions: "Above all, police and citizens may have a history of not getting along with each other. Especially in disadvantaged neighborhoods, there too often is a record of antagonistic relationships between residents and the police, who may be perceived as arrogant, brutal, and uncaring—not as potential partners."

In such communities, disorder and crime may flourish. In a classic article, "Broken Windows," Wilson and Kelling (1982, p. 31) contend:

> Social psychologists and police officers tend to agree that if a window in a building is broken *and is left unrepaired,* all the rest of the windows will soon be broken. This is as true in nice neighborhoods as in run-down ones. Window-breaking does not necessarily occur on a large scale because some areas are inhabited by determined window-breakers whereas others are populated by window-lovers; rather, one unrepaired broken window is a signal that no one cares, and so breaking more windows costs nothing. (It has always been fun.)

*The broken window that remains unfixed gives the impression that no one cares. Crime is likely to flourish in such an environment.*

◆

The **broken window phenomenon** suggests that if it appears "no one cares," disorder and crime will thrive.

◆

Wilson and Kelling based their *broken window* theory, in part, on research done in 1969 by a Stanford psychologist, Philip Zimbardo. Zimbardo arranged to have a car without license plates parked with its hood up on a street in the Bronx and a comparable car on a street in Palo Alto, California. The car in the Bronx was attacked by vandals within ten minutes, and within twenty-four hours it had been totally destroyed and stripped of anything of value. The car in Palo Alto sat untouched. After a week Zimbardo took a sledgehammer to it. People passing by soon joined in, and within a few hours that car was also totally destroyed. According to Wilson and Kelling (p. 31): "Untended property becomes fair game for people out for fun or plunder, and even for people who ordinarily would not dream of doing such things and who probably consider themselves as law-abiding."

Broken windows and smashed cars are very visible signs of people not caring about their community. Other less subtle signs include unmowed lawns, piles of accumulated trash and graffiti.

When considering community policing, it is imperative to determine if a sense of "we-ness" and ownership exists in the community. Establishing police-community partnerships is a challenge because, as Mastrofski (p. 65) stresses, the police face a continuous struggle with "the dilemmas of governing communities that are, in fact, complex, ambiguous, diverse, and highly stratified."

This challenge is also emphasized by Weisburd and McElroy (1991, pp. 100–01): "The community is often identified as a resource waiting to be mobilized. Yet, as our findings suggest, community policing police officers are often confronted with settings of severe social disorganization. Such disorganization is not easily transformed into the kind of community organizations envisioned by the community policing philosophy."

It is extremely difficult to maintain community policing when the values of groups within a given area clash. For example, controversy may exist between gay communities and orthodox Christian or Jewish communities in the same area. Do each of these communities deserve a different style of policing based on the "community value system"? Do "community" police officers ignore behavior in a community where the majority of residents approve of that behavior, but enforce sanctions against the same behavior in enclaves where that behavior causes tension? These are difficult ethical questions.

Another factor that negates a sense of community is the prevalence of violence. We live in a violent society. The United States was born through a violent revolution. The media emphasizes violence, constantly carrying news of murder, rape and assault. It seems that if a movie or television program is to succeed, at least three or four people must meet a violent death or suffer some physical injury. The average cartoon that children watch contains more violence than most adults realize. Children learn that violence is acceptable and justified under some circumstances. It is not surprising that violent crimes are increasing more quickly than the size of the population. Citizens expect the police to prevent such violence, but the police cannot do it alone. Individuals must come together to help stop violence and in so doing can build a sense of community.

Saville (1996, p. 1) describes a theory called the "ecology of crime" which explains how criminal opportunities are created in neighborhoods. He suggests that every neighborhood has a crime "threshold" (p. 7): "The basic idea is that just like a natural ecosystem, a neighborhood has the capacity to hold only a certain number of things. Add too many and the system will collapse because it exceeds its carrying capacity."

This is close in concept to the "tipping point" described by Gladwell (1996). The tipping point is that point at which an ordinary, stable phenomenon can turn into a crisis. He uses the analogy of a health epidemic, which he stresses is a nonlinear situation, that is, small changes can have huge effects and large changes can have small effects—in contrast to linear situations where every extra increment of effort will produce a corresponding improvement in result. He uses as another example, the experience of pouring ketchup:

> Like all children encountering this problem for the first time [pouring ketchup], I assumed that the solution was linear; that steadily increasing hits on the base of the bottle would yield increasing amounts of ketchup on the other end. Not so, my father said, and he recited a ditty that, for me, remains the most concise statement of the fundamental nonlinearity of everyday life: "Tomato ketchup in a bottle—None will come and then the lot'll."

How does this relate to neighborhoods? Gladwell (1996, p. 5) explains that this principle of nonlinearity can be applied to the phenomenon of "white flight":

> A racist white neighborhood, for example, might empty out when blacks reach 5 percent of the population. A liberal white neighborhood, on the other hand, might not tip until blacks make up 40 or 50 percent.

Communities need to recognize when they are approaching the "tipping point" or the "threshold" in a given situation. In addition to understanding the complex concept of community, it is also important to assess the demographics of the area.

## COMMUNITY DEMOGRAPHICS

**Demographics** refers to the characteristics of the individuals who live in a community.

◆

Demographics includes a population's size, distribution, growth, density, employment rate, ethnic makeup and vital statistics such as average age, education and income.

◆

Although people generally assume that the smaller the population of a community, the easier policing becomes, this is not necessarily true. Small communities generally have fewer resources. It is also difficult to be the sole law enforcement person being, in effect, on call twenty-four hours a day. A major advantage of a smaller community is that people know each other. A sense of community is likely to be greater in such communities than in large cities such as Chicago or New York.

When assessing law enforcement's ability to police an area, density of population is an important variable to consider. Studies have shown that as population becomes more dense, people become more aggressive. In densely populated areas, people become more territorial and argue more frequently about "turf."

Rapid population growth can invigorate a community, or it can drain its limited resources. Without effective planning and foresight, rapid population growth can result in serious problems for a community, especially if the population growth results from an influx of immigrants or members of an ethnic group different from the majority in that area.

The community's *vital statistics* are extremely important from a police-community partnership perspective. What is the average age of individuals within the community? Are there more young or elderly individuals? How many single parent families are there? What is the divorce rate? What is the common level of education? What is the dropout rate? What is the ratio of blue collar to professional workers in the community? How does the education of those in law enforcement compare? What is the percentage of latchkey children? Such children may pose a significant challenge for police.

Income and income distribution are also important. Do great disparities exist? Would the community be described as affluent, moderately well-off or poor? How does the income of those in law enforcement compare? Closely related to income is the level of employment. How much unemployment exists? How do those who are unemployed exist? Are they on welfare? Do they commit crimes to survive? Are they homeless?

The ethnic makeup of the community is another consideration. Is the community basically homogeneous? A **homogeneous** community is one in which people are all quite similar. A **heterogeneous** community, in contrast, is one in which individuals are quite different from each other. Most communities are heterogeneous. Establishing and maintaining good relations among the various subgroups making up the community is a challenge. Usually one ethnic subgroup will have the most power and control. Consider the consequences if a majority of police officers are also members of this ethnic subgroup.

The existence of *ghettos* in many of our major cities poses extreme challenges for law enforcement. A **ghetto** is an area of a city usually inhabited by individuals of the same race or ethnic background who live in poverty and, to outsiders, apparent social disorganization. According to Pace (1991, p. 43): "Since ghettos house more than 70% of racial or ethnic minorities, the ghetto, minorities, and crime become interrelated and are the focus for most of the anti-crime efforts of the criminal justice system." This is often perceived as a clear bias by law enforcement against members of racial or ethnic minorities.

Poverty, unemployment, substandard housing and inadequate education have all figured into theories on the causes of crime. They are often part of the underlying problems that are manifested in crime.

*Hungry ghetto-dwellers search through trash bags for food on West Houston Street in New York City.*

## A RAPIDLY CHANGING POPULATION

Communities have been undergoing tremendous changes in the past quarter century.

> People of different races, cultures, and languages are coming into closer contact with each other and enormous demands are being made on their understanding and tolerance. Forecasters expect that by the end of the decade, less than 50 percent of the population of the United States will be white. . . .

> North America is faced with uncertain economies, overburdened social services and declining educational standards at a time when increasingly complex technology demands greater knowledge and sophistication. There are widening class divisions, more broken families and homelessness, growing anger on the part of the disadvantaged, a rise in violent crime and the unpredictable destruction of the international terrorist to contend with (Inkster, 1992, p. 28).

In addition, as noted by McCord and Wicker (1990, p. 30): "The United States is becoming a bifurcated society with more wealth, more poverty, and a shrinking middle class. The gap between the 'haves' and the 'have nots' is widening."

Trojanowicz and Carter (1990, pp. 6–11) note the following changes in the United States and predict they will continue:

- White dominance will end; minorities will increase.
- The elderly population will increase.
- The number of legal and illegal immigrants will increase.

United States Census Bureau projections suggest that non-Hispanic whites will account for only about half of the U.S. population by the middle of the next century. In addition, the past decade has had an estimated 23 percent increase in the number of Americans aged 65 and older. Further, the growing number of both legal and illegal immigrants "flooding into this country," say Trojanowicz and Carter (p. 6), "are of different races, ethnic groups, religions, and cultures. Many do not have even a rudimentary knowledge of the English language." They conclude (p. 11): "Today's challenge is to find new ways for law enforcement to contribute to make the United States a place where all people have an equal chance to secure a piece of the American dream for themselves and their children."

Challenges raised by dealing with members of minority groups, the elderly and immigrants are discussed in detail in Section 2.

In addition, twentieth century sociologists have been describing for decades either the loss or the breakdown of "community" in modern, technological, industrial, urban societies such as ours. Proponents of community policing in some areas may be missing a major sociological reality—the absence of "community"—in the midst of all the optimism about police playing a greater role in encouraging it.

*Understanding Community Policing* (1994, p. 3) notes: "The social fabric of our country has changed radically. The family unit is not as stable as it once was. Single working parents find it extremely difficult to spend enough time with their children, and churches and schools have been unable to fill this void. Immigrants, ethnic groups, and minorities, while adding to the diverse nature of American communities, often have different interests and pursue disparate goals."

## ORGANIZATIONS AND INSTITUTIONS

In addition to understanding the demographics of the community and being able to relate to a great variety of individuals, police officers must also be knowledgeable of the various organizations and institutions within the community and establish effective relationships with them. Brown (1990, p. 8) stresses that effective policing "requires the involvement of agencies other than the police—social services, education, clinics, businesses, employment offices, trash collection—anyone involved in community service."

As noted by Hubert Williams, President of the Police Foundation (1990, p. iv): "A strong network of community organizations and institutions contributes to a system of shared values that does not tolerate criminal behavior. This type of cohesiveness encourages the cooperation of citizens in ways that engender crime control and increase the likelihood that the commission of illegal acts will be detected."

✦

Organizations and institutions can play a key role in enhancing community safety and quality of life.

✦

Sulton (1990, p. 3) stresses that: "Community institutions are the basic fabric from which our complex society is woven." Thus, it is society itself that encourages or discourages conditions related to crime. According to Sulton (p. 1):

All theories of causes of crime share common threads. They assume that crime is a socially defined phenomenon caused by the failure of community institutions to constrain behavior so that it conforms to the law and does not threaten the rights, safety, and lives of others. According to this perspective, crime reduction depends on eradication of the social conditions that produce crime.

A good relationship between the schools in the community and the police is vital to maintaining order. Other organizations and institutions that police officers should interact effectively with include the Department of Human Services, health care providers, emergency services providers and any agencies working with youth. Communities may also have libraries, museums and zoos that would welcome a good relationship with the police. Such cooperation often poses problems, however, as noted by Wilson and Kelling (1989, p. 52):

The problem of interagency cooperation may, in the long run, be the most difficult of all. The police can bring problems to the attention of other city agencies, but the system is not always organized to respond. In his book *Neighborhood Services,* John Mudd calls it the "rat problem": "If a rat is found in an apartment, it is a housing inspection responsibility; if it runs into a restaurant, the health department has jurisdiction; if it goes outside and dies in an alley, public works takes over." A police officer who takes public complaints about rats seriously will go crazy trying to figure out what agency in the city has responsibility for rat control and then inducing it to kill the rats.

In other words, if responsibility is fragmented, little gets accomplished.

## THE PUBLIC-PRIVATE POLICING INTERACTION

A good relationship between the private security industry and the police is also becoming more important. As noted by Trojanowicz and Bucqueroux (1990a, p. 131): "Almost invisibly, private for-profit and nonprofit corporations have been assuming roles that were once almost exclusively the province of the public criminal justice system." They caution that many businesses are turning to private security for their protection and ask: "Does this portend a future where those who have the option choose to ignore the public police in favor of hiring private firms to provide them as much help as they want and can afford?"

Cameron (1991, p. 1) describes the phenomenal growth of the private security industry:

> According to a new study by the National Institute of Justice, private security already outspends public law enforcement by 73%—and employs two and a half times the workforce, and is expected to increase even more over the next decade. The facts are, spending for private security is $52 billion vs. our $30 billion. And private security agencies employ 1.5 million people vs. our estimated 600,000. The average annual rate of growth in private security is predicted to be 8%, double that of public law enforcement.

◆

Private policing has two and one-half times the workforce of public policing and outspends law enforcement by 73 percent.

◆

Many communities and even police departments are using **privatization,** contracting with private security agencies or officers to provide services typically considered to be law enforcement functions. Examples of privatization include prisoner transport and prisoner housing. Many police departments are also relinquishing responsibility for responding to home security alarms to private security firms.

The number of false alarms generated by private alarm systems is staggering and severely depletes the resources of many police departments. Jones (1991, p. 24) suggests that the Philadelphia experience proved the usefulness of having private alarm companies respond to most such alarms.

> The Central Police Division has enlisted the support of all those in the private security industry in central Philadelphia—uniformed and non-uniformed security, guards and officers, the hotel industry, alarm companies and the Building Owners and Managers Association. The Philadelphia Parking Association has also joined the Security Watch program. . . .
>
> As a result, tangible gains have been made in reducing violent crime, decreasing calls for service involving order-maintenance problems and identifying and eliminating repeat unfounded alarms.
>
> The private security sector and the Philadelphia Police Department have formed a true partnership to establish and maintain order in the Center City area.

The need for public and private police forces to establish good working relationships was recognized by the National Institute of Justice in the early 1980s when it began urging cooperation between the agencies and established the Joint Council of Law Enforcement and Private Security Association.

*Using multi-image closed-circuit TV sets, a security guard monitors a large high-tech manufacturing facility in Irving, California. Security officers can serve as additional eyes and ears for the police department.*

Unfortunately, as noted by Mangan and Shanahan (1990, p. 19): "Police have traditionally viewed private security employees as inadequately trained and ill-paid individuals who could not find other work but were nevertheless allowed to carry a gun." Derogatory names such as "rent-a-cop" and "cop-in-a-box" contribute to this negative perception of private security. Despite this image, Mangan and Shanahan contend: "Private security has emerged as a major player in the safeguarding of Americans and their property." They call for a "growing partnership between police professionals and private security specialists in a highly technical and changing environment."

## THE POWER STRUCTURE

Most communities have both a formal and an informal power structure.

◆

The **formal power structure** includes divisions of society with wealth and political influence such as federal, state and local agencies and governments, commissions and regulatory agencies.

◆

*This group of New York City planners is part of the city's power structure.*

The public can usually readily identify the formal power structure. Often policy decisions made at the federal and state level directly affect local decisions. In addition, federal and state funding can directly influence local programs.

◆

The **informal power structure** includes religious groups, wealthy subgroups, ethnic groups, political groups and public interest groups.

◆

The public cannot as readily identify the informal power structure. The informal power structure includes banks, real estate companies and other large and influential businesses in a community.

The informal power structure is not merely a few people controlling the masses; rather, the control groups are entire subcultures that influence other subcultures. It has been alleged that four hundred families control the wealth of the United States. Every other subculture is directly affected by this small subgroup (Pace, 1991, p. 121).

Awareness of the way informal groups, especially wealthy and political groups, exercise their ideologies is important for the community relations functionary. The way in which informal group pressure is forced into the formal structure of an organization is a key to understanding why the community at large is often in conflict with the criminal justice system (Pace, pp. 123–24).

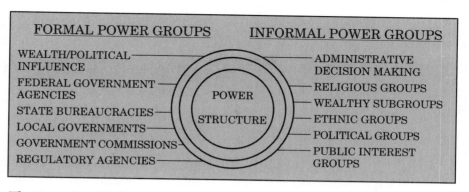

*Figure 2.1*    **The Formal and Informal Power Structure**

SOURCE: Denny F. Pace. *Community Relations Concepts.* Incline Village, Nev.: Copperhouse
Publishing Company, 1991: 116. Reprinted by permission.

Wilson and Kelling (1982, p. 34) suggest: "The essence of the police role in
maintaining order is to reinforce the informal control mechanisms of the community itself. The police cannot, without committing extraordinary resources,
provide a substitute for that informal control."

The formal and informal power structure is illustrated in Figure 2.1.

Law enforcement personnel must understand the different subgroups within
their jurisdiction and the power struggles that occur among them. Pace (p. 34)
suggests: "While democracy may promise equality, the reality is that the majority demands conformity." He further notes: "The reality is that most cultures do
not readily adapt to the white, middle-class style of living," but in most communities that is where the power lies.

Each community is a distinct social system and, as such, has certain elements that cause and influence needs and affect ways in which needs are served
and problems are solved. The elements of a community social system include
the following:

- *Goals, ends and objectives.* What members of the community social system
  expect to accomplish or gain from being a part of the system.

- *Norms.* The written and unwritten rules that describe what is socially
  acceptable and what is not.

- *Status roles.* The expectations for the various positions that exist in the
  system, including perceptions of employment and family roles of men
  and women.

- *Power.* Control over people or resources. In a community social system
  different types and levels of authority and influence affect how the system
  operates.

- *Social rank.* The subtle and not-so-subtle rankings of worth attached to individuals in the system, often based on wealth, education, church affiliation and group membership.
- *Facilities and resources.* The means available to a system for use in attaining its ends.

## THE CRIMINAL JUSTICE SYSTEM

Most people will equate policing or law enforcement with the criminal justice system when, in fact, it is only one part of this system. The other two components, courts and corrections, are much less visible in most communities.

◆

The three components of the criminal justice system are law enforcement, the courts and corrections.

◆

Law enforcement is only one segment of the vast criminal justice system which includes the courts and corrections. Because the police are the most visible component of the system, they often become *the* criminal justice system in the eyes of the community.

Many people have a limited understanding of the role the courts and corrections play in crime control. When the perception or the reality is that criminals are not being convicted or are being released early from prison, some people demand more police and ask why they are not doing "their job."

Members of the law enforcement community typically become frustrated and confused by such incidents. Officers become cynical and wonder why they work so hard to make arrests when they see cases dismissed or plea bargained. Officers may also become frustrated when those who are convicted are given a light sentence or perhaps even probation.

Most officers know many career criminals whose behavior has not improved even after they have been through prison, probation, parole, halfway houses and rehabilitation programs. At times various components of the criminal justice system seem to work against each other. It is important, however, to remember that law enforcement is only one part of the criminal justice process.

In the criminal justice process it is the task of the police to receive reports of, or on their own initiative to detect, law violations, to apprehend those reasonably believed to be responsible for such violations, and to present those apprehended before a court of law for a determination of guilt or innocence. The court, through a time-honored procedure, weighs the charge and the evidence as presented both by an officer of the court who represents the people of the community and by an officer of the court who represents the person accused. If found to be guilty of the charge, the accused either is sentenced by

*A witness gives testimony in a criminal trial as the court reporter makes a verbatim record.*

the court to a term of confinement in a county or state (or, in the case of violations of federal statutes, a federal) facility or is permitted to return to the community under close, formal supervision (Garmire, 1989, pp. 22–23).

This system is a "carefully contrived procedure of checks and balances, designed to ensure that no person is accused of a crime and subsequently deprived of freedom of movement without every reasonable step being taken to guarantee fairness and equity in the process" (Garmire, p. 23). In other words, these checks and balances are consistent with and are provided to assure fairness and equity through the "due process" and "equal protection" clauses.

Those who become critical of judges usually do so based on whether they agree with a judge's procedures and sentencing practices. Critics should remember that the system is designed to work the way it does. After all, if we assumed that everyone arrested by the police is guilty of a crime, there would be no need for prosecutors, judges, juries or courtrooms. The accused could be taken directly to prison.

According to Pace, the public has a negative opinion of the courts because of their failure to process cases promptly, their inconsistency in plea bargaining and the long tenure accorded to judges. Many believe that the courts provide "assembly-line" justice, and the legal process is filled with delays. Pace (p. 133) notes: "Justice is an abstraction that may be given a person if he or she is affluent enough to hire the right attorney and outlast the system."

Aspects of the correctional system that have impeded good public relations include failures to reform offenders, the early release of prisoners who are recidivists and the growing prison population. What constitutes good criminal justice administration and a good court system is open to debate. Many issues related to the effectiveness of the criminal justice system are controversial and will affect police-community partnerships. Although many issues are outside police officers' appropriate sphere of action, they affect the system as a whole. Therefore, police officers need to be aware of these issues and their potential impact on the profession.

✦

Controversial issues in the criminal justice system that affect police-community partnerships include plea bargaining, diversion, sentencing, rehabilitation, community alternatives to prisons, victim's rights and capital punishment.

✦

*Plea Bargaining.* **Plea bargaining** is a practice by which prosecutors charge a defendant with a less serious crime in exchange for a guilty plea, thus eliminating the time and expense of a trial.

*Diversion.* **Diversion** is a system operating in most states that "diverts" juvenile status offenders and delinquents from the jurisdiction of the courts, whenever possible. This practice evolved because once juvenile delinquents are labeled they tend to act out and perpetuate that negative role.

*Sentencing.* Judges often have considerable discretion in sentencing. When the community perceives sentences as too lenient, it sparks controversy. Police officers often believe that sentences are too light for serious crimes.

*Rehabilitation.* One objective of the correction process is rehabilitation, an objective that many have come to believe is an unattainable goal. The **recidivism,** or repeat offense rate of criminal behavior, is very high. Greenfeld (1992, p. xvi) reports on a study on prisoners released in 1988. The prisoners were followed for three years. After three years 63 percent had been rearrested for felonies or serious misdemeanors.

*Community Alternatives to Prison.* Among the alternatives to prison are community supervision programs, including probation or parole, halfway houses and house arrest. Community supervision is a method of helping offenders become productive, law-abiding members of the community while not adding to the overcrowding of our correctional facilities and the expense of incarceration. These alternatives become especially controversial when a community must determine the location of the facilities. Citizens often have the **NIMBY syndrome,** that is, "not in my backyard."

*Victim's Rights.* As violent crime increases, a growing number of people are protesting the treatment of victims by the criminal justice system. The law enforcement community has responded to this protest in a number of ways. Interacting with victims is the focus of Chapter 12.

*Capital Punishment.* The debate continues on the merits and effectiveness of capital punishment as a deterrent to crime and a form of retribution.

Another controversial issue in the criminal justice system is that it has concentrated its efforts on fighting crime to keep the "public peace." Many perceive police officers as armed social workers.

> It is hard to understand why the American criminal justice system has concentrated its efforts almost solely upon the recognition of individual crimes and the discovery of specific procedures and policies to eliminate each crime. The system has been remiss in developing methods that attack the syndromes of crime (Pace, 1991, p. 5).

A **syndrome of crime** is a group of signs, causes and symptoms that occur together to foster specific crimes. The syndromes of crime are central to problem-solving policing, discussed in detail in Chapter 4.

Another shift within the criminal justice system has been a shift in basic philosophy from a *medical model* to a *justice model.*

◆

The **medical model** sees those who break the law as victims of society; the **justice model** views lawbreakers as responsible for their own actions.

◆

No longer will society take the blame for individual criminals. Justice is served by having individuals be responsible for their own actions and suffer the consequences when they break the law. This change in philosophy is likely to enhance relations between those in the criminal justice system and law-abiding citizens.

A relatively new approach being taken by some in the criminal justice system is that of *restorative justice.* Robinson (1996, p. 6) explains:

> Restorative justice is based on an ancient form of justice that traces its roots to the Code of Hammurabi in 2000 B.C. It holds the offender accountable—not to the state but to the victim who has been harmed and to the community that has been disrupted. Restorative justice seeks not to punish for punishment's sake but to right the wrong, to repair the damage to the extent possible, and to restore both the victim and the community.

◆

**Restorative justice** advocates a balanced approach to sentencing that involves offenders, victims, local communities and government to alleviate crime and violence and obtain peaceful communities.

◆

Table 2.1 summarizes the difference between the traditional retributive approach to justice and restorative justice.

*Table 2.1*    **Paradigms of Justice—Old and New**

| Old Paradigm Retributive Justice | New Paradigm Restorative Justice |
|---|---|
| 1. Crime defined as violation of the state | 1. Crime defined as violation of one person by another |
| 2. Focus on establishing blame, on guilt, on past (did he/she do it?) | 2. Focus on problem solving, on liabilities and obligations, on future (what should be done?) |
| 3. Adversarial relationships and process normative | 3. Dialogue and negotiation normative |
| 4. Imposition of pain to punish and deter/prevent | 4. Restitution as a means of restoring both parties; reconciliation/restoration as goal |
| 5. Justice defined by intent and by process: right rules | 5. Justice defined as right relationships; judged by the outcome |
| 6. Interpersonal, conflictual nature of crime obscured, repressed; conflict seen as individual vs. state | 6. Crime recognized as interpersonal conflict; value of conflict recognized |
| 7. One social injury replaced by another | 7. Focus on repair of social injury |
| 8. Community on sidelines, represented abstractly by state | 8. Community as facilitator in restorative process |
| 9. Encouragement of competitive, individualistic values | 9. Encouragement of mutuality |
| 10. Action directed from state to offender: <br> • victim ignored <br> • offender passive | 10. Victim and offender's roles recognized in both problem and solution: <br> • victim rights/needs recognized <br> • offender encouraged to take responsibility |
| 11. Offender accountability defined as taking punishment | 11. Offender accountability defined as understanding impact of action and helping decide how to make things right |
| 12. Offense defined in purely legal terms, devoid of moral, social, economic, political dimensions | 12. Offense understood in whole context—moral, social, economic, political |
| 13. "Debt" owed to state and society in the abstract | 13. Debt/liability to victim recognized |
| 14. Response focused on offender's past behavior | 14. Response focused on harmful consequences of offender's behavior |
| 15. Stigma of crime unremovable | 15. Stigma of crime removable through restorative action |
| 16. No encouragement for repentance and forgiveness | 16. Possibilities for repentance and forgiveness |
| 17. Dependence upon proxy professionals | 17. Direct involvement by participants |

SOURCE: Howard Zehr. *IARCA Journal* (March 1991): 7. Used by permission of the International Association of Residential and Community Alternatives.

# CITIZEN/COMMUNITY INVOLVEMENT

Once upon a time, when food resources in a village were seemingly gone, a creative individual—knowing that each person always has a little something in reserve—proposed that the community make *stone soup*.

After the stone was set to boil, people in the community were asked if they had "just a little something" to improve the soup. One person found a carrot, another brought a few potatoes, another a bit of meat and so on. When the soup was finished, it was thick and nourishing.

Such is the situation in our communities today. Because resources are stretched to the limit, we tend to hold on to our time, talent or money. These self-protective actions leave most groups without enough resources to effectively handle community problems. Perhaps it is time to adopt the "stone soup" stance of cooperation!

As noted in *Understanding Community Policing* (1994, p. 4): "Community policing is democracy in action. It requires the active participation of local government, civic and business leaders, public and private agencies, residents, churches, schools and hospitals. All who share a concern for the welfare of the neighborhood should bear responsibility for safeguarding that welfare."

Givens (1993, p. 6) observes that the most likely areas police might expect immediate citizen involvement include:

- Crime prevention information requests that most likely will increase.
- Good Samaritan requests—flat tire, car trouble, etc.
- Lost and found property.
- Missing children.

◆

Citizen/community involvement has taken the form of civilian review boards, crime watch programs and citizen police academies.

◆

## Civilian Review Boards

"Civilian Review Boards (CRBs), intended to boost public confidence in the process of investigating complaints made by citizens against police, are an increasingly visible feature on the American law enforcement landscape," according to *Law Enforcement News* ("Police Increasingly Face. . . ." April 15, 1991, p. 7). The article quotes Samuel Walker, criminal justice professor at the University of Nebraska, Omaha, who predicts that "increased public attention on police brutality and misconduct because of the videotaped beating of motorist Rodney King by Los Angeles police will result in the establishment of still more civilian review boards."

In a survey of the fifty largest cities in the United States, 60 percent had some form of civilian review (Brown, 1991, p. 6). In contrast, a survey of chiefs of police in towns with populations of 25,000 or less showed that 79 percent did not have such boards and do not want them (Sharp, 1990, p. 98).

Supporters of civilian review boards believe it is impossible for the police to objectively review actions of their colleagues. They emphasize that the police culture demands that police officers support each other, even if they know something illegal has occurred.

Opponents of civilian review boards stress that civilians cannot possibly understand the complexities of the policing profession and that it is demeaning to be reviewed by an external source. As noted by Sharp (1990, p. 6): "People unfamiliar with police procedures can be stumbling blocks to harmonious civilian-police relations. . . . As most police administrators would agree, their jobs are tough enough without having the additional burdens of civilian review boards looking constantly over their shoulders."

Civilian review boards may be good in theory, but are often poor in reality. Pace (1991, p. 250) suggests two problems with citizen review boards:

> The first problem was that the persons who were pushing for representation on the board were not representative of the community. They were generally the vocal rabble rousers who wished to impose their values upon the community. The second difficulty was, they were operating in a legal vacuum. They could make recommendations, but no one had authority to carry out their decisions. . . .
>
> Theoretically, the Citizen Review Board is an ideal vehicle to seek out misdeeds and to reconcile them to the satisfaction of the community at large. In practice, they do not function with objectivity, they do not have impartial or specialized investigators to conduct necessary investigations, and they have no power to carry out their decisions.

Civilian review boards are one of the most controversial issues in police work today. Most departments handle officer discipline internally. Complaints against officers are investigated by department personnel who determine whether misconduct occurred.

Police maintain it would be unfair to allow those outside police work to judge their actions, because only police officers understand the complexities of their job and, in particular, how and when force must be used. They stress that few citizens understand such concepts as "command presence" and "verbal force" so often necessary in high-risk encounters. As one police sergeant put it: "The public should walk a mile in our combat boots before they judge us."

Citizens who demand to be involved in the review process maintain that internal police discipline is tantamount to allowing the "fox to investigate thefts in the chicken coop." According to these citizens, police protect each other and cover up improper or illegal conduct. Citizens believe that this perpetuates abuses and sends a message to brutal officers that their behavior will be shielded from public scrutiny.

In some larger cities, police have lost the power to investigate complaints against fellow officers. The trend is toward more openness and citizen involvement in these matters. Officers should assume that they will be required to be more accountable for their actions. Officers may be held to a higher standard and will need to be prepared to justify their use of force in certain situations.

Successful resolution of this issue requires that the concerns of both the community and the police are addressed. The desired outcome would be that the police maintain the ability to perform their duties without the fear that they will be second-guessed, disciplined or sued by those who do not understand the difficulties of their job, *and* that citizens are not brutally or disrespectfully treated by officers.

## Citizen Patrol

As Murphy (1995, p. 8) says: "Community policing . . . is based on the reality that the police depend upon the eyes, ears, information and influence of the public to exert social control."

Nonetheless, as Harman (1996, p. 44) suggests: "It has not been easy for the volunteers to win the respect and support of the average police officer. Officers have definite ideas about civilians involving themselves in what they see as 'police business.'" Harman also notes: "Our experience shows that all it takes for an officer to become a champion of the program [citizens' crime watch] is for the volunteers to effectively provide information that leads to an arrest."

The Fort Worth Police Department has instituted a citizen patrol program called Code Blue. Windham and Ely (1994, p. 52) describe the program's major goals:

- To reduce crime, with a specific focus on violent crime.
- To improve the quality of life for all citizens.
- To increase direct citizen involvement in crime prevention efforts.
- To involve children in crime prevention and self-esteem development efforts.
- To become a focal point through which other crime prevention programs could be developed and promoted to the public.

## Police Citizen Academies

Another type of community involvement is through citizens' police academies, a relatively recent innovation designed to familiarize citizens with law enforcement and to keep the department in touch with the community. For example, the Farmington (Connecticut) Police Department established such an academy in 1993 designed to accomplish two ends (Enns, 1995, p. 133):

First, it improved communication with the community and served as a valuable problem-solving resource. Second, it gave individuals who have the potential to influence public opinion an appreciation for the challenges facing law enforcement.

The Minneapolis Police Department's Citizens' Academy was established as "a way to offer residents and business owners a peek into the world of law enforcement—one filled with split-second decisions that are often misunderstood by the public" (Graves, 1995, p. B1).

The San Luis Obispo County Sheriff's Citizen Academy provides community members with an inside look at the sheriff's office, law enforcement ethics, criminal law, investigations, patrol procedures, communications, crime prevention, drug enforcement and drug education.

A twist on the citizens' academy is the Teen Citizen Academy of the Arroyo Grande Police Department. Designed for youth thirteen to eighteen years of age, the academy provides an overview of topics such as gangs, drugs, weapons safety and personal safety.

## SUMMARY

Community policing must begin with an understanding of what communities are and how they function. Citizens of the United States have established the "public peace" through the U.S. Constitution and Bill of Rights, as well as through federal and state statutes and local ordinances. They also adhere to a social contract. The social contract states that for everyone to receive justice, each person must give up some freedom.

*Community* refers to the specific geographic area served by a police department or law enforcement agency and the individuals, organizations and agencies within that area. Community also refers to integration, shared values and a sense of "we-ness." The broken window phenomenon suggests that if it appears "no one cares," disorder and crime will thrive.

Understanding a community requires police to know about its demographics. Demographics includes population or size, distribution, growth, density and vital statistics such as average age, average education, average income as well as employment rate and ethnic makeup. Three important changes that will alter the demographics of our communities are: (1) white dominance will end; minorities will increase, (2) the elderly population will increase, and (3) the number of legal and illegal immigrants will increase.

Organizations and institutions can play a key role in enhancing community safety and quality of life. The private security industry can also play an important role in improving a community's well-being. Private policing has two and a half times the workforce of public policing and outspends law enforcement by 73 percent.

Operating within each community is a power structure that can enhance or endanger police-community relations. The formal power structure includes those with wealth and political influence: federal, state and local agencies and governments, commissions, regulatory agencies and power groups. The informal power structure includes religious groups, wealthy subgroups, ethnic groups, political groups and public interest groups.

Also operating within communities and affecting the police-community relationship tremendously is the criminal justice system. The three components of the criminal justice system are law enforcement, the courts and corrections. Controversial issues in the criminal justice system that affect community policing include plea bargaining, diversion, sentencing, rehabilitation, community alternatives to prisons, victim's rights and capital punishment. The criminal justice system is moving away from a medical model of criminality to a justice model. The medical model sees those who break the law as victims of society; the justice model views lawbreakers as responsible for their own actions.

Restorative justice advocates a balanced approach to sentencing that involves offenders, victims, local communities and government to alleviate crime and violence and obtain peaceful communities. Other forms of citizen/community involvement include civilian review boards, crime watch programs and citizen police academies.

## Discussion Questions

1. How would you describe your community?
2. What instances of *broken windows* have you seen in your neighborhood? Other neighborhoods?
3. Can you give examples of the NIMBY syndrome?
4. What major changes have occurred in your community in the past ten years? In your state?
5. Who is included in the power structure in your community?
6. Do you favor the medical model or the justice model for dealing with criminals? Why?
7. How extensively are the services of private security used in your community? Do they cooperate with or compete against the local police?
8. Do you favor use of civilian review boards? Why or why not?
9. Which seems more "just" to you: retributive justice or restorative justice?
10. What factors are most important in establishing a "sense of community"?

## References

Brown, Lee P. "The Civilian Review Board: Setting a Goal for Future Obsolescence." *The Police Chief.* (July 1991): 6.

Brown, Lee P. "The Police-Community Partnership." *The Police Chief.* (December 1990): 8.

Cameron, Bruce W. "Goodbye Cops—Hello Security Officers?" *Law and Order.* (December 1991): 1.

"Census Bureau Predicts Large Scale Changes in U.S. Population's Makeup." (Minneapolis/ St. Paul) *Star Tribune.* (March 25, 1996): A5.

Enns, Tracy. "Citizens' Police Academies: The Farmington Experience." *The Police Chief.* (April 1995): 113–35.

Garmire, Bernard L. (ed.) *Local Government Police Management.* 2nd rev. ed. Washington, D.C.: Published for the Institute for Training in Municipal Administration by the International City Management Association, 1989.

Givens, Greg. "A Concept to Involve Citizens in the Provision of Police Services." *American Journal of Police.* (Vol. XII, No. 3, 1993): 1–9.

Gladwell, Malcolm. "The Tipping Point." *Subject to Debate.* (October 1996): 1, 4–6, 11.

Goldstein, Herman. *Problem-Oriented Policing.* New York: McGraw-Hill Publishing Company, 1990.

Graves, Chris. "Understudying a Difficult Role." (Minneapolis/St. Paul) *Star Tribune.* (April 5, 1995): B1, B3.

Greenfeld, Lawrence A. *Prisons and Prisoners in the United States.* Washington, D.C.: Bureau of Justice Statistics, April 1992.

Harman, Alan. "Citizens' Crime Watch." *Law and Order.* (December 1996): 41–44.

Inkster, Norman D. "The Essence of Community Policing." *The Police Chief.* (March 1992): 28–31.

Jones, Lee A. "The Alarm Industry: Friend or Foe to Police Officers?" *The Police Chief.* (August 1991): 24–27.

Klockars, Carl B. "The Rhetoric of Community Policing." In *Community Policing: Rhetoric or Reality,* edited by Jack R. Greene and Stephen D. Mastrofski, 239–58. New York: Praeger Publishing, 1991.

Mangan, Terence J. and Shanahan, Michael G. "Public Law Enforcement/Private Security: A New Partnership?" *FBI Law Enforcement Bulletin.* (January 1990): 18–22.

Manning, Peter K. "Community Policing as a Drama of Control." In *Community Policing: Rhetoric or Reality,* edited by Jack R. Greene and Stephen D. Mastrofski, 27–45. New York: Praeger Publishing, 1991.

Mastrofski, Stephen D. "Community Policing as Reform: A Cautionary Tale." In *Community Policing: Rhetoric or Reality,* edited by Jack R. Greene and Stephen D. Mastrofski, 48–67. New York: Praeger Publishing, 1991.

McCord, Rob and Wicker, Elaine. "Tomorrow's America: Law Enforcement's Coming Challenge." *FBI Law Enforcement Bulletin.* (January 1990): 28–32.

Murphy, Patrick V. "Community Policing: The Only Proper Policing Method in a Free Society." *Law and Order.* (January 15, 1995): 8, 11.

Pace, Denny F. *Community Relations Concepts.* Incline Village, Nev.: Copperhouse Publishing Company, 1991.

"Police Increasingly Face Public Scrutiny Through Civilian Review Boards." *Law Enforcement News.* (April 15, 1991): 7, 11.

Robinson, Laurie. "Linking Community-Based Initiatives and Community Justice." *National Institute of Justice Journal.* (August 1996): 4–7.

Saville, Gregory. "Searching for a Neighborhood's Crime Threshold." *Subject to Debate.* (October 1996): 1, 7.

Seagrave, Jayne. "Defining Community Policing." *American Journal of Police.* (Vol. XV, No. 2, 1996): 1–22.

Sharp, Arthur G. "Civilian Review Boards May Be a Thing of the Past." *Law and Order.* (September 1990): 97–100.

Skogan, Wesley G. "The Community's Role in Community Policing." *National Institute of Justice Journal.* (August 1996): 31–34.

Sulton, Anne Thomas. *Inner-City Crime Control. Can Community Institutions Contribute?* Washington, D.C.: The Police Foundation, 1990.

Trojanowicz, Robert and Bucqueroux, Bonnie. "The Privatization of Public Justice: What Will It Mean to Police?" *The Police Chief.* (October 1990): 131–35.

Trojanowicz, Robert C. and Carter, David L. "The Changing Face of America." *FBI Law Enforcement Bulletin.* (January 1990): 6–11.

*Understanding Community Policing.* Washington, D.C.: Bureau of Justice Assistance, August 1994.

Weisburd, David and McElroy, Jerome E. "Enacting the CPO Role: Findings from the New York City Pilot Program in Community Policing." In *Community Policing: Rhetoric or Reality,* edited by Jack R. Greene and Stephen D. Mastrofski, 89–101. New York: Praeger Publishing, 1991.

Williams, Hubert. Preface. In *Inner-City Crime Control. Can Community Institutions Contribute?* Washington, D.C.: The Police Foundation, 1990, iv.

Wilson, James Q. and Kelling, George L. "Making Neighborhoods Safe." *The Atlantic Monthly.* (February 1989): 46–52.

Wilson, James Q. and Kelling, George L. "The Police and Neighborhood Safety: Broken Windows." *The Atlantic Monthly.* (March 1982): 29–38.

Windham, Thomas R. and Ely, Randy P. "Code Blue: Citizens on Patrol." *The Police Chief.* (May 1994): 52–54.

*Chapter 3*

# The Police

*The strength of a democracy and the quality of life enjoyed by its citizens are determined in large measure by the ability of the police to discharge their duties.*
—Herman Goldstein

## Do you know

- How the makeup of the police force has changed in recent years?
- What characteristics are attributed to the police subculture? Which is the dominant characteristic?
- Where the police image comes from?
- What a negative contact is?
- What the public expects of the police?
- What dilemma faces law enforcement?
- What police spend the majority of their time doing?
- When officers or agencies exercise discretion?
- How discretion fits into the community policing philosophy?
- What three ethics checks are?

## Definitions

Can you define these terms: discretion, negative contacts, paradox, selective enforcement.

# *Introduction*

Although "police officers" are the professionals discussed in this chapter, the concepts reviewed apply equally to police with different titles such as deputies or sheriffs. While this chapter focuses on police officers as professionals, always remember that police officers are first and foremost individuals. They are sons, daughters, mothers, fathers, brothers, sisters, aunts, uncles, neighbors and friends. They may belong to community organizations. They may attend local churches. They may be active in politics. Their individual attributes have a great influence on who they are as police officers.

This chapter begins by describing who the police are and some characteristics of their subculture. This is followed by a discussion of the police image and public expectations of the police. Next the two sometimes conflicting roles of law enforcement and service to the public are examined. Then the role of police discretion and use of force are discussed. The chapter concludes with an examination of ethics and policing.

## WHO ARE THE POLICE?

Traditionally, police officers were a fairly homogeneous group: white, male, with a high school education and a military background. This has changed; police officers have become a more heterogeneous group.

◆

Today police departments have more minority and female officers. The educational level of the officers is much higher, and fewer have military experience. Police also are as interested in helping people as they are in fighting crime.

◆

As noted by VanBlaricom (1989, p. 7): "The bright, well-educated, and (at least initially) service-oriented young men and women who are recruited into police departments today want to do something about crime besides taking reports of it."

Such changes in the makeup of the police force are fundamental to the community policing philosophy. As police departments become more representative of the communities they serve, they will be better able to understand the problems they must address. As officers become better educated, they will be better equipped to devise solutions to community problems.

Although the makeup of the police force has changed considerably, police officers still have several things in common that affect how they perceive themselves and their role in society.

## THE POLICE SUBCULTURE

The police are a distinct subgroup in their community. They have tremendous power over the citizens they serve and protect. They may face a life-threatening situation at any time. Their lives may depend on each other. They experience situations others would not be likely to understand. As a result, they have developed their own subculture or value system. According to Goldstein (1990, pp. 29–30):

> The strength of the subculture grows out of the peculiar characteristics and conflicting pressures of the job: the ever-present physical danger; the hostility directed at the police because of their controlling role; the vulnerability of police officers to allegations of wrongdoing; unreasonable demands and conflicting expectations; uncertainty as to the function and authority of officers; a prevalent feeling that the public does not really understand what the police have to "put up with" in dealing with citizens; a stifling working environment; the dependence that officers place on each other to get the job done and to provide for their personal safety; and the shared sense of awareness, within a police department, that it is not always possible to act in ways in which the public would expect one to act.

In addition, police work is often unpleasant. Police often have to deal with ugly situations and antisocial behavior. Police are lied to, spit upon and sworn at. They see unspeakable atrocities. Because of their shared experiences and unique exposure to their community, many police officers develop negative characteristics as coping mechanisms.

Ortiz and Peterson (1994, p. 70) list the following attributes of the police subculture:

Adherence to SOPs

Conformity

Discipline

Elitism

Formal interoffice memos

Inflexible organization

Interest in technology

Interest in weaponry

Lateral transfers

Maintenance of distance from citizens

Militarism

Negative perception of innovation

Numerous meetings

Organization as family

Organizational loyalty to employees

Orientation toward sworn officers

Physical fitness

Recruit training

Reluctance to share credit for results

Selective recruitment

Specialized police language

Territorialism

Union strength

Cynicism is a characteristic frequently associated with police officers. Pitter (1994, p. 57) explains:

> Police officers tend to be cynics, a trait that is acquired over the years as a result of numerous stressors that affect the officers' disposition. Distorted accounts of police events by the news media, the constraints of fiscal austerity, unfavorable court decisions, outdated equipment, a perceived lack of appreciation, the adverse effects of shift work on the lifestyle of the officer and his family, inadequate reward and reinforcement systems, increased workloads and the lack of job security all contribute to a growing sense of cynicism.

Conroy and Hess (1992) describe the responses police officers in a large metropolitan police force gave to the question: "What price did you pay to become a police officer?" The "prices" of becoming an officer are often described as characteristics of the police subculture.

◆

The police subculture has been characterized as including a loss of innocence, cynicism, loneliness, isolation and a constricted and inappropriate affect.

◆

Police officers have described each characteristic as follows:

- *Loss of Innocence.* I never in a million years would have guessed there was so much violence, so much sadness, so much bitterness, so much anger, so much ugliness out there. It was beyond my comprehension. I would not have guessed it existed to the extent it does. (p. 81)

- *Cynicism.* I can take this uniform off and put it in my locker when I go home, but I've only got one brain. It's the brain I brought with me the first day I came to work, and it's the same brain I got everyday. I don't trust you because you might hurt me. I don't trust you because you're standing out in front of that store because you're a lookout. You're a bad guy until

I know otherwise. That's what I learned, and for the last twenty-eight years that's what I've practiced. (p. 95)

- *Loneliness.* I am the loneliest man in the world, the loneliest man in the world. I still had friends, still had people that cared for me, but I was lonely. Nobody was in there with me where it was really terrible. (p. 107)
- *Isolation.* I wasn't close to anybody because I saw myself being in a situation where nobody knew what it was like for me and nobody would understand even if I told them. I thought I was pretty different in my pain and agony. I wasn't close to anybody now that I think about it. (p. 117)
- *Constricted and Inappropriate Affect.* You're required to be very cool and calculating when you dispense your emotions. You can't do it impulsively. I would have a calculated response to any occurrence. (p. 131)

A recurrent theme among the officers interviewed was the inability of the public to understand the police role and a tremendous reliance on the "police family." Social inbreeding often occurs when police families sometimes limit their socializing to other police families and, thus, gain constant reinforcement for their beliefs. In such situations, they are not usually exposed to ideas and opinions different from their own.

◆

Two dominant characteristics of the police subculture are isolation and a "them v. us" world view.

◆

This "them v. us" mentality can also be seen in the phenomenon of police solidarity. As Winfree et al. (1996, p. 26) suggest: "Solidarity, or fellowship arising from common responsibilities and interest, is a common feature of many occupational subcultures. However, there is an unusually high degree of social cohesiveness and solidarity among police officers."

The isolation experienced by police is enhanced by the emphasis on patrolling in squad cars. As Conroy and Hess (1992, p. 121) note: "As you drive around in your squad car with the windows up, in the winter to stay warm, in the summer to stay cool, you are isolated in your 'cocoon.' Cocoons, however, serve not only to isolate caterpillars as they change to butterflies, but to protect them from predators as well."

Such isolation and "them v. us" world view conflicts with a community-oriented philosophy of policing. Unfortunately, as Ortiz and Peterson (1994, p. 68) note: "The irony of culture is that, like the air people breathe, its powerful effects normally escape the attention of those it most affects."

As communities move toward a return to foot patrol and to an emphasis on improving police-community relations, police isolation and their world view is likely to change.

Having looked at how the police often see themselves, now focus on how the public often views the police.

*A police sergeant takes time to gather his thoughts after the successful conclusion of a hostage shootout.*

## THE POLICE IMAGE

How does the public view the police?

- The handsome, fashionable, invincible undercover cops of *Miami Vice?*
- The laid-back, bumbling police department of Mayberry and its two officers, Andy Griffith and Don Knotts?
- Unselfish, fearless heroes who protect the weak and innocent? Dirty Harrys?
- Hard-hearted, brutal oppressors of the underclass?
- Corrupt abusers of power, who become part of the criminal world?

Our society has varied images of law enforcement professionals. As noted in Chapter 1, that image is greatly affected by how the public perceives the criminal justice system within which the police function. Many Americans believe in an ideal justice system in which fairness and equality are guiding principles; truth and justice prevail, and the accused is innocent until proven guilty. Law enforcement professionals are part of this idealized vision; many view police officers and sheriff's deputies as unselfish, fearless, compassionate protectors of the weak and defenseless, who can uncover the truth, bring the guilty to justice and make things "right."

In contrast, others in our society see a criminal justice system that is neither fair nor just. Some individuals point out that the system employs officers who are overwhelmingly white, middle-class males. They also believe that some officers abuse their power and, in some cases, also abuse those with whom they come in contact in the line of duty.

Walchak (1996, p. 7) cites the annual Gallup Poll which rates the honesty and ethical standards of more than two dozen occupations. He notes that police officers have rated in the top seven for the past sixteen years, along with members of the clergy and medical doctors. Referring to the Gallup Poll, Walchak notes: "Americans asked to express their confidence in public institutions ranked the police number two—right behind the military and ahead of the church, the Supreme Court, newspapers, Congress and big business."

A national survey conducted in 1993 by Mark Clements Research ("Criminal Justice Survey," 1993, p. 53) posed the question: "In general, do you have a positive or a negative attitude towards the police?" The response was 82 percent positive, 18 percent negative. And this was well after the highly publicized Rodney King incident. Those who responded positively gave the following reasons for their attitude:

- 34.1 percent—Tough job/They do their best
- 17.4 percent—They're here to help/protect
- 16.0 percent—Overall they are fair/good people
- 10.7 percent—Never/rarely had bad experience with them

Those who responded negatively gave these reasons for their attitude:

- 23.4 percent—Misuse others
- 12.9 percent—Their attitude towards others
- 11.0 percent—They are racist/prejudiced
- 9.1 percent—Police brutality

In response to the question, "How often do you think the police use excessive force when arresting?" the responses were: 18.1 percent frequently; 79.6 percent occasionally; and 2.3 percent never. To the question, "Have there been instances of police brutality in your community?" 28.7 percent responded "yes," and 71.3 percent responded "no."

## Sources of the Police Image

An individual's opinion of the police is based on many factors. Among the factors that contribute to the police image are television programs, movies, newspapers, magazines, books, the opinions of friends and family, your education, where you live, your economic status, whether you are handicapped, your sex, whether you are a member of a minority group and, most importantly, your contact with the criminal justice system.

◆

The police image is affected by individual backgrounds, the media and personal experiences with the criminal justice system.

◆

The media has an enormous impact on public opinion. The police image is affected by the manner in which television and newspaper stories present crime and law enforcement activities. Improving police-media relations is the focus of Chapter 13.

An additional source of the police image is the folklore surrounding citizen interaction with police. People tend to embellish their contacts with the police. In addition, many stories people tell about contacts with the police are actually not theirs, but a contact that a friend of a friend had. Unfortunately, few, if any, of these stories can be traced to their origin, but in the meantime, police end up with a negative image. Further, police seldom run in the same social circles where the stories are recounted and, therefore, have no means of defending themselves, their coworkers, their departments or their actions.

## Police Work Contributes to the Police Image

Police officers are charged with some of society's most distasteful and dangerous tasks and are allowed to use reasonable force to affect arrests. The nature of police work and the power they are legally permitted to use make the police extremely powerful. This contributes to their image.

According to Greene and Mastrofski (1991, p. 192): "In a society aspiring to achieve peace by peaceful means where that is not always possible, the police have been given the responsibility to use force and violence." The inherently negative associations coupled with the use of force are stressed by Klockars (1991, p. 240): "The police are not only fundamentally and irreconcilably offensive in their means to the core cultural aspiration of a modern society [using force to achieve peace], but an ever present reminder that all of these noble institutions, which should make it possible for citizens to live in nonviolent relations with one another and with the state, often come up very short."

*The police uniform with its badge, patches and gunbelt conveys authority.*

◆

The police image is also shaped by police actions and appearance.

◆

As Sheehan (1994, p. 19) stresses: "The image projected by a police officer is an important part of that officer's power and authority." Pilant (1992, p. 37) also notes: "Image can be everything in the law enforcement business. An officer who looks like an unmade bed does not present a reassuring, authoritative image to a recently burglarized homeowner or a stranded motorist."

The police image is also affected by the police uniform and equipment. The uniform most police officers wear is a very visible reminder of the authority and power bestowed upon police. In fact, officers know that the uniform plays a major part in their ability to gain cooperation and compliance from the public.

Much of their authority comes simply from what they are wearing. People recognize and react to visible symbols of authority.

The uniform and its trappings—patches, badges, medals, mace, nightsticks, handcuffs and guns—can be overwhelmingly intimidating and can evoke negative public responses. Reflective sunglasses and handcuff or gun tie tacks can add to this negative image.

The manner in which police exercise their authority also has an impact on the police image. The attitude of law enforcement officers, their education, their personal image of policing, discipline, professionalism and interaction with the community have enormous impact on the public's perception of the police.

Seemingly innocent and humorous police novelty items have caused major confrontations between police and the communities they serve. Some police product companies produce calendars, posters, T-shirts and mugs that support, encourage and make light of police brutality. Almost always meant to be humorous, the public may not share the same sense of humor. Such items can be immensely destructive to police-community relations. Particularly offensive examples include slogans such as "Brutality, the fun part of police work" and takeoffs on the Dirty Harry line, "Go ahead, make my day."

A few years ago, a black suspect died in police custody as the result of a carotid hold applied by police officers during a struggle. In response to the black community's anger and concern, the chief of police issued an order prohibiting the carotid hold. Already in severe conflict with their chief over several other issues, two officers produced and sold T-shirts within the department that said, "Don't choke'em, smoke'em." The T-shirts went on sale the day of the suspect's funeral. It is not difficult to understand how destructive this was to the police image and community relations in that city as well as in other cities where the media reported these events.

In contrast with this unfortunate incident is the Hug-O-Bear Program which many departments now use. Plush teddy bears are used to calm traumatized children officers encounter in the course of fulfilling their duties. The bears, sometimes donated to the department by community organizations, are often carried in patrol cars and have been invaluable at accident scenes, in child abuse situations and at the scene of fires. Programs such as this can reduce the effect of *negative contacts* people may have with the police.

## Negative Contacts

Another factor that contributes to the police image and the difficulty in maintaining good community relations is what police commonly refer to as negative contacts.

◆

**Negative contacts** are unpleasant interactions between the police and the public. They may or may not relate to criminal activity.

◆

While officers have many opportunities to assist citizens, much of what they must do causes people unhappiness. Many people have police contact only when something goes wrong in their lives. Citizens commonly interact with the police when they:

- Receive a traffic citation.
- Have an illegally parked vehicle towed.
- Have a loud party terminated.
- Have been victimized.
- Discuss a child who is in trouble with the law.
- Have a domestic "disagreement" broken up.
- Are arrested for driving while intoxicated (DWI) or some other offense.
- Receive a death notification.

Many more possible scenarios in which citizens become angry or disillusioned occur daily because of the actions police officers must take to perform their duties.

For the most part, the police have no way to eliminate negative contacts and still perform their duties. A major challenge of law enforcement is to build good community relations despite the often adversarial nature of the job. The fact that many negative contacts take place between police and noncriminal individuals, the so-called "average citizen," makes the task especially difficult.

## PUBLIC EXPECTATIONS

Otherwise law-abiding citizens who receive traffic tickets or who are arrested for DWI often believe they should be excused and that the police should concentrate on "real" criminals. Most police officers feel that citizens want the law enforced to the letter *except* when it comes to themselves.

The public often demands that the police crack down on crime, on drunk drivers and even on traffic violations. For many police departments, the majority of their complaints involve traffic problems. Citizens often demand that police enforce speed laws near their homes. Inevitably, when the police respond by issuing citations to violators, some of those who want the laws to be strictly enforced are ticketed; they often feel betrayed and angry. Somehow, they see their own violation of the speed law as different from that of "teenagers" or "outsiders," and they feel they deserve "a break." Most police officers have been asked, "Why don't you spend your time catching real criminals instead of picking on citizens?"

◆

People expect the law to be enforced, except when enforcement limits their behavior.

◆

Citizens become incensed when crime flourishes. They hold the police responsible for combatting crime. As noted by Wadman and Olson (1990, p. 27) there is a "dichotomy of the police being held responsible for crime but having little or no authority over its causes." According to Kelling (Morrow, 1991, p. 17): "The terms 'war on crime' and 'war on drugs' encourage and even demand an all-out attack by police upon criminals—no holding back, no quarter given. But like American soldiers in Vietnam, the police are fighting an unwinnable war, assuming large social responsibilities that belong more to politicians than to policemen."

◆

The police are placed in the dilemma of being expected to win the wars on crime and drugs but are given no control over the causes of these problems. The police cannot win these wars.

◆

This view is also held by Klockars (1991, p. 244):

The fact is that the "war on crime" is a war police not only cannot win, but cannot in any real sense fight. They cannot win it because it is simply not within their power to change those things—such as unemployment, the age distribution of the population, moral education, freedom, civil liberties, ambitions, and the social and economic opportunities to realize them—that influence the amount of crime in any society. Moreover, any kind of real war on crime is something no democratic society would be prepared to let its police fight. We would simply be unwilling to tolerate the kind of abuses to the civil liberties of innocent citizens—to us—that fighting any kind of a real war on crime would inevitably involve.

In addition, when citizens have a problem, they expect the police to help resolve it. In fact, police sociologist Egon Bittner (1974) states that we have police for just that reason—because *"something-ought-not-to-be-happening-about-which-something-ought-to-be-done-NOW!"* Klockars (1985, p. 16) notes that Bittner purposely did not refer to the situation as *illegal* because the police are called upon in many situations that do not involve an illegality. Bittner left the purpose of police involvement wide open: *something ought to be done.*

◆

People also expect the police to help them when they have a problem or when someone else is causing a problem.

◆

The *NOW* portion of Bittner's explanation refers to the police's unique ability to use force to correct a situation. How and when police actually use force is discussed later in this chapter.

Public expectations and the expectations of those in law enforcement are often at odds. Even within agencies police disagree about what their primary focus should be.

# LAW ENFORCEMENT V. SERVICE TO THE PUBLIC

Police departments are often divided on whether their emphasis should be proactive or reactive. Wilson and Kelling (1989, p. 52) reported on a study conducted by the Police Foundation which found that in every department they visited those who were incident-oriented (reactive) spoke "disparagingly of the problem-oriented officers as 'social workers'; some of the latter responded by calling the former 'ghetto blasters.'"

Is the best police officer the one who catches the most "bad guys"? Certainly police departments will continue to apprehend the "bad guys." The crimes they target may, however, contribute to negative police-community relations. The police usually focus on certain kinds of crime, particularly common crimes such as burglary, robbery, assault and auto theft. The police expect that offenders who commit these crimes might flee or try to avoid arrest in some other way. Police may need to use force to bring the offender to justice.

Police officers generally do *not* enforce white-collar crimes. They would not, for example, investigate or arrest a businessperson for insider trading, price fixing or cheating on income taxes. According to Garmire (1989, p. 8):

> Police noninvolvement in most crimes committed in connection with the conduct of business, in the practice of a profession, or in politics seems to be based on a policy choice that, even though not always articulated, is commonly understood among police agencies. According to this understanding, the police have refrained from developing enforcement capacities in these areas of criminal conduct because special enforcement agencies were created when the various crimes were defined in legislation.

White-collar crime involves those who are in business, the professions or public life—those who tend to be relatively well-to-do, powerful people.

Common crimes could conceivably be committed by anyone, rich or poor. The vast majority of these crimes, however, are committed by those from society's lowest socioeconomic level. Those at or near the poverty level include the majority of our minority populations.

As noted by Klockars (1985, p. 57), since the police officers' domain is the streets: "Those people who spend their time on the street will receive a disproportionate amount of police attention. . . . particularly people who are too poor to have backyards, country clubs, summer homes, automobiles, air conditioning, or other advantages that are likely to take them out of the patrolman's sight."

These facts contribute to the *impression* that the police are focused solely on the kind of crime poor people and minorities commit, hence, the *impression* that they are hostile to those who are poor or members of minority groups. This negative impression does little to foster good community relations.

Police work involves much more than catching criminals. It is a complex, demanding job requiring a wide range of abilities. Studies suggest that 80 percent

*A NYC officer taking childrens' fingerprints at a rural hospital "Health Fair" (Northern Dutchess).*

of police officers' time is spent on nonpunitive activities (Pace, 1991, pp. 20–21). According to Klockars (1985, p. 103): "Over 90 percent of all the problems police attend to are in response to citizen requests for service."

◆

The majority of police actions have nothing to do with criminal law enforcement, but involve *service* to the community.

◆

Service to the community includes:

- Peacekeeping.
- Preventing suicides.
- Looking for lost or runaway children or vulnerable adults.
- Protecting children and other vulnerable people.
- Maintaining public safety.
- Assisting motorists with disabled vehicles.
- Dealing with emergencies and crisis situations—accidents and natural disasters.
- Delivering death notifications.

- Resolving conflicts.
- Preventing crime.
- Educating the public.

In fact, defining exactly what police work entails is almost impossible. Most would agree, however, that people have always called the police for help. They call not only about criminal matters, but also about a myriad of situations where they perceive a need for government intervention. The police respond to such calls and usually take whatever action is needed.

It has been said that the police are the only social service agency available twenty-four hours a day, seven days a week, and they make house calls. What is reasonable to expect of them? One way to clarify the focus of a police department is for the department to adopt a clearly articulated mission statement.

## POLICE DISCRETION

According to Goldstein (1993, pp. 1–2): "The police have tremendous power—to deny freedom and to use force, even to take a life. Individual officers exercise enormous discretion in using their authority and in making decisions that affect our lives."

Police *do* have broad discretionary powers to enforce the law. Each agency exercises discretion when it establishes its mission, policies and procedures. Each officer exercises discretion when deciding whether to issue citations or make arrests when laws are violated. Klockars (1985, p. 93) provides a comprehensive definition of police discretion.

◆

A police officer or police agency may be said to exercise **discretion** whenever effective limits on his, her or its power leave the officer or agency free to make choices among possible courses of action or inaction.

◆

Officers make those choices based on a variety of reasons such as:

- Is there evidence to prove a violation in court?
- Will a good purpose be served by arrest or citation, or is police contact sufficient to end the violation?
- What type of crime and suspect is involved?
- What circumstances exist at the time?

Officers would probably not arrest a stranded motorist in a blizzard who, in danger of freezing to death, breaks into an alarmed commercial building. Nor

*Officers lead an arrested suspect to jail. Being arrested can change a person's life dramatically.*

would they be likely to arrest a driver who develops chest pain and breathing difficulty and drives through a stop sign in an attempt to maneuver off the road. In these cases the value of police discretion, or **selective enforcement,** is clear. It makes sense to most people not to enforce the letter of the law.

Police discretion also poses a problem for police, however, because citizens know that the officer can act subjectively. The person an officer tickets or arrests may feel discriminated against. The public is also concerned that discretion gives the police too much freedom to pick and choose when and against whom they will enforce the law. Citizens worry that discretion allows the police too much room to discriminate against some and overlook the violations of the wealthy and powerful.

Police agencies and officers have broad discretion in deciding which laws to enforce, under which circumstances and against whom. Some people believe the law should be enforced consistently and in every instance. Most officers, however, believe that such police action would soon be unacceptable, far too harsh and virtually impossible.

The police are not the only players in the criminal justice system to exercise discretion. Prosecutors exercise discretion when determining priorities for prosecution and in plea negotiations. Judges exercise discretion in sentencing, preliminary hearings and exclusionary rulings. Parole boards, parole officers, probation officers, corrections officials and prison guards all exercise discretion.

## Reasons for Police Discretion

Police departments are bureaucracies subject to rules and regulations that may contribute to irrational and inappropriate behavior. Such regulations limit an officer's ability to use common sense or act in a humane way in certain situations. Such limitations subject the officer to critical media coverage and adverse public opinion. For example, the police strictly upheld the law and towed a car containing a crying and screaming paraplegic girl because the vehicle was parked fifteen minutes too long in a restricted zone. Millions of Americans and Canadians viewed this episode on national television.

Discretion is necessary for a number of reasons:

- The statute books are filled with archaic or ambiguous laws.
- Some laws are almost never enforced and no one expects them to be.
- There are not enough police to act on every violation. They must select which laws they will enforce.
- Police prioritize the offenses they act upon: crime is of more concern than a violation of a regulation and serious crime is a greater threat than minor crime. The police act accordingly.
- Discretion is important to maintaining good community relations. If the police were to enforce the letter of the law, community resentment would soon follow. The police need community support if they are to succeed.
- Community standards influence how the police enforce laws. In most urban areas, significant changes have occurred in the past several years in the enforcement of drunk driving laws. Now violators are routinely arrested and charged; the police rarely overlook this kind of violation.

Morrison (1992, p. 100) notes: "Vague or ambiguous laws which regulate moral conduct standards too strictly for a majority of the community are another reason for officer discretion." He also notes that: "Discretion can be an effective tool of behavior modification. An untold number of juveniles have been turned around by a sympathetic cop who gave them a break. When used this way, it's good for the police image, too."

## Changes in Police Discretion

Law enforcement has responded to an increased public awareness of the dangers of tolerating drunk driving. Agencies, as well as individual officers, have a mandate from the public to strictly enforce DWI laws. Police discretion in this area is limited.

Similar changes have occurred in other areas as well. The public has ceased tolerating crimes that occur among family members. Once among the laws that the public knew the police would not enforce, many police strictly uphold laws against spouse beating and the physical and sexual abuse of children. Again, a significant change in police discretion has occurred in this area.

Community policing has also had a great impact on police discretion. According to Pratt (1992, p. 99): "Increasingly, police officers are being trusted to use good judgment on the streets in everyday enforcement activities while being subjected to ever-fewer limits and restricting rules. In effect, officers are increasingly being allowed to approach true 'professionalism.'"

◆

Community policing emphasizes wider use of officer discretion.

◆

In *Terry v. Ohio* (1968), the Supreme Court recognized the role that discretion plays in policing. As noted by Pratt (1992, p. 99), recent court decisions have continued this perspective, recognizing that police officers possess special training and experience that allow them to exercise "wide discretion" in several areas. Among the views expressed in recent decisions are the following:

- Officers are more knowledgeable than most people about human (particularly criminal) behaviors.
- Since officers wear a badge, the public must consider them honest. Police statements are more likely to be true than those made by a suspect.
- Specialized training and experience enable officers to recognize suspicious behavior not apparent to others.
- Based on training and experience, officers can and should take any action reasonably necessary to investigate suspicious activity.
- Officers are exposed to unusual dangers and must, at all times and under all circumstances, act to protect themselves from harm (Pratt, p. 99).

## The Downside of Police Discretion

Corrupt officers can wield their discretion in an illegal manner to obtain bribes or payoffs. Officers usually work independently without direct supervision and have tremendous power to decide what action they will take, who they will arrest and which laws they will enforce.

A corrupt officer can use his power of discretion to obtain payoffs for favorable treatment. As noted by Pollock-Byrne (1989, p. 83):

Discretion is a good thing and it is a necessary element of the law, but it also leads to a greater dependence on individual ethical standards in place of rules and laws. . . .

Unethical police behavior often arises directly from the power of discretion. Because police officers have the power to select and entrap suspects, they can also make that decision unethically, such as by taking a bribe in return for letting a suspect go. Since they have the power to decide how best to conduct an investigation, they may decide to use this power to entrap and select suspects in a biased or otherwise unfair manner rather than by probable cause.

### Discretion and the Police Image

Unless the police exercise their discretion with care, the community may complain about an actual or perceived abuse of power or discrimination in the way police enforce the law. If the community believes that the police overlook violations committed by a certain segment of society or strictly enforce laws against another, severe community relations problems will develop. As noted by Morrison (1992, p. 100): "The use of discretion by officers in the Jeffrey Dahmer case in Milwaukee resulted in an outpouring of criticism for both police and probation officers."

A police agency's policies, procedures and priorities and the manner in which it equips and assigns its officers indicates how that agency will exercise discretion. Individual officers have the greatest amount of discretion. Police officers often work alone, exercising wide discretion in matters of life and death, honor and dishonor in an environment that is tension filled and often hostile. In addition, within the police bureaucracy, discretion increases as one moves down the organizational hierarchy. Thus, patrol officers—the most numerous, lowest-ranking and newest to police work—have the greatest amount of discretion. All officers should be acutely aware of the power they wield and the immense impact the exercise of discretion has on the community and the police-community relationship.

While officers often operate independently, without direct supervision, it is important to remember that the community watches how officers perform their duties. The public notes how and when officers enforce the law. Citizens may form opinions about their police department and about all officers in that department based on an individual officer's actions. Perhaps the most critical discretionary decision an officer can make is when and how much force to use.

## USE OF FORCE

Police officers are trained for, and equipped to, overcome the resistance they can expect to encounter as they perform their duties. As noted by Garmire (1989, p. 8): "The mandate of the police is to deal with all problems in which force may have to be used, regardless of whether the problems arise out of the criminal law or some other context."

Certain types of criminals, usually those who commit common crimes, are likely to evade arrest, and require the police to find and forcibly take them into custody. Police deal with noncriminal situations which can also require overcoming resistance. Suicidal individuals may require forceful intervention. So might out-of-control mental patients.

The use of force by the police encompasses a wide range of possible actions, from the officer's mere presence to the use of deadly force. The police presence affects a majority of citizens. The police uniform and squad cars are symbols of the officer's power to enforce the law and bring violators to justice—by the use of force if necessary. The visual image of power and authority created by the uniform and equipment facilitates the officer's ability to gain public compliance. The police image is also affected, either positively or negatively, by whether a department develops an authority-heavy image. Care must be taken not to develop such an intimidating image that it alienates the community.

Think about extreme examples you have seen of the *intimidating* police image, perhaps in television programs or movies. Items such as mirrored sunglasses, helmets, billy clubs, handcuffs or gun tie tacks, and black leather sap-type gloves are likely to generate negative emotions and contribute to a sense of fear of or anger toward police.

Uniforms convey a message and often elicit a particular response from the public. For example, many officers feel strongly that wearing an American flag patch on the uniform reduces the number of assaults on police officers.

Controversy on the use of force by police is almost always discussed in terms of police brutality. "There is little doubt," says Pace (1991, p. 70), "that brutality is the criminal justice system's number one community relations problem." The nationally televised Rodney King beating certainly added to this perception.

Police brutality is considered a problem by a large segment of the public. The extent of the problem is perceived differently among urban and suburban, rich and poor, and minority and majority populations. There are valid reasons why different people have different perceptions of the problem. One reason is that the job the police are required to do differs from community to community.

First consider that because the police must intervene in crimes where apprehension is likely to be resisted, most of their enforcement efforts are directed toward "common" criminals. In contrast, white-collar criminals are unlikely to flee or resist. They tend to see their situation as a legal dilemma to be won or lost in court. White-collar criminals are relatively wealthy, have a career and have a place in the community; they have too much to lose to simply flee. Since police enforcement efforts focus on common criminals, who are frequently poor, the most use of force by the police will be directed against this part of the population.

Citizens in white suburban areas tend to see the police in different circumstances:

- When they report a crime and have been victimized.
- When they need assistance after an automobile accident, in a medical emergency, when their child is lost or when their car has run out of gas.
- When they have locked themselves out of a car or home—or want their home watched.

In each scenario, the police are there to lend assistance. Citizens in suburban areas may never see a police officer use force. The most negative experience they are likely to have with a police officer is receiving a traffic ticket.

When people from these widely separated communities talk about the police, it seems as though they are speaking of entirely different entities. On the one hand, police may be referred to as brutal, racist aggressors while others describe them as professional, helpful, efficient protectors. Which is the true picture of the police?

While the public has many stereotypes of the police, those stereotypes will be shattered or reinforced each time a citizen has personal contact with a police officer. Each individual police contact can have a positive or negative impact on police-community relations.

Most citizens understand and support law enforcement officers' obligation to enforce the law and to use appropriate force when necessary. All officers have a duty to the profession to encourage public support by professional behavior respectful of each citizen's rights. Sometimes, however, public support of the police does not exist in a community. Lack of support may be the result of the unique characteristics of coercion.

## The Paradoxes of Coercive Power

A **paradox** is a seemingly contradictory statement that may, nonetheless, be true. According to Klockars (1985, pp. 124–31) four paradoxes of coercive power affect policing:

- *The paradox of dispossession:* the less one has, the less one has to lose.
- *The paradox of detachment:* the less the victim cares about preserving something, the less the victimizer cares about taking it hostage.
- *The paradox of irrationality:* the more delirious the threatener, the more serious the threat; the more delirious the victim, the less serious the threat.
- *The paradox of face:* the nastier one's reputation, the less nasty one has to be.

**The Paradox of Dispossession.** This paradox suggests that the police have the most power over those who have the most to lose, usually people in the middle and upper classes who are afraid to lose their material possessions, careers and reputations. As noted by Klockars (p. 125): "So despite the fact that our possessions, resources, friendships, occupation, reputation, and position in the community appear to give us power to resist being coerced, they actually have the opposite effect." In contrast, "life's losers," those who have little or nothing to lose, cannot be easily coerced. Says Klockars: "To coerce the truly dispossessed, police are inclined to threaten to injure the only hostages that such unfortunate people offer: their freedom, such as it is, and their bodies."

**The Paradox of Detachment.** This paradox is frequently evident in domestic disputes. Things that were once important to those involved in domestic disputes are no longer important. A person's many possessions, career or reputation are of no importance if an officer cannot use them to coerce a violent spouse. In such instances police officers try to "reattach" the person to those possessions. As noted by Klockars (p. 127): "The crucial element is the officer's ability to find something that had once been important to the couple and to talk to them about it in a way that will re-attach them to the value it once had and the hope it represents for the future."

**The Paradox of Irrationality.** In the line of duty, police encounter many people who are so drunk, mentally ill, terrorized or traumatized, that they are, according to Klockars (p. 128), "virtually immune to coercive threats." He notes: "If they are so irrational they cannot comprehend a threat, short of actually using coercive force, they cannot be coerced." In such instances officers seek to make the person more rational. Sometimes, however, this is simply not possible. This paradox has further implications for police officers, notes Klockars (p. 120):

> If police wish to increase their power to coerce rational persons, the paradox of irrationality advises them to appear irrational in their willingness to carry through whatever threats they make. In the paradoxical world of coercive encounters, the police officer who is crazy enough to go any length to carry out a threat (e.g., who is willing to shoot to kill a motorist who refuses to move his car from a no-parking zone) is a police officer any rational person will obey!

This certainly would do little to foster police-community relations, however.

**The Paradox of Face.** Some police officers want to have a reputation for being extremely "tough." As one police officer put it: "I was very aggressive and very by-the-book and got the reputation for being an asshole. And knew it, and it didn't bother me. That was part of the job. It's easier to be known as an asshole than to have to be one" (Conroy and Hess, 1992, pp. 126–27).

With power and the authority to use force comes the responsibility to use that power and force not only legally, but also ethically.

# ETHICAL POLICING

The tremendous power that policing has over people's lives requires that police officers represent good over evil. To maintain the public trust, police must be men and women of good character who hold foremost the ideals of fairness and justice. The manner in which police use their discretion to enforce the law and solve problems will determine whether the public will view the police as ethical.

It is not always clear in many situations what is the ethical way to act. Officers frequently have their decisions reviewed and questioned after a crisis has passed. Unfortunately, the police have often not been given appropriate guidance in ethical decision making. Given the complexities of enforcing the law in a diverse population, it is inadequate to teach rookie officers the technical skills of policing and then send them into the community under the assumption they will do the "right thing."

Perhaps a move toward higher ethical standards is reflected by the decision of many police departments to require their police officers to have a college education. There is an increasing need to begin a dialog within the police community on ethics—what ethical behavior is, and how to achieve it in the profession. Incredibly, a discussion of ethics is not a standard part of the training and education of officers. If a prospective officer has a good record, the department assumes he or she meets ethical standards.

One simple adage, set forth by Blanchard and Peale (1988, p. 9), might serve as a starting point for a discussion on ethics: *"There is no right way to do a wrong thing."* They suggest (p. 20) three questions that can be used as personal "ethics checks."

◆

Three ethics-check questions are:

- Is it legal?
- Is it balanced?
- How will it make me feel about myself?

◆

The first question should pose little problem for most officers. Much time is spent on criminal and constitutional law in most law enforcement programs. The focus of the second question is whether the decision is fair to everyone involved, in the short term and long term. Does the decision create a win-win situation? The third question is perhaps the most crucial. Would you mind seeing your decision published in the paper? Would you feel good if your friends and family knew about your decision?

Blanchard and Peale (p. 79) suggest the following five principles of ethical power for individuals:

- *Purpose.* I see myself as being an ethically sound person. I let my conscience be my guide. No matter what happens, I am always able to face the mirror, look myself straight in the eye, and feel good about myself.

- *Pride.* I feel good about myself. I don't need the acceptance of other people to feel important. A balanced self-esteem keeps my ego and my desire to be accepted from influencing my decisions.
- *Patience.* I believe that things will eventually work out well. I don't need everything to happen right now. I am at peace with what comes my way.
- *Persistence.* I stick to my purpose, especially when it seems inconvenient to do so. My behavior is consistent with my intentions. As Churchill said, "Never! Never! Never! Never give up!"
- *Perspective.* I take time to enter each day quietly in a mood of reflection. This helps me to get myself focused and allows me to listen to my inner self and to see things more clearly.

Ethical behavior by individual officers and by the department as a whole is indispensable to effective police-community partnerships.

## SUMMARY

Today's police departments have changed. They have more minority and female officers. The educational level of the officers is much higher, and fewer have military experience than in years past. Most officers also are as interested in helping people as they are in fighting crime. The police subculture has been characterized as including a loss of innocence, cynicism, loneliness, isolation and a constricted and inappropriate affect. A dominant characteristic of the police subculture is isolation and a "them v. us" world view.

The police image is affected by individual backgrounds, the media and personal experiences with the criminal justice system. It is also shaped by what police do and how they look—their uniform and equipment.

Negative contacts are unpleasant interactions between the police and the public. They may or may not involve criminal activity.

People expect the police to enforce the law, except if it adversely impacts them. People also expect the police to help them when they have a problem.

The majority of police actions do not involve criminal law enforcement, rather they are community-service oriented.

Police use of discretion and force will profoundly affect police-community relations. A police officer or police agency may be said to exercise discretion whenever effective limits on his, her or its power leave the officer or agency free to make choices among possible courses of action or inaction. Community policing emphasizes wider use of officer discretion. Police discretion and authority to use power are balanced by the responsibility to act ethically. Three questions to check police ethical standards are: (1) Is it legal? (2) Is it balanced? and (3) How will it make me feel about myself?

## *Discussion Questions*

1. What is the image of the police in your community? What factors are responsible for this image? Could the police image be made more positive?
2. What expectations do you have of law enforcement agencies?
3. Does police discretion frequently lead to abuse of alleged perpetrators?
4. Are police officers now more violent and less ethical than their predecessors?
5. Does the image of law enforcement affect its ability to get the job done?
6. Why are so many of the characteristics of the police subculture negative?
7. What should be a department's ideal balance between fighting crime and service to the community?
8. Have you witnessed police exercise their discretion? How did it impress you?
9. Can you give examples of each of the four paradoxes of coercive power as they operate in police work?
10. What decisions commonly made by police officers involve ethical considerations?

## *References*

Bittner, Egon. "Florence Nightingale in Pursuit of Willie Sutton: A Theory of Police." In *The Potential for Reform of Criminal Justice,* edited by H. Jacob, 17–44. Beverly Hills: Sage, 1974.

Blanchard, Kenneth and Peale, Norman Vincent. *The Power of Ethical Management.* New York: Fawcett Crest, 1988.

Conroy, Dennis L. and Hess, Kären M. *Officers at Risk: How to Identify and Cope with Stress.* Incline Village, Nev.: Copperhouse Publishing Company, 1992.

"Criminal Justice Survey." *Law Enforcement Technology.* (November 1993): 53.

Garmire, Bernard L. (ed.) *Local Government Police Management.* Published by the International City Management Association, 1989.

Goldstein, Herman. *The New Policing: Confronting Complexity.* Washington, D.C.: National Institute of Justice Research in Brief, December 1993.

Goldstein, Herman. *Problem-Oriented Policing.* New York: McGraw-Hill Publishing Company, 1990.

Greene, Jack R. and Mastrofski, Stephen D. (eds.) *Community Policing: Rhetoric or Reality.* New York: Praeger Publishing, 1991.

Klockars, Carl B. *The Idea of Police.* Newbury Park: Sage Publishing Company, 1985.

Klockars, Carl B. "The Rhetoric of Community Policing." In *Community Policing: Rhetoric or Reality,* edited by Jack R. Greene and Stephen D. Mastrofski, 239–58. New York: Praeger Publishing, 1991.

Morrison, Richard D. "Police Discretion—Can We Afford It?" *Law and Order.* (August 1992): 100.

Morrow, Lance. "Rough Justice." *Time.* (April 1, 1991): 16–17.

Ortiz, Robert L. and Peterson, Marilyn B. "Police Culture: A Roadblock to Change in Law Enforcement?" *The Police Chief.* (August 1994): 68–71.

Pace, Denny F. *Community Relations Concepts.* Incline Village, Nev.: Copperhouse Publishing Company, 1991.

Pilant, Lois. "Enhancing the Patrol Image." *The Police Chief.* (August 1992): 37–61.

Pitter, Gordon. "Police Cynicism in the 1990s." *The Police Chief.* (May 1994): 57–59.

Pollock-Byrne, Joycelyn M. *Ethics in Crime and Justice: Dilemmas & Decisions.* Pacific Grove: Brooks/Cole Publishing Company, 1989.

Pratt, C. E. "Police Discretion." *Law and Order.* (March 1992): 99–100.

Sheehan, Kathy. "Image Projection." *Law and Order.* (April 1994): 19–22.

VanBlaricom, D. P. "Shaking the Pillars of Police Tradition." *Law Enforcement News.* (October 31, 1989): 7.

Wadman, Robert C. and Olson, Robert K. *Community Wellness: A New Theory of Policing.* Washington, D.C.: Police Executive Research Forum, 1990.

Walchak, David G. "Police Image and Ethics." *The Police Chief.* (January 1996): 7.

Wilson, James Q. and Kelling, George L. "Making Neighborhoods Safe." *The Atlantic Monthly.* (February 1989): 46–52.

Winfree, L. Thomas, Jr., Bartku, Gregory M., and Seibel, George. "Support for Community Policing versus Traditional Policing Among Nonmetropolitan Police Officers." *American Journal of Police.* (Vol. XV, No. 2, 1996): 23–50.

# Chapter 4

# Problem-Solving Policing

*A problem well stated is a problem half solved.*
—Charles Kettering

## Do you know

- Who is credited with originating problem-oriented policing?
- How efficiency and effectiveness differ? Which is emphasized by community policing?
- What the first step in Goldstein's problem-oriented policing is?
- What four stages of problem solving are used in the SARA model?
- What three areas problem analysis considers?
- What the magnet phenomenon is?
- What crime-specific planning is?
- What mental locks should be avoided?
- What killer phrases are?

## Definitions

Can you define these terms: creativity, crime-specific planning, decision, effectiveness, efficiency, innovation, killer phrases, magnet address, magnet phenomenon, magnet telephone, mental locks, problem, problem-solving policing.

87

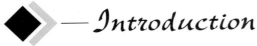

# Introduction

**Problem-solving policing** involves identifying problems and making decisions about how best to deal with them. A **problem** is a deviation from what is desired—a difficulty. A **decision** is a judgment or conclusion. Making a decision is the act of selecting from among alternatives. An all-important first step in community policing is to identify problems in a community.

A basic characteristic of community policing is that it is proactive rather than reactive. This involves recognizing problems and seeking the underlying cause(s) of the problems.

To illustrate, a man and his buddy, who could not swim, were fishing on a riverbank when a young boy floated past, struggling to stay afloat. The fisherman jumped in and pulled the young boy from the water. He resumed his fishing, but within a few minutes another person came floating by, again struggling to stay afloat. Again, the fisherman reacted by jumping in and pulling the person to safety. He then resumed his fishing and again, within minutes, another person came floating by. The fisherman got up and started heading upstream. His buddy called after him, "Where are you going?" To which the fisherman replied, "I'm going to find out who's pushing all of these people into the river!"

It is usually more effective to get to the source of a problem rather than simply reacting to deal with it. This chapter focuses on a problem-solving approach to policing. It begins with an examination of the relationship between community policing and problem solving. Next efficiency and effectiveness are described, followed by an explanation of the importance of addressing substantive problems. Next the four-stage SARA model for problem solving is described. Then problem solving and crime-specific planning are discussed. This is followed by a discussion of common mistakes in problem solving as well as the role of creativity in problem-solving efforts. The chapter concludes with a description of problem solving in policing and the benefits that can result from this approach.

## COMMUNITY POLICING AND PROBLEM SOLVING

Many practitioners equate community policing and problem solving. As noted by Wilson and Kelling (1989, p. 49): "Community-oriented policing means changing the daily work of the police to include investigating problems as well as incidents. It means defining as a problem whatever a significant body of public opinion regards as a threat to community order. It means working with the good guys, and not just against the bad guys." Wilson and Kelling suggest that community policing requires the police mission to be redefined "to help the police become accustomed to fixing broken windows as well as arresting window-breakers."

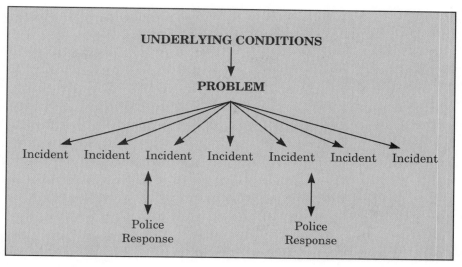

**UNDERLYING CONDITIONS**

↓

**PROBLEM**

Incident   Incident   Incident   Incident   Incident   Incident   Incident

Police
Response

Police
Response

*Figure 4.1*    **Incident-Driven Policing**

SOURCE: John E. Eck and William Spelman. *Problem Solving: Problem-Oriented Policing in Newport News.* Washington, D.C.: Police Executive Research Forum, 1987: 4. © 1987 Police Executive Research Forum. Reprinted with permission by PERF.

The differences between incident-driven, reactive policing and problem-driven, proactive policing are illustrated in Figures 4.1 and 4.2.

As noted by Eck and Spelman (1987, p. xix), the National Institute of Justice requires that problem-solving systems follow five basic principles:

- Officers of all ranks and from all units should be able to use the system as part of their daily routine.
- The system must encourage the use of a broad range of information, including but not limited to conventional police data.
- The system should encourage a broad range of solutions, including but not limited to the criminal justice process.
- The system should require no additional resources and no special units.
- Finally, any large police agency must be able to apply it.

◆

Herman Goldstein is credited with originating problem-oriented policing.

◆

Goldstein's problem-oriented policing (POP) model is a basic component of community policing. Throughout this chapter it will be referred to as a

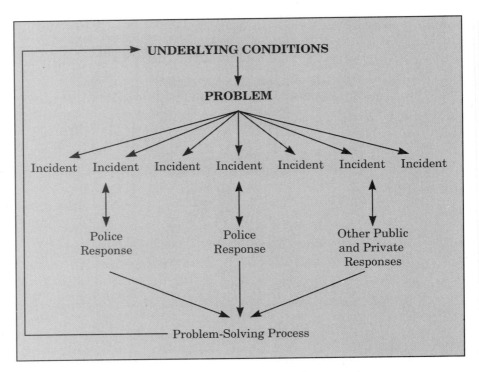

*Figure 4.2*    **Problem-Solving Policing**

SOURCE: John E. Eck and William Spelman. *Problem Solving: Problem-Oriented Policing in Newport News.* Washington, D.C.: Police Executive Research Forum, 1987: 4. © 1987 Police Executive Research Forum. Reprinted with permission by PERF.

problem-solving approach. Community policing combines this problem-solving approach and police/community collaboration.

Goldstein (Rosen, 1997, p. 8) draws a clear distinction between problem-oriented policing and community policing:

> I've always assumed that community policing, and the package of changes commonly conveyed by that term, is designed to place emphasis on one great need in policing, which is to engage the community, to emphasize the point that the job of social control essentially in our society depends upon networks other than the police, that the police can only facilitate those networks and support them. Problem-oriented policing, on the other hand, places the major emphasis on the need to reconceptualize what the police are doing more generally, to focus attention on the wide range of specific problems that police confront and to try to encourage a more analytical approach to those problems. Then, as a result of that analysis, to think through different strategies, one of which is to engage more intensively with the community in the context of dealing with that particular problem. There's a big difference, but I think the difference is primarily in emphasis. We need more engagement

*Calls coming to a 911 dispatcher provide raw data from which problems might be identified.*

in community; we also have a critical need for thinking differently about what the police are expected to do and investing heavily in systematic analysis of the various pieces of police business.

Goldstein (1990, pp. 14–15) cites five concerns that have most strongly influenced the development of problem-oriented policing:

1. The police field is preoccupied with management, internal procedures and efficiency to the exclusion of appropriate concern for effectiveness in dealing with substantive problems.

2. The police devote most of their resources to responding to calls from citizens, reserving too small a percentage of their time and energy for acting on their own initiative to prevent or reduce community problems.

3. The community is a major resource with an enormous potential, largely untapped, for reducing the number and magnitude of problems that otherwise become the business of the police.

4. Within their agencies, police have readily available to them another huge resource: their rank-and-file officers, whose time and talent have not been used effectively.

5.  Efforts to improve policing have often failed because they have not been adequately related to the overall dynamics and complexity of the police organization. Adjustments in policies and organizational structure are required to accommodate and support change.

A problem-solving approach to policing was developed in response to these concerns. The first concern that influenced the development of a problem-solving approach to policing was that of efficiency and effectiveness.

## EFFICIENCY AND EFFECTIVENESS

**Efficiency** involves minimizing waste, expense or unnecessary effort. Efficiency results in a high ratio of output to input. Efficiency is doing things right. **Effectiveness** has to do with producing the desired result or end goal. Effectiveness is doing the right thing. Ideally, both efficiency and effectiveness are present in policing.

◆

Efficiency, doing things right, has been the traditional emphasis in law enforcement. Effectiveness, doing the right things, is the emphasis in community policing.

◆

Unfortunately, too often police departments have emphasized efficiency, for example, rapid response to calls, number of citations issued and the like, rather than what will produce the desired outcomes of the department.

According to Goldstein (p. 32), a problem-solving approach to policing is "a comprehensive plan for improving policing in which the high priority attached to addressing substantive problems shapes the police agency, influencing all changes in personnel, organization, and procedures."

This focus on substantive problems (effectiveness) rather than on the smooth functioning of the organization (efficiency) is a radical change which is difficult for some departments to make. Those departments which have made the shift in focus have accomplished excellent results.

## ADDRESSING SUBSTANTIVE PROBLEMS

Traditionally police have responded to incidents, handled them as effectively as possible and then moved on to the next call. This fragmented approach to policing conceals patterns of incidents that may be symptomatic of deeper problems. Says Goldstein (p. 33): "The first step in problem-oriented policing is to move beyond just handling incidents. It calls for recognizing that incidents are often merely overt symptoms of problems."

*A citizen patrol member calls his volunteer center. Citizens are a major resource, with largely untapped potential to help reduce neighborhood problems.*

◆

The first step in problem solving is to group incidents as problems.

◆

The basic elements in a problem-solving approach combine steps a police department can take and theoretical assumptions to make the steps work. They include the following (Goldstein, pp. 32–49):

- Grouping incidents as problems.
- Focusing on substantive problems as the heart of policing.
- Seeking effectiveness as the ultimate goal.
- Using systematic inquiry.
- Disaggregating and accurately labeling problems.
- Analyzing the multiple interests in problems.

- Capturing and critiquing the current response.
- Adopting a proactive stance.
- Strengthening the decision-making processes and increasing accountability.
- Evaluating results of newly implemented responses.

Many departments have developed problem-solving approaches that incorporate these basic elements.

## THE SARA MODEL: A FOUR-STAGE PROBLEM-SOLVING PROCESS

Eck and Spelman (1987, p. 42) describe the four-stage problem-solving process used in the Newport News Police Department and known as the SARA Model.

◆

The four stages of the SARA problem-solving model are scanning, analysis, response and assessment.

◆

Scanning refers to identifying the problem. Analysis is learning the problem's causes, scope and effects. Response is acting to alleviate the problem, that is, selecting the alternative solution or solutions to try. Assessment is determining if the response worked.

This model is illustrated in Figure 4.3. Beck (1996, p. 9) describes this model:

SCANNING
Officers determine problems through personal experience, through communications with residents or through calls for service.

ANALYSIS
Officers learn everything possible about the players, incidents and actions that may have been used to deal with the problem. If an officer understands all of the components of a problem, the officer can create a customized response to fit the problem.

RESPONSE
Officers develop a goal based on careful analysis. The goal is reached using a customized response to fit the problem. Solutions are designed to:

- Eliminate the problem
- Reduce the problem
- Reduce the harm created by the problem
- Deal with a problem more effectively
- Remove the problem from police consideration. The officer locates an agency that can better handle the problem.

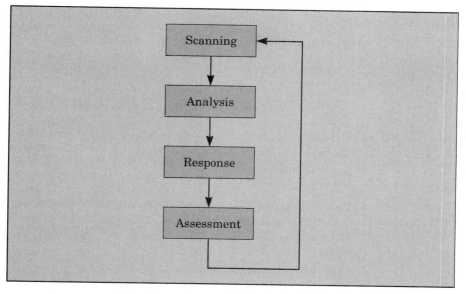

*Figure 4.3*    **The Four-Step SARA Problem-Solving Model**

ASSESSMENT

Officers evaluate the effectiveness of their response. Did the officers achieve their goal? Did the response to the problem:

• Reduce calls for service?

• Satisfy residents or businesses?

• Create a more manageable problem?

• Result in a noticed difference by policymakers in amount of complaints?

The SARA model of problem solving shows that there are no failures, only responses that do not provide the desired goal. When a response does not give the desired results, the officer can examine the results and try a different response.

Books (1995, p. 7) provides an example of the SARA model in action. Table 4.1 illustrates potential sources of information for identifying problems. To assist in problem analysis, the Newport News Police Department developed a problem-analysis guide that lists topic headings police should consider in assessing problems, illustrated in Table 4.2.

◆

Problem analysis considers the individuals involved, the incidents and the responses.

◆

Illustrated in Figure 4.4, their graphic representation of this problem-analysis guide highlights the complex interaction of individuals, incidents and responses occurring within a social context and a physical setting.

*Table 4.1*     **Potential Sources of Information for Identifying Problems**

**Crime Analysis Unit**—Time trends and patterns (time of day, day of week, monthly, seasonal, and other cyclical events), and patterns of similar events (offender descriptions, victim characteristics, locations, physical settings and other circumstances).

**Patrol**—Recurring calls, bad areas, active offenders, victim types, complaints from citizens.

**Investigations**—Recurring crimes, active offenders, victim difficulties, complaints from citizens.

**Crime Prevention**—Physical conditions, potential victims, complaints from citizens.

**Vice**—Drug dealing, illegal alcohol sales, gambling, prostitution, organized crime.

**Communications**—Call types, repeat calls from same location, temporal peaks in calls for service.

**Chief's Office**—Letters and calls from citizens, concerns of elected officials, concerns from city manager's office.

**Other Law Enforcement Agencies**—Multi-jurisdictional concerns.

**Elected Officials**—Concerns and complaints.

**Local Government Agencies**—Plans that could influence crimes, common difficulties, complaints from citizens.

**Schools**—Juvenile concerns, vandalism, employee safety.

**Community Leaders**—Problems of constituents.

**Business Groups**—Problems of commerce and development.

**Neighborhood Watch**—Local problems regarding disorder, crime and other complaints.

**Newspapers and Other News Media**—Indications of problems not detected from other sources, problems in other jurisdictions that could occur in any city.

**Community Surveys**—Problems of citizens in general.

SOURCE: John E. Eck and William Spelman. *Problem Solving: Problem-Oriented Policing in Newport News.* Washington, D.C.: Police Executive Research Forum, 1987: 46. © 1987 Police Executive Research Forum. Reprinted with permission by PERF.

The problems Newport News Police identified and how they approached them are discussed later in the chapter. Based on the Newport News experience, Eck and Spelman (1987, p. 3) offer twelve suggestions as to what a problem-oriented policing agency should do:

1. Focus on problems of concern to the public.
2. Zero in on effectiveness as the primary concern.
3. Be proactive.
4. Be committed to systematic inquiry as the first step in solving substantive problems.

*Table 4.2*    **The Problem-Analysis Guide (List of Topic Headings)**

**Actors**

*Victims*

Life style

Security measures taken

Victimization history

*Offenders*

Identity and physical description

Life style, education, employment history

Criminal history

*Third parties*

Personal data

Connection to victimization

**Incidents**

*Sequence of events*

Events preceding act

Event itself

Events following criminal act

*Physical context*

Time

Location

Access control and surveillance

*Social context*

Likelihood and probable actions of witnesses

Apparent attitude of residents toward neighborhood

*Immediate results of incidents*

Harm done to victim

Gain to offender

Legal issues

**Responses**

*Community*

Neighborhood affected by problem

City as a whole

People outside the city

*Institutional*

Criminal justice system

Other public agencies

Mass media

Business sector

*Seriousness*

Public perceptions

Perception of others

SOURCE: John E. Eck and William Spelman. *Problem Solving: Problem-Oriented Policing in Newport News.* Washington, D.C.: Police Executive Research Forum, 1987: xxi. © 1987 Police Executive Research Forum. Reprinted with permission by PERF.

5.  Encourage use of rigorous methods in making inquiries.

6.  Make full use of the data in police files and the experience of police personnel.

7.  Group like incidents together so that they can be addressed as a common problem.

8.  Avoid using overly broad labels in grouping incidents so separate problems can be identified.

9.  Encourage a broad and uninhibited search for solutions.

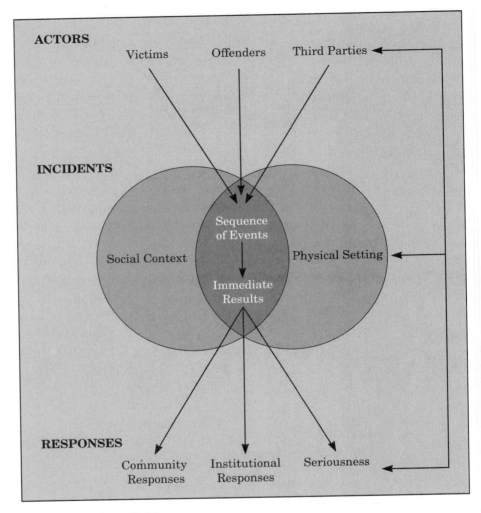

*Figure 4.4*    **Problem-Analysis Guide**
SOURCE: John E. Eck and William Spelman. *Problem Solving: Problem-Oriented Policing in Newport News.* Washington, D.C.: Police Executive Research Forum, 1987: 55. © 1987 Police Executive Research Forum. Reprinted with permission by PERF.

10. Acknowledge the limits of the criminal justice system as a response to problems.
11. Identify multiple interests in any one problem and weigh them when analyzing the value of different responses.
12. Be committed to taking some risks in responding to problems.

*Problem Solving in Action*

## Store No Longer a Hangout for Disorderly Teens

**By Jim Books**

Late in the 1993 to 1994 school year, the St. Petersburg, Fla., Police Department addressed a serious loitering problem at a local convenience store and its adjoining lot. Large groups of teenagers from the local middle and high schools were hanging out regularly at the Circle K convenience store at 54th Avenue North and 16th Street.

### Scanning

The problem, identified by the police department, community residents and businesses, was that patrons were having difficulty driving into the parking lot due to the large and disruptive groups of teenagers. Some also felt intimidated walking through the groups to enter the store. Employees from the business complex located next to Circle K complained about students parking on their lot, leaving their customers without parking spaces. Seventy-five to 100 students would congregate in the area on school days, particularly in the afternoon.

The following problems arose:

- disorderly juveniles,
- fights,
- aggravated batteries,
- thefts, and
- graffiti.

Circle K had a history of attracting loitering teens, but the problem had intensified within the last few years. Police had addressed the problem with traditional responses; calls to 911 had resulted in their temporarily dispersing the groups, without any long-term deterrent effects.

### Analysis

The problem was greatest between 1:30 and 2:30 P.M., although there was also a problem between 2:30 and 4:30 P.M. The before-school groups were small and the students did not stay on the property for very long. There was a small group of middle school students who arrived in the morning and needed encouragement to leave to be on time for school.

Some of the juveniles who went to Circle K in the afternoon were waiting for rides from friends or parents. Others were dropouts or gang members waiting for their friends to get out of school.

The peak activity period fell just before and during police shift changes, limiting the number of officers available to deal with the problem.

To address the problem, police officers met with business owners to come up with ways to keep the teens away from the area. The police also spoke with school administrators about options for tightening restraints on students leaving school grounds during afternoon classes.

*continued*

*Response*

The response was to make the area less appealing to the teens. The business owners' tolerance for the teens' loitering, combined with the lure of Circle K's video games, encouraged juveniles to gather there.

Once the factors contributing to the problem were identified, the Circle K store's managers were eager to cooperate. They helped the policed department by turning off the video games during peak hours, posting "no loitering" signs, issuing blanket trespass warnings, and keeping a book of Polaroid pictures of youths who had received trespass warnings. Businesses in the immediate area also posted "no loitering" signs, and issued blanket trespass warnings for their properties.

School resource officers further improved the situation by tightening attendance restrictions and increasing sanctions for cutting class.

*Assessment*

Through aggressive and innovative enforcement, police officers and their partners in the community eliminated the loitering problem within two weeks. Police continue to patrol the area regularly to prevent the problem from resurfacing. Although some of the teens have moved to other hangouts, the number of those who congregate is significantly lower.

Both business owners and their patrons are satisfied with the changes. The parking lots are available for patrons, and the environment is safer.

*Jim Books is a sergeant with the St. Petersburg, Fla., Police Department.*
*(Books, 1995.) Reprinted by permission of the Police Executive Research Forum.*

Note the similarities between these suggestions and the basic elements of problem-solving policing set forth by Goldstein on pp. 468–69.

When identifying problems, it is important to be aware of the *magnet phenomenon.*

◆

The **magnet phenomenon** occurs when a phone number or address is associated with a crime simply because it was a convenient number or address to use.

◆

A **magnet telephone** is one that is available when no other telephones are, for example, a telephone in a convenience store which is open all night and on weekends. Victims of or witnesses to a crime in the area may use that telephone to report the crime, even though the store was not the scene of the crime. Similarly, a **magnet address** is one that is easy for people to give, for example, a high school or a theater.

Buerger (1992, p. 127) describes how this phenomenon operated in a problem-solving approach being used by the Minneapolis Police Department with the city's bus depot:

After analyzing the calls, it became apparent that the depot was also a magnet address because it is easy for a caller to identify: "I need help; I am across the street from the Greyhound station." The dispatcher then entered the message to meet a party across from the Greyhound depot, and used that as the address-of-record for that call.

When specific crimes are identified during the first stage of problem solving, crime-specific planning may be appropriate.

## PROBLEM-SOLVING POLICING AND CRIME-SPECIFIC PLANNING

To maintain effective police-community partnerships, police must also fulfill their crime-fighting role. Police can approach this role with many of the problem-solving skills just discussed, using crime-specific planning. Cummings (1990, p. 63) notes: "While similar to problem-oriented policing in its process, crime-specific planning is more specific in that it approaches criminal justice problems by considering underlying problems that are categorized by the type of offense." Crime-specific planning involves reviewing the following factors (Cummings, p. 63):

1. Seriousness of the offense.
2. Frequency of the occurrence.
3. Public concern.
4. Impact on the community.
5. The drain on resources of the criminal justice system.
6. The susceptibility of each crime to control.
7. Whether the crime is one of opportunity or calculation.
8. The degree of concentration required to develop plans for the perpetration of the crime.
9. The *modus operandi* and patterns.
10. The violent characteristics that may be present.
11. The property that may be taken or damaged.
12. The victim's response.
13. The community's response.
14. The system's response.
15. The actual target.
16. Characteristics of the target.

17. When the target is attacked.
18. How the target is attacked.
19. Where the target is located in the environment.
20. The number of potential targets in each area.
21. The accessibility of the targets.
22. Transportation patterns surrounding the targets.
23. Offender characteristics.

◆

**Crime-specific planning** uses the principles of problem solving to focus on identified crime problems.

◆

A careful analysis of these factors will provide the basis for problem solving and deriving alternatives for approaching each specific crime problem.

## COMMON MISTAKES IN PROBLEM SOLVING

As noted by Bennett and Hess (1996, p. 179): "Common mistakes in problem solving and decision making include spending too much energy on unimportant details, failing to resolve important issues, being secretive about true feelings, having a closed mind and not expressing ideas. . . . Inability to decide, putting decisions off to the last minute, failing to set deadlines and using unreliable sources of information are other common errors in problem solving and decision making." Other mistakes commonly made during problem solving and decision making include:

- Making multiple decisions about the same problem.
- Finding the right decision for the wrong problem; that is, dealing with symptoms rather than causes.
- Failing to consider the costs.
- Delaying a decision.
- Making decisions while angry or excited.

Each of these common mistakes in problem solving and decision making has its positive counterpart. For example, rather than making decisions while angry or excited—make decisions calmly when you are in control of the situation. Bennett and Hess (1996, p. 180) offer the following checklist against which to evaluate decisions:

*Is the decision:*

- Consistent with the agency's mission, goals and objectives?
- A long-term solution?
- Cost-effective?
- Legal?
- Ethical?
- Practical?
- Acceptable to those responsible for implementing it?

## PROBLEM SOLVING AND CREATIVITY

Several structured approaches to problem-solving policing have been discussed. These approaches will be less than effective, however, unless creativity is incorporated into the approach. **Creativity** is a process of breaking old connections and making useful new connections. It is often synonymous with **innovation.** von Oech (1983, p. 7) stresses: "The creative mind has the power to transform one thing into another. By changing perspective and playing with our knowledge and experience, we can make the ordinary extraordinary and the unusual commonplace. *Discovery consists of looking at the same thing as everyone else and thinking something different.*"

### Thinking Outside the Dots

The following exercise (Figure 4.5) is frequently used in problem-solving seminars. Try to complete the exercise. If you cannot connect the dots, turn to Appendix A for the solution. Now, those of you who could connect the dots and those of you who had to look at the solution share the same knowledge: "You sometimes have to go outside the perimeters." As noted by von Oech (1983, p. 24): "Nothing is more dangerous than an idea if it is the only one you have." He describes several **mental locks,** or ways of thinking that prevent creativity, to be avoided.

♦

Mental locks that prevent creative thinking include:

- The right answer.
- That's not logical.
- Follow the rules.
- Be practical.
- Avoid ambiguity.
- To err is wrong.
- Play is frivolous.
- That's not my area.
- Don't be foolish.
- I'm not creative.

♦

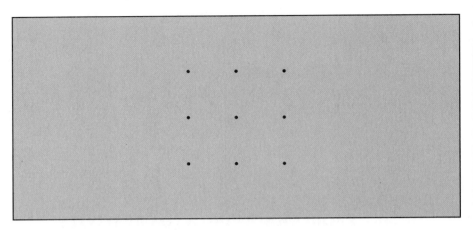

*Figure 4.5*    **Nine-Dot Exercise Instructions:** Using four straight lines, connect the 9 dots. You may start wherever you wish, but do not lift your pencil from the paper.

**The Right Answer.**  von Oech (1983, p. 22) notes that most people will take over 26,000 tests before completing their education. He suggests: "Children enter elementary school as question marks and leave as periods."

**That's Not Logical.**  Sometimes logic limits creativity. Both creative and logical thinking are usually needed for the toughest problems.

**Follow the Rules.**  How often do parents admonish their young children to "stay in the lines" when they color or tell them that they cannot color the chicken in their coloring book purple? Although patterns and rules *can* help in problem solving, they can also hinder the process.

**Be Practical.**  People have the unique and useful ability to imagine, to dream. As Walt Disney was fond of saying, "If you can dream it, you can do it." Practicality is also important when seeking solutions. However, when problem solving, practicality can limit creative solutions. von Oech (p. 54) calls the realm of the possible a "germinal seedbed." He encourages people to ask "what if" questions to stimulate the imagination.

**Avoid Ambiguity.**  von Oech (pp. 76–78) presents the following illustration: *Exercise:* In the following line of letters, cross out six letters so that the remaining letters without altering their sequence, will spell a familiar English word.
    B S A I N X L E A T N T E A R S
Try the exercise.

Many people approach this problem by focusing on the fact that there are sixteen letters here. People think that if they cross out six, they will have a ten-letter word, and they concentrate on which letters to cross out. In fact, one man who had a computer fed the problem in, confident that he would have the answer momentarily. Imagine his surprise when the computer generated a thirty-foot-long printout of possible solutions.

The minute he saw the list, he realized he had asked the computer the wrong question. The greatest computer in the world cannot resolve the wrong problem. To solve the problem, ask yourself, "What else could 'cross out six letters' mean?" von Oech (p. 78) suggests that instead of crossing out six letters, you literally crossed out the "S," the "I," the "X," the "L," and the "E," and so on. If you try this approach, you will be left with the word *banana*. When thinking creatively, ambiguity can help.

**To Err Is Wrong.** This fallacy is similar to the mental trap about "right answers." Risk taking is a necessary part of progress. To err is wrong only if you do not learn from the "mistake." Henry Ford once said, "Failure is the opportunity to begin again more intelligently."

**Play Is Frivolous.** People tend to take themselves too seriously. Take time out to play in your mental playground. Solutions to problems often come when you least expect them. Give them time in your "germinal seedbed" while you enjoy yourself doing something that gives you pleasure.

**That's Not My Area.** Our society has become so complex that specialization is often necessary. Sometimes, however, someone who is outside a specific field but who is genuinely interested in and perhaps affected by a problem can suggest the most brilliant alternative. This is, in fact, often true of citizens. Alternatives to crime-related problems may be generated by non–law enforcement professionals if given an opportunity.

**Don't Be Foolish.** Relax, have fun and brainstorm, allow all ideas to percolate—even those that may seem ridiculous.

**I'm Not Creative.** As the saying goes: "If you think you can or if you think you can't, you're right." Never demean yourself or your abilities, including your ability to be creative. You would not be this far into this text if you were not a capable individual. You have absorbed a great deal of information and you have years of experience to relate to that information. If you wish you can approach policing in creative ways.

Once you have considered "how to unlock your mind for innovation," consider next how others might deter you—or you might be deterring others—from creative solutions.

### Killer Phrases

◆

**Killer phrases** are judgmental, critical statements that are put-downs. Killer phrases stifle creativity.

◆

Among the most common killer phrases are the following (Buchholz and Roth, 1987, p. 136): "That's too radical. It's contrary to policy. That's not our area. It won't fit within the deadline. We'll never get help. That's too much hassle. It just won't work. It's too obvious. Get real. Be practical. Costs too much. We've never done it that way before. Get serious."

Avoid such phrases when you are thinking to yourself and in your discussions with others if you want creative solutions to the numerous problems you will encounter in policing. The alternative solutions to problems are waiting to be "discovered."

## PROBLEM-SOLVING POLICING AT WORK

The theoretical foundation of problem solving in Newport News was discussed earlier. During the problem identification process, the following problems became evident (Eck and Spelman, 1987, p. 44):

- Groups of workers from a large industrial complex engaged in drug dealing, drug usage and drinking during their lunch break.
- Thefts from vehicles in the downtown parking areas.
- Prostitution and robberies in District 1.
- Burglaries in New Briarfield Apartments.
- Business burglaries in District 9.
- Confrontations between students from rival high schools.
- Jefferson Avenue traffic accidents.
- Serial crimes.
- Disorder problem in a small area of bars and a motel, near a military base.
- Traffic congestion in the downtown area when day shift workers leave the industrial area.
- Non-reporting of suspicious circumstances by citizen witnesses.
- Disturbances around and near a meeting area of people looking for dates.
- Groups of youths drinking, using marijuana, making noise and littering near a residential community.

*Table 4.3* **Types of Problems**

| | *Citywide* | *Neighborhood* |
|---|---|---|
| **Crime problems** | Domestic homicides | Personal robberies (Central business district) |
| | Gas station driveoffs | Commercial burglaries (Jefferson Avenue business district) |
| | Assaults on police officers | Vacant buildings (Central business district) |
| | | Residential burglaries (New Briarfield Apts) |
| | | Residential burglaries (Glenn Gardens Apts) |
| | | Larcenies (Beechmont Gardens Apts) |
| | | Thefts from autos (Newport News Shipbuilding) |
| | | Drug dealing (32d and Chestnut) |
| **Disorder problems** | Runaway youths | Rowdy youths (Peninsula Skating Rink) |
| | Driving under the influence | Shot houses (Aqua Vista Apts) |
| | Disturbances at convenience stores | Disturbances (Marshall Avenue 7-Eleven) |
| | | Dirt bikes (Newmarket Creek) |
| | | Disturbances (Village Square Shopping Center) |

SOURCE: John E. Eck and William Spelman. *Problem Solving: Problem-Oriented Policing in Newport News.* Washington, D.C.: Police Executive Research Forum, 1987: 82. © 1987 Police Executive Research Forum. Reprinted with permission by PERF.

Table 4.3 illustrates how police categorized the problems so they could be analyzed.

The way the department addressed the problem of commercial burglaries illustrates the problem-solving approach. The patrol officers surveyed the area and found that some major streets had been barricaded due to a major highway construction project. This resulted in limited vehicle traffic, limited police patrol at night and a large increase in nighttime burglaries. To alleviate these problems, patrol officers were instructed to leave their squads and patrol the area on foot at night. The officers also persuaded the merchants to clean up the piles of trash and debris which could easily conceal the activities of burglars.

Besides dealing with the environment, Sgt. Quail, the officer in charge, also analyzed the specific problem (p. 83):

He collected offense reports of burglaries committed in the area. To help identify geographic patterns, he plotted them on a detailed spot map. To identify M.O. and repeat offender patterns, Quail recorded a description of the suspects, time of commission, type of property taken, and similar information on a specially designed form. Finally, he suspected that some of the offenders were using vacant apartments located above some of the businesses to conceal stolen property; he began to investigate this possibility.

*A Washington, D.C., police officer talks with a citizen representative of a
neighborhood safety organization.*

These efforts resulted in the apprehension of several burglars and a decrease
in the burglary rate. When the construction was completed and the barriers
removed, the burglaries decreased further. Since construction is frequent,
Sgt. Quail began to develop a policy and procedure statement so that police and
city agencies could communicate better regarding construction projects, street
closing and potential burglary problems.

The Tulsa Police Department has also adopted the problem-solving
approach to policing. Smith (1990, p. 62) notes that "Cuff 'em and stuff 'em" is
no longer their approach, quoting their chief of police who says: "We try to look
at the whole problem. Prevention is as important as apprehension." Their
approach, according to Smith, involves the following steps (p. 63):

- Identify the problem and analyze it to see if its cause is environmental,
  social, physical, ages of residents, economics, or a symptom of something
  else that is wrong.

- Set a goal and determine a direction on how to respond. Is there something that needs to be eliminated, reduced, or just improved? Sometimes
  the problem does not have to be totally eliminated to be successful.

- Analyze the result of the approach taken to see what worked and what
  didn't—and if changes should be made.

When the Tulsa Police Department shifted to this approach, they began to group their incident data to look for patterns. By doing so, they found that they had received sixty to eighty calls from one woman in thirty days. The calls had been answered by different officers on different shifts, and no one realized how much time was spent responding to her calls. They investigated the situation and found that the woman was lonely and had a drinking problem. They got her involved in some of the community's social service agencies and since that time have not received a single call from her.

Not all problems were solved as easily, however. When they assessed the drug problem in a local housing project, a solution involved much more probing. The department found that the residents were extremely frightened, that violence was so prevalent that fire and ambulance services were afraid to answer calls there and that the Housing Authority considered the drug problem the landlord's concern—not police business. The police persisted, however, and discovered some serious problems. First, many residents did not have telephones, and therefore had no means of communication with the outside world. Adding foot and horse patrol brought the officers and the outside world to them. Project managers and foot patrols were provided with radios or beepers so they could maintain contact with each other.

Another related problem was lack of transportation for the great majority of residents. Police enlisted the aid of the Community Partnership, a social service agency, which helped with the problem. As a result, several residents were able to attend school, participate in vocational programs or get jobs.

The Baltimore County department has also implemented a problem-solving approach. In 1981, they first implemented the approach, called Community Oriented Police Enforcement or COPE. The department's basic mission at that time was to fight the fear of crime by addressing the social problems that caused it. According to Taft (1986, p. 10): "'Citizen Oriented Police Enforcement' officers would engage in intensive patrol, develop close contacts with citizens, conduct 'fear surveys' (door-to-door canvassing to identify concerns) and use any means within their power to quell fear."

One early success was when COPE officers saw the potential for violence between two groups of black and white students who used adjacent bus stops. COPE officers convinced the County Board of Education to move one stop to a new location, eliminating the daily confrontations between the two groups.

In 1983, two COPE officers were called to Garden Village and warned to expect trouble because the citizens there hated the police. Using the problem-solving approach to the crime and violence existing in Garden Village, the officers conducted fear surveys, compiled crime statistics, took pictures of deteriorating areas and measured distances from housing projects to playgrounds. They then brainstormed for solutions to deal with the various problems they had uncovered. According to Taft (1986, p. 15):

> Using statistics to show that most Garden Village crime occurred after dark, the pair convinced Baltimore Gas and Electric to repair the broken street

*This alley in the Hill district of Pittsburgh might become a key target for a problem-solving police department.*

lights. Using photographs of potholes and cracked pavement, they persuaded the county roads department to patch up Garden Village's alleyways. Using the dimensions of other basketball courts and playgrounds, they badgered county park and recreation officials until a dormant rehabilitation and construction project was approved for a local park.

In another instance, officers were called to help with a panhandling problem that had gotten out of hand in Dundalk, a small neighborhood on the outskirts of Baltimore. Although vagrants had inhabited Dundalk for over twenty years, they had recently become a serious problem, accosting local shoppers for money. Plainclothes COPE officers helped the officers from that precinct make nineteen arrests, which reduced the panhandling. The officers knew, however, that the underlying problem was still there. Using the problem-solving approach, they accomplished the following (Taft, p. 18):

The officers convinced the county to trim shrubs and add lights in the park where panhandlers loitered. They helped the Chamber distribute 15,000 copies of a "Stop Panhandling" flyer . . . and visited liquor store owners to remind them that selling liquor to an intoxicated person is illegal. They researched panhandling laws from different cities and drafted a new version for Baltimore County, one that would make such aggressive panhandling a criminal offense.

But Fox and Grupp [the two COPE officers ] knew that even stiffer jail sentences would not prevent the vagrants from returning. So they turned their attention to a more radical solution: establishing Baltimore County's first detoxification and rehabilitation center.

They also succeeded in setting up a task force on the homeless, which continues to examine the remaining problems. As noted by Officer Fox (Taft, p. 19): "We changed the environment. We changed public attitudes. We verified the need for a detoxification facility. We asked for a task force and got it. COPE works."

According to Taft (p. 22): "The success of COPE suggests that modern police can play an even more active role than their historical counterparts—that in today's complex society police can, if they so choose, become active agents of change by identifying social problems and bringing to bear public and private resources to solve them."

## BENEFITS OF THE PROBLEM-SOLVING APPROACH

Kelling and Moore (1991, p. 19) suggest: "Police officers enjoy operating with a holistic approach to their work; they have the capacity to do it successfully; they can work with citizens and other agencies to solve problems; and citizens seem to appreciate working with police."

As noted by Bittner (1986, p. 30), a problem-solving approach is not really a radical new idea:

Problem-oriented policing is firmly rooted in the practical outlook of the 'street cop.' . . . Experienced, skilled and judicious officers have always known that, for example, the likelihood of violent teenage conflict in public housing depends upon the layout of the walkways, the locations of entrances and exits, and the distribution of transportation facilities. The best officers have always geared their capacities to intervene to the existence of such conditions. Problem-oriented policing . . . builds on the wisdom and on the perception of necessities as seen by these officers.

Bittner is speaking of the problem-oriented COPE project, but his comments can be applied in a much broader context. He notes: "It is the great strength of the COPE project that it makes explicit what was implicit and unrecognized in street practice; it makes routine what was exceptional." He concludes (p. 31): "I look forward to the day when the entire police profession recognizes problem-solving as a regular part of the job."

## SUMMARY

Herman Goldstein is credited with originating problem-oriented policing. One concern of such an orientation is differentiating between efficiency and effectiveness. Efficiency, doing things right, has been the traditional emphasis in law enforcement. Effectiveness, doing the right things, is the emphasis in community policing.

The first step in problem solving is to group incidents as problems. Four stages of problem solving are scanning, analysis, response and assessment. Problem analysis considers the individuals involved, the incidents and the responses. Such analysis should take into account the magnet phenomenon. This phenomenon occurs when a phone number or address is associated with a crime simply because it was a convenient number or address to use.

Crime-specific planning uses the principles of problem-solving policing to focus on identified crime problems. Both crime-specific planning and problem solving can be more effective if those working on the problem can approach it creatively. Mental locks that prevent creativity include "the right answer," "that's not logical," "follow the rules," "be practical," "avoid ambiguity," "to err is wrong," "play is frivolous," "that's not my area," "don't be foolish" and "I'm not creative." Killer phrases are judgmental, critical statements that serve as put-downs and stifle creativity.

### Discussion Questions

1.  How do you approach problems? Do you use a systematic approach?
2.  Do you think problem solving takes more time than the traditional approach to policing?
3.  Does your department use problem solving?
4.  Do you consider yourself to be creative? What helps you to be so? What hinders you?
5.  What difficulties can you foresee for a department that uses problem-solving techniques?
6.  How do problem-solving policing and crime-specific planning differ?
7.  Considering the list of mental locks on page 103, do you find yourself thinking in any of these ways? If so, what can you do to unlock your creativity?
8.  In what kinds of problems do you think a problem-solving approach would be most effective?
9.  What is the relationship between community policing and a problem-solving approach to policing?
10. How might computers help police in their problem-solving efforts?

### References

Beck, Brian. "Problem Solving for Police Officers." *Minnesota Cities.* (August 1996): 8–9.

Bennett, Wayne W. and Hess, Kären M. *Management & Supervision in Law Enforcement.* 2nd ed. St. Paul: West Publishing Company, 1996.

Bittner, Egon. "Afterword." In *Fighting Fear: The Baltimore County COPE Project,* 30–31. Washington, D.C.: Police Executive Research Forum, February 1986.

Books, Jim. "Store No Longer a Hangout for Disorderly Teens." *Problem-Solving Quarterly.* (Fall 1995): 7.

Buchholz, Steve and Roth, Thomas. *Creating the High-Performance Team.* New York: John Wiley and Sons, 1987.

Buerger, Michael E. (ed.) *The Crime Prevention Casebook: Securing High Crime Locations.* Washington, D.C.: Crime Control Institute, 1992.

Cummings, D. Brian. "Problem-Oriented Policing and Crime-Specific Planning." *The Police Chief.* (March 1990): 63–64.

Eck, John E. and Spelman, William. *Problem-Solving: Problem-Oriented Policing in Newport News.* Washington, D.C.: The Police Executive Research Forum, 1987.

Goldstein, Herman. *Problem-Oriented Policing.* New York: McGraw-Hill Publishing Company, 1990.

Kelling, George L. and Moore, Mark H. "From Political Reform to Community: The Evolving Strategy of Police." In *Community Policing: Rhetoric or Reality,* edited by Jack R. Greene and Stephen D. Mastrofski, 3–25. New York: Praeger Publications, 1991.

Rosen, Marie Simonetti. "A LEN Interview with Professor Herman Goldstein, the 'Father' of Problem-Oriented Policing." *Law Enforcement News.* (February 14, 1997): 8–10.

Smith, Charlotte Anne. "Tulsa PD Uses Multiple Solutions." *Law and Order.* (September 1990): 62–66.

Taft, Philip B., Jr. *Fighting Fear: The Baltimore County COPE Project.* Washington, D.C.: Police Executive Research Forum, February 1986.

von Oech, Roger. *A Whack on the Side of the Head.* New York: Warner Books, 1983.

Wilson, James Q. and Kelling, George L. "Making Neighborhoods Safe." *The Atlantic Monthly.* (February 1989): 46–52.

## *Chapter 5*

# Implementing Community Policing

*Change is the law of life. And those who look only to the past or the present are sure to miss the future.*

—John F. Kennedy

## Do you know

- What basis changes are required to make the transition to community policing?
- What a mission statement is?
- How law enforcement agencies have traditionally been organized?
- What participatory leadership is?
- What three levels of policing have been identified?

## Definitions

Can you define these terms: mission statement, participatory leadership.

# Introduction

According to Goldstein (1993, p. 1): "The policing of a free, diverse, and vibrant society is an awesome and complex task." And, as noted by Peak (1994, p. 29): "We must do all we can to determine what the future will bring—and what we are going to do about it. The citizens of America deserve our best analytical efforts, most imaginative solutions and most finely honed problem-solving abilities as we head into the turbulent 21st century." He might as well be describing community policing.

You have looked at the theory of community policing as well as at the key players—the community and the police. You have also considered a basic component of community policing—problem solving. The challenge of community policing is to move from theories about using problem-solving techniques to reduce crime and violence to actual implementation. According to Rodgers (1995, p. 116): "Approximately two-thirds of the police departments in the United States have, or are in the process of developing, Community Policing programs."

This chapter beings with a consideration of the basic nature of change and how it will influence implementation of community policing. This is followed by a discussion of how the community policing philosophy should be reflected in the mission statement and how it will probably affect the entire police organization. Next is a discussion of the importance of a participatory form of leadership rather than the traditional authoritarian approach. Then a discussion of various approaches to implementing community policing and promising targets is presented. The chapter concludes with a look at some of the obstacles to anticipate.

## CHANGE

It has been said that nothing is constant except change. Nonetheless, police administrators, supervisors and even line personnel are frequently resistant to change in any form, preferring the status quo. But change is occurring and will continue to occur. Police departments can resist or they can accept the challenge and capitalize on the benefits that may result. Bentz (1995, p. 14) suggests that certain issues are "propelling us into a whirlwind of change" including:

- Technological advances.
- Changing demographics.
- Fiscal constraints.
- Fear of crime.
- Shifting values.
- Global issues [such as environmental concerns and drug trafficking].

Mulder (1994, p. 55) suggests similar reasons underlying the need for change within police departments:

- Severe reductions in fiscal resources while demands for law enforcement services continue to increase.
- Highly publicized incidents of police misconduct or perceived incompetence.
- Political simplification of a highly complex profession.
- Increasing citizen fear of unabated and ruthless criminal gang violence.

Some changes have already occurred within many departments that should make the transition to community policing easier, including better educated police officers who are less inclined to accept orders unquestioningly, a shift in incentives with intrinsic, personal-worth type rewards becoming as important as extrinsic, monetary rewards and the necessity to provide more services with fewer resources. Enlisting the community has become not only more attractive, but necessary.

Other changes are needed to move from the traditional, reactive, incident-driven mode of policing to the proactive, problem-solving, collaborative mode typical of community policing.

◆

Community policing will require a change in mission statement, departmental organization, leadership style and the general approach to "fighting crime."

◆

As Peterson (1994, p. 50) suggests: "It is clear that tolerance to change will be one of the more valuable attributes for managers in the year 2001."

Nonetheless, resistance to change should be anticipated. As Rippy (1990, p. 136) cautions: "Perhaps the most significant resistance to change comes from the fact that leaders have to indict their own past decisions and behavior to bring about change."

In addition to their own resistance, police management may experience an internal backlash, described by Dolan (1994, p. 28) as "ranging from visible frustration to outright mutiny." This backlash is often encountered when chiefs attempt to impose innovations such as community policing on a department. To reduce or eliminate such backlash, Dolan (p. 32) suggests the following:

- Train the entire department in the community policing philosophy from the very beginning.
- Develop a management style and organizational structure that embraces input from all members of the department.
- Constantly stress to both the department and community that the agency will always perform traditional police duties.

- Go slowly. . . . In most cases, it will take 10 to 20 years to change our current incident-driven response to a community-oriented partnership.
- Stay focused on the fundamentals.
- Don't take it personally when members of the department demonstrate backlash.
- Most importantly, role model what you expect to see. Chiefs and managers have to literally walk the beat. We have to demonstrate to our officers that what they are doing is important and that we are all in the transformation together.

Change will take time. Traditions die hard. Most police officers will find any hint of proposed change to their culture extremely threatening. However, although the police culture is tremendously strong, remember that a huge ship can be turned by a small rudder. It just takes time and steadfast determination.

It is also helpful to be familiar with the five categories of "adopters" to expect within any organization, as shown in Figure 5.1.

The innovators are risk takers. They embrace uncertainty and change. The early adopters are opinion leaders, the ones to whom others come for advice. The early majority accept new ideas slightly ahead of the majority. The late majority is more skeptical. They can be persuaded, but usually require a great deal of peer pressure. The late adopters are the most difficult to convince. They tend to be suspicious of any innovations. Recognizing these individual characteristics may be helpful in developing strategies to "sell" community policing to the troops.

Finally, it is important to heed the comment of Goldstein (1993, p. 2): "Policing in the United States is much like a large, intricate, complex apparatus with many parts. Change of any one part requires changes in many others and in the way the parts fit and work together."

Usually, the first basic change that must be made to implement community policing is in the department's mission statement.

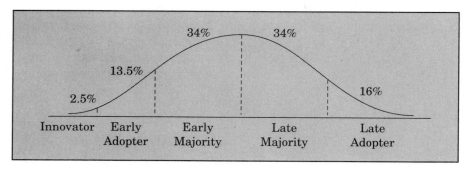

*Figure 5.1*    **Change Takes Time**

# MISSION STATEMENTS

Why do most law enforcement agencies exist? What is their *mission?* The answer is obvious to those who say the purpose is to catch "bad guys." Others believe that the purpose is to prevent crime, or maintain order or protect the public. Articulating the purpose for an agency's existence helps its members to focus on the same goals and determine how to accomplish their purpose.

◆

A **mission statement** is a written declaration of purpose.

◆

A mission statement is a road map that delineates how an agency will arrive at a desired destination. Without it, a law enforcement agency can wander, appearing inconsistent, inefficient and purposeless. According to VanMeter (1991, p. 65):

> Simply put, a mission is a reason to work. More than just an empty platitude, a mission statement is the standard against which administrators evaluate all decisions and actions. It is the legal foundation for legitimate decision making that affects employment. To be effective, it must be broad enough in scope and sufficient in depth to capture the philosophy, values and goals of the organization.

The mission statement will tell you what the agency's commitment is to the community it serves and how it views its relationship with the community. A mission statement can reveal, rather accurately, the state of police-community relations.

As noted in *Law and Order* ("Your Agency's Driving Force. . ." 1991, p. 65): "The mission answers the question of why things are done. If it is defined adequately, the agency's decisions and actions will be appropriate as long as they remain based on the mission."

A mission statement can focus a police department's energies and resources. Will the department continue to be reactive and focused on fighting crimes that have already occurred or proactive, focused on identifying problems and attacking those problems? As noted by Wilson and Kelling (1989, p. 49), a community-oriented policing philosophy requires redefining the police mission: "To help the police become accustomed to fixing broken windows as well as arresting window-breakers requires doing things that are very hard for many administrators to do."

Consider the following mission statement of the Madison, Wisconsin, Police Department:

> We believe in the dignity and worth of all people.
> We are committed to:
> • Providing high-quality, community-oriented police services with sensitivity
> • Protecting constitutional rights
> • Problem-solving

- Teamwork
- Openness
- Continuous improvement
- Providing leadership to the police profession

We are proud of the diversity of our workforce which permits us to grow and which respects each of us as individuals and we strive for a healthful workplace.

How are mission statements developed? A committee, comprised of members of the community and police officers, assesses various police functions. Why would a law enforcement agency include input from the community when it develops its mission statement? Community input improves police-community relations and increases the possibility of an agency accomplishing its missions.

As noted by VanMeter (1991, p. 65): "In public service organizations, the public determines the nature of the mission by identifying the services it expects from the organization. If the expectations go unmet, the public becomes dissatisfied. The organization generally suffers loss of financing, loss of political support and increased interference in day-to-day operations." Or, as Captain Michael J. Nila (1990, p. 43) of the Aurora (Illinois) Police Department states, the citizen-police committee that developed Aurora's mission statement had "to write a statement that would create a philosophy demanding that the community and the police become one—united by a common goal to enhance the quality of life for all of Aurora." The committee's efforts resulted in the following mission statement:

> We, the Aurora Police Department, exist to serve all people within our jurisdiction with respect, fairness and compassion. We are committed to the prevention of crime and the protection of life and property; the preservation of peace, order and safety; the enforcement of laws and ordinances; and the safeguarding of constitutional guarantees.
>
> With community service as our foundation, we are driven by goals to enhance the quality of life, investigating problems as well as incidents, seeking solutions and fostering a sense of security in communities and individuals. We nurture public trust by holding ourselves to the highest standards of performance and ethics.
>
> To fulfill its mission, the Aurora Police Department is dedicated to providing a quality of work environment and the development of its members through effective training and leadership (Nila, 1990, p. 43).

Developing a mission statement that reflects an agency's commitment to the community it serves can be the vehicle to positive, meaningful police-community relations as well as to a more effective police department. It is this mission statement that will, in large part, determine where the agency places its priorities.

Closely related to the mission statement are the goals and objectives set by a department. Rodgers (1995, p. 117) cautions: "History shows that programs emphasizing a 'kinder, gentler' philosophy or image don't sit well with police officers." He cites the Houston Police Department's Neighborhood Oriented Policing Program (NOP). According to Rodgers, officers perceived the program as more social work than police work and referred to it as "Nobody On Patrol." To avoid such perceptions, he suggests top management should emphasize that "our primary mission is the detection and apprehension of law violators and that our [community policing] program would enhance our ability to do so." In fact, community policing is tougher on crime than traditional policing because it is able to rely on the people helping the police. Citizens know they share the responsibility for their neighborhood.

## ORGANIZATION OF THE POLICE DEPARTMENT

The traditional law enforcement organization design has been that of a pyramid-shaped hierarchy based on a military model, as depicted in Figure 5.2. Command officers and supervisors had complete authority over subordinates, and there was

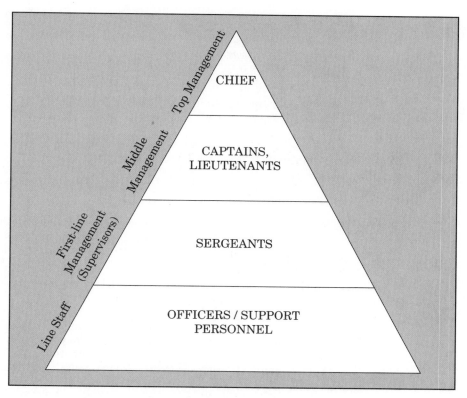

*Figure 5.2*    **Typical Police Department Management Structure**

*The local police chief addresses a town meeting—the chief is in a position of authority and can sway public opinion.*

little tolerance for ideas originating at the bottom of the pyramid. Communication flowed downward through the chain of command.

◆

The traditional law enforcement organizational structure has been a pyramid-shaped hierarchy based on a military model.

◆

According to Goodbody (1995, p. 12):

A bureaucracy takes on a life of its own, and will, along with the people who have a vested interest in it, resist and undermine all attempts at reform. This is especially true if the reform entails a complete reorganization of existing practices and procedures. . . .

Police bureaucracies differ in two essential ways from more conventional bureaucracies. First, supervision is based on a military system of rank that vests police supervisors with significantly more authority than their counterparts in the civilian sector. The quasi-military organization of policing, with uniforms and ranks as a visible component of every interaction, tends to make the police among the more rigid and authoritarian of bureaucracies. Second, police bureaucracies rely heavily on punishment to enforce rules.

This bureaucratic organizational structure worked well for decades. Recently, however, it has been called into question, with many looking to corporate American as a more appropriate organizational model.

For several years corporate American has been making changes in its organizational structure, eliminating tiers of management in an effort to speed decision making and implementation. Such streamlining might also benefit police departments, as noted by Harrison (1994, p. 55): "A recent study of a major law enforcement agency concluded that the paramilitary bureaucratic structure was the culprit for the agency's most destructive and intractable organizational problems. . . . Unnecessary bureaucracy impedes innovation and superior customer service, builds mediocrity into our workforce and makes it impossible to fire people who do not perform."

Mullen (1996, p. 8) describes how the organization of the Baltimore County (Maryland) Police Department changed: "Through a multiphased reorganization, the department moved from a traditional top-down command structure to a decentralized structure that provides the optimal conditions for working in and with the community."

## PARTICIPATORY LEADERSHIP

Yet another change is that community policing usually requires a different management style. According to Couper and Lobitz (1991, p. 16):

> Although many people believe that autocratic style was an effective method of leading workers from the industrial revolution into the 20th century, it will not have the same effect leading workers down the road to the 21st century. In today's workplace, autocratic leaders who reserve the sole right to decide not only where the organization is going, but also each step they will take along the way, have chosen a route that is difficult, if not impossible.

One viable alternative to the autocratic style of leadership is that of participatory leadership. This is different from democratic leaderships where each individual has a vote.

◆

In **participatory leadership** each individual has a voice in decisions, but top management still has the ultimate decision-making authority.

◆

What is important is that everyone has an opportunity to express their views on a given issue or problem. As Couper and Lobitz (1991, p. 23) stress:

> Employees are entering the police profession with a different set of job expectations and values than their predecessors held. They want—and expect—to be part of a team. They want their leaders to value their ideas and suggestions and to permit them to participate in organizational decision making. If we, as police leaders, do not attempt to meet these needs, we will find ourselves out of step with our employees as well as our community.
>
> This is the first time we have had an effective alternative to the way in which we have conducted business for so many years. The choice is up to using police

leadership. The time is right to mesh the needs of our employees and our communities to forge a new alliance—community-oriented policing.

Unfortunately, in some police departments, according to Zhao et al. (1995, p. 168): "Leadership turnover is more likely than conversion to new values to bring about management commitment to community policing, and recruitment for diversity is more likely than remaking traditional 'kick ass and take names' cops into community policing advocates."

## LEVELS OF POLICING

Dodd (1996) has identified three levels of policing that a department might evolve through on its way to community policing.

◆

Three levels of policing are peacemaking, peacekeeping and peace building.

◆

The first level, peacemaking, is the traditional reactive policing mode which is usually highly valued by the public. The primary purpose of this mode is to regain the state of stability. This mode, however, presents a difficulty illustrated by the reactive spiral shown in Figure 5.3. As citizens demand more and more, resources are stretched thin and activities must be concentrated on short-term efforts at crime fighting.

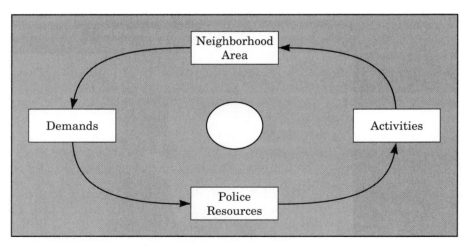

*Figure 5.3*    **The Reactive Spiral**
SOURCE: David Dodd. "Clarity of Purpose in Policing." *Law and Order.* (December 1996): 45–48. Reprinted by permission of the publisher and the author.

The second level, peacekeeping, is planned policing focused on reducing crime and disorder. This often includes specialized squad activity and intelligence-led policing.

The third level, peace building, is "real preventive policing" involving partnerships with others. It has the greatest potential for long-term results.

## APPROACHES TO IMPLEMENTING COMMUNITY POLICING

Tempe, Arizona, has a comprehensive model for community policing which involves numerous elements, as shown in Figure 5.4. As Chief of Police Brown notes: "We said community policing is going to be an evolution, not a revolution.

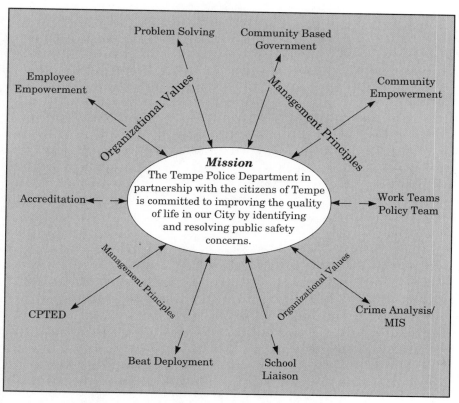

*Figure 5.4*    **A Model Said to Depict the Focus of the Tempe Police Department and the Elements That Drive Its Community-Based Policing Philosophy**
Used by permission of the Tempe Police Department.

*Neighborhood meeting with police to discuss crime, drug activity in northeast Austin, TX. Such meetings are critical to implementing community policing.*

We did not want to come in and say, 'Effective next Monday, we will be a community policing organization.' It's been a gradual change process for us, and it's growing every day (Rosen, 1994)."

Pratt (1995, pp. 57–58) describes a five-step approach to implementing community policing:

1. Problem Identification/Assessment. Consult civic, political, business, religious and media leaders, consult the public through town hall meetings or informally at educational, cultural and social activities within identifiable neighborhoods. Determine priorities, trying to place the public's needs ahead of the department's needs.

2. Plan Development. The overall objective of crime reduction must be kept in mind. Strategy obviously will depend upon the nature of the specific crime problem chosen for attack. Any program must consider ethnic, social, economic and other cultural factors in the area and will differ from one area to another. The strategy must fit the problem and the tactics must fit the neighborhood.

3. Personnel Selection/Development/Training. Strong ties between officers and citizens can best be formed by considering ethnic, religious, national origin or economic factors, with assignment of officers who are either representative of such groups or are empathetic with them.

4. Community Preparation. Include full information to the community of intended police action, how the residents will benefit from those actions and what role citizens may be expected to play, along with the legal and safety limits placed upon citizen actions.

5. Ongoing Evaluation and, Where Appropriate, Modification. It is vital to monitor progress, evaluating each phase and tactic so that timely modifications can be made as appropriate.

A ten-step implementation plan used in the Pueblo County Sheriff's Department is described by Corsentino (1996, pp. 2, 8):

1. Developed a strategic plan.
2. Leadership planted community policing seeds with officers and support units so that they would take ownership.
3. The department incorporated team policing into all sectors and encouraged deputies to go beyond basic law enforcement decisions to problem solving.
4. The department decentralized decision making where and when possible and encouraged officers to work on critical issues as they determine a need.

5.  The department changed its organizational culture to a customer orientation and used this approach to interact with citizens.

6.  Designed a new approach to strategic planning that involves officers and citizens more closely in the organizational changes required to support community policing.

7.  Designed and rebuilt the system for better operating efficiency.

8.  Established community outreach programs such as DARE, GREAT, and DFSZ (Drug Free School Zone).

9.  Personnel encouraged good relations with the media, and the media in turn were instrumental in improving the department's image.

10. Trained, trained, trained—taught, taught, taught—coached, coached, coached.

Hart (1996, p. 19) suggests that police departments implement a presentation on the Web. This might include a "virtual tour" of the department, a photo gallery of the officers or continuously updated crime statistics. Hart (p. 20) concludes: "A Web site poses some intriguing possibilities for imaginative administrators who want to add a high-tech aspect to their community policing strategies. Administrators should keep in mind the potential pitfalls, however—including interest, funds and ability to maintain the site."

*Understanding Community Policing* (1994, p. 33) stresses; "Timing is an important factor in the implementation process. Implementation that moves too slowly may dampen enthusiasm and reduce momentum, while implementation that moves too quickly may create confusion and resentment and may threaten the success of the project through the use of hurried and ill conceived methods."

This monograph (p. 42) also suggests: "Media involvement ensures a wide dissemination of the community policing message and encourages the media to stay involved in future community policing events."

## PROMISING STRATEGIES FOR COMMUNITY POLICING

A national survey of police chiefs conducted in 1993 by the Division of Governmental Studies and Services at Washington State University found that the majority of police departments across the nation had implemented some type of community policing strategies within the past three years (Zhao et al., 1995, p. 16). Table 5.1 summarizes the type of community policing strategies used.

*City of Poughkeepsie (New York) policewoman explains part of new community policing program to city residents at meeting. Citizens are vital to implementing any new community policing strategy.*

*Table 5.1*   **Frequency Distribution of Externally Focused Change: COP Programs**

|  | | *Yes* | *No* |
|---|---|---|---|
| 1. | Community newsletter | 49.8% | 52.2% |
| 2. | Foot, horse patrol | 88.4% | 11.6% |
| 3. | Storefront station | 41.4% | 58.6% |
| 4. | Special task unit | 91.6% | 8.4% |
| 5. | Victim contact program | 62.8% | 37.2% |
| 6. | Education of public | 98.1% | 1.9% |
| 7. | Fixed assignment | 87.0% | 13.0% |
| 8. | Citizen survey | 62.3% | 37.7% |
| 9. | Block watch | 97.7% | 2.3% |
| 10. | Business watch | 65.1% | 34.9% |
| 11. | Block meeting | 86.5% | 13.5% |
| 12. | Volunteer program | 68.4% | 31.6% |
| | | n = 215 | |

SOURCE: Zhao et al. "Community-Oriented Policing Across the U.S.: Facilitators and Impediments to Implementation." *American Journal of Police.* (Vol. XIV, No. 1, 1995):11–28. Used by permission of MCB University Press.

## BENEFITS THAT MIGHT BE ACHIEVED

Matthews (1995, p. 37) cites the following benefits that might be achieved by departments that implement community policing:

- The philosophy is embraced by the entire department.
- There is no animosity based on job description; everyone performs community policing initiatives.
- All officers are trained in community policing and problem solving.
- There is a single agenda: to resolve community concerns about crime and disorder by responding to calls for service, mobilizing the community and building partnerships.
- All officers are responsible for taking action and empowered with authority to make decisions.
- Entrepreneurial problem solving with action and creativity is encouraged.
- Pooling of common resources is encouraged, making them accessible to everyone.
- Community police officers are integrated throughout the organization.
- Officers work on all types and sizes of problems.
- The documentation is shared, department-wide.

## ERRORS TO AVOID

Matthews (1995, p. 34) describes what he calls "cop flops" or mistakes in implementing community policing. At the top of his list is adopting a specialized unit or task force approach to community policing: "When an organization divides itself into 'those who serve the public' and 'those who do real police work,' barriers of animosity are created." He lists the following implementation problems when a task force approach is used to implement community policing (p. 37):

- Acceptance of the philosophy is isolated to individuals in the community policing unit.
- Employee resentment exists because of job description, "real police" vs. "social worker" mentality.
- Only selected officers are trained in concept.
- The dual/competing agenda: primary responsibility results in calls for service and other police activities to be neglected.
- Officers are responsible for taking action, but decision making authority resides with management.

- Bureaucratic entanglements occur due to agency restrictions.
- Specialized resources are permitted strictly for community policing unit.
- Community-based officers are segregated from others.
- Specific problems are targeted.
- Documentation is limited to isolated, special projects.

Walker (1993, pp. 36–37) suggests that those implementing community policing should take some lessons from what was learned from the team policing programs instituted during the mid-1960s to mid-1970s. Both community policing and team policing had a neighborhood focus, decentralized decision making, community input and a new police role. But the basic goals of community policing differ radically from team policing, with community policing rejecting the crime attack model in favor of an emphasis on order maintenance and quality-of-life problems. In addition, the team policing effort faced three major obstacles (pp. 41–44):

Opposition from middle management—captains and lieutenants resented their loss of authority as greater responsibility was placed on sergeants and police officers.

Trial by peers—where it was a success, or reputed to be a success, there was resentment on the part of other officers, often as the result of unequal workloads.

Problems with dispatching technology—dispatching technology remained centralized, with team members spending as much as half their time outside their team area.

The most important lesson to be learned from team policing according to Walker (p. 44), was the problems associated with unclear definition of goals. He (p. 54) notes:

The problem of unclear goals is probably greater in community policing than in team policing. . . . Community policing . . . represents a radical role redefinition, eschewing crime control in favor of attention to problems that have traditionally been defined as not part of the police role. . . .

Redefining the police role in such a radical fashion introduces a number of problems. The most important is socializing the various actors and publics into the new role. Resocializing police officers is a major change. . . . Equally difficult is the task of resocializing the public.

Walker (p. 48) notes yet another hazard associated with community policing: "If community policing has the potential for unleashing the untapped creativity of officers on the street, it also has the danger of allowing them to revert to the gross abuses of a previous era in policing."

Walker (p. 51) also cautions against the hazards of inflated expectations: "Community policing places a heavy burden of responsibility on rank-and-file officers to develop creative, neighborhood-specific programs. This is an enormous burden indeed and the unpleasant truth may be that it is unrealistic to expect that much creativity among the police rank and file."

## POSSIBLE IMPEDIMENTS TO OVERCOME

Sadd and Grinc (1996, pp. 1–2) report on a National Institute of Justice survey of eight cities implementing innovative neighborhood-oriented policing (INOP). This study revealed the following:

- The major implementation challenges were resistance by police officers to community policing and the difficulty of involving other public agencies and organizing the community.
- With the exception of one site, the involvement of other public agencies was limited.
- Police officers generally did not understand community policing. They saw INOP assignment as conferring an elite status; perceived INOP as less productive, more time-consuming, and more resource-intensive than traditional policing; and felt their powers, particularly to enforce the law, were restrained.
- Average citizens had less knowledge than community leaders about INOP and were reluctant to participate.

This survey (p. 13) also looked at the "untested assumptions of community policing that residents really want closer contact with the police and want to work with them to reduce crime." The survey found that many citizens didn't want to become involved in community policing efforts because of "outright hostility—the historically negative relationship between the police and residents of economically disadvantaged communities."

Another implementation problem the survey identified (p. 14) was the nature of the target neighborhoods:

> The economically disadvantaged urban areas that generally serve as testing grounds for community policing tend to be highly disorganized, characterized by poverty, unemployment, inadequate educational services, and high crime rates. In areas encumbered by such an array of problems it is often difficult to find well-organized community groups that are attempting to address quality-of-life issues.

The survey also identified conflict among community leaders and residents regarding what issues should be addressed (p. 14): "In reality the community is often an aggregate of competing groups."

Zhao et al. (1995, p. 19) cite several factors impeding implementation of community policing, as summarized in Table 5.2.

*Table 5.2*   **Factor Analysis: Impediments to COP Implementation***

| Factor** | Loading | | | Mean Rating*** (SD) |
|---|---|---|---|---|
| | I | II | III | |
| **1. Organizational Impediments (IMP1)** | | | | |
| **a.** Resistance from middle-management | .75 | −.03 | .05 | |
| **b.** Line officers' resistance | .75 | .16 | .08 | |
| **c.** Departmental confusion of what COP is | .68 | .15 | .31 | |
| **d.** Problem in line-level accountability | .66 | .25 | .22 | |
| **e.** Officers' concern: COP is "soft" on crime | .63 | .46 | −.18 | |
| **f.** Lack of COP training | .55 | .24 | .41 | |
| **g.** Union resistance | .52 | .51 | −.18 | 2.41 (.76) |
| **2. Community Impediments (IMP2)** | | | | |
| **a.** Community resistance | .07 | .71 | .16 | |
| **b.** Community concern: COP is "soft" on crime | .11 | .69 | −.00 | |
| **c.** Civil service rules | .13 | .64 | .10 | |
| **d.** Pressure on chief to demonstrate COP reduces crime in short term | .23 | .59 | .34 | |
| **e.** Lack of support from local government | .22 | .56 | .36 | 1.96 (.87) |
| **3. Transition Impediment (IMP3)** | | | | |
| **a.** Problems in balancing increased foot patrol activities while maintaining emergency response time | .11 | .15 | .84 | 2.98 (1.10) |

*Alpha level of first two factors>.70.
**% of variance (Eigen Value) of three factors are: 36.9 (4.8), 10.7 (1.4), and 8.0 (1.0) respectively.
***Mean Ratings: 1=no obstacle, 2=slightly, 3=moderate, 4=serious obstacles.
Zhao et al. "Community-Oriented Policing Across the U.S.: Facilitators and Impediments to Implementation." *American Journal of Police.* (Vol. XIV, No. 1, 1995):11–28.
Used by permission of MCB University Press.

## ASSESSING THE EFFECTIVENESS OF COMMUNITY POLICING EFFORTS

Dempsey (1995, pp. 60–61) lists the following areas that might be used to evaluate the effectiveness of community policing efforts:

1.  A statistic review of reported crime rates in target area. (Certain types of crime seem to be good targets for community policing: domestic violence, residential and commercial burglary, vandalism [graffiti], street-level drug related crimes and gang activity.)

2.  A comparative review of complaints filed against officers in the targeted communities.

3.  A comparative review of commendations of officers from either citizens or supervisors,.

4.  A review of follow-up calls for service at the same address or to the same identified problem.

5.  Survey tools should be developed to measure the perception of specific groups with regard to crime and police effectiveness.

Gnagey and Henson (1995, p. 25) describe a survey divided into five components: fear of crime, neighborhood disorder, police service evaluation, demographic information and open-ended response.

To assess fear of crime, the survey asked questions such as whether a person feels crime has decreased, increased or remained the same; whether they have limited or changed their activities due to fear of crime; and if their neighborhood is dangerous enough that they have considered moving.

To assess neighborhood disorder, citizens were asked to indicate whether certain factors were a big problem, somewhat of a problem or no problem in their neighborhood. The factors included such items as abandoned/burned-out buildings, cars speeding/screeching tires, drug dealers operating openly, loud music from homes, parking/traffic problems, prostitutes/"johns" roaming neighborhood, run-down buildings, stray/noisy animals, vandalism/graffiti, dilapidated streets/sidewalks, poor street lighting, public drinking, strangers trespassing, striped/abandoned cars, unsupervised children and juvenile delinquency.

To assess police service, citizens were asked to rate the protection provided their neighborhood as excellent, good, fair or poor. The final questions asked respondents if they have any suggestions for improving police service.

*Understanding Community Policing* (1994, p. 45) suggests that since one core component of community policing is community partnerships, an early measure of effectiveness could be the number and type of community partnerships that are formed. Other means of assessment include (pp. 46–47):

- The number and type of problems solved and the creativity and scope of the solutions.
- Increased levels of community participation in crime reduction and prevention efforts.
- Commitment of an increased level of community resources devoted to crime reduction efforts.

Trojanowicz and Bucqueroux (1994, pp. 27–32) have developed an extensive self-assessment checklist which includes most of the philosophy, concept, totality and reality of community policing. It looks at the department as a whole, top command, first-line supervisors, line officers, problem solving, quality of life and ethical and legal concerns.

## SUMMARY

Community policing will require a change in mission statement, departmental organization, leadership style and the general approach to "fighting crime."

The first change is usually in the traditional law enforcement organizational structure which has been a pyramid-shaped hierarchy based on a military model. To implement community policing, the pyramid might be inverted.

Another change might be in leadership style, with a preference for participatory leadership where each individual has a voice in decisions, but top management still has the ultimate decision-making authority.

Three levels of policing are peacemaking, peacekeeping and peace building. Only the peace-building level involves true partnerships and community policing.

### Discussion Questions

1. What do you consider the greatest obstacles to implementing community policing?
2. If you had to prioritize the changes needed to convert to community policing, what would your priorities be?
3. Find out what your police department's mission statement is. If it is not community policing focused, how might it be revised?
4. How would you assess whether community policing efforts are working?
5. Does your community have agencies and/or organizations that could become partners with the police department?
6. Why might citizens not want to become involved in community policing efforts?
7. Discuss the similarities between team policing and community policing and describe the most important lessons to be learned from team policing.
8. How would you go about assessing your community's needs regarding efforts to reduce crime and violence?

9. How would you enlist the support of the media? What resources are available in your community?

10. Are there conflicting groups within your "community"? Does one group have more political power than another?

## References

Bentz, David E. "Leadership with an Eye on the Future." *The Police Chief.* (February 1995): 14–17.

Corsentino, Dan L. "A 10-Step Transformation Plan." *Community Policing Exchange.* (Spring 1996): 2, 8.

Couper, David C. and Lobitz, Sabine. "The Customer Is Always Right: Applying Vision, Leadership and the Problem-Solving Methods to Community-Oriented Policing." *The Police Chief.* (May 1991): 16–23.

Dempsey, Tom G. "Evaluating Community-Based Efforts." *Law and Order.* (October 1995): 54–55, 60–62.

Dodd, David. "Clarity of Purpose in Policing." *Law and Order.* (December 1996): 45–48.

Dolan, Harry P. "Coping with Internal Backlash." *The Police Chief.* (March 1994): 28–32.

Gnagey, John and Henson, Ronald. "Community Surveys Help Determine Policing Strategies." *The Police Chief.* (March 1995): 25–27.

Goldstein, Herman. *The New Policing: Confronting Complexity.* Washington, D.C.: National Institute of Justice Research in Brief, December 1993.

Goodbody, William L. "A Square Peg in Bureaucracy's Round Hole." *Law Enforcement News.* (June 30, 1995): 12, 14.

Harrison, Bob. "Integrating the Focus of Law Enforcement's Future." *The Police Chief.* (February 1994): 52–61.

Hart, Fran. "How—and Why—to Implement the World-Wide Web for Community Policing." *The Police Chief.* (December 1996): 19–20.

Matthews, John. "Department-Wide Versus 'Task Force' Implementation." *Law and Order.* (December 1995): 34–37.

Mulder, Armand. "Resistance to Change." *Law and Order.* (February 1994): 55–59.

Mullen, Karen. "From 'C' to Shining 'C': Developing Community Policing Through Reorganization." *Community Policing Exchange.* (July/August 1996).

Nila, Michael J. "Defining the Police Mission: A Community/Police Perspective." *The Police Chief.* (October 1990): 43–47.

Peak, Ken. "Police Executives as Change Agents." *The Police Chief.* (January 1994): 27–29.

Peterson, Kenneth. "Management 2000: Providing the Resources." *The Police Chief.* (February 1994): 49–51.

Pratt, C. E. "Five Steps to Community-Based Policing." *Law and Order.* (October 1995): 54–58.

Rippy, Keith M. "The Politics of Being a Police Chief: The Ins and Outs of Implementing Change." *The Police Chief.* (April 1990): 135–40.

Rodgers, Todd. "A Blueprint for Community Policing." *Law and Order.* (March 1995): 116–121.

Rosen, Marie Simonetti. "A LEN Interview with Chief Dave Brown of Tempe, Arizona." *Law Enforcement News.* (May 1994): 8–11.

Sadd, Susan and Grinc, Randolph M. *Implementing Challenges in Community Policing: Innovative Neighborhood-Oriented Policing in Eight Cities.* Washington, D.C.: National Institute of Justice Research in Brief, February 1996.

Trojanowicz, Robert and Bucqueroux, Bonnie. *Community Policing.* Cincinnati: Anderson Publishing Company, 1994.

*Understanding Community Policing.* Washington, D.C.: Bureau of Justice Assistance, August 1994.

VanMeter, D. J. "Mission and its Value." *Law and Order.* (August 1991): 65–66.

Walker, Samuel. "Does Anyone Remember Team Policing? Lessons of the Team Policing Experience for Community Policing." *American Journal of Police.* (Vol. XII, No. 1, 1993):35–55.

Wilson, James Q. and Kelling, George L. "Making Neighborhoods Safe." *The Atlantic Monthly.* (February 1989): 46–52.

"Your Agency's Driving Force: Mission and its Value." *Law and Order.* (August 1991): 65.

Zhao, Jihong; Lovrich, Nicholas P.; and Gray, Kelsey. "Moving Toward Community Policing: The Role of Postmaterialist Values in a Changing Police Profession." *American Journal of Police.* (Vol. XIV, No. 3/4, 1995):151–71.

Zhao, Jihong; Thurman, Qunit C.; and Lovrich, Nicholas P. "Community-Oriented Policing Across the U.S.: Facilitators and Impediments to Implementation." *American Journal of Police.* (Vol. XIV, No. 1, 1995):11–28.

# Section

# Building Relationships

With the basic background supplied by Section 1, you are ready to look at the interaction occurring between the police and the publics they serve. At the most basic level, police-community relations begin with one-on-one interaction between a police officer and a citizen.

The section begins with a discussion of the interpersonal skills needed to interact effectively with average, mainstream adults (Chapter 6). Ensuing chapters discuss specific challenges in dealing with individuals who differ from this norm in some respect: members of minority groups (Chapter 7); people who are disabled (Chapter 8), including those who are visually or hearing impaired, mentally and emotionally disabled and those who have epilepsy; the elderly (Chapter 9), including those who have Alzheimer's disease and those whose quality of life is reduced because of fear of being victimized; youth (Chapter 10), including youth who are learning-disabled, who are in trouble with the law and who are members of gangs (Chapter 11). Interacting with victims of crimes or natural disasters is also discussed (Chapter 12).

Although these special populations are discussed separately, overlap often exists. The more differences an individual has from the "norm," the greater the challenge in establishing good relationships. It must always be remembered that each member of the specific group discussed is first an individual.

Last, the section discusses interaction with members of the media (Chapter 13), the constitutional issues involved and how such interactions can help or hinder community policing.

*Chapter 6*

# Basic Interpersonal Skills

*Public cooperation and voluntary compliance with law comes not through law but through positive human contacts.*

—Denny Pace (p. 69)

## Do you know

- How a person's world-view is largely created?
- Why two people may "see" the same thing differently?
- What the most basic rule of semantics is?
- What police officers must recognize in themselves?
- The difference between prejudice and discrimination?
- What empathy is?
- What networks are?
- What the communication process consists of?
- What individual characteristics are important in the communication process?
- What can improve communication?
- What are common barriers to effective communication?
- Why effective listening is often difficult?
- Why police officers may have more barriers to communication than other professionals?
- What the primacy effect is?
- What the four-minute barrier is?
- What two human relations practices used in business might be adopted for improving police-community relations?
- What networking is and how it functions?

## Definitions

Can you define these terms: bias, body language, communication, communication process, discrimination, empathy, extensional world, four-minute barrier, jargon, kinesics, networking, networks, nonverbal communication, perception, phenomenological point of view, preference, prejudice, primacy effect, self-fulfilling prophecy, semantic environment, semantics, sensorium, stereotyping, symbolic process, verbal world.

 *Introduction*

A woman executive at a shopping center discovered a minor theft of company property from her company car. The car had been parked outside a police office where several traffic officers took breaks between shifts. The office was not accessible to the public, but had an identification sign on the locked door.

The woman knocked on the door and asked the sergeant who opened it who was responsible for watching the parking area. She also commented on the officers she could see sitting in the room, and suggested they were not doing their jobs. The officers in the room stopped talking with each other and turned their attention to the conversation at the office door.

The sergeant and the woman never got around to discussing the missing item. Instead he responded to her comments with questions. "What do you mean by that?" "What are you trying to say?" She left to tell her supervisor, refusing to file a police report. She soon returned, however, and encountered another officer just outside the office. Their conversation, later characterized as "heated" by witnesses, centered on the woman's suggestion that the officers should do more to prevent theft in the parking lot. She implied they were lazy and shirked their responsibilities.

At this point the woman asked to file a police report, and the officer asked her to enter the police office with him to do so. They entered the office, but when the officer suggested they enter a private office away from the hubbub of the break area, she refused to do so. She later said the officer intimidated her by slamming drawers, moving quickly and ordering her into the room. She feared being alone with him.

The officer's perception of the incident was entirely different. He commented that the woman had a "chip on her shoulder" and an "attitude." She was demanding and impossible to deal with.

After refusing to enter the office to file the report, the woman sat down on a chair in the break area. She was told to either go into the other room and file the report or leave. When she refused to do either, she was escorted from the office and left outside the locked doors. The woman filed a complaint against the police department.

With better communication, this problem and thousands like it could be avoided. Effective communication with the public is vital to good police-community relations. In fact, at the heart of police-community relations are one-on-one interactions between officers and citizens. "Human relations is the thread that holds civilized people together" (Pace, 1991, p. 237).

The following discussion assumes that those involved in the interaction are adults with no serious physical or mental disabilities. Interactions involving individuals with disabilities are discussed in later chapters.

This chapter begins with a discussion of understanding oneself—a prerequisite for effective interpersonal relationships. This is followed by an explanation of understanding others and the nature of the interaction between police and citizens. Next the communication process is described, including nonverbal communications and body language, communication enhancers and communication barriers. Then the chapter discusses the primacy effect and the four-minute barrier. The chapter concludes with lessons learned from business and some human relations guidelines.

## UNDERSTANDING ONESELF

Officers who seek to build effective relationships with the citizens they serve first need to understand themselves and potential barriers to such relationships. They need to recognize their own level of self-esteem as well as the roles they play. Officers need to understand how their view of the world has been shaped and how it affects their interactions with others.

◆

Your world-view is largely created by what you see and hear as you experience events.

◆

### Perception—What Is Seen

What is "seen" may not always be trusted as illustrated by the common phenomenon of optical illusions as shown in Figure 6.1. One critical aspect of a person's world-view is individual *perception*. According to Hageman (1985, p. 39), **perception** is "the process of giving meaning or organization to experience." Hageman (p. 40) notes that perception is "a complex, dynamic, interrelated composite of processes that involves the human nervous system." Two primary components of this process are the eye and the **sensorium,** that part of the brain that interprets what the eye takes in. Says Hageman (p. 40):

> The eye takes the energy of certain wavelengths of light and converts it into nerve impulses. It is not the eyes that see. Rather, it is the "perceiver" in the brain, commonly called the sensorium. While the eye can handle stimuli of

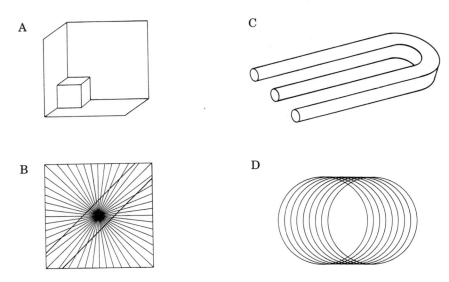

*Figure 6.1*    **Optical Illusions**
   A. Is the box inside a room or are there two boxes?
   B. Are the lines pulled apart at the center or are they parallel?
   C. Where is the center group?
   D. Which end is out?
   (A. Either is correct; B. Parallel; C. Unknown; D. Either one.)

nearly five million bits per second, the sensorium has limited abilities. The sensorium's resolving power is limited to approximately five hundred bits per second. In short, some stimuli are labeled by the person as important and others as not important. Some stimuli, needless to say, fall by the wayside. The perception is in the "eyes" of the beholder.

◆

The discrepancy between what the eye takes in (five million bits per second) and what the person actually processes (five hundred bits per second) accounts, in part, for why two witnesses can see the same thing differently.

◆

Two witnesses' sensoriums process different portions of what the eye "sees." According to Hageman (p. 44): "As a general rule, the more objective we are, the more our perceptions mirror the perceptions of others." She gives as an example the fact that if a group of people were given a standard ruler and asked to measure the size of something, they would probably all come up with the same measurement. When no such standard ruler exists, people rely on their limited experiences. Reliance on past experiences may result in prejudices and stereotyping. Later in this chapter you will consider the problems prejudice and stereotyping present to police-community relations. Another aspect of perception is the manner in which people typically categorize and classify their experiences by generalizing in their thoughts and in their language.

## Perception—What Is Heard v. What Is Said

In addition to what individuals see, the language they use also shapes their "reality." Individuals in the field of **semantics** research and study the meaning of language. According to Hayakawa (1949, pp. 21–22):

> Words—the way he uses them and the way he takes them when spoken by others—largely shape his beliefs, his prejudices, his ideals, his aspirations. They constitute the moral and intellectual atmosphere in which he lives—in short—his **semantic environment**. . . .
>
> It will be the basic assumption of this book [the classic, *Language in Thought and Action*] that widespread intraspecific co-operation through the use of language is the fundamental mechanism of human survival. A parallel assumption will be that when the use of language results, as it so often does, in the creation or aggravation of disagreements and conflicts, there is something wrong with the speaker, the listener, or both. Human "fitness to survive" means the ability to talk and write and listen and read in ways that increase the chances for you and fellow-members of your species to survive together.

The following are some key assertions of Hayakawa:

- The process by means of which human beings can arbitrarily make certain things *stand* for other things may be called the **symbolic process.** We are, as human beings, uniquely free to manufacture and manipulate and assign values to our symbols as we please (p. 25).

- Of all forms of symbolism, language is the most highly developed, most subtle, and most complicated. . . . Symbols and things symbolized are independent of each other; nevertheless, we all have a way of believing as if, and sometimes acting as if, there were necessary connections (p. 27).

- The symbol is NOT the thing symbolized. The four-legged animal that goes "moo" and gives milk is represented in English by three letters arranged to form the word *cow*. Other languages have very different words for the actual animal. The word is NOT the thing; the map is NOT the territory. There is a sense in which we all live in two worlds. First, we live in the world of happenings about us which we know at first hand. But this is an extremely small world. . . . Most of our knowledge, acquired from parents, friends, schools, newspapers, books, conversation, speeches, and radio, is received *verbally*. Call this world that comes to us through words the **verbal world,** as opposed to our own experience, called the **extensional world.** Now this verbal world ought to stand in relation to the extensional world as a *map* does to the *territory* it is supposed to represent (pp. 21–32).

- Classification. What we call things and where we draw the line between one class of things and another depend upon the interests we have and the purposes of the classification . . . Many of us, for example, cannot distinguish between pickerel, pike, salmon, smelts, perch, crappies, halibut, and mackerel; we say that they are "just fish, and I don't like fish." To a seafood connoisseur, however, these distinctions are real. . . . To a zoologist, even finer distinctions become of great importance. . . . When we name something, then, we are classifying. The individual object or event we are naming, of course, has no name and belongs to no class until we put it in one . . . (pp. 209–10).

There are few complexities about classifications at the level of dogs and cats, knives and forks, cigarettes and candy, but when it comes to classifications at high levels of abstraction, for example, those describing conduct, social institutions, philosophical and moral problems, serious difficulties occur. This can be a major source of conflict. When one person kills another, is it an act of murder, an act of temporary insanity, an act of homicide, an accident, or an act of heroism? As soon as the process of classification is completed, our attitudes and our conduct are to a considerable degree determined. We hang the murderer, we lock up the insane man, we free the victim of circumstances, we pin a medal on the hero. Unfortunately, people are not always aware of the way in which they arrive at their classifications (pp. 211–12).

How do we prevent ourselves from getting into such intellectual blind alleys, or, if we find we are in one, how do we get out again? One way is to remember that practically all statements in ordinary conversation, debate and public controversy taking the form, "Business is business," "Boys will be boys," and so on, are *not* true. . . .

A simple technique for preventing classification from harming our thinking is the suggestion made by Korzybski to add "index numbers" to our terms, thus: Englishman$_1$, Englishman$_2$ . . .; cow$_1$, cow$_2$, cow$_3$ . . . The terms of the classification tell us what the individuals in that class have in common; **The index numbers remind us of the characteristics left out.** A rule can then be formulated as a general guide in all our thinking and reading: Cow$_1$ is NOT Cow$_2$ Politician$_1$ is NOT Politician$_2$, and so on. This rule, if remembered, prevents us from confusing levels of abstraction and forces us to consider the facts on those occasions when we might otherwise find ourselves leaping to conclusions which we may later have cause to regret (pp. 212–14).

◆

The simplest and most basic rule of semantics is: Cow$_1$ is NOT Cow$_2$.

◆

Once aware of how perceptions are formed, consider the natural tendency to have preferences and the danger it presents to effective police-community relations.

## Preferences, Prejudice, Bias, Stereotyping and Discrimination

It is important to recognize that no one can be completely objective. Everyone, consciously or unconsciously, has certain preferences and prejudices.

◆

It is critical to self-understanding to recognize preferences, prejudices and stereotypes.

◆

A **preference** is selecting someone or something over another. You may, for example, prefer to interact with people of your own ethnic background, your own age or your own economic level.

A **prejudice** is a negative judgment not based on fact; an irrational, preconceived negative opinion. Prejudices are often associated with a dislike of a particular group, race or religion.

Prejudices are often the result of the classifications discussed earlier. They represent *overgeneralizations,* a failure to consider individual characteristics. According to Hageman (1985, p. 51):

We as human beings, as part of processing information, have a tendency to prejudge—to classify information into meaningful categories. Prejudgments are natural for human beings, whose eyes are able to receive more bits of stimuli than their brains are able to process. Thus, each one of us is carrying around "preconceived notions" of specific persons or groups of persons. . . .

These prejudgments do not always involve minority groups, such as blacks and American Indians. Prejudgments can also center on the categories developed and labeled as "old people," "teenagers," "the handicapped," "gay people," and "women."

Prejudices are also referred to as **bias,** a belief that inhibits objectivity. Taken to an extreme, a bias becomes hatred. It is important for law enforcement to understand bias and its extreme form—hate—in order to deal with the increase in bias and hate crimes. The manner in which police should deal with hate crimes is discussed in the next chapter. Prejudices or biases are the result of overgeneral classification or stereotyping.

**Stereotyping** assumes that all people within a specific group are the same; they lack individuality. Simply because a person is a member of a specific group, that person is thought to have certain characteristics. Common stereotypes associated with nationalities include the French being great lovers, the Italians being great cooks, the Scotch being thrifty and American Yankees being ingenious.

Often the stereotype of Americans is very negative, as illustrated by an article date-lined *Marne-la-Vallee, France,* when Euro Disneyland opened in France in the spring of 1992:

Writer Jean Cau dismissed the theme park as "a horror made of cardboard, plastic and appalling colors, a construction of hardened chewing gum and idiotic folklore taken straight out of comic books written for obese Americans. . . ."

Another writer . . . said the park was "a terrifying giant's step toward world homogenization." . . .

A novelist said Euro Disney represented the transformation of culture from craft into industry. "If we do not resist it," he warned, "the kingdom of profit will create a world that will have all the appearance of civilization and all the savage reality of barbarism."

Many people have stereotyped police officers. As noted by Conroy and Hess (1992, p. 82), one officer described the television cop syndrome: "They don't see you standing on the street corner in late January directing traffic after an accident. . . . They don't see you down at the medical center with a bite in your arm from some hooker who didn't want you to arrest her. . . . What they see is the TV cop doing all sorts of neat things."

Police officers may also stereotype those with whom they come in contact. As noted by Trojanowicz and Carter (1990, p. 8): "The temptation to generalize from the few to the many is a particularly critical problem for the police." In the traditional mode of policing, officers spend a considerable amount of time dealing with criminals and their victims. Some officers may begin to categorize certain types of individuals as perpetrators. Trojanowicz and Carter (p. 9) note: "Police officers so often see people at their worst, not their best. And because police officers focus so much attention on crime, there is always the danger that they will have a distorted view of who the 'bad guys' are and how many there are of them. This temptation to generalize from a few to the many is a particularly critical problem for the police in the case of immigrants."

An additional danger of stereotyping is that it may become a **self-fulfilling prophecy.** Psychologists tell us that if a person is labeled as being a certain way long enough, the person may come to actually be that way. For example, if you frequently tell a child he is a delinquent, that child may accept the label and actually become a delinquent.

It is a very natural tendency to stereotype people, but a tendency that can be fatal to effective police-community relations. Police officers must first recognize that those they deal with may have formed a stereotype of police officers. It is important for police officers to determine if this is true and, if so, to determine if it is a positive or negative image. Officers must also recognize their own prejudices and be certain they do not lead to discrimination on the job.

Prejudices may lead to **discrimination,** showing a preference or prejudice in treating individuals or groups. Some male traffic officers, for example, are known to issue warnings to females who violate traffic laws and to issue tickets to males for the same violation. Oran (1995, p. 99) defines *discrimination* as: "The failure to treat equals equally; in particular, illegally unequal treatment based on race, religion, sex, age, etc." It is often alleged that members of minority groups receive rougher treatment from police officers than a white person would receive.

◆

 Prejudice is an attitude; discrimination is a behavior.

◆

Hageman (1985, p. 55) notes:

The difference between the *attitude* reflected in the word "prejudice" and the overt behavior of prejudice, as in the word "discrimination," was summed up by an English judge in his comments to nine youths convicted of race rioting in the Notting Hill section of London:

Think what you like . . . But once you translate your dark thoughts into savage acts, the law will punish you, and protect your victim.

In the United States, the 1964 Civil Rights Act and the 1972 amendment to the Act make it illegal for agencies with fifteen or more employees to discriminate in education, housing and employment on the basis of race, religion, national origin or sex. It is critical that police officers understand their own prejudices, biases and stereotypes and that they avoid any form of discrimination.

## UNDERSTANDING OTHERS

As noted by Parker et al. (1989, p. 78): "To engage in professional work in many areas of life one needs to understand the behavior and motivation of individuals." Understanding others is particularly important in police work. Understanding others does not, however, mean that you sympathize with them or even that you agree with them. Parker et al. suggest: "Understanding involves sensing the view of others in attempting to grasp a feeling of what their world is like." It is synonymous with *empathy*.

◆

 **Empathy** is understanding another person.

◆

To empathize with someone is to see things from their perspective or, as the saying goes, to put yourself in another's shoes. Parker et al. (p. 83) describe three levels of empathy: low, moderate and high:

*Low Empathy*—The communicator shows little or no understanding of the most basic part of what the other has communicated, seems out of touch with what the other has said, and responds only from her or his own frame of reference. In *Low Empathy* the first person subtracts from the interpersonal encounter.

*Moderate Empathy*—The communicator grasps at least the essential part of the message, and sends a message that fits well with what the other is saying and is essentially interchangeable. The communicator shares with the other an understanding of at least the surface feelings and main content of the message.

*A Detroit police lieutenant talks with a citizen.*

This communicator has not completely missed the point as in *Low Empathy*, where there may not be even the slightest acknowledgement of what the person has communicated.

*High Empathy*—In deep empathy there is a consistent communication on the part of the communicator that indicates that she or he not only hears the surface message, but is able to sense the underlying feelings and concerns that are barely hinted at in the overt communication of the second person. In *High Empathy*, the communicator's responses are additive or expand on what the person has stated, and thus allow the second person to explore his or her feelings. In deep empathy, the recipient has a feeling of being able to elaborate on the discussion, and feels truly understood. Communication is opened up; there is an air of excitement about really being heard by the other. This is most important when the police officer or corrections counselor must communicate with distressed persons.

Parker et al. (p. 84) give the following example of the levels of empathy when responding to an irate husband involved in a domestic dispute:

Husband: I know damn well she's whoring around, she's never around here when I come home. She's tired, she never prepares supper, doesn't give a crap about me.

(Low Empathy) Officer: When does she come home at night?

(Moderate Empathy) Officer: It really makes you angry that she seems to be fooling around with other men.

(High Empathy) Officer: It makes you madder'n hell to think she's screwing around, but it also hurts a lot because the message is, "I don't care about you."

High empathy does not always require a response. Sometimes knowing when just to listen is important. Parker et al. (p. 85) stress: "Frequently, just listening attentively allows people to fully express their concerns, which may be extremely helpful in and of itself." Situations perceived as real, are real in their consequences. One secret to effective communications is to attempt to see the world from the other person's perspective.

To empathize with others, you need to adopt the **phenomenological point of view,** which stresses that reality is different for each individual. This point of view is used by Noose (1992, p. 101) in his conceptualization of *networks.*

◆

**Networks** are the "complex pathways of human interaction that guide and direct an individual's perception, motivation and behavior."

◆

Such networks are vital to effective communication, including interviewing individuals. According to Noose:

Networks represent relationships, links between people, and between people and their beliefs. Without an understanding of these relationships, these networks, it is often quite difficult, and sometimes even impossible, to understand an event or the circumstances that led to it. The answers obtained may have very little in common with the questions asked.

All human beings act to create a personal reality, one that allows them to predict and control the world around them. Their associations with others and their own fundamental beliefs all become part of this unique construction of reality. In this way these networks determine how people act and what they will relate when they are questioned. . . .

Networks produce the context within which a statement from a complainant, victim, witness or suspect can be most clearly understood.

Among the most important networks are those that are social: family, neighbors and friends. Sometimes legal relationships help to form networks such as those between children and their parents or between spouses. In addition to these social networks, there are occupational and professional, political, cultural and religious networks. Any of these networks can affect how a person views reality as well as what they are willing to communicate about that reality. As noted by Noose (p. 102): "Networks are critically important whenever perception is being questioned." He stresses (p. 103): "Staying informed about the networks that operate within a community is vital for officers who hope to be effective interviewers."

## IDENTIFYING THE NATURE OF THE INTERACTION

When making contact with individuals, it is important to know what the purpose of the interaction is. This will, in large part, determine the most effective tone to establish and image to project. Is the contact primarily social—an effort to create good public relations? Is the contact made primarily to seek information—about what? A person? A problem? An incident? Is the contact primarily persuasive—to get an individual to comply with a request? What role must you play? What roles are others playing?

Sometimes, of course, a contact may serve more than one purpose. It may begin as a social contact and turn into one that is persuasive or provides information. Without a clear purpose in mind, however, your communication may not be effective.

Once you consider with whom you are interacting (your audience) and why (your purpose), then focus on how the interaction generally occurs, that is, through communication.

## THE COMMUNICATION PROCESS

According to George (1985, p. 64): "A **communication** is simply the transfer of information and understanding from one person to another." Depending on the situation, the communication process involves four or five components.

◆

The **communication process** involves a sender, a message, a channel, a receiver and sometimes feedback.

◆

Communication involves transferring thoughts from one person's mind to another person's mind. The people involved, how well the message parallels the sender's thoughts and the channel used will all affect the communication.

The sender *encodes* the message in words—spoken or written—and then transmits the message by telephone, fax, letter, in person or in some other way. The receiver *decodes* the message. The receiver may then provide the sender with some kind of feedback that indicates the message has been received. Many factors will influence the message.

◆

Individual characteristics that are important in communication include age, education, sex, values, emotional involvement, self-esteem and language skills.

◆

Imagine, by way of illustration, that people see the world through tinted glasses. The tint represents their particular world view. If the sender of a message sees the world through yellow glasses and the receiver of the message sees the world through red glasses, the message received will be a mixture of the world views of both and will result in a different color—orange.

In addition to the message conveyed through words, a large part of communication occurs as the result of nonverbal communication and body language. UCLA sociologist Albert Mehrabian's research found that the effectiveness with which a face-to-face communication is received depends on the communicator's (Berglund, 1992, p. 2D):

- Look     55 percent
- Sound    38 percent
- Message   7 percent

Our educational system concentrates on the communication skills of reading and writing. Some time is devoted to speaking, and little or no time is devoted to listening. It is simply assumed that everyone knows how to listen.

Sheehan (1996, p. 38) observes: "It is a fact that most officers need training in advanced communication skills. While the concept of spending valuable training time to teach officers "how to talk" may seem unwarranted, consider how much of the job involves communicating, in direct personal conversation as well as over the radio, telephone, or computer. Clear communication is important with victims, witnesses, suspects, supervisors, residents and each other."

## NONVERBAL COMMUNICATION AND BODY LANGUAGE

Adams (1996, p. 46) stresses the importance of nonverbal cues: "In both business and personal dealings, it's your silent signals that often matter most." He quotes statistics that indicate that a mere 7 percent of what's understood between two people derives from the spoken word, 38 percent from the tone of the voice, and a full 55 percent from non-verbal cues—or "silent speech."

**Nonverbal communication** includes everything other than the actual words in a message such as tone, pitch and pacing. Sometimes the tone in which something is said makes it obvious the person is being sarcastic. A person who is nervous may speak rapidly in a high-pitched voice. Nonverbal communication also includes a person's appearance—how well groomed an individual is and the type of clothing a person wears.

**Body language** refers to messages conveyed by how a person moves. To test the power of body language, consider what the following say about a person:

Walking—fast, slow, stomping

Posture—rigid, relaxed

Eye contact—direct, indirect, shifting

Gestures—nod, shrug, finger point

Physical spacing—close, distant

## Nonverbal Communication and Body Language of Police Officers

The police communicate with the public most obviously through the uniform they wear, the way they wear it and the equipment they carry.

Police uniforms resemble military uniforms. Frequently navy blue or black, they have accessories such as silver or gold badges, name plates, collar brass and patches. Police wear leather belts loaded with equipment: handgun, radio, handcuffs, nightstick, mace and ammunition. Through their uniforms, police officers convey many messages without ever speaking.

The type of uniform is almost universally recognized as that worn by police because, despite variations, police look the same all over the world. Wearing a uniform may be called the ultimate in *power dressing*. Uniforms are authoritative and professional and have an impact on the behavior of the public.

Officers find that they can gain compliance and cooperation from most people very easily on request, even when people would prefer not to cooperate. The public is likely to ignore the same officer who makes the same request while wearing blue jeans and a T-shirt.

Of course, there are ways to change the message the police uniform gives to the public and, consequently, the image the public develops of the department. Consider what the following factors might communicate:

- Worn, faded, torn or unkempt looking uniforms.
- Scuffed shoes.
- Mirrored sunglasses.
- Dirty, dented squad cars.
- Handcuff or handgun tie tack.
- Black leather sap gloves.

*The nonverbal message of the police officers at this pro-choice rally is clear: Don't cross this line.*

- Overweight officers.
- Facial hair or long, shaggy, greasy hair.
- Several rings or earrings.
- Long, painted fingernails.
- Chewing gum.
- Playing with nightstick.
- Reading the newspaper while on duty.
- Smoking or eating in the squad car.

Obviously, even if officers wear identical uniforms, individuals will communicate their own messages about their competency, professionalism and personality.

In addition to understanding such nonverbal messages, many police officers develop their abilities to interpret body language, also called **kinesics,** to such an extent that they can tell when a person is lying or about to become aggressive or flee. They learn to take control of situations by using voice command and authoritative body language.

Other forms of body language are equally important. How officers stand, how they look at those to whom they are talking, whether they smile or frown—all convey a message. A warm smile is said to be the universal language of kindness.

Even a handshake conveys messages. A limp handshake sends one message, a firm handshake another message. Touching, too, can be used to an officer's advantage or disadvantage, as noted by Pace (1991, p. 229):

> Touching is an important means of communicating willingness to assist, warmth, and sincerity. This gesture has limited use in police communications. Most official situations do not lend themselves to this type of communication. In fact, touching has many negative connotations and is often the catalyst to violent reaction.

It is worth some time and thought to make sure your appearance and demeanor convey a professional, competent image. Try to eliminate any mannerisms that may give the public the wrong impression about you.

Usually police officers want to convey the impression that they "know their way around." This may actually interfere with effective communication. Noose (1992, p. 105) gives as an example the person who asks directions about how to find a certain store in Boston. If the person is from Boston, the directions given are likely to be brief, with obvious landmarks omitted. If the person is from out of town, however, the directions are likely to be much more detailed. Noose suggests that when interviewing a truthful witness, police officers may want to modify their body language and soften up their "official" language, in a sense pretending to be from out of town. A relaxed manner may result in more in-depth communication and better understanding.

In a confrontational situation, communication skills are also essential. According to Klockars (1985, p. 145): "The police officer's most important tool is his mouth." He notes (p. 146): "The ability to talk in strong, subtle, and sensitive ways, the art of effective rhetoric is essential to the skillful exercise of coercion."

## Reading the Nonverbal Messages and Body Language of Others

Police officers, with time and experience, learn to "read" the nonverbal messages and body language of suspects, victims and witnesses. It is what some call a "sixth sense," and it alerts officers when something is not as it appears or when someone is suspicious, untruthful, afraid or hesitant. Officers will sometimes call it a "gut feeling" or a nagging suspicion. As many officers have discovered, acting on such inarticulable feelings can pay off.

Criminals are often apprehended because an officer thought they looked suspicious or because something did not "feel right" about a traffic stop or other contact. Many law enforcement officers develop an uncanny ability to spot stolen cars in traffic based on a driver's movements, actions and driving maneuvers. Officers also learn to read their own "hunches," a very illusive form of communication. Acting on a hunch can save lives, however, as illustrated in the rescue of a driver by an alert, "tuned in" officer.

Officer James Northagen of the Silver Bay Police Department on Lake Superior was on his way to work on a late November night when he noticed tire tracks leading into a snowbank along the edge of the lake. He later said it looked like a vehicle had slipped into a ditch and then driven out. Northagen continued on his way to work, but he kept thinking about the tracks and decided to go back after he started his shift. More than an hour after he first saw the tracks, Officer Northagen looked over the snowbank and saw the wreckage of a pickup truck 60 feet below, in the icy cold water of Lake Superior. The lone occupant was conscious, but pinned in the truck. It took an hour to rescue the man whose head was just barely out of the water for the three hours he was trapped in his truck.

Police officers can tell story after story of nagging and intuitive feelings which they acted on, with similar results.

The REID School of Interviewing and Interrogation trains officers to understand intuitive feelings and the truthfulness of what people communicate. The REID School teaches police officers reliable techniques to determine if a subject is telling the truth based on body language and verbal responses to questions asked by trained interrogators. The REID School's research indicates that certain responses to key questions are very accurate indicators of deception. Police investigators have found such training invaluable; it often results in confessions from guilty people whose lies do not fool the police.

## COMMUNICATION ENHANCERS

Over twenty years ago, the National Advisory Commission on Criminal Justice Standards and Goals: Police (1973, p. 407) emphasized the importance of interpersonal communication skills: "Every police agency should immediately develop and improve the interpersonal communications skills of all officers. These skills are essential to the productive exchange of information and opinion between the police, other elements of the criminal justice system, and the public; their use helps officers to perform their tasks more effectively."

According to Buchholz and Roth (1987, pp. 82–85), six behaviors can enhance communication.

♦

Behavioral communication enhancers include describing, equality, openness, problem-orientation, positive intent and empathy.

♦

These behavior modes are typical of individuals with a positive self-image.

*Describing.* "I see it like this." "I hear you saying. . . ." The message sender presents feelings or perceptions that do not judge others as wrong or needing to change.

*Equality.* "We're on the same team. We're in this together." People's differences are recognized and respected. "Differences in talent, ability, power, and status often exist," say Buchholz and Roth, "but the person who encourages communication seems to attach little importance to these distractors."

*Openness.* "What do you think? Who has an idea? You've got a good point there. You may be right!" Investigating options rather than steadfastly clinging to the solution greatly enhances communication. People work together toward solutions rather than choosing sides to debate the "best" solution. If people are open, they agree to disagree without being disagreeable.

*Problem-orientation.* "We're going to have to work this out. We're on the spot and need to come up with an answer." People are encouraged to share their perspectives on a problem. This is an important part of community policing.

*Positive Intent.* "Here's why I'm asking you to do this." Honest, open, candid, sincere behavior promotes communication. People react positively to situations they believe are represented accurately. People usually resent being used or subjected to hidden agendas.

*Empathy.* "I understand how you feel. I appreciate your concern." Empathy, as discussed previously, is synonymous with understanding others.

Other behaviors that can enhance communication, according to Buchholz and Roth, are: "leaning forward, smiling, nodding, having direct eye contact, sticking to the subject under discussion, and paying full attention." These are also effective *listening* skills, and being an effective listener is an important way to enhance communication.

## Active Listening

Officers can use several techniques to improve listening effectiveness. Strother (1987, p. 628) cites the following ten keys to effective listening suggested by the Sperry Corporation:

- Listen for ideas, not facts.
- Judge content, not delivery.
- Listen optimistically.
- Avoid jumping to conclusions.
- Adjust your note-taking to the speaker.
- Concentrate.
- Use excess listening time to summarize the speaker's ideas.
- Work at listening.
- Keep your mind open and your emotions in check.
- Exercise your mind.

Another set of suggestions is made by Fritz (1988):

- Periodically clarify what's being said to you.
- Look for the main points and draw conclusions from them.
- Offer encouragement.
- Separate fact from opinion.
- Avoid interrupting.
- Listen between the lines.
- Notice body language.

Johnson (1996, p. 45) offers the following additional suggestions for being a good listener:

- Watch your body language. Open your arms to appear receptive. Lean forward. Don't fold your arms across your chest and lean back in your chair.
- Nod at appropriate times. Look at the speaker. Take care not to glance at the clock on the wall, your watch, those reports you have been meaning to get to, or worse yet, the newspaper open on your desk.
- Make frequent use of conversation enablers such as, "Uh-huh go on. I see," etc. But do not fake attention.
- Do not interrupt.
- Minimize distractions. Have your calls held. Close the door to your office. Meet somewhere quiet to talk.
- Be aware of the tendency to formulate replies in your mind while the speaker is still talking. When in this process, you are not hearing what is being said.

Harris (1994, p. 42) suggests: "The resourceful listener draws upon two principal control factors to keep distractions out: containment and conscious convergence." His suggestions for using these control factors follow.
*To contain concentration:*

- Look at the speaker.
- Get in a calm frame of mind.
- Reposition the body.
- Remember to balance the listener's "thought speed" with the speaker's "talk speed."
- Hear the *meaning* of the words, not just the words themselves.

*To consciously converge:*

- Ask questions.
- Summarize.
- Take notes.
- React responsively.
- Listen for completion.
- Listen between the lines.

Harris concludes: "Articulate listening takes work, but it's worth the effort. Good listening is a mark of distinction, and a true index of professionalism."

Carroll S. Price, in reviewing the manuscript for this book, noted that the primary process of active listening involves a projection: the ability of listeners to project themselves into the shoes of the speaker, so to speak, to not only understand what is being communicated, but *why* the speaker is verbalizing the information and feelings at a specific time.

## BARRIERS TO EFFECTIVE COMMUNICATION

Because effective communication is so critical to police-community relations, officers should be aware of barriers to effective communication.

◆

Common communication barriers include:
- Prejudices and stereotypes.
- Lack of time.
- Use of jargon.
- Lack of feedback.
- Failure to listen.

◆

Prejudices and stereotypes can greatly interfere with an officer's ability to communicate. Preconceived ideas about a person's truthfulness or "worth" can result in strained relationships with individuals and little or no interchange of ideas. The very language used to refer to others can interfere with communication. For example, would you rather be called a *victim* or a *survivor?* A *cripple* or *physically disabled?*

Lack of time is another barrier to effective communication. Police officers and members of the public are busy. Often neither want to take the time to communicate fully and to establish high empathy. Bad timing can also interfere with communication. Police officers frequently are interrupted by calls for service and need to cut short conversations with others.

The use of **jargon,** the technical language of a profession, is another barrier to communication. Law enforcement has its own special terminology, for example, *alleged perpetrator, modus operandi* and *complainant.* Officers should avoid using such terms when talking with the public. Officers should also avoid using them in written reports. As noted by Pomerenke (1991, p. 39): "No other profession uses so much jargon and so many acronyms in reports that must be read by people outside the profession than police officers. Many readers, frustrated and confused, ultimately conclude that law enforcement reports are incomprehensible." She gives as an example, the following:

> R/P informed R/O that VI found apt. entered. A/O and S/O assisted R/O at scene. COMPL/VI (w/f 25yoa 8/15/1945 dob) was taken to Mercy Hosp. TOT was 1135 hrs. VI's veh was transported by TCR.

Excessive use of jargon and abbreviations can greatly hinder communication.

Lack of feedback can also reduce effective communication. *I know that you believe that you understand what you think I said, BUT I am not sure you realize that what you heard is not what I meant.*

A failure to *listen* is one of the most common and most serious barriers to effective communication. According to Strother (1987, p. 626): "Research has shown that 45% of the total time devoted to communication is spent in listening." Although we spend a great amount of time listening, most people are *not* good listeners. In fact, very few people know how to truly listen. Our educational system develops reading, writing and speaking skills. The system takes listening skills for granted. Consequently, few people are as good at listening as they could and should be.

One reason for poor listening is the difference between how quickly the human brain can process words and how rapidly most people talk.

♦

Effective listening is difficult because of the gap between how rapidly people talk (125 words per minute) and how rapidly the brain can process those words (500 words per minute). The difference between the speed of speech and the speed of thought creates a false sense of comprehension and promotes mental tangents.

♦

The sense of hearing, like the sense of sight, is physically tremendously slower than the brain's ability to process the information received through the senses.

Other barriers to communication are certain behaviors people can exhibit. Buchholz and Roth (1987, pp. 80–82) note six behaviors that tend to hinder communication.

♦

Behavioral barriers to communication include judging, superiority, certainty, controlling, manipulation and indifference.

♦

Note that these behavioral barriers to communication are the opposites of the communication enhances discussed earlier.

Buchholz and Roth suggest: "These behavior modes are often engaged in innocently and unconsciously, certainly not deliberately by well-meaning people." Often, these behavior modes are trademarks of individuals with low self-esteem.

*Judging.* The opposite of describing. "You're wrong." Judging seriously interferes with listening. Rather than focusing on the potential of what someone says, a judgmental person focuses on discrediting what is being said. A person who is quick to judge usually is quite opinionated.

*Superiority.* The opposite of equality. An "I'm-more-important-than-you-are" attitude can seriously hinder communication. Flaunting a position of authority hinders communication. Central to this attitude is the feeling that what *I* have to say is ultimately much more important than what is being said by others.

*Certainty.* The opposite of openness. "My mind's made up. Don't confuse me with the facts." A person who is convinced of the truthfulness or accuracy of his or her information is generally unable to recognize the possibility of making a mistake.

*Controlling.* The opposite of problem-orientation. "Let me tell you how this should be done." Few people appreciate being told how to act or what to do. Of course, in certain situations, police officers *must* take control. When officers must have effective personal interaction, however, such control is usually inappropriate and counterproductive.

*Manipulation.* The opposite of positive intent. "Gotcha." It is manipulative to communicate with hidden motives to get people to unknowingly agree or act in a certain way. The manipulator "uses" people.

*Indifference.* The opposite of empathy. "You're not important. What you think doesn't matter." A person who acts superior often has an indifferent attitude. An officer can convey indifference by the simple act of answering a call for service while talking to someone. To avoid misinterpretation, the officer must take care to explain the necessity of answering the call.

According to Buchholz and Roth (p. 82), other behaviors that inhibit communication include: "facial expressions such as frowning or raising eyebrows, shaking the head, yawning, sighing, leaning back, avoiding eye contact, gazing around the room, taking irrelevant notes, or changing the subject."

◆

Police officers may have more barriers to communication because of the image they convey, their position of authority and the nature of their work.

◆

When speakers realize officers listen to and evaluate what they say carefully, they generally make sure their output is factual and accurate and that their responses are appropriate under the circumstances.

The ability to listen and to assess the situation when communicating can help officers make the best first impression possible.

# THE PRIMACY EFFECT AND THE FOUR-MINUTE BARRIER

According to Reece and Brandt (1987, p. 268): "The way you are treated in this world depends largely on the way you present yourself—the way you look, the way you speak, the way you behave. Although human contact is a challenge, you can learn to control the first impressions you make on others. The key is to become fully aware of the impression you communicate to other people." The first few moments of a personal contact are critical.

♦

The tendency to form impressions of people quickly is called the **primacy effect.**

♦

You can test the primacy effect by asking yourself a few questions. Have you ever walked into a store, been approached by a salesperson, and known almost immediately that you will probably buy something—or will probably *not* buy anything? Have you ever been seated on an airplane next to a stranger and almost immediately wanted to talk to the person—or wanted to get a magazine and bury yourself in it?

First impressions will tend to set the tone for a positive or negative interaction. As Will Rogers so astutely put it, "You never get a second chance to make a first impression."

How long does it take for the primacy effect to occur? Usually in the first four minutes according to Leonard and Natalie Zunin. They have developed the concept of the four-minute barrier.

♦

The **four-minute barrier** is the point in an initial meeting at which most people have formed a positive or negative opinion about the individual with whom they are communicating.

♦

If you can get past the first four minutes of an initial interaction with a person on a positive note, your relationship is likely to be positive. As noted by Reece and Brandt (p. 267): "The general principle is that first impressions establish the mental framework within which a person is viewed, and later evidence is either ignored or reinterpreted."

# LESSONS FROM BUSINESS

Changes in technology and in our society have had a profound effect on business. Many businesses have changed their basic approach toward their employees as well as toward their customers. Businesses recognize the importance of service and of good customer relations.

◆

Law enforcement might adopt two practices used successfully in business: networking and seeking customer satisfaction.

◆

## Networking

Personal networks were discussed earlier in this chapter as connections individuals have with others in their lives. Consciously establishing such networks has become popular in the business world, with *networking* a popular buzzword. According to Adams (1991, p. 64), networking involves more than simply trading business cards—it requires skill. He cites the definition of networking used by Belinda Plutz, a consultant in New York City.

◆

**Networking** is the building and keeping of professional relationships for mutual interest and mutual help.

◆

Just as police officers need to communicate with the people in their jurisdiction, they also need to communicate with the institutions and agencies in the area. These include:

- Churches, schools and business associations such as the Lions, Rotary and Kiwanis.
- Social service agencies, storefront organizations and shelters.
- Hospitals, clinics and emergency care providers.
- City inspectors and licensors.
- Courts and corrections personnel.
- Politicians and members of advisory councils.
- Special interest groups such as MADD.

Finn and Sullivan (1988, p. 1) note:

The public repeatedly calls on law enforcement officers for assistance with people who are mentally ill, drunk in public, and homeless. . . . One way of expanding the options for handling these populations is to share responsibility for them with the social service system. Networks between law enforcement agencies and human services agencies can yield substantial benefits not only for the agencies involved, but for individuals who need help.

As suggested earlier, community policing creates a partnership between the police and groups of concerned individuals to address specific community problems. Those involved in the problem may also be part of its solution.

## The Citizen as Customer

A *customer* is one who buys good and services. Indeed, it is the citizens of a community who pay for the services provided by law enforcement. This dates back to the early days when citizens were expected to take their turn serving as watchmen and decided they would rather pay someone to do that job.

Police officers do not traditionally think of the members of their community as customers. In fact, one police fraternal organization had T-shirts printed up with the slogan "In my business, the customer is always wrong." Many officers think of criminals as their customers and the public as those who should just stay out of the way. Some officers consider the time they spend dealing with law-abiding citizens as wasted time or something that gets in the way of "real police work."

Law enforcement, like business, might benefit by emphasizing the value of customer service and the time-tested adage "The customer is always right." According to Hart et al. (1991, p. 75): "Customers who have bad experiences tell 11 people about it; customers who have good ones tell six."

In a very real sense, citizens are the customers of law enforcement agencies. Couper and Lobitz (1991, p. 17) illustrate this customer-oriented approach: "We will be a police department devoted to maintaining customer satisfaction and getting closer to the people we serve."

As Osborne and Gaebler (1992, p. 172) suggest: "The customers are the most important people for an organization; those who serve customers directly are next; and management is there to serve those who serve customers." This is a customer-service orientation. Osborne and Gaebler describe how customer-driven policing was instituted in the Madison (Wisconsin) Police Department. They surveyed the citizens to determine their perception of how well the police were meeting their needs. The final question on the survey was: "How can we improve the quality of our service in the future?"

According to Griffith (1993, p. 37): "Citizens in Clearwater, Florida, are considered "customers" of the police department. . . . With this business-world edict in mind, the police department developed a 'customer satisfaction' survey to better serve the needs of the citizenry."

Leland and Bailey (1996, pp. 73–74) offer the following suggestions for treating citizens as consumers:

- Make customer service the most important part of your job.
- Fulfill your customers' basic needs. Go beyond giving your customers what they ask for by satisfying their six basic needs: fairness, friendliness, understanding and empathy, control, options and alternatives, and information.
- Make direct eye contact with your customers.
- Give your customers easy access to you, e.g., a card with your phone number on it.

- Treat your co-workers as customers. Your co-workers are your internal customers and need special attention too.

Leland and Bailey (p. 74) also note that how you say something can make a big difference in customer satisfaction. For example:

| *Don't Say:* | *Do Say:* |
|---|---|
| That's not my job. | This is who can help you. |
| I don't know. | I'll find out. |
| No. | What I can do is . . . |
| You want it by when? | I'll try my best. |
| I'm busy right now. | I'll be with you in just a moment. |

In addition to external customer service, it is also important to consider your internal customers—for example, detectives, patrol, records and dispatch. Customer service is not just how the police work with the public, it is also how they help each other.

The organization must train the people who interact directly with customers, and then it must empower them. That is, it must give them the authority, responsibility and incentives to recognize, care about and attend to customer needs. Empowering the bottom of the organizational pyramid can be threatening, especially to middle-level managers, who may view such empowerment as an erosion of their own authority. Empowerment of all members of an organization is absolutely essential to good service recovery. Employees close to the customer are the first to know about problems and are in the best position to determine what can be done to satisfy the customer (Hart et al., 1991, p. 76).

Law enforcement agencies, like many successful businesses, would benefit from having an empowered workforce. It is vital to community policing to give patrol officers the authority and training necessary to make decisions and to reward them when they do so.

## HUMAN RELATIONS GUIDELINES

The ability to listen and understand, to speak and be understood, to communicate the message you intend—both verbally and nonverbally—is at the heart of effective public relations.

Effective human relations goes further than interpersonal communication. The context in which the communication occurs is important. Coffey et al. (1982, pp. 180–81) suggest the following guidelines to help police officers make a positive impression and improve interpersonal relationships (reprinted by permission):

1. Don't be trapped into unprofessional conduct by a threat or a challenge.

2. Make sure everything you do is calculated to enhance your reputation as a good officer—one who is firm, but fair and just.

3. When you are faced with a threat and you can't tell how serious it is, try to "buy time" in which to size up the situation by engaging the person in conversation. Make a comment or ask a question to divert his attention if possible.

4. Don't show hostility even if the other person does. Often a calm and reasonable manner will cause hostility to evaporate, or at least to simmer down.

5. Reduce your "threat" potential. Avoid a grim or expressionless countenance. Be an approachable human being. Too many officers habitually appear gruff and forbidding.

6. Cultivate a pleasant, friendly manner when making nonadversary contacts. Be ready with a smile, a pleasant word, a humorous comment when appropriate.

7. Let your general demeanor, and especially your facial expression and tone of voice, indicate that you respect the other person as a human being.

8. Let other people know by your reception of them that you don't expect trouble from them and that you don't consider them a nuisance. (Maybe you do, but don't let it show.)

9. Show an interest in the other person's problem. Maybe you can't do anything about it, but often it is a great help just to be a good listener.

10. Go out of your way to improve police-community relations. Even though your department may have a unit that specializes in community relations, never forget that you are the real key. The essence of good working relations between the people and the police is to be found in the way you handle yourself.

11. Always leave the people you deal with feeling that they have been treated fairly. When you render a service or react to a request, show some interest and give some explanation. This will promote good feelings, which, if carried on consistently by the entire force, will have the cumulative effect resulting in vastly improved human relations.

12. Try in every way you can to encourage people to work with the police for their own protection. Let the average citizen know that, far from being a threat, you are interested in being of help. Drive home the point that the citizen is threatened by crime and disorder, not by the police.

## SUMMARY

A person's world-view is largely created by what they see and hear as they experience events. The discrepancy between what the eye takes in (five million bits per second) and what the person actually processes (five hundred bits per second) accounts, in part, for why two witnesses can see the same thing differently.

Perception is also affected by the words people use to communicate. The most basic rule of semantics is: Cow$_1$ is NOT Cow$_2$, that is, each item within a specific class also has individual characteristics.

Effective police-community relations depend on an understanding of oneself and of others. Critical to self-understanding is recognizing preferences, prejudices and stereotypes. Prejudice is an attitude; discrimination is a behavior. Empathy is understanding another person. Empathy depends, in part, upon determining the other person's networks, the "complex pathways of human interaction that guide and direct an individual's perception, motivation and behavior."

The quality of police-community relations depends largely on the communication process. The process involves a sender, a message, a channel, a receiver and sometimes feedback. Individual characteristics that are important in communication include age, education, sex, values, emotional involvement, self-esteem and language skills. Behavioral communication enhancers include describing, equality, openness, problem-orientation, positive intent and empathy. Common communication barriers include prejudices and stereotypes, time, use of jargon, lack of feedback and failure to listen. Behavioral barriers to communication include judging, superiority, certainty, controlling, manipulation and indifference. Police officers may have more barriers to communication because of the image they convey, their position of authority and the nature of their work.

Effective listening is difficult because of the gap between how rapidly people talk (125 words per minute) and how rapidly the brain can process those words (500 words per minute). The difference between the speed of speech and the speed of thought creates a false sense of security and promotes mental tangents.

When seeking to improve human interactions, officers should keep in mind the tendency to form impressions of people quickly, that is, the primacy effect. The four-minute barrier is the point in an initial meeting at which most people have formed a positive or negative opinion about someone.

Law enforcement might benefit by adopting two practices used successfully in business: networking and seeking customer satisfaction. Networking is the building and keeping of professional relationships for mutual interest and assistance.

### Discussion Questions

1. What are some of your strong preferences? Might they be called prejudices?
2. Do you prefer to communicate by speaking or writing?
3. Who is included in your network?

4. Do you have a hobby that has a specialized language (jargon)? What words might most people not understand?

5. Three umpires were discussing balls and strikes in baseball. The first said, "I call them like I see them." The second said, "I call them like they are." The third said, "They aren't anything 'til I call them." How does this relate to the study of semantics?

6. What role do euphemisms ("soft" words) play in communication?

7. Give examples illustrating the basic rule learned from semantics: $Cow_1$ is not $Cow_2$. Why is the rule important in police work?

8. How does empathy differ from sympathy? When is each appropriate?

9. Can you think of examples of when the four-minute barrier and the primacy effect operated in your life?

10. In what ways might the general public be perceived as "customers" of a police department? What implications does this have?

## References

Adams, Michael. "Every Move You Make." *Successful Meetings.* (May 1996): 46–50.

Adams, Michael. "Exchanging Circles." *Successful Meetings.* (April 1991): 64–65.

Berglund, Bob. "Your Message Is Not the Most Important Part of Your Speech." (Minneapolis/St. Paul) *Star Tribune.* (July 1, 1992): D2.

Buchholz, Steve and Roth, Thomas. *Creating the High-Performance Team.* New York: John Wiley & Sons, Inc., 1987.

Coffey, Alan; Eldefonso, Edward; and Hartinger, Walter. *Human Relations: Law Enforcement in a Changing Community,* 3rd ed. Englewood Cliffs: Prentice-Hall, Inc., 1982.

Conroy, Dennis L. and Hess, Kären M. *Officers at Risk: How to Identify and Cope with Stress.* Incline Village, Nev.: Copperhouse Publishing Company, 1992.

Couper, David C. and Lobitz, Sabine. "The Customer Is Always Right." *The Police Chief.* (May 1991): 17–23.

Finn, Peter E. and Sullivan, Monique. *Police Response to Special Populations: Handling the Mentally Ill, Public Inebriate, and the Homeless.* Washington: National Institute of Justice. January 1988.

Fritz, Roger. *Rate Your Executive Potential.* New York: John Wiley & Sons, Inc., 1988.

George, Claude S., Jr. *Supervision in Action: The Art of Managing Others,* 4th rev. ed. Reston: Reston Publishing Company, 1985.

Griffith, Douglas L. "Citizen Feedback Line." *Law and Order.* (December 1993): 37–40.

Hageman, Mary Jeanette. *Police-Community Relations.* Beverly Hills: Sage Publications, 1985.

Harris, Richard M. "Articulate Listening." *Successful Meetings.* (May 1994): 42.

Hart, Christopher W. L.; Heskett, James L.; and Sasser, W. Earl, Jr. "Surviving a Customer's Rage." *Successful Meetings.* (April 1991): 68–79.

Hayakawa, S. I. *Language in Thought and Action.* New York: Harcourt, Brace & World, Inc., 1949.

Johnson, Robert Roy. "Listening." *Law and Order.* (February 1996): 43–46.

Klockars, Carl B. *The Idea of Police.* Newbury Park: Sage Publishing Company, 1985.

Leland, Karen and Bailey, Keith. "Customer Service: Happy Holidays." *Successful Meetings.* (December 1996): 73–74.

Marne-la Vallee, France. "Ooh, la, la! Disney's First Theme Park in Europe Opens Near Paris." (Minneapolis/St. Paul). *Star Tribune.* (April 13, 1992): A1, A5.

National Advisory Commission on Criminal Justice Standards and Goals. *Task Force on Police.* Washington: U.S. Government Printing Office, 1973.

Noose, Gregory A. "Basic Investigative Interviewing Skills: Networking an Interview." *Law and Order.* (March 1992): 101-07.

Oran, Daniel. *Law Dictionary for Nonlawyers,* 2nd rev. ed. St. Paul: West Publishing Company, 1985.

Osborne, David and Gaebler, Ted. *Reinventing Government.* New York: A Plume Book, 1992.

Pace, Denny F. *Community Relations Concepts.* Incline Village, Nev.: Copperhouse Publishing Company, 1991.

Parker, L. Craig, Jr.; Meier, Robert D.; and Monahan, Lynn Hunt. *Interpersonal Psychology for Criminal Justice.* St. Paul: West Publishing Company, 1989.

Pomerenke, Paula J. "Jargon Dangers in Law Enforcement." *Law and Order.* (March 1991): 39.

Price, Carroll S. Letter to author, reviewing the manuscript, 1992.

Reece, Barry L. and Brandt, Rhonda. *Effective Human Relations in Organizations,* 3rd rev. ed. Boston: Houghton Mifflin Company, 1987.

Sheehan, Kathy M. "Critical Police Communications." *Law and Order.* (February 1996): 37–41.

Strother, Deborah Burnett. "On Listening." *Phi Delta Kappan.* (April 1987): 25–28.

Trojanowicz, Robert C. and Carter, David L. "The Changing Face of America." *FBI Law Enforcement Bulletin.* (January 1990): 6–12.

Zunin, Leonard and Zunin, Natalie. *Contact—The First Four Minutes.*

# Chapter 7

# Dealing Effectively
# with Diversity

*If one were to offer men to choose out of all the customs in the world such as seemed to them the best, they would examine the whole number, and end by preferring their own; so convinced are they that their own usages surpass those of all others.*

—Herodotus, The Persian Wars, Book III, Chapter 38

## Do you know

- What ethnocentrism is?
- What are the three schools of thought on what happens when more than one culture inhabits the same territory?
- What is one of the main barriers frequently associated with ethnic/racial diversity?
- What strategies might be used to communicate more effectively with those who do not speak English?
- What types of diversity are found in the United States?
- What the three basic socioeconomic classes are? What they are based on?
- What the poverty syndrome is?
- What the multi-cultural trap is?
- What has been the dominant culture in the United States?
- What a bias or hate crime is?

## Definitions

Can you define these terms: acculturation, assimilation, bias crime, cultural conflict, cultural pluralism, cultural window, culturally literate, culture, ethnocentrism, ghetto syndrome, hate crime, hyphenated American, multi-culturalism trap, poverty syndrome.

# Introduction

Police officers need to be aware of the role diversity plays in the community they serve. Law enforcement traditionally has tried to maintain the *status quo*. Diversity is a source of stress for many officers. This need not be the case if officers realize that diversity involves issues that are extremely delicate, sensitive and important. The questions diversity raises do not have simple answers.

"People of different races, cultures and languages are coming into closer contact with each other and enormous demands are being made on their understanding and tolerance," says Inkster (1992, p. 28). He notes: "There are widening class divisions, more broken families and homelessness, growing anger on the part of the disadvantaged, and a rise in violent crime." This social unrest presents a significant challenge to police-community relations. It requires "enlightened" police officers, perhaps somewhat like Gulf War commander, General Arnold Schwarzkopf.

During the Gulf War (1991), General Schwarzkopf insisted on American soldiers respecting Islam's religious and cultural values. He was as familiar with the subtleties of Islamic law as he was with the high-tech weaponry and military strategies of the United States. He epitomized the ideal leader— educated, thoughtful, articulate, culturally sensitive and knowledgeable in several disciplines.

> These must be the qualities of our police officers if we are to maintain peace, order and a sense of security in society. They must act from a base of knowledge about their profession, about the cultural values of the community in which they work, about people individually and collectively, and about the larger world in which they live. This includes a sensitivity to different cultures and language skills that allow them to communicate with and understand their clients (Inkster, 1992, p. 30).

Dealing effectively with diversity is important to community policing because community outreach, communications, trust and activism are all necessary to community partnerships, and none of these can be achieved without accepting—indeed, embracing—diversity.

This chapter begins with an in-depth discussion of cultural, racial and ethnic diversity. This is followed by an examination of problems encountered with language and cultural barriers to communication and legal issues pertaining to cultural diversity. Next religious diversity and socioeconomic diversity are described. The availability of the American Dream is explored, followed by an explanation of the majority versus the minority world-view. The chapter concludes with a look at racism, sexism and bias/hate crimes and the diversity-related challenges facing the police department of the twenty-first century.

# CULTURAL, RACIAL AND ETHNIC DIVERSITY

**Culture** is defined as a collection of artifacts, tools, ways of living, values and language common to a group of people, all passed from one generation to the next. The specific items that make up a culture fall into two broad categories: material and nonmaterial. Material elements of one culture are readily borrowed or adopted by another culture if they are an obvious improvement. This is not the case, however, with the nonmaterial elements involved in "ways of living."

"Ways of living" includes religion, political beliefs, kinship roles, values and laws, both moral and legal. Diversity is most obvious and sometimes most problematic when different "ways of living" coexist in the same community.

The previous chapter discussed how language (which is an element of culture) shapes the way individuals view the world. The culture itself also provides a framework or world-view, a **cultural window** through which events are interpreted. Recall the reaction of some of the French nationals to the opening of Euro Disneyland. Houston (1996, p. 124) suggests:

> America has always been a country at war with itself. Our history is one of self-conflict. Perhaps our most profound wars have been our cultural wars— the ones fought for the soul of our nation. . . . Perhaps we are, at once, the most generous nation to have ever existed—and the most selfish. We are the most inclusive society that the world has ever known, and at the same time we have become the most exclusive in our attitudes towards others. We are a kaleidoscope of cultures.

◆

**Ethnocentrism** is the preference of one's own way of life over all others.

◆

People are naturally attracted to others who are similar to themselves. If we surround ourselves with others similar to us, we minimize uncertainty regarding how people will respond to us and we maximize the likelihood we will be in agreement. Minimization of uncertainty motivates people because uncertainty is cognitively uncomfortable. Ethnocentricity and segregation are consequences of our desire to avoid uncertainty.

Several different cultures came to the "New World" and established the United States. As noted by Clement (1992, p. 25): "In a sense, all of us who are not Native Americans are boat people." The United States is a nation of individuals with varying ethnic and racial backgrounds. The sociological literature on ethnic and racial diversity has three schools of thought on the consequences of two or more cultures inhabiting the same geographic area: assimilation, cultural pluralism and cultural conflict.

◆

**Assimilation** theorists suggest that our society takes in or assimilates various cultures in what is commonly referred to as a "melting pot."

◆

Assimilation, also referred to as **acculturation**, was, indeed, what happened to the early colonists. Initially the colonists came from various countries with different religions. They settled in specific geographic areas and maintained their original culture, for example, the Pennsylvania Dutch.

The seemingly unlimited resources available and the mutual struggle for survival in the "New World" encouraged colonists to assimilate. Over time, the triple forces of continued immigration, urbanization and industrialization soon turned the United States into a "melting pot" with diverse cultures from the various colonies merging. The "melting pot" was accomplished relatively painlessly because of the many similarities among the cultures: they looked quite similar physically, they valued religion and "morality," most valued hard work and, perhaps most important, there was plenty of land for everyone. The "homogenization" of the United States was fairly well accomplished by the mid-1800s. The formerly distinct cultures blended into what became known as an American culture, which was a white, male-dominated, culture of European origin.

Unfortunately, some groups were not as easily assimilated as others. In fact, one group, the Native Americans, were precluded from the developing American culture. Like animals, they were herded onto reservations. Native Americans have only recently begun to enter into the mainstream of American life. Some Native Americans no longer want to be assimilated—they seek to maintain their culture and heritage. The same is true of many African Americans. It is likely, therefore, that cultural diversity will continue to exist in the United States. Assimilation does not always occur.

An alternative to assimilation is for diverse cultures to peacefully coexist.

◆

**Cultural pluralism** suggests there are many melting pots. Some groups are comfortable in one pot, other groups are comfortable in another.

◆

One example of cultural pluralism is the Native American. American Indians are in reality a nation of tribes. There are over 450 recognized Indian tribes and bands in this country with populations ranging from less than 100 to more than 100,000.

Prior to colonization of the United States, the Indian tribes had distinct territories, languages and cultures. Later, as the settlers took their lands, they joined together in self-defense. In the 1990s, Native Americans are often referred to as a single entity, although the individual tribes still maintain their unique identities.

Cultural pluralism is particularly noticeable when new immigrants arrive in the United States. Usually, instead of attempting to assimilate into the mainstream of America, immigrants seek out others from their homeland, resulting in Chinatowns, Little Italys, Little Greeces and, most recently, Hmong communities. This has resulted in what is sometimes referred to as the **hyphenated American:** the Italian-American, the Polish-American, the Afro-American, the Asian-American and so forth.

Cultural pluralism rests on the assumption that diverse cultures can coexist and prosper. In the 1990s the view that diversity strengthens a society is widely held by members of the public. In Oakland, California, for example, members of the community consider the social studies textbooks antihistorical because they describe the United States as a "common culture," created by waves of immigrants. As noted by Epstein (1992, p. 636): "Once you have decided that the story of America is the story of Europeans escaping events like the potato famine and seeking a better way of life, then you are only telling that part of American history which fits that version. The story of African-Americans and Native Americans is not that story; they were not voluntary immigrants seeking a better life. Our story is the story of a continuous, never-ending struggle for justice and human values within this country."

Indeed, peaceful coexistence, is not always the reality.

◆

The **cultural conflict** theory suggests that diverse cultures that share the same territory will compete with and attempt to exploit one another.

◆

Such cultural conflict was common between the early settlers and the Native American tribes. Conflict was also common between the white immigrants and the black slaves they imported from Africa. From 1619 to 1860 more than six million Africans were involuntarily transported to the American colonies.

The hostile treatment of Japanese Americans during World War II was also rooted in cultural conflict. Following the attack on Pearl Harbor, many Americans believed that the Japanese Americans were a national threat. Over 110,000 Japanese, the great majority of whom were American-born citizens, were forced by the government to sell their homes and businesses and then placed in internment camps.

Cultural conflict can currently be seen in growing tensions between specific ethnic groups as they compete for the limited remaining resources available. In Minnesota, for example, only Native Americans are allowed to harvest wild rice or to spear fish. The Mille Lacs band of Chippewa has sued Minnesota, claiming treaty rights allow them to fish outside their reservation without state regulation. Native Americans are also currently lobbying to be allowed to take motorboats into the wilderness area to enhance their guide business.

*Asian children gather on a sidewalk in San Francisco's Tenderloin district, home to many Asian refugee families.*

A report from the U.S. Census Bureau ("Census Bureau . . . ," 1996, p. A14) suggests that the United States is experiencing "one of the most dramatic shifts in its racial and ethnic makeup since the slave trade transformed the racial composition of the South." This report predicts that non-Hispanic whites will account for only about half of the U.S. population by the middle of the next century. Hispanics will make up 24.5 percent, up from 10.2 percent. Asians will make up 8.2 percent, up from 3.3 percent. The African-American population will remain relatively stable at about 12 or 13 percent.

The *New York Times* ("The Changing Face . . . ," 1996, p. A5) summarizes the projected ethnic makeup of the U.S. population in Table 7.1.

Organizations working for women's rights, grey power and gay power make it clear that the United States is, indeed, a culturally pluralistic nation. Assimilation, cultural pluralism and cultural conflicts are all realities in the 1990s in the United States, presenting a formidable challenge for those who must maintain the "public peace." It is a greater challenge to develop "communities" and to enlist their aid to maintain the peace if there is a language barrier.

*Table 7.1*    **The Ethnic Composition of the United States (Projected)**

| Year | Asian | Hispanic | Black | White |
|------|-------|----------|-------|-------|
| 1980 | 1.5% | 6.4% | 11.5% | 80.0% |
| 1995 | 3.3% | 10.2% | 12.0% | 73.6% |
| 2030 | 6.6% | 18.9% | 13.1% | 60.5% |
| 2050 | 8.2% | 24.5% | 13.6% | 52.8% |

# NON-ENGLISH OR LIMITED ENGLISH SPEAKING INDIVIDUALS

In some parts of the country it is common for officers to deal with non-English speaking people or those who speak English as a second language. Try to imagine performing a car-stop on a vehicle filled with people who do not understand anything you are saying and you cannot understand them. The language barrier can make just getting the job done safely very difficult, to say nothing of maintaining positive police-community relations.

The language barrier is a major problem in police interactions with some ethnic/racial groups.

◆

As noted by Sharp (1991, p. 95): "Roughly two-thirds of the departments responding recently to a poll focusing on language barrier problems indicated that they encounter difficulties from time to time." Sharp notes: "A cardinal maxim affecting police work is that emergencies can happen anywhere, at any time. All emergencies are bad. They grow worse when the responders and victims do not speak the same language."

In addition, as noted by Hinkle (1990, p. 23), when police interact with those who do not speak English, the officer is in a difficult situation:

A citizen (or even a non-citizen) who speaks no English is protected by the same constitutional guarantees as anyone else. This means that delays in the judicial process, delayed response to emergencies, apparent unconcern or lack of proper attention (medical and otherwise) or any of the other problems that may arise from lack of communication place the officer and every one of his supervisors at risk of a lawsuit.

Hinkle suggests that ideally officers would be bilingual, speaking English and the language of the main ethnic minority in the area. It is usually not possible, however, for officers to be bilingual. An alternative is to learn the words and phrases used most frequently in policing in the other language. Hinkle notes that soldiers in foreign countries have little trouble issuing simple commands to the locals. If you were to learn ten new words a day, in one year your working vocabulary would be 3,650 words. This vocabulary would be sufficient to understand most communications and to convey your own messages in most situations.

Officers could also benefit from a plasticized guide of the most common words and phrases along with their pronunciations. One such guide, *Speedy Spanish for Police Personnel,* includes words and phrases needed for, among other situations, routine traffic stops, D.U.I., burglary/theft reports, victim/witness interrogation, Miranda Warning & Waiver, domestic disputes, medical care and booking/body search. Table 7.2 is a page from this guide.

Until recently, Spanish was the primary language officers needed to learn. In the past few decades, however, refugee influxes from the former Soviet Union, Ethiopia, Poland, Romania and, of course, Asia, have added to the challenge. As one physician noted: "The result is waiting rooms that sound like Towers of Babel, clinics that look like U.N. lobbies and doctors who don't know where to begin" (Clement, 1992, p. 25). Police officers may also be frustrated by the same situation.

Clement (p. 26) describes a physician's difficulty dealing with a Hmong patient and her interpreter who also spoke limited English. The doctor wanted to draw blood for a test. The interpreter, however, could not make the distinction between "test" and "taste." Said Clement: "For a long time, we had to fight the myth that our doctor wanted to drink the blood. And when we asked for urine and stool specimens, they just laughed." Police officers could encounter a similar difficulty in a D.U.I. incident.

◆

Strategies to help improve communication with non-English speaking individuals include (1) learning the language or at least common words and phrases, (2) using a language guide, (3) having a list of local language teachers who could serve as interpreters and (4) subscribing to the Language Line.

◆

In an effort to improve communications with non-English speaking individuals police could maintain a list of teachers of various foreign languages at local high schools, colleges and universities. Another option is to subscribe to AT&T's *Language Line.* According to Sharp (1991, p. 99):

This service, which is the only one of its kind in the world, allows police to get immediate translations of 143 different languages 24 hours a day, seven days a week, 365 days a year. . . . They can place calls from any phone to seek assistance via an 800 number.

Police departments that subscribe to the Language Line service are issued language identification cards listing all the languages the service can translate.

*Table 7.2*  **Communication Aid for Officers Interacting with Spanish-Speaking Individuals**

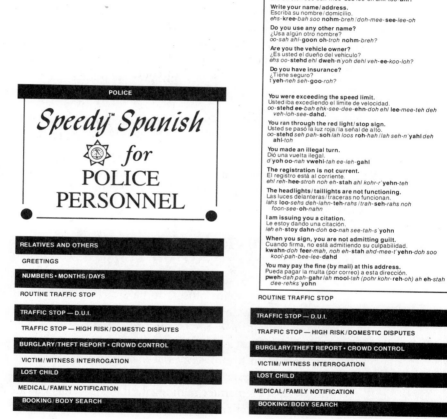

**ROUTINE TRAFFIC STOP**

**Turn off the engine.**
Apague el motor.
*ah-***pah**-*gheh ehl moh-***tohr**

**Step out of the vehicle.**
Salga del vehículo.
**sahl**-*gah dehl veh-***ee**-*koo-loh*

**May I see your driver's license?**
¿Puedo ver su licencia de manejar?
**pweh**-*doh vehr soo lee-***sehn**-*see-ah deh mah-neh-***hahr**?

**Take it out for me.**
Sáquela.
**sah**-*keh-lah*

**May I see the vehicle registration?**
¿Puedo ver el registro del vehículo?
**pweh**-*doh vehr ehl reh-***hee**-*stroh dehl veh-***ee**-*koo-loh*?

**Is this your current address?**
¿Es este su domicilio actual?
*ehs* **eh**-*steh soo doh-mee-***see**-*lee-oh ahk-too-***ahl**?

**Write your name/address.**
Escriba su nombre/domicilio.
*ehs-***kree**-*bah soo* **nohm**-*breh/doh-mee-***see**-*lee-oh*

**Do you use any other name?**
¿Usa algún otro nombre?
*oo-sah ah!-***goon** *oh-troh* **nohm**-*breh*?

**Are you the vehicle owner?**
¿Es usted el dueño del vehículo?
*ehs oo-***stehd** *ehl* **dweh**-*n yoh dehl veh-***ee**-*koo-loh*?

**Do you have insurance?**
¿Tiene seguro?
*t***yeh**-*neh seh-***goo**-*roh*?

**You were exceeding the speed limit.**
Usted iba excediendo el límite de velocidad.
*oo-***stehd** *ee-bah ehk-see-dee-***ehn**-*doh ehl* **lee**-*mee-teh deh veh-loh-see-***dahd**.

**You ran through the red light/stop sign.**
Usted se pasó la luz roja/la señal de alto.
*oo-***stehd** *seh pah-***soh** *lah loos* **roh**-*hah/lah seh-n'***yahl** *deh* **ahl**-*toh*

**You made an illegal turn.**
Dió una vuelta ilegal.
*d'yoh oo-nah* **vwehl**-*tah ee-leh-***gahl**

**The registration is not current.**
El registro está al corriente.
*ehl reh-***hee**-*stroh noh eh-***stah** *ahl kohr-r'***yehn**-*teh*

**The headlights/taillights are not functioning.**
Las luces delanteras/traceras no funcionan.
*lahs* **loo**-*sehs deh-lahn-teh-rahs/trah-***seh**-*rahs noh foon-see-***oh**-*nahn*

**I am issuing you a citation.**
Le estoy dando una citación.
*leh eh-***stoy** *dahn-doh oo-nah see-tah-s'***yohn**

**When you sign, you are not admitting guilt.**
Cuando firma, no está admitiendo su culpabilidad.
*kwahn-doh* **feer**-*mah, noh eh-***stah** *ahd-mee-t'***yehn**-*doh soo kool-pah-bee-lee-***dahd**

**You may pay the fine (by mail) at this address.**
Pueda pagar la multa (por correo) a esta dirección.
**pweh**-*dah pah-***gahr** *lah* **mool**-*tah (pohr kohr-***reh**-*oh) ah eh-stah dee-rehks* **yohn**

ROUTINE TRAFFIC STOP

---

**POLICE**

*Speedy™ Spanish*
*for*
**POLICE
PERSONNEL**

**RELATIVES AND OTHERS**

GREETINGS

**NUMBERS • MONTHS/DAYS**

ROUTINE TRAFFIC STOP

**TRAFFIC STOP — D.U.I.**

TRAFFIC STOP — HIGH RISK/DOMESTIC DISPUTES

**BURGLARY/THEFT REPORT • CROWD CONTROL**

VICTIM/WITNESS INTERROGATION

**LOST CHILD**

MEDICAL/FAMILY NOTIFICATION

**BOOKING/BODY SEARCH**

TRAFFIC STOP — D.U.I.

TRAFFIC STOP — HIGH RISK/DOMESTIC DISPUTES

BURGLARY/THEFT REPORT • CROWD CONTROL

VICTIM/WITNESS INTERROGATION

LOST CHILD

MEDICAL/FAMILY NOTIFICATION

BOOKING/BODY SEARCH

Reprinted by permission from *Speedy Spanish for Police Personnel*, Santa Barbara: Baja Books.

The cards are written in the native script of each language so non-English speakers can indicate their language to officers.

An article in *Law Enforcement News* ("Parlez-vous Miranda Warnings?" 1990, p. 3) described a typical instance in which the Language Line was invaluable to police:

> Officers in San Jose who arrived at the home of a Vietnamese woman found her badly beaten on the kitchen floor and found a man cowering behind furniture. Neither spoke English. The officers did not jump to conclusions, but dialed the Language Line Service instead. As a result, they were able to learn from the woman that she had been beaten by her husband. The man hiding was her brother, who had been frightened by the fight and hid himself.

Police departments must recognize and plan for the language barrier because, as noted by Sharp (p. 99): "There are currently between 12 and 22 million non-English speaking people living in the United States. Another 40 million visit the country every year. Immigration quotas account for approximately 800,000 more entering each year." Rachlin (1992, p. 101) notes:

> Although a police agency may never have a need for Maihili or Waray-Waray or Azerbaijani, it can never be sure when it will need Toyshanese or Linqala or . . . Punjabi. With its battery of professional interpreters, the Monterey-based AT&T Language Line Services operations center can readily identify virtually any language presented to them and have an interpreter on the line before you can say "Peter Perpetrator picked a pocket of pickled peppers."

## CULTURAL DIVERSITY AND OTHER BARRIERS TO COMMUNICATION

It is important for police officers to be aware of other cultural differences. For example, in some Asian cultures, only the oldest family member will deal with the police on behalf of the entire family. In the last few years many immigrants have come from Southeast Asia. Often victims of discrimination and crime, there is a tendency for them to not seek police assistance or report crimes. Many, in fact, especially the elderly, fear the police. In one Texas community, for example, an officer was giving a Vietnamese man involved in an accident a ride home. Sensing the man's fear, the officer smiled and tried to put him at ease. The man just stared at him and said in his broken English, "Police very mean. Police in Vietnam. . . ." and then shaped his hand like a gun and held it to his own head (Rachlin, 1992, p. 100).

Cultural norms often dictate that family problems be solved within the community. One good illustration exists among the Hmong people of Southeast Asia. If a Hmong woman is raped, she is unlikely to report it because in her culture the custom is that the rapist, if discovered, is forced to marry his victim. There is, however, great trust among the Hmong people. Such trust can lead to difficulties as noted by deFiebre (1992, p. A1): "Thriftiness, traditions of trust and a lack of financial sophistication lead many immigrants from Asian and other Third World nations to avoid mainstream American banks and rely on other vehicles to save money." The cultural backgrounds of these people leave them extremely vulnerable to scams.

Other examples of cultural barriers to communication come from the Native American culture. According to Day (1992, p. 15), making direct eye contact in the Ojibwa culture is a sign of disrespect or outright defiance. He notes: "To show respect they may appear disinterested, present a flat affect, avoid eye contact, say very little and offer only tangential or indirect responses." A police officer could easily misinterpret such a response.

Eye contact, in fact, varies greatly among different cultures. Most African Americans prefer indirect eye contact while listening and direct eye contact while speaking as a sign of attentiveness and respect. The opposite is true of most people of European descent, who prefer direct eye contact during listening and indirect eye contact during speaking as signs of attention and respect. To Hispanics, avoidance of direct eye contact is sometimes a sign of attentiveness and respect, but sustained direct eye contact may be interpreted as a challenge to authority.

Other cultural differences in nonverbal communication can result in misunderstanding. For example, hissing to gain attention is common for Hispanics, but to whites hissing is usually considered impolite and indicates contempt. A slap on the back in the white culture usually indicates friendliness; a slap on the back in Asian or Vietnamese cultures is usually insulting.

The American "okay" sign—thumb and forefinger forming a circle, fingers pointing up—is considered an obscene gesture in Brazil. This same gesture means *money* in Japanese and *zero* or *worthless* in French. There is great potential for miscommunication between members of different groups.

Police officers should determine what racial/ethnic minorities reside in their jurisdiction and learn what cultural values they might misunderstand. Indeed, what is legal in some cultures may be illegal in the United States.

## CULTURAL DIVERSITY AND THE LAW

A few specific examples will show how legal problems might result from cultural diversity. According to Dr. Thomas W. Day (1992, p. 15): "More than one Southeast Asian family has been investigated for child abuse after health professionals noted the skin lesions caused by traditional coin rubbing treatment." The practice of "coining" involves rubbing warm oil and coins across the skin and often results in long, red bruises.

According to deFiebre (1991, p. B1): "Many Asians are frustrated by child-abuse laws that prohibit severe corporal punishment and a juvenile-justice system that shies away from jailing first offenders."

Another cultural difference that causes problems is that the Hmongs have no age restriction on marriage. Gustafson and Prince (1991, p. A1) described the situation of a Hmong man who married a twelve-year-old girl after paying her parents $2,000. He was charged with third-degree criminal sexual conduct for having sexual relations with a minor because state law prohibited anyone under sixteen to be married, even with parental consent. According to his lawyer, "I think he's having some difficulty understanding why something accepted in Hmong culture is wrong to do here."

Before considering more problems that result from cultural differences, consider two other forms of diversity in the United States, religious diversity and socioeconomic diversity.

◆

In addition to cultural diversity (including racial/ethnic diversity), the United States also has religious and socioeconomic diversity.

◆

## RELIGIOUS DIVERSITY

Many of those who came to America did so to escape religious persecution. The colonists' desire for religious freedom is inherent in our Bill of Rights. The First Amendment protects, among other freedoms, freedom of religion. The First Amendment was drafted and adopted to protect the segregated turfs of different religious communities in the early colonies: Congregationalism in New England, Quakerism in Pennsylvania and Catholicism in Maryland. Over the years, these distinctions have become much less important, with "Christians" becoming a sort of religious melting pot for people of quite similar religious beliefs. Innumerable religions now exist in the United States.

In recent years, devil worship or Satanism has come to the attention of police departments in some areas. The First Amendment protects such practices. Police become concerned, however, when those engaged in Satanism desecrate churches, steal religious artifacts or sacrifice their neighbor's dog.

Sometimes there is a very fine line between religious freedom and illegal activity. For example, the Supreme Court will consider whether a Florida city's ban on animal sacrifice in religious ceremonies violates the constitutional guarantee of religious freedom ("Religious Animal Sacrifice. . . ," 1992, p. A1). In 1987 the city of Hialeah adopted an animal-sacrifice prohibition after members of Santeria, an ancient African religion which practices animal sacrifices, made plans to open a church there. In this case, *Church of the Lukumi Babalu Aye v. City of Hialeah,* those who challenge the ban argue that the law is specifically aimed at animal slaughter for religious purposes. The city has not made it a crime to kill animals, but rather a crime to kill animals in a religious ceremony.

Santeria has an estimated 50,000 to 60,000 followers in South Florida. Santerians sacrifice animals at rites celebrating birth, marriage and death and also during ceremonies to cure the sick. Opponents of the ban argue: "Hialeah has not interfered with the sale of lobsters to be boiled alive and the record does not show that it has interfered with the practice of feeding live rats to pet snakes. . . . Religion is almost the only unacceptable reason for killing an animal in Florida."

In Oregon a similar situation existed when a group lobbied for an exception to the general drug laws to make it legal for American Indians to smoke peyote during their rituals. In this case, the Supreme Court ruled that such an exception need not be granted. Smoking peyote was illegal across the board; the American Indians were not a special group that had been singled out.

## SOCIOECONOMIC DIVERSITY

Even the casual observer recognizes that social and economic class factors create diversity in the United States. Sociologists typically divide individuals within the United States into three basic classes.

◆

The three basic socioeconomic classes, based primarily on income and education, are the lower, middle and upper classes. These basic classes may be further subdivided.

◆

According to Teepen (1995, p. A6): "The gap between the rich and poor is now wider in the United States than in any other industrial nation. . . . The top 1 percent of U.S. households owns 40 percent of the nation's wealth; the top one-fifth owns 80 percent. The lowest-earning fifth takes in just 5.7 percent of the after-tax income and has virtually no assets."

When considering the socioeconomic classes, do not forget the maxim that "Cow$_1$ is not Cow$_2$." Each person has unique, individual characteristics. Each socioeconomic class will also have members of all the diverse groups discussed in the previous section. Some groups, however, are more numerous in certain classes. As previously discussed, in their traditional role of crime fighter, the police interact most frequently with those from the lower socioeconomic class.

### The Lower Socioeconomic Class

Certain races and ethnic groups are frequently equated with poverty and crime. Pace (1991, p. 102) describes the interaction of these factors as the *poverty syndrome*.

◆

The **poverty syndrome** includes inadequate housing, inadequate education, inadequate jobs and a resentment of those who control the social system.

◆

*Members of the Philadelphia, PA, Anti-Drug Network who live in neighborhoods threatened by the trade in illegal drugs gather and then march through their neighborhoods to let both the drug dealers and the police know of their opposition to the drug trade.*

Pace notes: "The poverty syndrome has a powerful psychological influence on how a person views society and how he views those who control society." He notes that poor people are in contact with the criminal justice system more frequently because they are on the streets and highly visible.

A poor person who drives an old car will get a repair ticket whereas a wealthier person is more likely to drive a newer car that does not require repairs. In addition, the repair ticket issued to the poor person is likely to be a much greater hardship for that person than a similar ticket would be to someone in the middle or upper classes.

Often members of the lower socioeconomic class live in ghettos. Pace (p. 44) notes: "Approximately 69% of the Black population lives in metropolitan areas, with about 56% of that number living in the inner city. . . . If society were to integrate totally, about 95% of all Blacks would have to relocate."

Indeed, getting out of the ghetto is difficult for many. Pace (1991, p. 45) notes that the **ghetto syndrome** is a vicious circle of failure: poverty, poor education, joblessness, low motivation to work, welfare and poverty. . . . In addition, according to Pace (p. 43): "Since ghettos house more than 70% of racial or ethnic minorities, the ghetto, minorities and crime become interrelated and are the focus for most of the anti-crime efforts of the criminal justice system." This accounts, in part, for charges of racism against some police departments, as discussed in Chapter 6.

Thirty years ago ghettos were more commonly referred to as *slums*. At that time internationally known scholar, scientist, educator, author and former president of Harvard University, James B. Conant, wrote *Slums and Suburbs*. In this classic study of American education in the late fifties and early sixties, Conant (1961, p. 18) expressed a belief that mixing Negro (the socially accepted term in the 1950s and 1960s) children into purely white schools was not the solution to the problem of the inferior quality of the schools in the Negro slums: "I believe the evidence indicates that it is the socioeconomic situation, not the color of the children, which makes the Negro slum schools so difficult; the real issue is not racial integration but socioeconomic integration."

Conant (p. 3) noted that suburban schools spent $1,000 a year per student; the slum schools less than half that amount. Suburban schools were modern, spacious facilities with 70 staff per 1,000 pupils; slum schools were unattractive dilapidated schools staffed by 40 or fewer professionals per 1,000 pupils. Conant (p. 2) cautioned: "I am convinced we are allowing social dynamite to accumulate in our large cities." He (p. 18) also sent a warning:

> What I should like to do is to create in the reader's mind a feeling of anxiety and concern. For without being an alarmist, I must say that when one considers the total situation that has been developing in the Negro city slums since World War II, one has reason to worry about the future. The building up of a mass of unemployed and frustrated Negro youth in congested areas of a city is a social phenomenon that may be compared to the piling up of inflammable material in an empty building in a city block. Potentialities for trouble—indeed possibilities of disaster—are surely there.

Not long after Conant wrote these words, riots occurred in the same slums. Much of the rioting erupted out of a sense of frustration at being denied the American Dream. Blacks trapped in the ghettos saw no way of getting out. Whites who attended schools in the suburbs seemed to have a fast track to college and a share of the Dream. In many areas, the situation has not changed that much.

Homelessness is a major problem for many in the lower socioeconomic class.

## The Homeless

Glensor and Peak (1994, p. 101) note: "As first responders, the police walk a fine line between being compassionate to the needs of the homeless and protecting the public from interference with its rights."

The police must interact with the three million homeless people sleeping on our nation's streets. Among the homeless are women and children, alcoholics and drug addicts, the retarded and the mentally ill. Carrying their worldly goods and

*A homeless man, who would only give his name as John, walks his belongings through the flooded China Basin area of San Francisco on Thursday, Jan. 2, 1997. Homeless advocates say the city will push the homeless out of China Basin when they start construction on the new ballpark.*

camping everywhere from laundry rooms to train and bus stations, the homeless pose a challenge for the police who often look after their safety while attempting to minimize their public presence.

The homeless population includes:

*Veterans*—mainly from Vietnam, veterans in some cities comprise 50 percent of the homeless male population.

*Mentally ill*—before the 1970s, an estimated quarter million of today's homeless would have been institutionalized, a problem discussed in the next chapter.

*Physically disabled or chronically ill*—those who cannot work and have no means of support.

*Elderly*—their fixed incomes are often inadequate.

*Men, women, families*—on the street after losing a job.

*Single parents*—usually women, without resources or skills.

*Runaway children*—often victims of abuse.

*Immigrants*—legal and illegal.

*Traditional transients*—those who have taken to the road, and prefer to be there—sometimes referred to as the "hard core homeless."

Many homeless are also alcoholics and drug abusers. Although being homeless is not a crime, the average citizen is uncomfortable around and may feel threatened by those who are homeless. Whether motivated by guilt or fear, they want the homeless people "removed."

The police must somehow try to deal with the homeless, a problem that society has thus far been unable to solve. The needs of the homeless are as varied as the people who comprise the homeless population. To address the problems of and presented by the homeless, the police need to draw on many resources, from detoxification facilities to children's shelters, from hospital crisis units to county social services.

In those communities where sleeping on the streets is illegal, what begins as a social problem becomes a problem of criminal justice. The officer on the beat is, of course, the person expected to enforce the law.

The notice in Figure 7.1 illustrates how homelessness can, in effect, be made illegal. Such notices are being contested in court in some areas of the country. Miami has demonstrated a "malicious abuse" of the Constitution in arresting thousands of homeless people living in parks and under bridges, an attorney argued in the trial of a federal lawsuit. The central question "is whether the government can lock you up for being outside when you have no place to go," attorney Valerie Jonas said in her opening statement on behalf of the city's estimated 6,000 homeless (*Star Tribune*, June 16, 1992, p. A7).

# NOTICE

## The following is illegal in My Town U.S.A. and you will be arrested for:

- ■ Begging

- ■ Trespassing on private property

- ■ Trespassing on state property

- ■ Drinking in public

- ■ Urinating in public

- ■ Unlawful assembly (gathering in groups of three or more)

- ■ Interfering with pedestrians or vehicle traffic (touching, causing fear, etc.)

**Parks are closed from 10:00 p.m. to 7:00 a.m.**

*Figure 7.1*    **Notice of Illegal Actions in City Parks**

In addition, the homeless more often end up as victims of crime than as perpetrators. They are robbed and assaulted and have no phone from which to call 911.

Sometimes when the police deal with homeless individuals both the homeless and the neighborhood can benefit. This was the case in a community where a group of homeless men were hanging around a business district, worrying the local merchants. When the business owners complained to the police, the officer on that particular beat talked to those involved and they worked out a solution. The homeless men swept the sidewalk and kept the area litter free in return for food and a place to sleep.

A New York City police officer, Fran Kimkowski, developed another innovative approach to the homeless problem for a particular group of homeless men in the Long Island City section of Queens, New York. Assigned to calm the fears of residents when the Salvation Army opened a shelter for homeless veterans in the neighborhood, Kimkowski wanted to show the residents that the homeless men could and would contribute to the community if given a chance. She organized V-Cops in 1988 to help prevent crime in the neighborhood. Members of V-Cops, who volunteer their time, are all homeless veterans who volunteer "not only to help prevent crime in the neighborhoods, but also to aid in his [the veteran's] recovery from drug abuse or alcoholism and to regain a sense of self-esteem" (*Law Enforcement News*, September 30, 1991).

V-Cops use anticrime foot patrols to deter, detect and report crimes to the police. About 200 homeless veterans have been members of the V-Cops since it began. In the first nine months of 1991, for example, twenty-seven men had donated 8,000 hours of patrol in the Queens, Bedford-Stuyvesant and Brownsville sections of New York. The V-Cops patrol local banks, particularly when people cash social security and welfare checks. The number of robberies and scams against customers has fallen according to Officer Kimkowski, and V-Cops would like to believe they had something to do with that. Some banks are so pleased with the V-Cops that they provide free lunch for them on the days they patrol.

The V-Cops program has many other components, including crime prevention presentations to organizations, talks to high school students and patrol of subways and "play streets" for neighborhood youth during the summer months. Beyond the obvious benefits to the community, the participating homeless veterans have an opportunity to make a contribution while getting their lives back on track. Simultaneously, the role of the police department in the program fosters good community relations. Tentative plans are being made for landlords in high-crime areas to offer V-Cops housing in exchange for patrol and other services.

## The Privileged

At the opposite end of the socioeconomic scale are the privileged and celebrities. In the traditional role of crime fighter the police seldom interact with the upper class, but when they must, problems can arise. With regard to community policing, however, the personal and financial resources of those in the upper socioeconomic level can be invaluable.

When police officers share a common background and education with the citizens they serve, officers and citizens understand each other and good community relations are fairly easy to achieve.

Imagine for a moment a community where the majority of residents are better educated than the police. Or where they earn five or six times as much money as police officers. In that community, it may take a special effort to develop and maintain respect and confidence in the police department's credibility and expertise. There it would be important for the department to find ways to minimize the cynical or negative attitudes officers may develop toward the privileged class. Police officers may become bitter if powerful people misuse their political connections to obtain special privileges from the police or to circumvent the law.

A police officer from Los Alamos, New Mexico, a highly educated population, commented that the police constantly deal with problems resulting from the differences between the officers and the educated community. Officers refer to citizens as "coneheads" in discussions among themselves, not helping matters. Likewise, the citizens use the term "town clowns" to describe the police. This term has remained with the citizens of Los Alamos for at least the past forty years, despite the fact that the Los Alamos Police Department has one of the highest educated departments in the state.

How can police departments address such situations? Perhaps the most effective way is for citizens to be involved in some area of the police department. Many departments have crime prevention programs, reserve officer organizations and crime reward funds, all of which need citizen volunteers.

Some departments have educational incentive plans to pay the tuition of officers who go to college and give a salary increase to those who graduate. Educational achievement can be considered in the promotional process; officers with the most education should benefit.

Officers should also receive regular, up-to-date inservice training to help them maintain and update professional skills. Well-trained officers will have confidence in their own abilities and that inspires confidence and respect in others.

Officers' equipment, uniforms and physical condition all affect their image in the community and their own self-image. Departments with dirty and ill-equipped or damaged vehicles on the streets prevent officers from feeling professional, respected or competent. Officers who are poorly equipped are less likely to act in a professional manner.

## Celebrities

Interacting with celebrities and other well-known citizens such as national politicians, especially if the interaction is a negative contact, can be very difficult for the police. Often media hounds will use a minor incident for publicity. On the other hand, they may try to exert undue influence on an officer by mentioning rich and powerful "close friends" who allegedly have the power to negatively affect the officer's career. Officers need some measure of assurance from their department that they can do their job professionally and not be subject to reprimand because they happen to take appropriate action against someone with powerful connections.

*Former Hall of Fame football star O.J. Simpson is shown in his official Los Angeles Police Department booking photo following his arrest for two murders, his ex-wife, Nicole, and acquaintance Ronald Goldman, June 1994. Simpson was arrested following a two-hour chase across Los Angeles area freeways. He was under 24-hour surveillance as police feared he would commit suicide. Simpson was found not guilty by the jury.*

The manner in which the criminal justice system treats celebrities can also affect how the public views the police. The trials of evangelist Jim Baker and, more recently, that of Mike Tyson may have had an impact on the public's perception of the police.

The privileged and celebrities are embodiments of the American Dream. They represent the promise America held in the past and continues to hold in the future. But is the American Dream truly available to all? And at what price?

## AVAILABILITY OF THE AMERICAN DREAM

The movement from one class to another is a cultural change that requires not only access to opportunities but the willingness and ability to pursue them. Since the 1960s there has been debate over whether it is better for individuals from different cultures or ethnic groups to learn English, retain their own language or become bilingual. The debate becomes especially heated when talking about "Black English." There are those who argue adamantly that black students should be allowed to speak and write their particular style of English without being penalized. Many black parents, however, insist that allowing their children to speak "Black English" is a ploy to keep them in the lower class—that their children will never succeed in the United States without good standard English skills.

Quite often entrance into colleges depends on test scores such as the Scholastic Aptitude Test. These tests assume facility with standard English. In addition, according to Hirsch (1988, p. xiii), to succeed, students must also be culturally literate:

> To be **culturally literate** is to possess the basic information needed to thrive in the modern world. The breadth of that information is great, extending over the major domains of human activity from sports to science. . . . Cultural literacy constitutes the only sure avenue of opportunity for disadvantaged children, the only reliable way of combating the social determinism that now condemns them to remain in the same social and educational condition as their parents.

Cultural literacy, however, can be carried too far and result in the *multi-culturalism trap*.

◆

The **multi-culturalism trap** occurs when people get so involved with their own cultural concerns they ignore the rest of the society in which they live.

◆

This differs from ethnocentrism which views one's culture as superior to all others. The multi-culturalism trap, in contrast, is often encountered by minority groups who want to bring their culture "up to the level" of the mainstream culture. Pace (1991, p. 45) suggests: "Multi-culturalism, while strengthening sub-group cohesiveness, can be deadly to the integration of the community at large."

> Groups that retain cultural ideals that are different or out of step with laws, mores and customs, of the rest of society must change. These groups must strike a balance between service to their own culture and a contribution to the services of the rest of the community. Unless this self-centeredness of the minority groups is rejected by the groups themselves, they will never foster public support from the rest of society nor will they develop rapport with the criminal justice system because this system represents the majority society (p. 67).

## THE MAJORITY V. THE MINORITY WORLD-VIEW

Whenever cultural pluralism exists in a society, a majority and minorities will also exist. Which group one belongs to will greatly influence how one views the world.

### The Majority World-View

The Minnesota Peace Officer Standards and Training (P.O.S.T.) Board (1991, p. 110) has identified the following as elements of the majority world-view:

- The majority view that its philosophy and ideas are most legitimate and valid.
- Minority viewpoints, while their expression may be tolerated, lack the force and power of the majority, therefore, are less valid than and secondary to the majority viewpoint.
- The minority members have the option of leaving the society if they cannot abide by majority rule.
- Alternative viewpoints are often considered disruptive or disloyal.
- Power, status and wealth are the result of hard work and/or genetics.

◆

Traditionally the majority culture in the United States has been defined and controlled by a white, male, European world-view.

◆

Given current population trends, however, the majority culture is rapidly changing, as noted earlier.

Any group that does not fall within the majority world-view can be considered a minority.

### The Minority World-View

The P.O.S.T. Board (p. 110) identified the following elements as common to the minority world-view:

- Minorities must perform better to be accepted as average.
- Majority groups have the power and control major institutions.
- Minority groups lack power to control their own destiny.
- The minority views fairness as being more valid than power, status and wealth.
- The minority views success as being achievable by working through the rules set by the majority.
- The minority views the criminal justice system as biased against minorities.

Sometimes cultural conflicts between minority groups or between the majority and minority groups become so intense that they lead to racism, sexism and bias crimes.

## RACISM, SEXISM AND BIAS CRIMES

Racism has been a problem almost since the beginning of the United States. Many people feel threatened by simply coming into contact with those who are culturally different. As noted by Bodinger-deUriarte (1991, p. 4): "Americans often are poorly informed and suspicious of cultures and lifestyles outside their own." What people do not understand they tend to fear and what they fear, they tend to hate.

### Racism

Racism has been likened to carbon monoxide. It may be silent, you may not see or hear it, but uncontrolled, it can kill. Monk (1991, p. 160) suggests: "Traditionally, America has been a racist society. Blacks, it is well known, were exploited and oppressed in virtually every aspect of social, economic, and political life. Today they are often not thought of as *victims* of crime but as criminals." Monk notes that some black sociologists and economists argue that blacks are economically deprived because of *class* rather than race—the same contention set forth by Conant in 1961. The fact remains, according to Monk, that: "Crime and color are linked in both official statistics and public perceptions." Because this is the case, racism is common in our society.

Although our society has improved in several areas, it would appear from the statistics that racism is still a problem as described in the article, "Crime's Impact on Blacks Makes for a Bleak Picture."

- Blacks are both the victims and the perpetrators of violent crime in disproportionate numbers.
- The incarceration rate for black males in the United States is four times that of South Africa.
- While 41 percent of those arrested on drug charges in 1989 were black, just 15 percent of the drug-using population is black (1991, p. 1).

Of grave concern is racism and bigotry found within the police department itself.

Plummer (1995, p. 1) believes: "Behavior motivated by bigotry and hate is endemic to the law enforcement profession." He suggests (pp. 1, 6): "Our ability to serve people of all races and backgrounds hinges on making sure that our organizations, and all that we do, are firmly grounded in and supported by key values, the most critical of which are honesty and true appreciation for diversity." He concludes (p. 7): "Recent public attention to police bigotry and hateful behavior, however painful to us and to those we serve, clearly represents an opportunity . . . . We must work together to ensure universal adoption of values, policies and practices that lead to truly equal treatment for all citizens."

## Sexism

Although women outnumber men in the United States, they are still often classified as a "minority." The reason for their minority status is that when it comes to having true power, women are still in the minority. Berglund (1992, p. 9) suggests that when dealing with bias: "We are dealing with deep-seated attitudes formulated in a culture dominated by white males."

Rosen (1992, p. 7) interviewed then Houston Chief of Police, Elizabeth Watson, appointed by a female mayor who was later defeated. Watson noted: "Very often I would take a very hard stand on things that I believe in. Whereas in a man that might be called strength and determination, in me it was called arrogance and stubbornness." While testifying at a sexual harassment trial of a female sergeant, the former chief described the male officers in the department as "indefatigable sexual predators, libidinous in the extreme" (Hodges, 1992, p. 5B).

Sometimes racism, sexism and other forms of prejudice are carried to the extreme and result in bias or hate crime.

## Bias or Hate Crimes

"Wherever such statistics are kept across the United States," says Bodinger-deUriarte (1991, p. 2), "bigotry cases have become more commonplace. . . . The incidents have ranged from anonymous spray-painting of slurs to cross burnings to murder. What they have in common is their motivation: fury directed at those who are different because of their race, their religion, or their sexual orientation."

The Southwest Regional Laboratory (SWRL) defines hate crimes as follows:

◆

A **hate** or **bias crime** is any act, or attempted act, to cause physical injury, emotional suffering or property damage through intimidation, harassment, racial or ethnic slurs and bigoted epithets, vandalism, force, or the threat of force motivated all or in part by hostility to the victim's real or perceived race, ethnicity, religion or sexual orientation.

◆

"Hate crimes are designed to intimidate the victims and other members of the victims' community in an attempt to leave them feeling isolated, vulnerable and unprotected by the law" (Lieberman, 1994, p. 21).

The FBI received 7,947 reports of hate crimes in 1995, most of which were of racial bias. This was an increase of 37 percent from 1994. The most commonly reported hate crime was intimidation ("FBI . . .," 1996, p. 5).

Morris (1997, p. 16) reports that of the 4,831 crimes in which race was the primary motivator, blacks were victimized 61.9 percent of the time. Religious bias was the second most common motivator of hate crimes, followed by the victims' sexual orientation.

According to Martin (1996, p. 465), the majority of hate crimes are against the person, including assault (the most common), harassment, menacing/reckless endangerment and robbery. Crimes against property include vandalism/criminal mischief (most common), arson/cross burning and burglary.

Homosexuals and lesbians are frequent targets of *gay-bashing*, a form of hate crime. Police officers should recognize when crimes might be the result of bigotry and seek the causes for a particular incident. Several states have passed mandatory reporting laws that require police departments to keep statistics on the occurrence of bias and hate crimes. In 1990 the Federal Hate Crime Statistics Act was passed mandating the justice department to secure data on crimes related to religion, race, sexual orientation or ethnicity.

Walker and Katz (1995, p. 29) suggest: "The creation of bias crime units is part of a national response to the problem of hate-motivated violence that includes state and federal legislation. By 1994 all but four states (Alaska, Nebraska, Utah, Wyoming) had some form of legislation."

As Lieberman (1994, p. 21) says: "Under these laws, no one is punished merely for bigoted thoughts, ideology or speech. But when prejudice prompts an individual to act on these beliefs and engage in criminal conduct, a prosecutor may seek a more severe sentence."

While there is considerable variation among these laws, the most common elements include (1) enhanced penalties for common-law crimes against persons or property that are motivated by bias based on race, ethnicity, religion, gender or sexual orientation; (2) criminal penalties for vandalism of religious institutions; and (3) collection of data on bias crimes.

Nelson (1994, p. 50) lists several criteria to help determine if a particular act or incident is bias related:

- Is the motivation of the alleged offender known?
- Was the incident known to have been motivated by racial, religious, ethnic or sexual orientation bias?
- Does the victim perceive the offenders's action to have been motivated by bias?
- Is there no other clear motivation for the incident?
- Were any remarks reflecting racial, religious, ethnic or sexual orientation bias made by the offender?
- Were there any offensive symbols, words or acts that are known to represent a hate group or other evidence of bias against the victim's group?
- Did the incident occur on a holiday or other day of significance to either the victim's or the offender's group?
- What do the demographics of the area tell you about the incident?

Hate crimes present a unique opportunity for community policing, as noted by Lieberman (1994, p. 18): "Law enforcement officials can advance police-community relations by demonstrating a commitment to be both tough on hate crime perpetrators and sensitive to the special needs of hate crime victims."

## FACING THE CHALLENGE

Keeping the peace, "serving and protecting" in a society as diverse as the United States presents an extreme challenge to police officers. To meet the challenge, police might consider the following guidelines:

- Each person is, first and foremost, an individual.
- Each group, be it racial, ethnic, religious or socioeconomic, consists of individuals who share certain values. Knowing what these values are can contribute greatly to effective police-community interactions.
- Communication skills are vital. Empathy, listening and overcoming language barriers are crucial to effective police-community interactions.
- An awareness of personal prejudices and biases can guard against discrimination.
- An awareness of the language used to talk about different groups is extremely important.

Hare (1991, p. 157) calls for a change in the terminology the public uses to refer to different cultures and ethnic groups of people. Although Hare is speaking of terminology used at American universities, police departments could benefit from Hare's guidelines (reprinted by permission):

The term "minority," for example, is laden with stereotypic images. The term fosters expectations of inability and pathology. . . .

We hold that in our multiethnic and multicultural university there are no minorities and there is only one race: the human race.

Hare suggests the following changes in terminology:

- Abandon the use of racial designations such as "black" and "white" in favor of continental, ethnic and cultural heritage based identifiers such as African American, American Indian/Native American, Asian American, Latino-Hispanic American and European American. Beyond gross "continental dividers," national identifiers such as Italian American, Polish American, Japanese American, Brazilian American, [and] Nigerian American, may also be used. When such designations prove too laborious, such phrases as "traditionally underrepresented groups" or "targeted populations" should be used when appropriate. In most instances, groups should be referred to respectfully—with the terms they prefer and not summarily put in a "minority" box. In addition, we should avoid the term "minorities," with its subtle secondary, if not caste status, that implies the antithesis to "majority," which is frequently polite code for "white." "People of color," given its antithetical relationship to "whiteness," should also be avoided. "Third world" should additionally be avoided as it is simply an international "non-European" and "non-white" euphemism. The continental, geographical, regional, or national areas of concern should simply be named.
- All publications, media advertising and reports should reflect a new sensitivity to terminology.
- All offices and programs in the university system that carry such labels as "Department of Minority Affairs" and "Office for the Disadvantaged" should be required to change their titles to more inclusive titles such as "Multicultural Affairs" or "Pluralistic Development" while enhancing their functions.

Whether you follow all of the preceding suggestions is not the main concern. It is important that officers consider the terms they use and how they might be perceived by those who are being "labeled." Of course, in an emergency when officers need to communicate with each other rapidly, a descriptive term such as *black* or *white* is appropriate and, indeed, necessary to rapid response. It is important for officers to know when to use certain terminology.

Himelfarb (1991, p. 53) suggests: "Few in policing today would dispute the important role that training must play in improving the relationship between police and the ethnocultural and visible minority communities they serve." He suggests six key principles that promote culturally sensitive, responsive policing:

- Respect for and sensitivity to the diverse communities served is essential for effective policing.
- Respect for and sensitivity to ethnocultural communities can best be achieved through a broad-based multicultural strategy.
- Training must be an essential element of such a strategy.
- Training must be ongoing and built into the experience of policing; that is, it must be more than a course or two on multiculturalism.
- A multicultural strategy and the training that supports it will be most effective if they are perceived as integrated aspects of the philosophy and operations of policing.
- A multicultural strategy and training program must be created in consultation with the ethnocultural communities served by the police.

Himelfarb (p. 55) concludes: "Multicultural training is only one element of multicultural policing and multicultural policing is only one element—though a crucial one—of community-policing. While specialized courses may still be necessary to supplement such an integrated approach, they are more likely to achieve their objectives when they are seen as reflecting an overall philosophy of multicultural policing."

 *Problem Solving in Action*

Murphy (1993, p. 5) describes how problem solving was used to help stop burglaries in his community.

## Homeless Men Help Stop Burglaries

### By Larry Murphy

*Tempe, Arizona*—One afternoon on patrol, I was dispatched to Shurguard Storage regarding a burglary. While at the scene, I contacted the manager Bob Naugle. The storage facility had over 128 units and coded gates that allowed 24-hour access to the complex. Naugle advised me that the complex had no security between the hours of 10:00 P.M. and 8:00 A.M. An attendant only worked part time at this location.

*continued*

Burglaries had been historically high at Shurguard Storage. There were 18 burglaries throughout 1992. For several months, the police department received the majority of its calls for burglaries from this facility. Rock bands practiced in different units at night and a lot of their music equipment and personal items from other units were stolen. In the past, the department had taken reports about incidents and put extra patrols in the area; but these measures had no effect on the problem. Due to a recent rash of thefts and burglaries, I advised Naugle that the complex needed full-time security.

Talking with Naugle, I also learned that some of the storage units had electricity. I suggested he employ a transient person and supply a heater and bed in a unit so a person could live there comfortably. I learned that transients are territorial and will protect their area from other transients. Naugle said he would check with his district manager about the suggestion.

The next day Naugle said his manager approved of housing someone in the complex at night. As I was leaving the complex, I saw Cowboy, a transient who had lived in my beat area for the past five years. Cowboy was living outside near Hudson Park. I asked him if he'd be interested in living inside a storage unit in exchange for making periodic checks of the complex. Cowboy agreed and said his friend Sparky was also interested.

I introduced Cowboy and Sparky to Naugle the next morning. Several days later, I contacted Naugle, who reported the two men had spent the previous nights at the complex. Cowboy and Sparky each monitored one end of the storage facility. Naugle was happy with their performance. He also implemented new policies of closing at 10:00 P.M. and not giving rock bands access to the facility.

This arrangement successfully reduced thefts and burglaries at the storage complex. All of the units are fully occupied, which had not been the case previously. Since the new measures, there has been only one attempted burglary. Cowboy is also doing light maintenance for Shurguard now and has another job with a Shurguard tenant. Shurguard is even considering using transients for security at their other facilities across the country.

*Reprinted by permission of the Police Executive Research Forum.*

## SUMMARY

Ethnocentrism is the point of view that one's own way of life is better than all others. Assimilation theorists suggest that our society takes in or assimilates various cultures in what is commonly referred to as a "melting pot." Cultural pluralism suggests there are many melting pots. Some groups fuse into one pot and other groups into another. The cultural conflict theory suggests that diverse cultures that share the same territory will compete with and attempt to exploit one another.

A major problem in police interactions with some ethnic/racial groups is the language barrier. Strategies to help improve communication with non-English speaking individuals include (1) learning the language or at least common words and phrases, (2) using a language guide, (3) having a list of local language teachers who could serve as interpreters and (4) subscribing to the Language Line.

In addition to cultural diversity (including racial/ethnic diversity) the United States also has religious and socioeconomic diversity. The three basic socioeconomic classes, based primarily on income and education, are the lower, middle and upper classes. These basic classes may be further subdivided. Those in the lower class are often trapped by the poverty syndrome. This syndrome includes inadequate housing, inadequate education, inadequate jobs and a resentment of those who control the society.

The multi-culturalism trap occurs when people get so involved with their own cultural concerns they ignore the rest of the society in which they live.

Traditionally the majority culture in the United States has been defined and controlled by a white, male, European world-view. A hate or bias crime is any act, or attempted act, to cause physical injury, emotional suffering or property damage through intimidation, harassment, racial or ethnic slurs and bigoted epithets, vandalism, force or the threat of force, motivated all or in part by hostility to the victim's real or perceived race, ethnicity, religion or sexual orientation.

## Discussion Questions

1. What is your ethnic background? What is the background of your classmates?
2. How diverse is your community?
3. Have you ever tried to communicate with someone who does not speak English? What was it like?
4. How would you define the American culture?
5. Do you believe your generation can achieve the American Dream?
6. Have there been any instances of hate crimes in your community? Your state? Does your state have mandatory reporting laws for hate crimes?
7. Do you believe the "multi-culturalism trap" is a valid concern in the 1990s?
8. Would you favor eliminating the word *minority* when talking about diversity? If so, what term would you use instead?
9. Do you consider yourself "culturally literate"? Why or why not?
10. Have you encountered instances of ethnocentrism? Explain.

## References

Berglund, Judy. "Bias: Tearing the Fabric of Minnesota Nice?" *Advocate (Journal of the Minnesota Education Association).* (March 27, 1992): 8–9.

Bodinger-deUriarte, Cristina. *Research Bulletin: Hate Crime. The Rise of Hate Crime on School Campuses.* Bloomington: Phi Delta Kappa, December 1991.

"Census Bureau Predicts Large-Scale Changes in U.S. Population's Makeup." (Minneapolis/ St. Paul) *Star Tribune.* (March 14, 1996): A14.

"The Changing Face of the U.S." (Minneapolis/St. Paul) *Star Tribune.* (March 25, 1996): A5.

Clement, Douglas. "Border Crossings: Refugees Travel Difficult Road to Health Care." *Minnesota Medicine.* (March 1992): 24–29.

Conant, James B. *Slums & Suburbs.* New York: McGraw-Hill, 1961.

"Crime's Impact on Blacks Makes for a Bleak Picture." *Law Enforcement News.* (February 14, 1991): 1, 9.

Day, Thomas W. "Cross-Cultural Medicine at Home." *Minnesota Medicine.* (March 1992): 15–17.

deFiebre, Conrad. "St. Paul Police Hope Focus on Asian Culture Will Help Communication." (Minneapolis/St. Paul) *Star Tribune.* (May 27, 1991): B1.

deFiebre, Conrad. "Tradition of Trust Makes Hmong Targets of Scams." (Minneapolis/St. Paul) *Star Tribune.* (March 30, 1992): A1, A6.

Epstein, Kitty Kelly. "Oakland Moves to Create Its Own Multicultural Curriculum." *Phi Delta Kappan.* (April 1992): 635–38.

"FBI Recorded Nearly 8,000 Hate Crimes Last Year." *Criminal Justice Newsletter.* (November 15, 1996): 5.

Glensor, Ronald W. and Peak, Ken. "Policing the Homeless: A Problem-Oriented Response." *The Police Chief.* (October 1994): 101–03.

Gustafson, Paul and Prince, Pat. "Hmong Man Faces Charges for Marrying Underage Girl." (Minneapolis/St. Paul) *Star Tribune.* (May 16, 1991): A1.

Hare, Bruce R. "Beyond 'Black' Students and 'White' Universities." *The NEA Higher Education Journal.* (Fall 1991): 157–59.

Himelfarb, Frum. "A Training Strategy for Policing in a Multicultural Society." *The Police Chief.* (November 1991): 53–55.

Hinkle, Douglas P. "Street Spanish." *Law Enforcement Technology.* (April 1990): 22–23, 44.

Hirsch, E. D., Jr. *Cultural Literacy: What Every American Needs to Know.* New York: Random House, 1988.

Hodges, Jill. "Was She Harassed or Not? Ex-Officer's Suit Leads to Trial." (Minneapolis/St. Paul) *Star Tribune.* (April 1, 1992): B5.

Houston, Paul. "For Whom the Bell Tolls." *Phi Delta Kappan.* (October 1996): 124–26.

Inkster, Norman D. "The Essence of Community Policing." *The Police Chief.* (March 1992): 28–31.

*Learning Objectives for Professional Peace Officer Education.* St. Paul: P.O.S.T. Board, July 1991.

Lieberman, Michael. "Enforcing Hate Crime Laws: Defusing Intergroup Tensions." *The Police Chief.* (October 1994): 18–28.

Martin, Susan E. "Investigating Hate Crimes: Case Characteristics and Law Enforcement Responses." *Justice Quarterly.* (September 1996): 455–80.

Monk, Richard C. *Taking Sides: Clashing Views on Controversial Issues in Crime and Criminology.* 2nd rev. ed. Guilford: The Dushkin Publishing Group, Inc. 1991.

Morris, Cole. "FBI Releases Hate Crime Stats." *Police.* (January 1997): 16.

Murphy, Larry. *Problem-Solving Quarterly.* (Summer 1993, Vol. 6, No. 3): 5.

Nelson, Marshall W. "A Multifaceted Approach." *The Police Chief.* (October 1994): 49–50.

Pace, Denny F. *Community Relations Concepts.* Incline Village, Nevada: Copperhouse Publishing Company, 1991.

"Parlez-Vous Miranda Warnings?" *Law Enforcement News.* (September 30, 1990): 3.

Plummer, Larry C. "The Problem of Bigotry and Hate Requires a Collective, Intentional Response." *Subject to Debate.* (October/November 1995): 1, 6–7.

Rachlin, Harvey. "Meeting the Demands of Foreign Languages in Small- and Medium-Sized Communities." *Law and Order.* (September 1992): 99–102.

"Religious Animal Sacrifice to Be Reviewed by Court." (Minneapolis/St. Paul) *Star Tribune.* (March 24, 1992): A1, A6.

Rosen, Marie Simonetti. "An Interview with Chief Elizabeth Watson of Houston, Tex." *Law Enforcement News.* (February 29, 1992): 6–7.

Sharp, Arthur G. "Are We All Speaking the Same Language?" *Law and Order.* (July 1991): 95–99.

Teepen, Tom. "We Can't Shrug Off the Income Gap that Divides America." (Minneapolis/St. Paul) *Star Tribune.* (May 1, 1995): A6.

Walker, Samuel and Katz, Charles M. "Less than Meets the Eye: Police Department Bias-Crime Units." *American Journal of Police.* (Vol. XIV, No. 1, 1995): 29–48.

## *Resources*

American Association of Retired Persons (AARP), Criminal Justice Services, 601 E. Street N.W., Washington, DC 20049; (202) 434-2222.

American Indian Movement (AIM), Peacemaker Center 2300, Cedar Ave. S., Minneapolis, MN; (612) 724-3129.

Anti-Defamation League of B'nai-Brith, 823 United Nations Plaza, NY 10017.

Bureau of Indian Affairs (BIA), 1849 C Street N.W., Washington, DC 20240; (301) 208-3711.

Indian Human Development Services, 200 Independence Avenue S.W., Washington, DC 20201; (301) 245-2760.

League of United Latin American Citizens (LULAC), 777 N. Capitol Street N.E., Washington, DC 20002; (301) 408-0060.

Mexican American Legal Defense and Education Fund (MALDEF), 634 S. Spring Street, 11th Floor, Los Angeles, CA 90014; (213) 629-2512.

Mexican Chancery, 1911 Pennsylvania Ave., N.W., Washington, DC 20007; (301) 728-1600.

National Association for the Advancement of Colored People (NAACP), 4805 Mount Hope Drive, Baltimore, MD 21215; (212) 481-4100.

National Association of Blacks in Criminal Justice (NABCJ), P.O. Box 66271, Washington, DC 20035; (215) 686-2961.

National Organization of Black Law Enforcement Executives (NOBLE), 908 Pennsylvania Avenue S.E., Washington, DC 20003; (202) 546-8811.

National Rehabilitation Information Center, 8455 Colesville Road, Suite 935, Silver Spring, MD 20910-3319; (301) 588-9284.

National Urban League, 500 East 62nd Street, New York, NY 10021; (212) 310-9000.

State Department of Human Rights—locate in phone book.

# Chapter 8

# Interacting with the Physically and Mentally Disabled

*It is more important to know what sort of a patient has a disease [or disability] than what sort of disease [or disability] a patient has.*

—Sir William Osler

## Do you know

- How many people in the United States have disabilities?
- What *the* most important guideline is for interacting with an individual with disabilities?
- What disabilities police officers might frequently encounter?
- What method of communication most individuals who are deaf prefer?
- What effect deinstitutionalization of the mentally ill has had on communities?
- What behaviors police most frequently encounter in contacts with mentally disabled individuals?
- What mental health is? Mental illness?
- How serious the problem of suicide is in the United States?
- What the four civil criteria for detainment and commitment of mentally ill individuals are?
- What dispositions are available when dealing with mental illness or mental retardation?
- How epilepsy can imitate intoxication or a drug high?

## Definitions

Can you define these terms: ADA, Ameslan, crisis behavior, deaf, deinstitutional-ization, delusional (paranoid) disorder, disability, epilepsy, hearing impaired, mental health, mental illness, mental retardation, mood disorders, personality disorders, psychotic symptoms, schizophrenia, seizure, TAB, TDD.

 *Introduction*

A police officer asks an individual to perform some field sobriety tests and the person cannot do so even though she is not under the influence of any drug, including alcohol. Another person ignores the direct order of a police officer to step back on the sidewalk. Yet another person approaches an officer and attempts to ask directions, but his speech is so slurred he is unintelligible. These common occurrences for police officers can often be misinterpreted. In each of the preceding instances, the individual interacting with the officer has a disability: a problem with balance, a hearing impairment, a speech disability.

A **disability** is a physical or mental impairment that substantially limits one or more of an individual's major life functions.

◆

In the United States 43 million people have disabilities.

◆

The estimated number of disabled people in the United States is probably conservative. According to Burden (1991, p. 11): "Depending on how 'disabled' is defined, there are between 40 million and 70 million in the U.S.—easily the nation's biggest 'minority.'"

Concurring, Cushing (1992, p. A19) suggests: "People with disabilities are the largest minority group in the United States. Just as with other minority groups, individuals are identified by stereotypes rather than ability, by how they are different rather than how they are like the able-bodied majority. They are identified as a what, rather than a who."

Greater recognition of this "minority" came on July 26, 1990, when President Bush signed into law the Americans with Disabilities Act (**ADA**). President Bush called it "another Independence Day, one that is long overdue" (News Services, 1990, p. A1). Under the ADA, a disabled person is anyone who:

- Has a physical or mental impairment that substantially limits one or more major life activities;

- Has a record of such an impairment; or
- Is regarded as having such an impairment.

All of the policies that apply to people with disabilities also apply to people with communicable and infectious disease.

The ADA guarantees that persons with disabilities will have equal access to any public facilities that are available to persons without disabilities. It also guarantees that people with disabilities will have equal access to communication services available to those without disabilities. This includes certain types of telephones and television service.

Because the ADA guarantees access to government services, it helps in building partnerships for community policing. Under the ADA, all brochures and printed material must be available in braille or on audiotape if requested. To include people with disabilities in community partnerships, the police must be able to communicate with them and should conduct their meetings in barrier-free places.

The ADA regulates bias against those with disabilities. The law is likely to increase the number of disabled individuals who are "out and about" in the community. As stressed previously, and as aptly expressed by Burden (1991, p. 11):

> People with physical and mental disabilities are people first, disabled second.
> They have the same needs and desires of those (all the rest of us) they call
> **TAB**'s—the Temporarily Able-Bodied—but they have some special needs too.
> Often these needs are poorly understood by TAB's, including police officers.

How officers deal with the most vulnerable in our communities has a positive or negative effect on police-community relations. Many people in our communities have made the treatment of the disabled a priority and are available and willing to work with law enforcement agencies to ensure that people with disabilities are treated respectfully and protected from those who would victimize them. The outcome of increased awareness and service in this area will not only make police officers' jobs easier when they encounter disabled people, but will help reduce the disabled's fear and vulnerability. The focus on the disabled will make the community a better and safer place for everyone and help to build excellent police-community relations. To increase their comfort level when dealing with the disabled, officers should spend time with them, listen to them and learn to see them as individuals.

This chapter begins with discussions of the prevalence of disabilities in the United States, the likelihood of victimization and general guidelines for dealing with the disabled. Next specific conditions are described: the mobility impaired, the vision impaired, the hearing impaired, the mentally disabled and individuals with epilepsy. This is followed by an explanation of crime prevention for the disabled. The chapter concludes with a brief discussion of dealing with individuals with disabilities who break the law.

As you read the chapter keep in mind that the focus is on the role of the police in dealing with individuals with disabilities. Community support and other resources are assumed to be an integral part of law enforcement's efforts in this area. The listing of resources at the end of the chapter provides some insight into the variety of joint efforts that might be possible.

## FACTS ABOUT DISABILITY IN AMERICA IN THE 1990s

The National Institute on Disability and Rehabilitation Research has provided the following facts about disability in America today:

- More than one-sixth or 17 percent of our population has a physical or mental disability—the largest minority in America.
- Disability knows no political, economic, educational, sexual, age, ethnic, religious, social or geographic distinctions.
- An estimated 1 million Americans use wheelchairs.
- 2.5 million people are severely visually impaired and are unable to read a newspaper. Of those, 120,000 are totally blind and 600,000 are legally blind.
- 22 million Americans are hearing impaired. Two million of them are deaf.
- More than 6 million Americans are mentally retarded. Mental retardation affects more people than blindness, muscular dystrophy, polio, cerebral palsy and rheumatic heart disease combined.
- Approximately 2 million people with disabilities reside in institutions, including nursing homes, mental hospitals, residential facilities and mental retardation facilities.
- More than 46 percent of all people over age sixty-five have chronic impairments. (The elderly are discussed in Chapter 9.)
- On average, people with disabilities have less education, less income, fewer job opportunities and fewer social contacts than others.
- People with disabilities are the most welfare-dependent minority in the United States.
- More than 25 million people with disabilities are registered voters, an emerging political force.

In addition to being victims of a particular accident or disease, disabled individuals are also frequently victims of crime.

## VICTIMIZATION

The disabled are very frequent victims of crime. While the sex, race and age of crime victims are known, generally no information is compiled on victims' disabilities. As noted by Burden (1991, p. 11): "The few limited studies that have been done by police and social scientists indicate that the disabled are frequent crime victims, which is not surprising since many are easy prey for muggers and some are patsies for con games."

Criminals often prey on the disabled, assuming they cannot readily protect themselves. The disabled may, like many of us, develop predictable patterns of activity that make them vulnerable to victimization. The disabled need the help of law enforcement personnel to feel safe and to learn means to protect themselves. Retarded individuals, for example, often use public transportation. They are often easily identified as vulnerable and because of their dependency and often trusting nature, they are particularly prone to becoming victims.

The first steps a police department can take to better serve this segment of the community is to identify who the disabled are, what types of disabilities they have and where and under what circumstances officers are likely to encounter them.

Police officers encounter disabled individuals in group homes, school special education programs, sheltered work programs, mental hospitals, detention facilities, private homes, apartments, trailer homes or among the homeless. Disabled people can be average citizens, crime victims or the perpetrators of crime. In other words, the disabled are not a homogeneous group. Some are obviously disabled, while others are not.

Most veteran officers can tell stories about criminals who have cruelly taken advantage of disabled people. Unfortunately, however, most officers are not aware of how much they can do to reduce the vulnerability of the disabled. Their vulnerability can be reduced through special programs in which police personnel effectively participate. These programs should include officers teaching disabled people what they can do to protect themselves.

## GENERAL GUIDELINES FOR DEALING WITH THE DISABLED

◆

The most important guideline for interacting with disabled people is to treat them as individuals with the same needs and desires as any other citizen.

◆

In addition, the following guidelines apply to interactions with most individuals with disabilities:

- Do not shout.
- Be empathetic.
- Do not prejudge what a person with a disability can or cannot do. You do not know.
- Do not coddle individuals with disabilities. They need to be challenged just like everyone else.

◆

Disabilities police officers frequently encounter include mobility impairment, vision impairment, hearing impairment, mental or emotional impairment and impairment as a result of epilepsy.

◆

Now consider each of these disabilities and the recommended police response to each.

## THE MOBILITY IMPAIRED

*An estimated one million Americans use wheelchairs.*

Not all people who are mobility disabled use wheelchairs. Also included within this group are those who are entirely dependent on walkers, canes and other mobility aids. Many are victims of accidents. Many have such diseases as muscular dystrophy or multiple sclerosis. Others were born with birth defects which make mobility difficult or impossible.

Sometimes the appearance of those with cerebral palsy or muscular dystrophy makes people believe they are mentally retarded. This is often *not* the case. Officers should not assume that a severely physically disabled individual in a wheelchair is also mentally disabled.

### The Police Response

The following guidelines are suggested by an individual who was once able-bodied and is now disabled and uses a wheelchair (Ehlert, 1991, p. E3):

- Focus on the similarities you have with a disabled person, not on the differences.
- Don't lean on a disabled person's wheelchair. It's part of his/her space.
- Don't presume someone wants to tell you how they became disabled. Respect their privacy.

- Allow your kids to ask questions of disabled persons, though. Most disabled persons understand natural curiosity and don't mind explaining.
- Speak directly to disabled persons. Don't ask an able-bodied person present to intervene.
- Don't assume that disabled persons need to be "taken care of." Most can negotiate routine obstacles, such as getting in and out of their cars. If you think there is an unsurmountable barrier, ask them if they would like assistance—before you provide it.
- Get down at eye-level and converse with people in wheelchairs. Don't shout at them.
- Don't use words and phrases such as "a victim" of MS, "confined" to a wheelchair. Wheelchairs actually liberate the disabled.
- Don't misuse the word "normal," which is a good way to describe objects, but not people.

If mobility is the only disability an individual has, you can communicate with the person as you would with any other individual.

In addition, police officers should be alert to physical conditions that might make access difficult for those with mobility impairments. Police can also make certain that handicapped parking spaces are provided and that nonhandicapped individuals who park in these places are either severely warned or ticketed.

Community relations programs that place mobile individuals, including business owners and police officers, in a wheelchair for a day are an excellent way to demonstrate the difficulties those with mobility impairments encounter.

## THE VISION IMPAIRED

*2.5 million people are severely visually impaired.*

This figure represents only those who are *severely* visually impaired. According to the National Society to Prevent Blindness (Zehring, 1990, p. 33) over 11.5 million people in the United States are visually impaired.

Sometimes the visually impaired are very noticeable because of their white canes or their seeing-eye dogs. Other times, however, the disability is not readily apparent. Many people can see well enough to get around, but not well enough to read signs. Consequently, they may unknowingly break the law.

### The Police Response

The natural tendency is to talk louder than usual to a visually impaired person. Refrain from doing this, unless, of course, you have determined they are also hearing impaired, a common combination.

*A San Francisco police officer helps a blind woman across the street.*

When interacting with a blind or severely visually impaired person, allow the person to feel your badge or arm patch to establish your identity and authority.

The Mesa Public School District and the Mesa Police Department collaborated to adapt Stranger Danger and Officer Friendly programs to meet the needs of visually impaired elementary age students. The program helps children to recognize dangerous situations as well as to recognize police officers and their squad cars. As noted by Zehring (p. 34):

> The design of the Mesa Police Department's patch allowed the children to feel three points at the top of the patch and the points in each of the lower corners. The children were not allowed to touch the officer's service revolver, but they happily settled for touching his handcuffs, portable radio, wallet badge and other items on the officer's duty belt. The children also learned to identify the sounds of the police radio and specific items on the police car, such as door shields, overhead light bars, the cage between the seats and the antenna on the trunk.

## THE HEARING IMPAIRED

*22 million Americans are hearing impaired. Two million are deaf.*

The **hearing impaired,** commonly called *hard of hearing,* are those who have some residual hearing; that is, sounds may be audible, but not clear. For the hearing impaired, words are not just softer, they are garbled. **Deaf** people have such extreme hearing loss they cannot understand spoken words. They may respond to loud noises, but need visual communication clues. The deaf may or may not use sign language.

According to Dr. King, Director of Deaf Education at the University of Southern Mississippi (1990, p. 98):

> Deaf people can do anything hearing people can—except hear. . . . It may be surprising to learn that deaf people are much more *like* hearing people than *un*like them. . . . They are, however, cut off from both the spoken and written forms of the English language. . . .
>
> To most deaf people, English is a second language, if not a foreign one; their first language is American Sign Language. . . . For this reason, the average deaf person has a difficult time interacting with the written form of English; in fact, the average reading level of the deaf is between third and fourth grade. This is the result of a linguistic deficit caused by not being able to hear the English language, not by a mental deficiency on the part of the deaf person.

Dr. King says that deaf people communicate differently depending on the age when they became deaf, the type of deafness and the person's language skills, intelligence, personality and education. Many hearing impaired individuals are undereducated.

Most deaf people cannot lip-read. According to Hageman (1985, p. 116), 60 percent of English words look exactly like some other word when formed with the lips.

◆

Most deaf people prefer to communicate by means of sign language.

◆

The sign language deaf people use most often is **Ameslan** (American Sign Language). Consequently, interpreters are often of great assistance for police to communicate with the hearing impaired, just as language interpreters assist police to communicate with non-English speaking people.

It is important to distinguish between an interpreter, that is, one who knows Ameslan and a signer. Interpreters have special training and are registered. A list of interpreters can be obtained from the State Commission for the Hearing Impaired, the state chapter of the National Association of the Deaf (NAD) or the Registry itself.

Other people who can sign are considered "signers." Officers who are interested should consider taking "signing" classes so they can communicate more effectively with hearing impaired individuals. Signing skills can also be used in other aspects of police work, as noted by Gallo (1992, p. 54):

> Officers who can sign can communicate over long distances when there is too much noise to use a radio, such as during a parade or demonstration. It is also useful if you do not wish a suspect to know what you are saying.

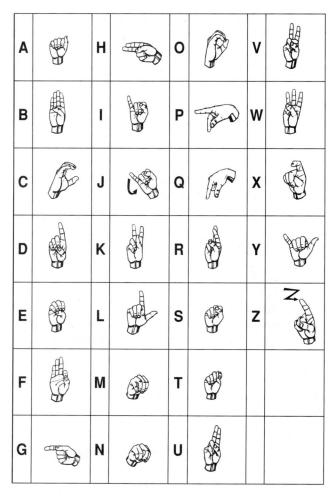

*Figure 8.1*   **Finger Spelling**

Youngblood and Lynch (1995, p. 52) recommend: "Police officers should learn at least simple signs and finger spelling (spelling with the manual alphabet)." See Figure 8.1.

Lesce (1996, p. 81) suggests that public safety employees, including police officers, learn to sign necessary words and phrases such as "ambulance," "blood," "medicine," "Can I help you?" "Did you see what happened?" "Sign slow," "Do you understand?" and "You're welcome."

An important consideration for police officers dealing with hearing impaired individuals who use signing is that sign language has a grammar and syntax all its own. Gallo (1992, p. 53) notes:

As a result, when officers try to communicate using notes passed between themselves and a deaf individual, they often experience messages that are more like baby talk than English. For example, in answer to an officer's written question "Where have you been tonight?" the answer might be, "I go there friends house finish, come here home sleep."

Such an answer could, understandably, lead an officer to believe that he is dealing with a mentally deficient individual. But this may be far from the truth.

Because sensitive or confidential information may be involved when dealing with hearing impaired individuals and interpreter/signers, it is important to use certified signers. Their code of ethics requires that they keep all information strictly confidential, use the appropriate mode of communication while conveying the full message and not inject personal opinions into the situation.

Some police departments and some police officers have distinguished themselves in developing skills and services for the disabled. Dan Levin of the Chicago Police Department is one such officer. As the only known certified law enforcement sign language interpreter, he has a unique niche. He now works exclusively for the department's senior and disabled service division where he spends approximately 70 percent of his time assisting communications between deaf people and police officers. He teaches recruits how to deal with deaf individuals as well as other handicapped people, assists on cases involving deaf victims or suspects and is also on cases that involve other types of disabled people. Levin sometimes gets called to assist a field unit who has a deaf victim or arrestee. Deaf people get arrested; they commit crimes as anybody does. He has been involved in everything from questions about parking tickets to murder.

Police officers who interact with hearing impaired individuals who are suspects must consider that if the individual needs to be handcuffed, the suspect will have no means of communication. Gallo (p. 54) suggests: "This is synonymous with gagging a hearing person."

Technological advances have greatly improved communicating with the deaf. Telecommunications devices for the deaf (**TDD**) consist of a receiver and a keyboard used to transmit and receive written communication using the telephone. Often civic organizations such as the Lions or Rotary are willing to purchase such equipment for a police department and for the hearing impaired individuals residing in a community.

According to King (1996, p. 47): "The acronyms TDD and TTY are used interchangeably to mean 'Telecommunication Device for the Deaf.' However, the adult deaf community seems to prefer the term TTY."

Another improvement in communications with the hearing impaired is close-captioned television whereby the words being spoken are displayed on specially equipped monitors for those who have impaired hearing.

When interacting with those who are hearing impaired, police should consider the potential for other difficulties in their lives. As noted by Hull (1985, p. 1):

> Violence in deaf families is greater than it is for families without this limitation. Family violence may be more common among deaf people because of the many frustrations they encounter every day in their lives.
>
> Violence against deaf women is inflicted by deaf men as well as by hearing men. The rate of abuse among couples with only one deaf partner may be greater because of increased communication problems. However, 85–90% of hearing impaired women are married to hearing impaired men. It can be assumed that a higher number of abusers against deaf women are themselves deaf.

## The Police Response

King (1990, p. 98) suggests: "The key is to determine how that particular deaf person communicates and use whatever combination of techniques is necessary to facilitate communication." He recommends the following (pp. 98–100):

- Get the deaf person's attention. [gently tap shoulder, wave]
- Make sure the deaf person understands the topic of discussion.
- Speak slowly and clearly, but do not over-enunciate or over-exaggerate words. Speak in short sentences.
- Look directly at the deaf person.
- Do not place anything in your mouth when speaking.
- Maintain eye contact.
- Avoid standing in front of a light source. [window, car's headlights, any other bright light]
- Don't hesitate to communicate by paper and pencil, but keep it simple. [third to fourth grade level]
- Use pantomime, body language and facial expressions.
- If possible, learn sign language.
- Do not assume the deaf person has understood the message just because he nods his head in acknowledgement.

Other recommendations when dealing with deaf or hard of hearing individuals include the following:

- Use normal rate—not too fast nor so slow that the natural rhythm is lost. The thought should come as a whole.
- Change the wording if it is not understood. Do not keep repeating the same phrase over.

- Move away from noises such as TVs, radios, etc.
- Avoid statements such as, "Did you hear that?" "Did you understand that?"
- If you have a mustache, keep it trimmed.

Siegfried (1996, pp. 20–21) offers a five-step approach to open the lines of communication with individuals who are hearing impaired:

1. Identify the signs and symptoms. In deaf culture, it is common for deaf people to touch people to get their attention. They may try to touch you. Do not interpret this as hostility.
2. Start writing. Offer them a pencil and paper.
3. Don't be fooled by lip readers. Even the best lip readers can only get partial information from lip reading.
4. Know the law. Know your state and local laws. In most states, when issuing the Miranda advisal, you must use a certified interpreter.
5. Ask for help.

If an interaction involves a group, arrange the chairs in a semicircle if possible. If tables are used, small tables are better than large ones. If there is a speaker or discussion, have all questions repeated from the front of the room.

**When Using an Interpreter.** King (p. 100) suggests the following guidelines when using an interpreter to interact with a hearing impaired individual:

- Treat the interpreter as a professional.
- Provide good lighting.
- Speak directly to the deaf person, not the interpreter.
- Remember that the interpreter will be a few words behind the speaker.
- Permit only one person to speak at a time.
- Speak clearly and in a normal tone.

Sometimes written communication is most effective. When using written communication, write notes as you normally would, assuming the person can understand. Indications that the person does not understand include the following: an inappropriate or no response, quizzical or blank expression, smiling or nodding at inappropriate times. If any of these behaviors occur, rephrase your note.

King (p. 100) echoes a recurring theme of this textbook: "Perhaps the most important thing the officer can communicate is respect and dignity, remembering that deafness is not a defect, but a cultural difference and that each deaf person is unique."

# THE MENTALLY DISABLED

Historically society decided to institutionalize the mentally disabled, whether mentally ill or mentally retarded. In the mid-1960s, however, institutionalization was replaced with treatment in the community. This was the result of several factors including the development of medications to control mental illness; research showing that institutionalized individuals did not receive adequate treatment and could do better in the community; federal programs to build and operate mental health centers; and patients' rights litigation and state legislation.

◆

**Deinstitutionalization** refers to the release of thousands of mentally ill individuals into society to be cared for by family or a special network of support services.

◆

Community-based mental health service rests on the premise that people have the right not to be isolated from the community simply because they are mentally ill. This premise works as long as a support system for them exists. Unfortunately, the network of support services has developed slowly. As a result, thousands of mentally ill people are on the street, homeless. Hundreds of others are in family situations where the family is totally ill-equipped to provide necessary care and assistance. In both such situations, the mentally ill individuals are likely to have encounters with the local police. This is usually as a result of some bizarre behavior rather than committing a crime. According to Finn and Sullivan (1988, p. 1): "Handling the mentally ill is perhaps the single most difficult type of call for law enforcement officers."

DeCuir and Lamb (1996, p. 99) note: "From law enforcement's point of view, if the system were working as planned, the alleys and bus stations would not be filled with homeless mentally ill people and state jails would not be holding thousands of psychotic misdemeanants."

As Louis (1997, p. 82) suggests: "A long-standing rift exists between law enforcement and those who provide public and private mental health treatment and resources. Issues of bed availability, jurisdiction, and accountability, cost considerations, and the whole issue surrounding behavior related to mental illness vs. criminal activity have all been a source of contention."

## Mental Illness

Flynn (1996, p. 44) defines mental illness as "a psychiatric disorder characterized by abnormal functioning of the centers of the brain responsible for thought, perception, mood and behavior."

The following discussion is a condensation of information Murphy presents in *Managing Persons with Mental Disabilities* (1989). Reprinted by permission.

**The Nature of the Problem.** One in ten people suffer from some type of mental illness. Between one and four million people are seriously mentally ill. They live in a variety of settings such as private residences with families or alone, halfway or group houses, bed and board homes, nursing homes, single room occupancy hotels, jails and prisons, homeless shelters and on the street.

**Factors Surrounding Police Responses.** The police become involved with mentally ill people because they have the only twenty-four-hour, seven-days-a-week, mobile emergency response capacity. Also, police officers have the authority to detain, arrest and use force if needed. Any citizen who feels threatened by the bizarre behavior or the mere presence of a mentally disabled person may call the police to "make the problem go away."

◆

When police are called to manage mentally ill persons, the behaviors most frequently encountered include:

- Bizarre, unusual or strange behavior.
- Confused thoughts or action.
- Aggressive actions.
- Destructive, assaultive or violent behavior.
- Attempted suicide.

◆

Police most frequently encounter mentally ill individuals during the evening shift. Police also receive frequent calls regarding the mentally ill during weekends and holidays. The mentally ill individuals police encounter are frequently unattached and lack social support; they are difficult to manage and may have complications such as alcohol or drug abuse.

**Mental Health v. Mental Illness.** *Mental health* is a relative term that means different things to different people. Generally speaking, those who are mentally healthy have a positive self-image and can successfully relate to others.

◆

**Mental health** is the ability to integrate one's self with one's environment. **Mental illness** is a severe disturbance in thinking, feeling and relating that results in substantially diminished capacity to cope with the ordinary demands of life.

◆

Basically, there are two broad categories of mental disabilities: disorders that cause a person to suffer from psychotic symptoms and those that do not. It is helpful for police officers to be familiar with the kinds of mental illnesses they may encounter and the terminology used by mental health professionals.

**Psychotic symptoms** demonstrate a significant loss of contact with reality and include illogical thought, incoherent speech, disorientation, extreme mood fluctuation, social withdrawal, hallucinations and delusions and neglect of family and occupational obligations. These symptoms are beyond the person's control. Psychotic behavior may be a nuisance, a burden or an outright danger. The public is generally threatened by such behavior.

The most chronic and disabling mental illness is **schizophrenia,** a deterioration in one's personality to the point where feelings, thoughts and behavior are not coherent. This is *not* the same as a split personality. Common symptoms of schizophrenia include social isolation or withdrawal; bizarre, meaningless, inappropriate behavior; prominent hallucinations; peculiar behavior such as collecting garbage, talking to oneself in public, hoarding food; rapid shift in subject matter when speaking; confusion and ambivalence.

Another mental illness with psychotic symptoms police commonly encounter is **delusional (paranoid) disorder**. This illness is characterized by nonbizarre delusions focused on a single theme or a series of connected themes. Common themes include persecution, jealousy and grandiosity.

**Mood disorders,** severe depression, mania or cycles of depression and mania are also of concern to police officers. Suicide is the most serious complication associated with depression, although not all those who suffer from clinical depression are suicidal.

Three disorders do not cause psychotic symptoms: anxiety disorders, dissociative disorders and personality disorders. There are three types of *anxiety disorders:* simple phobias (fears), panic disorders (characterized by sweating, dizziness, palpitations, trembling, nausea and severe, frightening episodes of apprehension and feelings of impending doom) and obsessive compulsive disorders.

*Dissociative disorders* are also of three types: multiple personalities, psychogenic fugue (sudden, unexpected travel away from one's home, assumption of a new identity and inability to recall previous identity) and amnesia.

*Personality disorders* are the form of mental illness most often encountered by police officers. This is because many habitual offenders have character or **personality disorders,** that is, inflexible and maladaptive personality traits and significant impairment of social and occupational functioning. Common elements of a personality disorder include lack of self-control, inability to learn from past experience, lack of good judgment and lack of moral or ethical values. Individuals with personality disorders provoke trouble, think of themselves first, are prodigious liars and are adept at manipulating others.

Police in one midwestern city shot and killed a suspect who had just robbed a gas station after a short foot chase through dark parking lots. The suspect turned out to be a mentally disturbed female whom they had dealt with often over the past year. After robbing the gas station, she ordered the clerk to call "911" and she stayed there until he had done so. The confrontation and subsequent shooting seemed orchestrated, forced by the woman who was depressed and suicidal. She claimed to have a gun, threatened to shoot the officers and advanced toward one with an object in her hand. The object turned out to be a comb. It is difficult to imagine a different outcome in this case; however, police should understand that motives of people, particularly of the mentally disturbed, may not be logical. Some suicidal people arrange to die at the hands of the police.

## Mental Retardation

*More than six million American children and adults have mental retardation.*

Mental retardation is the nation's fourth ranking disabling condition, affecting 3 percent of the U.S. population. Essentially, **mental retardation** means that normal intellectual development fails to occur. Unlike mental illness, mental retardation is permanent. It is diagnosed when the following three criteria exist:

- Significant subaverage general intellectual functioning (as measured by IQ tests).
- Resulting in, or associated with, defects or impairments in adaptive behavior, such as personal independence and social responsibility.
- With onset by age eighteen.

Mental retardation can be caused by biological or environmental factors or a combination of both. Mental retardation may be mild, the most common level, with IQ just below that of average normal intellectual functioning; moderate; or severe and profound. The differences between mental illness and mental retardation are summarized in Table 8.1.

In addition to individuals who have mental illnesses or mental retardation, police officers may have to interact with individuals who have extreme emotional problems, including crisis behavior and suicidal behavior.

## Crisis Behavior

**Crisis behavior** results when a person has a *temporary* breakdown in coping skills. Such people often fear they are going crazy and say such things as, "I must be losing my mind." Anyone can suffer from a crisis, and what may constitute a crisis for one person may not for another person.

## Suicidal Behavior

Although the mentally ill may attempt to commit suicide, not all those who attempt suicide are mentally ill.

Lerner (1994, p. 45) reports: "Suicide is the eighth leading cause of reported deaths in the United States. Many deaths as a result of suicide are reported as something else, nonetheless, it ranks just behind vehicular deaths and ahead of AIDS-related deaths. While 33,000 suicide deaths are reported each year, there are also five million living Americans who have attempted suicide."

*Table 8.1*    **Differences between Mental Retardation and Mental Illness**

Many people make the common mistake of confusing the mentally retarded with the mentally ill person. However, it is most important to understand that these disorders are separate and distinct conditions. The following chart compares the differences between the two.

| *Mental Retardation* | *differs from* | *Mental Illness* |
|---|---|---|
| **A.** Retardation refers to subaverage intellectual functioning. | | **A.** Mental illness has nothing to do with IQ. A person may be a genius or subaverage. |
| **B.** Retardation refers to impairment in social adaptation. | | **B.** A mentally ill person may be very competent socially but may have a character disorder or other aberration. |
| **C.** Retardation usually occurs during the period of development or is present at birth. However, a brain injury or toxemia may cause retardation in anyone at any age. | | **C.** Mental illness may strike at any time. |
| **D.** In mental retardation, the intellectual impairment is permanent, but can be compensated through education and development. | | **D.** Mental illness is often temporary. |
| **E.** A retarded person can usually be expected to behave rationally at his operational level. | | **E.** A mentally ill person may vacillate between normal and irrational behavior. |
| **F.** A retarded person will not be violent except in those situations that cause violence in non-retarded persons. | | **F.** A mentally ill person may be erratic or even violent. |
| **G.** A mentally retarded person has a learning disability and uses the skills of educators, psychologists and vocational rehabilitation therapists. | | **G.** A mentally ill person uses the services of psychiatrists, psychotherapists or psychologists. |

SOURCE: Gerard R. Murphy. *Managing Persons with Mental Disabilities: A Curriculum Guide for Police Trainers.* Washington: Police Executive Research Forum, 1989. Reprinted by permission.

◆

Suicide is the tenth leading cause of death among adults and the second leading cause of death among adolescents.

◆

Two-thirds of all suicides each year are committed by white men over thirty-five years of age. Women attempt suicide three times more often than men, but men kill themselves four times more often than women.

For every "successful" suicide, there are eight to ten attempts that "fail," or about 300,000 attempts annually. Persons who attempt suicide *must* receive professional counseling—they must not be placed in a holding or jail cell.

In one study 158 individuals who had a close friend or relative commit suicide were asked about the danger signs given by the 110 people who had killed themselves. The following summarizes their answers:

| | |
|---|---|
| Statements about hopelessness | 72% |
| Statements about helplessness | 68% |
| Statements about worthlessness | 64% |
| Talk about suicide | 57% |
| Preoccupation with death | 51% |
| Were suddenly happier, calmer before death | 41% |
| Lost interest in things they cared about | 40% |
| Visited or called people they cared about | 38% |
| Set their affairs in order | 30% |
| Gave away prized possessions | 15% |

Major indications of suicidal behavior include a suicide plan, history of past attempts, internal and external resources, recent loss, physical illness, drinking and other substance abuse, physical isolation, dramatic changes in mood or behavior, mental illness, saying good-bye to loved ones or taking steps to finalize plans by giving away possessions. A suicide can occur without these signs, but an officer should not hesitate to consider a person suicidal if only one or two of the signs are present.

Geberth (1996, p. 163) suggests: "The psychology of the suicide is rooted in depression. Therefore, investigators must take into account the clinical considerations as well as the investigative facts." He lists three basic considerations to establish if a death is suicide (p. 165):

- The presence of the weapon or means of death at the scene.
- Injuries or wounds that are obviously self-inflicted, or could have been inflicted by the deceased.

- The existence of a motive or intent on the part of the victim to take his or her own life.

## Statutory Requirements and Implications

In handling calls involving mentally ill persons, officers often misinterpret civil criteria for detaining and committing those who are dangerous. This misinterpretation usually leads to unnecessary, time-consuming delays in disposition. With a solid understanding of the common civil criteria for detainment and commitment, officers will be better able to manage this population.

◆

The four civil criteria for detainment and commitment of mentally ill individuals are:

- Mental illness.
- Dangerousness.
- Gravely disabled.
- In need of (mental health) treatment.

◆

These criteria are quite subjective. Usually mental illness and one other criterion must be present for someone to be committed.

*Mental illness* is the undisputed first criterion for an involuntary civil commitment. None of the other criteria will be accepted as grounds for commitment unless the person is also mentally ill. *Dangerousness* may be in relation to oneself or to others.

The *commitment process* usually involves four steps: (1) the police officer determines a person needs a mental health examination; (2) a psychiatrist or mental health professional determines if the person needs to be examined—if not, the person is released; (3) a psychiatrist conducts the examination and may detain the person for seventy-two hours; (4) a civil hearing is conducted where both sides (the state and the individual) present arguments for or against short-term commitment.

## Responding to the Call—On-Scene Management

When officers are called to a scene where an individual exhibits bizarre behavior, they must first try to assess whether the individual is mentally ill, mentally retarded or suicidal. Himmelsbach established the following guidelines for handling such encounters.

### Guidelines for Handling Frequently Encountered Situations*

1. **Subject Is Compulsive Talker.** Persons engaged in compulsive talking produce a stream of sometimes meaningless chatter at a rapid, almost

*SOURCE: Himmelsbach, in Arnold P. Goldstein, *Police Crisis Intervention* (Elmsford: Pergammon Press, 1979), reprinted in Gerard R. Murphy, *Managing Persons with Mental Disabilities: A Curriculum Guide for Police Trainers.* Washington: Police Executive Research Forum, 1989.

non-stop rate. These are understandable communications, but bear little or no relation to the problem at hand. This behavior indicates high levels of anxiety. If your requests to slow down are not effective, you can interrupt the compulsive speech pattern by asking the individual specific concrete questions. For example, ask his birth date or address; ask him to give the full name of his children or his parents; or ask him where he works or goes to school. Your goal is to interrupt the speech in order to break its pattern and bring it somewhat under control.

2.  **Subject Is Conscious but Non-responsive.** This happens in cases in which the person may be catatonic or severely depressed. You should never assume that because a person is not responding to your statement, he is not hearing what you say. In these situations, there is the temptation to begin acting and talking as if the subject were not present. This is a mistake. Mental illness does not render a person deaf. Therefore, you should make every effort to obtain a response from the individual. This can be done by quietly asking questions and being sensitive to any types of reply, such as a head nod.

    If this is not successful, you should attempt to understand the person's thoughts or feelings and communicate that understanding to him. These "guesses" can be based on the information which you acquire at the scene, as well as on the body posture and emotion the individual may be displaying. By making this effort, you communicate to the subject that you wish to understand his situation. The subject may then feel less threatened about discussing his difficulties with you.

3.  **Subject Is Hallucinatory.** Hallucinations are very frightening for the person who is experiencing them. Difficulties emerge when the person is actively hallucinating in the presence of the officer. The first response you must give is to validate the hallucinatory experience for the individual, but, at the same time, indicate that the hallucination does not (objectively) exist. If an individual is seeing or hearing things, you must indicate that you understand that those experiences are real and frightening for the subject, but that they do not exist in reality. Second, you must firmly and empathetically indicate that those sensations are due to the extreme emotional stress that the person is experiencing and that once the stress is lessened, the hallucinations will disappear. You may have to repeat this reassuring message many times before the individual can begin to respond to it.

4.  **Subject Exhibits Paranoid Tendencies.** Paranoia often involves very serious delusion. You must be very sensitive (both verbally and physically) when you respond to such individuals. Paranoid persons are marked by their extreme suspiciousness and tension. They can appear to be very frightening to others.

You must be acutely aware of any indications that the paranoid person is feeling threatened by you. If you detect this fear, you should become as non-threatening as possible, giving the person a feeling that he is in control of the situation. You should neither pick up on any verbal challenge, nor agree that you know anything more about the subject than he tells you. Many paranoid people may say things like, "You know what has been happening to me." Or, "You're a police officer, you have those secret records on me." You must not confirm that you have any special knowledge about the person.

When you're moving into or around a room in which a paranoid person is present, it is good practice to announce your actions before initiating them. Telling the subject that you are moving across the room to sit in a chair reduces the probability that he will think you are about to attack him. This telegraphing of your actions assumes that your goal is not to subdue the individual physically. Except in situations in which the person must be physically detained, avoid any physical contact with the person.

5. **Subject Is Psychotic and Aggressive.** This is probably the most troublesome situation for any police officer to respond to effectively. If the subject is in the act of attacking you or another individual, there is no question that you should respond with your police control skills. However, in many instances, the subject will not be acting out, but will be threatening someone. He may be waving his fists, or a knife, or yelling. If the situation is secure and if no one can be accidently harmed by the individual, you should adopt a non-threatening, non-confrontative stance with the subject. You may point out that you do not like to get injured or beaten up, that there is no need for the individual to threaten you because you are going to "listen" to him, that getting into a pitched battle with you may cause more problems than it will solve.

You should then begin talking to the subject as outlined above, allowing the individual to vent some of his hostility. You can also indicate this low-threat, low-offensive style by sitting down, removing your hat or otherwise trying to put the person at ease. Sit a comfortable distance from the subject, move the chair so that its back faces the subject and straddle it. This permits you to use it as a protective block if the person suddenly charges you. It's essential that you appear relaxed and non-threatening, but you must also be on your guard.

6. **Delusional Statements.** Delusions are unique ways of viewing the world, and delusional statements frequently come into conflict with the views of others. There are three possible responses to delusions:

   • agree with them;
   • dispute them; or
   • defer the issue.

If you agree with the mentally disturbed person's delusion, you put yourself in a position of being ineffective in your attempts to provide the person with help. The individual could legitimately ask, "Why do you want me to go to the hospital, since you agree that what I say is true?" Such agreement can also have the effect of increasing the subject's upset state, since the delusion is only a means for him to reduce his anxiety. To have others begin to believe in "his world" may be more frightening than helpful.

The next option, disputing the delusions, is equally ineffective. A direct confrontation with the subject over his disordered thinking may well result in his withdrawing from the person making the attack. He will become inaccessible, or arguments may ensue. This might result in the individual's acting out aggressively due to the threat he experiences.

This leaves the third option, deferring the issue. In this response, you do not agree with or dispute the person's statement; rather, you acknowledge the person's view of the world, indicate that it is not your own and follow with a statement of how you understand the person's feelings. An example of this type of response would be:

Subject:  There are many people who want me dead. There is an organization on T.V. which had my name on T.V.

Officer:  I can see you're worried about someone harming you. I don't know of anyone who wants to hurt you, but I really would like to assist you in any way I can to help you feel safer.

By this response, you neither confirm nor dispute the person's view of the world. Rather, you give the person a message of the availability of help.

**Recognizing and Handling Persons with Mental Illness.**  Officers do not usually need to diagnose the type of mental disorder a mentally ill person has. In specific situations, however, such as a hostage situation or a barricaded subject, inappropriate remarks or gestures toward the mentally ill could prove tragic. For example, pointing out to a depressed person or one with a personality disorder that his or her behavior is an indication of personal failure could cause that person to kill hostages and/or commit suicide. For this reason, police hostage negotiators and others with certain crisis intervention training should learn the specific behavioral characteristics typical of mental illness. Police hostage negotiators should also know how to deal with each type of mental illness.

Most officers, however, need only determine whether there is a reason to believe the subject has a mental disorder. Depending on the severity of the disorder, mentally ill persons can be difficult to identify. They can be intelligent, perceptive and articulate. The mentally ill can be employed and have strong family relationships. With the onset of a mental disorder, however, their thoughts and actions are not based in reality and their ability to think clearly is impaired.

General characteristics that indicate an individual has a mental illness include behavior and mood inappropriate to the setting and inflexible or impulsive behavior. Specific indicators of mental illness can include sudden changes in lifestyle; major changes in behavior; extreme anxiety, panic or fright; paranoia; hallucinations; delusions; depression; obsessions; unexplained loss of memory; confusion; and hypochondria.

Often people who suffer from mental illness are on medication to counteract a chemical imbalance. These medications, however, may cause side effects such as the following: minor stiffness; a rigid shuffling gait; an at rest, hand jerk; acute muscle spasms; tilted head; a constant, fine, fast tremor; blurry vision; rhythmic motion of the jaw or lips; a clucking of the tongue; smacking of the lips; or—in severe cases—facial distortion.

The following questions will help officers assess whether an individual may have a mental health problem:

1. Is the subject using or threatening to use violence?
2. Is the subject threatening suicide?
3. Is the subject acting dangerously toward himself or others?
4. Has the subject neglected personal care or bodily functions?
   —Mutilated himself?
   —Neglected to bathe in the past few days?
   —Neglected to eat in the past few days?
   —Neglected to take prescribed medications in the past few days?
   —Been sleeping irregularly?
5. Has the subject recently suffered a traumatic experience?
6. Does the subject have a history of mental illness? If yes, specify illness.
7. Does the subject feel that his behavior is controlled or influenced by outside forces?
8. Does the subject claim to receive messages from strangers, radio or television?
9. Does the subject ever hear voices when others do not?
10. Does the subject ever see things when others do not?
11. Does the subject indicate that others are plotting against him or are after him?
12. Does the subject claim that others can read his thoughts?
13. Does the subject claim that he can read others' thoughts?
14. Is the subject overly concerned with religion or death?
15. Is the subject oriented to his environment, that is, time, place and person?

16. Did the mood of the subject drastically change during the course of the interview or conversation?

17. Was the mood of the subject appropriate to the nature of the call?

18. Does it appear that the subject is under the influence of alcohol or illegal drugs?

If this assessment reveals that the person is likely to be mentally ill, the following guidelines are suggested.

**General Guidelines.** When handling a mentally ill person, gather as much information as possible about him or her before arriving on the scene. In the presence of a mentally ill person, be discreet and avoid attracting attention. Be calm, avoid excitement and have a take-charge attitude. Remove as many distractions from the scene as possible, including bystanders and disruptive friends or family members. Gather as much information as possible from helpful witnesses, family members and friends.

**Steps to Take When First Encountering a Mentally Ill Person.** The following steps are generally appropriate:

- Introduce yourself and explain the reason for your presence. Establish a helping and caring tone.

- Be aware that your uniform, gun, handcuffs and nightstick may frighten the person. Explain how your equipment will keep away the person's enemies.

- Be aware of the potential for violence.

- If the person is acting dangerously, but not directly threatening any other person or himself, give the person time to calm down. Violent outbursts are usually short.

**Keys to Successful Management.** *Communication* is essential. It allows officers to gain valuable information. It also allows officers and the individual to understand each other and may reduce tensions. *Firm gentleness* is also effective. The person should be treated gently and with care. With a take-charge attitude and an insistence on your orders being followed, gently indicate that your only intention is to help the person. Remain *professional*. Empathize with the individual without sympathizing.

**What Not to Do.** Do not excite, confuse or upset a mentally ill individual. Do not abuse, belittle or threaten the individual either. Do not use inflammatory language when addressing the individual. Do not lie to or deceive the person. Do not cross-examine the person. Do not dispute, debate or invalidate the person's claims. Do not rush the person or crowd his personal space. Avoid being a "tough guy." Do not let the person upset or trick you into an argument.

**If the Person Must Be Restrained or Force Must Be Used.** If the person is so dangerous or violent that he or another person is likely to be harmed, use the least amount of force necessary to restrain the person. If restraint is needed, two or more officers should be present. Such a show of force could dissuade the person from resisting. If not, however, increased adrenaline and insensitivity to pain enable mentally ill people to resist a "normal" amount of restraint.

Police should not always use handcuffs because they can injure the person or be broken. The ideal restraint would be a gurney with four-point restraints and body bands.

## Dealing with Mentally Retarded Persons

The mentally retarded are usually aware of their condition and may be adept at concealing it. Thus, it may be more difficult for police officers to determine mental retardation than mental illness. Certain communication problems, interaction problems, inability to perform tasks and personal history can help officers to make this determination.

*Communication problems* officers should look for that would indicate mental retardation include the following: an inability to communicate at the level of others of the same age; difficulty in understanding questions; difficulty in answering questions, for example, overreliance on "parroted" responses or offering standard responses; speech defects or impediments, including poor pronunciation; an inability to use abstract reasoning; and a limited vocabulary or limited grammatical skills.

*Interaction problems* that might indicate mental retardation include a preference by the person to associate with younger people; an excessive desire to please; reliance on a special person to provide help; behavior noticeably on a level below the person's age; crowding the personal space when interacting with others; a tendency to be easily persuaded or influenced by others.

*Inability to perform tasks* may also indicate mental retardation. Officers might ask the individual to read or write, identify money or make change, tell time or use the telephone.

*Personal history* can also help the officer to identify someone as mentally retarded. Find out if the person has attended a vocational education center or a sheltered workshop. See if the person is listed in the telephone book.

**Guidelines for Interacting if the Person Appears to Be Mentally Retarded.** If the person appears to be mentally retarded, avoid asking questions rapidly or attempts to unnerve or intimidate the person. Be aware of the person's reluctance to discuss the matter and that they are likely to attempt to please. If possible, use visual aids, pictures or diagrams and be firm and purposeful.

## Responding to Suicide Attempts

To effectively deal with a suicidal person use a calm, matter-of-fact tone; genuine concern for the person is best indicated through communication. Officers should insist, but not in a threatening manner, that the individual obtain some type of mental health help. Officers should talk about the finality of the act and use the terms *suicide, death* and *kill yourself.* The belief that talking about suicide will prompt the person to do so is a myth. The best way officers can help a suicidal person is to discuss the person's problems, the suicide plan and realistic alternatives. The following are suicide prevention guidelines:

- Obtain necessary personal data immediately.
- Bring the subject of suicide into the open. Also discuss the person's feelings of depression and that they are only temporary.
- Remove the means.
- Notify and meet with significant others.
- Offer realistic hope.
- Establish a specific plan of action.

## Dispositions

After responding to the call and effectively interacting with the suicidal individual, officers must make a disposition.

◆

The two formal dispositions are arrest or a civil commitment. Many informal dispositions are also available.

◆

To determine an appropriate disposition, officers should continuously evaluate the person and the nature of the incident. Dispositions that *should* be available to officers include the following:

- Counsel, release and refer the individual to a mental health center.
- Counsel, release to family, friends or some other support network and refer to a mental health center.
- Consult with a mental health professional.
- Obtain the person's agreement to seek voluntary examination.

- Detain for involuntary examination.
- Arrest.

Police officers protect and serve society and, in that capacity, serve as only one of the gatekeepers to the mental health system. Officers should be able to determine when someone needs referral to mental health professionals and should know how to gain access to those resources. They should be familiar with the resources available in the community, including the location of community mental health centers and hospitals that conduct mental health examinations, the services provided by those facilities, hours of operation and staff to be contacted. They should also know the procedures to be followed at the facilities and what to do when the facilities are closed.

## Programs for the Mentally Impaired

The Police Executive Research Forum undertook a study of treatment of the mentally ill in the community. During the course of this study they identified a number of elements that appear to be essential to the effectiveness of any program or involving the police in the handling of mentally disturbed individuals (Murphy, 1986, p. xiv):

- Each program maintains a 24-hour, on-site response capability, so there is less "slippage" in resolving cases involving the mentally ill.
- Each program maintains a 24-hour access to the needed resources, which also forestalls delays in resolution.
- Each program either provides trained mental health professionals (police or civilian) or provides line officers with thorough and appropriate training, which is necessary for the expeditious and appropriate handling of cases.
- Each program clearly delineates the separation of duties and responsibilities among the key actors from different agencies.
- Each program has developed procedures that reduce the time officers need to spend handling mentally ill persons.
- Each program includes close and regular liaison between the participating agencies to ensure that operational information is shared, feedback is provided and minor problems are addressed.

In Memphis, where officers respond to 4,000 calls a year involving "disturbed persons," a Crisis Intervention Team (CIT) of specially trained officers now responds around the clock to calls involving mentally disturbed people. Their primary objective, according to Crews and Cochran (1989, p. 67), is to "minimize the use of force without relinquishing safety in potentially violent situations related to mentally disturbed persons."

The Memphis Police Department was concerned about the growing number of potentially violent confrontations officers were having with mentally ill individuals as a result of deinstitutionalization. The department was also concerned that the incidents might increase the potential for lawsuits alleging brutality and result in negative press and a loss of community support. The department began to search for a better way to deal with the mentally ill and still provide for officer safety. Intensive training of the CIT officers has been crucial to the program's success. Officers learn how to use the Taser gun, a protective shield and Velcro leg wraps, all important equipment in interacting with a potentially dangerous mentally ill person. Understanding that mental illness is a disease rather than a crime makes the crisis intervention approach a sensible alternative that often has a positive outcome for everyone involved.

During the first eight months of operation, there have been fewer serious injuries to individuals, and injuries to officers handling mental disturbance calls have decreased by 50 percent. Dr. Gilliland, a professor at Memphis State University, CIT instructor and former FBI agent says: "The CIT concept saves lives and it saves the police a heck of a lot of bad press, embarrassment and legal entanglement" (Crews and Cochran, 1989, p. 70).

Police officers are probably least trained in this area, yet they are likely to spend a great deal of time interacting with individuals who are mentally disabled.

DeCuir and Lamb (p. 100) describe a coordinated effort of the Los Angeles Police Department and the Los Angeles County Department of Mental Health called SMART (Systemwide Mental Assessment Response Team). The team consists of one detective, an officer-in-charge, four police officers, four mental health clinicians and one mental health supervisor. The team is deployed seven days a week and is available sixteen hours a day. DeCuir and Lamb (p. 102) report: "The team saves needed county hospital and jail bed space. In many instances, it can divert the subject to a private hospital, substance abuse center or outpatient mental health program."

## INDIVIDUALS WITH EPILEPSY

Another population police officers should be prepared to interact with are individuals who have epilepsy. The following discussion is a condensation of the program *Epilepsy: A Positive ID* (1991), developed by the University of Minnesota Epilepsy Foundation and reprinted by permission.

**Epilepsy** is a disorder of the central nervous system. Epilepsy is not contagious, and it is not an indication that a person is mentally retarded. Known causes of epilepsy include head injuries, infectious diseases such as meningitis, encephalitis and brain abscesses. A person with epilepsy tends to have recurrent seizures.

A **seizure** is a sudden, uncontrolled event or episode of excessive electrical activity in the brain. It may alter behavior, consciousness, movement, perception and/or sensation. There are many types of seizures and an individual's behavior differs according to the type of seizure.

Police officers need to be able to recognize seizures, administer the proper first aid procedures and be responsive to the sensitivities and pride of people with epilepsy. Police officers' chances of encountering a seizure are probably greater than they may think.

The most common types of seizures are simple partial seizures, complex partial seizures, generalized tonic clonic seizures and absence seizures.

A *simple partial seizure* consists of changes in a person's motor function or sensations *without* accompanying alteration of consciousness. It may be characterized by stiffening or jerking in one or more extremity, a strange feeling in the stomach, tingling or an alteration of taste or smell. In some cases this type of seizure may progress to a generalized tonic clonic seizure.

A *complex partial seizure* impairs consciousness. The following behaviors may occur during a complex partial seizure: incoherent speech, glassy-eyed staring, aimless wandering, chewing or lip smacking motions and picking at clothing. The person may be confused or need to rest after the seizure.

◆

A complex partial epileptic seizure may be mistaken for a drug or alcohol-induced stupor because the person may have incoherent speech, glassy-eyed staring and aimless wandering.

◆

This type of seizure may last a few seconds to several minutes.

A *generalized tonic clonic seizure,* formerly called the grand mal seizure, is what most people commonly associate with epilepsy. *Tonic* means stiffening; *clonic* means jerking. In this type of seizure the following may occur: loss of consciousness, falling, stiffening and jerking, tongue biting and, sometimes, drooling and loss of bowel and bladder control.

The *absence seizure,* formerly called the petit mal, is often mistaken for daydreaming or staring. Absence seizures can occur up to 100 times a day or more and are most common in children and adolescents.

## The Police Response

It is important that police officers do not confuse the symptoms of an epileptic seizure with those of being high on drugs or alcohol. Table 8.2 summarizes the distinctions between an epileptic seizure and a drug reaction.

If the person is having a complex partial seizure it can last from thirty seconds to three minutes. The person may be confused or disoriented after the seizure. If possible, guide the person to a safe place to sit and let the seizure run its course. Keep the person calm and do not restrain him or her in any way. Determine the level of consciousness by asking the person's name, where he or

*Table 8.2*   **Drug/Alcohol Abuse or Epileptic Seizure?**

| *Complex Partial Seizure Symptoms* | *Drug/Alcohol Abuse Symptoms* |
|---|---|
| • Chewing, lip smacking motions | not likely |
| • Picking at clothes | not likely |
| • Should regain consciousness in 30 seconds to 3 minutes, except in the rare case of a complex partial status (when seizure continues) | a drunk/high person will not recover in 3 minutes or less |
| • No breath odor | a drunk will smell like alcohol |
| • Possibly wearing an epilepsy I.D. bracelet/tag | not likely |

**Symptoms Common to Both**

| | |
|---|---|
| • Impaired consciousness | • Incoherent speech |
| • Glassy-eyed staring | • Aimless wandering |

SOURCE: *Epilepsy: A Positive I.D.* Epilepsy Education, University of Minnesota, 1991. Reprinted by permission.

she is and what day it is. Check for a medical-alert bracelet or tag. Do not leave an individual who appears confused alone.

In the case of a generalized tonic clonic seizure: cushion the person's head, if he or she is wearing glasses remove them, loosen the collar and tie and clear the area of any hard objects he or she may hit. Do NOT put anything in the person's mouth—this may damage the teeth or jaw. After the seizure has subsided, turn the person on his or her side, allow the saliva to flow from the mouth and keep the airway open. Determine the individual's level of consciousness and check for a medical-alert bracelet or tag.

Call an ambulance if the person has hit his or her head, if you suspect injury, if there is no medical-alert bracelet or tag, if the seizure lasts between five to ten minutes or if the seizures occur one after another. If the person has hit his or her head, it is a life-threatening situation that requires immediate action.

Police officers should also be familiar with the medications people with epilepsy may take so that they are not mistaken for illegal drugs. Figure 8.2 illustrates the most common antiepileptic medications.

## CRIME PREVENTION FOR THE DISABLED

Disabled people, for the most part, can take responsibility for protecting themselves against crime once they are taught the correct responses to dangerous or suspicious circumstances. Programs should include community awareness, how

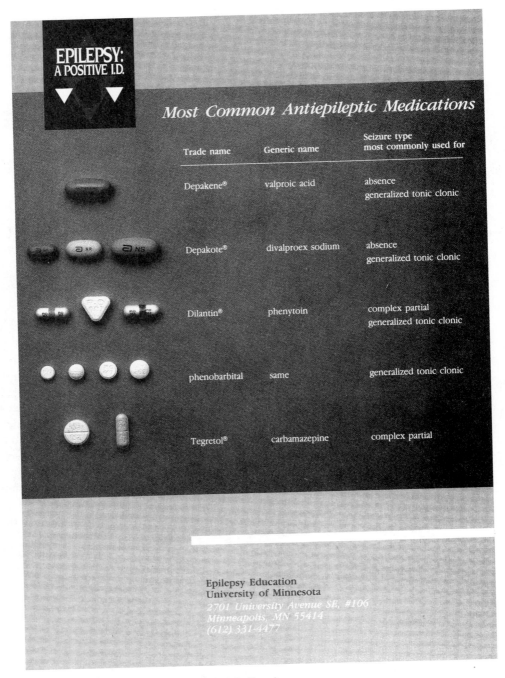

*Figure 8.2*   **Most Common Antiepileptic Medications**
Reprinted by permission.

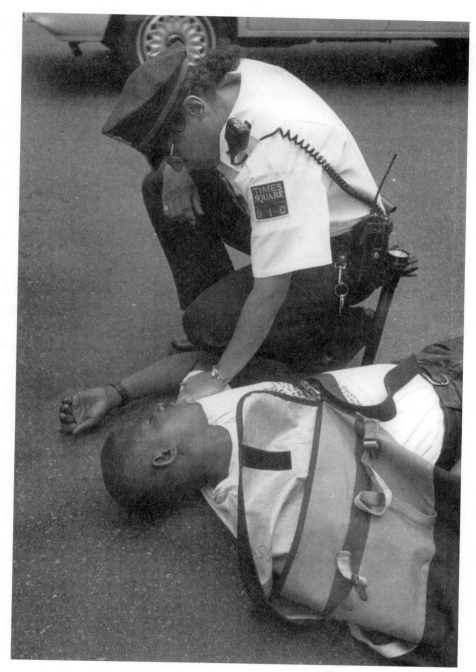

*Police officers may be the first at the scene of an emergency and are trained to assist.*

to deal with strangers, shopping awareness, how to report crime and resources available. Law enforcement can build positive relationships with the community by providing this vital assistance to some of our most vulnerable citizens.

### Crime Prevention Tips for the Disabled

Crime prevention programs geared toward the disabled should incorporate most of the following "tips" in some way:

- Consider your limitations and decide what you are prepared to do if an assailant confronts you.
- Use direct deposit for government payments to you.
- Know your neighbors and decide which ones you could rely on in an emergency.
- Let family or friends know where you are going and what time you expect to return home.
- Never let telephone callers know you are alone or disabled.
- When using public transportation, ride as near to the operator as possible.
- Travel with someone you know whenever possible.
- Be aware of body language. Transmit confidence and certainty.
- Carry enough money for telephone and emergency use, but never carry or display large amounts of cash.
- Be involved. Help your Neighborhood Watch with newsletters or telephone calls.
- Help a neighbor who has been a recent victim of crime. The more active you are, the safer you will be and the safer your neighborhood will be.

The basic premise to teach the disabled is that almost everyone can take responsibility for protecting themselves and their communities from crime. We all feel safer and *are* safer when we understand that we have some power over what happens to us. Of course, differences in disabilities require different approaches to crime prevention, but surprisingly, what works for most people will usually work for disabled people too.

Some law enforcement departments have developed programs specifically for disabled individuals. In addition, some existing programs developed for the general population work well for those who are disabled. Neighborhood Watch, for example, is a program that has a built-in component designed to enhance safety for the most vulnerable in the neighborhood. Block club members are encouraged to look after the elderly or disabled on their blocks, to be aware of suspicious activity around their residences, to check on them regularly and to assist the disabled and elderly to participate in block activities. This might be described as old-fashioned neighborliness, but in some neighborhoods, it is a practice that needs to be renewed and encouraged.

### Emergency ID for "Special Persons"

One program developed to fill a particular need of the disabled is the Emergency ID for "Special Persons," developed by Sheriff William M. Lanzaro of Monmouth County, New Jersey. Sheriff Lanzaro became aware of the need in 1987 when the director of a school for handicapped children told him the children needed some form of identification in case they were off school grounds or suffered some medical emergency. Sheriff Lanzaro, working with the Monmouth County Department of Human Services, the Office of the Handicapped and the Association for Retarded Citizens, developed the "Special Persons" ID card program for disabled and handicapped students. According to Freeman (1990, p. 91):

> The blue card, which measures 2¼ × 3½ inches, is available in two versions, one of which features the universal handicap logo for physically handicapped individuals. The card includes the individual's name, address and telephone number, as well as the names and telephone numbers of three emergency contacts. The back of the card lists the doctor's name and phone number, social security number, a place for special remarks and a photo of the individual. The cards are laminated at the presentation site and supplied with a 30-inch neck chain so that the cards may be worn and easily found in case of an emergency.

As noted by Freeman (p. 91), the cards not only address the identification needs of the handicapped and disabled, the program also "provides high visibility for the police department or sheriff's office and creates an opportunity for community service presentations."

## DEALING WITH INDIVIDUALS WITH DISABILITIES WHO BREAK THE LAW

It is natural for an officer to assume that individuals with disabilities are victims, not victimizers. This is not always true, however. The severely physically or mentally disabled are highly unlikely to be among those who break the law. Those with less limiting handicaps, however, are certainly represented among lawbreakers. When handicapped individuals violate the law, they should be treated as much like an able-bodied person as their disability will allow.

Do not make the mistake of thinking that physically disabled or mentally ill people cannot also violate the law. An individual's behavior, of course, will often be limited by his or her physical ability, but most officers encounter disabled offenders and must be prepared to recognize them as offenders when appropriate. Officers are acutely aware that the public will usually react critically toward any type of force used by police against a physically disabled person. As one officer noted:

> Man, a whole career goes on the line when you deal with a mental person. Criticize . . . that's all they do. They don't understand what we have to do, but they criticize (Crews and Cochran, 1989, p. 67).

Nonetheless, it is imperative that officers never forget that disabled criminals can pose as much of a threat to safety as an able-bodied criminal can.

As Kardasz (1995, p. 91) notes: "People with mental problems are regularly involved in crimes ranging in seriousness from the benign (shoplifting, trespassing) to the macabre (suicide, assault and homicide)." He suggests (p. 92): "In general, criminal matters take precedence over civil procedures. A mental patient involved in a crime usually travels through the criminal justice system and can be concurrently treated for mental illness until a judicial determination is made about the patient's sanity."

Consider the following scenario which happened in a midwestern city. The police were called to the courtyard of an apartment complex where a woman was being threatened by a man with a knife. When officers arrived, they encountered an hysterical female victim and a suspect who refused to drop the knife as ordered to at gunpoint. What the officers did not yet know was that this confrontation was between deaf spouses. The wife had just returned home to discover her husband had stabbed to death their young daughter, whose body lay in their nearby apartment. The confrontation ended with the arrest of the suspect and discovery of the child's body. Several different outcomes were possible because of the disabilities of the couple and the confusion they caused the officers.

It is critical that police officers differentiate between someone who is high on drugs or alcohol and someone who is suffering from an illness. Thurber and Yorgensen (1995, p. 104) caution that a suspected DWI may, in fact, be suffering from carbon monoxide (CO) poisoning. They list as signs of CO poisoning ringing in the ears, inability to think, confusion, lethargy, stupor and possibly loss of coordination.

In some instances large groups of individuals with disabilities have staged sit-ins and other types of civil disobedience to call attention to their needs. Law enforcement agencies should be prepared to deal with civil disobedience on a large scale, as described by Monahan (1997, p. 46): "Incidents of civil disobedience involving large numbers of persons with disabilities not only stretch the resources of a police agency to its limits, but also expose a department and municipality to civil liability, as well as penalties for violations of the ADA."

Monahan (p. 47) suggests that transporting arrestees with disabilities is a difficult logistical problem and that jail and detention facilities are also a concern.

Rubin and Dunne (1995, p. 1) caution: "Criminal justice agencies are required to accommodate persons who are deaf or hard of hearing in arrest and detainment situations. Likewise, it is critical that agencies charged with the responsibility of administering a community's emergency response service accommodate citizens with disabilities."

## A FINAL NOTE

Cushing (1992, p. A19) recommends:

> Just as the Americans with Disabilities Act requires us to build ramps, let our own commitment to inclusive communities require us to build attitudinal ramps. We can't really fight attitudes of discrimination and exclusion unless we do an end-run against ingrained beliefs.
>
> Perhaps individuals with disabilities will eventually serve as the unifiers of society. People with disabilities come from all races, socioeconomic groups and religions. The smartest and the strongest can be laid low as easily as all others.
>
> Perhaps if we begin to look at a disability as an equalizer, we'll understand that the greatest disability is what we do to our nation by preventing others from achieving their potential.

Adapting law enforcement duties and services to accommodate the millions of disabled Americans will not only help accomplish law enforcement's objectives in a more efficient and safe manner, but will also help to provide the services all citizens need and deserve. When that happens, excellent police-community relations are a likely by-product.

St. Louis Officer Fran Krupp discussed two projects she had undertaken to address the often frustrating and time-consuming crime and disorder problems related to people with mental illness. In one case, by informing family members of the extremely high number of unfounded calls for service placed by an elderly relative, Krupp completely eliminated the calls. In another instance, she eliminated repeated shoplifting by a person with mental illness by locating an agency that would manage his disability income and ensure that he received medication to moderate the symptoms of his illness. ("Celebrating Success and Working for the Future." *Subject to Debate.* [November 1994]: 1, 4–5.)

## *Problem Solving in Action*

### St. Louis Officers Address Crime and Disorder Problems Related to Citizens with Mental Illness

#### *Disturbance Calls*
**Scanning**
Last October, Seventh District Officers Fran Krupp and Laure Lamczyk received a call to 5876 Kennerly in the Wells-Goodfellow neighborhood for burglars in the building. They met the caller, Mrs. R., who is in her late eighties and legally blind. Mrs. R. complained that people had broken into her basement and that she could hear them talking while they did their laundry.

*continued*

The officers found no signs of intruders. Mrs. R., however, was convinced that people had entered her basement, but for the time being, she was satisfied with the officers' inspection. Krupp later recalled having heard several other assignments to that same address in the past.

### Analysis

Krupp checked the CAD system and found records of 188 police calls to 5876 Kennerly. This address was listed as the tenth highest call location in the Seventh District. Over the past three years, police had been dispatched to this address almost 300 times for either "burglars in the building" or "disturbances." Krupp also discovered that no police reports had ever been completed on these calls; they had all been designated as unfounded, requiring no further action.

Talking with other officers who handled calls at this location, Krupp heard the same story over and over—an elderly female called the police because she heard noises coming from her basement. In all cases, the calls were designated unfounded.

The police department had already spent an estimated 240 staff hours handling the previous calls and it was obvious that if something weren't done, these calls for service would continue.

### Response

As an interim step, the supervisors agreed that every time a call was dispatched to this location, the precinct sergeant would call the complainant to determine whether the police were really needed. If not, the sergeant would call off the responding officers.

Later, it was learned that Mrs. R. lived with her nephew. Krupp contacted him and described the problem. He was aware that his grandmother occasionally called the police but he was shocked when he heard the actual numbers. With his cooperation, a meeting between the family and the officers was arranged. Krupp, Lamczyk and Sergeant Greg Wurm met with the family. During the 30-minute meeting, the family agreed that something had to be done. They assured the officers that they would work with Mrs. R. to eliminate the unnecessary calls for police service.

### Assessment

Following up several weeks later, Krupp found that no calls had been dispatched to 5876 Kennerly. Concerned for Mrs. R's well-being, Krupp and Lamczyk went to Mrs. R's house to make sure she was all right. When they arrived, Mrs. R. greeted them at the door and told them that her family had forbidden her to call the police without first checking with them. Over the next three months, only one call was dispatched to 5876 Kennerly.

### *Shoplifting*

### Scanning

In February of this year, Seventh District Officer Fran Krupp was working secondary employment at Dillards department store in the St. Louis Center, a downtown shopping complex, when she arrested a 39-year-old man for shoplifting. The man, Marion G., was caught stealing an alarm clock.

After taking Marion to the security office, Krupp began filling out a summons release form. When Marion realized he was not going to be booked, he started crying and begged Krupp to take him to jail, where he would be fed and given a place to sleep for the night.

### Analysis

Krupp was curious why arrest, far from being a deterrent, had actually become the incentive for the man to commit a crime.

Marion explained to Fran that he stole from the St. Louis Center almost daily and sold the goods on the street. He used the money for food and transportation to the Veterans Administration Hospital, where he was receiving outpatient care for a mental illness.

As Krupp continued the interview, she learned that without medication, Marion hears voices that tell him to do weird things. Several years before, he had been judged incompetent to handle his own affairs, and consequently, his disability checks were delivered to a payee, in this case his mother, who lived in Illinois. Within the past year, Marion's mother had put him out of the house, but she had continued to cash the checks.

Krupp realized there was little she could do that evening, but she gave Marion enough money for food and transportation to the hospital and instructed him to meet her at the shopping center the following day.

The next day, Krupp contacted a counselor from the Harbor Light Shelter and explained Marion's situation. The counselor told Krupp that the Harbor Light could become the payee for Marion and help him recover from his illness. They would provide room and board for as long as he needed it, and through their pharmacy program, he would always have a supply of his medication.

### Response

When Marion returned to Dillards the following afternoon, Krupp arranged for the two of them to go to the Harbor Light Shelter. The counselor started the paperwork that would allow Marion to reassign a payee for his disability check.

### Assessment

Several months have passed, and Krupp reports that Marion has not been seen in the St. Louis Center.

"*St. Louis Officers Address Crime and Disorder Problems Related to Citizens with Mental Illness.*" Problem-Solving Quarterly. *(Winter/Spring 1994): 9–10.*
*Reprinted with permission from the Police Executive Research Forum.*

# SUMMARY

The United States has 43 million people with disabilities. The most important guideline in interacting with people with disabilities is to treat them as individuals with the same needs and desires as you have. Disabilities police officers might frequently encounter include mobility impairment, vision impairment, hearing impairment, mental or emotional impairment and impairment as a result of epilepsy. Most deaf people prefer to communicate by means of sign language.

Deinstitutionalization refers to the release of thousands of mentally ill individuals into society to be cared for by family or a special network of support services. When police are called to manage mentally ill persons, the behaviors most frequently encountered include bizarre, unusual or strange behavior; confused thoughts or action; aggressive actions; destructive, assaultive or violent behavior; and attempted suicide.

Mental health is the ability to integrate one's self with one's environment. Mental illness is a severe disturbance in thinking, feeling and relating to other people that results in substantially diminished capacity to cope with the ordinary demands of life. Suicide is the tenth leading cause of death among adults and the second leading cause among adolescents.

The four civil criteria for detainment and commitment of mentally ill individuals are mental illness, dangerousness, being gravely disabled and being in need of (mental health) treatment. The two formal dispositions are arrest or a civil commitment. Many informal dispositions are also available.

In addition to interacting with individuals with mental disabilities, police officers may also interact with individuals who have epilepsy. Police should know how to respond properly. A complex partial epileptic seizure may be mistaken for a drug- or alcohol-induced stupor because the person may exhibit incoherent speech, glassy-eyed staring and aimless wandering.

## Discussion Questions

1. Do you know anyone with a physical disability? How do you feel around them?
2. Do you know anyone with a mental disability? How do you feel around them?
3. Do you support the deinstitutionalization movement of the late 1960s? Why or why not?
4. Has the local media covered any stories of individuals with mental disabilities coming into conflict with police officers? What was the outcome?
5. What are the criteria for commitment in your state? How do they compare to other states—are they more or less restrictive?
6. Are you aware of resources in your community available for the mentally ill? The physically handicapped?
7. What impact might the Americans with Disabilities Act have on the hiring of police officers?
8. Is it reasonable to require very small businesses to be handicap-accessible?

9. Which type of disability do you feel would pose the greatest challenge for effective police-community relations?

10. How might individuals with disabilities suffer from stereotyping?

## References

Burden, Ordway P. "Making a Difference in Police Response to the Disabled." *Law Enforcement News.* (July/August 1991): 11.

Crews, Walter and Cochran, Sam. "Memphis Police Department's Crisis Intervention Team." *Law and Order.* (August 1989): 66–70.

Cushing, Marty. "Attitudes about the Disabled Need Repair, Along with Buildings." (Minneapolis/St. Paul) *Star Tribune.* (October 10, 1992): A19.

DeCuir, Walter J., Jr. and Lamb, Richard H. "Police Response to the Dangerous Mentally Ill." *The Police Chief.* (October 1996): 99–106.

Ehlert, Bob. "Suggestions on How to Deal with Disabled." (Minneapolis/St. Paul) *Star Tribune.* (November 7, 1991): E3.

*Epilepsy: A Positive ID.* Minneapolis: Epilepsy Education, University of Minnesota, 1991.

Finn, Peter E. and Sullivan, Monique. *Police Response to Special Populations: Handling the Mentally Ill, Public Inebriate, and the Homeless.* Washington: National Institute of Justice, January 1988.

Flynn, Michael P. "Mentally Ill and Dangerous." *Police.* (November): 44–48, 75.

Freeman, Ted. "Emergency ID for 'Special Persons.'" *The Police Chief.* (October 1990): 91.

Gallo, Francis J. "The Silent Community We Serve." *Law and Order.* (February 1992): 53–55.

Geberth, Vernon J. "The Psychology of Suicide." *Law and Order.* (October 1996): 163–66.

Hageman, Mary Jeanette. *Police-Community Relations.* Beverly Hills: Sage Publications, 1985.

Hull, Bev. "Hearing Impaired Battered Women." *Minnesota Coalition for Battered Women News.* (February 1985): 1, 3.

Kardasz, Frank. "Apprehending Mental Patients." *Law and Order.* (November 1995): 91–92.

King, Jess Freeman. "Dispatching for the Deaf." *Law and Order.* (February 1996): 47–48.

King, J. Freeman. "The Law Officer and the Deaf." *The Police Chief.* (October 1990): 98–100.

Lerner, Carole J. "Suicide: A Follow-Up Program." *Law and Order.* (December 1994): 45–47.

Lesce, Tony. "Cop Talk: Sign Language for Police Officers." *Law and Order.* (July 1996): 79–83.

Louis, Richard, III. "Collaboration Builds Bridges: Police Work with Health Professionals to Assist the Mentally Ill." *Law and Order.* (February 1997): 82–83.

Monahan, Tom. "Civil Disobedience and the ADA." *The Police Chief.* (February 1997): 46–49.

Murphy, Gerard R. *Managing Persons with Mental Disabilities: A Curriculum Guide for Police Trainers.* Washington: Police Executive Research Forum, 1989.

Murphy, Gerard R. *Special Care: Improving the Police Response to the Mentally Disabled.* Washington: Police Executive Research Forum, 1986.

News Services. "Bush Signs Disabilities Act as 3,000 Cheer at Last." (Minneapolis/St. Paul) *Star Tribune.* (July 26, 1990): A1.

Rubin, Paula N. and Dunne, Toni. *The Americans with Disabilities Act: Emergency Response Systems and Telecommunication Devices for the Deaf.* Washington: National Institute of Justice Research in Action, February 1995.

Siegfried, Michael. "Breaking the Silence with Deaf Citizens." *Police.* (April 1996): 20–21.

Thurber, Cameron and Yorgensen, Richard W. "Dead Drunk: Mistaking Medical Problems for Intoxication." *Law and Order.* (March 1995): 103–06.

Youngblood, Suzanne M. and Lynch, Thomas W. "Officer, I Can't Hear You!" *Law and Order.* (February 1995): 51–53.

Zehring, Timothy. "New Insights for the Visually Impaired." *Law and Order.* (December 1990): 33–35.

### *Resources*

American Psychiatric Association, 1400 K Street, N.W., Washington, DC 20005; (202) 682-6000.

American Psychological Association, 1200 17th Street, N.W., Washington, DC 20036; (202) 955-7660.

Epilepsy Education, University of Minnesota, 5775 Wayzata Boulevard, Suite 255, Minneapolis, MN 55416; (612) 525-1160.

International Center for the Disabled (ICD), 340 East 24th Street, New York, NY 10010; (212) 679-0100; (212) 889-0372 TDD.

Muscular Dystrophy Association, 3300 E. Sunrise Drive, Tucson, AZ 85718; (602) 529-2000.

National Alliance for the Mentally Ill, 1901 North Fort Meyer Drive, Suite 500, Arlington, VA 22209; (703) 524-7600.

National Association for Hearing and Speech Action (NAHSA), 10801 Rockville Pike, Rockville, MD 20852; (301) 897-8682; (800) 638-8255.

National Association of the Deaf, 814 Thayer Avenue, Silver Spring, MD 20910; (301) 587-1788.

National Council on the Handicapped (NCH), 800 Independence Avenue, S.W., Suite 814, Washington, DC 20591; (202) 267-3846; (202) 267-3232 TDD.

National Easter Seal Society, 2023 West Ogden Avenue, Chicago, IL 60612; (312) 243-8400; (312) 243-8880 TDD.

National Head Injury Foundation (NHIF), P.O. Box 567, Framingham, MA 01701; (617) 879-7473.

National Information Center for Handicapped Children and Youth (NICHCY), P.O. Box 1492, Washington, DC 20013; (703) 522-3332 (Voice/TDD).

National Institute of Mental Health, Public Inquiries Branch, 5600 Fishers Lane, Rockville, MD 21784; (301) 443-4515.

National Institute on Disability and Rehabilitation Research, National Rehabilitation Information Center, 8455 Colesville Road, Suite 935, Silver Spring, MD 20910; (301) 588-9284.

National Mental Health Association, 1021 Prince Street, Alexandria, VA 22314; (703) 684-7722.

National Society to Prevent Blindness (Formerly the National Society for the Prevention of Blindness), 500 E. Remington Road, Schaumburg, IL 60173; (708) 843-2020.

Registry of Interpreters for the Deaf, Inc., P.O. Box 1339, Washington, DC 20013.

"Tips for Disability Awareness." National Easter Seal Society, 2023 Ogden Avenue, Chicago, IL 60612; (312) 253-8400; (312) 243-8880 TDD.

"Together We Can Make A Difference." Pennsylvania Commission on Crime and Delinquency.

United Cerebral Palsy Fund, 1522 K Street, N.W., Suite 1112, Washington, DC 20005; 1-800-872-5827.

Local chapters of the organizations listed above.

# Chapter 9

# Communicating with the Elderly

*The first forty years of life give us the text; the next thirty supply the commentary on it.*

—Schopenhauer

## Do you know

- What the "graying of America" refers to?
- What causes some older Americans to be prisoners in their own homes?
- How likely the elderly are to be crime victims?
- What effect the increasing age of our population is likely to have on crime?
- What elder abuse is? How prevalent it is?
- What the usual police response should be in cases of elder abuse?
- What Alzheimer's disease is? How prevalent it is? What its symptoms are?
- What behaviors Alzheimer's sufferers have that may bring them into contact with the police?
- How Alzheimer's disease can resemble intoxication?
- What the cardinal rule in dealing with an Alzheimer's victim is?
- How police departments can benefit from senior citizens?

## Definitions

Can you define these terms: AARP, Alzheimer's disease (AD), catastrophic reactions, elder abuse, granny bashing, granny dumping, graying of America.

# Introduction

Older, retired people are one of the fastest growing segments of our population. Projections by the U.S. Census Bureau estimate that retired people will comprise more than 25 percent of the total population by the year 2025 (Enter, 1991, p. 67). During their careers, police officers have and will continue to have extensive contact with senior citizens. Police contact with older people rarely involves criminal activity; such contact usually arises from their vulnerability and the effects of the aging process.

Godwin (1992, p. 68) suggests that most gerontologists, those who study the elderly, do not focus solely on age to determine who is "old." Rather, they consider the following factors:

1.  Physical function—is the person able to get around easily and still physically active?
2.  Employment status—is the person retired or still engaged in some business or work, even on a part-time basis?
3.  Life activities—how socially active is the person?
4.  Self-perception—does the person view himself or herself as being old?

Some fifty-year-old individuals can seem as if they are eighty years old, and *vice versa.* To determine if someone is "elderly," police officers should consider the preceding factors and the individual's chronological age.

To have effective relationships with older citizens, officers must develop ways to serve their needs, reduce their victimization rate and gain their cooperation. Older people are especially reluctant to report crime to the police. The elderly tend to admire and respect authority; they are often grateful for any assistance the police may offer them.

Older people are usually in contact with the police if they become victims of crime, are involved in an automobile accident or are stopped for a traffic violation. Some elderly people do, however, suffer from Alzheimer's disease, a progressive, irreversible disease of the brain which adversely affects their behavior. Many elderly people have other serious medical problems for which they may require emergency medical assistance from a police officer. Older people may also have one or more of the disabilities discussed in the preceding chapter.

This chapter begins with a discussion of the graying of America, followed by some of the attendant concerns: driving problems, victimization, elder abuse, Alzheimer's disease and senility. Next crime prevention, community relations programs and using older volunteers in law enforcement are discussed. The chapter concludes with a description of some exemplary programs and recommendations of the Police Foundation.

# THE GRAYING OF AMERICA

Enter (1991, p. 67) notes: "America has traditionally been a youth-oriented nation. This tradition, however, is beginning to change. The maturation of the 'baby-boomers,' smaller nuclear families, and an extended life expectancy are contributing to that change."

◆

The **graying of America** is a metaphor that reflects the fact that our population is aging. The average American is living longer, the general population is becoming older and the percentage of elderly in the general population is increasing.

◆

Table 9.1 illustrates the age distribution of the U.S. population.

The implications for America's police are profound. As Miller (1992, p. 56) notes: "The senior element—those elderly citizens who presently make up between 12 and 30 percent of our communities—often express or exhibit heightened fears. Unnecessary fear undercuts effective police-citizen interaction and community life. This age group will make up an increasingly large, influential and active segment of society in the very near future."

As Lemmon (1996, p. 31) contends: "Enhancing the delivery of police services to the elderly is a worthwhile objective, but the changing demographics makes it an absolute must. Police and older citizens may not have had the opportunity to interact in the past, but as the baby-boomers reach senior status, the picture changes."

**Table 9.1   Age Distribution in the United States**

| Age | Percent of Population 12 or Older |
|---|---|
| **Total** | 100% |
| 12 to 15 | 7 |
| 16 to 19 | 7 |
| 20 to 24 | 8 |
| 25 to 34 | 20 |
| 35 to 49 | 28 |
| 50 to 64 | 16 |
| 65 or older | 14 |

SOURCE: Craig Perkins and Patsy Klaus. *Criminal Victimization 1994.* Washington: Bureau of Justice Statistics, April 1996: 6.

*Square dancing provides a fun form of activity and an opportunity to socialize.*

## THE ELDERLY AND DRIVING PROBLEMS

"By the year 2020, 50 million people in the U.S., half of them over 75, will be eligible to drive. Many will still be driving" (Bowes, 1992, p. 13). Many states require people over a specific age to retake their driving test. More states are likely to follow as the number of elderly drivers increases.

Bowes (1992, p. 13) suggests that police officers should understand some of the problems the elderly have that can affect their driving:

- Slower reaction time—resulting in more rear-end collisions, a greater number of traffic signal and yield violations and more pedestrian accidents.
- Decreased visual acuity—road direction signs are harder to read, and the ability to judge speed and distance is reduced.
- Narrowed peripheral vision—resulting in accidents at intersections.
- Loss of strength—limits the ability to steer quickly, brake suddenly or accelerate rapidly.
- Longer glare recovery time—an older person's glare recovery time can be as much as 50 percent longer than a younger person's. Glare from automobile headlights can be fatal to an elderly driver.

Bowes notes that elderly pedestrians with physical impairments such as arthritis can also pose problems to motorists because they walk slowly.

*Driving represents independence to young and old alike.*

## THE ELDERLY AND VICTIMIZATION

The elderly fear crime more than any other segment of our population.

◆

In some communities, the elderly's fear of crime makes them prisoners in their own homes.

◆

Brunswick and Wolfe (1992, p. A16) interviewed a sixty-seven-year-old woman who had not gone to church for the past two months, since three teenage boys harassed her while she was riding home on the bus:

I'm not some wishy-washy person. I take the bus all over. I have for years. But now only on weekdays. I never go out nights unless somebody picks me up at the door. I don't walk in strange neighborhoods. I don't open my door at night except for somebody I'm expecting. I have friends who have been bruised and pushed around by somebody grabbing a purse, and I just won't put myself in dangerous situations if I can help it.

Although the elderly have a heightened fear of crime, they are less likely to be victims of crime than younger people, as shown in Table 9.2.

◆

People aged sixty-five and older have the lowest rate of victimization in the United States both in violent and property crimes.

◆

*Table 9.2*    **Rates of Violent Victimizations by Age of Victim, 1992–1994**

| Type of Crime by Age of Victim | Victimization Rates per 1,000 | | | Percent Distribution | | |
|---|---|---|---|---|---|---|
| | 1992 | 1993 | 1994 | 1992 | 1993 | 1994 |
| **All violent crime** | 49 | 51 | 51 | 100% | 100% | 100% |
| 12 to 15 | 114 | 121 | 115 | 16 | 17 | 16 |
| 16 to 19 | 107 | 117 | 122 | 15 | 15 | 16 |
| 20 to 24 | 98 | 94 | 99 | 18 | 16 | 17 |
| 25 to 34 | 58 | 59 | 61 | 24 | 23 | 23 |
| 35 to 49 | 39 | 43 | 40 | 21 | 23 | 22 |
| 50 to 64 | 13 | 17 | 15 | 4 | 5 | 5 |
| 65 or older | 5 | 6 | 5 | 2 | 2 | 1 |
| **Robbery** | 6 | 6 | 6 | 100% | 100% | 100% |
| 12 to 15 | 13 | 14 | 12 | 15 | 16 | 14 |
| 16 to 19 | 11 | 12 | 12 | 12 | 12 | 13 |
| 20 to 24 | 14 | 11 | 11 | 21 | 15 | 16 |
| 25 to 34 | 8 | 7 | 8 | 27 | 24 | 24 |
| 35 to 49 | 4 | 5 | 5 | 16 | 22 | 23 |
| 50 to 64 | 2 | 3 | 2 | 6 | 8 | 6 |
| 65 or older | 2 | 1 | 1 | 5 | 3 | 3 |
| **Aggravated assault** | 11 | 12 | 12 | 100% | 100% | 100% |
| 12 to 15 | 20 | 23 | 22 | 13 | 14 | 14 |
| 16 to 19 | 27 | 30 | 34 | 16 | 16 | 19 |
| 20 to 24 | 23 | 27 | 27 | 19 | 20 | 20 |
| 25 to 34 | 13 | 15 | 14 | 23 | 24 | 23 |
| 35 to 49 | 10 | 9 | 8 | 23 | 20 | 18 |
| 50 to 64 | 3 | 4 | 3 | 4 | 5 | 5 |
| 65 or older | 1 | 1 | 1 | 2 | 1 | 1 |

SOURCE: Craig Perkins and Patsy Klaus. *Criminal Victimization 1994*. Washington: Bureau of Justice Statistics, April 1996: 6.

When elderly people *are* victimized, however, the crime tends to be violent. Older people are physically vulnerable and are likely to be hurt when they become victims of crime. According to the National Crime Prevention Council (1988):

Elderly violent crime victims are more likely to face offenders with guns, and are more likely to be attacked by strangers than younger victims. Violent crimes against the elderly are more likely to occur at or near their homes than offenses involving younger victims. About 45% of violent crimes against the elderly were robberies, compared with 17% of violent crimes against teenagers and young adults, and 18% of violent crimes against all victims under the age of 65.

Many of the crimes perpetrated against the elderly are purse snatchings and street robberies. Snatching the typical purse involves grabbing the purse with one hand, shoving the victim down with the other and running away. Broken bones are common in this type of crime—often more serious than the loss of the contents of the purse.

As Brunswick and Wolfe note: "When older people are victims of crime, they present special problems. Many have frailties, such as poor eyesight or memory, which make testimony at a trial difficult. Others are fearful of retaliation and decline to help prosecute their assailants." In addition, the elderly may have frailties such as osteoporosis. If the elderly are pushed, fall or are beaten, they may suffer broken bones and other serious injuries a younger person is not likely to sustain.

## The Police Response

Police department crime prevention programs aimed specifically at the elderly can help immensely. The police need to remind the elderly:

- To have their social security checks deposited directly in their bank.
- Not to carry much cash or other valuables on their person.
- To let go of a purse if it is grabbed.

Too many senior citizens have tried to hold on to their purses and been dragged along, suffering broken bones and other injuries.

To help the elderly population, police officers might start a block or building watch, set up a daily telephone contact program or enroll the elderly in Operation I.D. These programs will prevent crime and develop excellent police-community relations, not only among the elderly, but also the rest of the community who will appreciate the professional concern the police department shows for its elderly citizens.

## Crime Trends and the Effect on the Elderly

According to Enter (1991, p. 72): "By the year 2025, more than one-quarter of the population will be 60 or older. Therefore, it would be logical to assume that victimization of this age group will substantially increase, simply because the elderly will represent the greatest target population for the criminally minded."

◆

The increasing age of the population in the United States suggests that the elderly will be victimized more often simply because they will be a large target population, some very vulnerable, some very wealthy.

◆

Although the elderly presently constitute only one-sixth of our population, they "own one-third of all household net worth and 40 percent of financial assets" (Naisbitt and Aburdene, 1990, p. 45).

Criminal activity has generally been attributed to the young; however, as our population ages, according to Enter (p. 71): "The incidence of the 'geriatric delinquent' will undoubtedly become a greater problem for the criminal justice system."

◆

The number of elderly people who commit crimes will probably increase and present a great challenge to the criminal justice system, particularly corrections.

◆

Enter (p. 71) suggests:

One of the dilemmas that the criminal justice system will face concerns the processing of the older criminal through our present system. Arrest and detention policies, culpability issues, and sentencing options of today are limited in their ability to deal with the unique problems posed by elderly criminals. This gap will be especially apparent in issues concerning long-term incarceration of the elderly who will require extensive medical and psychological care beyond the present capabilities of most corrections institutions.

Another increase likely to result from the graying of America is an increase in what Enter (p. 72) calls **"granny bashing"** or domestic violence against the elderly.

## ELDER ABUSE

One evening in March of 1992 television news programs included a story that involved a confused and helpless eighty-two-year-old man who had been abandoned in his wheelchair at a dog racing track. Viewers were saddened by images of him in a hospital bed clutching a teddy bear. He was wearing slippers and a sweatshirt that read "Proud to be an American" and was holding a bag of diapers. Pinned to his sweatshirt was a typewritten note that said he was "John King, an Alzheimer's patient in need of care." All labels had been removed from his new clothing, and all identifying marks had been removed from his wheelchair. Egan (1992, p. A4) warns:

The face, that of an elderly person who does not even know his name and was left on society's doorstep, could become a face of the future. . . .

Increasingly, families pinched by the rising medical costs of aging parents and the strain of raising their own children are taking the radical step of abandoning the elderly. . . .

Although precise numbers are not available, the American College of Emergency Physicians surveyed hospitals and concluded that up to 70,000 elderly parents were abandoned last year by family members who were unable or unwilling to care for them any longer.

Such **granny dumping,** abandoning of the elderly, is only one form of elder abuse, however.

◆

**Elder abuse** encompasses physical and emotional abuse, financial exploitation and general neglect. The extent of elder abuse is unknown.

◆

According to Fox (1995, p. 95): "The abuse of seniors has been described as a 'hidden' or 'silent' crime, because cases often go unreported or undetected."

Most police agencies do not keep separate statistics on elder abuse. Agencies classify offenses by their traditional name (for example, assault, fraud or neglect) but not by age, so it is impossible to determine the extent of the problem. Further, many police officers believe elder abuse cases are "family matters" in which police should not interfere.

According to an **AARP** (American Association of Retired Persons) survey, in almost half the cases police did not know how the cases came to their attention, as illustrated in Table 9.3. As might be expected, a very low percentage of the reports came from family members.

Because most states now have mandatory reporting laws regarding elderly abuse, it is important that police officers recognize the signs of physical abuse of the elderly, summarized in Table 9.4.

*Table 9.3*    **How Majority of Cases Are Brought to Police Attention**

| | |
|---|---|
| Don't know | 43 % |
| Call from concerned individual (e.g., neighbor) | 12 |
| Referred from social service agency or other organization | 11 |
| Call from elder victim | 9 |
| Discovered while investigating a complaint or disturbance | 9 |
| Call from family member | 2 |
| (Had no reported cases) | 14 |

SOURCE: Martha R. Plotkin. *A Time for Dignity: Police and Domestic Abuse of the Elderly.* Washington: Police Executive Research Forum and the American Association of Retired Persons. 1988:22. Reprinted by permission.

### *Table 9.4*   **Signs of Physical Abuse of the Elderly**

- Any injury incompatible with explanation.
- Burns (possibly caused by cigarettes, caustics, acids, friction from ropes or chains).
- Cuts, pinch marks, scratches, lacerations or puncture wounds.
- Bruises, welts or discolorations:
  - bilaterally on the upper arms;
  - clustered on trunk, but may be evident over any area of the body;
  - unexplained bruises/welts in various stages of healing;
  - presence of old and new bruises at the same time;
  - injury reflects shape of article used to inflict injury (electric cord, belt buckle).
- Dehydration and/or other malnourishment without illness-related cause; unexplained loss of weight.
- Poor skin hygiene; pallor; sunken eyes, cheeks.
- Eye injury.
- Absence of hair and/or hemorrhaging beneath the scalp.
- Soiled clothing or bedding.
- Lack of bandages on injuries or stitches where needed; or evidence of unset bone fractures.

Injuries are sometimes hidden under the breasts or on other areas of the body normally covered by clothing. Repeated skin or other bodily injuries should be noted and careful attention paid to their location and treatment.

Frequent use of the emergency room and/or hospital or health care "shopping" may also indicate physical abuse.

SOURCE: Martha R. Plotkin. *A Time for Dignity: Police and Domestic Abuse of the Elderly.* Washington: Police Executive Research Forum and the American Association of Retired Persons. 1988:F-24 © 1988, AARP. Reprinted with permission.

Police must also watch for signs of extortion or fraud and the other forms of elder abuse.

## The Police Response

The issue of elder abuse is extremely sensitive. Often those who care for the elderly are ill equipped and lack resources themselves. Further, the arrest of the only caregiver could leave the elderly person in an even more precarious position. The victim of elder abuse may be extremely embarrassed by the treatment being given by "family." It is in the best interests of the elderly and the caregiver if the police can help work out a solution. Improving the care of the elderly does, however, involve more than just police intervention.

An effective response to elder abuse must incorporate the resources and expertise of many professional groups, of which the police are just one. Table 9.5 summarizes the agencies that police departments might work with.

*Table 9.5*    **Coordination with Non-Police Agencies**

| | |
|---|---|
| Social workers | 72% |
| Mental health workers | 60 |
| Victim services | 58 |
| Elder protective services | 40 |
| Hospital workers | 35 |
| Transportation services | 14 |
| Shelters for the elderly | 13 |

SOURCE: Martha R. Plotkin. *A Time for Dignity: Police and Domestic Abuse of the Elderly.* Washington: Police Executive Research Forum and the American Association of Retired Persons. 1988:50. Reprinted by permission.

◆

The police response in cases of elder abuse should be one of concern and empathy for all involved. The solution should involve appropriate professional support services.

◆

The AARP survey identified several model programs that deal with elderly abuse. Three such programs are summarized as follows.

**Charleston, South Carolina.** A specific elder abuse unit in the police department handles the casework, but all street supervisors are trained to handle complaints of elder abuse. The department uses a large network of agencies that assist with elder abuse cases: the Red Cross, home health agencies, nursing facilities and churches. The department provides training for agencies that work with the elderly, as well as workshops and lectures for senior citizens' groups and other interested local and national organizations. They have an Elder Supportline, a telephone support project that provides the community with a direct contact for reporting cases of elder abuse and neglect.

**Beaumont, Texas.** A departmental policy requires police officers to leave their patrol cars for at least ten minutes every hour to meet the public. The policy provides officers with an opportunity to spend time checking on the safety and well-being of the elderly and homebound. To identify seniors interested in and in need of such police services, letters soliciting this information were sent to city churches and other organizations in contact with the elderly population. The beat officer visits each elderly participant in the program weekly, and volunteers telephone the participant once a day except on the visitation day. If the participant does not answer the telephone or the officer finds no one home, the police investigate the situation.

**New York City.** New York City has a Crimes Against Senior Citizens Unit in each borough. These units emphasize preventing and investigating crimes against senior citizens, especially indoor robberies. The department produces an Older New Yorkers pamphlet which discusses city and police department assistance available to the elderly, crime prevention techniques, the courts and legal process, and provides a list of important telephone numbers.

In addition to being the victims of crime or of elder abuse, senior citizens are often the victims of disease. An especially devastating disease that affects the elderly is Alzheimer's disease.

## ALZHEIMER'S DISEASE: A POLICE PROBLEM TOO

This discussion is a condensation of the information provided in *Victim, Not Criminal: The Alzheimer Sufferer,* and the Alzheimer's Association Police Training materials. Reprinted by permission.

Imagine living in a world where every minute of your life is erased from memory as it passes. You can recall certain events from your childhood, school days, young adulthood, middle-age—but nothing from the past three years, five years or five minutes. You are unable to recall things you have known most of your life: your neighborhood, home, children, friends and spouse are all strange and foreign to you. This is the empty world of an Alzheimer's victim.

An estimated four million Americans have Alzheimer's disease (AD). AD afflicts about 10 percent of individuals over sixty-five and almost 50 percent of those over eighty-five. AD also afflicts more women than men. One out of three families has a close relative or family member with Alzheimer's disease. More than 50 percent of all nursing home patients are victims of the disease or a related disorder.

As the population of the United States ages, the number of people afflicted with AD will grow—along with the likelihood that police officers will encounter AD victims in the line of duty.

◆

**Alzheimer's disease (AD)** is a progressive, irreversible brain disease affecting four million elderly Americans. The classic symptom of Alzheimer's disease is loss of memory.

◆

Pronounced *Altz´-hi-merz,* the disease affects individuals of all social, economic and racial groups. It is the fourth leading cause of death in adults, causing 100,000 deaths per year. An estimated $40 to $50 billion is spent each year caring for Alzheimer's patients.

Alzheimer's victims may look perfectly healthy and may be well dressed. Those with Alzheimer's may be very adept at concealing their disease. Because police officers are likely to encounter individuals who suffer from Alzheimer's disease, and because there are no visible characteristics of the disease, officers should know the symptoms.

♦

Symptoms of Alzheimer's disease include gradual memory loss, impairment of judgment, disorientation, personality change, decline in ability to perform routine tasks, behavior change, difficulty in learning, loss of language skills and a decline in intellectual function.

♦

AD patients forget, they forget that they have forgotten and will not be able to recall what they have forgotten. It will not help to ask if they have AD because they will forget whether they have the disease.

The cause of Alzheimer's is not known, and it is a difficult disease to diagnose. In fact, medical confirmation of the disease is usually only possible by autopsy. Doctors diagnose AD by ruling out other diseases and by symptoms and family history. There is no cure for AD. The progress of the disease cannot be stopped. The course of the disease averages eight years from the time symptoms first appear, but individuals have lived as long as twenty years with the disease. Unfortunately, AD is always fatal. Although doctors cannot cure individuals with the disease, they can manage their symptoms.

Research has dispelled several *myths* associated with Alzheimer's. We now know that Alzheimer's disease:

- Is *not* a normal part of the aging process.
- Is *not* caused by hardening of the arteries or lack of oxygen.
- Is *not* contagious.
- Is *not* a mental illness or a form of insanity.
- Is *not* precipitated by alcoholism or malnutrition.

## Behavior Patterns

A number of behavior patterns common to AD patients may bring them to the attention of police officers.

♦

Alzheimer's victims may wander or become lost, engage in inappropriate sexual behavior, lose impulse control, shoplift, falsely accuse others, drive erratically and appear intoxicated.

♦

Any of these behaviors may cause the police to interact with an AD patient. The behaviors are the result of an individual's memory loss—the inability to make associations.

**Wandering.** Wandering is a common behavior of people with Alzheimer's that can occur any time, although it seems to be more common at night. An AD patient can become hopelessly lost, even when close to home and other familiar places. An officer may become frustrated when attempting to help because AD patients may not remember where they have been, where they are going or where they live, even when driven past their homes. AD patients may make up a story rather than admit their confusion. They may be uncooperative or even hostile and combative.

**Inappropriate Sexual Behavior.** AD patients are fidgeters and often develop repetitive behaviors. They may fidget with their clothing, their buttons and zippers, usually without sexual intent. The AD victim who zips and unzips his pants or unbuttons her blouse in public may simply be fidgeting.

**Loss of Impulse Control.** AD patients also suffer the loss of impulse control and may do whatever occurs to them, regardless of whether it is appropriate or acceptable behavior. Loss of impulse control may lead the AD patient to remove clothing that is uncomfortable or too warm. It may also cause the patient to urinate or defecate when they feel the urge, wherever the person may be.

**Shoplifting.** AD victims may forget to pay for things, forget they have picked up merchandise or forget that they are even in a store. AD patients rarely steal. They will forget that they have not paid for an item and will sincerely believe they are being falsely accused.

**Falsely Accusing Others.** AD patients may also falsely accuse store personnel of stealing from them. AD patients forget their pocketbooks and wallets, how much money they had when entering a store or how much money they have already spent. Unable to sort out the reality, they may become suspicious and accuse people around them.

AD patients may inaccurately believe they have been victimized by friends and family, as well as strangers. They may report crimes that did not occur.

In addition, neighbors may report that AD patients who live alone scream and yell at night. "Kidnap" or "adult abuse" reports may result from caregivers' attempts to limit an AD patient's behavior in public.

**Appearance of Intoxication.** AD victims may appear intoxicated because many symptoms of the disease are identical to those of drunkenness. Alcohol and AD both diminish brain function—alcohol temporarily, AD permanently.

◆

Many of the symptoms of intoxication and AD are identical: confusion and disorientation; problems with short-term memory, language, sight and coordination; combativeness and extreme reactions; and loss of contact with reality.

◆

**Victimization.** People afflicted with AD are easy prey for con artists, robbers and muggers. Police may become aware of AD patients as a result of legal actions such as evictions, repossessions and termination of utility service due to the patients' forgetfulness or inability to make payments.

**Poor Driving/Auto Accidents.** AD victims are often physically able to drive a car long after the time when their memory, judgment and problem-solving ability make it safe. Understandably, drivers who have Alzheimer's can have one or more of the following difficulties: "losing" their car and reporting it stolen; leaving the scene of an accident because they can actually forget it has happened; and "wandering" in the car because they are lost or have forgotten their destination. Sometimes drivers with AD are found several hundred miles from home. In such instances, the police should convince the AD patient to relinquish the car keys.

## The Police Response

Police officers' encounters with AD patients usually fall into two categories: (1) those involving behavior due to the primary symptoms of AD such as loss of memory and communication skills or (2) behavior due to resulting symptoms of AD known as catastrophic reactions.

**Problems Due to Memory Loss.** Officers called to the scene of an incident such as shoplifting or indecent exposure may arrive to find that the AD sufferer has completely forgotten the incident. There may be a dozen witnesses of the incident, but the subject will deny it occurred. The implications of such memory impairment are tremendously complex for police officers. If the patient did, indeed, commit a serious crime, the officer must take legal action. Usually, however, it is a minor incident such as shoplifting or misunderstood sexual behavior. If at all possible the officer should try to resolve the situation informally.

**Problems with Communication.** An AD patient who cannot remember or communicate what actually occurred may fabricate a story. Police officers could easily believe the subject is lying. The story may conflict so much with reality that the subject may appear to be taunting the officer.

**Is It Alzheimer's?** The following signs can help police officers determine if the person they are dealing with has Alzheimer's disease:

- Identification bracelet or other item indicating memory impairment (usually the bracelet will *not* indicate Alzheimer's disease, but will state memory impairment). Such a bracelet is the clearest way to identify an AD patient. Unfortunately, not all AD victims wear such identification.

- Confusion—an inability to grasp even the simplest sight, sound or situation.
- Facial expressions that are blank or inappropriate to the situation.
- Inappropriate dress. (Heavy clothing on a hot day, for example, or no shoes or coat in the winter.)
- Forgetfulness, especially short-term memory loss.
- Communication problems—difficulty remembering and understanding the meaning of words, keeping thoughts clear, speaking logically and following simple instructions.
- Age (most are over the age of sixty-five, but the youngest documented AD patient was twenty-eight years old).

**Catastrophic Reactions. Catastrophic reactions** occur when a situation overloads the AD patient's ability to act rationally and the patient reverts to impulsive behavior. AD may short-circuit an individual's ability to think, and the result is like a blown fuse. Behavior resulting from a catastrophic reaction can be relatively mild such as sudden mood changes and restlessness, or rapidly deteriorate into suspiciousness, stubbornness, inconsolable crying, anger and combativeness. During a catastrophic reaction, AD patients often lash out, verbally and/or physically, at people who try to help them.

## Guidelines

Although Alzheimer's disease is quite complicated, police officers can follow certain guidelines when they suspect or know they are dealing with an AD patient:

◆

The cardinal rule for police officers who deal with an Alzheimer's patient is to avoid the catastrophic reaction.

◆

The following guidelines should help an officer interact with an AD patient:

- Look for an I.D. bracelet or other identification.
- Identify yourself and explain what you are or will be doing, even if it is obvious.
- Avoid lectures or confrontation. Not only will they be ineffective, they are likely to aggravate the situation.
- Speak softly and slowly in a low-pitched voice. AD victims are not necessarily hard of hearing. Speaking loudly could be mistaken for anger and lead to a catastrophic reaction.
- Keep communication simple. Use short, familiar words and simple sentences.

- Use distraction to end inappropriate behavior; sometimes just your presence is sufficient.

- Maintain eye contact with the AD victim when speaking.

- Try to maintain a calm atmosphere. Any situation that may be mildly stressful for the average citizen can be extremely difficult for the AD victim. AD patients will often mimic your mood and respond more to the "climate" of an encounter than anything else. A nonaggressive posture and reassuring tones will help the officer to elicit the most helpful response from an AD patient.

- Do not overload the AD victim. When possible talk one-on-one, away from crowds and noise; ask simple questions one at a time.

- Avoid restraints, if possible. The use of handcuffs and physical restraint methods are almost certain to cause a catastrophic reaction, virtually eliminating chances of a simple solution to the situation.

The Alzheimer's Disease and Related Disorders Association (AD Association) suggests that, if at all possible, officers should avoid using handcuffs on an AD victim. Officers should, however, recognize that AD victims are unpredictable when frightened or upset, and they may need to be restrained for their own safety and the safety of others.

## Additional Police Response

Police departments can prepare to deal more effectively with AD victims by educating officers about the disease and encouraging families to get hard-to-remove I.D. bracelets for AD patients.

The AD Association's *Police Training Kit* is an excellent resource containing a fifteen-minute video, *Innocent Offender,* a curriculum manual with objectives, suggested activities and sample presentation plans for training sessions of ten, thirty or sixty minutes. The objectives of the training kit are that, through training, police officers will:

- Become sensitized to the physical and behavioral consequences of Alzheimer's disease.

- Identify situations where the person with Alzheimer's may be encountered.

- Learn specific intervention techniques for managing the Alzheimer person in crisis.

- Become familiar with the AD Association's resources for families in the community.

Included in the *Police Training Kit* is a Law Enforcement Officers Pocket Response Guide for Alzheimer's Victims. (See Figure 9.1, reproduced by permission

# LAW ENFORCEMENT OFFICERS POCKET RESPONSE GUIDE
## FOR ALZHEIMER'S VICTIMS

Made possible through
the generosity of . . .

KENTUCKY STATE LODGE
FRATERNAL ORDER OF POLICE

## TO USE THIS GUIDE:

Review this side for general recommendations when you first encounter a potential Alzheimer's victim.

## REVIEW SIDE 2:

For a brief description of the most common type of law enforcement encounters associated with individuals suffering from Alzheimer's Disease.

1. The primary symptoms of Alzheimer's Disease are memory loss, impaired judgment, carelessness in appearance especially with over/under dressing, disorientation, absent-mindedness, inability to communicate, and poor concentration abilities especially in response to the officer's kind of questioning. A neurological disorder, where the victim asks same questions over and over again, is quite common.

2. Since Alzheimer's Disease affects primarily the individual's mental functioning, there may not be any overt or recognizable physical characteristics of the disease.

3. Specific law enforcement encounters increase the likelihood that the individual may be suffering from Alzheimer's Disease. These encounters include wandering, auto accidents/traffic violations, indecent exposure, victimization/false reports, shoplifting, intoxication and homicide/suicide cases.

4. Bracelets indicating memory impairment, worn by the individual, may alert the officer that the subject is suffering from Alzheimer's Disease. Usually the words "memory impaired" distinguish this individual from other types of medic-alert categories. Some individuals will wear other forms of identification such as patches sewn to their clothing. If your area has a local Alzheimer's Chapter, it is recommended that it be contacted in case someone is missing, as well as to check with the Missing Persons Bureau.

5. When encountering a possible Alzheimer's victim, employ a non-threatening tone of voice. Maintain a calm environment and be cognizant of voice level so as to not give a false perception of anger or threat. Do not assume the individual is hearing impaired unless otherwise indicated.

6. Attempt to remove individual from noisy, stressful environmental situations. Excess stimuli may trigger a catastrophic reaction which is exhibited by increased symptoms of restlessness, pacing, agitation and anxiety. Sirens should be turned off, if possible, and radio volume and squelch turned down.

7. The ability to communicate (both sending and receiving messages) is greatly impaired with Alzheimer's victims.

   a) First, identify yourself as a law enforcement officer and state purpose of your being there no matter how obvious it may seem.

   b) Speak slowly — maintain low-pitched voice.

   c) Use short familiar words.

   d) Ask "yes" or "no" questions.

   e) Ask one question at a time allowing plenty of response time.

   f) If necessary, repeat question with exact previous wording. Victims may grasp only parts of initial question.

   g) Maintain good eye contact while communicating.

   h) Substitute non-verbal with verbal communication.

8. Avoid, if possible, the use of restraints or handcuffs. This action may trigger an increase in the victims' symptoms. Restraints should be used only as a last resort or when necessary for the safety of the individual and others.

*In Memory of Mike Cain*                    *©1990 Cain Consulting Associates*

*Figure 9.1*     **Side 1 of the Pocket Response Guide**

# LAW ENFORCEMENT OFFICERS POCKET RESPONSE GUIDE
### FOR ALZHEIMER'S VICTIMS

Typical behaviors associated with Alzheimer's Disease increase the likelihood of specific law enforcement encounters. Officers called to the scene, or who are confronted with a probable Alzheimer's victim, may very well find themselves dealing with a subject who has no recollection of an alleged incident.

Because Alzheimer's Disease affects that part of the brain where memory is stored, subjects may be unable to comprehend the seriousness of the issue and may be unable to effectively communicate and respond to the officers' line of questioning.

Officers may find themselves confronted with individuals who appear to be uncooperative and in denial of verifiable events.

## WANDERING

Alzheimer's Disease destroys the victim's ability to associate and recognize familiar landmarks. The individual's ability to retrace directional road maps and recall familiar driving routes becomes diminished.

Wandering behavior often increases at night and may pose serious safety concerns, especially if the victim wanders off during inclement weather, into remote areas or into an area of high traffic intensity.

## AUTO ACCIDENTS - TRAFFIC VIOLATIONS

Rules and regulations as they relate to highway safety are forgotten by Alzheimer's victims resulting in the failure to obey street signs, traffic lights and the maintenance of safe driving speeds. Individuals involved in accidents may even flee the scene unaware of any mishap.

## SEXUAL BEHAVIOR - INDECENT EXPOSURE

Societal norms associated with dress and impulse control are erased or forgotten.

Repetitive behavior exhibited by Alzheimer's victims such as fidgeting with zippers or buttons may be misinterpreted as deviant behavior.

Because judgment is often impaired with Alzheimer's Disease victims, undressing in public or leaving one's household without proper attire are common occurrences. The officer should be alerted when individuals are dressed inappropriately for summer or winter.

## SHOPLIFTING

Memory impairment will likely hinder the ability of Alzheimer's victims paying for merchandise. Victims may casually walk out of a store without paying, unaware of any wrongdoing.

Confrontation with the victim is not recommended and the officer is encouraged to work this out with the store owner if given the latitude to do so.

## VICTIMIZATION - FALSE REPORTS

Alzheimer's victims fall easy prey to con artists; however, lost or misplaced items also may be reported stolen. Often burglary attempts or strange intruders turn out to be long-time spouses or family members whom the victim has forgotten.

## INTOXICATION — D.U.I.

Erratic driving and failure to obey traffic signs may be caused by Alzheimer's Disease. Failure of the officer's assessment to identify any positive signs of alcohol or drug use may warrant the need to recognize the possibility of Alzheimer's Disease.

## HOMICIDE - SUICIDE

Unfortunately, without a cure for Alzheimer's Disease, caregivers may find themselves unable to bear the burden of dealing with this devastating disease and may choose to take the law into their own hands.

Several cases of homicide/suicide involving Alzheimer's victims are reported each year.

*Figure 9.1* **Side 2 of the Pocket Response Guide**
Used by permission of Cain Consulting Associates, Pewee Valley, KY.

of Cain Consulting Associates, P.O. Box 545, Pewee Valley, KY 40056.) This double-sided, laminated guide summarizes the key training concepts.

The kit is endorsed by the Fraternal Order of Police and is available for a modest charge from your local AD Association. Training is also available from your local chapter of the AD Association.

A program started in 1991, the Helmsley Alzheimer's Alert program, provides information on missing patients to public safety agencies. When a person with Alzheimer's is reported missing, the Alzheimer's Association faxes an alert and identifying information to a fax service which transmits simultaneously to hundreds of locations, including police, hospital emergency rooms and shelters. When the patient is found, another fax is sent to inform the agencies that the search is over. More than 275 patients have been assisted since the program began ("Alzheimer's Alert," 1993, p. 52).

## SENILITY

Senility is another disabling condition often associated with aging. Godwin (1992, p. 70) notes: "Senile dementia, organic brain syndrome (OBS), is the disorientation or change in the mental abilities and personality because of generalized brain damage." Factors commonly associated with the onset of senility include head injuries, infection, drug reactions, toxic chemicals and other problems such as multiple sclerosis. Senility can also be caused by alcoholism, anemia, malnutrition, congestive heart failure, diabetes and chemical reactions (Godwin, p. 70).

According to Godwin, common characteristics of OBS include:

> Disorientation of time, place or persons; memory loss; impairment of judgment with occasional auditory and visual hallucinations; and inappropriate behavior or emotional instability.

Godwin suggests:

> When dealing with a confused person, an officer should ensure the person is receiving information. He should attempt to establish a familiar environment, communicate slowly, reinforce reality by not reacting to their delusions and maintain a tolerant, calm and unflustered manner.

## CRIME PREVENTION AND COMMUNITY RELATIONS PROGRAMS

The older population's fear of crime, coupled with their unique vulnerabilities make them a logical target for crime prevention programs. The elderly are often cooperative and enthusiastic about participating in a police department's special efforts and programs.

Police departments across the United States have developed many effective programs for older citizens. Such programs can be easily adapted to other communities and are successful because they can reduce victimization, reduce the unrealistic fear of crime and improve police-community relations.

Honolulu, for example, has a Senior Citizen Watch Program. Members of authorized programs are issued official Senior Citizen Watch Program Identification Pins and are encouraged to wear them when going to and from planned club functions and other activities. As noted in their brochure: "The concept of the program is to utilize members of organized senior citizen groups to assist the police by becoming the eyes and ears for the department." The opening statement by Gibbe, the Chief of Police, notes: "Senior citizens offer much in the way of crime prevention. They are mature, dependable, trustworthy, observant and above all, enthusiastic."

Several similar programs are discussed in Section 3.

## OLDER VOLUNTEERS WITH LAW ENFORCEMENT

The police are not solely responsible for or even capable of reducing or preventing crime. Crime prevention is a community responsibility shared by the young and the old. Recently, law enforcement executives have sought citizen involvement and support in programs designed to reduce and prevent crime. Volunteers are currently involved in neighborhood watch block clubs, anonymous reporting and court watch programs.

❖

Seniors make excellent volunteers. Police departments across the country staff innovative programs with elderly citizens.

❖

Among the community volunteers are large numbers of older retired people who tend to be dependable, experienced, stable, available, trainable, committed, skilled, conscientious and service oriented. In addition, older volunteers have fewer accidents, are more careful of equipment than younger volunteers, use good judgment, follow directions, like to avoid trouble, have good attendance records and tend to be team players.

Benefits to the police department and the community that use older volunteers include:

- Increased service delivery.
- Increased cost-effectiveness.

- Improved public image.
- Relieving sworn personnel for other duties.
- Provision of new program opportunities.
- Increased political support.
- Restored community responsibility.
- Enhanced understanding of police functions.
- Reduced crime.
- Increased property values.

In addition, the volunteers may receive the following benefits:

- Reduced fear of crime.
- Use of their skills and expertise.
- The opportunity to help others.
- Enrichment of their daily lives.
- A greater sense of belonging and worth.

These lists, compiled by the AARP, are by no means exhaustive, but illustrate the many benefits to all involved in certain programs. Police-sponsored programs that use elderly volunteers have, however, raised some concerns.

## Concerns about Using Seniors as Volunteers

One frequently expressed concern is that volunteers may accomplish police officers' duties, and thereby affect future departmental hiring decisions. Other concerns are that volunteers need to be supervised while working in the department or that they may come in contact with sensitive or confidential material.

Volunteer programs can be tailored to address most objections. Volunteers rarely perform actual police functions. They frequently work in programs the department could not otherwise afford to provide such as fingerprinting children, distributing literature, maintaining equipment, entering computer data, organizing block groups, conducting department tours and translating.

Volunteers do, however, need supervision and recognition, and volunteer programs need a coordinator to handle those tasks. In some cases a member of the staff can act as coordinator. Where an extensive volunteer program is anticipated, a department may need to hire a volunteer coordinator.

Assistance and direction in managing seniors in volunteer programs is available from the AARP. This organization has, for example, developed a checklist to use when implementing a program of volunteers in law enforcement, shown in Figure 9.2.

## ✓ CHECKLIST

_____ Is there executive level commitment?

_____ Has a need been identified?

_____ Are volunteers the answer?

_____ Have you prepared departmental personnel to accept this concept?

_____ Will there be Union objections?

_____ What kind of unit is needed?

_____ Where will the unit be placed in the organization?

_____ Who will supervise the unit?

_____ Are the supervisory lines clear?

_____ Will you have a volunteer to coordinate the activities?

_____ Who will set work schedules?

_____ How will you recruit the volunteers?

_____ Do you know how many you will need to start the program?

_____ Will you develop screening criteria?

_____ Who will interview volunteers?

_____ Will you prepare job descriptions?

_____ What kind of paperwork will be needed?

_____ Can you identify specific tasks?

_____ Can the volunteers perform the tasks in the time offered?

_____ What will be the training needs?

_____ How much time for training?

_____ In the classroom? On-the-job?

_____ Will volunteers work specific shifts?

_____ Will you need back-up for occasional absenteeism?

_____ Do you plan group assignments?

_____ What hours will you want them to work?

_____ Will they log in and out on time sheets?

_____ Will you be able to keep backlogs from developing?

_____ Will there be adequate workspace?

_____ Comfort? Lighting?

_____ Will you have supplies available?

_____ Will you provide transportation?

_____ Will you pay out-of-pocket expenses?

_____ Will volunteers be assigned parking spaces?

_____ What will be the direct costs?

_____ Indirect costs?

_____ Have you considered liability?

_____ Will the department provide insurance?

_____ Must the volunteer provide insurance?

_____ How will you recognize their performance?

_____ Will you have criteria for measuring their performance?

_____ What termination procedures would be necessary when service is completed?

_____ How will the public be informed about these activities?

_Figure 9.2_ **Volunteer Checklist**
SOURCE: © 1988, American Association of Retired Persons. Reprinted with permission.

# EXEMPLARY PROGRAMS

Several departments have developed programs focused on elderly concerns. The following are a few of the many exemplary programs.

**Cleveland's Community Re-Entry Program.** Community Re-Entry is a church-sponsored, community-based corrections program that seeks to reintegrate ex-offenders into the community by entering into a contract with the Public Housing Authority to provide care to the elderly. Ex-offenders are hired by Community Re-Entry to serve as Care Team members. Sulton (1990, pp. 37–38) describes the responsibilities of the Care Teams:

> The Care Teams assist and protect the elderly who live in low-income, high-rise apartment buildings, and who are physically unable to complete basic tasks like cashing their checks, shopping for food and clothing, or traveling to doctors' offices. Because many of them are lonely, the Care Teams also provide companionship. In addition, the teams have established a resident grocery-variety store for the elderly to facilitate their purchase of small items.
> Security services are provided because the elderly requested it after several burglaries occurred. No elderly person has been victimized when a Care Team was on duty. The teams are effective, in part, because those most likely to cause disorder respect team members. . . .
> According to Re-Entry staff, none of the ex-offenders who are Care Team members has returned to prison.

**Detroit's Junior Police Cadet Section.** Sulton (1990, p. 74) notes that this program's approach "is to intervene and restore an attitude of caring and sharing among youth, senior citizens, and public and private institutions." A pilot project to assist the elderly was established in 1979 and involved 200 youth. By 1980 over 1,600 high school students participated in the program. Cadets wear uniforms and provide escort services to the elderly. Says Sulton (p. 76): "The senior citizen escort service is designed to permit the elderly to move freely throughout the community without fear of being victimized. Cadets ride buses and walk with the elderly while they shop, bank and visit physicians."

**San Antonio's Operation Blue.** One area in which the elderly are vulnerable is when they do their banking. They often walk away from the counter holding the cash in plain view. As Worrell (1993, p. 27) suggests: "These actions [check-cashing procedures], coupled with the somewhat slowed and helpless nature of the elderly, have made them prey for those in need of quick cash." In response, the San Antonio Police Department instituted Operation Blue. In this program police transport a temporary banking facility to the elderly who reside in the city-owned housing projects. The officers not only cash government checks, they also help seniors purchase money orders to pay their bills.

**Hartford's Senior Volunteer Assistance Program.** The Hartford, Connecticut, Police Department has instituted a Senior Volunteer Assistance Program to help senior citizens combat consumer fraud. The program has a toll-free hotline operating Monday through Friday. During its first three months, more than 1,000 seniors called for assistance. In addition, the seniors publish a monthly newsletter, *The Senior Advocate,* offering consumer tips and warnings on scams.

**Triad—A Coordinated Approach.** A joint resolution has been adopted by the AARP, the International Association of Chiefs of Police (IACP) and the National Sheriff's Association (NSA) (see Figure 9.3). As noted by Miller (1991, p. 96):

> These organizations expressed concerns about criminal victimization of older people and agreed to work effectively together to bring about interjurisdictional approaches and programs designed to reduce the victimization of older persons, assist those who have been victimized, and generally enhance law enforcement services to older adults and the community at large.

This three-way partnership, called TRIAD, seeks to provide support, including specific information such as the following (Miller, p. 96):

- Crime prevention materials: brochures, program guides and audiovisual presentations on crime prevention and the elderly.
- Policies and exemplary projects relating to law enforcement response to the older community and the formation of senior advisory councils to advise departments on the needs of seniors.
- Training for police about aging, communication techniques with elderly citizens, victimization of the elderly and management programs using older volunteers.

As noted by Miller: "Concern for older people is neither radical or new. However, the idea that law enforcement leaders should form a partnership with leaders of the elderly in their communities is new and is a concrete example of community policing."

Leadership is provided by an advisory group of older persons and those providing services to the elderly. This group is called S.A.L.T. (Seniors and Law Enforcement Together). This group helps law enforcement departments determine the crime and public safety-related needs and concerns of the elderly and suggests services to meet those needs.

The organizational structure of S.A.L.T. is illustrated in Figure 9.4.

**Joint Resolution**

| | |
|---|---|
| WHEREAS, | the proportion of senior citizens in the population is increasing at a significant rate in Illinois and the entire United States, and |
| WHEREAS, | the State's rapidly increasing senior population has special needs, especially relating to certain types of crime and the resulting feelings of vulnerability and fear of victimization, directly affect their quality of life, and |
| WHEREAS, | older Americans present unique challenges, as well as an important source of support to the law enforcement community, and |
| WHEREAS, | in many communities the needs of the elderly are only partially being met by law enforcement agencies' policies and programs, and |
| WHEREAS, | it is incumbent upon law enforcement agencies to formulate and execute policies and programs to enhance the service and protection for the safety and welfare of the older citizens in their communities, and |
| WHEREAS, | the National Sheriff's Association, the International Association of Chiefs of Police, and the American Association of Retired Persons have agreed to undertake joint activity, renewing their emphasis on the needs and concerns of senior citizens, and have adopted a resolution encouraging the formation of senior advisory councils to be called S.A.L.T. (Senior and Law Enforcement Together) groups |
| THEREFORE, | BE IT RESOLVED that the **Illinois Association of Chiefs of Police**, the **Illinois Sheriff's Association**, and the **Illinois State Leadership Council of the American Association of Retired Persons** agree to work jointly to develop and implement policies and programs to reduce criminal victimization of senior citizens, serve the special needs of older victims, and enhance the delivery of law enforcement services to the elderly. |
| ADOPTED, | this 11th day of July in the year of our Lord nineteen hundred and ninety at Chicago, Illinois. |

State Director, Illinois
American Association of Retired Persons

President
Illinois Association of Chiefs of Police

President
Illinois Sheriff's Association

***Figure 9.3*** **Joint Resolution**

SOURCE: © 1988, American Association of Retired Persons. Reprinted with permission.

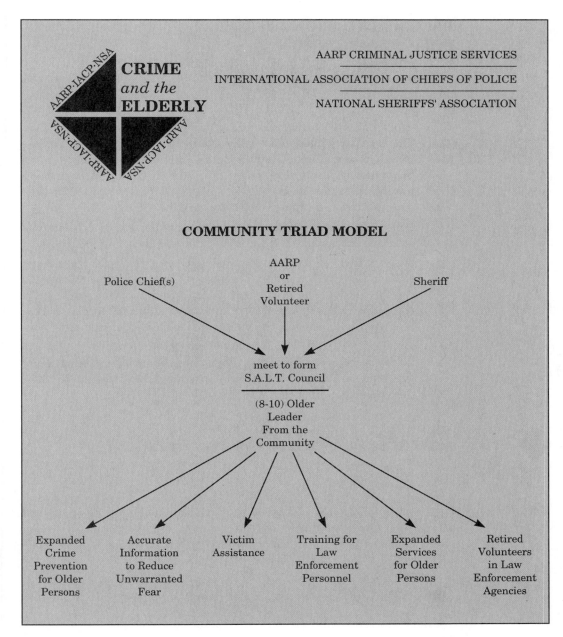

*Figure 9.4*    **Community Triad Model**
SOURCE: *Crime and the Elderly,* AARP Criminal Justice Services. Reprinted by permission.

## RECOMMENDATIONS OF THE POLICE FOUNDATION

The Police Foundation (Sulton, 1990, p. 104) has made the following recommendations for combatting crimes against the elderly. Reprinted by permission.

- Programs similar to Cleveland's Community Re-Entry and the Detroit Police Department Junior Police Cadet Section should be adopted by inner-city communities. Such programs raise public awareness concerning crimes against the elderly; foster an attitude of help, safety and caring toward the elderly; form partnerships and alliances to protect the elderly; and teach youth to appreciate and respect the elderly.
- Police should help reduce senior citizen fear of crime by providing them with information about the extent of crime in their neighborhoods.
- Senior citizen advisory councils should be established. These councils should: (a) provide support systems for the elderly; (b) encourage the elderly to participate in community activities; (c) operate programs that reduce the elderly's victimization and fear of crime; (d) match senior citizens with youth who will assist them with shopping, banking, letter writing and other activities; and (e) advise service providers of the elderly's needs.
- Public agencies and private organizations should provide financial and personnel resources to help senior citizens develop programs to increase their participation in community life.

 *Problem Solving in Action*

As suggested earlier, seniors often express great fear of crime. Many become virtual prisoners in their own homes or apartments, afraid to be out on the streets alone. The following account shows how the Kansas City (Missouri) Police Department used a problem-oriented approach to reduce fear of crime for apartment residents (Bennett et al., Fall 1994, pp. 1–2, 5).

## Due to Police Response, Apartment Residents No Longer Live in Fear

**By Robert Bennett, John Bryant and Jenifer Degen**

*Scanning*
Over the past several years, incidents of violent crime at the Creston Apartments in Kansas City (MO) increased dramatically.

The police department received numerous complaints and calls for service from residents and neighbors about drug dealing, homicides, assaults, robberies, prostitution and theft. In addition to these calls, the department also received verbal and written requests from city, state and federal officials to address the growing problem of violence at the Creston.

As of July 1993, the Creston was the number one location within the division of calls for police service, averaging 55 calls per month. Police officers spent hundreds of hours answering these calls every month. The calls not only caused problems for the officers, but also deprived citizens in other areas of the city of routine police patrol.

As time passed, offenders became more bold and violent, putting responding officers in greater danger each time they went to the location. Because the number of violent acts and assaults on police officers grew, the department began sending four police officers on each call. Two officers remained outside, ensuring the safety of their vehicles, while two officers responded inside to the call.

Residents of the Creston Apartments, especially those raising children, were the primary victims of the crime and disorder. These residents lived in an environment unfit for human occupancy—a building infested with mice, rats and roaches. They also had to coexist with drug dealers making transactions 24 hours a day, seven days a week. For the residents, unfit living conditions, drugs, violence and criminal activity were part of daily life.

Other area residents were also affected by the problems in the apartment complex. The area around the Creston Apartments consisted mostly of three-story Victorian-style homes with occupants in the medium-income bracket. Families with small children occupied many of the homes. The violent acts, gunfire and drug activity originating from the Creston often took place right in front of their homes. This illegal activity, along with an increase in residential burglaries, drove real estate values down and homeowner's insurance up. The residents felt like prisoners in their own homes, building privacy fences and buying watch dogs to protect their families. They refused to allow their children to play outside without supervision.

With these problems in mind, the police started a problem-oriented policing project at the Creston Apartments, with the objective of stopping drug sales and use, ending the violent crime and allowing residents to live in a better environment.

*Analysis*

The officers collected information from a variety of sources, including apartment residents, police records, tax and ownership records, and observations of the apartments.

The first step was to collect reports taken by officers at the Creston in the previous six months, and to obtain a computer printout detailing the nature of the calls. Thus, the most frequent types of calls and the people involved were identified. The majority of calls dealt with drug dealing in and around the building.

The officers went to the residents of the Creston and the surrounding community for help in gathering information on drug activity. Residents and neighbors received business cards with a pager number where police could be reached 24 hours a day. The police officers' candor with residents gave them confidence in the police, and the residents agreed to provide information. As people called, officers identified subjects involved and the times of heaviest activity.

*continued*

Over several weeks, the officers collected and forwarded this information to the Street Narcotics Unit, to assist them in making undercover narcotics buys.

The police contacted the owner of an abandoned building across the street from the Creston and requested his help. He agreed to allow officers to conduct surveillance from his building; however, the only way in was the front door. This posed a problem, as even the most naive drug dealer would notice uniformed police officers carrying video equipment into an abandoned building. The police department called on the fire department for help. The fire department staged an emergency call, sending pumpers, ladder trucks and fire personnel to the abandoned building. In the midst of this activity, police officers entered the building and set up video equipment without being noticed.

The officers videotaped numerous drug transactions, with the dealers unaware that the police were just 75 feet away, watching and taping their every move. After a transaction, officers conducted pedestrian checks or car checks on the parties involved.

The resulting videotape not only helped the police to respond to drug dealing, but also helped to mobilize other parties in response to the problem. Local television stations broadcast portions of the tape as part of their coverage of the problems at the Creston.

To address the physical decay of the apartments, officers contacted the owners of the building, who were uncooperative and unwilling to work with the police. Tax records revealed that the Creston was a HUD-subsidized facility. A HUD lien on the building made HUD just as responsible as the owners.

### Response

The video surveillance allowed for better identification of drug dealers, and thus facilitated the arrest and/or eviction of the people primarily responsible for drug activity at the Creston.

The police department provided the Jackson County Drug Abatement Response Team (DART), the fire marshal and the health inspector with copies of reports from the Creston and a copy of the videotape. After they inspected the building, they served the owners with numerous fire code and health code violations.

The department also contacted the regional director for HUD and advised him of the situation. He attended meetings with DART and the Longfellow Community Association (which included Creston residents), and was in constant contact with HUD's Washington office about the deplorable conditions at the Creston. An inspection by HUD officials soon followed. Engineers determined that the building had deteriorated to a point beyond repair.

The department solicited support from Rep. Alan Wheat and Sen. Christopher Bond. Bond met with the police, the community association, HUD and DART and promised to cut through the red tape as soon as he returned to Washington.

The HUD regional director then advised the police that HUD had allocated funds to improve living conditions at the Creston, and requested assistance in devising a plan of action.

The project's initial goal was to restore the Creston to a safe living environment, but engineers determined that repairs to make the building structurally sound would be too expensive. Basic improvements would make the building safe to live in until relocation of occupants was complete and the building destroyed.

HUD officials replaced the managers of the Creston with a management group willing to cooperate with the police. The new managers corrected all fire code violations, fumigated for insects and rodents and made cosmetic repairs to the building. HUD also provided 24-hour security, consisting of two off-duty police officers and four armed security guards patrolling the interior and exterior of the building. Security was also increased with the installation of a metal detector at the main entrance and the reinforcement of all other entrances. People entering the building had to pass through the metal detector and display picture identification.

### Assessment

The Creston Apartments are now closed and the building scheduled for demolition. HUD successfully relocated all residents.

Before the apartments were shut down, life at the Creston improved dramatically. The known drug dealers were jailed on narcotics charges or moved from the apartments after receiving eviction notices. Calls for police service dropped over 60 percent. Drug dealing ceased, and violent crime in the surrounding community was nearly nonexistent. The residents of the building and neighborhood were finally able to live without fear of violence and drugs, and happily adjusted to their new way of life.

The officers who once spent hundreds of hours answering calls at the Creston Apartments are now able to devote their time to other areas.

*Robert Bennett, John Bryant and Jenifer Degen are police officers with the Kansas City (MO) Police Department.*
*Reprinted by permission of the Police Executive Research Forum.*

## SUMMARY

The *graying of America* is a metaphor that reflects the fact that our population is aging. The average American lives longer than previous generations, the general population is becoming older and the percentage of elderly people in our society is increasing. The fear of crime among the elderly in some communities makes them prisoners in their own homes. Yet people aged sixty-five and older have the lowest rate of victimization in this country both in violent and property crimes.

The increasing age of our population suggests that the elderly will be victimized more often simply because they will be a large target population, some very vulnerable, some very wealthy. The number of elderly people involved in committing crime is also likely to increase, presenting a great challenge to the criminal justice system, particularly corrections. Likewise, elder abuse may increase.

Elder abuse involves physical and emotional abuse, financial exploitation and general neglect. The extent of elder abuse is unknown. In cases of elder abuse the police should express concern and empathy for all involved. The solution should involve appropriate professional support services.

The elderly may also be victims of Alzheimer's disease (AD), a progressive, irreversible brain disease affecting four million elderly Americans. Symptoms of Alzheimer's disease include gradual memory loss, impairment of judgment, disorientation, personality change, decline in ability to perform routine tasks, behavior change, difficulty in learning, loss of language skills and a decline in intellectual function.

Alzheimer's victims may wander or become lost, engage in inappropriate sexual behavior, lose impulse control, shoplift, falsely accuse others, drive erratically and appear intoxicated. Many of the symptoms of intoxication and Alzheimer's are identical: confusion and disorientation; problems with short-term memory, language, sight and coordination; combativeness; and in extreme reaction cases, loss of contact with reality. The cardinal rule police should follow when dealing with an AD patient is to avoid the catastrophic reaction.

The existence of a growing number of elderly individuals within a community has many benefits. One such benefit is that seniors are excellent volunteers. Police departments across the country use elderly volunteers to staff innovative programs.

## Discussion Questions

1. Do you know individuals who are caring for aging parents? How are they coping?
2. Have any cases of elder abuse been reported in your community recently? In your state?
3. What problems might police officers encounter when working with the staffs of nursing homes?
4. What resources does your community have for the elderly?
5. Do you know anyone who has Alzheimer's disease? What changes have they experienced?
6. Does your police department use elderly citizen volunteers? If so, how?
7. Does your police department provide support for retired officers?
8. In what specific ways might individual officers improve their interactions with the elderly?
9. Has the graying of America affected your community? If so, how?
10. What do you think your main concerns will be when you are a "senior citizen"?

## References

"Alzheimer's Alert." *Law Enforcement Technology.* (January 1993): 52.

Bennett, Robert; Bryant, John; and Degen, Jenifer. "Due to Police Response, Apartment Residents No Longer Live in Fear." *Problem-Solving Quarterly.* (Fall 1994): 1–2, 5.

Bowes, William B. "The Problems of Older Drivers." *Law and Order.* (May 1992): 13, 16.

Brunswick, Mark and Wolfe, Warren. "Reality of Crime Against Elderly Not as Great as Fear it Prompts." (Minneapolis/St. Paul) *Star Tribune.* (April 2, 1992): A1, A16.

Egan, Timothy. "Society's Doorstep Becomes Dumping Ground for Elderly." (Minneapolis/St. Paul) *Star Tribune,* citing *The New York Times.* (March 27, 1992): A4.

Enter, Jack E. "Police Administration in the Future: Demographic Influences as They Relate to Management of the Internal and External Environment." *American Journal of Police.* (Vol. X., No. 4, 1991): 65–81.

Fox, Christopher. "Shattering the Silence of Senior Abuse." *Law and Order.* (March 1995): 95–99.

Godwin, David W. "Police Services and the Elderly." *Law and Order.* (June 1992): 68–71.

Lemmon, Kathryn. "S.A.L.T.: Seniors and Lawmen Together." *Law and Order.* (December 1996): 29–31.

Miller, William D. "The Graying of America: Implications Towards Policing." *Law and Order.* (October 1991): 96–97.

Naisbitt, J. and Aburdene, P. *Megatrends 2000: Ten New Directions for the 1990s.* New York: William Morrow and Company, 1990.

National Crime Prevention Council. *Topics in Crime Prevention.* October 1988.

Sulton, Anne Thomas. *Inner-City Crime Control: Can Community Institutions Contribute?* Washington: The Police Foundation, 1990.

"Victim, Not Criminal: The Alzheimer Sufferer." Chicago: The Alzheimer's Disease and Related Disorders Association, Inc., 1987.

Worrell, Ann. "Operation Blue: Cops Become Bankers to Aid Elderly Citizens." *Law and Order.* (December 1993): 27–30.

## *Resources*

Alzheimer's Disease and Related Disorders Association, Inc., 70 E. Lake Street, Chicago, IL 60601-5997; (312) 853-3030, (800) 572-6037, (800) 372-3900.

American Association of Retired Persons (AARP), 601 E. Street N.W., Washington, D.C. 20049; (202) 434-2277.

*Chapter 10*

# Communicating with Youth: Victims and Offenders

*The moral test of government is how it treats those who are in the dawn of life, the children.*

—Hubert H. Humphrey

## Do you know

- At what age most states consider an individual an adult?
- What *parens patriae* is?
- What three kinds of youth are combined into one "jurisdictional pot"?
- What status offenses are?
- What the *Big D*'s of juvenile justice are?
- How a welfare model and a justice model differ? Which is most often used in the 1990s?
- What street justice is?
- What crimes youth might be victims of?
- What a police officer's first concern is with an abused or neglected child?
- What youths with special needs police officers should be familiar with?

## Definitions

Can you define these terms: attention deficit hyperactivity disorder, Big D's of juvenile justice, crack children, decriminalization, deinstitutionalization, diversion, due process, EBD, ephebiphobia, fetal alcohol syndrome (FAS), justice model, learning disability, "Norman Rockwell" family, one-pot jurisdictional approach, *parens patriae,* station adjustment, status offenses, street justice, welfare model.

285

# ◆ *Introduction*

A frequently overlooked segment of the population that is important to police-community relations is youth. Youth lack economic and political power; therefore, their problems may not command the attention they deserve. Many of our nation's youth are victimized; many others commit violent crimes. A community's youth poses significant challenges to law enforcement. The police should adopt a proactive approach toward the potential problems of the young.

> Of all minority groups, the most important one is the young. Their importance is emphasized because they represent all segments of society. The future of this nation depends upon the values they are forming. They obviously will be the future decision-makers of our society. . . .
>
> The law, to a young person, is often considered a "necessary evil." They do not understand the law, nor do they usually wish to learn about it. Rebellion against most laws, and especially those concerning the control of traffic, generates much hostility and animosity among the young.
>
> This hostility to law is naturally projected to police officers because they represent the negative forces that impose impossible sanctions. It is often said that the young do not like the police and the feeling is often mutual (Pace, 1991, pp. 108–09).

This chapter begins with a definition of youth, a look at the importance of the preschool years and a brief discussion of "good kids." This is followed by an overview of juvenile justice in the United States and the challenges faced by youth who are victims and those who have special needs. Distinctions are drawn between status offenders and youth who commit serious, often violent, crimes. The chapter concludes with a discussion of whether the juvenile justice system needs to be overhauled to meet the changing youthful population and community policing strategies that might prove effective in dealing with youth.

## YOUTH DEFINED

Each state establishes its own age defining youth, ranging from sixteen to nineteen years. Table 10.1 summarizes the age at which young people are officially considered adults in each state.

◆

The most common age for an individual to legally become an adult is eighteen.

◆

One state (Michigan) and perhaps others are moving toward lowering the age at which a person is considered an adult for prosecution purposes. One bill

*Table 10.1*    **Age at Which U.S. Criminal Courts Gain Jurisdiction over Young Offenders**

| Age 16 | Age 17 | Age 18 | | Age 19 |
|--------|--------|--------|--------|--------|
| Connecticut | Georgia | Alabama | Nebraska | Wyoming |
| New York | Illinois | Alaska | Nevada | |
| N. Carolina | Louisiana | Arizona | New Hampshire | |
| | Massachusetts | Arkansas | New Jersey | |
| | Michigan | California | New Mexico | |
| | Missouri | Colorado | N. Dakota | |
| | S. Carolina | Delaware | Ohio | |
| | Texas | D. of Columbia | Oklahoma | |
| | | Florida | Oregon | |
| | | Hawaii | Pennsylvania | |
| | | Idaho | Rhode Island | |
| | | Indiana | S. Dakota | |
| | | Iowa | Tennessee | |
| | | Kansas | Utah | |
| | | Kentucky | Vermont | |
| | | Maine | Virginia | |
| | | Maryland | Washington | |
| | | Minnesota | W. Virginia | |
| | | Mississippi | Wisconsin | |
| | | Montana | Federal Districts | |

SOURCE: Linda A. Szymanski. "Upper Age of Juvenile Court Jurisdiction Statutes Analysis." Washington: National Center for Juvenile Justice (March 1987).

currently in the legislature defines an adult at age fourteen. The public is becoming less tolerant of juvenile crime, which is increasingly assaultive and vicious as compared to fifty years ago.

## The Critical Preschool Years

Frequently, the only contact police have with the young is with those who create problems or break the law. Consequently, police officers may stereotype youth, especially teenagers. Since the police do not interact with many preschool children, they are not considered a problem. Yet it is during the preschool years that many of our youth's problems begin.

According to Hodgkinson (1991, p. 10) the following examples illustrate the "spectacular changes" in our society that affect our youth and have implications for law enforcement:

- One-third are at risk of school failure even before they enter kindergarten.
- Since 1987, one-fourth of all preschool children in the United States have been in poverty.
- Every year, about 350,000 children are born to mothers who were addicted to cocaine during pregnancy. Those who survive birth become children with strikingly short attention spans, poor coordination and much worse.
- Today, 15 million children are being reared by single mothers, whose family income averages about $11,400 in 1988 dollars.
- Twenty percent of America's preschool children have not been vaccinated against polio.
- The **"Norman Rockwell" family**—a working father, a housewife mother and two children of school age—constitutes only 6% of U.S. households today.
- One-fourth of pregnant mothers receive no physical care of any sort during the crucial first trimester of pregnancy. About 20% of handicapped children would not be impaired had their mothers had one physical exam during the first trimester, which could have detected potential problems.
- At least two million school-age children have no adult supervision at all after school. Two million are being reared by *neither* parent.
- On any given night, between 50,000 and 200,000 children have no home.
- In 1987, child protection agencies received 2.2 million reports of child abuse or neglect—triple the number received in 1976.
- Today, more than 80% of America's one million prisoners are high school dropouts (costing taxpayers upwards of $20,000 each per year).

Hodgkinson (p. 16) contends: "America's children are truly an 'endangered species,'" a fact society must address.

Children enter school with ingrained habits, attitudes, psychomotor skills, cognitive abilities, social interaction patterns and health characteristics. The following are some differences in five-year-olds entering school (source unknown):

- Some can count, say the alphabet and recite the colors; others cannot.
- Some can skip, throw a ball and build a block tower; others cannot.
- Some can play together, share and cooperate; others cannot.
- Some have strong bodies, good nutrition habits and healthy teeth; others do not.

- Some have an understanding of the community and the world; others do not.
- Some are eager to learn, enthusiastic and lively; others are not.
- Some know about music, books and the wonder of exploration; others do not.
- Some know what it is like to be loved and accepted; others do not.

In effect, what has happened to a child *before* entering school is likely to have a profound influence on how well the child will do in school.

### "Good Kids"

As you read this chapter, do not become discouraged about the future of our youth. Most young people (95 percent according to FBI statistics) have not been in trouble with the law. Of the 5 percent of juveniles who were arrested in 1992, about 9 percent were arrested for a violent crime, as shown in Figure 10.1. The overwhelming majority of "good kids" should not be forgotten in community

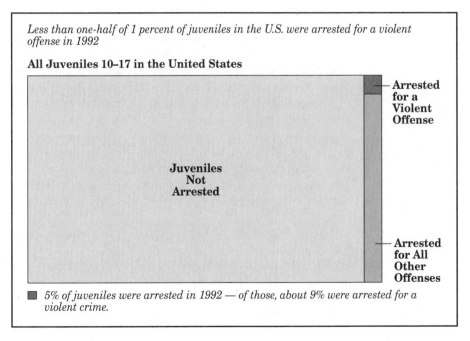

*Less than one-half of 1 percent of juveniles in the U.S. were arrested for a violent offense in 1992*

**All Juveniles 10–17 in the United States**

— **Arrested for a Violent Offense**

**Juveniles Not Arrested**

— **Arrested for All Other Offenses**

■ *5% of juveniles were arrested in 1992 — of those, about 9% were arrested for a violent crime.*

*Figure 10.1*    **Arrest Rates of Juveniles in the United States**
SOURCE: FBI (1993) *Crime in the United States 1992.*

*Youth in Austin, Texas, receive an anti-drug message from a police officer.*

policing efforts. They can be valuable as volunteers and, if provided opportunities to become active in areas of interest, will most likely continue to be good citizens. This chapter, however, focuses on those youth with whom law enforcement most often interact: youth who are victims and those who are victimizers.

According to Johnson (1996, p. 1): "In America, the relationship between police and youths can be described on a continuum of positive to very negative—even deadly. Some common problems between police and youths have been a lack of trust, little or no contact between line officers and youths except in negative contexts, high levels of anger and emotions, and racial and cultural differences. There is almost a natural adversarial relationship between police, who must control behaviors, and youths, who are anxious to experience new behaviors."

According to Astroth (1994, p. 411): "It is common today to hear that almost half of all young people between the ages of 10 and 17 are at risk of school failure, substance abuse, delinquency, and teenage pregnancy." He goes on to note, however: "It should come as a shocking surprise to learn that U.S. teenagers today are, by nearly every important measure, healthier, better educated, and more responsible than teens of the past."

Unfortunately, adults appear to be suffering from **ephebiphobia**—a fear and loathing of adolescents. Astroth (p. 412) suggests: "Nearly every generation of young people has been chastised for being 'out of control' or aberrant in some way."

Such attitudes need to be replaced with the view that these adolescents are the future of the country and need to be nurtured.

Freeh (1997, p. 26) stresses: "Crime prevention is like health prevention: if we don't inoculate children against diseases, we have epidemics that take a terrible toll. Prevention is one of the most valuable tools in the anti-crime arsenal, and we must use it to help reduce the pandemic of crime that now exists."

It is important that law enforcement officers, as first responders, assist in identifying the possible causes of juvenile activity, behavior or dangerous conditions and forward this information to those involved in the community policing efforts.

"At-risk behaviors include habitual truancy, incorrigibility, gang activity, drug abuse, alcoholism, suicide, promiscuity, criminal activity, tattooing or self-mutilating behaviors, vandalism, possession and use of weapons" (Doyle, 1996, p. 90).

Before addressing the specific challenges youth present to law enforcement, consider how the juvenile justice system affects the way police officers interact with youth.

## A BRIEF OVERVIEW OF JUVENILE JUSTICE IN THE UNITED STATES

For police officers to effectively interact with their community's youth, it is important for officers to understand how the juvenile justice system differs from the adult system and the implications such differences have.

The basic assumption upon which the juvenile justice system rests is that of *parens patriae.*

◆

**Parens patriae** refers to the government's right to take care of minors and others who cannot legally take care of themselves.

◆

The concept of *parens patriae* originated in thirteenth century England where common law established that the king was truly the "father of his country." As such the king was the guardian of all children. Children were considered wards of the state. The common-law notion of *parens patriae* is firmly entrenched in our system of juvenile justice. Krisberg (1992, p. 152) describes the evolution of the juvenile justice system:

Early reformers envisioned a special prison system for wayward youth that would emphasize education, industry, and moral training. . . . Throughout the nineteenth century, the practice of incarcerating wayward youth expanded. . . .

The following were significant events in the history of our juvenile justice system:

- 1818 Juvenile delinquency defined.
- 1825 First House of Refuge established in the United States.
- 1847 State reform and industrial schools founded.
- 1850–1890 Child-savers movement.
- 1869 First official use of probation (Massachusetts).
- 1870 First use of separate trials for juveniles (Massachusetts).
- 1880 First probation system applicable to juveniles instituted.
- 1898 Segregation of children under age sixteen awaiting trial.
- 1899 First juvenile court established in Illinois.

According to Krisberg and Austin (1993, p. 16):

Although early nineteenth-century philanthropists relied on religion to justify their good works, their primary motivation was protection of their class privileges. Fear of social unrest and chaos dominated their thinking. The rapid growth of a visible impoverished class, coupled with apparent increases in crime, disease, and immorality, worried those in power.

In 1818 the term *juvenile delinquency* was first used. The term was equated with pauperism, that is, being poor. In 1825, delinquency was equated with poverty when the New York House of Refuge was opened to house juvenile delinquents. Its charter defined juvenile delinquents as "youths convicted of criminal offenses or found in vagrancy."

In the second half of the nineteenth century a group of reformers called the "child-savers" became active, establishing centers in urban areas to distribute food and clothing and to provide temporary shelter for youth who were homeless. Like reformers before them, however, Krisberg and Austin (p. 21) note: "They viewed the urban masses as a potentially dangerous class that could rise up if misery and impoverishment were not alleviated."

The link between delinquency and poverty was strengthened by the first juvenile court act, passed in Illinois in 1899. The purpose of this act was to regulate the treatment and control of dependent, neglected and delinquent children, again equating poor children and those in need of protection with children who committed crimes and treating them in essentially the same way.

As further noted by Krisberg and Austin (p. 17): "From the outset, the first special institutions for juveniles housed together delinquent, dependent, and neglected children—a practice still observed in most juvenile detention facilities today."

◆

Our juvenile justice system uses a **one-pot jurisdictional approach**: children who are abused or neglected, those who are status offenders and those who are truly criminal are all treated the same way.

◆

According to Springer (1986, p. 45):

One of the major failings in the juvenile court system is what can be referred to as the "one-pot" jurisdictional approach—putting poor, rebellious, and criminal children in the same jurisdictional pot. . . .

All three kinds of children were thought to be the products or victims of bad family and social environments; consequently, it was thought, they should be subject, as wards of the court, to the same kind of solicitous, helpful care.

At the end of the nineteenth century the "child-savers" believed that "troublesome" youth could be "saved" by removing them from their homes and placing them in a "proper" environment. Their efforts led to legislation that authorized widespread governmental family intervention. This form of intervention continued for several decades.

By 1900 the juvenile justice system was very distinct from the adult system. Table 10.2 presents the current similarities and differences between the juvenile and adult justice systems.

Table 10.3 compares the different terminology used in juvenile and adult courts. The differences in terminology evidence a very basic difference in philosophy and approach.

## Status Offenses

An extremely important aspect of the juvenile justice system is its establishment of status offenses.

◆

**Status offenses** are actions by a juvenile that would not be considered criminal acts if done by an adult, for example, truancy or smoking cigarettes.

◆

Status offenses are certain actions considered crimes if done by those under legal age. They are not crimes if committed by adults. In most states, status offenses include truancy, running away, curfew violations, smoking cigarettes, drinking alcoholic beverages and "incorrigibility."

The philosophy of the first juvenile courts was to view children as basically good and in need of help—this approach is commonly referred to as the **welfare model.**

*Table 10.2*    **Similarities and Differences between the Juvenile and Adult Justice Systems**

| Similarities | Differences |
|---|---|
| 1. Discretion in decision making is used by police officers, judges and correctional personnel in both adult and juvenile systems. | 1. The primary purpose of juvenile procedures is protection and treatment; with adults, the aim is punishment of the guilty. |
| 2. Search and seizure law and the Fourth Amendment apply to juvenile and adult offenders. | 2. The jurisdiction of the juvenile court is determined chiefly by age; in the adult system, jurisdiction is determined primarily by the nature of the offense. |
| 3. The right to receive the *Miranda* warning applies to juveniles as well as to adults. | 3. Juveniles can be held responsible for acts that would not be criminal if they were committed by an adult (status offenses). |
| 4. Juveniles are protected, as are adults, from prejudicial lineups or other identification procedures. | 4. Juvenile proceedings are not considered criminal, whereas adult proceedings are. |
| 5. Procedural safeguards similar to those of adults protect juveniles when they make an admission of guilt. | 5. Juvenile court procedures are generally informal and private; those of adult courts are more formal and open to the public. |
| 6. Prosecutors and defense attorneys play an equally critical role in juvenile and adult advocacy. | 6. Courts cannot release identifying information to the press concerning a juvenile, but must do so in cases involving adults. |
| 7. Juveniles, like adults, have the right to counsel at most key stages of the court process. | 7. Parents are highly involved in the juvenile process; with adults, this would not be the case. |
| 8. Pretrial motions are available in juvenile and criminal court proceedings. | 8. The standard of arrest is more stringent for adults than for juveniles. |
| 9. Negotiations and plea bargaining are used with juvenile and adult offenders. | 9. As a practical matter, juveniles are released into parental custody, whereas adults are generally given the opportunity for bail. |
| 10. Children and adults have a right to a trial and appeal. | 10. Plea bargaining is used in most adult cases, whereas most juvenile cases are settled by open admission of guilt. |
| 11. The standard of evidence in juvenile delinquency adjudications, as in adult criminal trials, is that of proof beyond a reasonable doubt. | 11. Juveniles have no constitutional right to a jury trial; adults do have this right. |
| 12. Like adults, children waived from the juvenile court can receive the death penalty. | 12. Juvenile dispositional decisions are ordinarily based on indeterminate terms, whereas adults' sentences include proportionality and definiteness. |

*Table 10.2*  **Continued**

| Similarities | Differences |
|---|---|
| | **13.** The procedural rights of juveniles are based on the concept of "fundamental fairness"; those of adults are based on the constitutional right to due process under the Bill of Rights and the Fourteenth Amendment. |
| | **14.** Juveniles have the right to treatment under the Fourteenth Amendment; adult offenders have no such recognized right. |
| | **15.** A juvenile's record is sealed when the age of majority is reached; the record of an adult is permanent. |

SOURCE: Joseph J. Senna and Larry J. Siegel. *Introduction to Criminal Justice,* 5th rev. ed. St. Paul: West Publishing Company, 1990: 633. Reprinted by permission.

*Table 10.3*  **The Language of Juvenile and Adult Courts**

| Juvenile Court Term | Adult Court Term |
|---|---|
| Adjudication: decision by the judge that a child has committed delinquent acts. | Conviction of guilt |
| Adjudicatory hearing: a hearing to determine whether the allegations of a petition are supported by the evidence beyond a reasonable doubt. | Trial |
| Adjustment: the settling of a matter so that parties agree without official intervention by the court. | Plea bargaining |
| Aftercare: the supervision given to a child for a limited period of time after he or she is released from training school but while he or she is still under the control of the juvenile court. | Parole |
| Commitment: a decision by the judge to send a child to training school. | Sentence to imprisonment |
| Delinquent act: an act that if committed by an adult would be called a crime. The term does not include such ambiguities and noncrimes as "being ungovernable," "truancy," "incorrigibility," and "disobedience." | Crime |
| Delinquent child: a child who is found to have committed an act that would be considered a crime if committed by an adult. | Criminal |
| Detention: temporary care of an allegedly delinquent child who requires secure custody in physically restricting facilities pending court disposition or execution of a court order. | Holding in jail |
| Dispositional hearing: a hearing held subsequent to the adjudicatory hearing to determine what order of disposition should be made for a child adjudicated as delinquent. | Sentencing hearing |

*continued*

*Table 10.3* **Continued**

| Juvenile Court Term | Adult Court Term |
|---|---|
| Hearing: the presentation of evidence to the juvenile court judge, his or her consideration of it and his or her decision on disposition of the case. | Trial |
| Juvenile court: the court that has jurisdiction over children who are alleged to be or found to be delinquent. Juvenile delinquency procedures should not be used for neglected children or for those who need supervision. | Court of record |
| Petition: an application for a court order or some other judicial action. Hence, a "delinquency petition" is an application for the court to act in a matter involving a juvenile apprehended for a delinquent act. | Accusation or indictment |
| Probation: the supervision of a delinquent child after the court hearing but without commitment to training school. | Probation (with the same meaning as the juvenile court term) |
| Residential child care facility: a dwelling (other than a detention or shelter care facility) that is licensed to provide living accommodations, care, treatment, and maintenance for children and youths. Such facilities include foster homes, group homes and halfway houses. | Halfway house |
| Shelter: temporary care of a child in physically unrestricting facilities pending court disposition or execution of a court order for placement. Shelter care is used for dependent and neglected children and minors in need of supervision. Separate shelter care facilities are also used for children apprehended for delinquency who need temporary shelter but not secure detention. | Jail |
| Take into custody: the act of the police in securing the physical custody of a child engaged in delinquency. The term is used to avoid the stigma of the word "arrest." | Arrest |

SOURCE: Reprinted by permission from Harold J. Vetter and Leonard Territo. *Crime and Justice in America: A Human Perspective*, St. Paul: West Publishing Company, 1984. All rights reserved.

During the 1960s a series of major U.S. Supreme Court decisions fundamentally changed the Court's character. . . . A consensus emerged on behalf of limiting formal court intervention in children's lives. . . . From the late 1970s, a very different and more conservative political agenda dominated the juvenile justice policy arena. . . . As the juvenile court moves toward a punishment model, more attention must be paid to issues of due process, equal protection, and proportionality of sanctions (Krisberg, 1992, pp. 153–59).

In the 1960s and early 1970s the national emphasis on civil rights greatly affected the juvenile justice system. The following milestone cases in juvenile justice continue to shape the manner in which law enforcement responds to youthful offenders:

- 1966—*Kent v. United States* established that if a juvenile court waives jurisdiction and transfers a case to adult court, it must follow the dictates of due process and fair treatment.

- 1967—*In re Gault* established that juveniles have the same constitutional rights as adults: notice of charges, right to counsel, right to cross-examine and to confront witnesses and privilege against self-incrimination.
- 1970—*In re Winship* established that in a juvenile court hearing, the youth must be proven guilty beyond a reasonable doubt, just as in adult criminal court. (The former standards were preponderance of evidence, clear and convincing proof and reasonable proof.)
- 1971—*McKeiver v. Pennsylvania* established that juveniles do *not* have the right to a jury trial in the juvenile court system.

The 1970s focused on the four Big D's as described by Drowns and Hess (1995, p. 56).

◆

The **Big D's of juvenile justice** are diversion, decriminalization, deinstitutionalization and due process.

◆

**Diversion** means finding alternatives to placing juveniles into detention facilities. A major rationale underlying diversion was that not placing offenders into the justice system would avoid the danger assumed to be associated with criminal stigmatization and criminal association, thereby reducing the likelihood of subsequent crime by the offender.

**Decriminalization** refers to the efforts to make status offenses noncriminal actions. **Deinstitutionalization,** as the name implies, refers to efforts to release incarcerated youth through parole and community programs. **Due process** suggests that the advances made in the rights of youth continued to be important considerations in the 1970s.

Another important case involving juveniles is *Schall v. Martin* (1984). This case established the state's right to place juveniles in preventive detention, to protect both the youth and society.

## A Change from the Welfare to the Justice Model

The 1980s brought reform in the juvenile justice system; a change from the welfare model to a justice model. As noted by Springer (1986, p. 2):

> The first step in doing justice for juveniles is to revise juvenile court acts throughout the country so that when juvenile courts deal with delinquent children, they operate under a justice model rather than under the present treatment or child welfare model. By a justice model is meant a judicial process wherein young people who come in conflict with the law are held responsible and accountable for their behavior.

◆

**A justice model** views youth as responsible for their actions. Under the justice model, the good of society takes precedence over society's responsibility to take care of its children as in the welfare model.

◆

Springer (p. 2) contends: "Except for certain mentally disabled and incompetent individuals, young law violators should not be considered by the juvenile courts as being 'sick' or as victims of their environment. Generally speaking, young criminals are more wrong than wronged, more the victimizers than the victims." Springer (p. 33) further notes: "It is time that we recognize the impossible double bind our juvenile judges are placed in when they, judicial officers, are commanded to diagnose the 'problem' of some young offender, when in most cases it is obvious that the criminal youth does not have a problem—he or she *is the problem*."

This "get tough" attitude has been criticized by some, however, such as Brodt and Smith (1991, p. 176), who suggest:

In practice, getting tough means "let's get tough" with the following groups: (1) blacks; (2) Chicanos; (3) the poor; (4) the uneducated; (5) youth from single parent families; (6) the unemployed; (7) illegitimate youth; (8) welfare families; and (9) abused children.

This criticism might be addressed, in part, by making the changes Springer proposes in the juvenile justice system. Springer (p. 40) calls for the juvenile justice system to be divided into two categories: civil and criminal. Two subcategories would be within the civil category: (1) children who are endangered, abused or neglected; and (2) youth who commit status offenses. It is important for police officers to understand that the current juvenile justice system makes no such distinction. Consequently, police officers often use their discretionary powers and make the distinction themselves.

◆

**Street justice** occurs when police officers use their discretionary powers to simply talk to or warn youthful offenders rather than taking them into custody.

◆

Street justice may also involve talking to the youth's parents and/or making referrals to a social service agency.

## THE CHALLENGE OF YOUTH WHO ARE VICTIMS

Police officers need to be informed about the various ways in which youth can be victimized. Officers should understand why young people may act as they do and the type of assistance they might need.

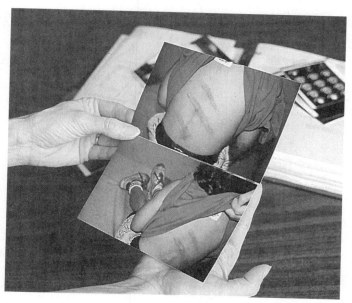

*Photographs of a child abuse victim beaten with a broomstick by his father.*

♦

Youth may be victims of abuse, homelessness or lead poisoning.

♦

Cowley (1991, p. 18) notes: "Nearly one child in four is born into poverty, a formidable predictor of lifelong ill health, and a growing number lack such basic advantages as a home, two parents and regular access to a doctor. Every year thousands die violently, from abuse or preventable accidents. Millions go unvaccinated against common childhood diseases. Millions more are poisoned by cigarette smoke or household lead."

Briscoe (1994, p. 26) asserts: "In 1994, an American child is abused or neglected every 13 seconds, born to an unwed mother every 26 seconds, born into poverty every 30 seconds, born to a teen mother every 59 seconds, arrested for a violent crime every five minutes and killed by guns every two hours." Briscoe (p. 28) also notes: "On a national basis, reports of neglect are three times as high as those for abuse. What's worse, unless there is neurological damage from the abuse, neglect has a longer term, more damaging impact to the development of the child."

Table 10.4 summarizes the rates of violent victimizations of youth.

Widom (1992, p. 1) reports the following based on detailed studies sponsored by the National Institute of Justice:

- Childhood abuse increased the odds of future delinquency and adult criminality overall by 40 percent.

*Table 10.4*  **Rates of Violent Victimizations by Age of Victim, 12–24, 1992–94**

| Type of Crime by Age of Victim | Victimization Rates per 1,000 | | | Percent Distribution | | |
|---|---|---|---|---|---|---|
| | 1992 | 1993 | 1994 | 1992 | 1993 | 1994 |
| **All violent crime** | 49 | 51 | 51 | 100% | 100% | 100% |
| 12 to 15 | 114 | 121 | 115 | 16 | 17 | 16 |
| 16 to 19 | 107 | 117 | 122 | 15 | 15 | 16 |
| 20 to 24 | 98 | 94 | 99 | 18 | 16 | 17 |
| **Robbery** | 6 | 6 | 6 | 100% | 100% | 100% |
| 12 to 15 | 13 | 14 | 12 | 15 | 16 | 14 |
| 16 to 19 | 11 | 12 | 12 | 12 | 12 | 13 |
| 20 to 24 | 14 | 11 | 11 | 21 | 15 | 16 |
| **Aggravated assault** | 11 | 12 | 12 | 100% | 100% | 100% |
| 12 to 15 | 20 | 23 | 22 | 13 | 14 | 14 |
| 16 to 19 | 27 | 30 | 34 | 16 | 16 | 19 |
| 20 to 24 | 23 | 27 | 27 | 19 | 20 | 20 |

SOURCE: Craig Perkins and Patsy Klaus. *Criminal Victimization 1994*. Washington: Bureau of Justice Statistics, April 1996.

- Being abused or neglected as a child increased the likelihood of arrest as a juvenile by 53 percent, as an adult by 38 percent and for a violent crime by 38 percent.
- It is not only violence that begets violence, but also neglect.

Such statistics highlight what Widom (1995, p. 1) refers to as the "cycle of violence" or the "intergenerational transmission of violence." Says Widom: "The research clearly revealed that a childhood history of physical abuse predisposes the survivor to violence in later years, and that victims of neglect are more likely to engage in violent criminal behavior as well."

There is a correlation between children who have been abused and those who commit criminal acts. A national expert on child abuse and neglect, Robert ten Bensel, has gathered a large body of evidence linking child abuse and neglect to later violent criminality (Springer, 1986, p. 76):

Studies have shown that virtually all violent juvenile delinquents have been abused children, that all criminals at San Quentin prison . . . studied had violent upbringings as children, and that all assassins . . . in the United States during the past twenty years had been victims of child abuse.

The FBI ("What's Killing America's Children," 1995, p. 14) suggests: "Children have far more to fear from their own families than from 'strangers.'" As noted by Craig (1992, p. 67): "For some children, family violence is so severe that it results in intervention by public authorities. For many other youngsters, it remains a secret destroyer that slowly permeates the fabric of self and distorts the content of all relationships."

Wexler (1996) reports that murder is the second-leading cause of death among teens, after auto accidents. He also reports on a Justice Department announcement that homicides by youths under seventeen years of age tripled between 1984 and 1994. Over the same time period, the number of juvenile murderers using guns quadrupled, underscoring the part that availability of firearms appears to be playing in the mayhem ("Number of Young Killers. . . ," 1996, p. A4).

A study conducted by canvassing 14,000 inmates imprisoned for violent crimes ("Direct from the Source," 1996, p. 1) found that two-thirds of sex offenders victimized a child, and that one-third raped or sexually assaulted their own child or stepchild.

Greenfield (1996, p. 17) reports: "In 1994 over 70 percent of the murders of infants were carried out by a family member. By contrast, among victims age 15 to 17, family members accounted for 3 percent of the murders."

The Department of Health and Human Services ("Report: 1 Million Cases of Child Abuse," 1996, p. A4) reports that "More than 1 million cases of child abuse or neglect were documented by the states in 1994, but the actual number of children mistreated may have been three times that." In this report 53 percent of the children studied suffered neglect.

The Centers for Disease Control and Prevention ("Which Is the Most Violent Nation. . . ," 1997, p. Al) reports that nearly three-quarters of all the murders of children in the industrialized world occur in the United States. The United States has the highest rates of childhood homicide, suicide and firearms-related deaths of any of the world's twenty-six richest nations.

Another group of youthful victims are those who are homeless, either because they are runaways, throwaways (their family has kicked them out) or their entire family is homeless. Stevens and Price (1992, p. 18) note that more than 300,000 school-age children are homeless each year.

Stevens and Price also note that three to four million children have been exposed to damaging levels of lead. The seriousness of this problem is reflected in the declaration of the Public Health Service that "lead poisoning remains the most common and societally devastating environmental disease of young children" (Needleman, 1992, p. 35). Needleman notes that:

> Being poor increases a child's risk radically. The ATSDR [Agency for Toxic Substances and Disease Registry] estimates that 7% of well-off white children have elevated blood lead levels; for poor whites, the proportion is 25%. Of poor African-American children, 55% have elevated levels. More than half of African-American children who live in poverty begin their education with this potentially handicapping condition. Lead exposure may be one of the most important—and least acknowledged—causes of school failure and learning disorders.

## The Police Response

Several service providers are mandated by law to report incidents of suspected child abuse and neglect: healing arts, social services, hospital administration, psychological treatment, psychiatric treatment, child care, education, law enforcement and the clergy.

The following conditions might lead a police officer to place a child in protective custody (Minnesota P.O.S.T. Board):

- Maltreatment in the home which could cause the child permanent physical or emotional damage.
- Although the child is in immediate need of medical or psychiatric care, the parents refuse to obtain it.
- Child's age or physical or mental condition renders the child incapable of self-protection.
- The physical environment of the home poses an immediate threat to the child.
- The parents cannot or will not provide for the child's basic needs.
- The parents may flee the jurisdiction.
- The parents abandon the child.

◆

The primary responsibility of police officers who deal with abused or neglected children is to protect the child, remove him or her from the home if necessary and collaborate with social service agencies to assure that the needs of the child are met.

◆

The dedication in *Deprived Children: A Judicial Response* notes: "The efforts of skilled and committed judges, legislators, law enforcement officers, health and child care workers, doctors, teachers, attorneys, volunteers and others involved in the lives of deprived children can do little without a rekindled national awareness that the family is the foundation for the protection, care and training of our children."

*Combating Violence . . . Action Plan* (1996, p. 10) suggests the following collaborative efforts which might break the cycle of violence:

- Improve juvenile and family court handling of child abuse and neglect cases by disseminating information to communities on model dependency court programs and protocols.
- Strengthen at-risk family support services and fund comprehensive health, educational, nutritional, social and other services that give children a healthy start.

- Support community-based services that reduce family violence and victimization.
- Provide training and technical assistance to strengthen agencies serving children and their families.
- Improve services to children who are victims of abuse and other crimes by continuing to provide support for the development and enhancement of local CASA's (Court Appointed Special Advocate for Children) and funding for multidisciplinary teams at children's advocacy centers.

Notice that several of these efforts will require the support of the municipality, the main source of funding. Community policing advocates might also seek federal grants for innovative programs in this area.

## YOUTH WITH SPECIAL NEEDS AND THE POLICE OFFICER

Police officers may have to deal with children who have very special needs.

◆

Children with special needs include those who are emotionally/behaviorally disturbed, who have learning disabilities, who have an attention deficit hyperactivity disorder or who have behavior problems resulting from prenatal exposure to drugs, including alcohol, or to HIV.

◆

### Emotionally/Behaviorally Disturbed Children

One group of young people police will encounter are emotionally/behaviorally disturbed children, often referred to as **EBD.** Usually EBD youth exhibit one or more of the following behavioral patterns:

- Severely aggressive or impulsive behavior.
- Severely withdrawn or anxious behavior such as pervasive unhappiness, depression or wide mood swings.
- Severely disordered thought processes that are reflected in unusual behavior patterns, atypical communication styles and distorted interpersonal relationships.

Parents and teachers in some communities have expressed concerns that children labeled as EBD have fewer coping skills to deal with police contacts than other children and may be traumatized by such contacts. Suggestions that police not interview or contact such children unless an EBD specialist is present have, for the most part, not been implemented because it is usually impossible for the police to know who is EBD and who is not.

Police may assume that a large percentage of children who are suspects in crimes are EBD and that condition is one of the causes of their unlawful behavior. It is not possible, however, to arrange for an EBD specialist to be present at all police contacts because a majority of contacts are unplanned, unscheduled events that occur on the street.

## Youth with Attention Deficit Hyperactivity Disorder

**Attention deficit hyperactivity disorder** (ADHD) is one of the most common disruptive behavior disorders in children. It is estimated that 5 to 10 percent of all children have the disorder; boys are four times more likely than girls to be diagnosed with it. This disorder is characterized by the following behaviors:

- Heightened motor activity (fidgeting and squirming).
- Short attention span.
- Distractibility.
- Impulsiveness.
- Lack of self-control.

Such behaviors are likely to be very unnerving for parents, teachers and other adults who must deal with children who have this disorder.

The *Washington Post* (1993, p. A7) notes: "Children with ADHD . . . often do poorly in school, have low self-esteem, and try the patience of parents and friends. The condition is treated with behavior modification and often with a drug called Ritalin." Although the condition often disappears by adulthood, by then former ADHD children often have other behavior problems including drug abuse, alcoholism or personality disorders.

## Youth with Learning Disabilities

An estimated five to ten million children suffer from some form of learning disability in the United States. The Association for Children with Learning Disabilities (ACLD) (p. 4) describes a learning disabled child in the following way:

◆

A person with a **learning disability** is an individual who has one or more significant deficits in the essential learning processes.

◆

The federal government, in The Education of All Handicapped Children Act, defines a learning disability as follows:

> Specific learning disability means a disorder in one or more of the basic psychological processes involved in understanding or in using language, spoken or written, which may manifest itself in an imperfect ability to listen, think, speak, read, write, spell, or to do mathematical calculations. The term includes such conditions as perceptual handicaps, brain injury, minimal brain dysfunction, dyslexia, and developmental aphasia. The term does not include children who have learning problems which are primarily the result of visual, hearing or motor handicaps, of mental retardation, of emotional disturbance or of environmental, cultural, or economic disadvantage.

According to the ACLD (p. 3): "The most frequently displayed symptoms are short attention span, poor memory, difficulty following directions, inadequate ability to discriminate between and among letters, numerals, or sounds, poor reading ability, eye-hand coordination problems, difficulties with sequencing, disorganization and numerous other problems." Such children are often discipline problems, are labeled "underachievers" and are at great risk of becoming dropouts.

Although learning disabilities are usually discussed in an educational context, as noted by the ACLD (p. 8): "The consequences are rarely confined to school or work." Characteristics that may bring a learning disabled youth into conflict with the law include the following:

- Responds inappropriately in many instances.
- Says one thing, means another.
- Forgets easily.
- Is impulsive.
- Needs immediate gratification.
- Has an overabundance of frustration resulting in disruptive behavior.

Other behaviors that are common to youth with learning disabilities include the following (ACLD, p. 8):

- Inability to read and interpret environment and people.
- Inability to adequately interpret their problems and needs.
- Little thought about the consequences of their actions—poor judgment.
- Inability to set realistic priorities and goals.
- Inappropriate conclusions due to deficient reasoning ability.
- Illogical reasons for their actions—sometimes even contradicting what was previously stated.

- Inability to develop meaningful social relationships with others; usually these children are loners.
- Inability to draw appropriate conclusions due to poor reasoning.
- Childish and bossy behavior.

Those who interact with such children need to be patient and communicate effectively. Youth with learning disabilities look like their peers. Inwardly, however, most are very frustrated, have experienced failure after failure and have extremely low self-esteem.

## Youth Exposed to Drugs or HIV Prenatally

Noted pediatrician T. Berry Brazelton (1990, p. 1) suggests: "Intrauterine exposure to drugs is the epidemic of the 1990s. Drug abuse is not new. . . . But the threat today is like a tidal wave." Sautter (1992, p. K2) cites the following statistics from the National Institute on Drug Abuse:

- The number of drug-exposed children born each year ranges from 375,000 to 739,000—possibly 18% of all newborns in the United States.
- Nearly 5% have been exposed to cocaine, from which crack is derived.
- Nearly 17% have been exposed to marijuana.
- Nearly 73% have been exposed to alcohol.
- By the year 2000 as many as *four million* drug-exposed children will be attending school.

The term **crack children** is sometimes used to refer to children who were exposed to cocaine while in the womb. They may exhibit social, emotional and cognitive problems.

Griffith (1992, p. 30) cautions against stereotyping such children, however, noting that: "[T]he media have sensationalized the problems these children present and have shown worst-case scenarios as if they were the norm."

Another pressing problem is that of **fetal alcohol syndrome (FAS).** Burgess and Streissguth (1992, p. 24) suggest: "Fetal alcohol syndrome (FAS) is now recognized as the leading known cause of mental retardation in the western world." They estimate that approximately one in 500 to 600 children is born with FAS and one in 300 to 350 children has FAS effects, including the following:

- Impulsivity and poor communication skills.
- Inability to predict consequences or to use appropriate judgment in daily life.
- Small children may exhibit a high level of activity and distractibility.
- Adolescents may suffer frustration and depression.

Tyler (1992, p. 711) cites the following "classic symptoms of drug-damaged children":

- Attention deficit disorder (the child has difficulty concentrating and is easily distracted).
- Hyperactivity (the child is unable to sit still, to be quiet or to control movement).
- Poor coordination (the child is clumsy, unable to control crayons or scissors).
- Low tolerance level (the child is easily frustrated by tasks and gives up quickly).
- Unpredictability (the child has mood swings, temper tantrums).
- Poor memory (the child has trouble following three-step directions).
- Indications of drug use in the home.

Police officers should be aware of these classic symptoms and recognize that they reflect a condition over which the youth has limited or no control.

Yet another group of children at risk and presenting special problems to law enforcement are children who were prenatally exposed to HIV. Such children may experience the following difficulties (Seidel, 1992, p. 39):

- Deficits in both gross and fine motor skills.
- Reduced flexibility and muscle strength.
- Cognitive impairment including decreased intellectual levels, specific learning disabilities, mental retardation, visual/spatial deficits and decreased alertness.
- Language delays.

Children with these special needs started entering grade schools in the early part of 1990 and will be adolescents in the latter part of the decade. Many are likely to be in contact with the police long before then, and many may become status offenders. Others may become more serious offenders. Many youth with special needs are likely to join gangs.

## STATUS OFFENDERS AND THE LAW

For centuries a double standard has existed for that which is expected of youth and of adults. Consider the "offenses" described in the following quote:

The children now love luxury. They have bad manners, contempt for authority, they show disrespect for elders, love chatter in place of exercise. They no longer

*Some behavior by youth is illegal only by virtue of age. Youth may feel guilty about such "illegal" actions as smoking, or they may view them as a way to flaunt the rules. Here thirteen-year-old girls are smoking next to a cigarette vending machine at the local county fair arcade.*

rise when their elders enter the room. They contradict their parents, chatter before company, gobble up their dainties at the table, cross their legs, and tyrannize over their teachers.

Many readers may nod in agreement. This quote, however, is not about the youth of today. It was written by Socrates in 500 B.C.

## The Police Response

Between 80 and 90 percent of children under eighteen commit some offense for which they could be arrested, yet only about 3 percent of them ever are. The reason for the low percentage of arrests is police discretion. Of those who do come into the juvenile justice system, 84 percent are from law enforcement referrals. Police most commonly release minor offenders, with or without a warning, and without making an official record or taking further action. This is called **station adjustment.** These children, many of whom desperately need help of some kind, are not referred to the proper social agency in the community where such help is available.

The police response usually is based on two factors: the specific incident and the "demeanor" of the youthful offender. If the incident is minor and the offender is respectful and appears contrite, the police will usually drop the matter. The older the offender, the more likely the police will be to take official action. Senna and Siegel (1990, p. 655), in discussing what to do with status offenders, state:

> Since its inception, the DSO [deinstitutionalization of status offenders] approach has been hotly debated. Some have argued that early intervention is society's best hope of forestalling future delinquent behavior and reducing victimization. Others have argued that legal control over status offenders is a violation of youth's rights. Still others have viewed status-offending behavior as a symptom of some larger trauma or problem that requires attention. These diverse opinions still exist today.

The *Action Plan* suggests that a system of graduated sanctions be used to provide immediate intervention and treatment for delinquent juveniles (p. 3):

- Intermediate intervention (community restitution, day treatment centers, diversion programs and protective supervision projects) for first-time delinquent offenders and many nonviolent repeat offenders.
- Intermediate sanctions (residential and nonresidential community-based programs, weekend detention, intensive supervision, probation, wilderness programs and boot camps) for many first-time serious and repeat offenders and some violent offenders.
- Secure confinement (community confinement in small, secure treatment facilities or, where necessary, incarceration in training schools, camps and ranches) for offenders categorized as violent or repeat serious offenders.

Again, community support is vital. If citizens have the NIMBY philosophy (not in my backyard) such efforts will be much more difficult.

Referral sources for juveniles will vary from community to community. Among the services commonly available are the following:

- Child welfare and child protection services.
- Community mental health centers.

- Community recreation activities often offered through local park and recreation departments.
- Churches.
- Crisis centers for high-risk/suicidal youths.
- Detox services that take youths.
- Drop-in centers or runaway shelters for youth.
- Groups that work with special needs of adoptive parents and youths.
- Human service councils which can provide brochures, information on food shelves, financial assistance, low-income housing and the like.
- Guardian ad litem programs.
- Juvenile probation/court services.
- Support groups (Alcoholics Anonymous, AlAnon, Adult Children of Alcoholics, Tough-Love Parenting, Emotions Anonymous, Sexual Addicts Anonymous, etc.).
- Victim/witness services.
- YMCA or YWCA programs.
- Youth service bureaus that often run diversion programs. Most counties have such bureaus.

## YOUTH WHO COMMIT SERIOUS CRIMES AND THE LAW

According to Regnery (1991, p. 165): "Juveniles do commit crimes at a rate significantly higher than the rest of the population. In fact, 16-year-old boys commit crimes at a higher rate than any other single age group. These are criminals who happen to be young, not children who happen to commit crimes."

The scene pictured in "Kids Who Kill" (Witkin et al., 1991, pp. 181–82) graphically portrays the deadliness of some youth:

> The datelines change daily, but the stories are chillingly similar. In Washington D.C., 15-year-old Jermaine Daniel is shot to death by his best friend. In New Haven, Conn., Markiest Alexander, 14, is killed in a drive-by shooting. In St. Louis, Leo Wilson, 16, is robbed of his tennis shoes and Raiders jacket and then shot dead. In New York, a 14-year-old boy opens up with a semiautomatic pistol in a Bronx schoolyard, wounding one youngster and narrowly missing another, apparently in a dispute over a girl. . . .

> During every 100 hours on our streets we lose more young men than were killed in 100 hours of ground war in the Persian Gulf. . . . Where are the yellow ribbons of hope and remembrance for our youth dying in the streets?

*This juvenile may learn a somber lesson from being taken into custody by police.*

In 1994, in Chicago, 11-year-old "Yummy" Sandifer killed a 14-year-old girl during a gun battle with a rival gang. When he became the object of a police search, his own gang members shot him down. The reaction from many was surprising:

- Thirteen-year-old who got into frequent fistfights with Yummy: "Nobody didn't like that boy. Nobody gonna miss him."
- A local grocer who had barred him from his store: "He was a crooked son of a bitch. He stood out there on the corner and strong-armed other kids. No one is sorry to see him gone."

Gibbs (1994, p. 56) reports that the mayor of Chicago admitted that Yummy had "slipped through the cracks."

> Chicago's authorities had known Yummy for years. He was born to a teenage addict mother and a father now in jail. As a baby he was burned and beaten. As a student he often missed more days of school than he attended. As a ripening thug he shuttled between homes and detention centers and the safe houses maintained by his gang. The police arrested him again and again and again; but the most they could do under Illinois law was put him on probation.

According to the Cook County public guardian: "If ever there was a case where the kid's future was predictable, it was this case. What you've got here is a kid who was made and turned into a sociopath by the time he was three years old."

Olson (1996, p. 1) offers a grim prediction: "We ain't seen nothin' yet. If we don't get a grip on this generation, there's going to be the devil to pay. They have no conscience, no morals, and they're living for today. They're hardened criminals by age 16 or 17."

The IACP Civil Rights Committee ("Broken Windows . . .," 1997, p. 23) warns: "We are facing a genuine—and growing—threat to our future: a criminal generation that is exceedingly self-centered, has weak empathy, no sense of the future and a radical present-orientation. . . . We pay now, or we pay later."

According to Snyder and Sickmund (1995, p. iv): "While juveniles may not be responsible for most violent crime, the growing level of violence by juveniles does not bode well for the future. If violent juvenile crime increases in the future as it has for the past 10 years, the authors of the *National Report* estimate that by the year 2010 the number of juvenile arrests for a violent crime will more than double and the number of juvenile arrests for murder will increase nearly 150%." See Figure 10.2.

One question frequently raised is whether the contribution of juveniles to the growth of violent crime is a recent phenomenon. According to the National Center for Juvenile Justice: "The juvenile contribution to the violent crime increase is far greater than their contribution to the increases seen in the past. In summary, juveniles are not driving the violent crime trends; however, their responsibility for the growth in violent crime in the U.S. has increased."

Martin (1994, p. 36) suggests: "The two main factors for the rise in teen violence . . . are a shift in adolescent attitudes toward the value of life and the ready availability of handguns." Martin concludes (p. 42): "While community policing cannot in and of itself eliminate violent teen crime, or any crime for that matter, in combination with other efforts on the part of community organizations, government agencies and the schools it can provide a counterbalance to the forces leading to violence."

Blumstein (1995, p. 5) cites the following drug-crime connections:

- Pharmacologically/psychologically driven crime, induced by the properties of the drug.

Juvenile population growth foreshadows increases in violent crimes by juveniles

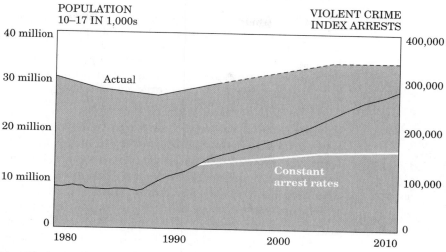

*Figure 10.2*    **Juvenile Population and Arrest Rates**

DATA SOURCE: Analysis based on UCR arrest data and Census Bureau population estimates and projections.

SOURCE: *Combatting Violence and Delinquency: The National Juvenile Justice Action Plan.* Washington: Coordinating Council on Juvenile Justice and Delinquency Prevention, March 1996: 1.

- Economic/compulsive crimes, committed by drug users to support their habit.

- Systemic crime, which includes the crimes committed as part of the regular means of doing business in the illicit drug industry.

The reasons for the increase in serious crimes committed by youth are complex. Eitzen (1992, p. 585) states: "Some children are angry, alienated, and apathetic. A few are uncooperative, rude, abrasive, threatening, and even violent. Some abuse drugs. Some are sexually promiscuous. Some belong to gangs. Some are sociopaths." Eitzen goes on to state: "My strong conviction is that children are *not* born with sociopathic tendencies; problem children are socially created."

The theory that environment has the most effect on a child's development is, however, becoming increasingly controversial. Studies conducted at the University of Minnesota of identical twins separated at birth and raised apart seem to indicate that heredity plays a larger role than previously thought in temperament and behavior. This view is also supported by some studies of adopted children. It would seem that criminals are made *and* born. This view is supported by Harvard Professor James Q. Wilson (1983, p. 86):

> [W]e now have available an impressive number of studies that, taken together, support the following view: Some combination of constitutional traits and early family experiences account for more of the variation among young persons in their serious criminality than any other factors, and serious misconduct that appears relatively early in life tends to persist into adulthood. What happens on the street corner, in the school, or in the job market can still make a difference, but it will not be as influential as what has gone before.

Eitzen (1992, p. 584) notes: "Some young people act in antisocial ways because they have lost their dreams." He contends that families and the youth within those families are shaped by their economic situation and that our economy has changed dramatically. Eitzen uses the analogy of a boat and the traditional argument about the economy that "a rising tide lifts all boats." This was true from 1950 to 1973 when the average standard of living rose steadily. In the past twenty years, however, the "rising tide" analogy has not been accurate.

Eitzen notes: "But since 1973 the water level was not the same for all boats, some boats leaked severely, and some people had no boat at all." The American Dream is fading for many. A home and a college education, things formerly taken for granted, are now out of reach for millions of Americans. In addition, says Eitzen (p. 587): "Children, so dependent on peer approval, often find the increasing gap in material differences between themselves and their peers intolerable. This may explain why some try to become 'somebody' by acting tough, joining a gang, rejecting authority, experimenting with drugs and sex, or running away from home."

An unfortunate result of our changing economy is the rise in poverty in our country.

> Poverty is especially damaging to children. Poor children are more likely to weigh less at birth, to receive little or no health care, to live in substandard housing, to be malnourished, and to be exposed to the health dangers of pollution. . . . Poor children are much more likely than others to be exposed to lead from old paint and old plumbing fixtures and from the lead in household dust. Sixteen percent of white children and 55% of black children have high levels of lead in their blood, a condition that leads to irreversible learning disabilities and other problems.

Eitzen (p. 588) also notes the changes that have occurred in American families: "These trends indicate widespread family instability in American society—and that instability has increased dramatically in a single generation."

Further, the cultural milieu of America greatly affects our youth. Eitzen (p. 588) suggests:

> The highly valued individual in American society is the self-made person—that is, one who has achieved money, position, and privilege through his or her own efforts in a highly competitive system. Economic success, as evidenced by

material possessions, is the most common indicator of who is and who is not successful. Moreover, economic success has come to be the common measure of self-worth.

Competition is pervasive in American society, and we glorify the winners. . . . What about the losers in that competition? How do they respond to failure? How do we respond to them? How do they respond to ridicule? How do they react to the shame of being poor?

. . . They may respond by working harder to succeed, which is the great American myth. Alternatively, they may become apathetic, drop out, tune out with drugs, join others who are also "failures" in a fight against the system that has rejected them, or engage in various forms of social deviance to obtain the material manifestations of success.

## The Police Response

The report of the Coordinating Council on Juvenile Justice and Delinquency Prevention (*Combating Violence and Delinquency: The National Juvenile Justice Action Plan,* 1996, p. 1) stresses: "The Nation must take immediate and decisive action to intervene in the problem of juvenile violence that threatens the safety and security of communities—and the future of our children—across the country."

The *Action Plan* (p. 13) provides the following suggestions for implementing an aggressive public outreach campaign on effective strategies to combat juvenile violence:

- Disseminate public service announcements that help to influence young people's choices to live healthy lifestyles and make all residents aware of the critical roles they can play in reducing delinquency and youth violence.
- Develop a document on ways community residents can reduce juvenile violence.
- Produce a videotape and CD-ROM on reducing juvenile violence.
- Produce a media message on reducing gun violence.
- Link successful local initiatives with a national public information campaign.

Funding for some of the informational pieces might be obtained from corporate sponsors. Communities can also apply for federal grants to pursue these efforts.

*Combating Violence* (p. vii) outlines the following goals of the National Juvenile Justice Action Plan:

1. Provide immediate intervention and appropriate sanctions and treatment for delinquent juveniles.

2. Prosecute certain serious, violent and chronic juvenile offenders in criminal court.

3. Reduce youth involvement with guns, drugs and gangs.
4. Provide opportunities for children and youth.
5. Break the cycle of violence by addressing youth victimization, abuse and neglect.
6. Strengthen and mobilize communities.
7. Support the development of innovative approaches to research and evaluation.
8. Implement an aggressive public outreach campaign on effective strategies to combat juvenile violence.

Objectives 4 and 6 would provide a good starting point for police departments engaged in community policing. Copies of the *Action Plan* can be obtained by calling the Juvenile Justice Clearinghouse at (800) 638-8736. The *Action Plan* can also be ordered via the Internet by sending an e-mail to askncjrs@apensys.com.

Collaborative efforts to provide opportunities for children and youth include the following:

- Provide mentoring opportunities for youth.
- Provide guidance in implementing school-based conflict resolution programs.
- Increase school safety to improve opportunities for youth academic success.

To reduce youth involvement with guns, drugs and gangs, the *Action Plan* (p. 6) makes these recommendations:

- Support interagency gun and drug interdiction and suppression strategies.
- Get guns out of schools by providing guidance and technical assistance on enforcement of the Gun-Free School Act of 1994 and providing alternative education programs to keep youth who are suspended or expelled for weapons law violations off the street.
- Advance youth-focused community-oriented policing through community demonstration projects and technical assistance.
- Provide information on effective curfew programs for juveniles.
- Support community partnership efforts to prevent substance abuse and help youth resist pressure to use drugs.

Kipper (1996, p. 26) suggests: "To address the rising problem of school-related violence, law enforcement officials must bring the community together on several basic issues. First, there must be the understanding that school crime and violence are community issues—not just school problems. . . . The second issue that must be faced by both law enforcement and school officials is the concept that the school is the community and the community is the school." Kipper (p. 31) concludes: "Law enforcement must proactively address the possibility of school crime and violence. By making the schools an integral part of our community policing objective, we will enhance our credibility within our cities and towns. The real winners, however, will be our children."

Revering and Campbell (1996, p. 5) describe their approach to juvenile delinquency using a citizens' anti-crime commission. In April 1994 the department started conducting police-family conferences. Offenders have the choice of appearing in court or participating in a conference. At the conference are the victim, the victim's family, the offender, the offender's family and a role model to the offender. A uniformed police officer first asks the offender to explain his or her actions. Then the victim expresses his or her feelings. Eventually, everyone who wants to talk can do so. By the end of the conference, everyone involved agrees on appropriate retribution. This model is based on seeing crime control as a cultural commitment to shaming and reintegrating offenders.

Koertge and Hill (1996, p. 26) describe a project sponsored by the Enforcement Foundation of Illinois, Inc., called Police and Children (PAC) camp project. "The project was evaluated and one item was statistically significant: 'Working together is a good way to accomplish something.' Clearly, camp 'veterans' viewed the idea of working together to accomplish something more favorably after their camp experience than prior to it." Koertge and Hill conclude (p. 34): "Based on interviews with the officer-counselors, we achieved what we set out to do—build bridges between police and kids." In addition, those attending camps did see the value of teamwork and might be more receptive to getting involved in community efforts to combat juvenile crime and violence.

A relatively recent approach is the use of boot camps for youthful offenders who might otherwise be incarcerated.

Bourque et al. (1996, p. 2) describe boot camps as "characterized by a strong emphasis on military structure, drill, and discipline." They note that the boot camp movement began with a single fifty-bed program in Georgia in 1983 and has since expanded to more than half the states as an intermediate sanction. According to Bourque et al. (p. 5): "Boot camps, in contrast to many other alternatives, offer a particularly attractive package—the chance to pursue rehabilitative goals in an environment that does not appear to coddle delinquents."

The three demonstration programs evaluated were the Cuyahoga County Court of Common Pleas, Cleveland, Ohio; The Boys and Girls Clubs of Greater Mobile, Alabama; and the Colorado Division of Youth Services in Denver, Colorado. Each camp incorporated a structured selection process, a three-month residential boot camp and a six- to nine-month aftercare phase.

Included within the programs were physical training, education, life skills, substance abuse education and counseling, other counseling or therapy, family involvement and community service. Aftercare was an important component of each program. The participants were described as at-risk males often from single-parent families, with low income, poor school attendance, delinquent siblings or peers, gang involvement, drug or alcohol use and a record of disciplinary problems at home or school.

According to Bourque et al. (pp. 79–80): "The [report] has presented some preliminary evidence that youths who entered the demonstration programs during their first year achieved physical fitness, educational, and attitudinal gains during the three-month boot camp."

In general, the programs were found to be successful. Only crude estimates of the programs' operating costs were possible, but data tends to indicate that those costs are lower than the daily costs of confinement in state or local facilities.

Siska and Shipley (1997, p. 33) write that the Adams County (Colorado) Sheriff's Department "has made a conscious decision to invest in the country's future. Community policing, DARE and the SRO programs are strategies designed to reach out and continually work with the youth of our community."

Burden (1994, p. 12) acknowledges the PAL program, celebrating its fiftieth anniversary in 1994, by doing proactive crime prevention for half a century.

The *Action Plan* (p. 11) suggests the following undertakings which might strengthen and mobilize communities:

- Support concentrated strategies to improve distressed neighborhoods and reduce violence citywide through programs such as Empowerment Zones and Enterprise Communities, Operation Weed and Seed and the like.
- Link federal and private initiatives at the community level, for example, by funding the SafeFuture program in selected jurisdictions.
- Advance communities' use of the public health approach to addressing and reducing violence.
- Hold satellite video teleconferences to share information on successful delinquency prevention and juvenile justice system programs that can be implemented at the local level.
- Encourage youth and adults to contribute to the safety of their communities.
- Improve the existing communications infrastructure with efforts such as Partners Against Violence Network (PAVNET) and utilize state-of-the-art technology to enable federal, state and local governments to share information about effective strategies and current research.
- Establish a center to coordinate the delivery of juvenile justice and delinquency prevention training and technical assistance.

- Promote collaborative funding for programs among federal agencies and public and private funding sources.
- Provide youth with activities that encourage positive youth development.
- Provide training and opportunities for youth employment through education, the Job Corps and programs focusing on high-technology skills.
- Establish and support family-based community centers that integrate service delivery through a range of promising prevention programs.
- Provide opportunities for youth to serve their communities.
- Coordinate and disseminate information about federal crime prevention programs.

"Youth Violence in America: Recommendations from the IACP Summit" (1996, pp. 21–29) makes the following recommendations:

- Strengthen the family. Increase services for troubled families and children. Provide enhanced support for parents who lack basic parenting and family management skills.
- Mobilize the community. Establish local delinquency councils to foster community prevention action.
- Reposition law enforcement. Augment or reprioritize police resources to increase the number of youth service school resource, DARE and GREAT programs. Increase the number of trained and equipped community policing officers.
- Recapture the schools. Keep troubled and trouble-making students out of classrooms and in alternative programs. Keep as many schools as possible open after hours as safe havens for students with expanded, extracurricular activities.
- Treat youth violence as an epidemic.
- Strengthen the delivery of justice. Employ a swift and sure justice model for all criminal acts that includes graduated local- and community-based sanctions.
- Strengthen multi-agency partnerships.
- Intensify public education. Encourage local and national media to balance coverage of youth issues by highlighting positive youth behavior and accomplishments. Demand that the electronic media be more accountable for deglamorizing violence and promoting nonviolent alternatives.
- Replicate programs that work. Increase funding for proven programs, like those of the Boys and Girls Clubs and Police Athletic Leagues.

- Improve information sharing. Establish systems to share information among police, justice, education, social services and community-based youth service agencies.

Eitzen (p. 588) underscores the role the community can play in influencing the media:

> [Another] aspect of culture that has special relevance here is the influence of the media, particularly the messages purveyed by television, by the movies, and by advertising. These media outlets glamorize—among other things— materialism, violence, drug and alcohol use, hedonistic lifestyles, and easy sex.

Witkin (p. 181) echoes this theme: "Today's kids are desensitized to violence as never before, surrounded by gunfire and stuffed with media images of Rambos who kill at will." Witkin notes another significant change in the cultural milieu: "By far the biggest difference in today's atmosphere is that the no-problem availability of guns in every nook of the nation has turned record numbers of everyday encounters into deadly ones."

This is *not* to suggest that society is completely to blame for our wayward youth. It is to suggest that for police and the community to deal effectively with delinquency mandates that they deal with underlying causes, a recurrent theme throughout this text. Specific programs aimed at youth are discussed in detail in Chapter 16. Unless police and the community effectively deal with juveniles and make them feel a part of the community, the problem of gangs is likely to grow. This is the focus of the next chapter.

 *Problem Solving in Action*

## Police, Parents Team Up to Teach Traffic Safety

### By Kenneth Bond and Scott Rastin

Bond and Rastin (1995, p. 8) describe how problem solving was used to teach children traffic safety.

The Hamilton Wentworth (Ontario) Regional Police Service's 750 sworn officers serve a population of about 500,000 citizens. The police service also has 500 non-sworn employees.

In 1991, the Hamilton Wentworth Regional Police Community Service Traffic Safety Branch became concerned about traffic accidents involving school children, and decided to evaluate traffic safety programs for school children. "Elmer's Safety Rules" was a program being delivered to children in first grade. This 30-year-old program had an elephant mascot and consisted of seven rules for children to follow around traffic.

### Scanning

Police first analyzed records of traffic collisions in 1990, focusing on children under the age of 16 who were pedestrians or cyclists. In 1990, there were 252 collisions involving the target group. Eighty percent of collisions involving children aged 6 to 8 were "dart-out" collisions, resulting from children darting into traffic from between parked cars. The result was surprising because one of Elmer's rules was not to play between parked cars.

To determine whether these results were an aberration or the norm, officers conducted further study. Records from 1985 to 1989 were evaluated, with similar results. In fact, the number of collisions involving the target group averaged 250 annually over the five years studied. Again, almost 80 percent of accidents involving 6- to 8-year-olds were dart-out collisions.

These data confirmed the need for a new traffic safety program, and officers began working on this task.

### Analysis

After several days' work, the officers involved realized that presenting Elmer's rules to first-grade children did not make them traffic safety experts. In retrospect, this realization was perhaps the most important step in the project. It meant that the officers had to look outside the police department for help.

The officers began by calling people in related organizations, such as city traffic, public health, early education and parents' groups. When advised of the problem, these organizations were surprised that the police were calling them for help. They thought the police were the experts! After many calls and referrals, in July 1991 the officers invited people from a number of disciplines to take part in an advisory committee on traffic safety for children.

The committee discovered that various groups, including public health nurses, teachers and the police, were teaching traffic safety. However, everyone was teaching a different program. This led to a scattered and inconsistent approach.

Based on their combined experiences and professional knowledge, members of the committee identified parents as the best teachers, because they had the most access to their children and were often willing to spend the time required for children to learn traffic safety. However, while parents may be willing to teach their children traffic safety, they often lack the proper information or knowledge to do so. The committee also recognized that in some family settings, due to economics, education and other factors, traffic safety would not be taught, no matter what information was provided.

These conclusions helped the committee to formulate two clear goals. First, parents and caregivers must take an active role in providing traffic safety training to their children. Second, a network of community organizations should assist parents, teaching the same message and reaching children whose parents might fail to educate them.

A study of traffic safety research confirmed the committees' conclusions: community agencies must work together to address traffic safety issues, police officers are not the best safety educators, dart-out collisions are a major cause for concern, parents often fail to become involved in teaching traffic safety, and parents are an important part of any safety program. The committee, not wanting to "reinvent the wheel," studied existing programs that incorporated these goals.

*continued*

The research unearthed a German program and book titled *Traffic Training: Parents Practice With Their Children* (English translation). The program included exercises that taught safe crossing at mid-block and between parked cars, thus addressing the dart-out problem. The committee obtained a copy of the program book and permission to use the material in developing a similar program.

### Response

Two volunteer authors from the committee worked with two police officers to develop the Canadian version of this book—the KIDestrian book and education program.

The KIDestrian program consists of a series of simple, fun exercises that parents or other caregivers teach their children. To address the committee's second goal, the book is also designed to assist community organizations in teaching traffic safety.

Parents can start using the exercises as soon as their children begin walking and playing outside. Important in the first exercises is the idea of stopping at the curb or, in the book's terminology, developing "Kid Brakes." This skill, once learned and made instinctive, becomes an important base from which to build further traffic safety skills.

To accommodate children as they mature and become more independent, the exercises can be adapted to each new stage. As children are allowed to venture out on their own, they tend to take shortcuts and forget safety rules. Rules such as always crossing at corners or never crossing between parked cars are forgotten when a friend is calling from across the street. The fact that children will often take the easiest route to get across the road explains, in part, the high number of dart-out injuries. To address this problem, the book includes exercises that teach crossing safely at mid-block and between parked cars.

The team of authors revised the book several times. After each revision, the book was either field tested or examined by safety experts. Therefore, the book incorporates not only the results of the committee's research, but also advice from traffic engineers, health department officials and educators. The field test included giving the books to parents at two local schools and asking for feedback. The results indicated that over 90 percent of parents and caregivers thought the book was outstanding. Their comments and suggestions were incorporated in each revision.

Public health nurses conducted field tests to determine the effectiveness of the program in communities where English is a second language. Older students took responsibility for explaining the program to parents and younger students. Once again, the study results were extremely positive.

Upon completion of field testing and revisions, the authors produced a very rough prototype of the book and solicited corporations for sponsorship. Corporate sponsorship would mean that the book could be provided free of charge. The committee thought this was important to get parents and others involved.

Canadian Tire, an automotive, sporting goods and hardware retailer with stores throughout Canada, is a leader in children's safety through its Child Protection Foundation. The foundation offered $19,000 to produce a quality prototype of the book. The prototype would be used to attract additional sponsors.

Canadian Tire made the book available in both English and French. The only thing missing was the money required for printing. It would cost approximately $25,000 to print 20,000 copies to initially reach community groups and parents and caregivers with children aged 2 to 9.

Fundraising was not the problem the committee expected it to be. Once organizations learned about the program, they became more than willing to assist, and ended up donating more than the required $25,000. Community members also expressed interest in helping to get the program running. This led to the development of the KIDestrian Team to incorporate community input in making administrative decisions relating to the program. The team included police and community members.

The national postal company, Canada Post, offered to package and distribute the materials at no cost. In addition to this support, Canada Post also mailed out a fundraising request, provided a cash donation, purchased sidewalk chalk to accompany the books and put KIDestrian advertising posters on all postal trucks.

Staff from a national publication called *Today's Parent* offered to print the books at a reduced cost, allowing the team to print 25,000 books instead of the original goal of 20,000. In addition to this support, they used their marketing expertise to enhance the book's layout, making it easier to read and more visually appealing.

As the books were fairly expensive, the team did not want to send them home with children and simply hope that they were used. They chose instead to target particular groups of people connected to children. Members of each group would know the best way to promote and distribute the book to others in their interest group. The team sent letters and order forms to school principals, recreation centers and neighborhood associations, day care centers and home care providers, home school organizations, parent associations, public health nurses, police officers and city traffic officials. In addition, the police video training branch produced a promotional video.

The team launched the KIDestrian program through a media event on April 13, 1994. Within two weeks, the 25,000 books were distributed, with demand exceeding expectations.

### Assessment

Parents eagerly requested the books, as did community organizations. In addition to the groups listed above, the books were purchased and used by senior centers (for training grandchildren), scouting and guide groups, school boards (for incorporating the program into gym classes), babysitter instruction trainers, pediatric physicians and the Canadian Red Cross Society.

Evaluation was an important part of the KIDestrian program from the beginning. The team has not yet been able to measure the program's effect on reducing child traffic injuries. Given the number of variables involved in such accidents, it is hard to make a correlation between a safety program and the number of accidents. The team also recognized that it would be very difficult to have an appropriate control group. So the evaluations focused on whether the KIDestrian program reached its intended audiences and whether those audiences found it useful.

The evaluations gathered information from parents, day care workers and teachers who used the program; other community groups; and the Canadian Association of Chiefs of Police. The evaluations revealed that the KIDestrian program was reaching its intended

*continued*

audiences and that people found it useful. Evaluators pointed out problems with the program, such as the need for a section on rural traffic safety and the fact that some sections were hard to follow.

As a result of the evaluations, the books have been redesigned, with new sections on rural and railroad-crossing safety. A KIDestrian community manual has also been developed, which helps community members publicize and disseminate the program through press releases and special events.

In March 1995, the Canadian Tire Child Protection Foundation launched the KIDestrian program nationally. Over 1 million books, in both English and French, have been circulated throughout Canada.

For those of you wondering about Elmer the safety elephant, he's still alive and well, but now he has help teaching traffic safety.

*Kenneth Bond and Scott Rastin are police officers with the Hamilton Wentworth Regional Police. Reprinted by permission of the Police Executive Research Forum.*

# SUMMARY

The most common age for legally becoming an adult is eighteen. *Parens patriae* refers to the government's right to take care of minors and others who cannot legally take care of themselves. Our juvenile justice system uses a one-pot jurisdictional approach, treating abused or neglected children, those who are status offenders and those who are truly criminal in the same way. Status offenses are actions by a juvenile that would not be a crime if committed by an adult, for example, truancy or smoking cigarettes.

The Big D's of juvenile justice are diversion, decriminalization, deinstitutionalization and due process. A justice model views youth as responsible for their own acts. Under the justice model, the good of society takes precedence over society's responsibility to take care of its children as in the welfare model. Street justice occurs when police officers use their discretionary powers to simply talk to youth who are status offenders rather than taking them into custody.

Youth may be victims of abuse, homelessness or lead poisoning. The primary responsibility of police officers who deal with abused or neglected children is to protect the child, remove him or her from the home if necessary and collaborate with social service agencies to assure that the child's needs are met.

Children with special needs include those who are emotionally/behaviorally disturbed, have learning disabilities, have an attention deficit hyperactivity disorder or have behavior problems resulting from prenatal exposure to drugs, including alcohol, or to HIV. A person with a learning disability is an individual who has one or more significant deficits in the essential learning processes.

## Discussion Questions

1. At what age do individuals become adults in your state?
2. When you were a teenager, did you get into any trouble with the law?
3. Do you feel the juvenile justice system should change from a welfare model to a justice model?
4. Do you agree with Springer's proposals to revamp the juvenile court?
5. What examples of street justice have you witnessed? Do you think street justice is fair?
6. Do you know anyone with a learning disability? How has it affected their lives?
7. At what age did you feel you should be considered an adult?
8. Do you feel youth are becoming more violent?
9. Have youth committed any violent crimes in your community within the last few months?
10. Do you feel status offenses should be decriminalized?

## References

Association for Children with Learning Disabilities. "Taking the First Step to Solving Learning Problems." Pittsburgh: Association for Children with Learning Disabilities.

Astroth, Kirk A. "Beyond Ephebiphobia: Problem Adults or Problem Youths?" *Phi Delta Kappan.* (January 1994): 411–13.

Blumstein, Alfred. "Violence by Young People: Why the Deadly Nexus?" *National Institute of Justice Journal.* (August 1995): 2–9.

Bond, Kenneth and Rastin, Scott. "Police, Parents Team up to Teach Traffic Safety." *Problem-Solving Quarterly.* (Spring/Summer 1995): 8.

Bourque, Blari B.; Cronin, Roberta C.; Pearson, Frank R.; Felker, Daniel B.; Han, Mei; and Hill, Sarah M. *Boot Camps for Juvenile Offenders: An Implementation Evaluation of Three Demonstration Programs.* Washington: National Institute of Justice Research Report, 1996.

Brazelton, T. Berry. In *Identifying the Needs of Drug-Affected Children: 1990 Issue Forum.* Washington: Office for Substance Abuse Prevention, U.S. Department of Health and Human Services, 1990.

Briscoe, Judy. "The Cost of Child Abuse and Neglect." *Corrections Today.* (December 1994): 26–28.

Brodt, Stephen J. and Smith, J. Steve. "Public Policy and the Serious Juvenile Offender." In *Taking Sides: Clashing Views on Controversial Issues in Crime and Criminology,* 2nd rev. ed. edited by Richard C. Monk, 171–80. Guilford: The Dushkin Publishing Group, Inc., 1991.

"Broken Windows . . . Shattered Dreams." *The Police Chief.* (February 1997): 23.

Burden, Ordway P. "A PAL of Long Standing." *Law Enforcement News.* (October 15, 1994): 12.

Burgess, Donna M. and Streissguth, Ann P. "Fetal Alcohol Syndrome and Fetal Alcohol Effects: Principles for Educators." *Phi Delta Kappan.* (September 1992): 24–30.

*Combating Violence and Delinquency: The National Juvenile Justice Action Plan.* Washington: Coordinating Council on Juvenile Justice and Delinquency Prevention, March 1996.

Cowley, Geoffrey. "Children in Peril." *Newsweek.* (Special Issue, Summer 1991): 18–21.

Craig, Susan E. "The Educational Needs of Children Living with Violence." *Phi Delta Kappan.* (September 1992): 67–71.

"Direct from the Source: Sex Offenders Prey on Young Family Members." *Law Enforcement News.* (March 15, 1996): 1.

Doyle, Grey. "Juvenile Violence: Identifying the At-Risk Teenager." *Law and Order.* (June 1996): 90–92.

Drowns, Robert W. and Hess, Kären M. *Juvenile Justice,* 2nd ed. St. Paul: West Publishing Company, 1995.

Eitzen, Stanley. "Problem Students: The Sociocultural Roots." *Phi Delta Kappan.* (April 1992): 584–90. Used by permission of the author.

Freeh, Louis J. "Youth Programs that Work." *The Police Chief.* (February 1997): 26–28.

Gibbs, Nancy R. "Murder in Miniature." *Time.* (September 1994): 55–63.

Greenfield, Lawrence A. *Child Victimizers: Violent Offenders and their Victims.* Washington: Bureau of Justice Statistics and the Office of Juvenile Justice and Delinquency Prevention, March 1996.

Griffith, Dan R. "Prenatal Exposure to Cocaine and Other Drugs: Developmental and Educational Prognoses." *Phi Delta Kappan.* (September 1992): 30–34.

Hodgkinson, Harold. "Reform versus Reality." *Phi Delta Kappan.* (September 1991): 9–16.

Johnson, Tim. "Community Policing: America's Best Chance to End Youth Violence." *Community Policing Exchange.* (January/February 1996): 1.

Kipper, Bobby. "Law Enforcement's Role in Addressing School Violence." *The Police Chief.* (June 1996): 26–31.

Koertge, George F. and Hill, Janice R. "PACT: Bringing Police and Children Together." *The Police Chief.* (August 1996): 26–34.

Krisberg, Barry. "The Evolution of the Juvenile Justice System." In *Criminal Justice 92/93,* 152–59. Guilford: The Dushkin Publishing Group, Inc., 1992.

Krisberg, Barry and Austin, James F. *Reinventing Juvenile Justice.* Newbury Park, Calif.: Sage Publications, 1993.

Martin, Deirdre. "Teen Violence: Why It's on the Rise and How to Stem Its Tide." *Law Enforcement Technology.* (January 1994): 36–42.

Needleman, Herbert L. "Childhood Exposure to Lead: A Common Cause of School Failure." *Phi Delta Kappan.* (September 1992): 35–37.

"Number of Young Killers Triples in Past Decade." (Minneapolis/St. Paul) *Star Tribune.* (March 8, 1996): A4.

Olson, Robert. "What They Are Saying." *Law Enforcement News.* (September 15, 1996): 1.

Pace, Denny F. *Community Relations Concept.* Incline Village, Nev.: Copperhouse Publishing Company, 1991.

Regnery, Alfred S. "Getting Away with Murder: Why the Juvenile Justice System Needs an Overhaul." In *Taking Sides: Clashing Views on Controversial Issues in Crime and Criminology,* 2nd rev. ed. edited by Richard C. Monk, 164–70. Guilford: The Dushkin Publishing Group, Inc., 1991.

"Report: 1 Million Cases of Child Abuse." (Minneapolis/St. Paul) *Star Tribune.* (April 2, 1996): A4.

Revering, Andrew C. and Campbell, H. Allen. "Anoka Finds Alternative to Broken Juvenile Justice System." *Community Policing Exchange.* (January/February 1996): 5.

Sautter, R. Craig. "Crack: Healing the Children." *Phi Delta Kappan Special Report.* (November 1992): K1–K12.

Seidel, John F. "Children with HIV-Related Developmental Difficulties." *Phi Delta Kappan.* (September 1992): 38–56.

Senna, Joseph J. and Siegel, Larry J. *Introduction to Criminal Justice,* 5th rev. ed. St. Paul: West Publishing Company, 1990.

Siska, Paul and Shipley, David. "The Law Enforcement Alliance with Community: Reaching Out to Youth." *The Police Chief.* (February 1997): 30–33.

Snyder, Howard N. and Sickmund, Melissa. *Juvenile Offenders and Victims: A Focus on Violence.* Washington: National Center for Juvenile Justice, May 1995.

Springer, Charles E. *Justice for Juveniles.* Washington: U.S. Department of Justice, Office of Juvenile Justice and Delinquency Prevention, 1986.

Stevens, Linda J. and Price, Marianne. "Meeting the Challenge of Educating Children at Risk." *Phi Delta Kappan.* (September 1992): 18–23.

Tyler, Rachelle. "Prenatal Drug Exposure: An Overview of Associated Problems and Intervention Strategies." *Phi Delta Kappan.* (May 1992): 705–10.

*Washington Post.* "Attention Deficit-Hyperactivity Caused by Gene Defect, Study Says." (Minneapolis/St. Paul) *Star Tribune.* (April 8, 1993): A7.

Wexler, Sanford. "Adult Crime Is Down, But Youth Violence Is on the Rise." *Law Enforcement Technology.* (October 1996): 60–66.

"What's Killing America's Children." *Law Enforcement News.* (December 15, 1995): 14.

"Which Is the Most Violent Nation for Children? It's U.S." (Minneapolis/St. Paul) *Star Tribune.* (February 7, 1997): A1.

Widom, Cathy Spatz. *The Cycle of Violence.* Washington: National Institute of Justice Research in Brief, October 1992.

Widom, Cathy Spatz. *Victims of Childhood Sexual Abuse—Later Criminal Consequences.* Washington: National Institute of Justice Research in Brief, March 1995: 1–8.

Wilson, James Q. "Thinking About Crime." *The Atlantic.* (September 1983): 86.

Witkin, Gordon et al. "Kids Who Kill." *Criminal Justice 92/93:* 181–85.

"Youth Violence in America: Recommendations from the IACP Summit." *The Police Chief.* (December 1996): 21–29.

## *Resources*

Association for Children with Learning Disabilities (ACLD), 4156 Library Road, Pittsburgh, PA 15234; (412) 341-1515.

Office of Juvenile Justice and Delinquency Prevention (OJJDP), 633 Indiana Avenue N.W., Washington, DC 20531; (202) 724-7782.

*Chapter 11*

# Communicating with Gangs and Gang Members

*Street gangs prey upon their neighborhood much like a malignant growth which continues to spread through its host until only a wasted shell remains.*

—"Street Gangs of Los Angeles County"

## Do you know

- What the difference is between a gang, a street gang and a youth gang?
- Which term is preferred by most local law enforcement agencies?
- What two basic functions are served by youth gangs?
- How contemporary gangs can be classified?
- How gang activity can be identified?
- What approaches have been used with youth gangs in the past forty years?
- What five strategies for gang intervention were identified by the OJJDP?
- Which strategy best predicted a decline in the gang problem?
- What are keys to successful gang-reduction programs?

## Definitions

Can you define these terms: gang, graffiti, representing, street gang, turf, youth gang.

# Introduction

Gangs are now spreading through our society like a violent plague. Daily, countless news stories depict the tragedy of gang violence. The following document only the tip of the problem:

- A gang fight at a crowded park resulted in a seven-year-old girl being shot in the head, while picnicking with her family.
- Shot gun blasts from a passing car, intended for a rival gang member, strike a child.
- A shoot-out between rival gangs killed a high school track star as he jogged around the school track.

Gangs can have different characteristics. There are some gangs whose intent is violence. Other gangs focus on crime commission, and violence is a by-product. The same is true with a gang's relationship to drugs. Some gangs focus on doing drug business, and others engage in business for the purpose of meeting their own drug needs.

Dart (1992, p. 96) suggests: "Violence perpetrated by street gangs is a principal—if not the major—social affliction affecting American communities today. In the last decade of the 20th century, gangs exist in virtually every community—suburban, as well as inner-city—in every metropolitan area. Rather than seeking socially acceptable means of achieving influence, gangs use violence, harassment, intimidation, extortion and fear to control a neighborhood."

The California Attorney General's Report, March 1993, notes: "Criminal street gangs have become one of the most serious crime problems in California. Gang violence—particularly assaults, drive-by shootings, homicides, and brutal home-invasion robberies—accounts for one of the largest, single personal threats to public safety in this state." The report indicates that gang membership has seen a 280 percent increase over the past eleven years.

This chapter begins with a variety of definitions of gangs and a discussion of why some youths are attracted to gangs. This is followed by an explanation of the expansion of gangs, the gang structure, outward trappings of gangs, their symbols and indicators of gang activity. The chapter concludes with strategies for dealing with the gang problem and descriptions of programs specifically designed to combat the gang problem, including recommendations from the National Symposium on Community Institutions and Inner City Crime.

## GANGS, STREET GANGS AND YOUTH GANGS

Gangs are defined as "any ongoing organization, association, or group of three or more persons, whether formal or informal, having as one of its primary activities the commission of one or more of the criminal acts . . ., which has a common name or common identifying sign or symbol, whose members individually or collectively engage in or have engaged in a pattern of criminal gang activity" (California Penal Code Section 186.22[f]). A gang *member* is defined as "any person who actively participates in any gang with knowledge that its members engage in or have engaged in a pattern of criminal gang activity, and who willfully promotes, furthers, or assists in any felonious criminal conduct by members of that gang" (California Penal Code Section 186.11[a]).

The definitions of gangs, street gangs and youth gangs provided by Spergel et al., 1990) are central to the following discussion.

◆

A **gang** is a somewhat organized group of people for some duration with a special interest in violence for status-providing purposes.

◆

Gangs are identified by turf concerns, symbols, special dress and colors. A gang is recognized by both its members and by others.

◆

A **street gang** is a group of people who form an allegiance based on various social needs and engage in acts injurious to public health and public morals. This is the preferred term of most local law enforcement agencies.

◆

Dart (1992, p. 96) says:

A street gang is an association of individuals who exhibit the following characteristics, in varying degrees:
- A gang name and recognizable symbols.
- A geographic territory.
- A regular meeting pattern.
- An organized, continuous course of criminality.

Members of street gangs engage in (or have engaged in) gang-focused criminal activity either individually or collectively. Gangs create an atmosphere of fear and intimidation in a community. Most local law enforcement agencies prefer the term *street gang* because it includes juveniles and adults and designates the location of the gang and most of its criminal behavior.

◆

For criminal justice policy purposes, the **youth gang** is a subgroup of a street gang.

◆

Spergel et al. (1990, p. 3) suggest:

The notion of *youth gang* incorporates two concepts: often a more amorphous "delinquent group" (e.g., a juvenile clique within a gang), and the better organized and sophisticated "criminal organization." The latter may be an independent group or clique of the gang and usually comprises older youth and young adults primarily engaged in criminal income-producing activity, most commonly drug trafficking.

## WHY YOUTHS JOIN GANGS

As Dart (1992, p. 96) explains: "If kids are not getting the recognition they seek at home, at school or from their peer group, they may seize upon the chance to identify themselves with a gang. In a gang, troubled youths find the fellowship and sense of identity they lack; participation in gang activities leads to acceptance."

Gangs fulfill socialization and survival functions for youths in low-income, socially isolated ghetto or barrio communities and in transitional areas with newly settled populations. Often the gang takes the place of family.

◆

Gangs provide their members with a feeling of belonging as well as protection from other youth.

◆

Some experts estimate that more than 80 percent of gang members are illiterate and find it almost impossible to get a job. They may turn to gangs as a way to earn a living through drug trafficking, illegal weapons sales, robbery and theft.

According to Osman and Haskins (1996, p. 1): "Gangs are one of the results of poverty, discrimination and urban deterioration. Some experts believe that young people, undereducated and without access to good jobs, become frustrated with their lives and join gangs as an alternative to boredom, hopelessness and devastating poverty."

## THE DEVELOPMENT OF GANGS

Street gangs have operated in the United States since the 1820s. Irish Americans in five point districts of New York City organized the Forty Thieves and engaged in murder, robbery and street muggings. These gang members came from overcrowded areas with substandard housing, poor or nonexistent health care, broken homes and few opportunities to improve their situation.

Osman and Haskins (1996, pp. 1–3) trace the development of gangs from the beginning of the European settlement in America when gang-like activity could be observed. Gang members from the poorer classes and from the same race or ethnic background tended to band together for protection, recreation or financial gain.

During the nineteenth century "criminal" gangs began to form. Irish immigrants formed the first American criminal gangs in New York City.

Early in the twentieth century the U.S. economy worsened, the population grew rapidly and the gap between rich and poor widened. All across the nation gangs appeared where poor, hopeless people lived.

In the 1950s gang fighting rose to an all-time high with gang members using guns, knives and homemade weapons. The fights were usually over girls or turf. The 1960s saw a decline in gang violence, perhaps because drug use escalated and individuals were caught up in a new racial consciousness focusing on civil rights and Vietnam War protests. By the 1970s gangs were again making headlines. Membership grew and the potential for violence increased significantly.

Since the 1980s guns have decided gang arguments quickly in wars usually fought like guerrilla warfare with sniping from rooftops and quick shots from speeding cars. Frequently innocent bystanders are killed in the crossfire.

Despite all of the social and economic advances made since the 1820s, many of the same conditions still exist today and explain the continued existence of street gangs.

Street gangs now exist across the United States. Originating on the East Coast, they have flourished in California, particularly the Los Angeles area, Chicago and other major cities in the United States. Not content to confine their activities to the crime-ridden areas of the large cities and searching to expand their drug trade, the Los Angeles and Chicago gangs have invaded other previously untouched areas of the United States. As noted by Taylor (1991, p. 103): "The increase and spread of youth gangs in today's United States constitute a movement that must be recognized and understood. Gangs can no longer be defined in traditional, preconceived terms. Social and economic factors have redefined them, and their imperialistic spread is a multidimensional movement."

Miller (1991, p. 263) suggests: "Youth gangs in the 1980s and 1990s are more numerous, more prevalent, and more violent than in the 1950s, probably more so than at any time in the country's history." Table 11.1 indicates where gangs were a chronic problem and where they were an emerging problem as of 1990.

Gangs have been reported in all fifty states and come from diverse backgrounds. Members are usually male between the ages of thirteen and twenty-four.

The Internet may become a new avenue for gang expansion with gangs using the Web to reach new recruits and promote street gang alliance.

A new type of gang has emerged in the early 1990s: *party crews*. As Valdez (1997, p. 24) describes them:

The crews can contain both female and male members or can be just one gender. The flexible turf they claim is called the "party scene."

Although many of the crews have no specific dress style, crew members often dress in stylized clothing worn by street gang members, including baseball caps

*Table 11.1* **Type of Gang Problem by Area (City, County, Site)**

| *Chronic Problem Cities/Areas* | *Emerging Problem Cities/Areas* |
| --- | --- |
| Albuquerque, NM | Atlanta, GA |
| Chicago, IL | Benton Harbor, MI |
| Chino, CA | Cicero, IL |
| Detroit, MI | Columbus, OH |
| East Los Angeles, CA | Evanston, IL |
| El Monte, CA | Flint, MI |
| Inglewood, CA | Fort Wayne, IN |
| Long Beach, CA | Fort Worth, TX |
| Los Angeles City, CA | Hialeah, FL |
| Los Angeles County, CA | Indianapolis, IN |
| New York, NY | Jackson, MS |
| Oakland, CA | Louisville, KY |
| Pomona, CA | Madison, WI |
| Philadelphia, PA | Miami, FL |
| Phoenix, AZ | Milwaukee, WI |
| San Diego, CA | Minneapolis, MN |
| San Francisco, CA | Reno, NV |
| San Jose, CA | Rockford, IL |
| Santa Ana, CA | Sacramento, CA |
| Stockton, CA | Salt Lake City, UT |
| Tucson, AZ | Seattle, WA |
| | Shreveport, LA |
| | Sterling, IL |
| | Tallahassee, FL |

| *Chronic Problem—*<br>*Institutional Sites* | *Emerging Problem—*<br>*Institutional Sites* |
| --- | --- |
| California Youth Authority[a] | Ethan Allen School (WI) |
| Sunrise House (CA) | Glen Mills School (PA) |
| | McClaren School (OR) |
| | Paramount School (CA) |

[a]In much of the analysis, only the California Youth Authority is included as an area along with cities or county areas. It has also dealt with the youth gang problem since before 1980.

SOURCE: C. Ronald Huff. *Gangs in America.* Newbury Park: Sage Publications, Inc. 1990: 292. Reprinted by permission.

and oversize clothing. Some party crew members wear tattoos and use slang and hand signs for communication . . . Substance abuse is common and expected from party crew members. Rivalries begin when crews compete over who throws the biggest party. . . .

The use of alcohol, marijuana, nitrous oxide, sex and music are a critical part of the party . . . Of all the types of parties hosted by the party crews, the "house party" seems to be the most dangerous. The house will be physically located within a gang turf and local gang members have a tendency to "crash" the party.

## GANG DIVERSITY

According to Huff (1991), gang membership and activity is quite diverse. He notes (p. 28) that "new generation" research on gang activity documents the increasing diffusion and diversity of gangs as well as the relationship between gangs and drug use. In fact, drugs "represent a unifying economic force for gangs just as alcohol did for organized crime during Prohibition."

Contemporary gangs can generally be classified as one of three types.

◆

Contemporary gangs may be classified as scavenger, territorial or corporate.

◆

Taylor (1991, p. 105) describes the three types of gangs.

**Scavenger Gangs.** Members of these gangs often have no common bond beyond their impulsive behavior and their need to belong. Leadership changes daily and weekly. They are urban survivors who prey on the weak of the inner city. Their crimes are usually petty, senseless and spontaneous. Often acts of violence are perpetrated just for fun. They have no particular goals, no purpose, no substantial camaraderies. Scavenger gang members generally have the characteristics of being low achievers and illiterates with short attention spans who are prone to violent, erratic behavior. The majority come from the lower class and the underclass.

**Territorial Gangs.** A territorial gang, crew, group or individual designates something, someplace or someone as belonging exclusively to the gang. The traditional designation of territory as it relates to gangs is better known as turf.

When scavenger gangs become serious about organizing for a specific purpose, they enter the territorial stage. During this stage, gangs define themselves and someone assumes a leadership role. . . .

Gangs defend their territories in order to protect their particular business. The word is out on the street to everyone: "This is gang territory—stay away." . . .

Mobility through financial power is the distinguishing factor between the traditional definition of territory and the nontraditional concept of territory. . . . Prior to the windfall of illegal drug profits, territory as a concept was limited to the immediate neighborhood. Today, with the power of organized crime, technology and escalating wages, territory can be intrastate, interstate or international.

**Organized/Corporate Gangs.** These well-organized groups have very strong leaders or managers. The main focus of their organization is participation in illegal money-making ventures. . . . Discipline is comparable to that of the military, and goals resemble those of Fortune 500 corporations.

Spergel and Curry (1991) contend that the key problem components of gang formation are economic deprivation, lack of opportunities, social disorganization and the failure of community institutions.

## GANG STRUCTURE

The internal structure of some gangs tends to be formal, similar to any corporate structure. Because of their structure, gangs tend to be mirror images of each other. Usually led by small groups of hard-core members (approximately 10 to 15 percent of the membership), the structure is usually as follows:

President
Vice President
War Lord
   Gestapo or Goon Squad
   Armorer
Spokesman
Peacemaker
Advisor

The *president* (prez, king, general, prince) is the supreme leader of the gang and has unlimited authority. Usually the president is older and smarter than other members of the gang, shrewd, articulate, charismatic and, for some reason, often of small stature. The president must retain the gang's respect by warding off rivals for the position, resolving internal problems, successfully confronting rival gangs and demonstrating leadership through critical periods or crisis situations.

The *vice president* is a close, trusted follower of the president and supports him in all decisions. The vice president is in charge of gang rituals and sometimes of discipline.

The *war lord* or *war counselor* is usually the most aggressive member. When the gang is in conflict, the war lord may actually assume control of the gang until the situation is resolved.

The *gestapo* or *goon squad* work for the war lord. These hard-core members enforce the war lord's will, correcting internal and external problems by force. The *armorer* also works for the war lord and is responsible for securing the gang's weaponry and keeping it in working order. Only the armorer and a few trusted gang members know where the weapons are stored.

The *spokesman* (statesman or intelligence officer) often acts on behalf of the president. The spokesman knows all the details of the gang's activities, alliances, treaties, territorial boundaries and disputes.

The *peacemaker* position exists in large gangs and is usually held by an older member. The peacemaker has proven skill in dealing with other gangs to establish alliances and settle gang disputes inside and outside the group.

An *advisor* to the gang is an older, often "retired" gang member who may or may not have a direct affiliation with the group. The gang consults with the advisor out of respect for his beneficial advice in previous matters.

The hard-core members who hold these leadership positions pose a threat to the community and the police because (1) they typically possess guns and other weapons, and (2) they tend to be aggressively anti-social and are encouraged to be so by the gang as long as their behavior does not violate gang rules or discipline.

The *marginal membership* is a much larger group that surrounds the hard-core members. The marginal members are not privy to the inner activity of the gang and are relegated to follower roles. Hard-core members are recruited from the marginal membership.

Gangs use children ages nine to fifteen, called *Peewees,* to commit crimes such as shoplifting, burglaries, armed robberies and drug sales in schools. Their youthful appearance is used to advantage because they often do not arouse suspicion. If caught, the criminal justice system deals more leniently with juveniles than adults.

Females are used by gangs in a variety of ways. They may:

- Serve as lookouts for crimes in progress.
- Conceal stolen property or tools used to commit crimes.
- Carry weapons for males who do not want to be caught with them.
- Carry information in and out of prison.
- Provide sexual favors (they are often drug dependent and are physically abused).

Like juveniles, females arouse less suspicion than male adults. Figure 11.1 depicts one way of viewing gang organization.

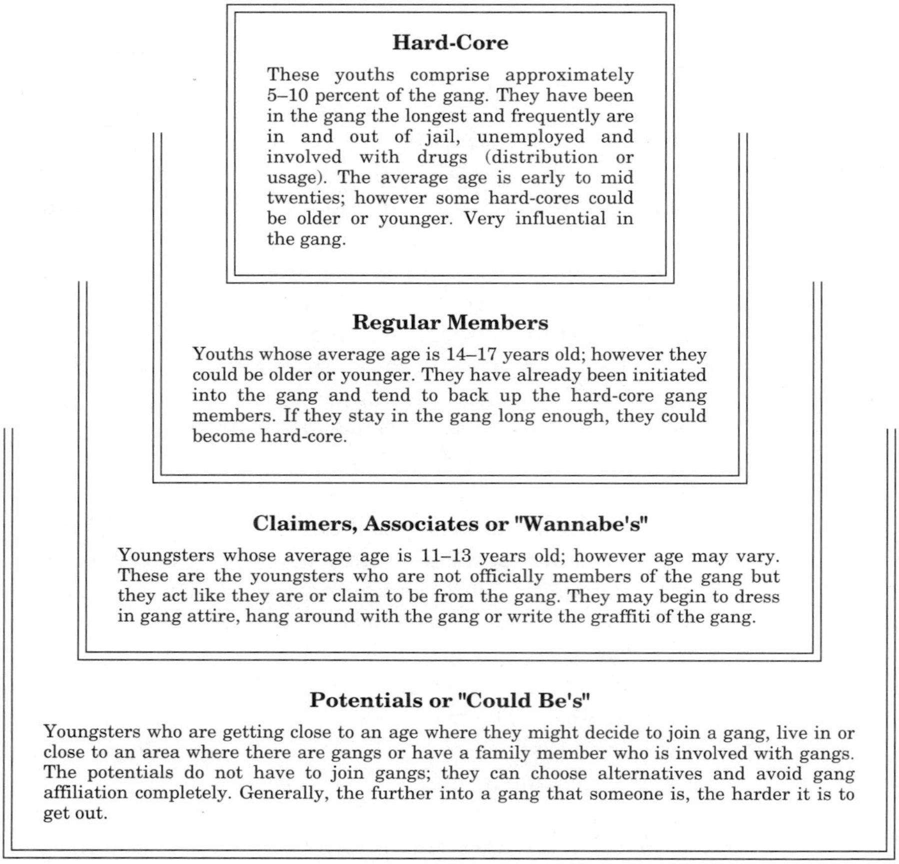

### Hard-Core

These youths comprise approximately 5–10 percent of the gang. They have been in the gang the longest and frequently are in and out of jail, unemployed and involved with drugs (distribution or usage). The average age is early to mid twenties; however some hard-cores could be older or younger. Very influential in the gang.

### Regular Members

Youths whose average age is 14–17 years old; however they could be older or younger. They have already been initiated into the gang and tend to back up the hard-core gang members. If they stay in the gang long enough, they could become hard-core.

### Claimers, Associates or "Wannabe's"

Youngsters whose average age is 11–13 years old; however age may vary. These are the youngsters who are not officially members of the gang but they act like they are or claim to be from the gang. They may begin to dress in gang attire, hang around with the gang or write the graffiti of the gang.

### Potentials or "Could Be's"

Youngsters who are getting close to an age where they might decide to join a gang, live in or close to an area where there are gangs or have a family member who is involved with gangs. The potentials do not have to join gangs; they can choose alternatives and avoid gang affiliation completely. Generally, the further into a gang that someone is, the harder it is to get out.

*Figure 11.1*    **Gang Organizational Chart**
SOURCE: Robert W. Drowns and Kären M. Hess. *Juvenile Justice,* 2nd ed. St.Paul: West Publishing Company, 1995: 258. All rights reserved.

## PROFILE OF A GANG MEMBER

A typical gang member is usually poor and often has a need for protection and a need to belong. A gang member often develops into an anti-social, aggressive, hostile person who rebels against society and who gets support for his feelings of anger and frustration from the gang structure.

Gang members are usually between the ages of nine and thirty. The majority are between thirteen and twenty-three.

The typical gang member is also male. Gangs are overwhelmingly male organizations; the male-female ratio is approximately twenty to one.

The ethnic/racial makeup of gangs has changed over the past few decades from predominantly white gangs to the majority of gangs now being African American, Hispanic and Asian. Some Native American gangs also exist in certain parts of the country. There seems to be a correlation between the racial makeup of gangs and the racial makeup of our society at or near the poverty level.

The lifestyle of a gang member is narrow and limited primarily to the gang and its activities. The typical gang member is a school dropout, unemployed and in trouble with the police. The gang provides its members with an identity and status. Members develop fierce loyalty to their respective gang and become locked into the gang's lifestyle, values, attitudes and behavior. It eventually becomes quite difficult for a member to break away from a gang.

## OUTWARD TRAPPINGS OF THE GANG

Gangs establish **turf,** territorial boundaries, within which they operate and which they protect at all costs from invasion by rival gangs. Turf begins at the meeting place which is the center of gang activity. This can be any place such as the backroom of a grocery store, the basement of a neighbor's home or a room in an abandoned building. The meeting place provides a sanctuary when a gang member is in trouble, a refuge when home life is intolerable, a hideout from the police, a hiding place for weapons, a place to plot future gang activities, a retreat and a safe haven.

A gang's turf is centered at its meeting place and spreads out through the community. Gangs are very territorial. Boundaries are well defined, and it is not unusual for boundaries to be clearly specified among gangs in written pacts. Rival gangs should never infringe upon these boundaries. If a gang does cross into another gang's territory it is understood that the response may be violent.

## GANG SYMBOLS

Like corporations, gangs use symbols or logos to identify themselves. In addition, a gang's choice of colors is important. The symbols and colors indicate whether the gang is an independent organization or a branch or affiliation of an already established group. Common gang symbols include the following:

- Pyramid.
- Ring of fire.
- Five- and six-pointed stars.
- All-seeing eye.
- Crossed pitchforks.

- Crown.
- Variations of the "Playboy" bunny.
- Champagne glass.

Gangs use graffiti to define their boundaries and mark their turf. Graffiti consists of painting gang symbols on walls, buildings, bridges, bus stops and any other available public surface. Graffiti has very specific meanings to gangs. (See Figure 11.5 on p. 347.)

Any misrepresentation or destruction of the gang's unique symbols could bring violent retribution against the offender, whether he knows the meaning of the symbols or not. Painting over graffiti on a building can result in dire consequences.

In addition to marking territory, gangs use graffiti to show opposition or contempt for rival gangs. Contempt is shown by displaying a rival gang's symbols upside down, backwards or crossed out. This is a very serious insult to the rival.

*Hand signs* are a means of showing allegiance or opposition to another group. Most hand signs duplicate or modify the sign language used by the deaf and hearing impaired. Occasionally, legitimate use of hand signs has jeopardized the safety of the users. For example, two deaf women signing to each other on a street corner were shot and killed by gang members who thought they were members of a rival gang.

**Representing,** like hand signs, is used to show allegiance or opposition to a gang. It is based on a manner of dress which uses an imaginary line drawn vertically through the human body. Anything to the left of the line represents left or "dress left," and *vice versa.* An example of right dress would be a hat cocked to the right side, right pants leg rolled up and a cloth or bandanna tied around the right arm.

Other important symbols are tattoos, certain hair styles, including cutting gang designs in the hair, gold jewelry in gang symbols and certain cars. The following symbols, used by the Disciples gang, create a snapshot of gang symbols:

- Refer to themselves as "folk."
- Major insignia is the six-pointed star.
- Dress to the right.
- Colors are black and blue.
- Earrings, if worn, are in the right ear.
- One glove may be worn on the right hand.
- One pocket, right side, is turned inside out, sometimes dyed one of the gang's colors.

- Right pant leg rolled up.
- Two fingernails on right hand painted gang colors.
- Hoods of sweatshirts dyed gang colors.
- Shoes or laces of right shoe are gang colors.
- Belt buckle worn loose on the right side.
- Bandanna in gang colors worn on right side.

The Disciple nation includes affiliates of the Simon City Royals, Ambrosse, Harrison Gents, Imperial Gangsters, Spanish Cobras, Latin Disciples, Latin Eagles, Satan Disciples, Latin Jivers, Two-Six Boys, etc. Their major rival, the Vice Lords, have a similar way of representing their gang symbols and also have many affiliates.

The primary problem with gangs is noted in *Street Gangs of Los Angeles County:* "Street gangs prey upon their neighborhood much like a malignant growth which continues to spread through its host until only a wasted shell remains." The largest of the Los Angeles gangs are the Bloods and the Crips. Offshoots of these gangs have penetrated most large cities west of the Mississippi.

## INDICATORS OF GANG ACTIVITY

Many signs indicate gang activity.

◆

Indicators of gang activity include graffiti, drive-by shootings, intimidation assaults, murders and the open sale of drugs.

◆

**Graffiti** may appear on neighborhood buildings and walls to mark gang turf. Drive-by shootings, intimidation assaults and murders are among the criminal activities of gangs. Gangs declare entire streets and neighborhoods as their turf. Gangs sell drugs openly. Children as young as eleven or twelve are identified by the pagers they carry constantly and become drug runners for gangs. Residents of neighborhoods in which gangs flourish become filled with fear. Some citizens become virtual prisoners in their own homes, afraid to get caught in the cross-fire of a gang gun battle.

Police-community relations in a gang-infested area are affected by the way local authorities respond to the threats posed by gangs. Typically, police chiefs in cities where gangs have recently arrived are slow to recognize the threat gangs pose to the community. If police chiefs deny the existence of a gang problem, despite mounting evidence to the contrary, the gang problem often grows to

*Gang members at a national gang summit held in Kansas City in May 1993 displaying two fingers held together as a symbol of togetherness.*

unmanageable proportions. On the other hand, if police publicly acknowledge the existence of gangs, this places the police administrator in a Catch-22. Publicly acknowledging gangs simply validates them and provides notoriety, whether named or not.

To effectively respond to gangs, police officers need to understand what gangs are and how they work. To some, gangs are merely a group of individuals in conflict with the establishment. The constant publicity of gangs on television and in the newspapers adds to their "Robin Hood Mystique." There is, however, nothing romantic about gangs. A youth who cannot break away from a gang is likely to have a future filled with continued criminal behavior, repeated arrests and ultimately prison—if he or she lives that long. Gang life is violent and dangerous for gang members and the rest of society.

Street gangs consist of individuals who group together in secret enclaves, yet defiantly identify themselves by signs, symbols and clothing. Gang members have a code of personal honor, yet as their major activity, they engage in a wide range of criminal activities.

To determine if an incident is street gang-related, investigators might analyze each case by the following criteria (Block and Block, 1993, p. 3):

- Representing—Offenses growing out of a signification of gang identity or alliance (such as hand signs, language and clothing).

- Recruitment—Offenses relating to recruiting members for a street gang, which include intimidating a victim or witness.
- Extortion—Efforts to compel membership or to exact tribute for the gang.
- Turf violation—Offenses committed to disrespect another gang's territory.
- Prestige—Offenses committed either to glorify the street gang or to gain rank within the gang.
- Personal conflict—Conflicts involving leadership or punitive action within the rank and file of a gang.
- Vice—Activities generally involving the street-level distribution of narcotics by street gang members.
- Retaliation—Acts of revenge for offenses against the gang by rival gang members.

## BRIEF DESCRIPTIONS OF REPRESENTATIVE GANGS

This section contains a brief history and description of the symbols, colors and affiliates of the B-Boys, the Disciples, the Latin Kings, the Naturals, the Vice Lords and cult-oriented gangs.

### B-Boys

Affiliates:  None

Colors:  None

Represent:  None

Symbols/Terms:  Bombers
                Bubble Letters
                Throw-Ups
                Characters
                Crews
                Hip Hop
                Kings
                Tags
                Toys

**Brief History.**  This group consists of talented juveniles and young adults who share a common interest in "tagging" and "graffiti." Publicity surrounding New York City subway art introduced a variety of visual styles in the 1970s which have since been popularized in such European cities as Amsterdam, Barcelona, Berlin, Bruhl, Copenhagen, Paris, Sydney and Vienna.

*Figure 11.2*    **Typical Examples of B-Boys Graffiti**

Members are committed to specific forms of self-expression and strive to display their statements in public places. Some are known to take their ideas from such publications as *Subway Art* (1984) and *Spraycan Art* (1987). See Figure 11.2.

## Disciples

Affiliates:  Black Disciples
            Black Gangster Disciples
            Black Gangsters
            Simon City Royals—white
            Crips

Colors:  Blue/White and Blue/Black

Represent:  Right
            "All is One"
            Folks

Symbols:  Six-Point Star
          Pitchforks
          Sword
          Winged Heart

*Figure 11.3*    **Typical Examples of Disciples Graffiti**

**Brief History.**  Based primarily in Chicago, the Disciples are known variously as the Black Gangster Disciples, Black Disciples or Black Gangsters. This group has the reputation of being one of the most feared and highly organized black street gangs.

Recruitment by hard-core members is selective and sophisticated, particularly in the prison setting. Allegiance to the "nation" is demanded and frequently tested. Members have rank and must follow a chain of command.

This group is frequently engaged in drug wars, and the members with rank are often heavily armed. See Figure 11.3.

## Latin Kings

Affiliates:  Latin Saints
             Vice Lords
             Bloods

Colors:  Gold/Black/Red

Represent:  None

Symbols:  Three-Point Crown
          Five-Point Crown

*Figure 11.4*   **Typical Examples of Latin Kings Graffiti**

**Brief History.** Latin Kings are typically young Hispanics who have settled in inner-city neighborhoods. Members are intensely loyal and follow codes of conduct which have been handed down orally within some families for generations. The chain of command is informal, and members remain close socially.

Latin Kings have been common in some Latino neighborhoods in Los Angeles since the 1940s. Today, Latin Kings exist in most large cities with Hispanic communities. Criminal activity varies among groups depending on neighborhood circumstances and the needs of the more powerful individuals in each group. See Figure 11.4.

## Club/Naturals/Crue

Affiliates:  None

Colors:  None

Represent:  None

Symbols:  Letter "N"

**Brief History.** Native Americans are members of this group. The group structure is somewhat casual, and individuals display strong social bonds. Individuals in this group tend to be neatly dressed and "natural" with few outward identifiers. Members are often associated with illegal drug activity and auto theft. See Figure 11.5.

*Figure 11.5*    **Typical Examples of Naturals Graffiti**

## Vice Lords

Affiliates:  Latin Kings
           Conservative Vice Lords
           Insane Vice Lords
           4 Corner Hustlers
           Micky Cobra Stones
           War Lords
           Bloods

Colors:  Red/Black
       Black/Gold

Represent:  Left
         "People All is Well"

Symbols:  Five-Point Star
        Martini Glass
        Crescent
        Pyramid
        Top Hat
        Cane

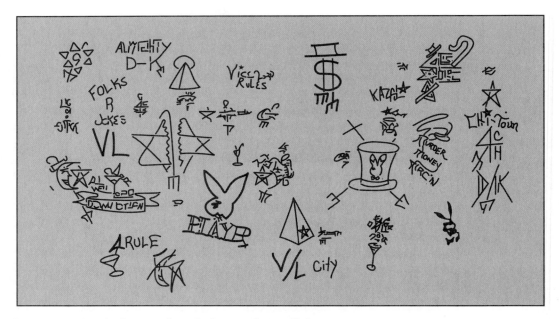

*Figure 11.6*    **Typical Examples of Vice Lords Graffiti**

**Brief History.** There are nineteen subfactions of this group in the City of Chicago as well as in the Illinois prison system. Vice Lords have existed in Minneapolis and Chicago since the 1950s, and the group now has factions throughout the South.

The membership tends to be young, and recruitment is aggressive in schools and on the streets. The imagery of this group tends to glamorize a lifestyle centered on drugs and predatory crime. The behavior patterns of the young members are patterned after the old and bolder Vice Lord members. See Figure 11.6.

### Cult-Oriented

Affiliation:  Stoners

Colors:  None

Represent:  None

Symbols/Terms:  Pentagram
                    Hexagram
                    Inverted Cross
                    Cross of Nero
                    "A" in Circle (Anarchy)
                    Black/White Candles

*Figure 11.7*    **Typical Examples of Cult-Oriented Graffiti**

Goat's Head
Sign of Beast (666)
Swastika

**Brief History.** While not commonly regarded as a street gang, cult-oriented youth tend to band together and participate in anti-social behavior which can conflict with others. The practice of Satanism has been combined with drugs and an interest in "heavy metal" music to produce bizarre behavior in some individuals.

Drug-induced rituals are popular and known to include systematic mutilations, grave robbing and desecration of religious places. Furthermore, some cult-oriented activity has included murder. See Figure 11.7.

## STRATEGIES FOR DEALING WITH THE GANG PROBLEM

The Office of Juvenile Justice and Delinquency Prevention (OJJDP) undertook a study to determine what has historically been done to address the problem of youth gangs as well as what is currently being done. The OJJDP study found a distinct difference in the approach used in the 1950s and 1960s compared to that used in the 1970s and 1980s.

◆

In the 1950s and 1960s law enforcement used a social services approach toward youth gangs. During the 1970s and 1980s law enforcement focused on a suppression approach.

◆

Neither approach to youth gangs is clearly superior. Some communities adopted a comprehensive approach that combines social services intervention and suppression strategies.

The OJJDP also surveyed 254 experts from forty-five cities and six special programs as to what strategies they were currently using. Those who were surveyed identified five strategies.

◆

The five strategies law enforcement currently uses to address the gang problem are as follows:

- Suppression.
- Social intervention.
- Social opportunities.
- Community mobilization.
- Organizational development or change.

◆

*Suppression* includes tactics such as prevention, arrest, imprisonment, supervision and surveillance. *Social intervention* includes crisis intervention, treatment for the youths and their families, outreach and referral to social services. *Social opportunities* include providing basic or remedial education, training, work incentives and jobs for gang members. *Community mobilization* includes improved communication and joint policy and program development among justice, community-based and grassroots organizations. Finally, *organizational development* or change includes special police units and special youth agency crisis programs.

According to the OJJDP survey, law enforcement most frequently used suppression as a strategy to address the gang problem; 44 percent of those reporting used it. This was followed by social intervention (31.5 percent), organizational development (10.9 percent), community mobilization (8.9 percent) and social opportunities (4.8 percent).

Although only a small percent of the reporting agencies used community mobilization, according to the OJJDP (p. 3): "Community mobilization was the factor that most powerfully predicted a decline in the gang problem."

◆

Community mobilization is the most effective strategy to address the gang problem.

◆

The OJJDP survey also found that providing gang members with basic social opportunities, including education and employment, were also important in combatting the gang problem.

Osman and Haskins (1996, p. 5) list the following strategies put forward by sociologists, social workers, law enforcement personnel and citizens from battered communities:

- Create jobs for young people.
- Develop community programs in the arts, sports, etc.
- Make sure young people receive a good education.
- Prevent children from joining gangs in the first place by providing other challenging opportunities.
- Create alternative living situations for children who cannot stay at home.
- Provide counseling services for families and young people.
- Society as a whole must look at problems of poverty and discrimination.
- Individuals can fight prejudice by beginning to appreciate cultural differences.
- Young people can do their part by being open to alternative activities.

Spergel and Curry (1991, p. 295) list the following community organization strategies for dealing with gang problems:

- Cleaning up graffiti in the community.
- Involving the schools.
- Mobilizing the community.
- Building community trust.
- Involving parent groups in community programs.
- Educating the community.
- Changing the community.

Spergel and Curry conducted a survey of forty-five cities or urban areas to determine the scope of the youth gang problem. They also examined the response of different types of agencies and cities to the problem. Their findings are as follows (p. 309):

> More resources alone for police or even human service programs would not contribute much to dealing effectively with the youth gang problem. It is more likely that community mobilization and more resources for and reform of the educational system and the job market, targeted at gang youth or clearly at-risk youth, would be more cost-effective as well as more effective in the reduction of the problem.

*A teen participant in a neighborhood cleanup project prepares to paint over gang-related graffiti on a bench in an inner-city park.*

> Police recommendations emanating from these findings would not necessarily require a renewed war on poverty, but rather a series of programs targeted specifically at the youth gang problem addressing not only issues of economic deprivation and lack of opportunities but social disorganization and the mobilization of community institutions in a concerted attack on the problem.

Furst (1991, p. A1, A3) describes a community project where eleven teenagers, most gang members, and two adult artists made ninety wooden lawn chairs for a neighborhood "plagued by crime and fear and crack." The two artists obtained funding from a local foundation and other sources to pay the neighborhood youth $4.50 an hour to build the chairs. To most of them, it was not the money, but the chance to do something positive that was important. As one gang member said: "It gave me something to do. . . . If there isn't anything to do, people walk up and down the street messing with people." Said another youth who claimed membership in two gangs, the Four Corner Hustlers and the Vice Lords: "It's cool. We did something for the block, and it was kind of fun. Everybody worked together."

Weston (1993, p. 80) describes the Community Action Team (CAT) approach to gangs used in Reno, Nevada: "Community policing normally means that the community is included as a partner with police in dealing with community issues, allocation of resources and problem solving. The Reno Police Department carried this philosophy a step further, designing the new CAT team with guidance from members of the local minority neighborhoods, community service agencies and political leaders." He concludes (p. 84): "A lesson learned early in Reno was that there is no aspect of policing that could not benefit from a collaboration with the community."

### Intelligence Gathering

An important strategy in most police departments is gathering information on gangs and their members.

Jackson and Gordon (1995, p. 48) note: "The Atlanta Police Department's new computerized Gang Intelligence System (GANGIS) has quickly demonstrated its effectiveness as a crime-fighting tool." They say: "Comprehensive suspect and gang profiles were instantly established on the basis of a partial name, a nickname, partial vehicle information or other skimpy details." They conclude (p. 53): "The implementation of GANGIS facilitates the development of more comprehensive and effective strategies that will deprive gang members of the anonymity they currently enjoy as they cross jurisdictional boundaries."

The article "Tracking Gangs . . ." (1997, p. 4) notes: "Community policing is about going back to grassroots. . . . This back-to-basics approach, however, doesn't mean that community policing only works if you use tools from the past. In fact, the entire concept is driven by innovative problem solving, and in today's world, innovation often requires technology." This article further notes: "A major force behind proactive gang enforcement is intelligence—knowing what gangs are out there, where they are, the names of the individual gang members and what gangs they belong to, where they have been seen, and who they've been seen with." The article describes a computer program for tracking gangs—called the General Reporting, Evaluation and Tracking (GREAT) system—as a "hot sheet, mug book and file cabinet all rolled into one." (Note: this program is not to be confused with the GREAT program used in the schools to teach children about resisting gangs.)

## PROGRAMS SPECIFICALLY DESIGNED TO COMBAT GANG PROBLEMS

Esbensen (1996, pp. 34–36) describes the Gang Resistance Education and Training Program (GREAT) and found: "Students completing GREAT reported lower levels of delinquency, impulsive behavior, risk-taking behavior and approval of fighting, and higher levels of self-esteem, parental attachment, anti-gang attitudes, perceived educational opportunities and positive school environments."

Los Angeles has a Community Reclamation program that targets sites plagued with gang and drug problems and capitalizes on the strengths and resources of the community. The program sets up a network among community-based organizations, law enforcement agencies, government and public agencies and concerned citizens. The program holds regular community meetings involving public and private agencies that work together to develop a cohesive plan and avoid duplication. It provides guidance and leadership to community members and assists them in identifying their concerns. If offers alternatives to gangs and drugs such as their graffiti-paint-outs; job workshops; "follow me, I'm gang and drug free" walks; and sports programs.

In Racine, Wisconsin, the police department has instituted a Gang Crime Diversion Program (GCDP). It began when the city's middle schools eliminated their sports programs. As a result they didn't have a gang problem in Racine, they had a nothing-to-do problem (Howell, 1997, p. 4).

Benson (1990) describes a program developed in Austin, Texas, by the police department and concerned citizens to combat an onslaught of graffiti and violence caused by gangs. They formed a group called Citizens Helping Austin Neighborhood Gang Environment (CHANGE). As noted by Benson (p. 66):

> CHANGE is a gang diversion program which uses a varied approach involving juveniles, their parents, churches and community-based organizations in an attempt to contain further gang violence and graffiti. A unique goal of CHANGE is to encourage the gangs to call a truce among themselves long enough to meet and discuss their differences. . . .
>
> Since inception of the program, gang members have filed charges, appeared as witnesses, and signed statements if they have been victimized instead of resorting to violence. . . .
>
> CHANGE approached area businesses with the idea of letting the gangs use their walls for murals instead of for random defacement. Officers are challenging the youths to make their community more attractive than a rivals' by getting rid of neighborhood refuse or helping older residents maintain their homes by helping them mow their lawns.
>
> CHANGE is also channeling the hostility the gangs have for one another into competitive sports [sponsoring a double elimination softball tournament twice a month]. . . . "It was a lot harder to shoot at somebody that you have tried to put out at second base." . . .
>
> The city council was so impressed with the volunteer efforts of the people involved with CHANGE and their remarkable results that they added an additional $240,000 in unsolicited funds to the police budget for the express use of the prevention of juvenile crime.

Philadelphia has developed a boystown called House of UMOJA which seeks to prevent youngsters from joining gangs. It works with youngsters who have gang affiliations or who are at risk of such affiliations. According to Sulton (1990, pp. 17–18), the House of UMOJA provides the following resources and services:

a surrogate family, food, shelter, emotional and spiritual support, life skills and job training, job placement, employment opportunities, counseling, reintegration planning, stress and aggression control training, values clarification and problem-solving skills, remedial reading, remedial math, GED preparation, vocational education, conflict resolution and communication skills, and recreational activities. Sulton notes (p. 18): "The House of UMOJA builds upon the *positive* characteristics of gangs—loyalty, trust, sharing and mutual respect among members."

Another exemplary program is Los Angeles' Community Youth Gang Services Project. According to Sulton (1990, p. 61): "Police estimate that 70,000 children and young adults belong to over 600 gangs [in Los Angeles]. Unofficial estimates indicate that over 100,000 young people belong to gangs and that 150,000 more are at risk of joining gangs." The Los Angeles Community Youth Gang Services Project (YGSP) is a grassroots community-based program aimed at reducing youth gang violence at the individual level through education, employment and involvement in positive activities.

◆

Keys to successful gang reduction programs are education, employment and involvement in positive activities.

◆

## RECOMMENDATIONS

Recommendations of the National Symposium on Community Institutions and Inner City Crime related to youth gang problems include the following (Sulton, pp. 100–01, used by permission):

1. Parents should be held accountable for their children's behavior and required to participate, with their children, in programs designed to prevent or discourage youth gang membership.
2. Schools and educational programs should develop curricula that discourages youth (grades 3 through 6) from joining gangs. These curricula should use a model similar to that employed by the community Youth Gang Services Project in Los Angeles.
3. Inner-city communities should be encouraged to establish urban boystowns similar to the model developed by the House of UMOJA in Philadelphia. In addition to providing housing, these boystowns should offer a variety of education, employment, and recreational services and maintain cooperative working relationships with juvenile justice agencies, businesses, and human service agencies.
4. Newspapers should exercise caution when publishing stories about youth gang violence. Gang members regularly read newspapers and often perceive articles concerning their violent activities as certificates of notoriety and success.

5. Federal, state, and local governments should expand summer youth employment programs and establish year-round job programs emphasizing community service and neighborhood improvement projects such as graffiti removal. These programs should employ gang members and youth at risk of becoming gang members. Ample supervisory positions also should be allocated.

6. A national task force on gangs should be established by a consortium of community-based organizations working to reduce youth gang violence. It should be funded by private foundations and corporations, and work with federal and local government agencies. It should (a) analyze youth gang violence, (b) develop a comprehensive plan to eliminate youth gang violence and gang warfare, and (c) provide technical assistance to public and private agencies working to eliminate these problems. The task force should consist of representatives of various community institutions and operate under the direction of a national coalition of community-based organizations.

7. A national research and training institute on gang violence and membership reduction should be established and operated under the auspices of a national coalition of community-based organizations. The institute should study the issue of conflict resolution without violence, and collect and analyze data pertaining to gangs, gang-related crime, and gang violence prevention programs. It also should periodically survey gang violence reduction programs, which should in turn submit questions for inclusion in the survey instruments. The institute should disseminate the findings to public and private agencies through publications and formal training programs. Juvenile and criminal justice officials should be encouraged to attend these training programs.

Other programs geared specifically for youth are discussed in Chapter 16.

According to Drowns and Hess (1995, p. 276): "Gangs are a community problem and a national challenge. Responding to gangs requires a systematic, comprehensive and collaborative approach that incorporates prevention, intervention and suppression strategies. While each strategy has a specific vision and pressing mandate, the greatest hope is on the side of prevention, for only by keeping children from joining gangs in the first place will we be able to halt the rising tide of terror and violence that gangs represent."

*Problem Solving in Action*

Bernardy (1995, pp. 1, 6–7) describes how problem solving was used to eliminate a gang problem in Reno, Nevada.

## Neighborhood Is Finally Free of Gang-Related Problems

**By Dave Bernardy**

Friendship Lane is a one-square-block area in the Northeast section of Reno, Nev. Ninety-five percent of the residents are non–English-speaking Hispanics. Most residents work at low-income jobs, and some have extended families living in two-bedroom duplexes. Local gangs found a criminal haven in this area by intimidating the residents.

Due to numerous calls for service based on gang-related incidents, including drive-by shootings, loud parties, drinking in public and drugs, the Reno Police Department began a problem-oriented policing project called the Friendship Lane Pilot Project.

### Scanning

Officers gathered information from a number of sources for the scanning and analysis phases of the project, including citizen meetings, calls for service, field interviews with gang members and officer observations.

A review of the calls for service in the area revealed that the department had received 255 calls from January to June 1994. Of these 255 calls, 11 percent were gang-related, as described by the complainant. Eleven percent of the total calls required a return visit by the officer; 9 percent of the calls involved crimes such as burglary, property destruction, auto theft and larceny; and 5 percent of the calls pertained to suspicious people and vehicles in the area.

The Reno Police Department has a Community Action Team (CAT) that works with local gangs. The CAT had conducted several field interviews with gang members in the Friendship Lane area. That information was reviewed for times, dates and circumstances of activity. Several officers on various shifts also drove through the area and made independent observations.

The gang that had "adopted" the area was a large Hispanic group called the Montellos (after a local street). According to the CAT's field interviews, none of the gang members lived in the area. The residents were easy prey for this gang, who threatened them if they called the police. Because of cultural and language barriers between residents and police, many incidents went unreported, and residents distrusted the police. The gang felt free to conduct all types of activities in the area, including stripping stolen vehicles, drinking in public and using abandoned apartments to take drugs and store weapons— presumably the weapons that they used in drive-by shootings.

### Analysis

To understand the root causes of the problem and come up with a response, officers used the above-mentioned information gathered from the CAT, crime data and officer observations, along with a series of community meetings that confirmed and added to this

*continued*

information. Those meetings resulted from the residents' growing concern about safety and the increase in drive-by shootings that threatened the safety of children and the whole neighborhood.

Police officers asked residents what they thought the problems were and what they wanted the police department to do about them. The residents listed several problems, but the number-one problem was the gang that had taken over their neighborhood. The gang's graffiti was ruining the appearance of the area, and residents were tired of the neighborhood's reputation as a gang-infested area. They also voiced serious concerns about the safety of their children. Because the streets were very dark due to lack of lighting, the gang members would drive their "low-rider" vehicles through the streets at high speeds and would not see the children playing.

Most gang activity took place between dusk and early morning. Inadequate street lighting meant that much of the activity went unnoticed.

Taken together, information from residents, police and the field interviews revealed two main factors that gave the gang opportunity to act in this neighborhood: (1) poor communication between residents and police, due to language and cultural barriers and intimidation of residents by gang members; and (2) environmental factors, such as poor lighting and streets well-suited for fast driving. It became apparent that the most effective and long-lasting solution would address those factors, thus eliminating the opportunity for criminal behavior.

### Response

In the past, the department had responded with a high level of visibility and enforcement. However, when the police had to direct their attention to other areas of the city, the problem would resurface in the Friendship Lane area. Officers decided that it would be more effective to build working relationships with community residents to gain their trust and support. They decided on several clean-up efforts, with the dual purpose of promoting better police-community relations and improving the area's physical appearance.

The police contacted the media at the beginning of the response phase. The officers did a walk-through of the neighborhood with the media, explaining their approaches to eliminating the gang problem. The public awareness and support received from the media stimulated businesses to assist in the project with donations.

The first step on the agenda was a community clean-up day. The local disposal service donated three large dumpsters. Rakes, shovels and brooms were also donated, and a local tow company loaned the community one of its trucks at no charge. The abandoned cars were towed from the area, the dumpsters were filled and removed, and the area was swept from one end to the other. These clean-up efforts were expanded with the painting over of all the graffiti on the buildings, in order to bolster the neighborhood's image. Through positive publicity, businesses donated enough paint and equipment for all the duplexes in the neighborhood to be painted.

The next phase of the project was lighting improvement. The local power company, with the city's cooperation, erected four large street lights in the darkest areas of the community. A local hardware store donated 30 motion-detector lights, enough for each of the duplexes. In addition, the streets were repaved and speed bumps added to thwart speeding vehicles, thereby reducing the likelihood of drive-by shootings and danger to residents, especially children. A local construction company was contacted and agreed to complete the work at no charge.

As a final step to long-term cooperation and public safety, police helped residents start a neighborhood watch group and plan regular monthly meetings to discuss crime issues. Police also developed a community advisory group that provided information on government services for residents.

This response phase was targeted to be completed in six months. During that time, the officers and community volunteers cleaned up the neighborhood, removed the graffiti, installed security lights, paved the street and established community awareness among the residents.

### Assessment

The residents were empowered to handle many of the problems themselves. They had gained trust in the police department.

The calls for service were compared between the first six months of the year and the second six months, which was the project period. Although calls for service increased during the project period, this may likely be attributed to the residents' increased trust in the police department. Calls regarding gang activity, however, decreased by 100 percent, while calls regarding unwanted people in the area decreased by 50 percent. Additionally, family disturbance calls decreased 50 percent, which may have been an unexpected benefit of the community cohesion the project created.

The officers also completed a resident survey to assess the project's impact. They went with translators to every house in the community and questioned at least one member of each household. The survey comprised 10 questions in both English and Spanish. Because the residents' number-one concern had been the gang problem, officers asked which of the activities completed seemed most successful at reducing the gang problem. Ninety percent said that the improved lighting made the most difference, while others listed the neighborhood watch and the clean-up projects as having the greatest effect. In addition officers asked residents to rate the department's performance in the neighborhood; all survey respondents gave the department the highest possible score. All the residents surveyed said they felt safer after the project.

These are the initial results of the project. The department is completing a second six-month evaluation to see if the project continues to have positive effects.

*Dave Bernardy is a sergeant with the Reno Police Department.*
*Reprinted by permission of the Police Executive Research Forum.*

## SUMMARY

A gang is a somewhat organized group of people with a special interest in violence for status-providing purposes. A street gang (the preferred term for local law enforcement agencies) is a group of people that form an allegiance based on various social needs and engage in acts injurious to public health and public morals. A youth gang is a subgroup of a street gang. Gangs provide their members with a feeling of belonging as well as protection from other youth.

Indicators of gang activity in a neighborhood include graffiti, drive-by shootings, intimidation assaults, murders and open sale of drugs.

Contemporary gangs may be classified as scavenger, territorial or corporate. In the 1950s and 1960s law enforcement used a social services approach to address the problems of youth gangs. In the 1970s and 1980s law enforcement efforts focused on a suppression approach. The five strategies currently being used to address the gang problem are suppression, social intervention, social opportunities, community mobilization and organizational development or change. Community mobilization has the most positive impact on the gang problem.

Keys to successful gang reduction programs are education, employment and involvement of gang members in positive activities.

### Discussion Questions

1. Are there gangs in your community? If so, do they cause problems for the police?
2. Have you seen any movies or television programs about gangs? How are gang activities depicted?
3. What do you think are the main reasons individuals join gangs?
4. How does a youth gang differ from a group such as a Boy Scout troop or a school club?
5. How does a youth gang member differ from other juvenile delinquents?
6. Should convicted youth gang members be treated like other juvenile delinquents, including status offenders?
7. What factors might influence you to become a gang member? To not become a gang member?
8. If you were to try to infiltrate a gang as an undercover agent, what factors would be important to you?
9. Are there efforts in your community to combat the gang problem?
10. Do you think the gang problem will increase or decrease during the 1990s?

### References

Benson, Carol. "Gang Diversion." *Law and Order.* (August 1990): 66–68.

Bernardy, Dave. "Neighborhood Is Finally Free of Gang-Related Problems." *Problem-Solving Quarterly.* (Spring/Summer 1995): 1, 6–7.

Block, Carolyn Rebecca and Block, Richard. *Street Gangs in Chicago.* Washington: National Institute of Justice Research in Brief, December 1993.

Dart, Robert W. "Chicago's 'Flying Squad' Tackles Street Gangs." *The Police Chief.* (October 1992): 96–104.

Drowns, Robert and Hess, Kären M. *Juvenile Justice,* 2nd ed. St. Paul: West Publishing Company, 1995.

Esbensen, Finn-Aage. "Gang Resistance Education and Training: The National Evaluation." *The Police Chief.* (September 1996): 34–38.

Furst, Randy. "2 Artists + 11 Kids = Something of Value." (Minneapolis/St. Paul) *Star Tribune.* (August 24, 1991): A1, A3.

Howell, Art. "Police Department Asks Ex-Gang Members for Help." *Community Policing Exchange.* (January/February 1997): 4–5.

Huff, C. Ronald. *Gangs in America.* Newbury Park: Sage Publications, Inc., 1991.

Jackson, Carter B. and Gordon, Jonathan S. "Atlanta's GANGIS Advances Fight Against Crime." *The Police Chief.* (May 1995): 48–54.

Miller, Walter B. "Why the United States Has Failed to Solve its Youth Gang Problem." In *Gangs in America,* edited by C. Ronald Huff, 263–87. Newbury Park: Sage Publications, Inc., 1991.

Osman, Karen and Haskins, James. *Street Gangs Yesterday and Today, West Side Story Home Page,* 1996: 1–5.

Spergel, Irving A.; Chance, Ronald L.; and Curry, G. David. "National Youth Gang Suppression and Intervention Program." *Juvenile Justice Bulletin.* June 1990.

Spergel, Irving A. and Curry, G. David. "Strategies and Perceived Agency Effectiveness in Dealing with the Youth Gang Problem." In *Gangs in America,* edited by C. Ronald Huff, 288–309. Newbury Park: Sage Publications, Inc., 1991.

Sulton, Anne Thomas. *Inner-City Crime Control: Can Community Institutions Contribute?* Washington: The Police Foundation, 1990.

Taylor, Carl S. "Gang Imperialism." In *Gangs in America,* edited by C. Ronald Huff, 103–15. Newbury Park: Sage Publications, Inc., 1991.

"Tracking Gangs the High-Tech Way." *Community Policing Exchange.* (January/February 1997): 4.

Valdez, Al. "Party Crews Adopt the Street Gang Lifestyle." *Police.* (February 1997): 24–25.

Weston, Jim. "Community Policing: An Approach to Youth Gangs in a Medium-Sized City." *The Police Chief.* (August 1993): 80–84.

## *Resource*

Office of Juvenile Justice and Delinquency Prevention (OJJDP), 633 Indiana Avenue N.W., Washington, DC 20531; (202) 724-7782.

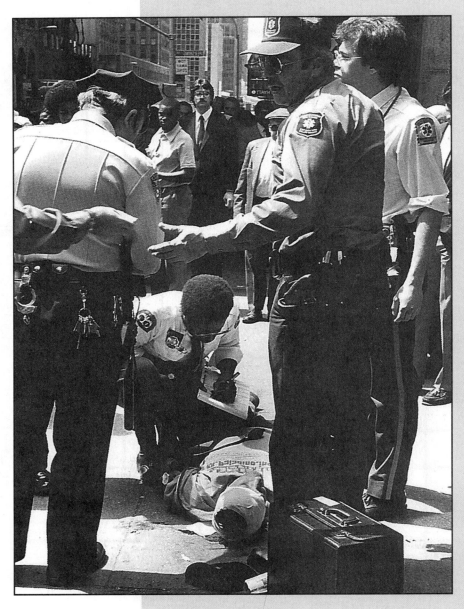

# Chapter 12

# Communicating with Victims and Witnesses

*In the Nation's ongoing fight against crime, statistics tell only part of the story. More than a violation of the law, every crime is a violation of the rights, property, person, or trust of another human being. Thus, behind every tally of offenses ranging from misdemeanors to aggravated felonies are innocent victims—individuals and families who must be recognized in the administration of justice.*

—President George Bush, April 22, 1991, Proclamation of National Crime Victims Rights Week

## Do you know

- How extensive victimization is?
- How victims may be affected?
- What a secondary victim is and who might become one?
- What victimology is and what it includes?
- Who is at most risk of being victimized?
- What second injury victims may suffer?
- What major legislation regarding victims has been passed?
- What a victim impact statement is?
- What national organizations exist to help victims?
- What two types of programs have been established to help victims? What services are most commonly provided in each?
- What rights victims have in most states?
- What special populations have been targeted for additional needs if victimized?

## Definitions

Can you define these terms: allocution, cognitive restructuring, culpability, post traumatic stress disorder (PTSD), primary victim, restorative justice, second injury, secondary victim, victim impact statement (VIS), victim service programs, victim statement of opinion (VSO), victimization, victimology, victim/witness assistance programs, vulnerability.

# *Introduction*

> If you haven't been there, you don't know the feelings of emptiness and fear, and how it changes your life. I was in a state of shock. I walked around in a daze for weeks. I wasn't functioning. No one really understood how I felt.
> —Sherry Price, rape victim.

"No one really understood how I felt." This sentiment, vividly expressed by Sherry Price, currently regional coordinator of the Sunny von Bulow National Victim Advocacy Center, Manhattan Office, and former president of the New York chapter of Victims for Victims, underscores the need of victims to be understood, to not be further victimized by the criminal justice systems.

As noted by Roberts (1990b, p. 13): "After decades of neglect, crime victims are finally being recognized as a vulnerable and forgotten group of people who have rights and are in need of services." Victimization is a much more extensive problem than is often realized.

DiIulio et al. (1993, pp. 8–9) see citizens as "co-producers of justice." They stress: "Citizens in a democracy must begin by holding themselves and their neighbors accountable for public affairs. A democratic vision of the justice system, therefore, is anything but a sop to public frustrations with crime and disorder. Citizens who expect judges, police, and other justice officials to solve society's crime problems are unrealistic; citizens should not expect the officials to succeed without the active cooperation and support of the community."

Strandberg (1997, p. 48) stresses:

> One of the most important things is for law enforcement to be sensitive to the needs of victims and witnesses. Witnesses are essential to the successful prosecution of any case, and working with witnesses to make them feel more comfortable and safe will certainly pay dividends. . . .
>
> Most experts feel that community policing is a major step in the right direction to curb implicit intimidation. When people know the police as members of their own community, they are much more willing to come forward.

This chapter begins by considering the importance of victims and witnesses and the results of being victimized. This is followed by a discussion of victimology, society and victims and the interaction of police officers and the criminal justice system with victims. Victim assistance programs and the police response are highlighted. The chapter concludes with a look at special populations, the response of the criminal justice system and recommendations for communicating with victims and witnesses. Although the material presented here focuses on communicating with victims, most of it also applies to communicating with witnesses to crime.

## THE EXTENT OF VICTIMIZATION

According to Monk (1991, p. 336): "Almost every American family contains one or more members who have been or will be victims of a serious crime. . . . Recently, the Bureau of Justice Statistics reported that 7 out of 8 Americans will be victims of personal theft three or more times within their lifetimes. Most Americans over the course of their lives will be victims of at least one assault."

The National Crime Victimization Survey for 1994 revealed the following (Perkins and Klaus, 1996, p. 1):

> In 1994 U.S. residents age 12 or older experienced approximately 42.4 million crimes. Thirty-one million (73%) were property crimes, 10.9 million (26%) were crimes of violence, and approximately a half million (1%) were personal thefts.

Table 12.1 summarizes criminal **victimization** in the United States in 1994. The violent crime rate has been essentially unchanged since 1992.

◆

National Crime Survey statistics estimate that 42.4 million victimizations were committed in the United States in 1994.

◆

In addition to dealing with victims of crime, police officers also frequently deal with victims of accidents and natural disasters. Law enforcement officials should be trained to assist victims of violent crimes, accidents and natural disasters.

### Victim and Witness Intimidation

According to Strandberg (1997, p. 42): "Victim and witness intimidation is suspected in up to seventy-five to one hundred percent of the violent crimes committed in some gang-dominated neighborhoods." He suggests: "One of the reasons that gangs manage to flourish is that they operate through intimidation." One area police must deal with is courtroom intimidation. Sometimes the court is "packed" with gang members who give threatening looks and suggestive signals to witnesses. Strandberg describes one department that countered this tactic by

*Table 12.1*    Criminal Victimization Experienced in the U.S. in 1994

| | Number in Millions | Rate per 1,000[a] | Percent of Measured Crime | Percent of This Crime Reported to Police |
|---|---|---|---|---|
| **All crimes** | 42.4 | — | 100% | 36% |
| **Violent crime** | 10.9 | 51 | 26% | 42% |
| Simple assault | 6.6 | 31 | 16 | 36 |
| Aggravated assault | 2.5 | 12 | 6 | 52 |
| Robbery | 1.3 | 6 | 3 | 55 |
| Rape/Sexual assault | .4 | 2 | * | 32 |
| **Personal theft[b]** | .5 | 2 | 1% | 33% |
| **Property crime** | 31.0 | 308 | 73% | 34% |
| Property thefts | 23.8 | 236 | 56 | 27 |
| Household burglary | 5.5 | 54 | 13 | 50 |
| Motor vehicle theft | 1.8 | 18 | 4 | 78 |

—Not applicable.
*Less than .1%.
[a]Per 1,000 persons age 12 or older, or per 1,000 households.
[b]Includes pocket picking and purse snatching.
SOURCE: Craig Perkins and Patsy Klaus. *Criminal Victimization 1994*. Washington: Bureau of Justice Statistics, April 1996: 1.

taking an entire class of police cadets into the courtroom: "Gang members, confronted with such a law enforcement presence, gave up and left."

## RESULTS OF BEING VICTIMIZED

The director of the Office for Victims of Crime, U.S. Department of Justice, Jane Nady Burnley (1990, p. 10), suggests: "As we begin the decade of the nineties, a growing and critical rediscovery of the impact of crime and the trauma of crime victims is in full stride in the United States." The results of victimization vary depending on the specific crime committed and the individual who is victimized.

♦

Victims of crime may suffer physical injury, financial and property losses, emotional distress and psychological trauma. Some suffer from **post traumatic stress disorder (PTSD),** a persistent re-experiencing of a traumatic event through intrusive memories, dreams and a variety of anxiety-related symptoms.

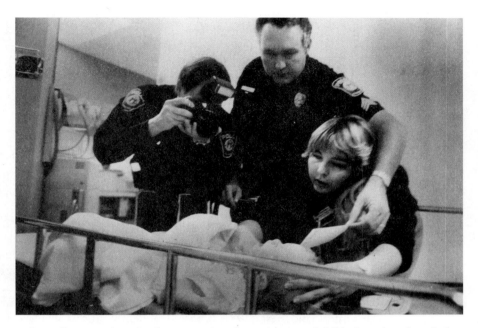

*Police officers and medical personnel gather evidence of child abuse in a hospital emergency room.*

According to Frederick et al. (1990, p. 106): "PTSD is nonselective, affecting professionals and nonprofessionals, males and females, and people of all races and socioeconomic backgrounds." The American Psychiatric Association (1985) presents the following diagnostic criteria for PTSD:

- Existence of a recognizable stressor that would evoke significant symptoms of distress in almost anyone.
- Re-experiencing of the trauma as evidenced by at least one of the following:
  - Recurrent and intrusive recollection of the event.
  - Recurrent dreams of the event.
  - Sudden acting or feeling as if the traumatic event were reoccurring, because of an association with an environmental or ideational (mental) stimulus.
- Numbing of responsiveness or reduced involvement with the external world, beginning some time after the trauma, as shown by at least one of the following:
  - Markedly diminished interest in one or more significant activities.
  - Feeling of detachment or estrangement from others.
  - Constricted affect.

- At least two of the following symptoms that were not present before the trauma:
  - Hyperalertness or exaggerated startle response.
  - Sleep disturbance.
  - Guilt about surviving when others have not, or about behavior required for survival.
  - Memory impairment or trouble concentrating.
  - Avoidance of activities that arouse recollection of the traumatic event.
  - Intensification of symptoms by exposure to events that symbolize or resemble the traumatic event.

Frederick et al. (p. 106) note that PTSD occurs in phases. Table 12.2 summarizes the phases victims are likely to experience as the result of a natural disaster, sexual abuse, physical assault or a hostage-taking situation. The table includes the psychological and physical symptoms of each phase.

Police officers may also experience these symptoms, including PTSD, after responding to shooting incidents or other especially grisly crimes. As noted by Conroy and Hess (1991, p. 65): "Frequently officers involved in shootings have recurrent nightmares. You may dream about a bullet leaving your gun in slow motion and falling ineffectively to the ground or about shooting a person repeatedly without effect." They cite the statement of one officer after a shooting incident:

> In some of the dreams I had been shot, people were holding me and stabbing me. I was being chased by crowds of people. I am being held and then shot by other parties. It is always a group. It is never one person just chasing me.
>
> In some of the dreams I shoot back, and the crowd keeps coming at me. It's like nothing is happening. And they just come up to me and grab me and stab me. The bullets don't seem to stop them. They just keep coming.

Waller (1990, p. 146) notes: "The emotional trauma, or 'invisible wound' is the least evident and understood, but it is often the most brutal effect of crime, not only on the direct victim, but on the victim's dependents and friends."

## Primary v. Secondary Victims

Two types of victims usually result from natural disasters and violent crime:

◆

A **primary victim** is a person actually harmed by an incident. A **secondary victim** is one indirectly affected by the trauma.

◆

In a rape, for example, the woman is, obviously, the primary victim. Her husband may be a secondary victim who also suffers from the trauma. A secondary

*Table 12.2* **Phases and Symptoms of Victimization**

|  | *Phases* | *Psychological Symptoms* | *Physical Symptoms* |
|---|---|---|---|
| **Natural Disaster** | Impact/shock | Anxiety, depression | Insomnia |
|  | Heroic | Depression | Nightmares |
|  | Honeymoon | Phobias | Anorexia |
|  | Disappointment | Hostility, resentment | Hypertension/hyperalertness |
|  | Reorganization | Loss of concentration, marital discord | Startle reaction, sexual inhibition |
| **Sexual Abuse** | Impact/shock | Fear of perpetrator, blunted emotions | Nightmares, stomachaches |
|  | Withdrawal | Shame, guilt, isolation | Diarrhea, startle reactions |
|  | Regression | Depression, marital discord | Sexual inhibition, fast heart |
|  | Compliance/anger | Intrusive thoughts, sexual confusion | Loss of appetite, urinary problems |
|  | Recovery | Irritability, anger, substance abuse | Increased blood pressure |
| **Physical Assault** | Impact/shock | Denial, disbelief, anxiety, muscle tension | Fast heart, dry mouth, enlarged pupils |
|  | Submission/withdrawal | Fear of perpetrator, depression, isolation | Sleeplessness, headaches |
|  | Ambivalence/anger | Fear, momentary anger | Sexual inhibition, chest pains, pale skin |
|  | Dependent aggression | Periodic fear, making mistakes | Increased blood pressure |
|  | Recovery | Guilt, isolation, fear | Loss of sexual interest, increased blood pressure |
| **Hostage Taking** | Impact/shock | Denial/disbelief, anxiety, muscle tension | Loss of appetite, dry mouth, fidgety, clammy palms |
|  | Interaction | Anxiety, phobias | Tension, pacing |
|  | Acceptance/acquiescence | Helplessness, depression, intrusive thoughts | Fitful sleep, nightmares |
|  | Ambivalence/anger | Phobias, loss of concentration | Diarrhea, fast heart, trembling, weight loss |
|  | Recovery | Tension, irritability | Stomach problems, skin disorders, increased blood pressure, startle reactions |

*Police officers may also be victims. This police officer was riding on routine patrol in Canton, Massachusetts, when a drunk driver sped down the road and struck the horse and officer. The impact crushed the horse's rear leg. The mortally injured horse was given a lethal injection.*

victim includes anyone who is close to the primary victim and can truly empathize with that victim. Riggs and Kilpatrick (1990, p. 133) state:

> Data suggest that individuals who are emotionally close to crime victims, particularly those of violent crime, should be assessed for psychological problems and counseled about the difficulties they may face.

> The development of psychological problems that are likely to appear among indirect victims of crime may exacerbate the symptoms of direct victims. For example, a husband faced with the news that his wife has been raped may respond with feelings of guilt, anger, and desire for revenge. These feelings are likely to make it more difficult for him to provide the emotional support that his wife needs to deal with her own response to the rape.

Riggs and Kilpatrick (p. 135) conclude: "It is important for the criminal justice system to recognize the difficulties faced by the friends and family members of crime victims. Those involved in the criminal justice system should help indirect victims find legal and psychological assistance and prepare them for the stress that might result from contact with the criminal justice system." In the case of police officers, as noted by Conroy and Hess (pp. 39–40):

The most obvious way officers become primary victims is through the physical dangers associated with the job. You may be assaulted, shot at, stabbed, or even killed in the line of duty. A much more subtle, more insidious way you become a primary victim, however, is through the psychological effects of your work.

This type of victimization is far less obvious, frequently contrary to established self-image, and until recently, denied to even exist by both officers and management. . . .

For the most part, however, officers seem to become secondary victims. You deal constantly with other people's victimization while the pain and blood are fresh and real.

Lurigio and Resick (1990, pp. 50–63) describe correlates of victim recovery following a traumatic incident. *Previctimization factors* include the following:

- Age—younger victims cope more effectively than older victims.
- Sex—women have been shown generally to be more distressed by crime than men.
- Education and income—victims with little formal education and low incomes are more traumatized than victims from higher socioeconomic and educational groups.
- Previctimization adjustment—a history of prior victimizations is associated generally with poorer adjustment.

Among the *victimization factors* are the following:

- Seriousness of the crime—severity of victim symptoms is related directly to the degree of violence or injury occurring in the incident.
- Relationship between victim and offender—some studies find no difference between victims of stranger and non-stranger offenders. Other studies indicate that women sexually assaulted by strangers were more anxious and depressed than those sexually assaulted by acquaintances.

*Post-victimization factors* that affect recovery include the victim's perception of the event and whether self-blame can be avoided. A victim's recovery is also affected by the ability to cognitively restructure what happened. As noted by Lurigio and Resick (1990, p. 69)

**Cognitive restructuring** is a coping mechanism in which victims reinterpret their experience to ameliorate the adverse effects of the incident. It can take several forms, such as finding meaning in the episode, engaging in downward comparisons (i.e., thinking about themselves as being better off than other real or imagined victims), comparing themselves to a hypothetical "worst world scenario" in that they are harmed to a much greater extent than in reality, and evaluating the event as occasioning personal growth or some other benefit.

The way individuals react to victimization is related to whether they report the incident to the police. As noted by Waller (1990, p. 139): "Given the importance of the victim to the police, one would expect police leaders to have ensured that victims are treated as 'privileged clients.'"

## Nonreporting of Being Victimized

Waller (1990, p. 141) notes that victims are the source of 60 percent of the common crime information known to police. He also notes that more than one-third of the robberies, aggravated assaults, burglaries and rapes reported in the National Crime Survey were *not* reported to the police. He lists the following reasons victims do not report crime (pp. 142–43):

- They believe the police will be unable to do anything. Statistics confirm the victim's view: 75 percent of robberies and 85 percent of burglaries will not be cleared.
- They consider the matter private.
- They fear reprisals and threats.
- They delay while discussing what action to take with a family member or neighbor.
- They fear the reception they might be given by the police.

Kelly (1990, p. 173) says: "A major reason for nonreporting was victims' apprehension as to how they would be treated and whether they would be believed." Waller (p. 144) notes that two out of five victims report crimes because they want to recover their property or file an insurance claim. One in three victims files a report to keep the crime from reoccurring. Less than 10 percent of victims report the crime to see the offender punished. Waller concludes: "The police could aid victims by giving greater emphasis on returning property to its owners and to crime prevention."

# VICTIMOLOGY

In the 1940s scholars became interested in the relationship between criminals and their victims. Benjamin Mendelsohn coined the term *victimology* and proposed that this be a new field of study, not simply a branch of criminology. Researchers in the 1940s and 1950s postulated that in a large percentage of cases, victims were partially responsible for their victimization. In *The Criminal and His Victim,* for example, von Hentig (1948) concludes that personality characteristics of some crime victims contributed to their victimization and that others became victims because of the community in which they lived.

◆

**Victimology,** the study of crime victims, includes the concepts of victims' vulnerability and culpability.

◆

**Vulnerability** suggests that certain groups of people are more susceptible to being victimized because of demographics rather than any unique, individual attributes. For example, are females or the elderly more likely to become victims than males or the young? Are people who live in certain neighborhoods or cities more vulnerable than those who live in other neighborhoods or cities? What about the victimization rate of children or teenagers, who some studies show are victimized far more than the elderly? Does race make a person more likely to be a target? Or does socioeconomic status influence the probability of being victimized? Table 12.3 summarizes answers to such questions for the year 1994.

◆

Bureau of Justice statistics show that those most at risk of being victimized are young, black males with low incomes who live in urban areas.

◆

Laub (1990, pp. 29-32) notes the following correlates of victimization:

- As age increases, the risk of victimization decreases.
- Males are victimized at twice the rate of females.
- The rate of violent victimization—especially aggravated assaults and robberies—is greater for blacks than whites.
- As income goes up, the risk of personal victimization goes down.
- Those who live in urban areas suffer more victimizations than residents of suburban or rural areas.

In addition to vulnerability, victimology also examines culpability. **Culpability** refers to any action of the victim that may in some measure contribute to their victimization. Do victims of auto theft share responsibility for theft if they left the keys in the ignition and the car unlocked? What about the person who continues to live with a violent spouse? Or the rape victim who was walking alone after dark when attacked? The concept of victim culpability is controversial because "blaming the victim" shifts some responsibility from the criminal onto the injured party.

## SOCIETY AND VICTIMS

The "blame-the-victim" syndrome is explained by Teresa Saldana, an actress who received nearly fatal stab wounds from a demented fan (Newton, p. 60): "They

*Table 12.3*  **Victimization Rates for Persons Age 12 or Older, by Type of Crime, Sex, Age, Race, Ethnicity, Income and Locality of Residence of Victims, 1994**

| | | | Victimizations per 1,000 Persons Age 12 or Older | | | | | |
| | | Crimes of Violence | | | | | | |
| | | | | | Assault | | | |
| Characteristics | All Crime | All Crimes of Violence | Rape/ Sexual Assault | Robbery | Total | Aggra- vated | Simple | Personal Theft |
|---|---|---|---|---|---|---|---|---|
| **Sex** | | | | | | | | |
| Male | 61.7 | 59.6 | .2 | 8.1 | 51.3 | 15.3 | 35.9 | 2.0 |
| Female | 45.1 | 42.5 | 3.7 | 4.1 | 34.7 | 8.1 | 26.6 | 2.5 |
| **Age** | | | | | | | | |
| 12–15 | 117.4 | 114.8 | 3.1 | 12.0 | 99.7 | 22.2 | 77.6 | 2.6 |
| 16–19 | 125.9 | 121.7 | 5.1 | 11.8 | 104.8 | 33.7 | 71.1 | 4.2 |
| 20–24 | 102.5 | 99.2 | 5.0 | 11.3 | 82.9 | 26.6 | 56.4 | 3.3 |
| 25–34 | 63.2 | 60.9 | 2.9 | 7.5 | 50.6 | 13.7 | 36.9 | 2.3 |
| 35–49 | 41.4 | 39.5 | 1.6 | 5.2 | 32.8 | 7.6 | 25.2 | 1.9 |
| 50–64 | 16.8 | 15.1 | .2* | 2.3 | 12.6 | 3.3 | 9.3 | 1.7 |
| 65 or older | 7.2 | 5.1 | .1* | 1.4 | 3.6 | 1.2 | 2.4 | 2.1 |
| **Race** | | | | | | | | |
| White | 51.5 | 49.4 | 1.9 | 4.8 | 42.7 | 10.9 | 31.8 | 2.1 |
| Black | 65.4 | 61.8 | 2.7 | 14.0 | 45.0 | 16.6 | 28.4 | 3.6 |
| Other | 49.1 | 47.6 | 2.5* | 9.0 | 36.1 | 11.9 | 24.2 | 1.6* |
| **Ethnicity** | | | | | | | | |
| Hispanic | 63.3 | 59.8 | 2.6 | 9.8 | 47.4 | 16.2 | 31.2 | 3.5 |
| Non-Hispanic | 51.9 | 49.8 | 2.0 | 5.6 | 42.1 | 11.1 | 31.0 | 2.1 |
| **Household Income** | | | | | | | | |
| Less than $7,500 | 88.3 | 83.6 | 6.7 | 11.1 | 65.8 | 20.5 | 45.3 | 4.7 |
| $7,500–$14,999 | 60.8 | 58.6 | 3.3 | 7.1 | 48.1 | 13.8 | 34.3 | 2.2 |
| $15,000–$24,999 | 51.7 | 49.9 | 2.3 | 5.9 | 41.7 | 13.2 | 28.5 | 1.8 |
| $25,000–$34,999 | 51.3 | 49.3 | 1.2 | 4.6 | 43.5 | 11.3 | 32.3 | 2.0 |
| $35,000–$49,999 | 49.3 | 46.8 | .9 | 4.8 | 41.1 | 10.1 | 31.0 | 2.6 |
| $50,000–$74,999 | 47.6 | 46.1 | .8 | 4.2 | 41.1 | 9.5 | 31.6 | 1.5 |
| $75,000 or more | 42.7 | 40.0 | .9* | 4.5 | 34.6 | 8.0 | 26.5 | 2.7 |
| **Residence** | | | | | | | | |
| Urban | 67.6 | 63.6 | 2.7 | 10.9 | 50.1. | 14.8 | 35.2 | 4.0 |
| Suburban | 51.8 | 49.6 | 1.8 | 5.1 | 42.7 | 11.0 | 31.7 | 2.2 |
| Rural | 39.8 | 39.2 | 1.7 | 2.6 | 34.9 | 9.2 | 25.8 | .6 |

Note: The victimization survey cannot measure murder because of the inability to question the victim.
*Estimate is based on about 10 or fewer sample cases.

SOURCE: Craig Perkins and Patsy Klaus. *Criminal Victimization 1994: A National Crime Victimization Survey.* Washington: Bureau of Justice Statistics, April 1996: 4.

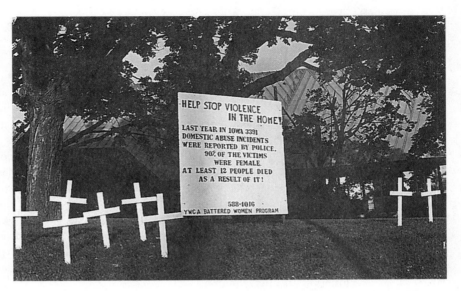

*A shelter for battered women in Iowa. Such shelters often also provide care for children and for abused husbands.*

said I had no business walking alone like that, or that actresses have to expect these things. It was unbelievably painful for me."

This sentiment is echoed by Colleen Davis, who says that becoming a victim "is like becoming a leper" (Newton, p. 60):

> Victims report being dropped by friends, who no longer invite them to parties for fear they'll cast a cloud of doom. Others have been fired by employers who became intolerant of time lost to medical or psychiatric care or time spent at court proceedings.
>
> When crime victims look for comfort, they report, friends advise them to just snap out of it, to brush themselves off and get back in the race.

Why does society treat victims badly? According to Martin Symonds, director of the Victim Treatment Center at the Karen Homey Clinic in New York: "People want to distance themselves from victims. It's a way of saying, 'If this can happen to you, I'm vulnerable.' That makes us uncomfortable." This may also partially explain why people do not want to get involved and, in fact, may not come to the aid of someone in distress.

Often police officers and the entire criminal justice system add "insult to injury" rather than assisting those who have been victimized.

## POLICE OFFICERS, THE CRIMINAL JUSTICE SYSTEM AND VICTIMS

During their careers, police officers deal with many more crime victims than criminals. Most officers feel some frustration, even exasperation with victims because their level of trauma, fear, anger or injury makes it difficult for them to be as cooperative as the officer needs them to be to obtain the maximum amount of information and evidence.

According to Karmen (1992, p. 48): "A relatively small percentage of privileged people harmed by street criminals might enjoy 'first class,' 'red carpet,' or 'VIP' treatment—their rights are scrupulously observed—while socially disadvantaged persons experience mistreatment as 'second-class complainants.'" Victims are often hurt by the physicians, nurses and police officers who interact with them immediately following their victimization. Victims often expect more warmth and assurance from these professionals than they can give. Professionals often assume businesslike attitudes to protect themselves emotionally and to function effectively in crises.

As noted by Waller (1990, p. 146): "Police officers may have difficulty in being sensitive to emotional reaction. In the course of their duties, they deal routinely with crimes and severe accidents in which victims have been physically injured and must handle such situations with professional detachment."

When victims interpret this necessary emotional detachment as a personal rejection, they receive what is commonly referred to as the second injury.

◆

The **second injury** often occurs to victims when they are treated badly by professionals who should assist them, including police officers.

◆

According to Skogan et al. (1990, p. 9): "Crime victims are the 'forgotten persons' of the criminal justice system, valued only for their capacity to report crimes and to appear in court as witnesses." People who have just been victimized may have to endure any or all of the following:

- The police may question the victim insensitively.
- There may be suspicion that the victim was somehow at fault.
- The victim may have difficulty learning what is going on in the case.
- Property is often kept for a long time as evidence.
- Wages may be lost for time spent testifying.
- Victims may find the authorities are indifferent to their fear of retaliation.
- Victims may be fearful of testifying in court.

As Geberth (1992, p. 91) suggests: "A homicide detective must guide the family through a complicated and confusing criminal justice system that is devoid of human compassion. In addition to pursuing the case, he also becomes the advocate for both the deceased and the surviving family throughout the entire process." He notes (p. 95): "Although the law enforcement community is fully aware of the inequities of the criminal justice system, most people are not prepared for a system that punishes the innocent by protecting the guilty. . . ."

Geberth also reports that research studies have found that "six out of ten family members (56%) thought that the criminal justice system treated the defendant better than it treated them. Some 61% said that they felt mostly or totally helpless while the case was in progress."

Victims may perceive the following rights of accused criminals as inequities:

- When arrested, they must be informed of their rights.
- They are represented by counsel—at the state's expense if they cannot afford a lawyer.
- They are fed, clothed and given medical care.
- They may be provided with psychological counseling or treatment for drug or alcohol problems.
- They can be present at all criminal proceedings and have the right to confront their accuser(s) in court.
- They may appeal to a higher court if found guilty.

In fact, the label "criminal justice" seems to place the emphasis on the rights of the criminal. The disparity between how criminals and victims are treated by the criminal justice system forces some victims to join together in support groups. The disparity also prompts others to try to better understand the victims of crime.

## PROGRESS IN ASSISTING VICTIMS

Society has made progress in assisting victims of crime. In 1981 President Ronald Reagan proclaimed National Victims of Crime Week, putting the full weight and influence of his office behind the victims' movement. In 1982 President Reagan created a Task Force on Victims of Crime to do an extensive study on crime victimization (Burnley, 1990, p. 11):

> The Task Force found that crime victims were often victimized twice—first by the crime itself, and then by the criminal justice system. Innocent victims were ignored, mistreated or even blamed for what happened. Traumatized by criminal and judicial proceedings they did not understand and relegated to serving as evidence at the convenience of the courts, the experience left victims unwilling to become involved again in the criminal justice system.

The Task Force's finding that more emphasis was put on the defendant's rights than on the rights of victims prompted it to call for a balancing of the rights of defendants and victims. The Task Force examined the Sixth Amendment clearly establishing the rights of suspects to a trial, to confront witnesses and to have an attorney present:

> In all criminal prosecutions, the accused shall enjoy the right to a speedy and public trial, by an impartial jury of the state and District wherein the crime shall have been committed, which districts shall have been previously ascertained by law, and to be informed of the nature and cause of the accusation; to be confronted with the witnesses against him; to have compulsory process for obtaining witnesses in his favor' and to have the assistance of counsel for his defense.

## Legislation

In 1982 Congress passed the Federal Victim and Witness Protection Act. Through this act, as noted by Kelly (1990, p. 174): "The Congress finds and declares that . . . without the cooperation of victims . . . the criminal justice system would cease to function."

◆

The Federal Victim and Witness Protection Act of 1982 (WPA) established the victim impact statement (VIS) as a formal part of the presentence report.

◆

Among the major provisions in the Victim and Witness Protection Act of 1982 are the following (Shriner, 1992, p. 2):

- Guidelines for ensuring the fair treatment of victims and witnesses in the Federal criminal justice system.
- Victim impact statements to be contained in presentence reports.
- Criminal penalties protecting victims and witnesses from intimidation or retaliation, including provisions for civil restraining orders.
- Restitution for victims.
- Consideration of victims' situations in bail determinations.

The WPA suggests that law enforcement officials should:

[E]nsure that the appropriate U.S. probation officer is fully advised of any information pertinent to the preparation of the victim impact statement . . . so that the report will fully reflect the effects of the crime upon the victims as well as the appropriateness and amount of restitution. The victim should be apprised that the probation officer is required to prepare a VIS that includes a provision on restitution. The victim should be advised as to how to communicate directly with the probation officer if he so desires.

◆

The **victim impact statement (VIS)** is a written report describing in detail the full effect of a crime on the victim. A VIS may influence the sentence passed by the judge.

◆

According to Wells (1991, p. 45): "The VIS can significantly benefit both the victim and the officer—it is the principle means for communicating with the court on issues such as emotional impact and financial loss; it helps to ensure that restitution amounts are accurate and reflect the total loss sustained by the victim; and it may influence final sentences imposed by the court. But perhaps its greatest benefit is the one most often overlooked; *it may promote psychological recovery of victims.*"

Other legislation attempts to reduce the financial hardships of victims. In 1984 Congress passed the Comprehensive Crime Control Act and the Victims of Crime Act, establishing a fund of up to $100 million for victims of crimes and the agencies that serve them.

◆

The Victims of Crime Act (VOCA), passed in 1984, established a fund making state grants available for victims' compensation, victim assistance programs and child abuse prevention and treatment.

◆

According to Shriner (1992, p. 2):

The Victims of Crime Act of 1984 (VOCA) (Public Law 98-473) is the most significant piece of Federal legislation for crime victims enacted to date. VOCA substantially contributed to the development and expansion of crime victim assistance and compensation programs across the United States by establishing an innovative funding mechanism that takes money away from convicted Federal criminals to support the provision of services to crime victims. The Crime Victims Fund (the Fund), which is financed by Federal criminals and not taxpayers, is derived from criminal fines, penalties, and bond forfeitures. Congress directed OVC, which it established under the terms of VOCA, to distribute the Fund proceeds principally to States and U.S. Territories so that a network of responsive victim assistance and compensation services would be immediately accessible for victims throughout the country.

According to Adams (1996, p. 1): "The Office for Victims of Crime (OVC) plays a pivotal leadership role in the victims movement. The Office supplements, reinforces and encourages the expansion of State compensation and assistance programs throughout the country."

As noted by Muraskin (1992, p. 13), in 1988 Congress reauthorized VOCA for another six years and appropriated $150 million for the VOCA fund.

Forty-five states and Washington, D.C., have established compensation programs to be eligible to receive VOCA funds and help crime victims recover financial losses incurred through medical bills. Table 12.4 summarizes the victim compensation programs and procedures in forty-two states.

According to Carrington and Nicholson (1991, p. 339):

> Legislatures of every state continued to respond enthusiastically to the victims' movement. Major initiatives were seen in such areas as victim impact statements, victims' rights to allocution at sentencing (and in some cases even at the plea bargaining stage), rape shield laws, extension of statutes of limitations in child sexual abuse cases, and other areas as well.

The Crime Control Act of 1990 (Public Law 101-647) strengthened the Victim and Witness Act by mandating services and rights that were to be accorded to all crime victims by employees of the federal criminal justice system engaged in the detection, investigation or prosecution of crime. These rights and protections were listed under Title V of the Act that, in effect, created a Federal Crime Victims' Bill of Rights and codified the services that are to be made available.

The Seventy-fourth Legislative session made a number of important changes to the Crime Victims' Compensation Act, including:

- Increasing the dollar amounts of certain benefits.
- Adding new types of benefits available through the Fund.
- Expanding the definitions of those eligible for benefits under the Act.

Franklin (1995, p. 153) observes: "The actions of the 103rd and 104th Congresses have propelled the victims' rights movement forward, helping to make victims feel whole again." One important provision is allowing the use of victim impact statements in the sentencing of convicted offenders in federal cases involving violent and sexual abuse crimes.

According to Parent et al. (1992, p. 4): "All states compensate crime victims for medical expenses, mental health counseling, and lost wages. In all states, survivors of deceased victims may be compensated for funeral expenses and loss of support. Thirty-seven states compensate for rehabilitation services; and thirty-five, for the cost of replacement services. Only eight states compensate for property losses, and then subject to strict limits on amounts and often only for elderly victims."

## Organizations

According to Burnley (1990, p. 10): "The notion of providing help to crime victims is a rather recent phenomenon. It originated in grassroots efforts in the 1960s and 1970s to assist victims of sexual assault and battered women."

The first national organization to support victims' rights was the National Organization for Victim Assistance (NOVA), founded in 1976 in Fresno, California, by a small group of victim advocates.

**Table 12.4**  Compensation Programs to Help Victims of Violent Crimes

| State | Use to Inform Victim | | | | | | Reporting Deadline (days) | Filing Deadline (days) | Processing Time (weeks) (avg. claim) | Processing Time (days) (emergency award) | Time Limit—Appeals (days) | Payment Method | | |
|---|---|---|---|---|---|---|---|---|---|---|---|---|---|---|
| | Police | Hospital/Emergency | Victim Assistance Programs | Prosecutor | Poster/Brochure | Public Service Announcements | | | | | | Lump Sum | Installments | Pay Vendors Directly? |
| Alabama | 2 | 3 | 1 | 1 | 4 | 5 | 3 | 365 | 16 | 2 | 30 | x | | x |
| Alaska | 1 | 3 | 5 | 2 | 4 | | 5 | 730 | 16 | 3 | 30 | x | x | |
| Arizona | 1 | 2 | 3 | 4 | 5 | 6 | 3 | 365 | 9 | 1 | | x | x | x |
| Arkansas | | | | | | | 3 | 365 | 10 | 22 | 30 | x | x | x |
| California | 2 | 3 | 1 | | 4 | | | 365 | 40 | 30 | 45 | x | | x |
| Connecticut | 1 | 3 | 2 | | 4 | 5 | 5 | 730 | 13 | 1 | 30 | x | | x |
| Delaware | 1 | 4 | 2 | 3 | 5 | | 3 | 365 | 13 | 12 | 30 | x | | |
| Florida | | | | | | | 3 | 365 | 16 | 15 | 60 | x | x | x |
| Hawaii | | | 1 | | | | | 548 | 40 | | 30 | x | | x |
| Idaho | 1 | 2 | 3 | 5 | 6 | | 3 | 365 | 9 | 10 | 145 | | x | x |
| Indiana | 3 | 2 | 1 | 4 | 6 | | 2 | 730 | 7 | 2 | 30 | x | x | |
| Iowa | 1 | 2 | 3 | 4 | 5 | | 1 | 180 | 16 | 42 | 30 | x | | |
| Kansas | 1 | 4 | 3 | 2 | | | 3 | 365 | 12 | | 30 | x | x | x |
| Kentucky | 4 | 3 | 1 | 2 | 5 | 6 | 2 | 365 | 20 | 30 | 30 | x | x | x |
| Louisiana | 1 | | | | | | | 365 | 45 | 6 | 5 | | x | |
| Maryland | 2 | 3 | 1 | 4 | 5 | | 2 | 180 | 10 | 10 | 30 | x | x | x |
| Massachusetts | 2 | | 3 | 1 | | | 2 | 365 | 32 | | 15 | x | | x |
| Michigan | 2 | 4 | 3 | 1 | 5 | | 2 | 365 | 22 | 30 | 30 | x | x | x |
| Minnesota | 1 | | 2 | 3 | 4 | | 5 | 365 | 14 | 12 | 30 | x | x | |
| Missouri | 1 | 3 | 4 | 2 | | | 2 | 365 | 30 | 30 | 30 | x | | |
| Montana | 1 | 2 | 3 | 5 | 9 | 6 | 3 | 365 | 7 | 7 | 30 | x | x | x |
| Nebraska | 1 | 5 | 2 | 3 | 6 | 4 | 3 | 730 | 6 | | 30 | x | x | |
| Nevada | 2 | 1 | 3 | 3 | | | 5 | 365a | 12 | 20 | 15 | x | x | x |
| New Jersey | 1 | 2 | 4 | 3 | 9 | 6 | 90 | 730 | 26 | 5 | 20 | x | x | x |
| New Mexico | | | | | | | 30 | 365 | | | | x | x | |
| New York | 1 | 2 | 4 | 5 | 3 | | 7 | 365 | 16 | 1 | 30 | x | x | |
| N. Carolina | 3 | 1 | 2 | | | | 3 | 365 | 13 | 3 | 60 | x | x | |
| N. Dakota | | | 1 | | | | 3 | 365 | 10 | | 30 | x | x | |
| Oklahoma | 2 | 3 | 5 | 1 | 4 | 7 | 3 | 365 | 15 | 12 | 30 | x | x | |
| Oregon | 1 | 2 | 1 | 2 | 3 | | 3 | 365 | 18 | 7 | 60 | x | x | |
| Pennsylvania | 2 | 4 | 1 | 3 | 3 | | 72 | 365 | 20 | 28 | 20 | x | x | |
| Rhode Island | | 3 | 2 | 1 | 4 | 5 | 10 | 1,095 | 104 | | 20 | x | | |
| S. Carolina | 3 | 4 | 1 | 2 | 9 | 5 | 2 | 180 | 9 | 2 | 30 | x | x | |
| Tennessee | 1 | 3 | 1 | 4 | 7 | | 2 | 365 | 12 | 15 | 30 | x | | |
| Texas | 2 | 1 | 3 | 4 | 9 | 5 | 3 | 365 | 22 | 3 | 20 | x | x | |
| Utah | 1 | | 4 | 2 | | | 7 | 365 | 4 | 4 | 20 | x | x | |
| Virgin Islands | 1 | 2 | 4 | 3 | 5 | | 1 | 730 | 27 | | | x | | |
| Virginia | 2 | 3 | 1 | 4 | | | 5 | 180 | 8 | 30 | 20 | x | x | x |
| Washington | 4 | 2 | 1 | 3 | 5 | | 3 | 365 | 4 | | 60 | x | x | |
| W. Virginia | 1 | 3 | | 2 | | | 3 | 730 | 4 | | 21 | x | | |
| Wisconsin | 1 | 2 | 3 | 4 | 3 | | 5 | 365 | 14 | | 30 | x | x | x |
| Wyoming | 2 | 5 | 4 | 3 | 1 | 6 | | 365 | 5 | 5 | | x | | x |

a—Minor sexual assault victims have until age 21 to apply.

SOURCE: Dale G. Parent, Barbara Auerbach, and Kenneth Carlson. *Compensating Crime Victims: A Summary of Policies and Practices.* U.S. Department of Justice, National Institute of Justice. Washington: U.S. Government Printing Office (January 1992).

◆

The National Organization for Victim Assistance (NOVA) was founded in 1976.

◆

NOVA has accomplished the following (Carrington and Nicholson, 1991, p. 342):

(1) Assistance in formulating and passing the Victims of Crime Act, the Victim and Witness Protection Act, the Justice Assistance Act, and bills of rights for victims; (2) providing through its advocates, crisis counseling, information, referral, and assistance; and (3) providing local victim assistance programs with updated information on how to serve the victims with whom they have contact.

In addition, victims of crime and those concerned about victims have become advocates for changes in the criminal justice system's response to victims. Grassroots victim organizations have been formed including such groups as Mothers against Drunk Driving, Parents of Murdered Children, the National Organization of Victim Assistance and Victims for Victims. In addition, victim compensation laws and victim advocacy and protection programs attempt to address what is widely perceived as the system's protection of the accused's rights to the victim's detriment.

The emergence of citizen groups concerned with victims' rights is well illustrated by the formation of the Stephanie Roper Committee. In 1982, Stephanie Roper, honors college student and daughter of Roberta and Vince Roper, was kidnapped, raped, tortured, then shot in the forehead and set aflame. During the trial of the two men accused of the atrocities, the Ropers were barred from the courtroom after they gave their testimony. They were allowed back into the courtroom when the accused were sentenced, but the court did not permit them to make a statement about how the crime had affected them. Outraged at the light sentence the two men received, the Ropers founded the Stephanie Roper Committee. Thousands of people joined and lobbied for tougher sentencing laws and better treatment of victims. In 1983 Maryland legislators passed the "Stephanie Roper legislation" which:

- Permits the use of written victim-impact statements to be submitted to the judge or at the sentencing hearing, which allow crime victims or their families to describe how the crime affected their lives.

- Increases the time before the convicted are eligible for parole in life sentences.

- Ensures the victim's right to remain in the courtroom after being called as a witness.

- Ensures the victim's right to be notified of parole release hearings and to give an updated impact statement.

- Gives victims the right to withhold their addresses and phone numbers to protect them from intimidation by defendants.

◆

A second national organization for victims, the National Victim Center, was founded in 1985.

◆

The National Victim Center was formerly the Sunny von Bulow National Victim Advocacy Center. This Center's broad-ranging programs include the following (Carrington and Nicholson, 1991, p. 342):

(1) Seminar training across the country of direct-line victim service personnel involved in such areas as rape crisis counselling, child protection activities, assistance with domestic violence cases, and counselling survivors of homicide victims; (2) work for constitutional amendments creating "Victims' Bills of Rights" in the several states; (3) information referral to individual crime victim service agencies; (4) maintaining a data base of some 13,000 pieces of legislation that concern victims' rights, directly or indirectly; and (5) maintaining another data base of the names and addresses of, and key individuals involved, with over 7,000 victim assistance agencies nationwide.

In 1986 NOVA established a Crisis Response Team (CRT) to assist communities that experienced disasters such as plane crashes, forest fires and shootings. As noted by Davis and Henley (1990, p. 164):

The CRT is a nationwide network of volunteers who have attended NOVA-sponsored training sessions throughout the country.

When a community requests help, NOVA staff members contact network members in the vicinity of the stricken community. Typically a specific team consists of a NOVA coordinator, member of the clergy, mental health professional, law enforcement representative, medical specialist, and press liaison.

Again, the cooperation of various professionals and community organizations is critical to the success of each CRT.

One trend in victimization is for victims or secondary victims to become spokespersons and work for victims' rights and tougher sentencing. Examples include Fred Goldman, Denise Brown and Patty Wetterling.

## Programs Implemented

Financial compensation is not the only type of assistance available from programs for victims. The most frequent services provided by victim/witness programs are summarized in Table 12.5.

◆

The two main types of programs provided for victims are **victim service programs** that provide crisis counseling, shelter and other specialized treatment and **victim/witness assistance programs** that seek to provide assistance to victims and witnesses as their case moves through the judicial process.

◆

*Table 12.5*    **Victim-Witness Program Services**

| | |
|---|---|
| **Emergency Services** | **Claims Assistance** |
| Medical care | Insurance claims aid |
| Shelter or food | Restitution assistance |
| Security repair | Compensation assistance |
| Financial assistance | Witness fee assistance |
| On-scene comfort | **Court-related Services** |
| **Counseling** | Witness reception |
| 24-hour hotline | Court orientation |
| Crisis intervention | Notification |
| Follow-up counseling | Witness alert |
| Mediation | Transportation |
| | Child care |
| **Advocacy and Support Services** | Escort to court |
| Personal advocacy | Victim impact reports |
| Employer intervention | **Systemwide Services** |
| Landlord intervention | Public education |
| Property return | Legislative advocacy |
| Intimidation protection | Training |
| Legal/paralegal counsel | |
| Referral | |

SOURCE: Peter Finn and Beverly Lee. *Establishing and Expanding Victim Witness Assistance Programs.* Washington: National Institute of Justice. (1988.) Reprinted by permission.

Programs should be based on identified needs of victims and witnesses. According to McClenahan (1990, p. 104):

> The most common needs among victims are access to case progress information, assistance with their safety concerns, compensation for losses, crime prevention information and feedback on how their feelings compare to those of others in similar situations.

> There are often many practical needs, as well. These include being in a safe environment, having funds to meet immediate expenses (e.g., bus fare, money for a meal) and having someone to talk to who is interested not only in their recollection of facts, but also in their experience and its emotional impact.

In addition to the formation of victims' organizations and the passage of legislation to provide funding and services for victims, progress has also been made in formalizing the rights of victims.

## Victims' Bill of Rights

"The struggle to gain formal, legal rights has been a powerful moving force throughout history. . . . The most well-known include civil rights, workers' rights, students' rights, children's rights, women's rights, gay rights and prisoners' rights. The victims' rights movement of the late 1970s and 1980s falls within this tradition" (Karmen, 1992, p. 46).

Thirty-six states have enacted victims' bills of rights, omnibus bills that, according to Newton (p. 61):

> [D]epending on the state, assert the right to be protected from intimidation, the right to access to information about a case, the right to submit a statement prior to sentencing, and the right to be consulted during plea bargaining.

Victims and witnesses have two basic rights: the right to obtain certain information from the criminal justice system and the right to be treated humanely by the system.

Senna and Siegel (1990, p. 178) note that comprehensive victims' bills of rights laws may also:

- Ensure the victim's right to continued employment.
- Provide medical or social support services.
- Require the appointment of an "ombudsman" to protect the rights of the victim during the trial period.

◆

Most victims' bills of rights include both informational and participatory rights.

◆

According to Karmen (1992, pp. 46-47), the most widely enacted *informational rights,* gained at the expense of criminal justice agencies and officials, include the following:

- To be read one's "rights": to reimbursement of losses—from state compensation funds, court ordered offender restitution, insurance coverage, civil lawsuits, or tax deductions; to referrals—to counseling programs, self-help support groups, shelters for battered women, rape crisis centers, and other types of assistance; and to be told of one's obligations—to attend line-ups, appear in court, be cross-examined under oath, and to be publicly identified and the subject of media coverage.
- To be informed of the whereabouts of the "accused" offender: at large; or in custody (jail or prison); escaped from confinement; or released back to the community (on bail, or due to dropped and dismissed charges, or because of acquittal after a trial, or out on appeal, probation, furlough, parole, or after an expired sentence).
- To be kept posted about key decisions: arrests, the granting of bail, rulings at evidentiary hearings, negotiated pleas, verdicts at trials, sentences, and parole board deliberations.

- To receive assistance in the form of intercession by an official on behalf of a victim with an employer or creditor; advance notification and facilitation of court appearances; and expeditious return of recovered stolen property.

Karmen (p. 47) lists the following *participatory rights,* gained at the expense either of offenders or agencies and officials:

- To be consulted when the terms and conditions of bail are being determined (as a protection against harassment and reprisals for cooperating with the prosecution).
- To be consulted about the offers made during plea negotiations.
- To be permitted to submit a victim impact statement, detailing how the crime caused physical, emotional, and/or financial harm, as part of the presentence report, and to submit a statement of opinion suggesting remedies, for the judge's consideration.
- To be permitted to exercise **allocution** rights in person, in court, detailing the harm caused by the offender and suggesting an appropriate remedy, before the judge imposes a sentence.
- To be permitted to bring to the attention of the parole hoard, either in writing or in person, information about the harm caused by the offender and an opinion about an appropriate remedy.

◆

Victims' rights bills commonly require the victim to be informed about available financial aid and social services; advised of case status and scheduling; protected from harassment and intimidation; provided with separate waiting areas during the trial; and a speedy return of property held as evidence.

◆

The International Association of Chiefs of Police (IACP, 1983) has defined the "incontrovertible rights of all crime victims" as follows:

1.  To be free from intimidation;
2.  To be told of financial assistance and social services available and how to apply for them;
3.  To be provided a secure area during interviews and court proceedings, and to be notified if presence in court is needed;
4.  To be provided return of stolen or other personal property when no longer needed as evidence;

5. To a speedy disposition of the case, and to be periodically informed of case status and final disposition; and, wherever personnel and resource capabilities allow, to be notified in felony cases whenever the perpetrator is released from custody;

6. To be interviewed by a female official in the case of rape and other sexual offenses, wherever personnel and resource capabilities allow.

### More Remains to Be Done

As noted by Elias (1991, p. 44):

> Victims have progressed significantly in the last quarter century, but they have not yet shaken their second-class status. When victimized, they lack confidence in receiving the aid they need, and for good reason—they often must tolerate inadequate services, cultural insensitivity, political insignificance, and official maltreatment.

One critical area in which to deter "official maltreatment" mandates that police improve their response to those who have been victimized.

## THE POLICE RESPONSE

Talking to victims and witnesses requires police to use specific skills to ensure that the victim or witness provides all available information for successful investigation, apprehension and prosecution of the perpetrator. At the same time, officers must treat victims and witnesses respectfully and take care of their immediate needs. Victims are frequently traumatized or injured. Crime victims might be frightened, injured, in shock, angry and confused when police expect them to submit to questioning and provide minute details of the crime and suspect. Occasionally a victim may have reason to lie about the events. The following interview skills will help to gain the victim's cooperation:

1. Take care of the victim's safety and medical needs first. Frightened people need to be assured that they are safe and that you will keep them safe. Any injuries or pain need to be attended to before they can be expected to provide any meaningful information.

2. Victims and witnesses need to be interviewed individually so they will not alter their recollections to match each other's. Victims sometimes trust another victim's memory more than their own.

3. Let the victim or witness know that what they tell you is very important and that you need their help. They may have a fear of retaliation or of testifying in court.

4. Provide the individual with resources that will help them to deal with the problems that result from being a victim or in some cases, a witness. They may need transportation, a place to stay, assistance in security for their house or business, the use of a telephone, a referral to counseling, or an advocate to help them.

The manner in which police officers interact with victims and witnesses makes a difference in how the officers and the department are perceived by the public. It also affects how they can develop informants, how many criminals the department can apprehend, how effectively they are prosecuted, how many complaints are lodged against officers and/or the department and how far officers are able to advance in their careers. It is critical that officers interact effectively with victims and witnesses.

According to Frederick et al. (1990, p. 106): "The outcome of effective police-victim interviewing can have a positive dual effect, aiding police in retrieving pertinent evidence and factual data relevant to the case, while protecting the immediate and potential future mental well-being of the victim." The first few moments of police contact with a victim or witness are critical. Frederick et al. (pp. 106–09) offer police officers the following victim/witness intervention techniques:

1. Display composure.
2. Try to put the victim at ease. ("I'm here with you and I want to help you.")
3. Give honest, accurate information (without being brutally frank or alarming).
4. Remove the victim temporarily from a stressful situation.
5. Begin interviewing and questioning the victim only after establishing psychological and physical equilibrium. (Lack of support and understanding from an official has been reported by some victims to be worse than the initial trauma.)
6. Proceed with a clear, unambiguous plan.
7. Contact and meet with available relatives and friends.
8. Use the victim's personal resources.
9. Encourage physical activity. (Simply suggesting that the individual get up and get a drink of water or accomplish some other useful act can be invaluable.)
10. Supply suitable advice and direction. (Every victim should be encouraged to seek psychological assistance from a skilled professional.)
11. Adapt to the needs of the victim, taking into account verbal facility, social background, age, sex and the like.

Waller (1990, p. 151) emphasizes:

> The police are well situated to initiate crisis support to victims. Because they are often the first officials to talk to the crime victim, they are able to reassure and refer the victim to appropriate services in the community. . . .
>
> The police could improve their support for crime victims by requiring the responding officer to provide the victim with a card that identifies the key telephone numbers of such services as the local distress center, locksmiths, criminal injuries compensation, the crime prevention unit, and a service that could help or refer the victim to other community services. Ideally, this card would identify both the file number of the case as well as the name of the police officer.

One important area in which police officers can help victims is in preparing the victim impact statement (VIS). Wells (1991, pp. 45–46) suggests these steps for law enforcement officers:

1. Let victims know that the opportunity to provide such a statement exists, and that they have the right to become active in the court case process. Remember, victims' rights are like offenders' rights were before the *Miranda* decision—if victims don't know these rights exist, in effect they do not exist.

2. Let victims know what procedures and policies are in place regarding the administration of the VIS program in your area. Do they simply send a letter to the judge? Do they complete a VIS form sent by the police department, the prosecutor, a victim advocate or the probation department? Do they talk directly to probation about the impact?

3. Encourage the victims' participation. Let them know that the information they have to offer can make a difference.

4. Let them know that you can answer their questions or concerns about the process and help them prepare their statements.

Wells (p. 46) notes that most of the forms used for VIS are directed "primarily toward meeting the needs of the system rather than the needs of victims." He suggests that police departments that use such forms should renew them and ask the following questions (pp. 46–47):

- Do the forms match victim and crime, or are they "one size fits all"? [Suggestion: develop separate forms and cover letters for violent, property and white-collar crime.]
- Do the forms enable the victim to express the crime's impact? [Suggestion: start the form with a simple, open-ended question such as "How are you and members of your family being affected by this crime?" and leave one page for the response.]

- Do the forms or cover letters use terms unfamiliar to many victims? [Suggestion: avoid such terms as "restitution," "deposition," "preliminary hearing," or "crime compensation," or explain them fully if they must be used.]
- Avoid using impersonal opening sentences such as: "We have been advised that a member of your family is deceased as a result of a crime." [Suggestion: say something like, "We are aware that you have been victimized by a crime and would like to know how you and members of your family have been affected by this crime."]

Many police departments are becoming more aware of the problem of officer insensitivity to victims and witnesses and are providing "consciousness-raising courses" to help officers understand and deal with victims empathetically.

Boston has an innovative approach to obtaining information about gang crimes—have a probation officer ride with a police officer. The probation officer can recognize most gang members on sight, many of whom are on probation and are violating that probation by being together. As noted by Butterfield (1997, p. 3): "When normally bystanders at a crime scene claim to have seen nothing, Mr. Steward [probation officer] was able to elicit information about a shooting from young people who faced having their probation revoked and going to jail, or—just as bad—spending more time on probation."

The Lincoln/Lancaster County Domestic Violence Coalition has instituted a cellular phone link with victims. As Larimer (1994, p. 57) notes, many lower-income crime victims do not have a telephone. In addition, with cellular phones there are no phone lines to cut and the phones can be preprogrammed with 911 and the general information numbers of the Lancaster County Sheriff's Office and the Lincoln Police Department. All other calling capability is locked out. Larimer describes how this program was funded:

> The Lincoln Police Department agreed to pay the monthly air time, the Lancaster County Sheriff's Office to pay for the telephones, the Justice Council Coordinator would find a college intern to help with the project, the Lincoln Telephone Company would program the telephones and the police department's Victim/Witness Unit would administer the project. After the project became public, many community organizations offered financial support. It was a total community effort. . . .
>
> The project empowered citizens to address risk factors and share problem solving among many diverse community groups. The project also inspired mutual accountability for public safety.

The Jefferson County Kentucky's Victim Information and Notification Everyday (VINE™) system is a fully automated notification system that alerts victims with a telephone call when an inmate is released from custody. As the article "Victims of Release Dates" (1996, p. 53) states: "Beyond saving lives through early alert, VINE gives crime victims a way to stay involved with the case." United States Attorney General Janet Reno has called VINE a model for the nation, commenting: "Technology needs to be utilized a lot more in order to protect crime victims."

### Civil Legal Remedies

One alternative available to crime victims is to seek civil legal remedies. As O'Brien (1992 p. 1) explains: "Victims of crime are now resorting to civil litigation, in addition to victim compensation and restitution, as a financial means for recovering from the ill effects of crime. Increasingly, victims are finding their way into civil courtrooms to recover from physical, psychological and financial injuries by recovering for lost wages, hospital costs, counselling expenses, property damages and all of the many other various costs incurred as a result of victimization." O'Brien suggests (p. 3): "It is likely that a victim wishing to vindicate his or her rights against a perpetrator or third party will find the civil court to be a much more agreeable forum than the criminal court."

## SPECIAL POPULATIONS

Interacting effectively with victims is a critical part of police officers' jobs that requires extreme skill and sensitivity. Some victims have additional medical and psychological needs that require officers to be quite sensitive.Officers should be aware of resources available for these "special" victims.

◆

"Special" crime victims who require additional services include battered or sexually assaulted women, abused children and elderly victims of crime or abuse.

◆

### Battered or Sexually Assaulted Women

Traditionally, police have not treated domestic violence as a crime except in extremely brutal cases. Police often considered domestic violence to be a "family matter." Wives had to press charges before the police could intervene. This requirement has been eliminated in most states. As noted by Friedman and Shulman (1990, p. 89): "As the result of womens' rights advocates lobbying efforts and the grave consequences to women in cases where they had been denied police protection after being assaulted, police departments now treat domestic violence as a crime."

In addition: "Only the state of West Virginia has failed to pass legislation that authorizes the police to make warrantless, probable-cause arrests and file complaints in domestic violence cases." No longer must the victim press charges, which, in effect, has shifted the burden of stopping the violence away from the victim. Friedman and Shulman (p. 91) stress: "Police departments have begun to develop policies on family violence that are guided by two principles: (1) domestic violence is a crime; and (2) victims of domestic violence require special considerations." They conclude (p. 100): "The staggering, but probably conservative statistics that indicate 2.1 million women are beaten each year, 3,000 die, and 20% of homicides are committed within the family demand that law enforcement and criminal justice agencies develop special responses to domestic violence cases to counteract years of reverse practices."

The Domestic Abuse Intervention Project is a national training project which includes seminars for law enforcement officers and trainers, prosecutors, legal advocates and police administrators. The seminars introduce two key wheels that can drive a relationship, the power and control wheel and the equality wheel, shown in Figure 12.1 and Figure 12.2.

In addition to explaining the dynamics of domestic violence, the seminars teach:

- State law and department policy regarding domestic violence.
- Establishing probable cause in domestic violence cases.
- Distinguishing between mutual assaults and self-defense.
- Making the decision to arrest, mediate between or separate spouses.
- Gathering evidence effectively and writing reports.
- Enforcing civil protection orders.
- Interviewing child witnesses.
- Maintaining officer safety and awareness of liability issues.
- Understanding the psychological dynamics of battering in relationships.

Such programs illustrate the progress that is being made to educate officers about domestic violence.

According to Roberts (1990a) recognition of the need for and establishment of crisis intervention for victims has increased dramatically since the mid-1970s.

The most common precipitating events that lead battered women to seek help from a domestic violence program are: "(a) an acute battering incident resulting in a serious physical injury, (b) a serious abusive injury inflicted on the woman's child and (c) a temporary impairment of hearing, sight, or thought process as a direct result of severe batterment" (Roberts and Roberts, 1990, p. 180).

Roberts and Roberts emphasize that it is essential for police to be familiar with referral sources that go beyond the immediate crisis. Such sources may include job training and placement, low-cost housing and child care needs. According to Roberts and Roberts (p. 202): "The most frequently used referral sources involved legal aid, medical care, Careers for Homemakers, Job Bank, day-

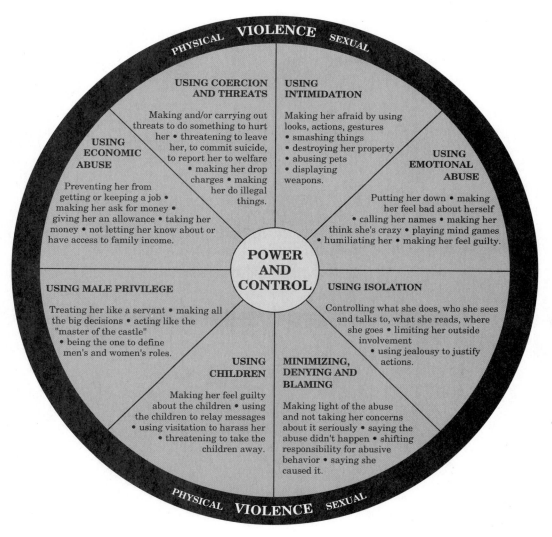

*Figure 12.1*   **The Wheel of Power and Control**

SOURCE: Domestic Abuse Intervention Project, 206 West Fourth Street, Duluth, Minnesota 55806. Reprinted by permission.

care programs, Women in Need (WIN, an agency concerned with long-term housing for single women), Alcoholics Anonymous, Women's Self-Help Center (providing counseling and support groups), and St. Pat's (a Catholic social service agency that finds low-cost housing and provides classes in budgeting money and other life skills)."

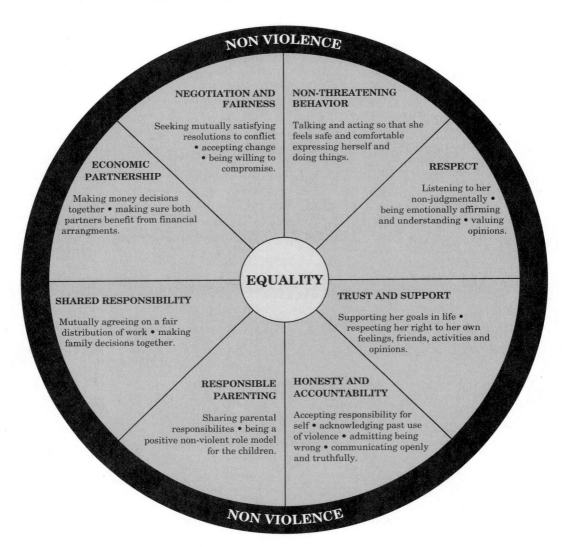

*Figure 12.2* **The Wheel of Equality**

SOURCE: Domestic Abuse Intervention Project, 206 West Fourth Street, Duluth, Minnesota 55806. Reprinted by permission.

As noted by Elias (1990, p. 230), progress has been made in legislation regarding battered women: "Better record-keeping, like monthly police reports are required to track abuse patterns. Other laws provide protective orders, assign possession of the residence, get the defendant to pay support and set custody and visitation rights. Thirty states authorize warrantless arrests for misdemeanor assaults, ten require it upon probable cause."

Women who have been sexually assaulted also have unique needs. Resick (1990, pp. 70–81) suggests the following:

> With very little effort on their parts, practitioners in the criminal justice system are in the position to help rape victims recover. . . . Although the police who investigate cases may disagree with the victims' appraisal of the imminent danger posed by the situation based on their experience, they should not disregard the victims' perceptions. . . . Investigators and other criminal justice system personnel should make a special effort to refer victims to counseling who describe the crime as an imminent death situation or who describe themselves as being terrified during the crime. . . .
>
> How a victim is treated by criminal justice practitioners may affect how the rape victim psychologically processes the event. Investigations can and should be conducted without implying that the victim brought on the crime . . . even when the investigator feels that the victim put herself at risk by her own behavior. . . . Teenagers are particularly naive and cannot always discriminate safe from potentially unsafe situations. Poor judgment is not an offense punishable by rape. . . .
>
> Police . . . need to be careful in their phrasing of questions. For example, "What happened next?" or "What did you do then?" are neutral questions, whereas, "Why did you. . . ?" implies blame and puts the victim on the defensive. . . .
>
> A few judicious statements by the criminal justice practitioner may help greatly in a victim's recovery. Statements about the normal course of recovery (months, not days or weeks) and normal symptoms, such as flashbacks, nightmares, intrusive memories, the desire to avoid reminders, sleeping problems, and roller-coaster emotions, may help victims know that their reactions are normal and that they are not crazy. Rape victims should be advised to take things one step at a time but to return to normal activities as soon as they are able rather than avoid non-dangerous "danger" cues that were conditioned during the crime. They should be encouraged to mobilize their social support network and tell their loved ones what they need. . . . Most often, families and friends want to be supportive but do not know what to do or say. . . .
>
> Finally, . . . they should be warned that they may be given bad advice from well-meaning but uninformed people . . . to subscribe to the "stiff-upper-lip school of psychology," to disregard their emotions, . . . put the event behind them, and get on with their lives.

According to Elias (1990, p. 230): "Sexual assault victims also receive special attention, with laws for services, such as hotlines and counseling, crime prevention and prosecution, and medical attention. At least one state requires sexual assault victims to be given information about AIDS."

## Abused Children

Dealing with abused children, especially those who have been sexually abused, is another very sensitive type of case and one that often involves considerable media attention. According to Smith (1990, p. 108): "It is important to empha-size that no arrest was made in nearly half of the cases in which the police believed sexual abuse had occurred." This statistic highlights the difficulty of investigating and prosecuting child sexual abuse cases.

According to Elias (1990, p. 220): "All but nine [states] try to make child tes-timony less traumatic, permitting a videotaped statement either alone (unsworn interrogatory) or under oath and cross-examination (deposition), or live testi-mony through closed-circuit television. . . . Nine states require everyone, and all states at least require professionals, to report suspected child abuse, backed by civil damages, or even criminal penalties."

Often child sexual abuse cases are jointly investigated by a child protection service agency and the police department. Smith (1990, pp. 114–55) suggests the following guidelines to make cooperative efforts successful:

- Maintain open communication.
- Conduct joint training.
- Conduct interagency staff retreats.
- Conduct regular interagency meetings.
- Establish specialized units.
- Balance the number of staff among the coordinated agencies.
- Exercise patience.

Professionals must receive extensive training to learn how to prevent and investigate child abuse. Abuse against children is one of the most underreported crimes in the United States. Serious attempts to reduce crime and violence in our society require that children be protected from abuse. Child abuse is a cyclical crime: those who have been abused tend to abuse others when they become adults. Many serious criminals were abused as children. The link between abuse as a child and adult criminal behavior was discussed in Chapter 10.

## Elderly Victims

Elderly victims of violent crimes often have unique problems and often are more drastically affected than younger victims. The elderly often live on a fixed, lim-ited income, so financial losses can be especially devastating. In addition, the elderly are frail, can be easily injured and take a long time to heal. The elderly may also be less emotionally able to cope with victimization.

Among services that a community might provide for the elderly are the fol-lowing suggested by Roberts (1990b, p. 78):

- Transportation and escort to stores, public health clinics, hospitals, and banks.

- Provision of a special police unit that responds to cases of senior burglaries, robberies, purse snatchings, and assaults.
- Training youth to help elderly victims.
- Establishment of neighborhood block watch programs and neighborhood building patrols.
- Arrangement for new locks on doors and windows of elderly burglary victims.
- Provision of 24-hour hotlines and daily telephone reassurance.
- Making information and referral services available.
- Installation of video monitors in elevators and corridors of large apartment buildings.

Roberts (p. 81) emphasizes: "The protection and provision of services for victims of elder abuse and neglect should be the joint responsibility of a network of community agencies, including victim assistance programs, family violence programs and shelters, police departments, visiting nurses' associations, in-home respite care programs, hospital senior care programs, and senior community centers." According to Elias (1990, p. 230):

> Elderly victims have elicited laws allowing the victim's age to be used in determining sentences, producing tougher penalties and probation denial. Some states criminalize the abuse or neglect of the elderly. Many states require elderly-abuse reporting, especially by professionals, with 26 states protecting all vulnerable adults and 22 protecting older adults over a certain age. Some states mandate ombudsmen, speedy trials, abuser registries, hotlines, food, clothing, shelter, medical care, and other social services.

Police officers must be sensitive to victims and understand the reasons they behave as they do. Police departments now emphasize victimology studies in police recruit training and continue to develop victim assistance programs.

## THE RESPONSE OF THE CRIMINAL JUSTICE SYSTEM

The entire criminal justice system should be sensitive to the needs of victims. According to Kelly (1990, p. 175): "Studies revealed that a sense of participation was more critical to victims' satisfaction with the criminal justice system than how severely the defendant was punished." Victim participation can occur in several ways.

### Plea Bargaining

Kelly (p. 176) notes that between 83 and 90 percent of all cases that remain in the criminal justice system are plea bargained. She also notes that the Federal Victim and Witness Protection Act of 1982 states that prosecutors should consult victims about the terms of a plea. Further, twenty-three states now allow or mandate some form of victim participation in plea bargaining.

### Victim Involvement in Sentencing

Kelly (p. 178) notes that 96 percent of the states allow some form of victim involvement in sentencing, with the two most common forms being the VIS and the **victim statement of opinion (VSO).** According to Kelly:

> The VIS allows victims to detail the medical, financial, and emotional injuries that resulted from the crime. . . .
>
> In contrast, the VSO is considered more subjective. VSO allows the victim to tell the court their opinion on what sentence the defendant should receive.

Hillenbrand (1990, p. 193) notes: "Virtually every state now also provides for some sort of victim impact statement prior to sentencing."

### Court Attendance

The Sixth Amendment to the Constitution establishes the right of the defendant to be in the courtroom, but crime victims often have no such rights. As noted by Kelly (1990, p. 180): "For many victims, to be relegated to a hallway or waiting room represents both the ultimate insult and the ultimate loss of control."

According to Elias (1990, p. 228): "Fifteen states allow victims in the courtroom (waiving sequestration rules) at the judge's discretion, and one state makes court attendance a victim right." In 1987 a national movement, the Victims Constitutional Amendment Network (VCAN), was organized to lobby for constitutional amendments to allow victims to be present and heard at all stages of the criminal justice process.

### Probation and Parole

According to Hillenbrand (1990, p. 193): "By the end of 1987, restitution was authorized or required in virtually every state as a condition of probation. In addition, at least 23 states authorized it as a condition of parole, 14 as a condition of suspended sentence, and 10 as a condition of work release. At least 26 states prodded for restitution in addition to, or in lieu of, other sentences."

## RECOMMENDATIONS

The National District Attorneys Association (p. 8) recommends that the following types of agencies be included in a victim/witness assistance referral network: community groups, day-care centers, domestic violence programs, food stamp distribution centers, job counseling and training programs, mental health care programs, physical health care programs, private sector allies, private and community emergency organizations, rape crisis centers, unemployment services, victim assistance or advocacy organizations, victim compensation boards, volunteer groups and welfare agencies.

Many criminal justice scholars and researchers are calling for an entirely new approach to "justice" in the United States—restorative justice.

## RESTORATIVE JUSTICE

Van Ness (1990, p. 62) notes: "The Western view of crime and justice has become skewed. Rather than admitting that crimes injure victims, our laws define them as only offenses against government. . . . Contemporary criminal justice is preoccupied with maintaining public order and punishing offenders. Victims are often ignored." One way to overcome this problem is known as *restorative justice*. **Restorative justice** seeks to use a balanced approach involving offenders, victims, local communities and government to alleviate crime and violence and obtain peaceful communities. Van Ness (p. 64) sees restorative justice as involving three basic principles:

- Crimes result in injuries to victims, communities and offenders; therefore, the criminal justice process must repair those injuries.
- Not only government, but victims, offenders and communities, should be actively involved throughout the entire criminal justice process.
- In promoting justice, the government should preserve order, and peace should be maintained by the community.

Zehr (1991, p. 4) also stresses that crimes should be viewed as violations against persons: "I would suggest that we define crime as it is experienced as a violation of one person by another. Crime is a conflict between people, a violation against a person, not an offense against the state."

Criminologists suggest that restorative justice is in effect a return to the justice of old. For centuries, in England, offenders had to repay their victims. This was written into the Germanic Tribal Laws, the Roman Law of the Twelve Tables and the first written laws—the Code of Hammurabi, 2000 B.C. As time went on, however, crimes were considered as offenses against the king—or in modern times, the government.

The article "Restore Victim. . . ."(1995, p. 4) presents two hypothetical cases to illustrate restorative justice:

> In the first, a neighbor complains about noise coming from his neighbor's house, where a party is being held. When the noise continues, he responds by destroying his neighbor's stereo speakers. Under normal circumstances, the act would end in a criminal or misdemeanor charge resolved by a negotiated plea

that probably would involve restitution for the speakers. In some jurisdictions, the offender might enter a diversion program. Under the restorative justice model, a mediation session would be held whereby the party-thrower would agree not to pursue criminal charges and to control the noise level if the perpetrator agreed to pay restitution for the speakers.

In another hypothetical case, a youth breaks into a neighbor's house and attempts to steal a stereo system. When he is caught by the owner, the young man strikes the victim with a baseball bat, breaking his arm. Under the standard system, the youth probably would be charged with a felony and sentenced to ten years or less in jail. Under the restorative model, he might be committed to a youthful offender program in which prosecution would be suspended if he agreed to undergo a substance abuse evaluation, become assigned to a mentor, submit to drug tests, comply with a curfew, take classes to obtain a high school equivalency degree, perform community service, and possibly make victim restitution.

Bazemore and Umbreit (1994, p. 4) summarize how the new roles involved in restorative justice would function within the juvenile justice system in Table 12.6. Bazemore and Umbreit (pp. 13–14) also suggest a restorative justice checklist adapted from Howard Zehr's *Changing Lenses* (Scottsdale, Pennsylvania: Herald Press, 1990, used by permission of the publisher):

1.  Do victims experience justice?
    - Do victims have sufficient opportunities to tell their truth to relevant listeners?
    - Do victims receive needed compensation or restitution?
    - Is the injustice adequately acknowledged?
    - Are victims sufficiently protected against further violation?
    - Does the outcome adequately reflect the severity of the offense?
    - Do victims receive adequate information about the crime, the offender and the legal process?
    - Do victims have a voice in the legal process?
    - Is the experience of justice adequately public?
    - Do victims receive adequate support from others?
    - Do victims' families receive adequate assistance and support?
    - Are other needs—material, psychological and spiritual—being addressed?
2.  Do offenders experience justice?
    - Are offenders encouraged to understand and take responsibility for what they have done?
    - Are misattributions challenged?

*Table 12.6*  **New Roles in the Balanced Approach**

**Accountability**—When a crime occurs, a debt incurs. Justice requires that every effort be made by offenders to restore losses suffered by victims.

**Juvenile justice system role:**
Direct juvenile justice resources to ensure that offenders repay victims and complete other relevant restorative requirements as a top system priority.

*Intended outcome:* Efficient, fair, and meaningful restorative justice practices; increased responsiveness to victims' needs.

**Offender role:** Actively work to restore victims' losses and participate in activities that increase empathy with the victim and victims generally.

*Intended outcome:* Understanding of consequences of offense behavior, increased empathy; feeling of fairness in justice process.

**Community role:** Assist in the process by providing paid work opportunities for offenders, helping to develop community service work projects and supporting victim awareness education.

*Intended outcome:* More participation in and support for the juvenile justice system; message that victims receive priority.

**Competency development**—Offenders should leave the juvenile justice system more capable of productive participation in conventional society than when they entered.

**Juvenile justice system role:** Assess youths' strengths and interests and identify community resources to build on those strengths in a way that demonstrates competency. Engage youth in these activities and provide necessary supports for successful completion. Build prevention capacity through productivity partnerships with employers, educators and other community agencies.

*Intended outcome:* More opportunities for youth competency development; improved image of juvenile justice; increased competency.

**Offender role:** Become actively involved in activities that make a positive contribution to the community while building life skills; make continuous progress in improving educational skills while using existing skills to help others.

*Intended outcome:* Increased sense of competency and self-esteem; exposure to and interaction with positive adult role models; improved public image of youth.

**Community role:** Become partner with juvenile justice system in developing opportunities for youth to make productive contributions to the community while learning positive civic and other values.

*Intended outcome:* Increased community involvement in and ownership of delinquency problem; new attitudes toward youth; completion of positive work in communities. Improved quality of life in the community.

**Community protection**—The public has a right to a safe and secure community; juvenile justice should develop a progressive response system to ensure offender control in the community and develop new ways to ensure public safety and respond to community concerns.

**Juvenile justice system role:**
Ensure that offenders are carefully supervised by staff and a range of community guardians and that offenders' time is structured in productive activities; develop a range of supervision restrictiveness options and alternative responses to violations and incentives for progress.

*Intended outcome:* Increased public support for community supervision.

**Offender role:** Become involved in building and restorative activities; avoid situations that may lead to further offenses.

*Intended outcome:* No offenses while on supervision; reduced recidivism when the period of supervision is over.

**Offender role:** Provide input to juvenile justice system regarding public safety concerns; share responsibility for offender control and reintegration.

*Intended outcome:* Increased feelings of safety in the community; increased confidence in juvenile community supervision.

- Are offenders given encouragement and opportunities to make things right?
- Are offenders given opportunities to participate in the process?
- Are offenders encouraged to change their behavior?
- Is there a mechanism for monitoring or verifying changes?
- Are offenders' needs being addressed?
- Do offenders' families receive support and assistance?

3. Is the victim-offender relationship addressed?
   - Is there an opportunity for victims and offenders to meet, if appropriate?
   - Is there an opportunity for victims and offenders to exchange information about the event and about one another?

4. Are community concerns being taken into account?
   - Is the process and the outcome sufficiently public?
   - Is community protection being addressed?
   - Is there a need for restitution or a symbolic action for the community?
   - Is the community represented in some way in the legal process?

5. Is the future addressed?
   - Is there a provision for solving the problems that led to this event?
   - Is there a provision for solving problems caused by this event?
   - Have future intentions been addressed?
   - Are there provisions for monitoring and verifying outcomes and for problem solving?

Quinn (1995, p. 3) contends: "In its fully developed form, restorative justice involves the community in much more meaningful ways, narrowing the gulf between citizens who trust the mechanisms of justice and those who view them as foreign to their life and interests."

As noted by Morales (1995, p. 1): "The heart of justice is the restoration of balance in our communities. In order to truly achieve justice, we must work to restore the victims and society in the aftermath of crime."

*Problem Solving in Action*

Plummer (1996, pp. 9–12) describes how problem solving was used to address the problem of domestic violence in Mountain View, California.

## "Predictability" of Domestic Violence Offers an Opportunity for Successful Problem Solving

**By Larry C. Plummer, Mountain View, Calif., Police Department**

The crime of domestic violence is different from virtually every other type of crime we investigate. It is, by the nature of its dynamics and parts, "predictable," and therefore preventable.

Unfortunately, in the past we associated cases of domestic violence—especially domestic homicides—with other types of crimes that involved "passion" as a motivating influence or causal factor. In doing so, we dismissed them as being unpredictable and therefore outside the realm of our ability to prevent.

Our problem in Mountain View was that we had been looking at the problem with blinders on. We had missed telltale signs and information that we now understand and use as indicators of predictability and the basis for the development of problem-oriented intervention and prevention strategies.

### Clues to Predictability

By examining the perpetrators of our domestic violence cases, their victims, the cyclical patterns of behavior associated with their violent relationships, and even the pattern of our own responses, we found an extraordinary amount of information. Generally, such information is available to us for other crime types only upon the conclusion or near conclusion of our investigations.

The following case illustrates the kind of information available when one asks who, what, where, when and how questions to analyze the nature of a domestic violence problem and the potential for more effective response.

**Who?** This case involved an estranged husband, just released from county jail for past violations of a restraining order; his wife; their two children; and the wife's male friend.

*Notes:* There was a pattern of escalating abuse and violence, and the main participants were known, having been principle parties in all previous cases.

**What?** This case involved domestic violence—in this instance, a multiple homicide. The husband returned to the home he was forbidden to approach as a condition of a restraining order, intent upon retaining "control" of his wife. She returned with the children and a friend to pick up belongings in anticipation of her husband's release and return. The husband and wife argued, the friend interceded, and the husband killed the friend, wife and then himself, all in front of the two children.

*Notes:* The crime type was the same as in previous cases involving this family—domestic violence. In this case however, the violence escalated to homicide. The involved parties were the same as in previous cases, with the exception of the innocent friend.

*continued*

**Where?** The crime took place at the "family" home, which had been the location for five previous police responses to complaints of domestic violence committed by the husband against the wife.

*Notes:* Where else? While domestic violence occurs in places other than the home, most crimes do occur behind the closed doors of the home. All previous cases involving this couple occurred at the home.

**When?** This case occurred several months ago. The "when" is the only component we can't fix with accuracy. However, whether domestic violence involves "simple" violence or homicide, we know that it is coming or may come at any time. Absent separation and treatment, the cycle of violence continues.

*Notes:* The husband had previously threatened to kill his wife should she ever try to leave him, and all of the previous cases occurred during a specific two-hour period on weekend evenings.

**How?** In this case, the husband used a handgun.

*Notes:* In previous cases the husband had struck his wife with his fists, but one case involved his brandishing a handgun and he had previously threatened to shoot and kill her.

### Inadequate Past Responses to the Problem

In the past, our responses to disturbance calls that did not involve actual domestic violence but that might be indicative of a domestic violence problem were rarely, if ever, captured on a "real" police report. As such, they could not be recovered for consideration as part of our domestic crime statistics and were never given a second look.

Minor domestic violence cases were often underinvestigated and underreported. In most cases, the substance of our responses and actions was captured on short form reports that sometimes lacked thorough information. Appropriate enforcement (arrest) and follow-up actions were not routine or consistent.

More serious domestic violence cases were usually appropriately investigated and documented, but our ability to support the victim ended with an arrest and/or provision of standard victim information and assistance cards. In general, our response to domestic violence probably mirrored that of many police agencies across the country. It followed the following pattern:

We began by responding to minor "disturbance only" calls that could have been recognized as activity associated with the cycle of domestic abuse. These were usually documented in ways that did not allow us to track or recover the data.

We would later respond to additional incidents at the same address. The incidents involved abuse or violence between the same two people, and the circumstances fit a predictable pattern. A female victim was abused or assaulted more seriously than she had been before, was now more cooperative with and trusting of police, and was more interested in her abuser's arrest and prosecution. The male suspect was calmer than the victim, denying his involvement, blaming the victim, or perhaps not at home when the police arrived. The children were once again witnesses to or victims of abuse (and perpetual scarring). We made a report, perhaps arrested the suspect and infrequently followed up on the investigation. We provided victim support information, but did not have any other means of supporting the victim or doing anything more to intervene.

Finally, in all too many cases, we responded one final time. This time, however, the case involved homicide and we took it very, very seriously. We arrested the suspect and did the most thorough form of investigation and reporting we knew how to do. The result, however, was merely one more arrest and closure, which did absolutely nothing for the victim or the domestic violence problem in general. And, as in all previous responses, we were, by virtue of our limited perspective and response, much too late.

### *Community Policing: A Change of Perspective*

A little over one year ago, Chief Michael Maehler committed our organization to institutionalizing and operationalizing the philosophy of community-oriented policing. Our new focus on "Policing with Partners" to solve problems that afflict our community led us almost immediately to reassess the way we viewed the problem of domestic violence and our response to the problem.

Our efforts were guided by the newfound perspective that we had to 1) be more proactive in addressing the problem, 2) approach it with a keen understanding of the issues involved, 3) seek long-term solutions and 4) be able to bring more resources to bear on the problem than we currently had at our disposal. We realized that success—reducing the incidence of domestic violence—would require the support and involvement of community partners.

The keys to our progress were our true belief that the problem's predictability provided opportunities for intervention, and our partnership with the Support Network for Battered Women (Network). The Network offered the support resource required to make eventual intervention strategies a reality.

### *Addressing Domestic Violence Using the SARA Model*

*Scanning.* The problem of domestic violence must be as old as humankind itself, and affects every jurisdiction in the world. We had lived with our problem for years, but despite rising media attention and public concern, our perspective remained quite traditional, this marked only by the changing of our protocol on the subject in 1993.

However, several things occurred in 1995 that led us to examine the problem from a fresh perspective and to change our methods. They were 1) our notice of a pattern of multiple, repeat police responses to several homes where domestic violence recurred; 2) our notice that responses to actual domestic violence at these locations had been preceded by one or more responses to "disturbances" (noise, arguments, yelling, bothering, abuse not amounting to a crime, etc.) that should have been indications to us that there existed a potential for future domestic violence; 3) our chief's commitment to community-oriented policing; 4) city involvement in a countywide conference on domestic violence, the outgrowth of which was the establishment of a city task force on domestic violence; 5) the fielding of several complaints about our poor response to domestic violence calls; and 6) the start of our relationship with the Network, our primary local support agency for battered women.

Our relationship with the Network did more than anything else to give us a newfound awareness and sensitivity, which led us to determine that our problem with domestic violence was masked and growing, that real intervention and reductions in the crime were possible, and that the problem deserved much more attention than we had previously given to it.

*continued*

*Analysis.* Investigative staff members responsible for addressing "persons" crimes noticed the problem with our response, as well as opportunities presented by our new relationship with the Network. They were responsible for forging a formal relationship with the Network and developing problem-solving strategies.

Their study of our statistics showed that while documentation of actual domestic violence cases had remained quite static over a period of time (35 cases per month), "disturbance" incidents that we might logically examine and connect to domestic relationships seemed to be escalating and were substantial in number. Investigators estimated their frequency at roughly twice that of actual domestic violence reports.

Interviews with our own officers supported their sense that the weight and importance of domestic violence-related disturbance calls was indeed substantial. Officers identified problem locations denoted by incidences of repeat responses and expressed their frustration at not having the time or resources to offer victims more than enforcement or referral information as a "solution."

Research conducted into what other agencies and individuals were doing and saying about the problem provided investigators with valuable insights, alternative response methods and potential for real intervention and abatement. They focused specifically, and with gratitude, on work conducted by the San Diego Police Department and Ann O'Dell, who had years before effectively addressed the predictability of domestic violence-related homicides.

Meetings with the Network were held to share information and obtain their feedback about the problem and our response methods. We learned through these meetings that victims and support agencies were unhappy with our response.

Victims saw the police as more of an impediment and threat than a source for support and resolution. Furthermore, they found it hard to accept police officers as both report takers/enforcers and support providers.

The Network also pointed to problems with the way we made reports on crimes of domestic violence and asked that we do a better and more consistent job in this arena. Finally, and most important, they expressed a strong desire to partner with us in developing problem-solving strategies designed to reduce the incidence of domestic violence.

Our analysis included consideration of the above-mentioned clues to predictability and the resulting belief that we could effectively predict future problems with domestic violence and then provide intervention services designed to prevent the likelihood of the actual occurrence.

Investigators thought we could do so by accurately documenting cases of domestic "disturbances," which we knew were sound predictors of a domestic violence problem. This could be followed by intervening with potential victims identified in those reports as well as reports of domestic violence, then offering them support services appropriate to their circumstances.

To proceed from this analysis, we knew that we had to change response and reporting methods, and also acquire additional personnel resources for adequate intervention and follow-up services.

*Response.* Investigators met with a variety of department personnel, members of the city task force and Network members to develop and choose a response plan. Listed on the following page are our goal and associated objectives. The objectives were constructed to incorporate the whole department in our response plan.

**Goal:** Reduce the incidence of domestic violence by providing intervention services to those documented as being victims of domestic violence and those predicted to be at risk of becoming domestic violence victims.

**Objective 1:** Enhance our reporting of domestic violence cases and create case documentation on other cases that could help predict the future incidence of domestic violence. We hoped to have members produce more complete, thorough and effective police investigations and to document as fully as we could the considerable number of disturbance cases occurring that might be predictors of domestic problems and future domestic violence incidents.

A range of alternatives was considered, including adding report forms, eliminating reporting forms and formats, increasing report review and changing data recovery mechanisms. We ultimately decided on the following actions. 1) Adopt a new domestic violence protocol endorsed by the county chiefs of police. The protocol required more complete reporting, more severe and consistent enforcement, and the provision of better "up front" and follow-up support to victims. 2) Create a new report classification of "Domestic Disturbance" and require hard-copy documentation of such cases. Doing so would capture those disturbance cases that might be predictors of a domestic problem and future violence. 3) Require review of disturbance cases by persons-crimes investigators. 4) Make statistics on the new disturbance category part of our monthly crime statistic reports.

**Objective 2:** Provide meaningful intervention services to victims of domestic violence or domestic disturbances as a follow-up to the original police responses and investigations. We hoped that doing so could effectively support victims to take actions to resolve their problems and reduce the likelihood of future violence.

The provision of intervention services required the dedication of personnel resources we didn't have at our disposal. We considered and rejected a plan to deliver such services through persons-crimes investigators—they were already taxed too heavily and felt that the provision of such services by people other than sworn officers would be better received. We also considered and rejected the use of nonsworn or volunteer members—budget, staffing and supervisory span of control were issues. True to our philosophy to "Police with Partners," we ultimately decided to create and implement a Victim Assistance Program (VAP) that would be staffed within the Persons Crimes Unit by volunteers from the Network. VAP volunteers would receive copies of each domestic violence and disturbance case report made, review the cases, contact victims, offer victim-support services, provide investigators with feedback from victims and on police reports/actions and, as appropriate, serve as a liaison between investigators and victims regarding further investigations.

New protocols to implement new reporting requirements and the VAP program were issued following delivery of training in June 1996.

*Assessment.* As we all know, the problem of domestic violence will take years to abate. In our case, the success of this first response plan will take several years to measure. We will by then have amended the plan, perhaps once or twice, in response to analysis of its effects, shortcomings and successes, as well as changes in the problem itself.

However, we have already had some successes based on our stated goal and objectives. Notable successes are as follows:

• The quality and effect of our investigations are much improved. This assessment is based on feedback from both internal and external review of case work.

*continued*

- Feedback from the Network, victims, citizens and our officers indicate that officers are showing more concern for victims of domestic violence and the problem itself.
- We are documenting an average of 66 domestic disturbance cases each month. These cases would previously have been buried, unnoticed or reflected only in statistics on the general category of "Disturbance Other" cases.
- The department and the Network are together issuing more emergency protective restraining orders and restraining orders than in the past.

We have contacted and offered services to an average of 50 victims of domestic violence or domestic disturbances each month through the VAP. While we average 97 cases of violence or disturbance each month and had set an objective of contacting a greater average number of victims (75+%), we have found this to be unattainable given the 20 hour per week volunteer allocation from the Network

Analysis of this shortcoming prompted the department to partner with the Network in submitting a grant request to the COPS Office for funding that would allow the Network to provide the department with a full-time, paid VAP employee for one year.

Comparison of the four-month period prior to the start of the plan with the four-month period following showed 1) a decrease in the incidence of actual domestic violence cases by two per month, but 2) an increase in arrests for domestic violence of almost 43 percent (21 vs. 30).

### Conclusion

We have been quite satisfied with the results of our response plan to date. Resistance we expected from line personnel on reporting changes and from persons-crimes investigators who might have perceived the VAP as an intrusion have never materialized. Rather, all members have been impressed by and appreciative of the support provided by the VAP. Furthermore, our general ethic and response to the problem of domestic violence and its victims has been elevated by the influence of the VAP and our partnership with the Network. We look forward to the program and our response evolving in the future.

*Reprinted by permission of the Police Executive Research Forum.*

## SUMMARY

National Crime Survey statistics estimate that 42.4 million victimizations were committed in the United States in 1994. Victims of crime may suffer physical injury, financial and property losses, emotional distress and psychological trauma. Some suffer from post traumatic stress disorder (PTSD), a persistent re-experiencing of a traumatic event through intrusive memories and dreams and a variety of anxiety-related symptoms. A primary victim is a person actually harmed by an incident. A secondary victim is one indirectly affected by the trauma.

Victimology, the study of crime victims, includes the concepts of vulnerability and culpability. Bureau of Justice statistics show that those most at risk of being victimized are young, black males with low incomes living in urban areas. A second injury often occurs to victims when they are treated badly by the professionals who should be helping them, including police officers and the criminal justice system.

Our society has made progress in helping crime victims. The Federal Victim and Witness Protection Act of 1982 established the victim impact statement (VIS) as a formal part of the presentence report. The victim impact statement is a report written by the victim that describes in detail the full effect of the crime. The VIS may influence the sentence passed by the judge. The Victims of Crime Act (VOCA), passed in 1984, established a fund making state grants available for victims' compensation, victim assistance programs and child abuse prevention and treatment. The National Organization for Victim Assistance (NOVA) was founded in 1976. A second national organization, the National Victim Center, was founded in 1985. Congress and many states have passed legislation to assist crime victims.

The two main types of programs provided for victims are victim service programs that provide crisis counseling, shelter and other specialized treatment, and victim and witness assistance programs that seek to provide assistance to victims and witnesses as they move through the judicial process

Most victims' bills of rights include both informational and participatory rights. Victims' rights bills commonly require victims to be informed about available financial aid and social services, notification of case status and scheduling, protection from harassment and intimidation, separate waiting areas and a speedy return of property held as evidence. Victims who require additional services include battered and sexually abused women, abused children and elderly victims of crime or abuse.

## Discussion Questions

1. Have you ever been victimized? How were you treated by those who "assisted" you?
2. How large a role do you believe culpability plays in victimization?
3. Did the "blame the victim" syndrome play a role in the Anita Hill—Clarence Thomas hearings?
4. Do police and other professionals who assist victims treat those victims who are wealthy differently than those who are poor?
5. How do you balance professional detachment and the need for empathy?
6. How large a role should victim impact statements play in sentencing?
7. What victim services are available in your community?
8. What services that are not currently available should be available in your community?
9. In what ways do police officers become victims?
10. What differences exist between assisting victims of crime and victims of accidents or natural disasters?

## References

Adams, Aileen. "Office for Victims of Crime." Washington: 1996, p. 1.

American Psychiatric Association. *Diagnostic and Statistical Manual of Mental Disorders,* 3rd rev. ed. Washington: American Psychiatric Association, 1985.

Bazemore, Gordon and Umbreit, Mark S. *Balanced and Restorative Justice.* Washington: Office of Juvenile Justice and Delinquency Prevention, 1994.

Burnley, Jane Nady. "Foreword." In *Helping Crime Victims: Research, Policy, and Practice,* edited by Albert R. Roberts, 10–12. Newbury Park: Sage Publications, 1990.

Butterfield, Fox. "In Boston, Nothing Is Something." *Subject to Debate.* (February/March 1997): 1, 3–4.

Carrington, Frank and Nicholson, George. "Victim's Rights? An Idea Whose Time Has Come—Five Years Later: The Maturing of an Idea." In *Taking Sides: Clashing Views on Controversial Issues in Crime and Criminology,* 2nd rev. ed., edited by Richard C. Monk, 338–43. Guilford: The Dushkin Publishing Group, Inc., 1991.

Conroy, Dennis L. and Hess, Kären M. *Officers at Risk: How to Identify and Cope with Stress.* Incline Village, Nev.: Copperhouse Publishing Company, 1991.

Davis, Robert C. and Henley, Madeline. "Victim Service Programs." In *Victims of Crime: Problems, Policies, and Programs,* edited by Arthur J. Lurigio, Wesley G. Skogan, and Robert C. Davis, 157–71. Newbury Park: Sage Publications, 1990.

DiIulio, John J., Jr.; Alpert, Geoffrey P.; Moore, Mark H.; Cole, George F.; Petersilia, Joan; Logan, Charles H.; and Wilson, James Q. *Performance Measures for the Criminal Justice System.* Washington: Bureau of Justice Statistics and the Princeton University, October 1993.

Elias, Robert. "The Politics of Victimization." In *Taking Sides: Clashing Views on Controversial Issues in Crime and Criminology,* 2nd rev. ed., edited by Richard C. Monk, 344–50. Guilford: The Dushkin Publishing Group, Inc., 1991.

Elias, Robert. "Which Victim Movement? The Politics of Victim Policy." In *Victims of Crime: Problems, Policies, and Programs,* edited by Arthur J. Lurigio, Wesley G. Skogan, and Robert C. Davis, 226–50. Newbury Park: Sage Publications, 1990.

Franklin, Sloane R. "New Legislation Makes Victims' Rights a Priority." *Corrections Today.* (July 1995): 153–54.

Frederick, Calvin J.; Hawkins, Karen L; and Abajian, Wendy E. "Beyond the Call of Duty? Victim/Witness Intervention Techniques." *The Police Chief.* (October 1990): 106–10.

Friedman, Lucy N. and Shulman, Minna. "Domestic Violence: The Criminal Justice Response." In *Victims of Crime: Problems, Policies, and Programs,* edited by Arthur J. Lurigio, Wesley G. Skogan, and Robert C. Davis, 87–103. Newbury Park: Sage Publications, 1990.

Geberth, Vernon. "Secondary Victims of Homicide." *Law and Order.* (September 1992): 91–96.

Hillenbrand, Susan. "Restitution and Victim Rights in the 1980s." In *Victims of Crime: Problems, Policies, and Programs,* edited by Arthur J. Lurigio, Wesley G. Skogan, and Robert C. Davis, 188–204. Newbury Park: Sage Publications, 1990.

International Association of Chiefs of Police. *Crime Victims' Bills of Rights.* Board of Officers. Arlington: Policy Center, 1983.

Karmen, Andrew. "The Implementation of Victims' Rights: A Challenge for Criminal Justice Professionals." In *Annual Editions: Criminal Justice 92/93,* 16th ed., 46–49. Guilford: The Dushkin Publishing Group, Inc., 1992.

Kelly, Deborah. "Victim Participation in the Criminal Justice System." In *Victims of Crime: Problems, Policies, and Programs,* edited by Arthur J. Lurigio, Wesley G. Skogan, and Robert C. Davis, 172–87. Newbury Park: Sage Publications, 1990.

Larimer, Peter. "Cellular Telephones Link Victims to Police." *Law and Order.* (September 1994): 57.

Laub, John H. "Patterns of Criminal Victimization in the United States." In *Victims of Crime: Problems, Policies, and Programs,* edited by Arthur J. Lurigio, Wesley G. Skogan, and Robert C Davis, 23–49. Newbury Park: Sage Publications, 1990.

Lurigio, Arthur J. and Resick, Patricia A. "Healing the Psychological Wounds of Criminal Victimization: Predicting Postcrime Distress and Recovery." In *Victims of Crime: Problems, Policies, and Programs,* edited by Arthur J. Lurigio, Wesley G. Skogan, and Robert C. Davis, 50–68. Newbury Park: Sage Publications, 1990.

Lurigio, Arthur J.; Skogan, Wesley G.; and Davis, Robert C. (eds.) *Victims of Crime: Problems, Policies, and Programs.* Newbury Park: Sage Publications, 1990.

McClenahan, Carol A. "Victim Services—A Positive Police-Community Effort." *The Police Chief.* (October 1990): 104.

Monk, Richard C. *Taking Sides: Clashing Views on Controversial Issues in Crime and Criminology,* 2nd rev. ed. Guilford: The Dushkin Publishing Group, Inc., 1991.

Morales, Dan. "A Message from Dan Morales: The Crime Victims' Institute." *CVD News.* (September 1995): 1.

Muraskin, Roslyn. "The Growth Industry of Victim Services." *Law Enforcement News.* (March 15, 1992): 13.

National District Attorneys Association. *A Prosecutor's Guide to Victim Witness Assistance.* Alexandria: National District Attorneys Association, n.d.

Newton, Edmund. "Criminals Have All the Rights." In *Criminal Justice 87/88,* edited by John J. Sullivan and Joseph L. Victor, 57–61. Guilford: The Dushkin Publishing Group, Inc.

O'Brien, Victoria. *Civil Legal Remedies for Crime Victims.* Washington: Office for Victims of Crime Bulletin, December 1992.

Parent, Dale G.; Auerbach, Barbara; and Carlson, Kenneth E. *Compensating Crime Victims: A Summary of Policies and Practices.* Washington: National Institute of Justice, January 1992.

Perkins, Craig and Klaus, Patsy. *Criminal Victimization 1994.* Washington: Bureau of Justice Statistics Bulletin, April 1996.

Plummer, Larry C. "'Predictability' of Domestic Violence Offers an Opportunity for Successful Problem Solving." *Problem-Solving Quarterly.* (Fall/Winter 1996): 9–12.

Quinn, Thomas J. "Righting Wrongs: Making the Case for Restorative Justice." *NCJA Justice Bulletin.* (September 1995): 4–5, 11–13.

Resick, Patricia A. "Victims of Sexual Assault." In *Victims of Crime: Problems, Policies, and Programs,* edited by Arthur J. Lurigio, Wesley G. Skogan, and Robert C. Davis, 69–86. Newbury Park: Sage Publications, 1990.

"Restore Victim, Assess Community Risk, NCJA Panelists Say." *NCJA Justice Bulletin.* (June 1995): 3–6.

Riggs, David S. and Kilpatrick, Dean G. "Families and Friends: Indirect Victimization by Crime." In *Victims of Crime: Problems, Policies, and Programs,* edited by Arthur J. Lurigio, Wesley G. Skogan, and Robert C. Davis, 120–38. Newbury Park: Sage Publications, 1990.

Roberts, Albert R. *Crisis Intervention Handbook: Assessment, Treatment and Research.* Belmont: Wadsworth, 1990a.

Roberts, Albert R. *Helping Crime Victims: Research, Policy, and Practice.* Newbury Park: Sage Publications, 1990b.

Roberts, Albert R. and Roberts, Beverly Schenkman. "A Model for Crisis Intervention with Battered Women and Their Children." In *Helping Crime Victims: Research, Policy, and Practices,* edited by Albert R. Roberts, 186–205. Newbury Park: Sage Publications, 1990.

Senna, Joseph J. and Siegel, Larry J. *Introduction to Criminal Justice,* 5th rev. ed. St. Paul: West Publishing Company, 1990.

Shriner, Susan. *Victim Programs to Serve Native Americans.* Washington: OVS Bulletin, February 1992.

Skogan, Wesley G.; Lurigio, Arthur J.; and Davis, Robert C. "Criminal Victimization." In *Victims of Crime: Problems, Policies, and Programs,* edited by Arthur J. Lurigio, Wesley G. Skogan, and Robert C. Davis, 7–21. Newbury Park: Sage Publications, 1990.

Smith, Barbara E. "The Adjudication of Child Sexual Abuse Cases." In *Victims of Crime: Problems, Policies, and Programs,* edited by Arthur J. Lurigio, Wesley G. Skogan, and Robert C. Davis, 104–19. Newbury Park: Sage Publications, 1990.

Strandberg, Keith W. "Victim and Witness Intimidation." *Law Enforcement Technology.* (February 1997): 42–48.

Van Ness, Daniel W. "Restoring the Balance: Tipping the Scales of Justice." *Corrections Today.* (February 1990): 62–66.

"Victims of Release Dates." *Law Enforcement Technology.* (November 1996): 52–55.

Waller, Irvin. "The Police: First in Aid?" In *Victims of Crime: Problems, Policies, and Programs,* edited by Arthur J. Lurigio, Wesley G. Skogan, and Robert C. Davis, 139–56. Newbury Park: Sage Publications, 1990.

Wells, Robert C. "Victim Impact: How Much Consideration Is it Really Given?" *The Police Chief.* (February 1991): 44–47.

Zehr, Howard. "Restorative Justice." *IARCA Journal.* (March 1991): 1–7.

## *Resources*

National Center for Missing and Exploited Children, 1835 K Street, N.W., Suite 700, Washington, D.C. 20006; (202) 634-9821. Hotline: (1-800) 843-5678.

National Organization for Victim Assistance (NOVA), P.O. Box 11000, Washington, D.C. 20008; (202) 232-NOVA.

National Victims Resource Center, Box 6000, Rockville, MD 20850; (800) 627-6872.

# Chapter 13

# Communicating
# with the Media

*The police work is very much an "us-and-them" kind of thing. They are the beleaguered minority who are out there protecting the citizens from themselves, and the citizens are not smart enough to appreciate them. And the newsies are out there lying in wait, and the moment they screw up, we're there to jump their throats and tell the world.*

—Kevin Diaz

## Do you know

- What organizations the "media" includes?
- What is the common goal of the police and the media?
- Why the police-media relationship can be called symbiotic?
- What amendment protects "freedom of the press"?
- What amendment guides the police in their relationship with the media?
- What conflicts exist between the media and the police?
- What are legitimate reasons for not giving information to the press?
- What "off the record" really means?
- How to enhance the safety of members of the media during explosive situations?
- How reporters and police generally differ in decision making?
- Whether conflict between the police and the press must be dysfunctional?
- Why reporters may foul up stories? What implications this has for law enforcement?

## Definitions

Can you define these terms: Pager Information Network (PIN), public information officer (PIOs), symbiotic.

415

# *Introduction*

"On any given day on any given newscast in any given city, law enforcement-related news—misdemeanors, felonies, traffic accidents—consumes approximately 30% of the available air time" (Gleick, 1991, p. 98). In addition: "The image of the entire criminal justice system is dependent upon what is said in the media about each of its components" (Pace, 1991, p. 244). Pace notes: "Good publicity is the life blood of a police agency."

Conversely, negative publicity can be extremely damaging, as evidenced by the "Rodney King Affair" aired internationally by CNN.

◆

The media includes newspapers, radio and television.

◆

The media can and should be a powerful partner in community policing efforts.

◆

The police and members of the media share the common goal of serving the public.

◆

In addition to sharing a common goal, they also rely heavily upon each other.

This chapter begins with a discussion of the mutual reliance of the police and the media and the inherent conflict between the guarantees of the First Amendment and the Sixth Amendment. This is followed by a description of the historical conflict between the press and the police as well as the importance of treating police officers and reporters as individuals. General polices regarding media relations and photographing and videotaping at crime scenes are reviewed, along with suggestions for improving relations with the media. Next the discussion turns to being professional when interviewed, the news conference and press information officers. The chapter concludes with recommendations for establishing cooperative relationships with the media and a proposed model police department program.

## MUTUAL RELIANCE OF THE POLICE AND THE MEDIA

Police departments and individual officers need the press. The press can shape public opinion, and most police agencies are concerned about their public image. Administrators know that crime and police activities are covered by the media regardless of whether the police provide reporters with information. Most police departments understand that the level of police cooperation will ultimately affect how the public views the police. As noted by Guffey (1992, p. 33):

> The police and the media are two organizations that interact regularly. The relationship can be described as symbiotic. The media need the police to supply them with information about crime and crime patterns that are of interest to their readers, listeners, or viewers. The police need the media to improve their image within the community, to publicize major crimes or crime patterns, to publicize wanted persons, and to seek witnesses from the community.

Garner (1995, p. 41) explains this mutual dependency: "The news business needs law enforcement as its largest single course of news that readers, viewers, and listeners want to know about. Law enforcement, meanwhile, needs the access to the public that the press can provide; to recognize good work by the frontline troops, enlist the citizenry's aid in solving a tough case or get the community's help with an important new police program or project." Garner further observes (p. 44): "Considering the many mutual benefits to be gained from getting along, cooperation is a win-win proposition for both sides."

◆

The police and the media share a **symbiotic** relationship; they are mutually dependent upon each other.

◆

The symbiotic nature of the relationship between the police and the media is described by news director Parrish (pers. com. 1992), who formed special bonds of friendship and respect with some officers. She was able to get extra information from the officers, and they "used" her when they needed to have information made public: "We both used each other, and we both knew it. I got some scoops. And the officers I worked with let it be known in the department that I was trustworthy, and it helped to open doors." Such relationships can be advantageous to all parties.

Unfortunately, relations between the police and the media are often strained. Weinblatt (1992, p. 32) asks: "Why would modern day police officers rather meet a hulking bad guy in a back alley than face a white-collar professional person armed with only a pen and note pad? . . . The trepidation and distrust comes from a lack of communication and a failure to understand just what each party's responsibilities are."

To understand the relationship between the police and the media, officers should be aware of what rights the media has, what their mission is and why law enforcement does not always appear in a positive light in the media.

## THE FIRST AMENDMENT AND FREEDOM
## OF THE PRESS

The First Amendment to our Constitution states: "Congress shall make no law
. . . abridging the freedom of speech or of the press."

According to Rosenthal (1996a, p. 19): "The free flow of information is one
of the cornerstones of our society. If the public asks (or if the media asks on
behalf of the public) then law enforcement is legally required to respond and
generally encouraged to do so (DOJ guidelines)."

◆

> The First Amendment to the Constitution guarantees the public's right to know,
> that is, freedom of the press.

◆

Our society deems the public's right to know so important that the media
operates without censorship, but is subject to legal action if it publishes untruths.

Police reporters are often eager and aggressive in carrying out their duty to
inform the public. Traditionally, police beat reporters are anxious to do well, to
be the first with information and, therefore, they gather and publicize police and
crime news as much as they can. According to Parrish (pers. com. 1992):

> Although traditionally green reporters were assigned to the police beat, more
> recently, the police beat is the prestige beat sought by the experienced, hungry,
> aggressive reporters. It has become the sexy beat, the way to get your face (or
> byline) on record just about every day. TV and movies have made cops big news
> and big box office fodder. The police beat has become the high visibility beat.
> Viewers and readers remember the reporters assigned to these stories. They
> never remember who did a story on the financial status of a school district.

As noted by Dunphy and Garner (1992, p. 47): "Most news media representatives are honest, up-front, hardworking types. They, too, are interested in seeing that an accurate accounting is given to the public."

Rosenthal (1996a, p. 18) describes the Freedom of Information Act (FOIA)
which governs what police can and cannot disclose: "The Freedom of Information Act establishes a presumption that records in the possession of agencies and
departments of the executive branch of the U.S. Government are accessible to the
people . . . the 'need to know' standard has been replaced by a 'right to know'
doctrine. The government now has to justify the need for secrecy." Rosenthal
cites the following exceptions, when the free flow of information can and should
be restricted:

- When anyone's safety could be jeopardized.
- When the integrity of an investigation and/or subsequent prosecution
  could be jeopardized.

- When a confidential source would be revealed.
- When limited internal personnel matters are involved.
- When release of such information jeopardizes the privacy rights of sex crime victims, juveniles or persons who are mentally ill.

Every state has a public records law that specifies what information a law enforcement agency must release, what information must not be released and what is up to the discretion of the particular agency. Such laws are enacted to protect the rights of citizens under suspicion of breaking the law.

## THE SIXTH AMENDMENT, SUSPECT'S RIGHTS AND CRIMINAL INVESTIGATION

The Sixth Amendment of our Constitution establishes that "in all criminal prosecutions, the accused shall enjoy the right to a speedy and public trial, by an impartial jury of the state and district wherein the crime shall have been committed. . . ."

◆

The Sixth Amendment guarantees suspects the right to a fair trial.

◆

In addition to assuring these rights, police officers are also responsible for investigating the crimes suspects are accused of committing. Law enforcement officers sometimes view reporters as an impediment to fulfilling their duties to the public. Law enforcement officers often try to protect information they deem imperative to keep out of the media and may, therefore, be at odds with reporters. Such conflicts arise when police try to prevent public disclosure of information that may tip off a criminal of impending arrest, make prosecution of a particular crime impossible or compromise privacy rights or safety of a victim or witness. Reporters are anxious to do well on their assignments while officers try to avoid weakening their case and reprimands for being too open with the press. The parties' conflicting interests may result in antagonism.

## CONFLICT BETWEEN THE PRESS AND THE POLICE

The press and the police are two powerful forces in our society that depend on one another but are often hostile toward and mistrust each other.

As Parrish (1993, p. 93) observes: "Police and media are natural adversaries, and probably always will be."

Lesce (1994, p. 98) provides the following comments by reporters and police officers about each other:

- Reporters never quote you right. They twist everything you say to suit themselves.
- Cops are just a bunch of secretive paranoids who are afraid of the press and everybody else.
- The cops in this town just hate your guts if the story you write doesn't make them look good in every way.
- Reporters are liberal cop-haters who try to make cops look bad every chance they get.

A basic source of the conflict is the competing objectives of the press and the police.

## A Conflict in Objectives

As noted by Pace (1991, p. 244): "The objectives of the police and the news services may not be compatible because their roles are different. . . . There is even an incongruity between constitutional guarantees."

♦

The First Amendment guarantees freedom of the press, yet the Sixth Amendment guarantees the right to a fair trial and protects the defendant's rights.

♦

The basic conflict is between the public's right to know and the individual's right to privacy and a fair trial.

Weinblatt (1992, p. 32) suggests some other internal conflicts that result from these differences:

Police officials with an active investigation in progress are very conscious of the dichotomy which exists in their mandate. On the one hand, cases are solved with information from the public. The police need the press to get to the masses. On the other, police concerns regarding next of kin notification, family suffering and investigation impairment are also bona fide issues and need to be addressed.

♦

Police may need to withhold information from the press until next of kin are notified, in the interest of public safety or to protect the integrity of an investigation.

♦

Although many police officers are keenly aware of the conflict between themselves and the press, they often do not understand how the need to withhold information contributes to the conflict and the resulting negative coverage and what officers can do to alleviate the problem.

## Complaints of the Press

To do their job, members of the media need information from the police. Press people say they have problems obtaining information they are entitled to because the police refuse to provide it. In some cases, reporters believe they have been singled out by the police for "punishment" in response to a negative story about the police.

Reporters tell of police who restrict information, refuse requests for interviews, disregard reporters' deadlines, hang up the telephone on reporters, provide inaccurate information, play dumb or even blackball a particular reporter in retaliation for a story they did not like.

Guffey (1992, p. 40) reports the following frequent media complaints about the police:

- They are not forthcoming.
- They cannot accept legitimate criticism.
- They withhold important information.
- They hide behind the shield of the Sixth Amendment too often.
- They are often uncooperative.
- They cannot accept that the media are a legitimate "check" on possible abuses of authority.

The police have a similar list of complaints about the press.

## Complaints of the Police

Complaints of the police regarding the press include the following (Guffey, 1992, p. 38):

- Interference with ongoing investigations.
- Insensitivity to legitimate privacy interests of victims.
- Insensitivity to the impact of their report on the police.
- Penchant for sensationalism even at the expense of accuracy.

Some police agencies or officers, who have had negative experiences with the media or believe they have been tricked into releasing information, react by becoming uncooperative, not giving information to which the press is entitled, playing favorites among reporters and even lying. The behavior of the police aggravates a difficult relationship.

Consider, for example, the "off the record" comments some public officials are inclined to make to reporters. Many have been unpleasantly surprised to be quoted in the next edition of the newspaper. Officers must learn to say only that

*CHP (California Highway Patrol Officer) Fred Bowes promotes their crackdown on drunk drivers in front of a wrecked car. Enlisting community support often depends on the media's cooperation.*

which they can accept attribution for and are prepared to read or hear reported in the media.

◆

> To speak to a reporter "off the record" does not guarantee that the information will not be reported. It may, in fact, make it more likely to be reported.

◆

In some cases, reporters promise to keep information "off the record" when they have no authority to do so.

Motivated by a desire to protect their case and the privacy of those involved, police complain that the press is critical and biased against the police, that reporting is often inaccurate, that reporters lack sensitivity especially toward victims and that the press releases sensitive material and betrays the trust of officers. As noted by Cook (1991, p. 88): "A sensitive investigation is a tough job. But often the toughest part is the confrontation from a pack of reporters bent on yanking something 'newsworthy' (i.e., 'controversial') out of your mouth." Cook contends: "Important cases are going to be tried in the press, with or without you." Often press coverage of important cases is sensationalist.

Many criminal justice scholars place the blame for the emphasis on crime directly on the media, noting that crime news has quadrupled in the past four years ("'Media Crime Wave . . . ,'" 1996, p. 3). In 1995 crime news increased by 32 percent over 1994 and 52 percent from 1993. Television coverage of murders, which averaged about 100 stories per year during the early 1990s, totaled 1,249 stories in 1995.

The way the public views crime depends in large part on what the media prints. Wright (1991, p. 114) suggests that the media presents a distorted, sensationalized view:

> Over dramatization is the norm rather than the exception in modern crime reporting.
>
> The media distorts its presentation of crime patterns by selecting particular incidents to report. Unusual, bizarre, violent, and macabre incidents receive more media attention. A recent review of research about patterns of crime reporting found that "without exception, violent individual crimes—particularly murders—are represented disproportionately in news media presentations."

Officers must remember, however, that the media consists of businesses, in fierce competition with each other for readers, listeners and viewers. What officers may consider sensationalism, reporters might consider the competitive edge.

Another source of conflict between law enforcement and the media is the danger members of the press may expose themselves to in getting a story and the police's obligation to protect them. A reviewer of this chapter, Parrish, wrote: "When I saw you on 5/6, I had no idea that the next night my news crew would be attacked during the riot in North Minneapolis. Julia, my reporter, is a patient at Sister Kinney and is still unable to walk because of her head injuries. It's been very scary." Parrish discussed the suggestion that this text address the issue of media safety:

> Maybe I'm a little sensitive right now, but the safety of the media at crime scenes or riots or potentially dangerous situations is important. Generally reporters and photographers will not cross yellow lines of police tape. But what about situations which are unfolding and the police and the media are both on the scene.
>
> Cops should not tell journalists to stay away. That is a red flag to most reporters who will run headlong into the area to get their story. But cops are better trained at reading dangerous situations. I would suggest that they urge reporters and photographers to leave an area if they deem it unsafe and tell them why. Don't just bark, "Get out of here."
>
> Since the KMSP incident, I have talked to cops who said they knew their first responsibility was to secure the area and calm things down, but they also felt a responsibility for the safety of the media. That angered them . . . that the media was "stupid" enough to be in the middle of the riot. My crew was told to leave and was doing so when attacked. But despite their supposed hatred of the media, the cops in North Minneapolis didn't want to see my people hurt, and they felt bad when they were.

Police should meet with local media representatives to explain about rules of safety. And this should be done before an incident arises. It might boil down to telling journalists that they have the right to make decisions about their own well-being, but that as officers, they will issue warnings to try and ensure the safety of news crews. I think that, with the ugly mood in this country right now, the matter of safety of news crews—and whether or not the police are responsible for that safety—will become a big issue.

◆

To help assure the safety of media personnel at explosive situations, police should meet with media representatives to explain the safety rules *before* an incident arises.

◆

## One Possible Factor Underlying the Conflict between the Press and the Police

Fundamental differences in personality type may be one reason for the conflict that sometimes exists between the police and the press. Hennessy (1992) studied the personalities of police compared to those of the population at large and specific groups, including editors and reporters. Hennessy used the Myers-Briggs test which divides individuals into four basic types, depending on how they make decisions and interact with others.

Individuals may prefer to rely upon how they *feel* about a situation or what they *think* about the situation. Some people are more emotional or more logical in their decision-making process. In addition, individuals may prefer to rely upon their senses (*sensing*) or on their *intuition* when making decisions. These preferences result in the following possible combinations:

ST Sensing/Thinking
SF Sensing/Feeling
NT Intuitive/Thinking
NF Intuitive/Feeling

Hennessy gave a sample of 23,557 individuals the Myers-Briggs test to establish what is "normal" for Americans. The same test was given to over 3,000 police officers and to over 100 editors and reporters. The test results of the three groups are summarized in Table 13.1.

Note that while the majority (58 percent) of citizens and reporters relied upon feeling in making decisions, the majority of police officers (80 percent) relied on thinking. Another very obvious difference between the two personality types is the reliance of police officers on sensing in contrast to reporters who rely heavily on intuition.

*Table 13.1*   **Preferred Cognitive Styles by Group**

|  |  | Citizens (N = 23,557) | Editors/ Reporters (N = 113) | Police Officers (N = 3,101) |
|---|---|---|---|---|
|  |  | Percent | Percent | Percent |
| Intuitive-Feeling | NF | 28.32 | 41.71 | 6.3 |
| Sensing-Feeling | SF | 29.34 | 16.82 | 14.0 |
| Intuitive-Thinking | NT | 17.56 | 27.43 | 16.6 |
| Sensing-Thinking | ST | 24.78 | 15.04 | 64.1 |
| Totals |  | 100.00 | 100.00 | 100.0 |

SOURCE: G. P. Macdaid, M. H. McCaulley, and R. I. Kainz, *Myers-Briggs Type Indicator Atlas.* Gainesville: Center for Applications of Psychological Type, Inc.,1986, and Stephen M. Hennessy, *Thinking Cop/Feeling Cop: A Study in Police Personalities,* Scottsdale: Leadership, Incorporated of Scottsdale, 1992.

◆

Police tend to rely on thinking and their senses in decision making, in contrast to editors and reporters who tend to rely on feeling and intuition.

◆

The specific percentages for each of the four ways to approach decisions are summarized in Table 13.2.

It is interesting to note that social workers had results within seven percentage points of the editors and reporters which may explain some of the communication problems police have with these professionals.

*Table 13.2*   **Comparison of Citizens, Reporters and Police Officers on the Myers-Briggs Test**

|  | Citizen | Editors/Reporters | Police Officers |
|---|---|---|---|
| Feeling | 58% | 58% | 20% |
| Thinking | 41% | 42% | 80% |
| Intuition | 46% | 69% | 23% |
| Sensing | 54% | 32% | 78% |

## POLICE OFFICERS AND REPORTERS AS INDIVIDUALS

Chapter 4 discussed the need for police to avoid stereotypes. Stereotypes can greatly impede good working relationships between law enforcement and members of the press. Parrish wrote a letter that was published in a law enforcement agency's union newsletter. Her letter illustrates the position held by many members of the media:

> As police, you despise being lumped together in a bad light. So do we. Not all journalists are out to get you. You are out to find justice; we are out to seek truth. If we find a story regarding questionable behavior by an officer, we cover it. But we also do stories on community meetings, the COP program, and DARE classes. We show you receiving medals for acts of heroism. We ride along with officers to get a better feel for the difficult job you do. We air composites when you need our help in finding a suspect. And we cover the funerals of your comrades who fall in the line of duty.
>
> You ask for more respect from us. I respond by saying you should give some respect in return. Be more open and honest with us when we are trying to get information on a story . . . hiding facts just makes us suspicious. And it's hard to do a "balanced" story when no one at [a law enforcement agency] will talk to you. We understand your need to keep some information confidential so it doesn't jeopardize your case. We work to *report* what you are doing, not to *thwart* it.
>
> Stereotyping is a dangerous habit these days. It is happening to you, and it is happening to us. We both work under the cloak of the U.S. Constitution. I firmly believe we could do more to open up the lines of good communication between our two groups and work together for the public good.

Understanding differences in personality can be a significant step toward changing a dysfunctional conflict into a healthy, beneficial conflict:

> [To] the police and the media, functional, or healthy, conflict is necessary. The media must avoid a close, bonding relationship with the police and vice versa. Each must remain distant enough to be able to criticize the other when necessary, but not to allow the criticism to end communication (Guffey, 1992, p. 35).

♦

Conflict need not be dysfunctional. In fact, healthy conflict between the press and the police is necessary and beneficial.

♦

Conflict can stimulate people to grow and change. It can diffuse defensiveness if those in conflict recognize that their roles are, by definition, conflicting yet complementary. Better understanding of each other may lead to a cooperative effort to serve the public. Most large law enforcement agencies recognize that a cooperative relationship with the media is to their benefit. Many have developed media policies which set forth for officers exactly what may and may not be released to the press, how information will be released and by whom.

Effective relationships between individual police officers and individual media personnel can greatly reduce the barriers involved. There can and must be a *trust factor* for this to be effective. For example, a radio newscaster who has the trust of the police department can be given confidential information, knowing that he or she will not release it until given the go-ahead. This one-on-one relationship can be of value to law enforcement and to the media.

## GENERAL POLICIES FOR MEDIA RELATIONS

Most agencies have developed written policies governing release of information to the press. These policies recognize the right of reporters to gather information and often direct officers to cooperate with the media. Lying to the press is always a bad idea. So is making promises that you cannot keep or misleading the reporter. Such actions usually haunt the individual or the agency in the form of negative press or lack of media cooperation when the police need help. It is better to honor commitments to the press and be straight forward when information is to be released.

Garner's "rules" for dealing with the press are as follows (1995, pp. 41–43):

- Maintain credibility.
- Keep in touch. Stay proactive in personal press relations. Remain accessible.
- Do unto others. Follow the Golden Rule.
- Check your ego. You are not the story.
- Watch your step. Treat all cameras and microphones as "live" at all times.

Additional guidelines are suggested by Dunphy and Garner (1992, pp. 46–47):

- Practice your presentation in advance. Anticipate questions and prepare responses.
- Treat every microphone as "live" and every camera as "on."
- Establish and maintain control.
- Make sure you understand the question.
- Defuse volatile questions by rephrasing them in softer, less emotional terms.
- Do your homework. Know your topic and your interviewer. . . . Never try to bluff your way through; admit that you do not have the answer and promise to get it if possible.
- Tell the truth. Never lie, even by omission.
- Know the reporters and their deadlines.
- Emphasize your interest to serve the public.

The Commission on Accreditation for Law Enforcement Agencies (CALEA), Chapter 54, governs standards dealing with media relations. According to Program Manager, Stephen W. Mitchell (1997): "Recent studies have determined that the Commission standards can be readily applied to any law enforcement agency operating under Community Policing principles."

# 54
# PUBLIC INFORMATION

Standards in this chapter relate to the establishment and maintenance of public information. Agencies have an obligation to inform the public and news media of events that affect the lives of citizens in the community with openness and candor.

To convey information, agencies often rely on the news media. Policies should be developed that govern what information should be released, when it should be released, and by whom it should be released. In large jurisdictions, where media contacts are frequent and often of a sensitive nature, a full-time public information officer may be needed to coordinate activities. Where the community served is small and media contacts infrequent, the assignment of the function to an individual as a part-time responsibility may suffice. Agencies should consider procedures for involving the media in the development of policies affecting the news media, and for determining when a public information officer should respond to the scene of a crime or other event.

A state-level agency must comply with those public information standards that are consistent with its mission. A state agency is not expected to perform public information activities that would interfere with those provided by local agencies. State agencies may wish to consult Commission staff about the applicability of these standards to their operations.

## 54.1 Public Information

**54.1.1** *The public information function shall include, at a minimum:*

a. *assisting news personnel in covering news stories at the scenes of incidents;*

b. *being available for on-call responses to the news media;*

c. *preparing and distributing agency news releases;*

d. *arranging for, and assisting at, news conferences;*

e. *coordinating and authorizing the release of information about victims, witnesses, and suspects;*

f. *assisting in crisis situations within the agency;*

g. *coordinating and authorizing the release of information concerning confidential agency investigations and operations; and*

h. *developing procedures for releasing information when other public service agencies are involved in a mutual effort.*

**Commentary:** The intent of this standard is to establish agency accountability for the public information function in writing. The function should be developed and operated to effectively meet the agency's needs. Placement of the function within the organizational structure is also addressed by standard 11.1.1. Proving compliance with this standard may be accomplished through a series of documents or a single, all inclusive directive.

The directive should also identify those within the agency authorized to make releases when the CEO/PIO is not available. All information released should be reported to the CEO/PIO as soon as practical.

Another intent of the standard is to provide specific guidance to personnel regarding the release of information about the prior criminal record, character, or reputation of the accused; mugshots of the accused, the existence of any confession, admission of guilt, or statement made by the accused or the failure or refusal by the accused to make a statement; the results of any examinations or tests conducted or refusal by the accused to submit to any examinations or tests; the identity, testimony, or credibility of any prospective witness; any opinion of agency personnel regarding the guilt or innocence of the accused; any opinion of agency personnel regarding the merits of the case or quality of evidence gathered, personal information identifying the victim; information identifying juveniles; and information received from other law enforcement agencies without their concurrence in releasing that information.

"Other service agencies" as used above is meant to refer to all public service agencies, e.g., fire departments, coroners' offices, and other outside agencies. Where more than one agency is involved, the agency having primary jurisdiction should be responsible for releasing, or coordinating the release of, information.

**54.1.2** *The agency involves the news media in the development of changes in policies and procedures relating to the public information function.*

**Commentary:** By allowing media representatives to participate in the process of developing policies and procedures relating to the public information function, agencies can receive input that should lead to more effective working relationships between agency and media personnel.

**54.1.3** *A written directive controls the access of news media representatives, including photographers, to the:*

a. *scenes of major fires, natural disasters, or other catastrophic events; and*
b. *perimeter of crime scenes.*

**Commentary:** News media representatives should not be in a position to interfere with law enforcement operations at the scene of an incident. The guidelines for news media access, including access by photographers, to the scene should be communicated to the media to help ensure their cooperation.

Reprinted by permission of the Commission on Accreditation for Law Enforcement Agencies.

*Interviews with police officers are often featured on local television programs.*

## POLICIES REGARDING PHOTOGRAPHING AND VIDEOTAPING AT CRIME SCENES

Police departments vary in whether they allow news cameras in or around crime scenes. According to Sharp (1991, p. 90): "To prohibit pictures gives a perception that cops have something to hide in their activities." Nonetheless, it is imperative that individuals not involved in an investigation *not* be allowed to contaminate the crime scene, as noted by one chief of police: "I feel the First Amendment right does not guarantee an individual the right to photograph or otherwise record a police scene at will. To the contrary, such activities must be controlled to preserve the scene's integrity. To do otherwise could compromise the criminal investigation beyond a salvageable point" (Sharp,1991, p. 91).

Another chief of police noted a different type of problem with photographing crime or accident scenes: "I perceive problems not from our standpoint, but from that of the victim or complainant, who might not want to be on someone's video, documentary or TV series and might not want cameras in his or her home" (Sharp, p. 92).

In addition, says Sharp (p. 92): "Training bulletins should include warnings to [police to] always be on their best behavior, lest they unwittingly star in a videotape shown on a local television or international network. . . . It never hurts to remind them to 'Smile, they may be on candid camera.'"

Finally, police officers should be aware of the news system called "file video" or "file photos" where pictures are kept indefinitely and can be reused at anytime. Parrish (pers. com. 1992) cites an example of how video taken during a ride with a police officer intended to promote police-community relations can also be used differently. In this case a photographer arranged to go with a squad on a high-risk entry into a crack house. The police department let the reporter come along to get some video of how they are working to curb drug traffic in the city. The reporter did the story, and the police were pleased with the resulting public image. Two years later, one officer involved in the high-risk entry unit faced an indictment by a federal grand jury for police brutality. The reporter mentioned to his boss that they had video of this officer breaking into the home of some poor black citizens on the north side. The editors decided that was just what they needed for the story. Video the police had at one time encouraged the media to take was used against an officer.

## IMPROVING RELATIONS WITH THE MEDIA

Rosenthal (1996d, p. 19) suggests: "With law enforcement suffering a number of body blows to its image in the last couple of years, the profession cannot afford to take media relations lightly or pass up any opportunity to improve its public image."

As an important first step to improve relations with the media, Cook (1991, p. 88) suggests that police officers be aware of three basic reasons why reporters often foul up a story.

◆

Reporters may bungle a story due to ignorance, time constraints or over-simplification.

◆

- Ignorance—Reporters may be ignorant of law enforcement procedures.
- Time constraints—Reporters work under severe deadline pressure.
- The need to simplify—Police deal in complex realities. . . . A reporter must turn a complicated investigation into a paragraph-long news story or a fifteen- to twenty-second story at the top of the hour.

If officers are aware of these three common problems they can more effectively deal with reporters.

◆

To improve police-media relations, inform the press of your department's procedures, simplify your information and respect reporters' deadlines.

◆

- Be a teacher—Provide background information to reporters.
- Simplify—Present complex matter in its simplest terms. Avoid police jargon and technical terminology.
- Respect the reporters' deadlines—Release information in a timely manner so that the press has a chance to fully understand the situation.

Rosenthal (1996c, p. 18) stresses: "Reporters live and die by deadlines. Deadlines are critically important to the media and therefore do demand an awareness and sensitivity on the part of law enforcement, if the two professions are to have a mutually effective relationship."

Weston (1996, p. 122) notes: "Improved media relationship has resulted in generally objective reporting and a heavy focus on community policing programs." He advises: "The media is to be treated as a customer, just as citizens are."

## BEING PROFESSIONAL WHEN INTERVIEWED

It has been said, "You don't argue with people who buy ink by the barrel." This may be helpful to keep in mind when preparing for an interview with a news reporter.

Garner (1995, p. 41) observes: "For too many law enforcement managers, a meeting with the press is anticipated with about as much enthusiasm as a trip to the dentist." Garner (1995, p. 51) provides a checklist for surviving an interview:

- Find out what you are to be interviewed about.
- Gather the facts you need to respond to anticipated questions.
- Realize it is all right to be a bit nervous.
- Look, sound and act like the professional you are.
- Always tell the truth—and nothing but.
- Remain courteous and in control of your emotions.
- Get to the point; do not wander or waste words.
- Know and follow your agency's media guidelines.
- If you do not know the answer, say so.
- If you cannot give the answer, say so and explain why.

Garner (1996, pp. 50–51, 111) offers several additional tips for getting a message across during an interview:

- Check your appearance. The look of a relaxed, confident, got-it-together professional is what you are after.
- Choose your words carefully. Steer clear of off-color terms or derogatory remarks.
- Keep it brief. It is precisely that kind of statement that is most likely to get on the air or into print.
- Stay in control.
- Remain courteous. Maintain good eye contact and do not hesitate to smile if appropriate.
- Stay on the record. Do not tell secrets to the press. Going "off the record" is extremely risky.
- Be clear. Offer to clarify anything that remains unclear.
- Do not play favorites.
- Clarify convoluted questions. Ask the interviewer to explain exactly what it is that is being asked.
- Beware of live electronics. Assume that every camera or microphone in your presence is live.
- Avoid "no comment." Provide a truthful explanation of why you can't respond.
- Defeat the interrupter. Speak over them if necessary.
- Correct the misinterpreter. Correct any incorrect information immediately.
- Live through dead air. Some interviewers will silently and expectantly stare at you when you have finished answering a question. Don't be pressured; simply stare back.

Rosenthal (1996e, p. 17) offers advice on how to respond if a reporter wants to report on a case of officer misconduct. He suggests that it is NOT advisable to simply say, "I cannot comment due to the fact that it is an ongoing investigation." He notes: "In an ugly situation your natural inclination may be to lock out the media and the public, but *never* do that. . . . *You must be accessible to the media and be as forthcoming as possible!*" Quoting Joel Chandler's classic "You can't run from trouble, there ain't no place that far," Rosenthal suggests the following:

> In general terms, you *empathize;* making a basic statement that you *care* about what's going on, that you are *disturbed* by the ugly situation, and are *determined* to set things right. . . . Give the offending officer a fair shake, but remember the best interests of your department, too. . . . Don't ever try to justify the unjustifiable, defend the indefensible or explain the inexplicable;

there's nothing in that for you or your department. Reporters won't stand for it, the public won't buy it, and you'll be creating an image nightmare for yourself and your department that won't go away.

Rosenthal (1996b, p. 89) offers the following suggestions for "hostile" reporters:

- First, commit your department to openness and fairness with the media.
- Whatever you do, don't lose your head.
- Talk with the reporter face-to-face and try to set the record straight.
- If the reporter persists, and continues the attack, respond right away with all your clout. Bring out your "big gun": the chief or sheriff should seek an immediate meeting with the reporter's publisher or general manager. . . . Your goal is to present the facts, counter the unfair reporting, get a correction and prevent future abuse. A publisher or general manager may well hear you, where an overly aggressive reporter has not.

Garner (1996, p. 43) also offers advice on handling bad news:

- Don't lie, ever.
- Don't hide from the press or refuse to see reporters. This raises suspicions.
- Don't dribble out bad news.
- Don't alter press policies to make them more restrictive during bad news.
- Don't lose your cool.

The press needs the police to provide them with necessary information. The press knows that bad relations between the media and the police can result in limited access to police information. Cooperation and mutual trust benefit both the press and the police.

## THE NEWS CONFERENCE

According to Garner (1996, p, 49): "There is no reason why a law enforcement professional who does not hesitate to confront an armed and dangerous offender should fear a news hound carrying only a notepad, recorder or camera." News conferences can keep the public informed and build positive relations with the media. Dunphy and Garner (1992, p. 45) offer the following guidelines for effective news conferences:

- Help select the site for the conference, preferably one with an exit near the speaker.
- Maintain good eye contact with the audience. Keep your gaze moving.

- Limit the opening statement to about 10 minutes maximum. Then answer questions.
- Repeat each question to the audience.
- Keep your responses short and to the point.
- Remain responsive and open to your audience, but be aware that every word you speak is now part of the public domain.
- Shift your attention. Try to involve the whole audience in the conference.
- Keep the conference on subject.
- Let your audience know that prepared copies of your statement or news release will be available at the conclusion of the conference.
- Provide an after-conference contact. Someone "in the know" should remain accessible by telephone for several hours after the news conference ends to field any questions reporters might have as they write up their stories.

## PRESS INFORMATION OFFICERS

Rosenthal (1996f, p. 43) recommends that the ideal situation is to have a full-time, well-trained public information officer on staff. However, this is impractical for many smaller departments. In such cases, Rosenthal advises: "An agency should at least have in place a public information standard operating procedure (SOP) which outlines the framework within which you will work with the media."

Some police departments feel comfortable allowing any member to talk to the press and provide information. The former chief of the Minneapolis Police Department, Tony Bouza, did not have press officers during his administration: "Every member of the department serves as a spokesperson. Reporters are free to call any member of the department and ask them any questions they want. And you will get an answer, regardless of the rank of the officer you speak to." Bouza was fond of saying that the Minneapolis Police Department had 714 public information officers.

Journalists complain that although any officer could speak on behalf of the police department, the police usually release far less information than such an open policy permits.

Some departments have **press information officers (PIOs)** who disseminate all information to the press and discourage individual officers from providing information to reporters. PIOs try to provide accurate information in a consistent manner while controlling leaks of confidential or inaccurate information.

Press officers are trained in public relations and are professionals in managing controversial or negative situations to the department's benefit. Pace (1991, pp. 244–45) lists the following responsibilities of most press relations officers:

- The officer speaks for the chief of police and for all persons throughout the department.
- The designated press relations officer will always be available to the press.
- Information about major cases will be made available to the media on a timely basis.
- Withholding information about a critical case is asked for by the police and is a voluntary act on the part of the news media.
- The officer provides all news media with facilities and holds press conferences as requested.
- The officer makes available data on the internal processes and procedures in a department and keeps the press informed about personnel investigations and any plans it may have for major operations.

The PIO has a significant amount of responsibility. When PIOs properly carry out their responsibilities they can improve police-media relations. In addition, Kelsey (1992, p. 35) offers the following suggestions for PIOs:

1. When notified respond directly to the scene, unless ordered otherwise. That is where you will be most effective.
2. Know who the incident commander is and take direction only from him.
3. If more than five media representatives are present, insist that a uniformed officer be assigned to assist you. You cannot control the movements of more than five individuals and do your job at the same time.
4. At your initial media briefing, introduce yourself and inform them that you will be the sole source of official information. (Members of your agency must accept that you are the only spokesman.) This will ensure that conflicting information is not issued.
5. Your main responsibility is to maintain order to ensure that the media representatives know that you are in charge. A fair but firm attitude will allow for mutual respect to be fostered.
6. Do not address any questions that you don't know the answer to and don't speak on any subject that would be better dealt with by another responding agency. If you don't know an answer, inform the questioner that you will get an answer and report back to them. THEN FOLLOW THROUGH. Don't promise anything that you can't deliver.

7. Inform the media representatives as to the time that you will hold your next briefing and then make sure you appear as scheduled.

Kelsey (p. 35) notes: "There is no faster way to reach the public than by way of the media, and it is to your advantage to be in control as the situation unfolds." As Parrish warns:

> Any Chief or PIO who thinks all the information will flow from that one mouthpiece is sadly mistaken. A good reporter will not stop with the official line. He or she will try to talk to investigators to get more on the story. If journalists all wrote their pieces based on the press conference or press release, all stories would sound the same. They don't because other avenues are explored. PIOs should be regarded as funnels or starting points, not the be-all and end-all for journalists. And Chiefs had better know that.

## ESTABLISHING COOPERATIVE RELATIONSHIPS WITH THE MEDIA

Training is one way to improve relationships and enhance the media's understanding of what police work involves. Lakewood (Colorado) Police Department, for example, invited the local newspaper and broadcast reporters to enroll in a citizens' police academy. The reporters were given laser guns and acted out different scenarios to demonstrate the difficult decisions police must make. Inviting members of the media to ride in squad cars is also an effective way to enhance the media's understanding of policing. Conversely, police officers could benefit from learning more about the media and its mission and responsibilities. Officers must remember that reporting is a highly competitive *business*.

In addition to improving community relations, a good rapport with the media can also help the police department accomplish its mission. Comments from police chiefs from across the country underscore this point (Weinblatt, 1992, p. 32):

> We need goodwill to be efficient. Without the press, we won't get witnesses. We won't get people dialing 911.
>
> We view the media as a messenger. We can't reach our residents without them.

According to Thompson: "Police haven't learned to market themselves. We will be better cops if the public sees what we do and knows how to assist us in our service to the community" (Weinblatt, 1992, p. 38).

One outstanding example of the police and media working together is described by Wolfgang (1992). Press information officers from the Albany Police Department, the New York State Police and other area law enforcement agencies as well as representatives from the media formed the Capital District Law

Enforcement/Media Group. This group, representing eighty different agencies as well as print and electronic media, meets bimonthly to discuss areas of mutual concern. One problem the group tackled was the need to get information to all the media rapidly. Most members of the media believed the practice of PIOs calling down through a media list was very inequitable. It also required a great deal of the PIOs' time. The group found a mutually acceptable solution to the problem: a **Pager Information Network (PIN).**

Pagers can display full text messages and also have printing capability. One phone call from a law enforcement agency can simultaneously notify all the media. The PIOs can call from the department, home or a pay or cellular telephone. The system is kept secure through use of passwords and identification codes. According to Wolfgang (1992, p. 30):

> A department can relay information to all the media in the Albany area by simply dialing an unpublished phone number. An operator employed by Airpage is on duty 24 hours a day. . . .
>
> Messages entered into the Airpage computer are time and date stamped, and transmitted within 30 seconds to the more than 50 pagers now assigned to the network. . . .
>
> Since the system began operating in May 1990, it has been used to warn people of major traffic obstructions on highways, announced hazardous conditions, notified reporters of shams and cons being carried out, described bank robberies, announced newsworthy arrests and arraignments, announced press conferences and countless other items of interest to the media.

The media can also be of assistance in public education programs. For example, an agency in California wanted to increase the accuracy of citizens' reports of suspicious and criminal activities. They enlisted the aid of the local newspaper to run a public announcement about what to include in suspect and vehicle descriptions.

In Chicago, the police use the media in their crime prevention efforts. The Federal Communications Commission (FCC) requires all media to set aside airtime or publication space for community projects. This is another excellent avenue for law enforcement agencies to convey educational messages to the residents of their communities.

Other media possibilities include talk shows, in which an agency spokesperson can discuss a controversy or a trend. Sometimes the editor of a local newspaper or publication will permit an organization a regular column. Letters to the editors may be written in response to other letters sent in to the editorial page.

As police departments adopt the community policing philosophy and implement some of its strategies, public support is vital. The media can play an important role in obtaining the support—or in losing it. Wexler (1997, pp. 2–3) offers the following suggestions for working effectively with the media:

- As media police guru Jerry Nachman has advised, more police chiefs will lose their jobs due to the barrel of a camera lens than the barrel of a gun. So

Nachman advises, get to know editors and reporters during non-stressful times. Take them to lunch and tell them what you and your department are doing. Ask them what types of stories they are interested in doing and how you and your staff can provide the information they need when they need it.

- Don't overlook the editorial boards and op-ed page editors of newspapers or television. Again, develop a relationship with them and let them in on the "big picture" of your department's goals and plans.
- Be careful about giving exclusive interviews to national correspondents while you bypass local reports. National correspondents will leave town and local reporters will feel like second-class citizens. These are the reporters who can help make you or break you in the local news.

Rosenthal (1997, p. 12) believes: "Good media relations is the best investment police administrators can make. There are good days and very bad days in police work. If you build up the trust and good will of the media during the good times they'll tend to be on your side when things turn tough."

## RECOMMENDATIONS

The National Symposium on Community Institutions and Inner City Crime (Sulton, 1990, p. 107) makes the following recommendations regarding the news media:

- News media should exercise caution when covering crime-related incidents. When publishing stories about victims and children who are runaways, news media should refrain from using their names and faces. The filing of criminal complaints and indictments should not be characterized as evidence of guilt. The media should report acquittals as well as indictments.
- News media should cover positive aspects of inner-city neighborhoods.

Police should work to establish a positive, mutually beneficial relationship with the media. Cook (1991, p. 93) suggests the following three-pronged, proactive plan for positive publicity from the media:

1. *Create a master calendar.* You're probably doing a lot of good work that never gets reported. How about those talks at the local elementary schools? The ride-along program? The baseball card give-aways? What about some of the community projects individual officers are involved in? Make a calendar of events and story ideas you'd like covered.
2. *Inventory the local media.* Are you overlooking any media? Company newsletters enjoy a loyal readership. So do supermarket bulletin boards. These are media, too.

3. *Develop an announcements/events plan.* Call reporters on a regular basis to provide story ideas. Draft an occasional press release. For a really big event, plan an open house or press conference. You can create positive news.

As noted by Weinblatt (1992, p. 32): "A host of police media experts underscore one clear principle—a working, proactive relationship with the press is an essential component in the success or failure of an agency in its service to the community. Communication is of paramount importance."

## MODEL POLICE DEPARTMENT PROGRAM

The results of a survey conducted in the San Francisco Bay Area as well as a national survey mailed to the police departments in the fifty largest cities in the United States led to the development of a proposed model police department program for dealing with the media (Guffey, 1992, pp. 45–48):

1. The model department should designate a public information officer (or someone designated to serve as such), including a part-time assignment in smaller departments.
2. "Ride-alongs" of reporters with patrol officers should be encouraged.
3. There should be training at all levels on proper police-media contacts.
4. A thorough media relations policy that has been reviewed by at least one local newspaper and, if available, one radio and one television station should be implemented.
5. Consider implementing one or more programs such as Secret Witness, Crime Stoppers, Green Light and Media Hotline.
6. Ideally, reporters should be allowed to read offense reports and traffic accident reports under supervised conditions.
7. Reporters should be allowed to use departmental telephones to call in news stories to their agencies.
8. Reporters should be allowed to talk with any police personnel having a part in the news story they are preparing.
9. Communication channels should be kept open constantly by telephone or bimonthly meetings at neutral, congenial settings such as police-media breakfasts.
10. Chiefs and PIOs should actively seek to appear on radio news talk programs to discuss current events and issues and to answer live questions from the listening public.

11. The PIO should be trained in use of conflict resolution techniques.

12. The department should issue press identification cards after a careful background investigation of reporters.

Although implementing every component of this model program may be unrealistic for some agencies, police departments should consider those that are feasible.

## SUMMARY

One important group with which the police interact is the media. The media includes newspapers, radio and television. The police and members of the media share the common goal of serving the public. They share a symbiotic relationship in that they are mutually dependent upon each other.

The press are guided by the First Amendment to the Constitution which guarantees the public's right to know, that is, freedom of the press. The police are guided by the Sixth Amendment which guarantees the right to a fair trial. The objectives of these amendments are sometimes in conflict. The First Amendment right to know must be balanced against the Sixth Amendment's guarantee of the right to a fair trial and the protection of the defendant's rights.

Police may need to withhold information from the press until next of kin are notified, in the interest of public safety or to protect the integrity of an investigation. When police do give information to the press, they should be aware that to ask to speak "off the record" does not guarantee that the information will not be reported. It may, in fact, make it more likely to be reported.

Another source of conflict between the press and the police is the danger members of the press may place themselves in trying to obtain a story. To help assure the safety of media personnel at dangerous situations, police should meet with media representatives to explain the rules of safety *before* an incident arises.

One possible explanation for the conflict between police and the press may be the different ways in which they tend to approach decisions. Police tend to rely on thinking and their senses in decision making, in contrast to editors and reporters who tend to rely on feeling and intuition.

Conflict between the police and the press need not be dysfunctional. In fact, healthy conflict between the press and the police is necessary and beneficial. A step toward mutual understanding is to recognize why reporters may foul up a story. Reporters may bungle a story because of ignorance, time constraints or oversimplification. To remedy this situation police need to be teachers, simplify the information they provide to the press and respect reporters' deadlines.

## *Discussion Questions*

1. Why should the police never lie to the press?

2. Does your police department have a press information officer?

3. How fairly do you feel the media in your community reports crime and violence?

4. How fairly do you feel national media (radio, television, magazines, newspapers) cover crime and violence?

5. What might make good topics for PIOs during crime prevention week?

6. Have you ever conducted a news conference or issued a press release? If so, what went well? What was difficult?

7. Why is it important to remember that the media is a for-profit business?

8. Do you feel the media is sometimes insensitive to victims and could also be part of the second wound injury of victimization? If so, can you give examples?

9. What media are available in your community to inform the public of police department operations?

10. Which media do you feel has the most impact on the public?

## *References*

Cook, Marshall J. "How to Handle the Press." *Law and Order.* (September 1991): 88–94.

Dunphy, Francis R. and Garner, Gerald W. "A Guide to Effective Interaction with the News Media." *The Police Chief.* (April 1992): 45–48.

Garner, Gerald W. "The Interview Game." *Police.* (August 1996): 49–111.

Garner, Gerald W. "Meeting the Press." *Law and Order.* (December 1995): 41–44.

Gleick, Richard H. "Public Information Officers: Trained to Deal with the Media." *Law and Order.* (August 1991): 98.

Guffey, James E. "The Police and the Media: Proposal for Managing Conflict Productively." *American Journal of Police.* (Vol. XI, No. 1, 1992): 33–51.

Hennessy, Stephen M. *Thinking Cop/Feeling Cop: A Study in Police Personalities.* Scottsdale: Leadership, Incorporated of Scottsdale, 1992.

Kelsey, Dean R. "The Crash of Flight 585: Working with the Media." *Law and Order.* (February 1992): 33–35.

Lesce, Tony. "Information Officers: Vital for Public Relations." *Law and Order.* (May 1994): 98.

"'Media Crime Wave' Continues—Crime News Quadrupled in Four Years." *Overcrowded Times.* (February 1996): 3.

Mitchell, Stephen W. Personal correspondence, March 17, 1997.

Pace, Denny F. *Community Relations Concepts.* Incline Village, Nev.: Copperhouse Publishing Company, 1991.

Parrish, Penny. Letter to author, October 7, 1991.

Parrish, Penny. Letter to author, May 26, 1992.

Parrish, Penny. "Media Alert: Ten Tips on How to Be Prepared." *Law and Order.* (September 1993): 91–93.

Rosenthal, Rick. "The Freedom of Information Act (FOIA)." *Law and Order.* (June 1996a): 18–19.

Rosenthal, Rick. "The IACP's PIO Section." *Law and Order.* (February 1997): 12–13.

Rosenthal, Rick. "Media Brutality." *Law and Order.* (July 1996b): 85–90.

Rosenthal, Rick. "Media Deadlines." *Law and Order.* (December 1996c): 18–19.

Rosenthal, Rick. "The Public Information Officer." *Law and Order.* (August 1996d): 19–20.

Rosenthal, Rick. "You Can't Run From Trouble." *Law and Order.* (October 1996e): 17–18.

Rosenthal, Rick. "Your Public Information S.O.P." *Law and Order.* (May 1996f): 43–44.

Sharp, Arthur M. "Picture This." *Law and Order.* (September 1991): 89–92.

Sulton, Anne Thomas. *Inner-City Crime Control: Can Community Institutions Contribute?* Washington: The Police Foundation, 1990.

Weinblatt, Richard. "The Police and the Media." *Law and Order.* (February 1992): 32, 36–38.

Weston, Jim. "Police and the Media: Exploring Some High-Tech Solutions to Some New Problems." *Law and Order.* (October 1996): 119–22.

Wexler, Chuck. "Rules for Reformers." *Subject to Debate.* (February/March 1997): 2, 4.

Wolfgang, Robert. "Working Together, Police and the Media." *Law and Order.* (February 1992): 29–30.

Wright, Kevin N. "The Overdramatization of Crime in America." In *Taking Sides: Clashing Views on Controversial Issues in Crime and Criminology,* 2nd rev. ed., edited by Richard C. Monk, 111–17. Guilford: The Dushkin Publishing Group, Inc., 1991.

### *Resources*

Parrish Institute for Law Enforcement and Media, 4900 Kingsdale Drive, Bloomington, MN 55437; (612) 835-0582.

Radio Television News Director's Association, 1000 Connecticut Avenue N.W., Suite 615, Washington, DC 20036; (202) 659-6510.

# Section

# Projects and Programs:
# Coordinated Efforts

Communities consist of individuals, organizations, businesses, agencies, the media, citizen groups, schools, churches and police departments. Effective interactions with the members of ethnic and cultural minorities, the disabled, the elderly, the young, victims and members of the media are critical to developing projects and programs to meet a community's needs.

This section begins by describing early experiments in crime prevention and community policing strategies (Chapter 14). Among the most common programs are those by which law enforcement agencies attempt to improve communication between the police and the public. Law enforcement is part of the criminal justice system. The other two components of this system, courts and corrections, also sponsor programs that may directly affect the image of the police. These programs also affect how well the entire criminal justice system serves the community, including those who break the law (Chapter 15).

Programs focused on youth are prevalent (Chapter 16). Community-based programs geared at crime prevention have been in existence for decades. The programs may be organized and operated by citizen groups, volunteers, businesses, churches, social service agencies or a combination of these organizations. They may focus on crime prevention in general or eradicating a specific type of crime such as the sale of drugs (Chapter 17).

The section concludes with a brief discussion of the future of community policing and how its effectiveness might be evaluated (Epilog).

*Chapter 14*

# Early Experiments in Crime Prevention and Community Policing Strategies

*Don't be afraid to take a big step if one is indicated. You can't cross a chasm in two small jumps.*

—David Lloyd George, former prime minister of England

## Do you know

- What was demonstrated in studies of community policing in Flint? Newark? Oakland? San Diego? Houston? Boston? Baltimore County?
- What the most common components of community policing have been?
- What was demonstrated in studies of community crime prevention programs in Seattle, Portland and Hartford?
- What the CPTED Commercial Demonstration Project in Portland found?
- How successful the McGruff national campaign was?
- How successful crime prevention newsletters are?
- What are characteristics of several exemplary police-community strategies?
- What impediments might hinder implementing community policing?

## Definitions

Can you define these terms: CPTED, cross-sectional analysis, empirical study, panel analysis, PSAs, qualitative evaluations, reciprocity, statistically significant.

# *Introduction*

"It is probably premature to pronounce community policing the wave of the future," says Ordway P. Burden (1992, p. 5), president of the Law Enforcement Assistance Foundation and chairman of the National Law Enforcement Council. "However, were I a betting man, I would give hefty odds that it is."

Community involvement with and assistance in accomplishing the mission of law enforcement is becoming widely accepted. The change toward community involvement is illustrated in a change in the Portland Police Department's mission statement. The old mission statement proclaimed:

> The Bureau of Police is responsible for the preservation of the public peace, protection of the rights of persons and property, the prevention of crime, and the enforcement of all Federal laws, Oregon state statutes and city ordinances within the boundaries of the City of Portland.

The new mission, in contrast, is:

> to work with all citizens to preserve life, maintain human rights, protect property and promote individual responsibility and community commitment.

The change from traditional policing to community involvement does require many chiefs of police and their officers to take risks. Are the results of the shift toward community policing worth the risks? This chapter reviews experiments conducted across the country to answer this question.

Although this chapter may appear somewhat dated, it is a necessary addition to document efforts during the 1980s to improve crime prevention strategies and to involve citizens in such efforts. Many lessons were learned from the experiments of this time period.

The chapter begins with a description of empirical studies in crime prevention conducted in the 1980s, followed by a comparison of fear-reduction strategies and crime prevention programs. Using the media in crime prevention is discussed as well as lessons learned from the 1980s. The chapter concludes with a discussion of qualitative evaluations and salient program features and impediments to community policing.

## EMPIRICAL STUDIES OF COMMUNITY POLICING

An **empirical study** is based on observation or practical experience. Greene and Taylor (1991, pp. 206–21) describe eight studies of community policing in major cities throughout the country, including Flint, Newark, Oakland, San Diego, Houston, Boston and Baltimore.

## Flint, Michigan

The classic *Neighborhood Foot Patrol Program* of Flint, Michigan, was conducted from January 1979 to January 1982. It focused on fourteen experimental neighborhoods to which twenty-two police officers and three supervisors were assigned. The officers were given great discretion in what they could do while on foot patrol, but communication with citizens was a primary objective.

◆

The Flint Neighborhood Foot Patrol Program appeared to decrease crime, increase general citizen satisfaction with the foot patrol program, reduce citizens' fear of crime and create a positive perception of the foot patrol officers.

◆

Mastrofski (1992) explains that the Flint study tried to document what police did on foot patrol and how that differed from motorized patrol. He notes (p. 24):

Looking at the department's daily report forms, the researchers found that foot officers reported many more self-initiated activities—such as home and business visits and security checks—than police in cars. Officers on foot averaged much higher levels of productivity across most of the standard performance measures: arrests, investigations, stopping of suspicious persons, parking citations, and value of recovered property. The only category in which motor patrol officers clearly outproduced their foot patrol counterparts was in providing miscellaneous services to citizens.

According to citizen surveys (Trojanowicz, 1986, pp. 165–67), 64 percent were satisfied with the project and 68 percent felt safer. When asked to compare foot patrol and motorized patrol officers, citizens rated the foot patrol officers higher by large margins on four of the six areas: preventing crime, encouraging citizen self-protection, working with juveniles and following up on complaints. Motorized patrol officers were rated superior only in responding to complaints. In addition, in the foot patrol neighborhoods crime rates were down markedly and calls for service were down more than 40 percent.

No statistical tests were done, however, and results across the fourteen neighborhoods varied greatly. Therefore, the results should be interpreted with caution. In addition, problems were encountered in the Flint Foot Patrol Program. For example, because the program was loosely structured some officers were not accountable and their job performance was poor. Nonetheless, according to Skolnick and Bayley (1986, p. 216):

Foot patrol . . . appears from our observations and other studies to generate four meritorious effects:

1. Since there is a concerned human presence on the street, foot patrol is more adaptable to street happenings, and thus may prevent crime before it begins.

*Chinese American police officer while on foot patrol capitalizes on the opportunity to talk with young women in the area characterized as "Chinatown."*

2.  Foot patrolmen may make arrests, but they are also around to give warnings either directly or indirectly, merely through their presence.

3.  Properly carried out, foot patrol generates goodwill in the neighborhood, which has the derivative consequence of making other crime prevention tactics more effective. This effectiveness in turn tends to raise citizen morale and reduce their fear of crime.

4.  Foot patrol seems to raise officer morale.

## Newark 1

The original Newark Foot Patrol Experiment was done between 1978 and 1979 and addressed the issues of untended property and untended behavior. This experiment used twelve patrol beats. Eight of the beats, identified as using foot patrol, were divided into pairs, matched by the number of residential and non-residential units in each. One beat in each pair dropped foot patrol. An additional four beats which had not previously used foot patrol, added foot patrol officers. As in the Flint experiment, officers had great flexibility in their job responsibilities while on foot patrol.

◆

In the first Newark Foot Patrol Experiment, residents reported positive results, while business owners reported negative results.

◆

In areas where foot patrol was added, residents reported a decrease in the severity of crime and evaluated police performance more positively. Business owners, however, believed that street disorder and publicly visible crime increased and reported that the neighborhood had become worse. Pate (1986, p. 155) summarizes the results of the first experiment:

> The *addition* of intensive foot patrol coverage to relatively short (8–16 block) commercial/residential strips during five evenings per week over a one-year period can have considerable effects on the perceptions of residents concerning disorder problems, crime problems, the likelihood of crime, safety, and police service. Such additional patrol, however, appears to have no significant effect on victimization, recorded crime, or the likelihood of reporting a crime.

> The *elimination* of foot patrol after years of maintenance, however, appears to produce few notable negative effects. Similarly, the *retention* of foot patrol does not prove to have notable beneficial effects.

## Newark 2

A second foot patrol experiment was conducted in Newark in 1983 and 1984. This experiment used three neighborhoods and a control group (which received no "treatment"). The foot patrol officers in the experimental neighborhoods engaged in one of three "treatments": coordinated foot patrol, which included conducting radar checks, bus checks, road checks and enforcement of disorderly conduct ordinances; coordinating a cleanup campaign; or distributing a neighborhood newsletter.

◆

The second Newark Foot Patrol Experiment included a coordinated foot patrol, a cleanup campaign and distribution of a newsletter. Only the coordinated foot patrol was perceived to reduce perception of property crime and improve assessments of the police.

◆

The cleanup effort and newsletter programs did not affect any of the outcome measures studied. In addition, the cleanup effort and newsletter programs did not reduce crime rates. Nonetheless, as noted by the Police Foundation (1981, p. 118): "If vulnerable and weak people feel safe as a result of specific police activity and if that feeling improves the quality of their life, that is terribly important."

## Oakland

In 1983 Oakland assigned twenty-eight officers to foot patrol in Oakland's central business district. In addition, a Report Incidents Directly program was established whereby local businesspeople could talk directly to the patrol officers about any matters that concerned them. Mounted patrol and small vehicle patrols were also used in the Oakland program.

◆

The Oakland program, using foot patrol, mounted patrol, small vehicle patrol and a Report Incidents Directly program, resulted in a substantial drop in the rate of crime against individuals and their property.

◆

The crime rate dropped in the Oakland treatment area more than citywide declines, but again, no statistical tests were reported for this experiment.

## San Diego

San Diego conducted a community profile project from 1973 to 1974 designed to improve police-community interactions. Twenty-four patrol officers and three supervisors were given sixty hours of community-orientation training. The performance of these officers was compared with twenty-four other patrol officers who did not receive the training.

◆

The San Diego Community Profile Project provided patrol officers with extensive community-orientation training. These officers became more service oriented, increased their non–law enforcement contacts with citizens and had a more positive attitude toward police-community relations.

◆

The project did not consider the effect of community profiling on crime or on citizens' fear of crime.

## Houston

Like the second Newark experiment, Houston conducted a fear-reduction experiment between 1983 and 1984, testing five strategies: a victim recontact program following victimization, a community newsletter, a citizen contact patrol program, a police storefront office and a program aimed to organize the community's interest in crime prevention.

◆

The victim recontact program and the newsletter of the Houston Fear Reduction Project did not have positive results. The citizen contact patrol and the police storefront office did, however, result in decreases in perceptions of social disorder, fear of personal victimization and the level of personal and property crime.

◆

As noted by Skogan and Wycoff (1986, pp. 182–83) the police storefront officers developed several programs, including monthly meetings, school programs, a fingerprinting program, a blood pressure program, a ride-along program, a park program and an anticrime newsletter. A comparison of these results to those achieved in the Newark experiment is made on p. 457.

## Boston

In 1983 Boston changed from predominantly two-officer motorized patrol to foot patrol. The Boston police department also shifted the responsibilities of the foot patrol and motorized one-officer patrol to less serious crimes and noncrime service calls. The experiment studied 105 beats to determine if high, medium, low, unstaffed or no change in foot patrol made a difference in calls for service by priority.

◆

The Boston Foot Patrol Project found no statistically significant relationship between changes in the level of foot patrol provided and number of calls for service or the seriousness of the calls.

◆

Violent crimes were not affected by increased or decreased foot patrol staffing. After the department shifted to foot patrol, the number of street robberies dropped, but the number of commercial robberies rose.

## Baltimore County

The Baltimore Citizen Oriented Police Enforcement (COPE) Project, started in 1981, focused on the reduction of citizens' fear of crime. This problem-oriented project focused on solving the community problems of fear and disorder that lead to crime. According to Taft (1986, p. 10): "'Citizen Oriented Police Enforcement' officers would engage in intensive patrol, develop close contacts with citizens, conduct 'fear surveys' (door-to-door canvassing to identify concerns) and use any means within their power to quell fear."

◆

Baltimore County's COPE Project reduced fear of crime by 10 percent in target neighborhoods. It also reduced calls for service and increased citizen awareness of and satisfaction with the police.

◆

A study conducted in 1985 indicated that the COPE Project "passed its first statistical test with flying colors" (Taft, p. 20). The results of the study are summarized in Figure 14.1.

## Summary and Implications of the Experiments

Greene and Taylor (1991, p. 215) note that "there is not much consistency in findings across studies." Regarding *fear of crime,* Newark 1 observed a reduction; Newark 2 observed a reduction in the **panel analysis** (where the data was analyzed by individuals responding). It did not show a reduction in the **cross-sectional analysis** (where the data was analyzed by area rather than by individuals responding). The Houston study had the opposite results: a reduction in fear

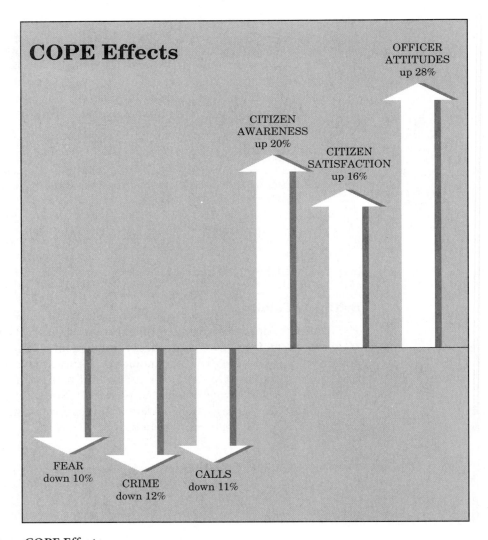

*Figure 14.1*    **COPE Effects**
SOURCE: Philip B. Taft, Jr. *Fighting Fear: The Baltimore County COPE Project.* © The Police
Executive Research Forum, 20. Washington: 1986. Reprinted with permission of PERF.

in the cross-sectional analysis, but not in the panel analysis. In the Flint study, citizen perceptions of the seriousness of crime problems increased. In Baltimore County it declined slightly. The San Diego, Oakland and Boston programs did not consider fear of crime. Greene and Taylor (p. 216) conclude: "Based on the problems associated with the evaluation of each of these programs, there is at present no consistent evidence that foot patrol reduces fear of crime."

Greene and Taylor also note inconsistent findings regarding crime rates. The Oakland study was the only one to demonstrate a reduction, but no statistical treatment was done. Again they conclude (p. 216): "Clearly, these studies do not point to decreases in crime or disorder as a consequence of community policing or foot patrol."

◆

The most common strategies used in community policing were foot patrol, newsletters and community organizing.

◆

Greene and Taylor discuss several problems with the research designs of the eight studies of community policing and suggest ways to improve the designs. This is *not* the view taken by Wycoff (1991, p. 103), however, who states that the fear-reduction studies conducted in Houston and Newark: "provide evidence of the efficacy of what the authors referred to as 'community-oriented' policing strategies for reducing citizen fear, improving citizens' attitudes toward their neighborhoods and toward the police and reducing crime."

## FEAR-REDUCTION STRATEGIES EXPERIMENTS COMPARED

Wycoff (pp. 107–08) summarizes the seven strategies tested in the Newark and Houston experiments as follows:

*Newsletters* (Houston and Newark). These were tested with and without crime statistics. They were police-produced and provided residents of the test area with information about crime prevention steps they could take, the police department, and police programs in their area.

*Victim Recontact* (Houston). Patrol officers made telephone contact with victims to inform them of the status of their case, inquire whether they needed assistance, offer to send crime prevention information, and ask whether victims could provide additional information.

*Police Community Station* (Houston). A neighborhood storefront operation was conducted by patrol officers. The station provided a variety of services for the area.

*Citizen Contact Patrol* (Houston). Officers concentrated their patrol time within the target area where they made door-to-door contacts, introducing themselves to residents and businesspeople, and asking whether there were any neighborhood problems citizens wished brought to the attention of the police.

*Community Organizing* (Houston). Officers from the Community Services Division worked to organize block meetings attended by area patrol officers. They organized a neighborhood committee that met monthly with the district captain and developed special projects ("safe" houses for children, identifying property, and a clean-up campaign) for the area.

*Signs of Crime* (Newark). This program focused on social disorder and conducted "random intensified enforcement and order maintenance operations" (e.g., foot patrol to enforce laws and maintain order on sidewalks and street corners; radar checks; bus checks to enforce ordinances and order; enforcement of disorderly conduct laws to move groups off the street corners, road checks for DWI, improper licenses, stolen vehicles). Addressing physical deterioration involved an intensification of city services and the use of juvenile offenders to conduct clean-up work in the target areas.

*Coordinated Community Policing* (Newark). This was the "kitchen sink" project that included a neighborhood community police center, a directed police-citizen contact program, a neighborhood police newsletter, intensified law enforcement and order maintenance, and a neighborhood clean-up.

Two types of samples were used: (1) cross-sectional analysis which gave data for each area and (2) panel respondents which gave data for individuals. The results of the testing are summarized in Tables 14.1 and 14.2. The checks in the table indicate that the results were **statistically significant** at the .05 level. This measurement means that the results would occur by chance only five times in one hundred. This level is most frequently used in such studies. A statistically significant finding at the .01 level means the results would occur by chance only one time in one hundred.

The programs were least effective reducing concerns about property crime and most effective reducing perceived social disorder. According to the data provided by individuals, the Newark Coordinated Community Policing study met the greatest number of goals.

## CRIME PREVENTION PROGRAM STUDIES IN THE 1980s

Several communities conducted crime prevention studies in the 1980s. Studies in Seattle, Portland and Hartford focused on citizen efforts to prevent residential crime; the study in Portland also focused on preventing crime in and around commercial establishments. Two studies examined the media and crime prevention: the McGruff national media campaign and the effectiveness of anticrime newsletters.

According to Heinzelmann (1986, p. 7): "In general, the results of these evaluations are favorable, indicating that community crime prevention programs can serve to reduce crime and fear, and at the same time improve the quality of life and the economic viability of urban neighborhoods and commercial settings."

### The Seattle Program

The Citywide Crime Prevention Program (CCPP) of Seattle, described by Lindsay and McGillis (1986, pp. 46–67), focused on residential burglaries and

Table 14.1 Effects of Fear-Reduction Programs (Cross-Sectional Results) (Area Results)

| Programs | Reduce Perceived Area Physical Deterioration | Reduce Perceived Area Social Disorder | Reduce Fear of Personal Victimization | Reduce Worry about Property Crime | Reduce Perceived Area Personal Crime | Reduce Perceived Area Property Crime | Improve Evaluation of Police | Increase Satisfaction with Area |
|---|---|---|---|---|---|---|---|---|
| Houston Newsletters with and without Statistics | n.a. | n.a. | | | | | | |
| Newark Newsletters with and without Statistics | n.a. | n.a. | | | | | | |
| Houston Victim Recontact Program | n.a. | n.a. | | | | | | |
| Houston Police Community Station | n.a. | ✔ | ✔ | | ✔ | ✔ | | |
| Houston Citizen Contact Patrol | n.a. | ✔ | ✔ | | ✔ | ✔ | | ✔ |
| Houston Community Organizing Response Team | n.a. | ✔ | | | | | ✔ | |
| Newark "Signs of Crime" Program | | | | ✔ | | | | |
| Newark Coordinated Community Policing | | ✔ | | | | ✔ | ✔ | |

✔ = Desired goal achieved; significant at .05 level

n.a. = Not applicable

SOURCE: A. M. Pate, W. G. Skogan, M. A. Wycoff, and L. W. Sherman. *Reducing the "Signs of Crime": The Newark Experience.* Washington: The Police Foundation, 1986. © The Police Foundation. Reprinted by permission.

Table 14.2   Effects of Fear-Reduction Programs (Panel Results) (Individual Results)

| Programs | Reduce Perceived Area Physical Deterioration | Reduce Perceived Area Social Disorder | Reduce Fear of Personal Victimization | Reduce Worry about Property Crime | Reduce Perceived Area Personal Crime | Reduce Perceived Area Property Crime | Improve Evaluation of Police | Increase Satisfaction with Area |
|---|---|---|---|---|---|---|---|---|
| Houston Newsletters with and without Statistics | n.a. | | | | | | | |
| Newark Newsletters with and without Statistics | n.a. | | | | | | | |
| Houston Victim Recontact Program | n.a. | | | | | | | |
| Houston Police Community Station | n.a. | | ✔ | | | | | |
| Houston Citizen Contact Patrol | n.a. | ✔ | | | ✔ | | ✔ | |
| Houston Community Organizing Response Team | n.a. | ✔ | | | | | ✔ | ✔ |
| Newark "Signs of Crime" Program | | ✔ | ✔ | | ✔ | ✔ | | |
| Newark Coordinated Community Policing | | ✔ | ✔ | ✔ | ✔ | ✔ | ✔ | ✔ |

✔ = Desired goal achieved; significant at .05 level

n.a. = Not applicable

SOURCE: A. M. Pate, W. G. Skogan, M. A. Wycoff, and L. W. Sherman. *Reducing the "Signs of Crime": The Newark Experience.* 28. Washington: The Police Foundation, 1986. © The Police Foundation. Reprinted by permission.

included three primary police services: property identification, home security checks and organizing neighborhood block watch programs.

◆

The Seattle Citywide Crime Prevention Program used property identification, home security checks and neighborhood block watches to significantly reduce the residential burglary rate as well as the number of burglary-in-progress calls.

◆

Fleissner et al. (1992, p. 9) note:

When citizens and police in South Seattle banded together to fight crime, quarterly crime statistics showed dramatic improvements in the quality of life. Citizen activity spread in the city's other three police precincts; now community policing is a going concern throughout Seattle—a citywide success.

According to Lindsay and McGillis (p. 65), not only did the burglary rate drop significantly, "burglary-in-progress calls as a proportion of all burglary calls to police increased significantly in treated areas, and their quality was relatively high as measured by presentation of suspect information and the occurrence of subsequent arrests."

## The Portland Program

Portland also instituted a burglary prevention program, described by Schneider (1986, pp. 68–86), which included providing citizens with information about locks, alarms, outside lighting around entrances, removal or trimming of hedges and precautions to take while on vacation. The program also encouraged citizens to mark property with identification numbers. Door-to-door canvassing and a heavy emphasis on neighborhood rather than individual protection were important components of the program.

◆

The Portland antiburglary program succeeded in reducing the burglary rate for those who participated.

◆

As noted by Schneider (p. 84): "In the high crime areas of Portland more than 20% of the homes could expect to be burglarized at least once a year. This was reduced to about 8% for participating households in those areas." Schneider (p. 85) also points out a class bias in this study: "Those attending meetings, engraving their property, and displaying the decals tended to be in the higher socioeconomic groups."

## The Hartford Experiment

The Hartford Experiment, described by Fowler and Mangione (1986, pp. 87–108), used a three-pronged approach to reduce crime and the fear of crime: changing the physical environment, changing the delivery of police services and organizing the citizens to improve their neighborhoods. This experiment centered on the interdependence of citizens, the police and the environment. As noted by Fowler and Mangione (p. 89): "The approach focuses on the interaction between human behavior and the (physically) built environment. It was hypothesized that the *proper design and effective* use of the built environment can lead to a reduction in crime and fear."

The program was based on four previous research efforts. First was that of Jacobs (1961) which found that neighborhoods which were relatively crime free had a mix of commercial and residential properties, resulting in many people on the streets and a great opportunity for police surveillance. In addition, a community with such mixed use property tended to have residents who cared about the neighborhood and watched out for each other.

Angel (1968) described similar findings in his concept of "critical density," which states that if quite a few people are present on the most frequently used streets, they will serve as deterrents to burglary. In addition, Newman's classic work (1972) suggests that crime can be reduced by redesigning buildings to increase the number of doorways and other spaces that could be easily observed. Finally, Repetto (1974), like Newman, found that opportunities for surveillance could reduce crime, and, like Jacobs, that neighborhood cohesiveness could have the same result.

Based on this research the Hartford Experiment focused on Asylum Hill, a residential area a few blocks from the central business district of Hartford that was rapidly deteriorating. It was found that due to the high rate of traffic, residents did not use their yards and felt no ties to the neighborhood. The physical design of the neighborhood was changed to restrict through traffic and visually define the boundaries of the neighborhood. Cul-de-sacs were built at a few critical intersections, and some streets were made one-way.

A second change in the neighborhood involved the assignments of patrol officers. Instead of using rotating assignments within a centralized department, Hartford began using a decentralized team of officers assigned permanently to the Asylum Hill area.

Finally, the Hartford Experiment caused the neighborhood to organize. Organization included setting up block watch programs, recreational programs for youth and improvements for a large neighborhood park.

As a result of these changes, according to Fowler and Mangione (p. 96): "Residents used their neighborhood more, walked more often both during the day and evening hours, used the nearby park more often, and spent more days per week outside in front of their homes."

◆

The Hartford Experiment restructured the neighborhood's physical environment, changed how patrol officers were assigned and organized the neighborhood in an effort to reduce crime and the fear of crime.

◆

Fowler and Mangione (p. 106) caution: "A crime control program such as this must be custom fit to a particular set of circumstances. What one would want to derive from the Hartford project is not a program design, but rather an approach to problem analysis and strategies to affect them."

## The Portland Commercial Demonstration Project

The Crime Prevention through Environmental Design (**CPTED**) Commercial Demonstration Project implemented in Portland from 1974 to 1979, described by Lavrakas and Kushmuk (1986, pp. 202–27), also built upon the research of Jacobs (1961) and Newman (1972) and the concept of "defensible space."

The CPTED Project incorporated four major strategies: motivation reinforcement, activity support, surveillance and access control, as described in Figure 14.2. The CPTED project developed seven specific strategies (Lavrakas and Kushmuk, pp. 206–07):

1. Creation of a "Safe Streets for People" component.
2. Creation of a Residential Activity Center and miniplazas along Union Avenue Corridor (UAC).
3. General promotion of UAC.
4. Improved transportation both into and out of UAC.
5. Security services provided by a UAC security advisor.
6. Increased law enforcement support throughout UAC.
7. Development of a "Cash Off the Streets" program.

The first two strategies of the CPTED Project involved redesigning some streets, improving roads, adding street lighting and generally making the area more attractive.

◆

The Portland CPTED Commercial Demonstration Project found that the most successful strategies were security services, organization and support of the business community and the street lighting program.

◆

According to Lavrakas and Kushmuk (p. 223): "Of moderate success were the economic development activities. Large-scale and comprehensive improvements

---

**MOTIVATION REINFORCEMENT**

*Design and Construction:* Design, build, and/or repair buildings and building sites to enhance security and improve quality.

*Owner/Management Action:* Encourage owners and managements to implement safeguards to make businesses and commercial property less vulnerable to crime.

*Territorial Identity:* Differentiate private areas from public spaces to discourage trespass by potential offenders.

*Neighborhood Image:* Develop positive image of the commercial area to encourage user and investor confidence and increase the economic vitality of the area.

---

**ACTIVITY SUPPORT**

*Land Use:* Establish policies to prevent ill-advised land and building uses that have negative impact.

*User Protection:* Implement safeguards to make shoppers less vulnerable to crime.

*Social Interaction:* Encourage interaction among businessmen, users, and residents of commercial neighborhoods to foster social cohesion and control.

*Police/Community Relations:* Improve police/community relations to involve citizens in cooperative efforts with police to prevent and report crime.

*Community Awareness:* Create community crime prevention awareness to aid in combating crime in commercial areas.

---

**SURVEILLANCE**

*Surveillance Through Physical Design:* Improve opportunities for surveillance by physical design mechanisms that serve to increase the risk of detection for offenders, enable evasive actions by potential victims, and facilitate intervention by police.

*Mechanical Surveillance Devices:* Provide businesses with security devices to detect and signal illegal entry attempts.

*Private Security Services:* Determine necessary and appropriate services to enhance commercial security.

*Police Services:* Improve police services in order to efficiently and effectively respond to crime problems and to enhance citizen cooperation in reporting crimes.

---

**ACCESS CONTROL**

*Access Control:* Provide secure barriers to prevent unauthorized access to building grounds, buildings, and/or restricted building interior areas.

---

*Figure 14.2*   **Commercial Environment Objectives of CPTED**

NOTE: The four key hypotheses are not mutually exclusive. Surveillance objectives also serve to control access; activity support involves surveillance; and motivation reinforcement provides support for the other three hypotheses.

SOURCE: H. Kaplan, K. O'Kane, P. J. Lavrakas, and S. Hoover. *CPTED Final Report on Commercial Demonstration in Portland, Oregon.* Arlington: Westinghouse Electric Corporation, 1978. © Westinghouse Electric Corporation. Reprinted by permission.

in the physical environment (with the exception of the redesign of Union Avenue itself), promotional events, and residential social cohesion were judged to have achieved, at best, low levels of success." The results are summarized in Figure 14.3.

Lavrakas and Kushmuk (pp. 223–24) suggest three important lessons learned from this project. First, it is essential to have a realistic time frame and strong political support. Second, the more groups that are involved, the more complicated and difficult the project will become. And third, changes in the social environment of a community are much more difficult to make than those in the physical environment.

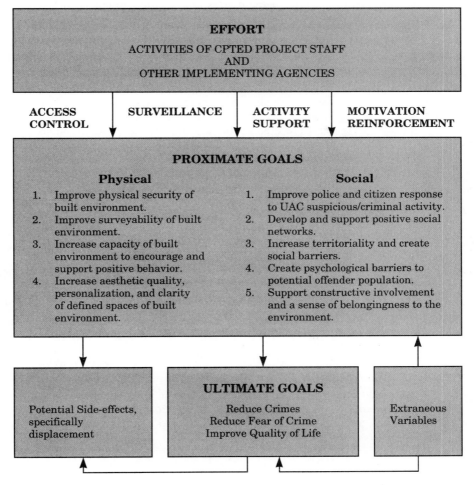

*Figure 14.3*    **CPTED Evaluation Design**
SOURCE: P. J. Lavrakas, J. Normoyle, and J. Wagener. *CPTED Commercial Demonstration Evaluation Report.* Evanston: Westinghouse Electric Corporation, 1978. © Westinghouse Electric Corporation. Reprinted by permission.

# USING THE MEDIA IN CRIME PREVENTION EFFORTS

Two different approaches to using the media have also been extensively studied: the "McGruff" media campaign and the use of police-community anticrime newsletters.

## The "McGruff" National Media Campaign

McGruff, the crime dog, is to law enforcement what Smokey the Bear is to the National Forest Service. A press release from the National Crime Prevention Council describes the creation of McGruff and the campaign:

> The concept of a national public education campaign to teach Americans that they could prevent crime (and how to do so) was first conceived in 1978. The Department of Justice supported the plan, as did distinguished civic leaders and such organizations as the AFL-CIO, the International Association of Chiefs of Police, and the National Sheriffs' Association. The Advertising Council, Inc. agreed to support the campaign. Research and program development advisory groups helped formulate a strategy. With the creative aid of the volunteer ad agency then known as Dancer Fitzgerald Sample (now Saatchi & Saatchi), the first McGruff public service ads were developed in 1979 and premiered in February 1980. . . .
>
> The Campaign's objectives were clear:
>
> 1. To change unwarranted feelings and attitudes about crime and the criminal justice system.
> 2. To generate an individual sense of responsibility for crime prevention.
> 3. To initiate individual action toward preventing crime.
> 4. To mobilize additional resources for crime prevention efforts.
> 5. To enhance existing crime prevention programs and projects conducted by national, state and local organizations.

This campaign, also known as the "Take a Bite Out of Crime" campaign, as described by O'Keefe (1986, pp. 252–68), was aimed at promoting citizen involvement in crime prevention activities through public service announcements (**PSAs**).

♦

The public has favorably received the "McGruff" format and content. The "McGruff" campaign has had a sizeable impact on what people know and do about crime prevention.

♦

As noted by O'Keefe (p. 259): "Most said they thought the ads were effective in conveying the message, that they liked the McGruff character and that they felt

*McGruff crime prevention posters cover a variety of areas. Used by permission.*

*A young girl holds the paw of a McGruff crime dog robot during an anti-drug rally at the Texas State Capitol building.*

the information in the ads was worth passing on to other people." In addition, people indicated that they felt more confident about their own ability to protect themselves from crime. Most importantly, almost one-fourth of the people took preventive action after exposure to the PSA, particularly to improve their own household security and work with neighbors in cooperative efforts—the two main themes of the McGruff promotions.

## Police-Community Anticrime Newsletters

Lavrakas (1986, pp. 269–91) reviews the results of three studies on a relatively new crime-prevention strategy, the police-community anticrime newsletter.

Included in Lavrakas' review are *ALERT*, the Evanston (Illinois) Police Department newsletter; the *Community Policing Exchange* newsletter of the Houston Police Department; and *ACT I*, the newsletter of the Newark Police Department.

One important finding of these three studies was that although readers were much more aware of crime, at a statistically significant level, their fear of crime did *not* increase. According to Lavrakas (p. 286): "In each of the cities, results indicated that residents were overwhelmingly positive in their assessments of the newsletters, especially the versions that included crime statistics. Not only was exposure greater to the version with crime statistics, but it was rated as significantly more interesting and more informative."

◆

Studies of three police-community anticrime newsletters found them to be highly effective, especially if crime statistics were included.

◆

Lavrakas (pp. 289–90) concludes that the three tests "suggest that such newsletters merit consideration elsewhere as one strategy in the arsenal in the fight against crime."

## LESSONS LEARNED

Yin (1986, pp. 294–308) analyzed eleven research studies of community policing/crime prevention and suggests that they "point to the desirability of joint police-citizen initiatives in successful community crime prevention efforts" (p. 304). Table 14.3 summarizes the research studies Yin analyzed and the results of each.

A key finding, according to Yin, is that any crime prevention strategy, taken singly, is likely to be ineffective. A second finding points to the importance of improving the police-community relationship. Yin (p. 306) suggests that the results of these studies provide a general pattern and a major lesson about crime prevention:

◆

Successful crime prevention efforts require joint activities by the residents and police and the presumed improvement of relationships between these groups.

◆

Skolnick and Bayley (1986, p. 212) describe this as police-community **reciprocity**: "Police-community reciprocity means that police must genuinely feel, and genuinely communicate a feeling, that the public they are serving has something to contribute to the enterprise of policing." Both parties can benefit from working together.

In addition to these relatively formal evaluations, other less quantitative evaluations have been conducted.

**Table 14.3  Summary of Eleven Evaluation Studies**

| Description of Intervention | Study Author(s) | Intervention Sites and Period | Type of Crime Addressed | Type of Outcomes Examined | Nature of Outcomes | Analytic Criteria Used in Test Outcomes |
|---|---|---|---|---|---|---|
| *Hartford Project:* physical redesign, police redeployment, and community organizing | Fowler & Mangione | Hartford, Connecticut 1973–1979 | residential | informal social control; burglary and robbery victimization rates; fear of crime | crime reduction when whole intervention in place | statistical significance |
| *Crime Newsletters:* distribution of community newsletters in target neighborhoods | Lavrakas | Evanston, Illinois, 1981 Houston, Texas, 1983 Newark, New Jersey, 1983 | residential | awareness of newsletter; perceived crime problem; fear of crime | positive changes at one of three sites | statistical significance |
| *Portland Project:* physical redesign, police assistance, and business organizing | Lavrakas & Kushmuk | Portland, Oregon 1974–1980 | commercial | reported burglaries; fear of crime; quality of life | burglary reduction | statistical significance |
| *Seattle Community Crime Prevention Program:* block watch, security inspections, and property engraving | Lindsay & McGillis | Seattle, Washington 1974–1975 | residential | burglary victimization rate | burglary reduction | statistical significance |
| *McGruff National Media Campaign:* information used in mass media and in pamphlets | O'Keefe | Nationwide campaign, 1979 | residential | awareness of announcements; reported learning; reported preventive actions | reported learning and actions increase | data in supplemental report |
| *Newark Foot Patrol:* foot patrols from 4 P.M. to midnight | Pate | Newark, New Jersey 1973–1979 | residential | reported crime victimization rates; perceived crime, safety, and satisfaction with police | no crime reduction; changed perceptions | statistical significance |
| *Urban Crime Prevention Program:* block watches and related neighborhood meetings | Rosenbaum, et al. | Chicago, Illinois 1983–1984 | residential | victimization rates; perceived crime; fear of crime; perceived efficacy; social disorder; physical deterioration | crime reduction at only one of four sites; increases at others | statistical significance |
| *Portland Anti-Burglary Program:* street lighting, property engraving, and community education | Schneider | Portland, Oregon 1973–1974 | residential | reported burglaries; victimization rates | burglary reduction | statistical significance |
| *Commercial Security Field Test:* security surveys undertaken by business proprietors | Tien & Cahn | Denver, Colorado, 1981 Long Beach, California, 1981 St. Louis, Missouri, 1981 | residential | burglary victimization rates; fear of crime | burglary reduction at one of three sites | statistical significance |
| *Neighborhood Foot Patrol:* foot patrol and community organizing | Trojanowicz | Flint, Michigan 1979–1982 | residential | reported crime; satisfaction with police | crime reduction; increase in satisfaction | descriptive data only |
| *Storefront Police Office:* location of storefront office, staffed by police, in local neighborhood | Wycoff & Skogan | Houston, Texas 1983–1984 | residential | fear of crime; perceived crime, safety, and satisfaction with police | fear reduction; improved perceptions | statistical significance |

SOURCE: "Community Crime Prevention, A Synthesis of Eleven Evaluations." In *Community Crime Prevention: Does It Work?* 297–99, edited by Dennis P. Rosenbaum. Beverly Hills: Sage Publications, 1986. © Sage Publications. Reprinted by permission.

## QUALITATIVE EVALUATIONS AND SALIENT PROGRAM FEATURES

**Qualitative evaluations** are more descriptive and less statistical. One large-scale qualitative evaluation, undertaken by the National Symposium on Community Institutions and Inner-City Crime Project, sought to identify model programs for reduction of inner-city crime. According to Sulton (1990, p. 8) almost 3,500 national organizations, criminal justice scholars and federal, state and local government agencies were asked to recommend outstanding local programs. This resulted in the identification of approximately 1,300 programs. Each was sent a request for detailed information, and 350 (27 percent) responded. From these, eighteen were selected for site visits.

Sulton (p. 10) notes that although each program was unique, they shared some common characteristics.

◆

Eighteen model programs shared the following characteristics. The program:

- Focused on causes of crime.
- Built on community strengths.
- Incorporated natural support systems.
- Had an identifiable group of clients.
- Targeted those who were less affluent.
- Had clearly stated goals and well-defined procedures.
- Had sufficient resources.
- Had a strong leader.

◆

Sulton (p. 10) observes that many of the problems focus on specific social problems of inner-city residents "identified as correlates with, if not causes of, inner-city crime, such as emotional or family instability, lack of education, absence of vocational skills, unemployment, drug and alcohol abuse, juvenile gangs and sexual abuse and exploitation." The programs have a clear focus, a clear audience and a clear idea of how to proceed. Several of these programs are described in the chapters that follow.

On a much smaller scale, but equally instructional, is the Newport News Police Department's reliance on data to identify a problem and to evaluate their solution (Guyot, 1992, p. 321):

The problem was that local hunters and other gun owners were doing target practice at a large pit where dirt had been excavated for I-64. Officer Ron Hendrickson found out that between April and September 1987, the department had been called 45 times to chase away shooters and that the problem had existed for at least 15 years. Most of the calls had come from a couple whose nearby home was bullet-riddled and who thought the police were doing a good job because each time they chased away the shooters.

When Officer Hendrickson decided, with the support of his sergeant, to end the problem, he interviewed shooters and learned that most were soldiers from nearby Ft. Eustis and that many others were sent to the pit by gun shop owners. The officer determined that the pit was close enough to I-64 to make any firearms discharge illegal there. Deciding to use education backed by legal sanctions, he first took photographs of damage and other evidence. These he used to persuade a judge to give anyone convicted of illegal shooting a suspended sentence and a small fine, with a warning that a second appearance would result in confiscation of the weapon and a jail sentence. The officer obtained from the property owners permission to arrest on their property and the same from the C & O Railroad for shooters crossing the tracks to reach the pit. In a crucial step, he wrote a pamphlet which defined the problem and the department's intended enforcement action. He distributed the pamphlet to the military base and to all gun shops in the area. Finally, he had no parking—tow zone signs erected on the shoulder where most shooters were parking.

The statistics on the results were simple. Officers issued 35 summonses to shooters in September, only 15 in October, and the last on November 12, 1987. The pit soon became so overgrown that it was uninviting for target practice.

Success in the preceding incident and others might indicate that community policing and problem-solving policing would be readily accepted by law enforcement officials and the communities they serve. Such acceptance is not, however, always the case.

## IMPEDIMENTS TO COMMUNITY POLICING

Recall from Chapter 5 the challenges facing implementation of community policing as described by Sadd and Grinc (1996, pp. 1–2):

- Resistance by police officers.
- Difficulty involving other agencies and organizing the community.
- Average citizens were reluctant to participate, either because of fear or cynicism.

Sadd and Grinc suggest (p. 8): "Community policing is a fight for 'hearts and minds' of patrol officers and the public . . . involving a shift in the culture of policing."

Another challenge noted by Sadd and Grinc is that projects were usually established as special units which some saw as elite: "The perception of elitism is ironic because community policing is meant to close the gap between patrol and special units and to empower and value the rank-and-file patrol officer as the most important agent for police work."

Resistance to change is common, especially in a tradition-oriented profession such as law enforcement. Skolnick and Bayley (1986, pp. 225–26) describe six impediments to implementing innovative community-oriented policing.

◆

Impediments to implementing innovative community-oriented policing include:

- The powerful pull of tradition.
- Substantial segments of the public do not want the police to change.
- Unions will continue to be skeptical of innovation.
- Innovation may prove costly.
- Lack of vision on the part of police executives.
- Police departments' inability to evaluate their own effectiveness.

◆

Despite these impediments, community policing appears to offer a realistic approach to reducing violence, crime and the drug problem. The remaining chapters discuss specific programs that use community policing and problem solving to address these issues.

## SUMMARY

Several studies in the 1980s assessed the effectiveness of community policing efforts. The Flint Neighborhood Foot Patrol Program appeared to produce a decrease in crime, an increase in general citizen satisfaction with the foot patrol program, a decline in the public's fear of crime and a positive evaluation of the foot patrol officers.

In the first Newark Foot Patrol Experiment, residents reported positive results, while business owners reported negative results. The second Newark Foot Patrol Experiment used coordinated foot patrol, a cleanup campaign and distribution of a newsletter. Only the coordinated foot patrol reduced the perception of property crime and improved assessments of the police.

The Oakland program, using foot patrol, mounted patrol, small vehicle patrol and a Report Incidents Directly program, resulted in a substantial drop in the rate of crime against individuals and their property.

The San Diego Community Profile Project provided patrol officers with extensive community orientation training. These officers became more service oriented, increased their non-law enforcement contacts with citizens and had a more positive attitude toward police-community relations.

The Houston Fear Reduction Project did not achieve desired results from the victim recontact program or the newsletter. Citizen contact and the police storefront operation did, however, result in decreases in the public's perception of social disorder, fear of personal victimization and the level of personal and property crime.

The Boston Foot Patrol Project found no statistically significant relationship between changes in the level of foot patrol provided and number of calls for service or the seriousness of the calls.

Baltimore County's COPE Project reduced fear of crime by 10 percent in target neighborhoods. It also reduced calls for service and increased citizen awareness of and satisfaction with the police.

The most common components of community policing experiments have been foot patrol, newsletters and community organizing.

Other studies have reviewed the effectiveness of community crime prevention efforts. The Seattle Citywide Crime Prevention Program, using property identification, home security checks and neighborhood block watches, significantly reduced the residential burglary rate as well as the number of burglary-in-progress calls. The Portland antiburglary program also succeeded in reducing the burglary rate for the participants. The Hartford Experiment restructured the physical environment, changed how patrol officers were assigned and organized the neighborhood in an effort to reduce crime and the fear of crime.

The Portland CPTED Commercial Demonstration Project found that the most successful strategies were security services, organization and support of the business community and the street lighting program.

The effectiveness of the media in assisting crime prevention efforts is another evaluation focus. The public has favorably received the "McGruff" format and content. The "McGruff" campaign has had a sizeable impact on what the public knows and does about crime prevention. Studies of three police-community anticrime newsletters found them to be highly effective, especially if they included crime statistics.

Some general conclusions can be drawn from the preceding studies, including the finding that successful crime prevention efforts require joint activities by the residents and police and the presumed improvement of relationships between these groups.

Eighteen model programs identified by the National Symposium on Community Institutions and Inner-City Crime Project shared the following characteristics: The programs (1) were focused on causes of crime; (2) built on community strengths; (3) incorporated natural support systems; (4) had an identifiable group of clients; (5) targeted those who were less affluent; (6) had clearly stated goals and well-defined procedures; (7) had sufficient resources; and (8) had a strong leader.

The implementation of community policing must be weighed against several impediments including the powerful pull of tradition; substantial segments of the public who do not want the police to change; the skepticism of unions with regard to innovation; the cost of innovation; lack of vision on the part of police executives; and the incapacity of police departments to evaluate their own effectiveness.

## Discussion Questions

1. Why is it difficult to conduct research on the effectiveness of community policing?
2. Which studies do you think have the most value for policing in the next few years? Which studies have the most promise?
3. Why would a police department want to reduce fear of crime rather than crime itself?
4. Which of the fear reduction strategies do you believe holds the most promise?

5. What do you think are the most reasonable aspects of the crime prevention through environmental design (CPTED) approach?

6. If you believe in the CPTED approach and see individuals ignoring its potential to reduce crime, do you think that if they are victimized the concept of culpability should be considered?

7. Has your police department conducted any research on community policing or crime prevention efforts? If so, what were the results?

8. Does your police department have its own McGruff? If so, how does the department use him?

9. What do you think are the most important questions regarding police-community relations that should be researched in the next few years?

10. How much of a police department's budget should be devoted to research? Which areas should be of highest priority?

### *References*

Angel, S. *Discouraging Crime through City Planning.* Berkeley: University of California Press, 1968.

Burden, Ordway P. "Citizens Spur Community-Based Policing." *Law Enforcement News.* (March 15, 1992): 5.

Fleissner, Dan; Fedan, Nicholas; and Klinger, David. "Community Policing in Seattle: A Model Partnership Between Citizens and Police." *National Institute of Justice Journal.* (August 1992): 9–18.

Fowler, Floyd J., Jr. and Mangione, Thomas W. "A Three-Pronged Effort to Reduce Crime and Fear of Crime: The Hartford Experiment." In *Community Crime Prevention: Does It Work?* edited by Dennis P. Rosenbaum, 87–108. Beverly Hills: Sage Publications, 1986.

Greene, Jack R. and Taylor, Ralph B. "Community-Based Policing and Foot Patrol: Issues of Theory and Evaluation." In *Community Policing: Rhetoric or Reality,* edited by Jack R. Greene and Stephen D. Mastrofski, 195–223. New York: Praeger Publishers, 1991.

Guyot, Dorothy. "Problem-Oriented Policing Shines in the Stats." In *Source Book: Community-Oriented Policing: An Alternative Strategy,* edited by Bernard L. Garmire, 317–21. Washington: ICMA, May 1992.

Heinzelmann, Fred. "Foreword." *Community Crime Prevention: Does It Work?* edited by Dennis P. Rosenbaum, 7–8. Newbury Park: Sage Publications, 1986.

Jacobs, J. *The Death and Life of Great American Cities.* New York: Vintage, 1961.

Lavrakas, Paul J. "Evaluating Police-Community Anticrime Newsletters: The Evanston, Houston, and Newark Field Studies." In *Community Crime Prevention: Does It Work?* edited by Dennis P. Rosenbaum, 269–91. Beverly Hills: Sage Publications, 1986.

Lavrakas, Paul J. and Kushmuk, James W. "Evaluating Crime Prevention through Environmental Design: The Portland Commercial Demonstration Project." In *Community Crime Prevention: Does It Work?* edited by Dennis P. Rosenbaum, 202–27. Beverly Hills: Sage Publications, 1986.

Lindsay, Betsy and McGillis, Daniel. "Citywide Community Crime Prevention: An Assessment of the Seattle Program." In *Community Crime Prevention: Does It Work?* edited by Dennis P. Rosenbaum, 46–67. Beverly Hills: Sage Publications, 1986.

Mastrofski, Stephen D. "What Does Community Policing Mean for Daily Police Work?" *National Institute of Justice Journal.* (August 1992): 23–27.

Newman, O. *Defensible Space: Crime Prevention through Urban Design.* New York: Macmillan, 1972.

O'Keefe, Garrett J. "The 'McGruff' National Media Campaign: Its Public Impact and Future Implications." In *Community Crime Prevention: Does It Work?* edited by Dennis P. Rosenbaum, 252–68. Beverly Hills: Sage Publications, 1986.

Pate, Anthony M. "Experimenting with Foot Patrol: The Newark Experience." In *Community Crime Prevention: Does It Work?* edited by Dennis P. Rosenbaum, 137–56. Beverly Hills: Sage Publications, 1986.

Police Foundation. *The Newark Foot Patrol Experiment.* Washington: The Police Foundation, 1981.

Repetto, T. A. *Residential Crime.* Cambridge: Ballinger, 1974.

Sadd, Susan and Grinc, Randolph M. *Implementation Challenges in Community Policing.* Washington: National Institute of Justice Research in Brief, February 1996.

Schneider, Anne L. "Neighborhood-Based Antiburglary Strategies: An Analysis of Public and Private Benefits from the Portland Program." In *Community Crime Prevention: Does It Work?* edited by Dennis P. Rosenbaum, 68–86. Beverly Hills: Sage Publications, 1986.

Skogan, Wesley G. and Wycoff, Mary Ann. "Storefront Police Offices: The Houston Field Test." In *Community Crime Prevention: Does It Work?* edited by Dennis P. Rosenbaum, 179–99. Beverly Hills: Sage Publications, 1986.

Skolnick, Jerome H. and Bayley, David H. *The New Blue Line: Innovation in Six American Cities.* New York: The Free Press, 1986.

Sulton, Anne Thomas. *Inner-City Crime Control: Can Community Institutions Contribute?* Washington: The Police Foundation, 1990.

Taft, Philip B., Jr. *Fighting Fear: The Baltimore County C.O.P.E. Project.* Washington: Police Executive Research Forum, 1986.

Trojanowicz, Robert C. "Evaluating a Neighborhood Foot Patrol Program: The Flint, Michigan, Project." In *Community Crime Prevention: Does It Work?* edited by Dennis P. Rosenbaum, 157–78. Beverly Hills: Sage Publications, 1986.

Wycoff, Mary Ann. "The Benefits of Community Policing: Evidence and Conjecture." In *Community Policing: Rhetoric or Reality,* edited by Jack R. Greene and Stephen D. Mastrofski, 103–20. New York: Praeger Publishers, 1991.

Yin, Robert K. "Community Crime Prevention: A Synthesis of Eleven Evaluations." In *Community Crime Prevention: Does It Work?* edited by Dennis P. Rosenbaum, 294–308. Beverly Hills: Sage Publications, 1986.

*Chapter 15*

# Criminal Justice Programs

*To perfect society, liberty is necessary to develop the faculties, both intellectual and moral, . . . but to preserve society it is necessary to guard the community against injustice, violence, and from anarchy within, and against attacks from without.*

—John C. Calhoun

## Do you know

- What changes have occurred in the criminal justice system in the past decade?
- What components of the criminal justice system can help reduce the crime problem?
- What the greatest obstacle to change within police agencies might be?
- What benefits might be derived from improving police-community relations?
- What opportunities are provided by calls for service?
- What services police might offer citizens?
- How effective citizen-police ride-alongs have been?
- What police-based programs have proven effective?
- What court-based programs have proven effective?
- What corrections-based programs have proven effective?

## Definitions

Can you define these terms: directed imbalance, experimental imbalance.

*Introduction*

The criminal justice system includes law enforcement, the courts and corrections. The way our courts and correctional facilities operate directly affects law enforcement. A major challenge to the criminal justice system is balancing liberty and security. As our society has changed, so must the criminal justice system that serves it. Many of the trends that affect the criminal justice system directly affect the type of programs police departments should implement to improve community relations.

❖

Trends in the criminal justice system include:

- Emphasis on police service to the community rather than fighting crime.
- Greater responsibility and discretion for line officers.
- Reliance on cooperative efforts of law enforcement, courts and corrections to accomplish the goals of the criminal justice system.
- Belief in a justice model rather than a medical model when dealing with offenders.

❖

As noted by Trojanowicz (1986, p. 177): "Though most young officers think their job will involve the 'gun-toting,' 'siren-wailing,' 'crook-chasing' portrayed in the media and reinforced by their academy training, they find on the job that they spend most of their time mediating disputes, stopping neighborhood fights, or responding to complaints about barking dogs. The majority of their work involves delivering services to the community, not law enforcement activities."

The police are the most visible component of the criminal justice system and have the most direct contact with the public. The day-to-day contacts of line officers are the most critical factor in police-community relations. The street-level officer is really "where it's at." As previously discussed, what occurs within courts and corrections facilities can also greatly affect police-community relations. It is vital that the three components of the system collaborate and develop programs to serve the needs of the public.

This chapter begins with a brief description of the components of the criminal justice system and the need for collaboration among these components and the public. Next the police function and police-community relations are reviewed and placed into the policing context. This is followed by a discussion of the resistence to change, the "traditional" police response (responding to calls for service) and how the traditional response is influenced by community policing. The chapter concludes with a look at innovative police-based programs, court programs and correction programs.

## COORDINATED EFFORTS

What happens in each component of the criminal justice system directly affects the other components of the system.

◆

A coordinated effort among law enforcement, courts and corrections is required to effectively deal with the crime problem and to elicit the support of the community in doing so.

◆

Over thirty years ago, such cooperation was successfully implemented in California (Price, pers. com., 1992):

In the 1960s the San Bernardino County Sheriff's Department had an exchange program where a combined committee of police departments, sheriff's officers, prosecutors, probation and parole officers, corrections, court officers and educators exchanged personnel on a limited scale for one month. Cooperation between departments increased measurably after the exchanges. Members of each agency became more aware of the duties, responsibilities and problems of all of the other criminal justice agencies in the area as a direct result of the exchanges.

## THE POLICE FUNCTION AND POLICE-COMMUNITY RELATIONS REVIEWED

In essence, everything the police do affects their relationship with the community. Even the uniforms they wear are a factor, as noted by Aaron (1992, p. 14): "Today, uniforms have become a tradition, but the role and image of the police has changed dramatically since the tradition began. Some research already indicates that by selecting uniforms which are not associated with the old military style of policing and past police brutality, police may appear less threatening to other citizens in the community." He stresses (p. 15): "The image portrayed by the police to citizens is an issue of growing importance as resources dwindle and more citizens are asked to cooperate in community-based crime preventing and policing efforts." Police often resist change regarding their uniforms and other issues.

## RESISTANCE TO CHANGE

According to Wadman and Olson (1990, p. 55), the lowest hurdle toward change to a community policing philosophy is selling the approach to the public. The next lowest hurdle is convincing the rest of city government. They state that "the highest hurdle of all will be the organizational resistance of the police agency itself."

◆

The greatest obstacle to change may be resistance from within the police agency itself.

◆

Sparrow (1988, p. 1) uses the example of a truck driver to illustrate resistance to change:

> The professional truck driver does not drive his 50-ton trailer-truck the same way that he drives his sports car. He avoids braking sharply. He treats corners with far greater respect. And he generally does not expect the same instant response from the trailer, with its load, that he enjoys in his car. The driver's failure to understand the implications and responsibilities of driving such a massive vehicle inevitably produces tragedy: if the driver tries to turn too sharply, the cab loses traction as the trailer's momentum overturns or jackknifes the vehicle.

> Police organizations also have considerable momentum. Having a strong personal commitment to the values with which they have "grown up," police officers will find any hint of proposed change in the police culture extremely threatening. Moreover, those values are reflected in many apparently technical aspects of their jobs—systems for dispatching patrols, patrol officers constantly striving to be available for the next call, incident-logging criteria, etc. The chief executive who simply announces that community policing is now the order of the day, without a carefully designed plan for bringing about that change, stands in danger both of "losing traction" and of throwing his entire force into confusion.

## Overcoming Resistance to Change

Resistance to change can be reduced by two kinds of imbalance within an organizational structure that can render it susceptible to change: **directed imbalance** and **experimental imbalance**.

**Directed Imbalance.** A physical comparison to describe directed imbalance is that of riding a bicycle. Think of how, when riding a bicycle, your body unconsciously shifts in the opposite direction of a turn to be made. Without this shift in balance, you are likely to tip over. You are also likely to fall if you shift in preparation for a turn and then do *not* turn. Sparrow (1988, p. 3) suggests: "Directed imbalances within a police organization will be those imbalances that are created in anticipation of the proposed change in orientation. They will be the changes that make sense only under the assumption that the whole project will be implemented, and that it will radically alter organizational priorities." He gives the following examples of directed imbalance:

- Movement of the most talented and promising personnel into the newly defined jobs.
- Making it clear that the route to promotion lies within such jobs.
- Disbanding those squads that embody and add weight to the traditional values.
- Recategorizing the crime statistics according to their effect on the community.
- Redesigning the staff evaluation system to take account of contributions to the nature and quality of community life.
- Providing inservice training in problem-solving skills for veteran officers and managers.
- Altering the nature of the training given to new recruits to include problem-solving skills.
- Establishing new communication channels with other public services.
- Contracting for annual community surveys for a period of years.

**Experimental Imbalance.** Experimental imbalance, as the name implies, creates an atmosphere of trial and error and of risk-taking. It encourages officers at all levels to be creative and seek innovative ways to approach community problems. Sparrow notes (p. 4): "The resourcefulness of police officers, so long apparent in their unofficial behavior, can at last be put to the service of the department. Creativity blossoms in an experimental environment that is tolerant of unusual ideas."

## CHANGES TO ANTICIPATE

Change is occurring as law enforcement agencies move toward community-oriented, problem-solving policing.

The managerial grid often used in business also fits the options facing police officers as they deal with the public, as illustrated in Figure 15.1. A (1,1) style of policing indicates low concern for control or for citizens' rights. It would be a removed, "do not rock the boat," style of policing. A (1,9) style of policing indicates low concern for control and high concern for citizens' rights. A (9,1) style, in contrast, would put little emphasis on citizens' rights and great emphasis on control. The grid illustrates the many options officers have when they perform their jobs.

The police work grid implies that different situations require different responses. For example, sniper or hostage situations usually do not call for community surveys. Although the emphasis on community service is increasing, police are still expected to serve as protectors when necessary. The skill with which they fulfill this role greatly affects police-community relations.

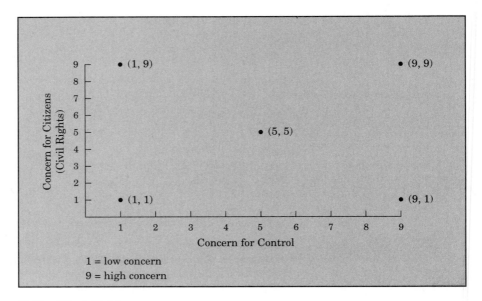

*Figure 15.1*    **Police Work Grid**

SOURCE: Mary Jeanette Hageman. *Police-Community Relations.* Beverly Hills: Sage Publications, 1985: 25. © 1985 Sage Publications. Reprinted with permission.

Another basic way the police role varies because of community policing is the manner in which the police interact with the public. Snelson and Oettmeier (1987, pp. 5–6) describe a number of objectives of the Houston Police Department's policing style, designed to facilitate interactive relationships between neighborhood residents and beat officers:

1. Establish trust and harmony between and among neighborhood residents and the beat officer by establishing a positive, cooperative and productive relationship between both parties;

2. Exchange information between neighborhood residents and beat officers which will strengthen rapport and enhance neighborhood safety;

3. Respond to the problem of crime and criminal activity by maximizing the efficient utilization of available department and community resources in enforcing the law;

4. Identify and resolve neighborhood problems which will reduce the fear of crime and enhance the quality of life within the neighborhoods;

5. Establish and improve communication linkages and working relationships between and among divisional and departmental personnel;

6. Establish an effective management structure which utilizes divisional and community input to define service needs, direct operational com-

mitments and clarify responsibilities on behalf of division personnel and the public in order to more efficiently respond to the concerns of neighborhood residents;

7. Facilitate the acquisition, analysis and utilization of information in order to identify neighborhood crime and non-crime problems capable of being resolved through mutual participation on behalf of police personnel and community residents;

8. Develop and implement programs, strategies and/or activities to efficiently use beat officers' uncommitted patrol time;

9. Provide safe and orderly traffic flow through the neighborhoods by enforcing violations and reducing the number of traffic accidents; and

10. Identify and utilize employee incentives conducive to improving employee morale.

These objectives balance concern for the officers with concern for the community while balancing the officers' crime-fighting and service roles.

### Benefits of Change

Wycoff (1991, p. 114) enumerates several benefits that are likely to result from this expanded view of policing. Officers should "have greater concern for citizens' problems, concern for victims, sense of independence, self-esteem, respect for their own skills, sense of 'ownership' of and responsibility for work, organizational commitment and a more positive view of citizens and of the way in which citizens view the police."

◆

Benefits of improved police-community relations might include greater police concern for citizens, including victims, as well as increased independence, self-esteem and sense of ownership in the police function.

◆

## RESPONDING TO CALLS FOR SERVICE

A potential conflict exists between responding to calls for service and community policing efforts because calls for service use up much of the time needed for problem identification and resolution efforts. Departments must set their priorities and determine if they will be driven by calls for service (reactive) or by a problem-oriented approach (proactive). Regardless of the selected approach, the manner in which police respond to calls is a critical factor in enhancing police-community relations.

As stressed throughout this text, the one-on-one interaction between police officers and the citizens they serve is critical.

*In many jurisdictions, bike patrols are being used extensively.*

◆

Responding to calls for service presents an excellent opportunity to foster good
police-community relationships.

◆

Officers' responses to service calls are critical to effective police-community
relations; therefore it is important to assess how effectively officers do respond.
Bondurant (1991, pp. 74–76) describes a citizen response questionnaire used in
Plainsboro, New Jersey, to assess the effectiveness of officer performance in the
field. The ten item questionnaire is mailed to citizens who request police service.
Citizens are asked to respond yes or no to the following (p. 75):

1. Did the officer respond quickly to your call for service? Approximately
   how long did it take for the officer to respond after being called?
2. Was the officer courteous?
3. Was the officer neatly attired?
4. Did the officer identify himself by name? If not, do you think he should
   have?
5. Did the officer speak clearly? Were you able to understand him?
6. Were you satisfied with the service provided by the officer?

7. Did the officer appear knowledgeable?

8. Did he obtain all information that would seem pertinent under the circumstances of this contact?

9. If applicable, did you feel satisfied with the supplemental investigation conducted by the officer?

10. Upon completion of this police contact, did you feel satisfied with the general quality of the service rendered?

11. Additional comments:

Respondents are asked to sign, date and mail the questionnaire back to the police department.

In addition to assessing how well officers respond to calls for service, most police departments have several other means to improve police-community relations. Indeed, any police department that adopts the community policing philosophy will make several internal changes and will also institute several community programs.

## INNOVATIVE POLICE-BASED PROGRAMS

It should be noted that programs identified in this chapter are *not* community policing, although community policing may incorporate the use of these and other programs. Too many police officials think that because they have a Neighborhood Watch Program or a ride-along program, they are doing community policing. In fact, some police chiefs and sheriffs state with pride that they are deeply involved in community policing because they have a DARE program. Such programs, in isolation, are more community relations or even public relations, not community policing.

Some simple services that police departments might provide for the community cost little and require limited personnel. Other services, however, may involve programs that are relatively expensive and must be staffed by many officers. The services and programs described in the following pages are a small sample of options available to law enforcement agencies to enhance the police-community partnership.

### The Houston Storefront Police Department

This experiment, evaluated by the Police Foundation and described briefly in Chapter 14, included several services to the community that were relatively inexpensive and involved limited personnel yet accomplished significant results (Skogan and Wycoff, 1986, pp. 182–83).

◆

Relatively inexpensive services include conducting monthly meetings, meeting with school administrators, conducting fingerprinting programs and blood pressure programs, participating in athletic contests, publishing newsletters and providing ride-alongs.

◆

The Houston Police Department held monthly meetings in a local church and discussed crime and other topics of community interest. Officers also met regularly with local school administrators to address the truancy problem. Their fingerprinting program for children began in the police department but was later moved to a local hamburger shop to reach more citizens. During the summer the department held softball, football, volleyball and horseshoe competitions in which residents played against police officers. The department's ride-along program involved citizens selected by area churches and civic organizations to ride with an officer patrolling their neighborhood. Ride-alongs are one very popular, yet controversial means to improve police-community relations.

## Ride-Along Programs

Ride-along programs are designed to give local citizens a chance to see what police work involves. According to Sharp (1990, p. 65), 96 percent of police departments polled across the country reported positive results from their ride-along programs, and 88 percent of the officers involved agreed with the findings.

◆

Ride-along programs are highly successful, with 96 percent reporting positive results.

◆

Many ride-along programs permit any responsible juvenile or adult to participate, but other programs have restrictions and may limit ridership. Participation by officers in a ride-along program is usually voluntary. Whether riders are allowed to use still or video cameras during a ride-along varies from department to department. Many departments also require their riders to dress "appropriately."

Sometimes a ride-along does more than foster police-community relations. In Denver, for example, officers who take clergy as riders will have help with death notifications, suicide situations, sexual assault investigations, runaway situations, emotionally disturbed persons, substance abuse investigations, significant conflagrations and child abuse victims (Sharp, p. 66).

Despite the numerous benefits of ride-along programs, Sharp (p. 67) notes: "There are departments which do not want to get involved in them for legitimate reasons such as insurance cost factors, liability considerations, concerns about the public's safety, officers not being in favor, administrative problems, the

*Rather than ride-alongs, some departments prefer to participate in youth sports programs in the community. Here two Minneapolis police officers prepare for a baseball game with local teens.*

potential to be disruptive, and cost." He cites the statement of Corporal Wilson, Georgia Highway Patrol (p. 67):

> The risk of injury to an untrained, nondepartmental civilian and the potential danger to our troopers resulting from the actions of an untrained, nondepartmental civilian will continue to contribute significantly to this department's decision not to sponsor civilian ride-along programs. An additional consideration is the unresolved question of civil liability of departmental members and the department.

Many departments ask those who participate in the ride-along program to sign a waiver that exempts the officer, the department and the city from liability.

## The Redondo Beach Civil Injunction Served on Gangs

One innovative way to combat gang crimes has been used by the Redondo Beach Police Department. In this award-winning experiment, the department got an injunction against the gang members who had essentially taken over a city park—sued them and won. This injunction resulted from a partnership between the community and the police department and exemplifies an innovative, creative, proactive approach to ensure public safety. The injunction restricted the following actions:

- Possessing, or remaining in the company of anyone with, dangerous weapons, including clubs, bats, knives, screwdrivers, BB guns, etc.
- Entering private property of another without prior written permission of the owner.
- Intimidating, provoking, threatening, confronting, challenging or carrying out any acts of retaliation.
- A gang member under (18) years of age cannot be in a public place after 8:00 P.M., unless going to legitimate business, meeting or entertainment activity.
- Gang members associating or congregating in groups of 3 or more in Perry Park or within 10 yards of the outside fence surrounding Perry Park.

## The Ft. Wayne, Indiana, Raspberry Barrier

While working on a comprehensive graffiti abatement initiative, a problem-solving group made up of police, businesses, the city park department and citizens pondered what to do about one particular wall which was the constant site of graffiti. The park department offered to donate some raspberry bushes if the group could get volunteers to plant them. This "raspberry barrier" effectively ended the graffiti at that location. The cost to the city was zero. This project won a 1996 National League of Cities Community Policing award.

## Model Police Programs

The National Symposium on Community Institutions and Inner-City Crime (the National Symposium) identified three police programs for inclusion in their project: the East Dallas Community-Police and Refugee Affairs Office, the Detroit Junior Police Cadet Section and the Houston Positive Interaction, Dispute Resolution and Inhalant Abuse Programs.

**East Dallas Community-Police and Refugee Affairs Office.**  As noted by Sulton (1990, p. 69) the primary goal of this office is "to reduce crime by decreasing refugees' fear of police, easing their transition into American society, and increasing area residents' willingness to cooperate with police." The program addresses the needs of Asian refugees who often do not speak English, have limited job skills, do not understand the American culture and may fear authority, including the police. Translation services is one of the office's primary focuses.

The office operates a storefront staffed by two officers, six community service officers and seventy-five volunteers. Although initially opened to serve Asian immigrants, it has expanded its services to include all residents of East Dallas, including African Americans, Hispanics and whites. The storefront provides not only food and clothing, but also fans, air conditioners and other needed items. In addition, staff helps individuals find housing, jobs and educational opportunities, and makes referrals to appropriate social service agencies in the community.

◆

The East Dallas Community-Police and Refugee Affairs Office operates a storefront that provides basic necessities to needy residents as well as assistance in finding housing, education and jobs and referral to other agencies.

◆

Sulton (1990, p. 72) notes: "This program does not require police to abandon their traditional order maintenance and crime control functions, but enhances their ability to detect crime and make arrests through mutual cooperation." According to the founder of the office, Corporal Ron Coward (pp. 72–73):

The program must target the community in greatest need of services and work hand-in-hand with other community institutions that address the oppression of inadequate housing, unemployment, illiteracy, lack of recreational opportunities for youth, and other social problems. Every squad car does not have to be a rolling social service agency. . . . but some of the officers should be especially sensitive to varying needs of a multi-cultural population. You need experienced officers willing to aggressively work to improve the community and advocate on its behalf. The community must know that the police care. The storefront must be more than a tourist booth which simply directs needy residents to some other agency. And it cannot be centralized; each storefront must be tailored to the neighborhood in which it is located.

The exemplary nature of this program was noted by a site-team member (p. 72): "This program is built upon an enduring spirit of cooperation and caring that transcends racial and cultural barriers and affirms the belief that in a democracy police are more than guardians of law and order."

**Detroit Police Department's Junior Police Cadet Section.** The program serves not only youth, but also the elderly in the community. Approximately 4,000 high school students and 100 college students participate in the program each year.

◆

Two services are provided by the Detroit Junior Police Cadets: school and community patrol and senior citizen escort.

◆

In addition, the program seeks to prepare young people who want to pursue a career in law enforcement. It also operates several other projects, including one that stresses academic excellence.

**Houston Police Department's Positive Interaction, Dispute Resolution and Inhalant Abuse Programs.** The Houston Police Department has developed

*A mobile police station. Such facilities are often used effectively in neighborhoods with high crime rates.*

three programs designed to improve police-community relations and to reduce crime and the fear of crime.

◆

A Positive Interaction Program, Dispute Resolution Program and Inhalant Abuse Program have proven to be successful in Houston.

◆

The *Positive Interaction Program* identifies community leaders who might join with the police to reduce crime and fear of crime and who might assist to mobilize communities in their crime prevention efforts. Basically, according to Sulton (p. 79), this program "organizes the organizers."

The *Dispute Resolution Program Implementation* is part of the Ingrando House Project which serves many African Americans. Its purpose is to reduce or prevent violence between family members, friends, neighbors and students by providing police officers trained in mediation and conflict resolution techniques.

The third program, the *Inhalant Abuse Program,* uses education and counseling to counter such harmful activities as glue sniffing. Program staff members educate other officers, school officials, social workers and parents about the extent of the problem, how to detect it and how to prevent it. Although officers are trained counselors, when they encounter youths who are inhalant abusers, they generally refer them to an appropriate treatment agency.

## Recommendations of the National Symposium for Police

The National Symposium recommends that police departments should (Sulton, pp. 107–08, used with permission):

1. Make crime prevention a priority.
2. Work with other community institutions to improve the quality of life of inner-city residents.
3. Adopt a style of policing that (a) presents opportunities for police to reinforce the concept of neighborhood and become part of it by sharing residents' problems; and (b) makes it possible for residents to work with police on order maintenance as well as crime problems.
4. Reduce the social distance between police and inner-city residents by organizing the department according to the needs of the community. Police departments should ascertain these needs through monthly meetings with police chief/community advisory committees and by recruiting and hiring minority group members sensitive to problems in the community.
5. Encourage use of civil remedies.
6. Enhance patrol officer crime prevention roles and provide the flexibility needed to develop innovative responses to inner-city problems.
7. Expand police training programs to include training in mediation techniques.

## INNOVATIVE COURT PROGRAMS

The way courts address the accused has a direct impact on the crime problem and on community policing efforts. The National Symposium identified two model court programs: Albany, New York's Community Dispute Resolution Centers and Madison, Wisconsin's Deferred Prosecution/First Offenders Unit.

◆

Model court programs include community dispute resolution centers and a deferred prosecution/first offenders unit.

◆

**Community Dispute Resolution Centers.** The thirty-two dispute resolution centers are independent, community-based, nonprofit organizations contracted by the Unified Court System of the State of New York, Albany, to do the following (Sulton, p. 83):

1. Provide dispute resolution resources for local communities.
2. Prevent the escalation of disputes into more serious civil or criminal matters.
3. Relieve the courts of matters not requiring the formalities of judicial intervention.
4. Teach individuals how to resolve their problems through mediation.

Police officers, probation officers, judges, district attorneys and legal aid offices can refer cases to a local dispute resolution center, or individuals may be self-referred. The mediation, conciliation or arbitration services provided by the center are free. The Chief Judge of the State of New York, L. H. Cook, stated the usefulness of this approach (Sulton, p. 87):

> The paths of dispute resolution are never set in concrete; they are for each age to establish for itself. But society, by its very nature and to avoid self destruction, requires adequate avenues to justice. In our time, mediation is one of them. . . . Mediation must in this decade be accorded its rightful place in society.

Dispute resolution is also used by the New York state government. Mediation rather than law enforcement or court intervention makes sense. The bottom line is saving tax dollars.

**The Deferred Prosecution/First Offenders Unit.**   This program, operated by the Dane County District Attorney's Office, Madison, Wisconsin, has as its purpose (Sulton, p. 88): "To prevent offenders' further involvements in crime by deferring prosecution upon the condition that they satisfactorily complete appropriate treatment and rehabilitation programs." The program recognizes the hazards of labeling individuals and the potential of treatment for first offenders who accept responsibility for their actions.

An offender's suitability for the program is based on several criteria including (Sulton, p. 90): the nature of the current offense, prior criminal record, admission of guilt, offender attitude, whether the offender is dangerous to self or community, likelihood of the offender repeating the crime, whether the offender will benefit from the treatment process, an agreement to participate in the treatment program prescribed, willingness to abide by the conditions of the diversion contract and payment of a $10 monthly fee for each month of program participation.

The program uses a large network of social service agencies and public and private organizations. Because a "substantial portion" of program participants are shoplifters, the staff conducts a one-day Saturday workshop on retail theft. Another integral part of the program is voluntary community service, not as a means of punishment, but as a way to repay the community for the crime committed and to change the offender's behavior patterns. Among the benefits of this program, according to Sulton (p. 91), are:

> [C]onservation of police, prosecutorial, judicial, and correctional resources. . . . Only a small number of program participants have failed to complete their diversion contracts. As a result, police officers are not required to spend countless hours waiting to testify, prosecutors can devote their time to preparation of more serious and complex cases, court dockets are relieved, and scarce jail space is reserved for the most dangerous offenders.

> Program staff also noted several other benefits. For example, sanctions for criminal conduct are administered closer to the time when the offenses

occurred. In addition, offenders' lives are minimally disrupted because they can continue to pursue their occupations and fulfill family obligations.

## Recommendations of the National Symposium for the Courts

Recommendations of the National Symposium for the courts include the following (Sulton, p. 108, used by permission):

1.  Court officials should educate the public about the operations and limitations of juvenile and criminal justice agencies and invite citizens to visit courts and meet with judges.

2.  When appropriate, prosecutors and judges should encourage criminal litigants to settle grievances outside court through mediation and other dispute resolution processes.

3.  Judges should continue to tailor sentences to individual offenders rather than rely totally on sentencing guidelines. Sentencing guidelines may discourage judges from fashioning appropriate sentences when such sentences are warranted by the presence of highly unusual mitigating or aggravating circumstances.

4.  Judges should use alternatives to incarceration, particularly when the offender is nonviolent. Community service, restitution, drug treatment and house arrest can be effective sentences. When it is unlikely that the offender will victimize additional community members or that public order or safety will be compromised, the least restrictive alternative should be selected.

5.  Prosecutors, defense attorneys and judges should encourage legislators to reevaluate statutory definitions of crimes. Legislative definitions of crimes frequently do not reflect the nature of the offense or extent of injuries to victims.

6.  Judges' performance should be evaluated on the quality of decisions rendered rather than on the quantity of cases disposed. Judges frequently are criticized because of the backlog of cases on their dockets. However, many of the cases handled by judges present complex legal issues requiring a great deal of time and effort to resolve. When judges' decisions are affirmed on appeal, credit should be given for the quality of work performed.

7.  Judges should work with community-based organizations and participate in activities to improve the quality of life of inner-city residents. For example, they can work to support community-based organizations by serving as members of the boards of directors, participating in public service events sponsored by the organizations or providing advice on how the organization can work more effectively with criminal justice agencies.

## INNOVATIVE CORRECTIONS PROGRAMS

How corrections deals with those who are sentenced to jail or prison terms also affects the crime problem as well as community policing efforts. Evans (1996, p. 124) provides the following definition: "Community corrections is that part of the justice system providing sanctions and services to enhance public safety and maintain offenders/defendants within the community."

Community-based corrections is gaining popularity in the 1990s, but is still resisted by many neighborhoods. Sometimes referred to as *intermediate sanctions*, community corrections may take many forms including halfway houses, prerelease centers, transition centers, work furlough and community work centers, community treatment centers, restitution centers and a host of other innovative approaches to involving the community in efforts to reintegrate offenders into the community *without* danger to the citizens.

Residents may live either part-time or full-time at such centers, depending on the other conditions set forth by the court. Evans (pp. 124–25) cites several elements of community corrections that must be taken for granted:

- Community corrections is part of the justice system, which involves both adults and juveniles and also includes a broader context containing elements of social justice.
- Community corrections agencies are involved in administering sanctions and providing services. Services are provided to victims, defendants and offenders.
- Community corrections agencies acknowledge that they exist to enhance public safety.
- Community corrections is effective and efficient when it works in partnership with local communities and other agencies interested in safer communities and justice.

Evans (p. 125) lists six important tasks that can help community corrections accomplish its goals while also enhancing public safety:

- Assessment of offenders for community placement.
- Responsibility of offenders for their behavior.
- Emphasis on reparative strategies for victims and communities.
- Provision of supervision and treatment interventions geared to reduce reoffending.
- The encouragement of citizens to join in the challenge of creating safer communities.

- Recognition of the importance of positive relationships between the community and the offender.

According to Evans (p.125), the goals of community corrections: "Are accomplished by selecting appropriate participants, holding offenders accountable, repairing the harm done to victims and the community, supervising and treating offenders/defendants, involving citizens, and maintaining positive ties between the community and the offender."

Community corrections can be viewed as a part of the broader justice system and represents a growing interest in what many are referring to as *community justice.*

The National Symposium identified one model corrections program, the Volunteers in Parole program of the State Bar of California, San Francisco, California.

◆

The model corrections program Volunteers in Parole provides a support system for young parolees and eases their transition from incarceration to productive citizenship.

◆

This program is designed to ease the caseload of parole officers, many of whom may have caseloads of up to 150 parolees. As noted by Sulton (p. 93):

Many of the individuals supervised are youthful offenders without family, friends, permanent housing, employment, or other resources. These teenagers and young adults are uneducated and illiterate, unmarried parents of small children, struggling with drug or alcohol dependency, stigmatized by lengthy criminal records, suspicious, fearful, and uncertain. They frequently commit new crimes or violate the conditions of their parole because adequate support systems are unavailable.

The program, modeled after the Big Brothers and Big Sisters programs, pairs youthful parolees, ages fifteen to twenty-three, with attorneys who volunteer their time. Attorneys are used because, as noted by Sulton (pp. 93–94), they: "1) understand the legal system; 2) are familiar with community resources and have referral skills; 3) are experienced in dealing with bureaucracies; 4) are not intimidated by the sophistication of parolees; and 5) have an office where they can conveniently meet with parolees and privately discuss their concerns." In addition, attorneys have undergone a licensing procedure that should assure they are of good moral character, and they will be able to answer the numerous questions parolees may have about the criminal justice system, governmental agencies, leases, contracts and other legal issues.

In addition to matching parolees with attorneys, the program conducts street law classes and informal lectures for the youthful parolees. Although no

*Juvenile delinquents make their beds at a detention home.*

studies have been conducted on the effectiveness of the program, given the high cost of incarceration, according to Sulton (p. 96): "Should only a small number of the matches result in a reduction of the number of youth being returned to detention facilities or prisons, the State of California probably saved millions of dollars by investing in this program."

## Recommendations of the National Symposium for Corrections

Recommendations of the National Symposium related to corrections include the following (Sulton, pp. 109–10, used by permission):

1. Correctional agencies, particularly community corrections, should provide opportunities for ex-offenders to fully participate in community life. Ex-offenders, who are a part of the crime problem, can become a part of its solution when provided encouragement and guidance by those charged with the responsibility of facilitating their reintegration into the community.

2. Because African Americans are disproportionately represented as prison inmates, corrections should recruit and hire more African Americans as corrections planners and correctional officials.

3. Alternatives to incarceration should be used whenever possible; imprisonment is very expensive, causes tremendous human suffering and is not very effective at rehabilitation.

4. Funds earmarked to build adult prisons and to support the growing "correctional-industrial complex" should be reallocated and spent on programs that prevent youth involvement in crime.

5. Correctional agencies, particularly community corrections, should provide personal direction, guidance and support services to ex-offenders. Typically, ex-offenders are supervised only via periodic telephone calls or office visits. Ex-offenders frequently need assistance in resolving personal problems that may be related to their involvement in crime. Correctional agencies may be the best source of this guidance because they have regular contact with ex-offenders and access to other social service agencies to which the ex-offender may be referred.

6. Prisons should prepare inmates for employment through training and work-release programs. The work-release placements should be appropriate to the knowledge and skill levels of the offenders, and offenders should be adequately supervised to ensure public safety and prevent further criminal victimization.

7. Parole boards should require prison inmates to complete the equivalent of a high school education as a condition of parole, particularly where they have been sentenced to lengthy prison terms and are capable of fulfilling this requirement. One must be able to read, write and count in order to participate in society. When offenders are illiterate, it is likely that they will recidivate. Therefore, the incentive of early release from prison should be used to encourage offenders to prepare themselves for participation in society.

8. Parole boards should discontinue the practice of returning parolees to prisons for technical violations of parole (e.g., changing jobs without notifying the parole officer) when no new crime has been committed.

9. Halfway houses should provide drug, family and job counseling services to ex-offenders. These houses also should work with state agencies, community-based organizations and inner-city residents to facilitate ex-offender participation in the community.

10. Juvenile justice agencies should establish diversion programs that permit nonviolent offenders to work in community service projects.

## SUMMARY

Trends in the criminal justice system include an emphasis on service rather than crime fighting; greater responsibility and discretion for line officers; reliance on cooperative efforts of law enforcement, courts and corrections to accomplish the goals of the criminal justice system; and belief in a justice model rather than a medical model when dealing with offenders. A coordinated effort among law enforcement, courts and corrections is required to effectively deal with the crime problem and to elicit the support of the community in doing so. The greatest obstacle to change in the criminal justice system may be resistance from within the police agency itself.

Benefits of improved police-community relations include greater police concern for citizens, including victims, as well as increased independence, self-esteem and sense of ownership in the police function.

Responding to calls for service is an excellent opportunity to foster good community relationships. Relatively inexpensive services include conducting monthly meetings, meeting with school administrators, conducting fingerprinting programs and blood pressure programs, participating in athletic contests, publishing newsletters and providing ride-alongs. Ride-along programs are highly successful; 96 percent of the programs report positive results. The National Symposium identified three model police programs. The first, the East Dallas Community-Police and Refugee Affairs Office, operates a storefront that provides basic necessities to needy residents as well as assistance in finding housing, education and jobs and referral to other agencies. Two services are provided by the Detroit Junior Police Cadets: school and community patrol and senior citizen escort. A Positive Interaction Program, Dispute Resolution Program and an Inhalant Abuse Program have proven to be successful in Houston.

Model court programs include a community dispute resolution center and a deferred prosecution/first offenders unit. The model corrections program Volunteers in Parole provides a support system for young parolees and eases their transition from incarceration to productive citizenship.

## Discussion Questions

1. What changes have been made in your police department in the last five years?
2. What police-community relations programs do you feel hold the most promise to accomplish the desired results?
3. What police-community relations programs does your police department participate in?
4. Does your department permit ride-alongs? If so, who can participate?
5. Do you believe the patrol officer's uniform should be changed? If so, how?
6. Do you feel the managerial grid "fits" the police situation? If so, how? If not, why not?
7. Do you feel mediation and arbitration are solutions to our crowded court dockets?
8. Do you believe first offenders should be treated differently than repeat offenders? Why or why not?

9.   What alternatives to incarceration would you support? For whom?

10.   Which recommendations would you support for the police, the courts and corrections?

## *References*

Aaron, Titus. "Police and the Uniform: We Need More Research." *Law and Order*. (April 1992): 14–15.

Bondurant, Elizabeth. "Citizen Response Questionnaire: A Valuable Evaluation Tool." *The Police Chief*. (November 1991): 74–76.

Evans, Donald G. "Defining Community Corrections." *Corrections Today*. (October 1996): 124–45.

Price, Carroll S. Letter to author, July 1992, reviewing manuscript.

Sharp, Arthur G. "Ride-Along with Me." *Law and Order*. (October 1990): 65–69.

Skogan, Wesley G. and Wycoff, Mary Ann. "Storefront Police Offices: The Houston Field Test." In *Community Crime Prevention: Does It Work?* edited by Dennis P. Rosenbaum, 179–99. Beverly Hills: Sage Publications, 1986.

Snelson, J. W. and Oettmeier, T. N. *Operational Plan for the Westside Command Station*. Houston Police Department, 1987.

Sparrow, Malcolm K. *Perspectives on Policing: Implementing Community Policing*. Washington: U.S. Department of Justice, National Institute of Justice, November 1988.

Sulton, Anne Thomas. *Inner-City Crime Control: Can Community Institutions Contribute?* Washington: The Police Foundation, 1990.

Trojanowicz, Robert C. "Evaluating a Neighborhood Foot Patrol Program: The Flint, Michigan, Project." In *Community Crime Prevention: Does It Work?* edited by Dennis P. Rosenbaum, 157–78. Beverly Hills: Sage Publications, 1986.

Wadman, Robert C. and Olson, Robert K. *Community Wellness: A New Theory of Policing*. Washington: Police Executive Research Forum, 1990.

Wycoff, Mary Ann. "The Benefits of Community Policing: Evidence and Conjecture." In *Community Policing: Rhetoric or Reality,* edited by Jack R. Greene and Stephen D. Mastrofski, 105–20. New York: Praeger Publishing, 1991.

# Chapter 16

# Programs for Youth

*If society wishes greater protection from juvenile crime, more attention has to be paid to the costly process of promoting moral order and of preventing crime.*

—Lamar Empey, criminologist (1978)

## Do you know

- What exemplary youth programs can promote positive police-community relations?
- What the focus of PAL is?
- What a police-school liaison program is? What its dual goals are?
- What the DARE program is?
- What group of professionals is of great importance in delinquency prevention programs?
- What youth program has been endorsed by the IACP?
- What the Teens on Patrol program is?
- What model programs for youth have been identified by the National Symposium on Community Institutions and Inner-City Crime Project?

## Definitions

Can you define these terms: DARE, *in loco parentis*, PAL, police-school liaison program.

*Introduction*

Many hope that the answers to crime, violence and substance abuse in our society lie in the numerous preventive programs for our youth. If we can somehow reach children before they become involved in drugs and its resulting life of despair, crime and poverty, perhaps we can prevent a significant amount of misery in our society and stem the escalating crime rate.

Given these hopes, it is especially tragic when one reads of events such as the killing of five elementary school pupils in a Stockton, California, schoolyard by a gunman. As noted by Okaty (1991, p. 39): "Crime and terror in schools is a harsh condition facing children, teachers and parents at all levels of the educational sector." Making schools safe for students to attend is another challenge for police officers.

On a less sensational level, but equally important, the National School Safety Center, Pepperdine University, California, has identified several studies that link truancy to daytime crime.* As noted by Okaty (p. 39): "Police administrators can be proactive in reducing community crime by working closely with schools and school districts to compare student absentee patterns and the neighborhoods where crimes are occurring."

Before reviewing specific programs for youth, consider how community policing and a problem-solving approach can be used to address common problems police encounter with juveniles.

This chapter begins with a discussion of a community policing approach for dealing with problems involving youth. This is followed by a description of traditional programs, school programs, programs aimed at preventing drug and alcohol abuse and programs designed to prevent child abuse. Next the chapter discusses programs focusing on building personal relationships, youth gangs in the schools, community-based youth programs and wilderness programs. The chapter concludes with descriptions of model programs for youth, including courts and corrections programs.

## A COMMUNITY POLICING APPROACH TO DEAL WITH PROBLEMS INVOLVING YOUTH

Police are often called to deal with groups of "rowdy" juveniles who are not breaking any laws but who are disturbing a neighborhood. Spelman and Eck (1992, p. 205) describe how police can use a problem-solving approach in such instances:

*Starred program descriptions on pages 502, 515, 517, 518, 519 and 520 are provided by the National School Safety Center.

The quiet nights of a middle-class Newport News neighborhood were spoiled when groups of rowdy teenagers began to frequent the area on Fridays and Saturdays. There had been no violence, and the kids' primary offenses were loud music, horseplay, and occasional vandalism. But residents felt the teenagers were unpredictable, particularly since they came from the city's mostly Black southeast side, several miles away. The neighborhood became a regular stop for officers working the evening shift.

Sergeant Jim Hogan recognized that responding to these calls took time but accomplished little except to irritate everybody involved. One Friday night he asked the beat officer, Paul Summerfield, to look into the problem and develop a better solution.

Summerfield suspected that the source of the problem might be a roller skating rink. The rink had been trying to increase business by offering reduced rates and transportation on Friday and Saturday nights. As he drove north toward the rink later that night, Summerfield saw several large groups of youths walking south. Other kids were still hanging around the rink, which had closed shortly before. Summerfield talked to several of them and found that they were waiting for a bus. The others, he was told, had become impatient and begun the three-mile walk home. Then Summerfield talked to the rink owner. The owner told him he had leased the bus to pick up and drop off kids who lived far from the rink. But he said there was always more kids needing rides at the end of the night than the bus had picked up earlier.

When Officer Summerfield returned to the skating rink early the next evening, he saw about fifty youngsters get out of the bus rented by the skating rink. But he saw others get out of the public transit buses that stopped running at midnight, and he saw parents in pajamas drop their kids off, then turn around and go home. Clearly the rink's bus would be unable to take home all the kids who would be stranded at closing time.

Summerfield consulted Sergeant Hogan. They agreed that the skating rink owner should be asked to bus the kids home. Summerfield returned to the rink Monday and spoke with the owner. When informed of the size of the problem he had unwittingly created, the owner agreed to lease more buses. By the next weekend, the buses were in use and Summerfield and Hogan saw no kids walking home.

Elapsed time from problem identification to problem solution: one week. Resources used: about four hours of an officer's time. Results: fewer calls, happier kids, satisfied homeowners.

This is a prime example of managing a problem by marshaling the necessary resources rather than simply continuing to respond to the calls about the problem—the essence of community policing. In other instances, programs have been developed in an attempt to prevent problems from occurring.

Agay (1997, p. 1) contends: "Too often the death of a young person is as a result of his or her being involved in activities that beget violence because there's a lack of more productive and satisfying activities in which he or she can participate." He asks: "Do we let children wander the streets at all hours where they will find something to do on their own, or do we develop and promote activities that are adult-supervised?"

Tortomasi (1996, p. 2A) quotes a juvenile who was recently arrested and is now on probation: "I think part of the reason I got in trouble with the police in the first place is because there is nothing to do around here."

## TRADITIONAL PROGRAMS FOR YOUTH

Police interaction with youth and several programs that focus on their needs were discussed in Chapter 10. Youth have traditionally been included in police-community relations efforts in several ways.

♦

Common programs aimed at youth are school safety programs, bicycle safety programs, the McGruff "Take a Bite out of Crime" program, the Officer Friendly program, police athletic leagues (PALs), the fingerprinting of young children and police explorer programs.

♦

In different localities, police have developed variations of many of these programs. The traditional *McGruff* as a crime prevention spokesperson program, for example, has expanded in some areas to include McGruff Houses, safe havens for young children. Another expansion is the McGruff crime dog robot developed by Robotronics. Operated by remote control, the robot winks, blinks, moves his hands and arms, tips and turns his head and has a two-way wireless voice system allowing the operator to talk and listen.

Police departments have also expanded upon the PAL program.

♦

The National Police Athletic League (**PAL**), now over fifty years old, was developed to provide opportunities for youth to interact with police officers in gyms or ballparks instead of in a juvenile detention hall.

♦

The Portland (Oregon) Police Department has adapted the PAL program to deal with escalating gang violence and street sale of drugs. As noted by Austin and Braaten (1991, p. 36), the goals of the Portland-area PAL are to:

* Reduce the incidence of juvenile crime, substance abuse and gang violence.
* Provide positive alternative activities for boys and girls.
* Guide boys and girls to make responsible decisions in life.
* Foster better understanding between youth and the police.

To accomplish their goals, the department has undertaken several activities. They have conducted a week-long Sport Quickness Day Camp for 600 at-risk

Officer Friendly *programs allow police officers to interact one-on-one with youngsters.*

youth, that keeps them productively occupied for eight hours a day in boxing, wrestling, football, soccer, martial arts, basketball, racquetball, track and field, volleyball and speed and quickness training.

The department also organizes events in which officers can participate with PAL youth, including a one-day fishing excursion, trips to Seattle Sea Hawks football games and scholarships to summer camps held throughout the state. According to Austin and Braaten (p. 38): "Through PAL, we are helping these kids build self-esteem, meet life's challenges, interact with positive role models, enhance their physical sports abilities and make friends with police officers."

*Officer Friendly* programs are designed for elementary school children and generally include a police officer who goes into classes to discuss good citizenship, responsibility and general safety. The program uses coloring books and a special activity book that teachers can use with their regular social studies curriculum. Pace (1991, p. 255–57) describes the Officer Friendly program in St. Louis, Missouri:

> This program is designed to establish constructive understanding between children in the primary grades and police officers.
>
> Public Affairs officers work with elementary school principals to establish a schedule for patrol officer visits. District commanders then assign the officer who patrols the area in which the school is located, to make two visits to each

kindergarten through third grade classroom in the school. An officer's job and equipment is described as well as safety. He utilizes picture reading books and electric street signals in his talks. Each teacher receives a manual for ongoing programs.

Following the second visit, the officer provides Junior Citizenship certificates for the children.

The officers then conduct "rap" sessions with older children in the school to explain the police function and answer questions in order to establish rapport with them.

The traditional police explorers program, an advanced unit of the Boy Scouts of America, also serves many communities. In Mesa, Arizona, for example, thirty-five explorers have been trained in various aspects of police work such as finger-printing, identification techniques, first aid and firearms safety. The minimum age for the program is fifteen, and the youths must have superior motivation and skill. As noted by Lesce (1991, p. 98): "The program demands a serious mind-set and dedication to public service, not self-serving ego satisfaction."

Explorers have a three to six-month probation; full membership is contingent on completing training and meeting proficiency standards as well as acceptable personal conduct. Lesce (p. 100) suggests that: "Explorer programs serve two purposes: favorable community relations and early recruitment for law enforcement agencies." Some departments, in fact, make even greater use of their explorer program. The Chandler (Arizona) Police Department, for example, used two eighteen-year-old Explorers in a sting operation involving a bar and liquor store's employees who sold alcohol to minors.

Many of the programs for juveniles involve the schools. Historically, the schools have been charged with instilling discipline in the students who attend.

## YOUTH AND THE SCHOOLS

The principle of *in loco parentis,* meaning "in place of parents," gives schools the authority to act as a parent might in situations requiring discipline or need. As noted by Pace (1991, p. 255): "Teachers, next to parents, are society's most important transmitters of values, mores, and cultures." He stresses:

> For many years, teachers, in internalizing their values, have been the most hostile group toward the police. Through their value system, they have consistently rated police officers low on acceptance scales. This is, in part, because police departments and school administrators have not maintained a proper liaison.

Educators and law enforcement groups often have difficulty distinguishing between what is a crime and what is a disciplinary problem. One program that strives to improve police-school relations, the National School Safety Center, brings teams from throughout the country together for a week of instruction and

*An officer explains bike safety to elementary school children.*

interaction. Each team has four people from the same community: the chief of police or sheriff, the school superintendent, the district attorney and the chief juvenile officer of the court. The teams spend the week working with each other on common problems.

**IPMP.** Toledo, Ohio, has established the Innovative Police Mentoring Program (IPMP). According to Boss (1996, p. 8), the program's purpose is: "To provide families in high-crime areas with role models, adolescent behavioral managers, community leaders, law enforcement informers, alternative behavior instructors, dysfunctional family assistants and parent educators." Boss says: "This partnership has dramatically improved the learning climate in the schools and has bridged and strengthened the teacher-parent-police-community relationship for the purpose of supporting and assisting in the lives of adolescent Toledo citizens" (contact: Dr. Marion Boss, University of Toledo, College of Education and Allied Professions, Toledo, OH 43606-3390; (419) 530-2185).

**Chicago Intervention Network.** The Chicago Intervention Network works with students of all ages and provides the schools with the following programs and services: (1) early intervention and prevention curriculum, including activities in anger management, impulse control and empathy training; (2) twenty-week delinquency prevention sessions in eighty schools; (3) attitude development sessions covering self-esteem, resisting peer pressure and understanding and managing conflict; (4) Safe School Zone Law presentations; (5) School Watch programs and Truancy follow-up; (6) assessments on gang problems in and around schools; (7) mediation and prevention of gang violence; (8) technical assistance and information for teachers and parents on how to identify gang activity through symbols, colors and signs; (9) help in securing Safe School Zone signs for schools; and (10) individual and group counseling for challenged youth (Department of Human Services, Youth Delinquency Prevention Division, 510 N. Peshtigo Court, Section 5B, Chicago, IL 60611-4375; (312) 744-0881 or (312) 744-1820).

**Safe City—Safe Campus.** The Monrovia, California, Safe City—Safe Campus Program is coordinated by a task force made up of representatives of all city departments, including city administration, police, fire, community service, community development and probation. The program includes a truancy ordinance as well as a school uniform policy. As Santoro says (1997, p. 3): "Monrovia's officers believe that truancy is habit forming and contributes to gang involvement, experimentation with drugs, crime and an increased student dropout rate." The program also has a student art program where student art is displayed at the police department (contact: Chief Joseph A. Santoro, Monrovia Police Department, 140 E. Lime Ave., Monrovia, CA 91016; (818) 359-1152).

## POLICE-SCHOOL LIAISON PROGRAMS

In 1958 Flint, Michigan, developed a highly publicized delinquency prevention program involving joint efforts of school authorities, parents, social agencies, the juvenile court, businesses and the police department. It became known as a school-liaison program and was widely replicated across the country.

◆

A **police-school liaison program** places an officer into a school to work with school authorities, parents and students, to prevent crime and antisocial behavior and to improve police-youth relationships.

◆

Goals of most police-school liaison programs include the following:

- To reduce crime incidents involving school-age youth.
- To suppress by enforcement of the law any illegal threats that endanger the child's educational environment.
- To improve the attitudes of school-age youths and the police toward one another.

According to Drowns and Hess (1995, p. 322): "The techniques used by school liaison officers involve counseling children and their parents, referring them to social agencies to treat the root problems, referring them to drug and alcohol abuse agencies and being in daily contact in the school to check the progress of behavior. Often school liaison officers deal with pre-delinquent and early delinquent youths with whom law enforcement would not have been involved under traditional programs."

Police-school liaison officers do not get involved in school politics or in enforcing school regulations. The school administrators are involved in these matters.

◆

The joint goals of most police-school liaison programs are to prevent juvenile delinquency and to improve police-youth relations.

◆

The police-school liaison programs can also do much to promote better relations among the police, school administrators and teachers. A number of organizations can focus attention on school-police relations and provide supportive programs both on the community and national levels, for example, the International Association of Chiefs of Police, the National Association of Secondary School Principals and the National Association of School Boards.

Drug use is often a target of police educational programs. Often officers help develop and promote programs aimed at preventing drug and alcohol abuse.

## PROGRAMS AIMED AT PREVENTING DRUG AND ALCOHOL ABUSE

Many police departments and schools work together to promote drug and alcohol abuse awareness. In Orange County, Florida, for example, the Sheriff's office broadcasts antidrug and antialcohol television programs directly into local elementary schools. According to Sarubbi (1991, pp. 41–42): "The video teaches children to deal with peer pressure and say 'No' by using the word STARS":

S—See the problem.

T—Think about your choices.

A—Ask for help.

R—Recognize the best choice.

S—Makes you a STAR if you stick to your good choice.

### The DARE Program

The Drug Abuse Resistance Education (DARE) program was developed jointly by the Los Angeles Police Department and the Los Angeles Unified School District.

◆

> The Drug Abuse Resistance Education (**DARE**) program is aimed at elementary age school children and seeks to teach them to "say no to drugs," to resist peer pressure and to find alternatives to drug use.

◆

The program uses a "self-esteem repair" approach consisting of seventeen classroom sessions taught by experienced police officers.

The City of Ridgecrest, California, initiated a DARE program and wanted a public relations program to help promote it. Ridgecrest used cards similar to baseball cards, each featuring numerous officers in different settings (see Figure 16.1). According to Narramore (1990, p. 23):

> The program is highly visible. We have put the DARE logo on everything possible. All of the students wear DARE T-shirts, their pencils say DARE, we even have DARE wrist bands. However, the newest and biggest success we have had in promoting the program are the new DARE cards.

**Ridgecrest Police**

Photo by Yvette Lovett

OFFICER HULL AND ASCO

*D.A.R.E.* TO KEEP KIDS OFF DRUGS.

**K-9 PROGRAM**

Asco was Ridgecrest P.D.'s first Police Dog. Asco has been in service for three years. Asco was purchased by the citizens of Ridgecrest. Asco is a full-blooded German Shepherd. He was raised and trained in Germany.

**SAFETY TIP        9**

SMART KIDS D.A.R.E. TO SAY "NO!" Drugs can hurt you. Besides, it's against the law to use drugs. Don't let anyone talk you into drugs. You're a smart kid . . . keep it that way.

This card comes to you as a gift from your friends at the Ridgecrest Police Department and the City Council.

Produced by: McDag Productions, Inc. P.O. Box 80826, Baton Rouge, LA 70898

*Figure 16.1*    **Ridgecrest Police DARE Card**
Courtesy of the Ridgecrest Police Department.

We even included photographs of the two police dogs and their handlers. Each card is numbered and has a safety tip on the reverse side of the card along with a job description of the person on the card, such as a definition of what a rangemaster does.

DARE is not without its critics, however. It has met with a great deal of opposition in some communities, and some of the research done on DARE is questionable.

## PEP Kids

PEP Kids is a program for parents, educators, police and kids, who work together to face the challenge of substance abuse among youth. The program was jointly conceived by the Tucson police chief and the superintendent of Amphitheater schools. The program focuses on preparing youth to not be influenced by a peer who tries to pressure them into trying drugs. As noted by Paterson and Schmoker (1992, p. 282): "Students hear first-hand about health, on the one hand, and the horrors of arrest, the destructive effects of drugs on the mind and body on the other. These anecdotes, some fairly grisly, underscore the reality that decisions have consequences, some unintended."

They stress (p. 283): "PEP Kids takes students beyond the cliches and into the real world they inhabit, where one day, alone or with friends, someone will offer them something they shouldn't accept. PEP Kids prepares them for that moment."

## Legislation Establishing Drug-Free Safe Zones Around Schools

Many states have passed legislation increasing the penalties for selling drugs around schools. They have also posted the areas and increased patrols during school hours.

## The Flying Fuzz

Patrol Officer Dennis Guth, also known as "The Flying Fuzz," has seventy national drag racing records and won the 1989 Drag Bike USA national championship. He is a fifteen year veteran of the Whitehall Township (Pennsylvania) Police Department and uses his drag bike and his racing records to reach out to youth. As noted by Krum (1990, p. 59): "During school demonstrations, Guth gets a message across to hundreds of youngsters every year. He speaks against the abuse of drugs and alcohol while lauding the positive aspects of athletics."

## COP'RZ

Bork (1991, p. 29) notes: "The term 'beat cop' has been redefined by five Dayton, Ohio, police officers." These cops entertain students, grades kindergarten through nine, with rock and roll music, promoting the message: "Say No to Drugs!" Since forming in the spring of 1990 the officers have made more than fifty performances, entertaining approximately 50,000 children and challenging them to be drug free. According to Bork (p. 30), they hit the stage "in uniform— to the accompaniment of a shrieking siren, blazing blue lights, and pounding drums. . . . Encouraging audience participation, COP'RZ launches into 'We Will, We Will Rock You,' their version being, 'We Will, We Will Say NO!'" They include in every program the National DARE theme song "Stand By Me," inviting the teachers to join them on stage.

◆

Teachers are among the most important professionals involved in making delinquency prevention programs work.

◆

As noted in Chapter 10, teachers greatly influence the youth with whom they work. Unfortunately, teachers often have negative attitudes about the police. Any efforts to improve relationships between teachers and officers should be applauded.

## Confiscated Vehicles

Many police departments have confiscated unusual and expensive automobiles used by drug dealers and have integrated them into their anti-drug campaigns. The Miami Police Department, for example, confiscated a $70,000 luxury Porsche 911 Carrera and redesigned it as a mock patrol car. Officers painted on the side of the car in capital letters: THIS CAR CONFISCATED BY THE MPD STREET NARCOTICS UNIT.

In their program, "Operation Hot Wheels," the Miami Police Department also has two, 33-foot long Gulfstream motor homes which have been redesigned as classrooms on wheels ("Vehicles Bought with Confiscated Monies. . . ," 1991, p. 35). Officers take the units to schools, parks and other community functions to relay the message that crime and doing drugs do not pay.

Ocean City, Maryland, has instituted an innovative program called Reducing the Availability of Alcohol to Minors (RAAM). As Massesy (1997, p. 8) explains: "The department identified key community stakeholders and asked their help and also that of the city's hotel, motel and rental property managers to help stop underage drinking. . . . The police created a special community policing zone comprising both the boardwalk and 25 other city blocks known for their number of disturbance-related calls for service." During the summer of 1996, police officers wrote more than 2,800 civil citations for underage drinking within the zone (contact: Chief David C. Massesy, Ocean City Police Department, 6501 Coastal Highway, P.O. Box 759, Ocean City, MD 21842-0759; (410) 723-6601).

### Teenage Drinking Task Force

The sheriff in Jim Wells County in South Texas and the chief of police of Orange Grove, a community in the northeast corner of the county, joined forces to tackle the problem of underage drinking. Alone, neither had the personnel to conduct an effective sweep, but together, their first sweep resulted in nearly fifty citations to minors in possession of alcohol and a dozen driving while intoxicated citations.

The efforts of these departments began the South Texas ad hoc teenage drinking task force. The task force has since expanded to include agencies from Live Oak, Kleberg, Nueces, Duval and Brooks counties as well as municipal forces from seven cities and towns. As noted by Reynolds (1991, p. 49): "The premise is simple—if you need help, call. Officers from whatever agencies have manpower to spare will be there to reinforce your officers. . . . Task force policy is either to cite and release juveniles and minors found in possession of alcohol, or to transport them to a central point, from which their parents are called to pick them up." Reynolds (p. 50) suggests that "a valuable byproduct of the task force is the high visibility given to police during a sweep. This has resulted in significant decreases in crimes against property and family violence calls on nights the force is operating."

## PROGRAMS TO PREVENT CHILD ABUSE

The "good touch, bad touch" child abuse prevention program has been highly successful in some areas. In such programs an officer comes into elementary classrooms to teach children where it is and is not all right to be touched. Some officers tell children that no one should touch them where their bathing suit would be.

### The "Soft Room"

Slahor (1992, p. 281) describes how the Palm Springs (California) Police Department set aside one room "just for kids" who for one reason or another were temporarily detained at the police station:

> A tall chest of drawers in one corner contains donations of toys, small games, books, diapers, baby supplies, fruit juices, clothing, and other "necessaries" for infants, toddlers, and children. A small-sized table and chairs decorate the room, and a television is ready with donated videotapes of cartoons and children's stories to help a youngster wile away the time. Stuffed toys are stored on a hammock-like shelf up in one corner. A quilt and playpen are also available.
>
> The room is painted in bright, primary colors and decorated with large decals of Walt Disney characters. . . . It is anticipated that about 100 children a year will use the new "just for kids" room.

### Officer Ollie

This program, instituted by the Geneva (Illinois) Police Department, teaches very young children about preventing child abduction, teaches skateboard and bicycle safety and provides latchkey and sexual abuse education. The Officer Ollie program is linked to the town's festivals and parades, with the Chamber of Commerce providing publicity. The director of the chamber notes (Hardy, 1990, pp. 19–20): "The Officer Ollie program lets the community know that the police department is aware, concerned, and involved in the community—not only as traditional officers, but also as a friend, willing to entertain and educate their children."

As noted by one officer (p. 21): "We're planting seeds with these children that the police are their friends, that we are there as helpers and not just ticket writers and arresters. If there's something going on they can come to us."

## PROGRAMS FOCUSING ON BUILDING PERSONAL RELATIONSHIPS

Departments across the country have developed programs to allow students and police officers to get to know and understand each other better. The Denver Police Department, for example, has a program called "Brown Baggin' with the Blues," in which children have lunch with police officers.

◆

The International Association of Chiefs of Police (IACP) has endorsed the Kops'n Kids program, a program bringing together children and officers to have fun.

◆

As noted by Brown (1991, p. 6): "The program brings officers and children together—not to deliver anti-drug or anti-crime speeches, but to have fun." Officers come with their motorcycles and their K-9s for demonstrations; they have lunch; they form running clubs; they do whatever helps to present police as positive role models and to present law enforcement as a career option.

The Greeley (Colorado) Police Department has a similar program, "Adopt-an-Officer," in which police officers volunteer to be "adopted" by fourth and fifth grade students. They share meals, write letters, exchange cards, visit the police station and, like the Kops'n Kids program, just have fun.

The Las Vegas Metropolitan Police has a unique program, "Shop with a Cop," which was designed to make the Christmas season happy for abused, neglected and disadvantaged children. As noted in the program description: "They wore badges, not beards. They drove squad cars, not sleighs. And none of them had bellies that shook when they laughed like bowls full of jelly. But to dozens of underprivileged Las Vegas youngsters, these officers were Santa Claus."

One hundred thirty police officers each took one underprivileged child on a shopping spree at the local Kmart. Each child had $75 to spend, the money contributed by local businesses.

The Joplin Police Department has also developed an innovative approach to reduce conflicts between youth and police. It resulted from a local program pairing each school in the district with a local business. One school, however, the Alternative School serving approximately ninety students who had difficulty adjusting to traditional schools, had no partner. During the initial year of the partnership program, the principal of the Alternative School and the new Joplin chief of police developed a good working relationship through their mutual involvement in various civic programs. They concluded that the police department would be a natural business partner for the Alternative School. According to Wrightman and Coburn (1991, p. 38:)

> The primary objective of this partnership was to provide the students with first-hand knowledge of a police officer's job through a positive encounter. Another goal was to let students see the officer as a caring individual whose job is service to others instead of the ultimate authority figure. It was felt this could only be accomplished by allowing individual relationships to be developed between students and officers. Individual ride-alongs helped break down the barriers of suspicion which existed both for the student and the officer. . . .
>
> In the three years this partnership program has been in existence, a formerly cautious, suspicious and doubting group of students and police officers have found acceptance with each other. . . . Attitudes have been changed and friendships developed. A greater understanding of the various lifestyles of the students and officers has been more closely examined, thereby contributing to a greater understanding of each partner's role in our community.

Stahr (1997, p. 7) describes how Bethlehem, Pennsylvania, has found new ways for juvenile offenders to make restitution: "Conferencing brings victims, offenders and their respective families and friends together for a face-to-face meeting. The program hold offenders accountable for their actions, addresses the victim's needs, and enables all conference participants to work out an agreement in which the offenders repair the harm caused by their unacceptable behavior" (contact: Lieutenant John Stahr, Bethlehem Police Department, 10 E. Church St., Bethlehem, PA 18015. (610) 854-7161).

The U.S. Department of Justice Community Relations Service specializes in conciliating and mediating race-related conflicts in any context—for example, on school campuses, between police and minority communities and in housing developments.* The Community Relations Service has been called in to ease tense transitions in school desegregations in Boston and New York and other related incidents. There are Community Relations Service regional offices in Boston, New York, Philadelphia, Atlanta, Chicago, Kansas City (Missouri), Denver, Dallas, Seattle and San Francisco. There are also field offices in Detroit,

Houston and Miami. Telephone numbers of branch offices should be listed under the U.S. Department of Justice, Community Relations Service in local telephone directories.

The Community Relations Service has a hot line that can be used to report incidents of racial harassment and hate violence and to request conflict resolution assistance. The hot line number is 1–800–347–HATE. The address and phone number of the main office is: 5550 Friendship Blvd., Suite 330, Chevy Chase, MD 20815; (301) 492-5929.

## YOUTH GANGS

Several prevention and intervention strategies can reduce problems with gangs and gang members.

*Behavior codes* should be established and firmly and consistently enforced. These codes may include dress codes and bans on showing gang colors or using hand signals. On the positive side, schools should promote and reward friendliness and cooperation.

*Graffiti removal* should occur in schools immediately. Graffiti is not only unattractive, it enables gang members to advertise their turf and authority. In some instances photographs of the graffiti may aid certain police investigations. School officials should give remaining paint cans and paint brushes that might be used as evidence to the police. As an alternative to graffiti, students might be encouraged to design and paint murals in locations where graffiti is most likely to occur.

*Conflict prevention strategies* are also important to address the problem of gangs in school. Teachers should be trained to recognize and deal with gang members in nonconfrontational ways. Staff should identify all known gang members. Staff must try to build self-esteem and promote academic success for all students, including gang members.

*Crisis management* is another important part of dealing with gangs. The police department and school officials should have a plan in place for dealing with crises that might arise. Included in the plan should be means for communicating with the authorities, parents and the public. The National School Safety Center (1988) recommends the following actions in a school crisis:

- Have a media policy worked out in advance. Spell out who will be the media spokesperson, and make it clear no one else should speak *officially* for the school or agency.
- Route all media inquiries to one person or, at least, to one office.
- Prepare an official statement responding to the particular crisis situation. Read from or distribute this statement when media inquiries are made. This will maintain consistency.

- Anticipate media questions and prepare and rehearse answers.

- Don't be afraid to say, "I don't know." This is better than lying or responding with the offensive phrase, "No comment." Volunteer to get the answer and follow up within a specified time.

- Start a rumor control center, if the situation warrants. Publish a number for media representatives to call if they hear a rumor or need information.

- Provide the news media with updates as events unfold, even after the initial crisis is handled.

- Keep calm and maintain a professional manner. Once calm has returned, it is imperative to begin work that will prevent a recurrence of the crisis.

*Community involvement* is also needed to effectively reduce and prevent gang activity. Parents and the general public should be made aware of gangs operating in the community, as well as of popular heavy metal and punk bands. They should be encouraged to apply pressure to television and radio stations and to book stores and video stores to ban material that promotes use of alcohol, drugs, promiscuity or devil worship. This approach may be considered a type of censorship.

### Gang Awareness Resource Program (GARP)*

The California State Office of Criminal Justice Planning provided grant funds for the Gang Awareness Resource Program (GARP). The Program is now in its fourth year. It places an Operation Safe Streets gang investigator deputy on the Carson High School campus in a highly visible "resident" capacity. The investigator serves the high school, as well as feeder junior high and elementary schools, through the following services: training and instruction of faculty, administrators, school police, parks and recreation personnel, community groups, parents and civic officials on gang awareness, and coordination of information between schools and between law enforcement and schools. The investigator also establishes a partnership with the business sector for their support in the effort to eliminate street gang violence.

The bridge that GARP has built between law enforcement and the schools (both faculty and students) has led to enhanced communications, reduced gang-versus-gang incidents and resulted in diminished gang activity on or about the high school campus. The GARP staff has developed and published a gang awareness pamphlet for community distribution and a pocket gang directory for school administrators and police.

The GARP deputy is in daily contact with many gang members and, as a result, has arrested many for crimes committed not only on the campuses, but also in the community. He has identified hundreds of new gang members who have not, as yet, entered the criminal justice system. He has assisted in the solution of many other crimes based upon his day-to-day contacts with students throughout the Carson city schools. The GARP deputy has made hundreds of gang awareness presentations before school staff, student assemblies and community groups. As a consequence, both school campuses and the community benefit from reduced gang violence.

## Gang Crime Section

The first formal gang unit in the Chicago Police Department was formed in 1967. Known by various names over the years, the unit was centralized in 1993 and is now known as the Gang Investigation Section. The unit's mission however, remains as it has always been, the suppression of criminal street gangs.

The Gang Investigation Section is composed of Gang Crime Specialists who are responsible for conducting long and short term investigations into the hierarchy of criminal street gangs. They monitor street gangs and gather intelligence that will be used in criminal cases. The successful presentation and prosecution of these cases in criminal court will result in the dismantling of street gangs which is the mission of this Section (Chicago Police Department, 943 W. Maxwell Street, Chicago, IL 60608; (312) 746-5884).

## B.U.I.L.D. (Broader Urban Involvement and Leadership Development)*

Non-profit B.U.I.L.D. works with gang members on the streets, trying to involve them in athletic or social recreational events and to encourage them to participate in education and job training programs. Many of the streetworkers are "graduates" of street gangs who the organization assisted.

B.U.I.L.D. also runs a prevention program for junior high and high school students at-risk for joining gangs. The program includes a weekly class session and after-school activities to teach kids about the dangers of joining gangs and offers positive alternative activities. The project is supported by Chicago's social, civic and corporate sectors (1223 N. Milwaukee Ave., Chicago, IL 60622; (773) 227-2880).

## Youth Development, Inc., Gang Intervention Program*

Youth Development, Inc. (YDI) is a social services organization offering more than thirty different programs to assist children, youth and families. The different components offer education, residential counseling, corrections, prevention, recreation and employment assistance to at-risk youth and their families.

The YDI Gang Intervention Program works on three levels: prevention, diversion and intervention. Puppetry, theater presentations and educational programs focus on preventing gang violence and activities. Diversion involves directing at-risk youth into positive activities and behaviors, while the intervention component works with gang members and court-ordered youth to stop self-destructive behavior.

A major project is a regular ten-week workshop for court-ordered gang members. Youths participate in community activities such as feeding the homeless, team-building events such as a ropes course and educational programs including visiting a medium-security prison. Each youth also has a counselor who works intensively with him or her on a one-to-one basis during the ten-week program.

The Gang Intervention Program is successful because it focuses on working with the youths as individuals, rather than as gang members. Also the YDI program is not against gangs per se, but against gang violence and illegal activities (6301 Central Ave. N.W., Albuquerque, NM 87105; (505) 831-6038).

### The Paramount Plan: Alternatives to Gang Membership*

The highly regarded Paramount Plan stresses disapproval of gang membership while working to eliminate the future gang membership base and to diminish the influence of gangs. The program sponsors neighborhood meetings and provides anti-gang curricula and posters on request. Community meetings are led by bilingual leaders and are held in neighborhoods identified by the sheriff's office as "under gang influence." The community meetings are aimed at parents and preteens.

A fifth-grade anti-gang curriculum emphasizes constructive activities available in the neighborhood (Human Services Department, City of Paramount, 16400 Colorado Ave., Paramount, CA 90723; (213) 531-3503).

## COMMUNITY-BASED YOUTH PROGRAMS

When youth have activities to occupy their time, they are much less apt to get into trouble. Participation in clubs, theater, sports and jobs can all be important. In Rochester, New York, each summer about 100 youths are hired to keep order in the city's parks.

◆

Rochester, New York's Teens On Patrol program hires youth to patrol the city's parks and recreational areas in the summer.

◆

Many youths employed to patrol parks in the summer pursue careers in the criminal justice field.

### Center for Urban Expression (C.U.E.)*

The Center for Urban Expression steers youth into structured, goal-oriented activities with a special focus on community organizing. The Common Ground prevention club, sponsored by the Center, brings youths of diverse ethnic backgrounds together to work on a variety of projects and performances.

Community service teams may shovel snow or clean garages for community residents; others may become involved in youth leadership programs. Common Ground groups have given song/rap performances in six states and have become very visible locally through their anti-drug audio and video public service media announcements (The Dorchester Youth Collaborative, 1514A Dorchester Ave., Dorchester, MA 02122; (617) 228-1748).

### Andrew Glover Youth Program*

A privately funded organization, the Andrew Glover Youth Program works to protect neighborhoods in New York's Lower East Side from crime. Another objective of the Program is to steer youth away from negative and illegal activities. The Program serves a large number of black and Hispanic young people by working with police, courts, youth services and social services to provide counseling, gang mediation, family counseling and housing assistance.

Youth workers are in contact with kids where they spend most of their time: on the streets. The youth workers also live in the community and are available for assistance twenty-four hours a day. The program was named after a local police officer who cared about and tried to help youth and who was shot to death in the line of duty by teenagers (100 Center St., Manhattan Criminal Court, Room 1541, New York, NY 10013; (212) 349-6381).

### Benton Harbor Learning Opportunities for Teens (LOFT)

Agay (1997, p. 1) describes the Benton Harbor Learning Opportunities for Teens (LOFT), which offers youth recreational and educational activities. In addition to a basketball league, youths can do their homework and practice computer skills (contact: Detective Lieutenant Milton A. Agay, Commander, Criminal Investigation Division, Benton Harbor Police Department, 200 E. Wall St., P.O. Box 648, Benton Harbor, MI 49022; (616) 927-8436).

### House of Umoja (Unity)*

Known as the first urban "Boys' Town," the house has taken in more than 2,500 youths since it began in 1968. At the time of the House of Umoja's inception, the deadliest phenomenon facing the youth of Philadelphia was gang warfare. The concern of Falaka and David Fattah over their own son's involvement led them to open their home in West Philadelphia to gang members. The House of Umoja quickly developed into a communal living facility, geared toward keeping young men off the streets and giving them the education and life skills necessary to enter into society and the workforce. Realizing that for many of these youths, a street gang acts as a surrogate family, providing a sense of belonging and self-worth, the Fattahs created a family system of their own.

The House of Umoja Boystown has since become one of the most acclaimed and successful youth service programs in the country. Now occupying most of the original block of Frazier Street, the stated purpose of the house is to "provide a non-traditional, community-based experience which offers a positive learning environment for young men who lack a sufficient family support structure." Umoja provides not only the basic amenities of food and shelter, but also educational and emotional support often lacking even in the most "stable" of American families.

The house's outreach program has sponsored the Black Youth Olympics, cultural exchange programs with boys from Belfast, Ireland, and local cultural programs. In the wake of the first Rodney King verdict in Los Angeles, Umoja cooperated with the Quaker Friends Society to call for peaceful response. The House also speaks on behalf of the community at local meetings, city hearings or any gathering where a concerned voice is required (1410 N. Frazier St., Philadelphia, PA 19131; (215) 473-5893).

## Young Adult Police Commissioners Program

This program was established in New Haven, Connecticut, after a needs assessment revealed that young people felt completely disenfranchised from the community and felt hostility toward the police. According to Morrissey (1997, p. 6): "The mayor, superintendent of schools, president of the board of police commissioners, corporation counsel and chief all signed a document establishing the New Haven Board of Young Adult Police Commissioners." This board consists of twenty-two high school students and meets once a month to discuss topics ranging from AIDS victims to drug abuse to communication between adults and youth (contact: Detective Tom Morrissey, Community Youth Coordinator, New Haven Police Department, One Union Avenue, New Haven, CT 06519; (203) 946-6276).

## Additional Award-Winning Programs

A 1996 National League of Cities award winner is the Community-Based Youth Program of Rock Falls, Illinois, which provides recreational evenings targeting at-risk youth. This town of 10,000 has significant diversity, and the police department has no money for youth programs. The chief, a school athletics coach and several police officers got the National Guard Armory donated for the program for three recreational evenings every week. Police officers and teachers volunteer their time to supervise the program which provides basketball, volleyball, badminton, ping-pong, weight lifting, games and music (Blake, 1996, p. A1).

The Office of Juvenile Justice and Delinquency Prevention (OJJDP) describes three programs that won OJJDP's 1995 juvenile excellence awards:

- The Utah Community Service and Restitution Program, which collected more than $1 million in restitution payments and logged more than 500,000 hours of community service, while demonstrating that youths who are required to assume responsibility for their actions are less likely to reoffend.
- The Arlington County (Virginia) Juvenile Sex Offender Program, which is a comprehensive treatment program involving the adolescent offenders and their families as well as others in the community.
- The Bridge, a residential psychiatric treatment program in Atlanta.

## WILDERNESS PROGRAMS

*Youth in Transition* is a wilderness program in Santa Fe, New Mexico, sponsored by Southwest Wilderness Challenge, Inc. As noted in their brochure, the program is "dedicated to the development and reorientation of teenagers through significant wilderness experiences." It is for youth ages thirteen to eighteen who exhibit any of the following traits: bright, but unmotivated; low self-esteem; insecure, lacking confidence; withdrawn; rebellious; depressed; runaways; alcohol or drug use; manipulative; expelled, suspended or dropped out; do not finish what they start.

Through a twenty-one-day wilderness expedition under the guidance of experienced staff, youth live and travel approximately 130 miles through the mountains and deserts in wilderness areas of the Southwest. Among the "aboriginal living skills" students have the chance to learn are fire-making (with bow drill and hand drill); wild edible plant identification, collection and preparation (seeds, roots and berries); water collection; shelter construction; deadfalls, snares and fish traps; tool-making (from stone, bone and sinew); cordage-making (from natural materials); animal tracking, sign tracking, following trails and runs; basic first aid and health maintenance; group dynamics and cooperative living.

Anticipated changes after completion of the program include enhanced self-esteem; self-discovery (new talents and capacities discovered); self-confidence; dependability; leadership; determination; self-discipline; and resourcefulness. Dr. Victor B. Cline, professor of psychology and author of *How to Make Your Child a Winner,* sent his son on the expedition and said of the experience:

> When Russ was 14 we noticed he had a tendency toward shyness, a reluctance to express his inner feelings, a certain apartness from the family. He was very smart and doing well in school, but he was struggling to find his own identity

and selfhood. He tended to be his own man and didn't accept suggestions from others, even his own parents. . . .

At first, Russ didn't want to go. . . . But in the end he went, shuffling and reluctant, but he went. . . . We went to pick him up from the wilderness area, and I witnessed a sight that can never be erased from my mind. As Russ got off the truck . . . in his eyes and on his face I saw a look of supreme triumph. He seemed to be walking six feet off the ground. He had found himself.

## MODEL PROGRAMS FOR YOUTH

The National Symposium on Community Institutions and Inner-City Crime Project (the National Symposium) has identified several projects focused on providing services for youth. Some of these projects were discussed previously.

◆

Included in the model programs for youth are:

- The Children of the Night (Hollywood).
- House of UMOJA Boystown (Philadelphia).
- Community Youth Gang Services Project (Los Angeles).
- Junior Police Cadet Section (Detroit).
- The School Program to Educate and Control Drug Abuse (SPECDA) (New York).
- Cabrini-Green Youth Options Program (Chicago).

◆

A discussion of the last two programs follows.

### The School Program to Educate and Control Drug Abuse (SPECDA)

This program, a joint venture of the New York City Board of Education and New York City Police Department, seeks to apprehend drug dealers who sell drugs close to schools. It also seeks to reduce the demand for drugs by educating students about the dangers of alcohol and drug use, by helping them resist peer pressure and by providing healthy alternatives.

The program has sixteen sessions, eight developed for fifth graders and eight for sixth graders. By 1987 this program had expanded to twenty-eight school districts and was using 100 full-time officers. According to police data, thousands of drug-dealer arrests have been made since the program began. In addition, a study conducted by the John Jay College of Criminal Justice found the following positive results (Sulton, 1990, p. 25): "The program has 1) increased student awareness of drugs and their dangers, 2) resulted in positive student attitudes toward SPECDA team members and 3) encouraged students to remain drug free."

### The Cabrini-Green Youth Options Program

Cabrini-Green is a public housing project for thousands of impoverished African Americans. Sulton (p. 56) says of Cabrini-Green:

> This decaying pocket of poverty has a reputation as being one of the most dangerous public housing projects in the United States. . . .
>
> Hundreds of second and third generation Cobra, Vice Lords, and El Rukn gang members roam the hallways and rooftops. Semi-automatic gunfire usually begins in the early afternoon and continues throughout the night. An average of three youngsters are killed each month as a result of gang-related violence. . . .
>
> Older, well-organized groups recruit younger members to compete in an environment of fear and mistrust, one which encourages economically rewarding criminal activity such as drug trafficking, burglary, and prostitution.

The Cabrini-Green Youth Options Program is sponsored by the Chicago Urban League and the Al Carter Youth Foundation. The purpose of the program is to deter gang recruiting by providing attractive alternatives. It provides educational counseling and employment services for youth as well.

### Recommendations by the National Symposium for the Schools

The National Symposium has made the following recommendations for schools (Sulton, p. 105, used with permission):

1. Schools and other community institutions should work to prevent youth from dropping out of school. They should stress the relevance of education as it pertains to employment opportunities, self-development, and one's ability to successfully negotiate his or her way through our complex social, economic, and political systems.
2. Schools should help students organize peer support groups or clubs that promote educational attainment, leadership development, and community service.
3. Schools should work with families and community-based groups to improve as well as to reinforce the importance and relevance of education.
4. Schools should establish advisory committees that comprise teachers, students, and parents who discuss and resolve school-related problems and develop alternative forms of discipline.
5. Schools should develop curricula that teach students about values, sexuality, career choices, drug abuse, practical law, conflict resolution without violence, mediation, and juvenile justice agencies.
6. Schools should teach students the disciplines of work as well as basic academic skills.
7. The federal government should encourage elementary and secondary schools to teach children life skills such as time management, goal setting,

*A Dallas police officer meets with his explorer troop in the city's Little Asia district. This East Dallas Community and Refugee Affairs Center was named "Best Inner-City Crime Reduction Project in U.S." by the Police Foundation, Washington, DC, in 1987.*

    decision-making, nutrition, physical fitness, parenting, the dynamics of family and community, and nonviolent conflict resolution.

8. Educational and training programs should be developed for police officers and social service professionals. These programs should teach about cultural differences and prepare participants to respond to the special needs of various population segments. Research is needed to develop effective educational and training programs.

## COURTS AND CORRECTIONS PROGRAMS

In Indiana, courts and corrections work together to create a system that will accommodate juveniles' needs. In Marion County, Indiana, as in other areas across the country, the court faces juvenile crimes ranging from vandalism and shoplifting to murder. Fortunately, as noted by Payne and Lee (1990, pp. 100, 102):

> Thanks to a unique public-private partnership and a broad spectrum of alternative programs, the county has opened a state-of-the-art detention center with *fewer* beds than the old one—an almost unheard-of phenomenon.
>
> The county's alternative programs range from a run-away shelter and a wilderness camp to electronic surveillance and community clean-up programs.

Together, they weave the fabric of a juvenile justice system that comprehensively evaluates youths in an attempt to steer them away from crime. The programs give juveniles positive options designed to foster responsibility and help mold them into contributing members of society.

The juvenile facility and alternative programs resulted from the work of a coalition formed of law enforcement officers, prosecutors, public defenders, community organizers, educators, probation officers and members of the court. The coalition talked with everyone in any way involved in the juvenile justice system in the county, "from cooks to commissioners." They also toured other juvenile facilities and hired consultants. The $16.6 million center opened in March 1989 and includes the following features (Payne and Lee, p. 105):

- a control desk opened to dayrooms that allows staff to watch and talk with the juveniles;
- private visitation areas for youths to spend time with parents, ministers and officers of the court;
- an area for court and detention center staff;
- a secured sally port for cars and vans;
- interior courtyards for outdoor recreation and visiting;
- a full-size gymnasium; and
- video display screens in the intake waiting rooms advising juveniles of their rights and highlighting available public services.

According to Payne and Lee (p. 106): "Collaboration is the key to successfully planning and building a new facility and to developing alternative programs for young men and women in trouble." They outline the following dispositional alternative programs developed by the Marion County Indiana system (pp. 103–04). Reprinted by permission of the American Correctional Association.

- *Project Challenge:* A six-week program aimed at breaking the behavior cycles that lead youths to trouble. It includes a three-week wilderness camp that encourages youths to trust themselves and their peers, and provides vocational, family and individual counseling.
- *Ivy Tech:* A part of the state's technical school system that offers vocational education for troubled youths who are functionally illiterate or in need of remedial education or extra attention in the classroom. Students learn skills such as auto mechanics, welding or how to use computers. Many students then find jobs in the community.
- *Electronic Surveillance:* For four years, electronic surveillance has allowed Marion County to make sure students are home when they are supposed

to be. The devices allow them to assume responsibility while ensuring community safety.

- *Run, Don't Run:* Aimed at youths who have literally run from encounters with law enforcement officers. Developed by the juvenile court with the Indianapolis Police Department and the Marion County Sheriff's Department, the program is intended to establish respect between young offenders and law enforcement officials. Youths learn from police officers and a judge or magistrate how fleeing, resisting and striking police officers influences the officers' actions.

- *Visions:* Designed for the serious first referral or repeat offender who comes into contact with the court system. Youths are admitted to the juvenile detention center for one night, followed by a morning lesson about the juvenile justice system. That afternoon juveniles tour the Indiana Boys/Girls School and the Marion County Jail.

- *Operation Kids CAN (Care About Neighborhoods):* Began in the summer of 1987, when more than 200 youths on probation picked up 3.5 tons of neighborhood trash. The program has now joined forces with the Indianapolis Clean City Committee. Youths spend mornings learning about the juvenile justice system. Then they work in structured community service projects such as cleaning vacant lots and picking up garbage.

- *Garden Project:* Youths and their parents plant vegetables and flowers during the summer. The program shifts in winter to craft projects.

- *National Corrective Training Institute:* Instructors have small group discussions with youths charged with misdemeanors. They talk with children about values, attitudes and behavior.

- *Paint It Clean:* Requires youths associated with destructive gang activities to paint over gang graffiti in local neighborhoods, parks and buildings. Under the supervision of court staff, Paint It Clean helps eliminate gang claims to territory and allows communities to reclaim their neighborhoods.

- *Summer Youth Program:* Gives youths the chance to go canoeing, horseback riding, camping, hiking, caving and on a field trip to the Indiana Amusement Park.

- *Basketball:* For eleven years the court and the Twilight Optimist Club have sponsored a basketball league for youths. This collaboration gives juveniles the chance to participate in structured recreation with positive role models.

- *Near Peer Tutoring:* Targets junior high school probationers having trouble in at least one class. High school honor students and adult volunteers tutor youths weekly at neighborhood probation offices.

Three programs under the auspices of the Texas Juvenile Probation Commission's Office have reached out effectively to troubled youth: Williamson County's

"Don't Choose Crime" program, Jefferson County's Foster Grandparent program and Hidalgo County's Juvenile Court Conference Committee Volunteer program.

The *"Don't Choose Crime"* program is aimed at children from prekindergarten through grade twelve to teach them to avoid drugs and delinquency. Young children are given coloring books that illustrate the consequences of crime. Youth in grades four through twelve attend audio-visual presentations, receive a bookmark listing crimes and their penalties and also receive book covers, news stories and posters. As noted by Briscoe (1990, p. 92): "More than 4,500 birthday cards have been distributed to 12th grade students warning them that, under Texas law, adulthood begins at age 17."

Several school districts in Texas take students to the detention center for a tour. In addition, the district judge, members of the district attorney's office, the adult probation department and the court clerk's office have staged mock trials for students.

Jefferson County's *Foster Grandparent* program focuses on high-risk juveniles with emotional problems or who have been physically abused or neglected. Senior citizens are given forty hours of training and then work with children in detention. The foster grandparents tutor students, talk with them about problems, counsel them and teach them arts and crafts or to play musical instruments.

Hidalgo County's *Juvenile Court Conference Committee Volunteer* program is a "neighbors helping neighbors" program. This program forms conference committees of local citizens who work with children who seem headed for serious trouble with the law. Conferences are held with the child and his or her parents, and the committee then makes a decision as to what would be best for the child involved. The parent and child are asked to sign a four-month contract with the committee which may include counseling, community service work, writing an essay, being tutored, referral to another agency, writing a letter of apology, a tour of the county jail or detention center or any number of other possible activities.

As noted by Briscoe, deputy executive director of the Texas Juvenile Probation Commission (p. 95): "If we are ever going to manage the problems of crime and juvenile delinquency, we must involve citizens and reach beyond our traditional jurisdictional boundaries. Professionals alone can't do it. We must be creative, and we must form alliances with the public. These three programs are good examples of local departments doing just that."

## A CALL FOR WIZARDS

Although the preceding projects and programs are successful and valuable to the participants, keep in mind the comments of Beyer (1991, p. 166):

> Most effective programs cannot be replicated. What comes to my mind when someone asks me about effective programs are not organization models—instead I see the faces of the talented wizards who have created them. . . .

I don't believe in successful treatment approaches per se. It is how the program's philosophy is put into action that matters.

Wizards are those insightful, motivated leaders who can maximize a program's effectiveness. Part of a wizard's magic is in selecting and training staff who truly love young people and can understand their values but who can also impart their own and the community's values. They do not label the youths with whom they work; they celebrate the diversity among the youths in any given program. As noted by Beyer (p. 174):

> Wizards' great genius is their appreciation of the chemistry between the staff and the young people. You can see the loving relationship between staff and youth in any effective program: the hand of an actor on a young person's shoulder, the look of achievement as a youth docks a boat, the pride of a young person taking a good grade to a tutor. . . .

> Wizards are the ultimate motivators. They are not bound by training or habit to one approach. They do what works. Their programs are driven by the needs of the young people.

## SUMMARY

Common programs aimed at youth are school safety programs, bicycle safety programs, the McGruff "Take a Bite out of Crime" program, the Officer Friendly program, the Police Athletic Leagues (PAL), the fingerprinting of young children and police explorer programs.

The National Police Athletic League (PAL), now over fifty years old, was developed to provide opportunities for youth to interact with police officers in gyms or ballparks instead of in a juvenile detention hall. A police-school liaison program places an officer into a school to work with school authorities, parents and students, to prevent crime and antisocial behavior and to improve police-youth relationships. The joint goals of most police-school liaison programs are to prevent juvenile delinquency and to improve police-youth relations.

The Drug Abuse Resistance Education (DARE) program is aimed at elementary age school children and seeks to teach them to "say no to drugs," to resist peer pressure and to find alternatives to drug use. Teachers are among the most important professionals in making delinquency prevention programs work.

The IACP has endorsed the Kops'n Kids program, a program bringing together children and officers to have fun. Rochester, New York's Teens On Patrol program hires youth to patrol the city's parks and recreational areas in the summer. Model programs for youth include the following: The Children of the Night (Hollywood), House of UMOJA Boystown (Philadelphia), Community Youth Gang Services Project (Los Angeles), Junior Police Cadet Section (Detroit), the School Program to Educate and Control Drug Abuse (SPECDA) (New York) and the Cabrini-Green Youth Options Program (Chicago).

## *Discussion Questions*

1. Which of the programs for youth do you feel are most effective?
2. What programs for youth are available in your community?
3. Does your community have a police-school liaison program?
4. Why do school administrators not consider drugs a security or crime problem?
5. What other major differences in philosophy often exist between school administrators and police?
6. When you were young, were you exposed to McGruff? If so, do you remember what you thought of him?
7. Do you think officers in police-school liaison programs should be uniformed? What are the advantages of wearing a uniform? The disadvantages?
8. On which age group do you think police-school programs should focus? Why?
9. Which of the strategies to combat gang activity in schools do you think seem most workable?
10. What are the advantages and disadvantages of expelling disruptive gang members from school?

## *References*

Agay, Milton A. "A Week without Violence." *Community Policing Exchange.* (January/February 1997): 1–2.

Austin, Dave and Braaten, Jane. "Turning Lives Around: Portland Youth Find a New PAL." *The Police Chief.* (May 1991): 36–38.

Beyer, Marty. "First, You Find a Wizard: The Best Juvenile Programs Start with Visionary Leaders." *Corrections Today.* (April 1991): 166, 172–74.

Blake, Tracy. "Passing Time at Teen Time." *Burlington-Rock Falls, Illinois.* (February 9, 1996): A1–A2.

Bork, Patricia. "COP'RZ." *Law and Order.* (December 1991): 29–32.

Boss, Marion. "An Innovative Police Mentoring Program." *Community Policing Exchange.* (September/October 1996): 8.

Briscoe, Judy Culpepper. "In Texas: Reaching Out to Help Troubled Youths." *Corrections Today.* (October 1990): 90–95.

Brown, Lee P. "President's Message: Making the Problems of Youth a National Priority." *The Police Chief.* (June 1991): 6.

Drowns, Robert W. and Hess, Kären M. *Juvenile Justice,* 2nd ed. St. Paul: West Publishing Company, 1995.

Hardy, Lynette. "Geneva, Illinois' Officer Ollie." *Law and Order.* (December 1990): 18–22.

Krum, Brad. "Flying Fuzz." *Law and Order.* (September 1990): 58–59.

Lesce, Tony. "Police Explorers: A Learning Experience." *Law and Order.* (September 1991): 97–100.

Massesy, David. "Underage Drinking: A Community Problem." *Community Policing Exchange.* (January/February 1997): 8.

Morrissey, Tom. "Young Adult Police Commissioners: A Model Program." *Community Policing Exchange.* (January/February 1997): 6.

Narramore, Randy. "Cards for Kids." *Law and Order.* (December 1990): 23.

National School Safety Center. *Gangs in Schools: Breaking Up Is Hard to Do.* Malibu: Pepperdine University Press, 1988.

Okaty, George J. "Kids at School/Kids at Risk: Cooperation Needed to Address Unique Aspects of Crime Prevention on Campus." *The Police Chief.* (May 1991): 39–41.

Pace, Denny F. *Community Relations Concepts.* Incline Village, Nev.: Copperhouse Publishing Company, 1991.

Paterson, James and Schmoker, Mike. "P.E.P. Kids: A Substance Abuse Prevention Partnership." *Law and Order.* (January 1992): 280–83.

Payne, James W. and Lee, Joe E. "In Indiana: A System Designed to Accommodate Juveniles' Needs." *Corrections Today.* (October 1990): 100, 102–03.

Reynolds, Phil. "Teen-Age Drinking Task Force." *Law and Order.* (December 1991): 49–50.

Santoro, Joseph and Miglia, Rick. "City Sees Schools as Focal Point for Change." *Community Policing Exchange.* (January/February 1997): 3.

Sarubbi, Doug. "Orange County Sheriff's Office Broadcasts Anti-Drug/Alcohol Television Programs Directly Into Local Schools." *Law and Order.* (December 1991): 41–42.

"Shop with a Cop." *Law and Order.* (December 1990): 42.

Slahor, Stephenie. "Just for Kids." *Law and Order.* (January 1992): 281.

Spelman, William and Eck, John E. "Sitting Ducks, Ravenous Wolves, and Helping Hands: New Approaches to Urban Policing." In *Source Book: Community-Oriented Policing: An Alternative Strategy.* 201–09. Washington: ICMA, May 1992.

Stahr, John. "City Finds New Way for Juvenile Offenders to Make Restitution." *Community Policing Exchange.* (January/February 1997): 7.

Sulton, Anne Thomas. *Inner-City Crime Control: Can Community Institutions Contribute?* Washington: The Police Foundation, 1990.

Tortomasi, Scott. "Rock Falls Police Using a Little Preventative Medicine." *Burlington-Rock Falls, Illinois.* (October 28, 1996): A2.

"Vehicles Bought with Confiscated Monies Help Miami Officers Reach Children." *Law and Order.* (December 1991): 35.

Wrightman, Michael and Coburn, Jim. "Reducing Youth/Police Conflicts: Joplin's Innovative Approach." *Law and Order.* (December 1991): 37–38.

"Youth in Transition," (brochure). Southwest Wilderness Challenge, Inc.

### Resources

National Association of School Boards (NSBA), 1680 Duke Street, Alexandria, VA 22314; (703) 838-6722.

National Association of Secondary School Principals (NASSP), 1904 Association Drive, Reston, VA 22091; (703) 860-0200.

National and Local Parent Teacher Associations (PTAs). National PTA, 700 North Rush Street, Chicago, IL 60611-2571; (312) 787-0977.

*Chapter 17*

# Community Policing and Crime Prevention: Collaborative Efforts

*In the last analysis, the most promising and so the most important method of dealing with crime is by preventing it—by ameliorating the conditions of life that drive people to commit crime and that undermine the restraining rules and institutions erected by society against anti-social conduct.*

—President's Commission on Law Enforcement and Administration of Justice, 1967

## Do you know

- What synergism is and how it relates to crime prevention efforts?
- What crime prevention programs are commonly implemented?
- Who the Guardian Angels are?
- What types of special crime watches have been used?
- What types of institutions have developed model crime prevention programs?
- How volunteers are used in crime prevention?
- What the four Rs of volunteer management are?
- What organizations concentrate their efforts on community crime prevention?
- What the two primary messages of most auto-theft programs are?
- What the CAT program is?
- What programs have been implemented to combat the drug problem in neighborhoods?

## Definitions

Can you define these terms: CAT, Guardian Angels, synergism, weed and seed.

 *Introduction*

Whose job is it to prevent crime? Many Americans, including the police, believe crime prevention is the responsibility of the police. Many of the programs already discussed seek to prevent crime, including many of those aimed at youth. When crime surges in a community, the usual public response is to demand that more officers be hired. Citizens often believe that a visible police presence will deter and reduce crime, although most studies indicate that this is not the case. For example, the classic study, *Kansas City Preventive Patrol Experiment,* found overwhelming evidence that decreasing or increasing routine preventive patrol within the range tested had no effect on crime, citizen fear of crime, community attitudes toward the police on the delivery of police services, police response time or traffic accidents.

In 1975, the FBI's *Uniform Crime Reports* noted:

> Criminal justice professionals readily and repeatedly admit that, in the absence of citizen assistance, neither more manpower, nor improved technology, nor additional money will enable law enforcement to shoulder the monumental burden of combating crime in America.

The broad nature of policing in the 1990s highlights the critical contributions citizens, community agencies and organizations can make to combat crime. For communities to thrive, citizens need a sense of neighborhood and to work together as a team. The resulting synergism can accomplish much more than isolated individual efforts.

**Synergism** occurs when individuals channel their energies toward a common purpose and accomplish what they could not accomplish alone.

The technical definition of *synergism* is "the simultaneous actions of separate entities which together have greater total effect than the sum of their individual efforts." A precision marching band and a national basketball championship team are examples of this synergism. Although there may be some outstanding solos and a few spectacular individual "dunks," it is the total team effort that produces the results.

The police and the citizens they serve must realize that their combined efforts *are* greater than the sum of their individual efforts on behalf of the community.

When police take a problem-solving approach to crime and include the community, what they are doing often falls under "crime prevention." Crime prevention is a large part of community policing. Community policing and crime prevention are, however, distinct entities.

As Horne (1991, p. 24) suggests: "Obviously, crime prevention and community policing are inextricably related. Crime prevention is the cornerstone of community policing." He notes: "One critical element common to both concepts is citizen input and participation; police crime prevention programs rely on the cooperation and voluntary involvement of individuals and groups in the community."

This chapter begins with a discussion of the national focus on community policing and crime prevention and a review of traditional approaches to crime prevention. This is followed by descriptions of special crime watch programs, National Night Out, model programs and using volunteers. Next the discussion turns to organizations focused on crime prevention including programs aimed at preventing auto theft, programs to deter prostitution and collaborative efforts to deal with the drug problem in public housing. The chapter concludes by stressing the importance of a comprehensive, coordinated approach to enhancing community safety.

## NATIONAL EMPHASIS ON COMMUNITY POLICING AND CRIME PREVENTION

The Violent Crime Control and Law Enforcement Act of 1994 authorized $8.8 billion over six years for grants to local police agencies to add 100,000 officers and promote community policing. To implement this law, Attorney General Janet Reno created the Office of Community Oriented Policing Services (COPS) in the Department of Justice.

The COPS office defines community policing as "a policing philosophy that promotes and supports organizational strategies to address the causes and reduce the fear of crime and social disorder through problem-solving and community-police partnerships" (Brann, 1997, p. 1). Brann stresses: "Just as we cannot expect our education system to be responsible for raising America's children, we cannot expect law enforcement to solve crime and disorder problems alone." Among the organizations that might provide assistance is the Community Policing Consortium.

The Community Policing Consortium is a partnership of five police organizations: the International Association of Chiefs of Police (IACP), the National Organization of Black Law Enforcement Executives (NOBLE), the National Sheriffs' Association (NSA), the Police Executive Research Forum (PERF) and the Police Foundation (PF). The Consortium is funded and administered by COPS within the Department of Justice. They provide training throughout the

United States, especially to agencies that receive COPS grants. The training materials emphasize community policing from a local perspective, community partnerships, problem solving, strategic planning and assessment. Their quick-read periodicals, *The Community Policing Exchange, Sheriff Times* and the *Information Access Guide,* relate real-life experiences of community policing practitioners across the country.

## REVIEW OF TRADITIONAL APPROACHES TO CRIME PREVENTION

When crime prevention became popular in the late 1960s and early 1970s, many communities undertook similar types of programs.

◆

Among the most commonly implemented crime prevention programs have been street lighting projects, property marking projects, security survey projects, citizen patrol projects and crime reporting, neighborhood watch or block projects.

◆

Claims of success should be carefully examined. Critics often say that the evaluations are flawed. Indeed, research within communities is extremely difficult because:

- Measuring what *did not happen* is nearly impossible.
- Crime is usually underreported.
- A reduction in reported crime could be the result of the crime prevention program or because the responsible criminal or criminals left town, went to jail on some other charge or died, and so on.
- Crime can be influenced by everything from seasonal and weather changes, school truancy rates and the flu, to road construction or even a change in a bus stop location. A drop in the crime rate does not necessarily mean a crime prevention program is working.

In addition, many of these programs are evaluated by people who have no training or experience in appropriate research methods and, consequently, they sometimes produce flawed results.

Some also argue that crime is not prevented by programs like Neighborhood Watch but instead it is displaced to neighborhoods where the residents are not as likely to report suspicious activity to the police. Even if this is true, such programs do raise community awareness and have a "chilling effect" on criminals who are inhibited by those who watch and call the police.

Use of crime data to evaluate crime prevention projects poses special problems. Crime data, obviously, is limited to *reported* crimes. Practitioners are aware of the *dark side of crime,* that is, the huge amount of crime that is *unreported.* When projects are instituted to enlist the community in preventing crime, the citizens' heightened awareness and involvement often results in an *increase in reported crime,* but this does *not* mean that crime itself has actually increased.

As you read this chapter, consider the difficulties in evaluating crime prevention projects or, indeed, any project involving many diverse individuals and problems.

## Street Lighting Projects

Since ancient times, lighting has been one means to deter and detect crime. Street lighting projects through environmental design (CPTED) efforts are often an important part of crime prevention. Most street lighting projects seek to not only improve the likelihood of deterring and detecting crime, but also to improve the safety of law-abiding citizens. Available research indicates that street lighting does *not* decrease the incidence of crime in participating target areas but that it is useful to reduce citizens' fear of crime and increase their feelings of security.

## Property Identification Projects

Often referred to as "Operation Identification" or "O-I" projects, property identification is aimed at deterring burglary and at returning property that is stolen when deterrence fails. Most property identification projects provide citizens with instructions, a marking tool and a unique number to be applied to all valuable items within a household. Stickers are provided to homeowners to display on windows and doors warning possible burglars that the residents have marked their valuables and they are on record with the police. In addition to its deterrent effect, the property identification program also helps police track the source of stolen goods and return stolen property to its rightful owners.

It is sometimes difficult to get people to participate in the program. In addition, although the burglary rate may drop for those enrolled in the program, it may not drop citywide. There is no evidence available to suggest a difference in the number of apprehended or convicted burglars in communities that do or do not participate in the program.

## Crime Prevention Security Surveys

Crime prevention security surveys are also usually an integral part of projects that focus on the environmental design of facilities and on "target hardening" as a means to deter or prevent crime. As noted by Crowe (1992, p. 22A):

> CPTED is based on the theory that the proper design and effective use of the built environment can lead to a reduction in the incidence and fear of crime and an improvement in the quality of life. Years of experiments and field

applications have demonstrated that CPTED works in all environments— that is, it applies to commercial, residential, transportation, recreational and institutional environments.

It has worked on scales as small as a single room and as large as an entire community.

Surveys used to determine the effectiveness of the existing "environmental design" are usually conducted by police officers specially trained in this area. They do comprehensive on-site inspection of homes, apartments and businesses. Of particular interest are doors, windows, locks, lighting and shrubbery that might be used to a burglar's advantage. The officer offers specific suggestions on how a location might be made more secure.

## Citizen Patrol Projects

Many variations of citizen patrol exist in the United States. Some are directed at a specific problem such as crack houses and sale of drugs in a neighborhood. Others are aimed at general crime prevention and enhanced citizen safety. Citizen patrols may operate throughout a community or may be located within a specific building or complex of buildings such as tenement houses.

The most successful patrols are affiliated with a larger community or neighborhood organization, sustain a working relationship with law enforcement and are flexible enough to engage in non–crime prevention activities when patrolling is patently unnecessary.

One hazard of citizen patrols is the possibility of vigilantism which has a long, often proud, history in the United States and, indeed, in the history of law enforcement and criminal justice. Now this hazard is quite serious because of the increase of readily available handguns in our country.

Probably the best known citizen patrol is the **Guardian Angels.** According to Clede (1990, p. 37): "The Alliance of Guardian Angels, Inc. is a non-profit, all volunteer organization whose purpose is to fight crime and provide positive role models for young children . . ."

◆

The Guardian Angels are private citizen patrols who seek to deter crime and to provide a positive role model for young children.

◆

As noted by Greenberg (1991, p. 42): "The Angels wear bright red berets and T-shirts imprinted with a flapping wing and badge insignia. They carry a pad, pen, whistle and—sometimes—handcuffs. Although they carry no weapons, they do attempt to arrest felony suspects and hold them for the police."

The Guardian Angels are now called the International Alliance of Guardian Angels. They are involved in training community groups to patrol their streets safely and to cooperate with police. Their crime prevention programs include

*A member of the Guardian Angels addresses a group of citizens concerned about rising crime and gang violence in their community.*

educating young people by teaching a no-gun, no-gang, no-drug philosophy. They also offer free self-defense courses and provide public speakers for college and community groups. Guardian Angels also offer reassurance, assistance, escorts and protection to anyone who needs it. Their long-term purpose is not only to provide a positive role model for young people but also to provide a realistic life opportunity for them to become crime fighters rather than criminals.

Members receive free training in self-defense/physical intervention, emergency first-aid, communications and negotiations, law, leadership skills and urban patrol procedures.

An innovative expansion of the Angels is their new all-volunteer Internet Safety organization. Membership in this group unites more than 1,000 users from thirty-two countries who "police the Internet" through what they call "Cyberspace Neighborhood Watch." Calling themselves CyberAngels, they focus on protecting children from online abuse by fighting child porn and advising online victims of hate mail.

The former mayor of Detroit told the Angels they were not welcome in his city and their organization efforts their failed.

In New York City, there is another type of private citizen patrol, called the Veterans Civilian Observation Patrol or V-COPS. According to Clark (1991, p. 8): "Each member is a homeless veteran of the U.S. armed forces who has volunteered his time and energy not only to help prevent crime in the neighborhoods, but also to aid in his recovery from drug abuse or alcoholism and to regain a sense of self-esteem."

Ironically, the V-COPS were born out of a neighborhood problem when the Borden Avenue Veterans Residence was opened by the Salvation Army to serve homeless veterans. Neighbors complained about noise and drinking at the shelter, but only a very small number of those living there were actually causing the problem. The police officer assigned to defuse the situation conceived the idea of the V-COPS, and it quickly became popular. About 200 homeless veterans have participated in the program since then.

V-COPS patrol bank areas on the days Social Security and welfare checks arrive, and the grateful bank officials often provide them with lunch. As noted by one V-COP (Clark, p. 8): "Our presence deters [criminals] from coming around the neighborhood. They know who we are. They know we're veterans. They think we're probably psycho or Rambo, and they walk away."

When on duty, V-COPS wear T-shirts with their emblem and march through neighborhoods military-style, silently, using hand signals. If the V-COPS find trouble or suspicious circumstances, they notify one of their group stationed in the precinct house who monitors their radio transmissions. This person then notifies on-duty patrol officers who respond.

Communities who want to develop a citizen street patrol will find assistance in a brochure developed by the Neighborhood Crime Prevention Council. The guide discusses how to recruit volunteers, how to structure patrols and what actions to take if one witnesses a crime. Citizen arrest procedures, a watch log and job descriptions are included.

## Citizen Crime Reporting, Neighborhood or Block Programs

Citizen crime reporting programs (CCRP) help to organize neighborhoods as "mutual aid societies" and as the "eyes and ears" of the police. Thousands of Neighborhood Watch programs exist in the United States, and many describe them as the backbone of the nation's community crime prevention effort. Typically local residents hold meetings of such programs in their homes or apartments. During the meetings, neighbors get to know each other and what is normal activity for their neighborhood. They receive educational information about crime prevention from the local police department and are told how to contact the police if they see something suspicious.

Signs are posted throughout the neighborhood warning possible offenders of the program. Often the programs provide safe houses for children to use if they encounter danger on their way to or from school.

Some programs work to enhance citizens' reporting capability. Whistlestop programs, for example, provide citizens with whistles which they can blow if they are threatened or see something requiring police intervention. Anyone hearing the whistle is to immediately call the police. Whistlestop programs are the modern-day version of the "hue and cry."

Some programs enlist the aid of ham radio operators who can report suspicious or illegal activity directly to the police without using public telephone lines. Other programs have implemented special hot lines whereby citizens can call a specific number with crime information and perhaps receive a monetary reward.

McLean (1991, p. 58) describes the citizen's watch program in Honolulu:

> Organized as fixed-location neighborhood watches, a remarkable 26,000 homes in nearly 300 separate neighborhoods are a direct extension of the Honolulu Police Department. If you factor in the 2.3 people per home in the Honolulu city/county jurisdiction, it's safe to say there are probably 58,000 sets of eyes and ears.
>
> • Honolulu PD's senior citizen watch has members in 44 registered groups within the county. They total roughly 830 individuals.
>
> • Business security watches, now being organized, number 321 commercial establishments, including the sprawling Ala Moana Shopping Center with 156 members.
>
> • The Neighborhood Security Watch is growing by 600 homes per month, with no end in sight.
>
> • Some 450 cars, trucks and buses have drivers who are, in a manner of speaking, "riding shotgun" with their cellulars and radios—trained and ready to accurately report crimes in progress.

Table 17.1 illustrates the types of activities engaged in by Neighborhood Watch programs and the relative popularity of each.

Very few of the programs concentrate on only the "neighborhood watch." Project Operation Identification and home security surveys are by far the most common activities of Neighborhood Watch programs. Street lighting programs, crime tip hot lines and physical environmental concerns are also quite common.

## SPECIAL CRIME WATCH PROGRAMS

In addition to the traditional types of crime watch programs commonly implemented throughout the country, some communities have developed more specialized types of crime watch programs.

◆

Specialized crime watch programs include mobile crime watch, youth crime watch, business crime watch, Realtor watch and carrier alert.

◆

Honolulu's mobile crime watch seeks to enlist the aid of motorists who have two-way communication equipment in their vehicles such as CBs, car telephones

*Table 17.1*    **Activities Engaged in by Neighborhood Watch Programs (Based on Program Survey Responses)**

| Activity | Number | Percent |
|---|---|---|
| **Neighborhood Watch Only** | 49 | 8.9 |
| **Crime Prevention Specific** | | |
| Project Operation Identification | 425 | 80.6 |
| Home security surveys | 357 | 67.9 |
| Street lighting improvement | 183 | 34.7 |
| Block parenting | 144 | 27.3 |
| Organized surveillance | 66 | 12.0 |
| Traffic alteration | 37 | 7.0 |
| Emergency telephones | 24 | 4.6 |
| Project Whistle Stop | 18 | 3.4 |
| Specialized informal surveillance | 18 | 3.4 |
| Escort service | 12 | 2.3 |
| Hired guards | 11 | 2.1 |
| Environmental design | 7 | 1.3 |
| Lock provision/installation | 4 | 0.7 |
| Self defense/rape prevention | 3 | 0.5 |
| **Crime Related** | | |
| Crime tip hotline | 197 | 37.5 |
| Victim witness assistance | 101 | 19.2 |
| Court watch | 17 | 3.2 |
| Telephone chain | 7 | 1.3 |
| Child fingerprinting | 2 | 0.4 |
| **Community Oriented** | | |
| Physical environmental concerns | 201 | 38.1 |
| Insurance premium deduction survey | 20 | 3.6 |
| Quality of life | 9 | 1.6 |
| Medical emergency | 4 | 0.7 |

SOURCE: James Garofalo and Maureen McLeod. *Improving the Use and Effectiveness of Neighborhood Watch Programs.* U.S. Department of Justice, National Institute of Justice/Research in Action Series. April 1988: 2.

or cellular telephones. Volunteers attend a short orientation session that trains them to better observe and report suspicious activity. Participants are also given Mobile Watch decals to place on their vehicles. They are advised to call 911 if they hear screaming, gunshots, breaking glass or loud explosive noises; if they see someone breaking into a house or car; if they observe a car driven in a dangerous or erratic manner; if they observe a person on the ground apparently unconscious; if they see anyone brandishing a gun or knife; or if they see an individual staggering, out of control or threatening others.

They are also trained to recognize and report other unusual behaviors such as:

- A child who appears to be lost.
- Anyone being forced into a vehicle, especially a child or female.
- Cars cruising erratically and repetitively near schools, parks and playgrounds.
- A person running, especially if carrying something of value.
- Parked, occupied vehicles at unusual hours near potential robbery sites.
- More than normal traffic in and out of a house or commercial establishment.
- Someone going door-to-door or passing through backyards.
- Persons loitering around schools, parks, secluded areas or in the neighborhood.

Pace (1991, p. 266) describes three other specialized watch programs implemented by the Miami-Dade Metro Police Department:

*Youth Crime Watch:* This program is available to all elementary and secondary students who will be trained in crime prevention and in observing and reporting incidents in their schools. Additionally, the youths may initiate and develop their own programs in order to make their neighborhoods safer.

*Business Crime Watch:* A general meeting of all businesses is held, similar to the "Primary Meeting." Crime prevention and crime watch training, however, applies to businesses, offices and stores rather than to residences.

*Realtor Watch:* Realtors throughout the county are trained to "crime watch" during their working hours in the neighborhoods and commercial areas in which they are selling.

Another specialized type of crime watch is the *Carrier Alert* program, initiated by the United States Postal Service. In this program letter carriers are asked to become aware of elderly citizens or citizens with special needs on their routes and to look out for them. They are to report any lack of activity or suspicious activity at their homes to the police.

Most successful community-based programs that focus on crime prevention or safety issues have a close partnership with law enforcement. The community and law enforcement have vital components to offer the other, making cooperation between the two highly desirable. It is difficult to imagine, for instance, an effective community-based Crime Watch program without input or cooperation from the local police agency. Crime Watch programs are built on the premise of mutual aid—citizens and police working together.

## NATIONAL NIGHT OUT

National Night Out is a program originated in Tempe, Arizona, and sponsored by the National Association of Town Watch and the Philips Lighting Company. Held in August, this nationwide program encourages residents to turn on their porch lights, go outside and meet their neighbors. Neighborhood Watch programs are encouraged to plan a party or event during National Night Out.

In 1996 this program involved more than 29.5 million people including law enforcement personnel; individuals from other units of government; members of business, education and community organizations; citizens; and youth in over 9,000 communities in all fifty states, U.S. territories and U.S. military bases around the world.

One crime prevention association's newsletter states: "The best deterrents for crime are good lighting and watchful, caring neighbors. The porch or yard lights are partly symbolic, partly crime prevention, but the neighborliness is the most important."

## PARTNERSHIPS IN ACTION

TRIAD was introduced in Chapter 9. According to Freeman (1995, p. 8), Monmouth County (New Jersey) has more than 120,000 senior citizens in fifty-three municipalities serviced by forty-nine police departments and one sheriff's office using the TRIAD program. Programs that have addressed the needs of the elderly in Monmouth County include senior citizen identification, scam prevention, citizen police academy, daily call-in for seniors, sensitivity training for police officers and senior safe walk.

The National Crime Prevention Council provides several examples of partnerships in action throughout the country.

### REDUCING CRIME IN NORFOLK, VIRGINIA

This city has cut homicides by more than 10 percent in each of the last 3 years and, even more impressive, has reduced overall crime rates citywide by 26 percent and in some neighborhoods by as much as 40 percent. A good share of the credit goes to Police Assisted Community Enforcement (PACE), a crime prevention initiative that works neighborhood by neighborhood in conjunction with teams of social, health, and family services agencies (the Family Assistance Services Team, or FAST) and public works and environmental agencies (Neighborhood Environmental Assistance Teams, or NEAT) to cut through red tape and help residents reclaim their neighborhoods.

### CAMPAIGNING AGAINST YOUTH VIOLENCE IN MINNESOTA

The Minnesota Crime Prevention Association enlisted the support of families, public officials, and 45 statewide and local organizations, including schools and churches, to wage a campaign against youth violence. Actions ranged from encouraging children and parents to turn off violent television shows to providing classroom training in violence prevention.

### PROVIDING SAFE HAVENS AFTER SCHOOL IN TRENTON, NEW JERSEY

A partnership of schools, parents, city leaders, and others led to a Safe Haven program in which the schools in the neighborhood became multipurpose centers after school hours for youth activities including sports, crafts, and tutoring. Children have flocked to the centers as a positive alternative to being at home alone after school or being at risk on the streets.

### PREVENTING CAMPUS CRIME IN COLUMBUS, OHIO

Crime near a college campus became an opportunity for a partnership formed by the City of Columbus, the State of Ohio, Ohio State University, the Franklin County Sheriff, and the Columbus Police. The Community Crime Patrol puts two-person, radio-equipped teams of observers into the neighborhoods near the campus during potential high-crime hours. A number of these paid, part-time observers are college students interested in careers in law enforcement.

### REDUCING CRIME IN PUBLIC HOUSING IN DANVILLE, VIRGINIA

A partnership approach to working with public housing residents resulted in a 53-percent reduction in calls about fights, a 50-percent reduction in domestic violence calls, and a 9-percent reduction in disturbance calls. The Virginia Crime Prevention Association worked with the Danville Housing Authority to bring public housing residents, local law enforcement, social services, and other public agencies together into an effective, problem-solving group. Residents were at the heart of the group, identifying problems that were causing high rates of aggravated assault in the community and working to provide such remedies as positive alternatives for youth, social services, and counseling for adults and children. Residents developed a code of conduct for the community, spelling out expectations for the behavior of those who live there.

### PROTECTING THE ELDERLY IN BOSTON

Boston's Neighborhood Justice Network, in partnership with the Council of Elders, the Jewish Memorial Hospital, the Boston Police Department, the Department of Public Health, and the Commission on Affairs of the Elderly, created a program to help reduce violence and other crimes against older people. It provides basic personal and home crime prevention education, assistance in dealing with city agencies, training in nonconfrontational tactics to avert street crime, and other helpful services that reduce both victimization and fear among the city's older residents.

These are just a few of a wide range of programs designed by community groups that are changing the quality of life in small towns and large cities, in neighborhoods and housing complexes, in schools and on playgrounds. These groups have proved that there is strength in numbers and that partnerships can provide the community basis for correcting the problems and conditions that can lead to crime. They achieved success because they developed the skills to work together effectively.

## MODEL PROGRAMS

The National Symposium on Community Institutions and Inner-City Crime Project has identified several model crime prevention programs.

◆

Model crime prevention programs have been developed by a hospital auxiliary, churches, foundations, businesses and civic groups.

◆

### Belleview Hospital Auxiliary, New York

**Special Project on Training of Professionals in Sexual Exploitation Prevention of the Developmentally Disabled.** The advisory committee of the project consists of crime victims, rehabilitation professionals and disabled individuals. Each year the project conducts seven or eight training sessions for twenty-five to thirty human service and criminal justice professionals. The training focuses on prevention of sexual exploitation, emphasizing that disabled people can be independent, assertive and able to defend themselves. Trainers are taught several techniques the disabled can use to avoid victimization or to cope with it should it occur. According to Sulton (1990, p. 29): "The project encourages local professionals to think about ways in which individuals and organizations can establish a local network of medical, psychological and legal services to which the disabled can turn before or after they have been abused . . . [promoting and facilitating] a local self-help approach to service delivery and education that continues after the training session ends."

### Ponce, Puerto Rico

**Centro Sister Isolina Ferre Programa Del Dispensario.** This church-based program seeks to help the poor of Puerto Rico's second largest city through "education, advocacy and revitalization at both the individual and community levels" (Sulton, p. 30). The center was founded in 1968 and is governed by a board of directors. It conducts educational programs, job-training programs, advocacy programs and community revitalization in the form of small business development.

The advocacy component seeks to foster community unity and spirit. Advocates are community residents who help "open doors to opportunities" for other residents. They represent troubled youth dealing with the justice system. They teach parents about their responsibilities and parenting skills. They also provide counseling to abused children, encourage handicapped children to participate in society to the fullest extent possible and encourage all children to remain in school.

### Lutheran Metropolitan Ministries Association of Cleveland, Ohio

**Community Re-Entry Program.** This church-sponsored, community-based corrections program focuses on "reintegration" of offenders through employment. Sulton (pp. 35–36) describes the concepts on which Community Re-Entry is based:

1.  People more readily act their way into a new kind of thinking, than think their way into a new kind of acting.

2.  Through community service one is able to explore one's talents and become more productive.

3.  Offenders must be integrated into the community for the good of society and themselves.

4.  People should be allowed to exercise self-determination.

Components of the program include Care Teams (discussed in Chapter 9), where ex-offenders help the elderly living in low-income, high-rise apartment buildings. The Denise McNair New Life Center is a storefront operation directed by ex-offenders that provides court-related advice, intervenes in family crisis situations, makes referrals to other community services and agencies and conducts home visits.

A Community Detention program is sometimes used in place of incarceration. During the day offenders do community service or work at their jobs, but they spend the night at the center. The program has also created jobs, operating such businesses as Paint Plus, Maintenance Plus, Fresh Lunch/Fresh Start, Creative Printing and the Wick Band. Yet another component of the program is the School Care Team, which provides drug and violence prevention counseling to high school students. Ex-offenders visit schools and talk with youth about the dangers of drug abuse and violence.

## Chicago, Illinois

**Sunbow Foundation, Inc.** This program is based on the belief that poor women should be trained for well-paying nontraditional jobs, specifically jobs in the construction field. The program is directed by an advisory board consisting of representatives from social services, building construction and the criminal justice system. Site-visit staff learned that 91 percent of the women enrolled in the program completed it and that 88 percent obtained jobs with Chicago-area construction and cable companies. As noted by Sulton (p. 43): "The program familiarized participants with drafting, blueprints, construction math, masonry, plumbing, electrical work, HVAC and the use and care of hand and power tools. Program participants attended workshops on safety, first aid, fitness, career planning and human relations."

## New York

**Wildcat Service Corporation.** Wildcat is a private, nonprofit transitional employment program that seeks to "break the cycles of poverty and welfare dependency by hiring and training the chronically unemployed for subsidized jobs and moving them into the regular workforce" (Sulton, p. 46). Approximately 2,000 individuals participate each year, the majority being African American or Hispanic.

The program operates like a traditional temporary help or job placement agency. In addition to this basic program, the Wildcat Service Corporation operates a Youth Literacy and Work Experience Program for juvenile offenders; an Enhanced Work Experience Youth Program for those receiving public assistance or from low-income families; a Clerical Work Experience/Classroom Training Program for adults who are on public assistance or unemployed; a Clerk-Typist Training Program for adults on public assistance; and a Supported Work Program for offenders currently in New York City-based state correctional institutions who are in work release programs and within six months of parole.

## Washington, D.C.

**Around the Corner to the World (ACW).** This program is located in Adams Morgan, which is, according to Sulton (p. 51): "the most densely populated and ethnically diverse neighborhood in our nation's capital." She notes:

> Around the Corner to the World is a neighborhood-based, grassroots response to the displacement, lost sense of community, and crime occurring in Adams Morgan. . . .
>
> ACW's primary goal is to stabilize and revitalize Adams Morgan through youth leadership development and economic development.
>
> ACW emphasizes personal empowerment (confidence and self-esteem), community empowerment (reinforcement of basic institutional relationships),

and means, and capacity to live positively and independent of destructive forces. It promotes self-sufficiency and economic development by teaching marketable skills and providing jobs to neighborhood residents.

### Newark, N.J.

**Soul-O-House Drug Abuse Program.** Soul-O-House is an outpatient, community-based drug prevention and rehabilitation center that seeks to reduce drug abuse and crime by helping citizens achieve productive, meaningful lives. According to Sulton (p. 67): "Program participants are counseled from an African-American perspective within an extended family. . . . Knowledge of one's culture and history and cultural pride are associated with positive self-concept." The program sponsors a latchkey program for elementary school children, parent meetings, health seminars on AIDS, field trips and athletic events for area residents.

## USING VOLUNTEERS

Many police departments make extensive use of volunteers. The importance of community volunteers is stressed by Leavy (1992, p. 69): "Volunteer resource pools, if enthusiastically used, can bring an enormous cachet of diversified expertise into a given situation. These volunteers are generally enthusiastic, committed and eager to contribute to the task. . . . Volunteer talent is a gift which if not fostered and utilized will be lost forever. Law enforcement cannot afford to lose the benefits a pool of volunteers can provide. The answer very simply is: USE THEM (to the maximum)—OR LOSE THEM."

◆

Volunteers may serve as reserve officers, auxiliary patrol, community service officers or on an as-needed basis.

◆

Reserve officers, auxiliary patrol or community service officers (CSOs) usually wear uniforms and badges but are unarmed. However, in some departments, reserve officers are armed and receive the same training as regular sworn officers. They are trained to perform specific functions that assist the uniformed patrol officers. They may be used to patrol watching for suspicious activity, to direct traffic, to conduct interviews with victims of and witnesses to crimes and to provide crime-prevention education at neighborhood watch meetings, civic groups, churches and schools.

CSOs may work with youths to prevent delinquency, refer citizen complaints to the appropriate agency and investigate minor thefts. They are usually heavily involved in public relations activities as well. Some CSOs are paid, but much less than police officers. Explorer programs, discussed in Chapter 16, and police cadet programs are other sources for volunteers.

Some communities use a volunteer officer program. According to Weinblatt (1991, p. 19), in some Massachusetts districts, volunteer officers are trained, armed and certified by the state. Volunteer officers alleviate severe personnel shortages in some areas. The program allows the department to have two-officer squads and also serves as a prescreening for potential paid officers. Weinblatt suggests: "Many volunteer officers are young people looking to make a career out of law enforcement and see volunteering as a way to get a foot in the door and test the waters."

Often departments ask professionals such as physicians, teachers and ministers, to volunteer their services, sometimes as expert witnesses. In Tempe, the Volunteers in Policing program has grown from three volunteers to 120. Their volunteer management philosophy is based on what they call the "Four Rs."

◆

The four Rs of volunteer management are research, recruitment, retention and recognition.

◆

The article "No Mere Paper-Pushers" (1991, p. 9) quotes the volunteer coordinator, Judy Bottorf, as saying: "Volunteers are really community-based policing, because they are in the community every day, they bring a different perspective. They have special problem-solving skills and feedback that we can use." The chief of police feels that the more than 1,000 volunteer hours a month are an excellent return on the investment they made in establishing Bottorf's position.

One Volunteers in Policing program, the Motorist Assist Program, helps stranded motorists and also assists in directing traffic at accident scenes. Volunteers in this program can also write civil citations for parking violations in handicapped zones and fire lanes.

Often volunteers perform office-type functions in police departments. Volunteers might perform crime analysis, conduct tours or answer telephone messages. They might also provide assistance to police at crime prevention programs and Neighborhood Watch meetings. Many departments use the AARP volunteer program, capitalizing on the experience and free time of the elderly citizens of the community.

## Advantages of Using Volunteers

Volunteers provide a communication link between the citizens and the police department. They can help establish the credibility of the department's public relations and educational efforts. Volunteers provide additional sources of information and perspectives.

Hogan (1995, p. 8) reports on the results of a survey of 1,000 law enforcement agencies and presents the following findings:

- Slightly more than one in ten police agencies use volunteers.
- Most respondents started volunteer programs because they needed help (61 percent).

The survey respondents reported the following benefits of using volunteers:

- Stability, reliability and dependability of workers (57 percent).
- Experience and knowledge (52 percent).
- Wisdom, maturity and leadership (47 percent).
- Work budget lifted from paid help (47 percent).
- Free labor (19 percent).
- Workers relate well to the community (5 percent).

## Disadvantages of Using Volunteers

Using volunteers does, however, cause certain problems. In fact, some police officers feel that volunteers are "more trouble than they are worth." The following are some reasons commonly given for not using volunteers:

1. People who are "joiners" or have time and/or money often lack sensitivity to minorities.
2. Citizen advisory committees lack direct policy-setting responsibilities.
3. Some citizens seek profit and gain for themselves and develop programs that are mere window dressing.
4. Some citizens lack qualifications and training.
5. Since volunteers receive no pay, they cannot be docked or penalized for poor performance.
6. Citizens lack awareness of the criminal justice system in general and specific agencies in particular.
7. Because of the use of volunteers and/or citizen participation, some communities and politicians fail to take responsibility for solving the larger social problem and/or refuse to hire adequate numbers of personnel or pay better wages.

In addition, some police unions have reacted negatively to volunteers who are sometimes viewed as competitors for police jobs. Reserve officers, in particular, tend to cause patrol officers to feel their jobs are threatened by those willing to do police jobs for free. Departments should be certain that the objectives of volunteer use are understood by the salaried police officers. Officers should know that programs using volunteers are those that could not otherwise exist due to lack of personnel and funding.

## ORGANIZATIONS FOCUSED ON CRIME PREVENTION

◆

Among the most visible organizations focused on crime are citizen crime prevention associations, Crime Stoppers and MADD.

◆

### Citizen Crime Prevention Associations

Among the many activities undertaken by citizen crime prevention associations are the following:

- Paying for crime tips.
- Funding for police-crime prevention programs.
- Supporting police canine programs.
- Raising awareness in the community through crime prevention seminars, newsletters, cable TV shows and booths.
- Providing teddy bears for kids.
- Raising money through sources such as:
    Business contributions;
    Membership fees;
    Charitable gambling; and
    Sales of alarms, mace, "Call Police" signs (usually sold as a service to community, not to raise any substantial money).
- Funding specific programs such as rewards to community members who call the hot line with crime information.

### Crime Stoppers

Crime Stoppers is a non-profit program involving citizens, the media and the police. Local programs offer anonymity and cash rewards to individuals who furnish to police information that leads to the arrest and indictment of felony offenders. Each program is governed by a local board of directors made up of citizens from a cross-section of the community, the businesses of the community and law enforcement. The reward money comes from tax-deductible donations and grants from local businesses, foundations and individuals.

When a crime-related call is received by Crime Stoppers, it is logged in with the date, time and a summary of the information given by the caller. Callers are given code numbers to be used on all subsequent calls by the same person regarding that particular case. Each week, one unsolved crime is selected for special treatment by the media. Over 850 programs throughout the United States, Canada, Australia, England and West Africa are members of Crime Stoppers International.

## Mothers Against Drunk Driving (MADD)

Mothers Against Drunk Driving (MADD) is a non-profit, grassroots organization with over 400 chapters nationwide. Its membership is open to anyone: victims, concerned citizens, law enforcement, safety workers and health professionals. As noted in their literature: "The mission of Mothers Against Drunk Driving is to stop drunk driving and to support victims of this violent crime."

MADD was founded in California in 1980 after Candy Lightner's thirteen-year-old daughter was killed by a hit-and-run driver. The driver had been out of jail on bail for only two days for another hit-and-run drunk driving crash. He had three previous drunk driving arrests and two convictions. But he was

*At a vigil sponsored by Mothers Against Drunk Driving, as a mother tells of her daughter who was killed by a drunk driver, her husband raises a picture of their daughter.*

allowed to plea-bargain to vehicular manslaughter. His two-year prison sentence was spent not in prison, but in a work camp and later a halfway house.

MADD differentiates between accidents and crashes:

> Those injured and killed in drunk driving collisions are not "accident victims." The crash caused by an impaired driver is a violent crime. Drunk driving involves two choices: to drink AND to drive. The thousands of deaths and injuries caused each year by impaired driving can be prevented . . . they are not "accidental."

MADD seeks to raise public awareness through community programs such as Operation Prom/Graduation, their Poster/Essay Contest, their "Tie One on for Safety" Project Red Ribbon campaign and a Designated Driver program. Their national newsletter, *MADD In Action,* is sent to members and supporters. MADD also promotes legislation to strengthen existing laws and adopt new ones. In addition, MADD provides victim services. Victims and their families may call 800-GET-MADD for emotional support and guidance through the criminal justice system. Annual candle-light vigils are held nationwide to allow victims to share their grief with others who have suffered due to drunk driving.

A current goal of MADD is to reduce by 20 percent alcohol-related traffic fatalities by the year 2000. To accomplish this goal, they are implementing measures in five major areas: youth issues, enforcement strategies, stronger sanctions, responsible marketing and service and self-sufficiency (funding for enforcement through DWI fines, fees and other assessments).

## PROGRAMS AIMED AT PREVENTING AUTO THEFT

Many police departments furnish citizens with information on how to prevent auto theft. Information may be provided in the form of pamphlets, newspaper stories, PSAs on television or speeches made to civic organizations. Such programs usually include tips such as the following from Honolulu's brochure:

- Never leave your keys in the ignition, not even at home or in a parking lot. It is an open invitation to theft.

- Hiding spare keys under the carpeting or over a sun visor is about as clever as leaving a house key under a doormat. Thieves know all the obvious places to look.

- Do not leave luggage, packages or other easily removed items in view inside your automobile. Lock your property in the trunk. Doctors should always conceal their bags while away from their vehicles.

- Automobile thieves frequent streets and parking areas in the vicinities of public gatherings. Do not take needless risks by leaving valuables in your car when it is not necessary to be transporting them.

- Avoid transferring items to the trunk of a vehicle at a location where it is to be parked. A thief may be watching. Checkbooks, credit cards or other credentials which a thief could use should not be left in the car.

- At night, park in a lighted area, preferably close to a corner where a potential thief may realize that he is more likely to be observed. (Thefts of automobile accessories have increased greatly since the introduction of bucket seats, car stereos and special wheels. These items, as well as hubcaps and other parts, should be marked as an aid to identification. Thousands of dollars worth of automobile parts are sold at auction every year by the police department because the rightful owners could not be located.)

- If your car is broken into or stolen, inform the police of the loss immediately. Stolen vehicles frequently are used in committing other crimes.

◆

The two main messages of anti-car theft programs are:

- Do not leave the keys in the car ignition.
- Lock the car.

◆

These messages are conveyed in a variety of ways from stickers to put on dashboards to posters warning that leaving keys in the ignition is a violation of the law if the car is parked on public property. In addition, leaving one's keys in the ignition is an invitation to theft, could become a contributing cause to some innocent person's injury or death and could raise the owner's insurance rates.

## The CAT Program

New York City has developed an anti-auto theft program that enlists the aid of motorists.

◆

The Combat Auto Theft (**CAT**) program allows the police to stop any car marked with a special decal between 1 A.M. and 5 A.M.

◆

The program is more a crime prevention program than a law enforcement strategy. Hildreth (1990, p. 92) describes the following key elements of the program:

- Participation is strictly voluntary. Car owners sign a consent form affirming that they do not normally drive between 1 A.M. and 5 A.M., the peak auto theft hours.

- Car owners are given a tamper-proof CAT Program decal to be affixed prominently on the inside of the car's rear window.

Those who participate in the program waive their rights against search and seizure protection. According to Hildreth (p. 93), New York's three-year-old CAT Program has registered 37,326 cars, of which only sixty-seven have been stolen. Further, says Hildreth: "New York City authorities have estimated that cars not enrolled in the CAT Program are 48 times more likely to be stolen than those that are protected by the program."

## PROGRAMS TO DETER PROSTITUTION

The Des Moines Police Department encourages citizens to send "Dear John" letters to registered owners of vehicles involved in prostitution. Citizens are told they can obtain the owner's name, address, make, year and color of the vehicle by taking the license number to the Iowa Department of Transportation. The information is free. Citizens are also given a sample letter they can send to the registered owner, like that which appears in Figure 17.1. Citizens are also instructed to send copies of the letter to the county attorney and to the vice squad.

## COLLABORATIVE EFFORTS TO COMBAT THE DRUG PROBLEM

In 1993, the U.S. illegal drug tab exceeded $47 billion. Americans spent:

$31 billion for cocaine

$7 billion for heroin

$9 billion for marijuana

New York Rep. Charles Rangel, a member of the House Committee on Narcotics Abuse, believes the figures are too low. He estimates that the figure is closer to $100 billion a year.

Communities have instituted many grassroots efforts to combat drug dealing. In Des Moines, for example, the police have provided citizens with a list of suspicious activities and common indicators of residential drug trafficking, illustrated in Figure 17.2. Police ask that citizens who suspect drug trafficking is occurring in their neighborhoods contact the vice/narcotics control unit.

In Minneapolis, Minnesota, police and property owners are using black and gold "No trespassing" signs in inner-city neighborhoods. "The distinctive signs," according to Gendler (1991, p. B1), "mark a new program intended to improve residents' security and deter street-level drug dealing by telling officers that they can enter the properties to question loiterers without a call from the property

Date: _____

_____

_____

_____

_____

Mr. and/or Mrs. _____ :

Your _____ was seen picking up a
                    (DESCRIPTION OF VEHICLE)

prostitute in the vicinity of _____ in
                                          (AREA)

Des Moines on _____ , at approximately_____ .
                      (DATE)                                    (TIME)

We hope you realize that by participating in such behavior you risk
criminal prosecution, as well as exposing yourself — and possibly your
family — to public humiliation and a host of diseases including the deadly
AIDS virus.

Prostitution is unacceptable and it will not be tolerated anymore in our
neighborhood.  A detailed description of your vehicle, complete with the
license number, has been circulated to area residents.

Sincerely,

North Side Neighbors

cc:  James Smith
      Polk County Attorney

      Vice Squad
      Des Moines Police Department

*Figure 17.1*     **Sample "Dear John" Letter**

SOURCE: Des Moines Police. *Drugs: A Municipal Approach, A Community Handbook:* 15.
Reprinted by permission.

1. A high volume of foot and/or vehicle traffic to and from a residence at late or unusual hours.
2. Periodic visitors who stay at the residence for very brief periods of time.
3. Alterations of property by the tenants, including the following:
   a. Covering windows and patio doors with materials other than curtains or drapes;
   b. Barricading windows or doors;
   c. Placing dead bolt locks on interior doors; and
   d. Disconnecting fire alarms.
4. Consistent payment of rent and security deposits with U.S. currency, especially small denominations of cash. (Large amounts of 20 dollar bills are commonly seized from drug dealers.)
5. The presence of drug paraphernalia in or around the residence, including, but not limited to, glass pipes, syringes, propane torches, paper or tinfoil bundles, folded shiny-slick paper (snow seals), large quantities of plastic baggies, scales, money wrappers and small glass vials.
6. The presence of unusual odors coming from the interior of the residence, especially the odor of pungent chemical substances and/or burning materials.
7. The presence of firearms, other than sporting firearms, including fully automatic weapons, assault weapons, sawed off shotguns, machine pistols, handguns and related ammunition and holsters.
8. The presence of tenant's possessions and furnishings which are inconsistent with the known income level of the tenant. This would include, but is not limited to, the following:
   a. New and/or expensive vehicles;
   b. Expensive jewelry and clothing; and
   c. Expensive household furnishings, stereo systems and other large entertainment systems.
9. Tenants who are overly nervous and apprehensive about the landlord visiting the residence.

Any of the indicators, by itself, may not be reason to suspect drug trafficking. However, when combined with other indicators, they may be reason to suspect drug trafficking. If you suspect drug trafficking in your neighborhood, please contact the police department at 555–5555.

*Figure 17.2* **Suspicious Activity and Common Indicators of Residential Drug Trafficking**
SOURCE: Des Moines Police. *Drugs: A Municipal Approach, A Community Handbook:* 26. Reprinted by permission.

*Children from an east side Detroit neighborhood march against crack houses in their neighborhood.*

owner." This expands the power of the police greatly and removes from landlords the sometimes threatening responsibility of signing a citizen's arrest form before the police can act.

In another area of the city, a group called HOPE (Homes on Portland Enterprise) marched near known crack houses, carrying signs and demanding that the dealers leave the neighborhood. As noted by Grow (1992, p. A1): "Living in a crack neighborhood means living in fear of both the bad guys (those involved in drugs) and the good guys (police). It means telling your child she can't play in the little park next door. It means friends won't come to visit. It means carrying a knife while waiting for the bus."

In March 1992, a group of women decided to take their neighborhood back from the drug dealers. They painted signs and marched near the crack houses. Grow states (p. A1): "They make an unusual group of drug warriors, these women marching with their kids. They've got no money, no political clout. They're scared to death. But they're determined to make their dreams come alive again. They're determined to live in a safe neighborhood." The march received much media attention and appears to have been successful.

The city of St. Paul also enlisted the aid of residents to force an alliance to fight drug dealers. The program, called FORCE (Focusing Our Resources on Community Empowerment), centered on getting longtime residents to permit narcotics officers to use their homes to monitor drug sales in the neighborhood. According to Lonetree (1992, p. B5):

> The FORCE team would work with a network of block club leaders to target drug dealers and to force the removal of, or improvements to ramshackle drug houses. Ramsey County would provide child protection services for youths found in drug houses. The Institute on Black Chemical Abuse also would advocate treatment programs for drug-addicted people who are caught selling or buying drugs.

Another grassroots effort has taken place in Price, Utah, a community with 10,000 people. The family services, school district, police and mental health professionals have established a volunteer interagency committee known as SODAA (Stop Our Drug & Alcohol Abuse). This committee coordinates prevention and education programs and strives to eliminate duplication of efforts.

The committee developed and promoted a Substance Abuse Awareness Sabbath. They developed a five-page informational factsheet and identified all churches in the community. They then distributed the factsheets through the forty-four churches which represented nineteen denominations. As noted by Shilaos (1990, p. 43), each church was asked to:

- Duplicate and distribute a copy of the handout to every adult member.
- Devote part of their Sabbath to substance abuse awareness.

The local newspaper also dedicated an entire page to the campaign. Every church that participated in the Substance Abuse Awareness Sabbath received recognition in the article.

Another very successful crime prevention program was developed in Wilson, North Carolina. Their program, "Operation Broken Window," was rooted in the broken window philosophy discussed earlier. The 500 block in Wilson was their "broken window," an open-air drug market widely known as a place where drugs could be easily bought. Undercover police operations had been unsuccessful in reducing the problem. The Wilson Police Department turned to problem-oriented policing as a possible solution. According to Yonce (1992, p. 67), in the planning process, "the department used all of the available resources of the city, including direct input from citizens who worked and lived in the target area."

The department formulated a four-pronged attack: undercover operations, increased uniform police presence with more officers and a satellite police station in the target area, two K-9 units assigned to drug interdiction at the local bus station and attention to social and environmental conditions. Yonce (pp. 68–69) notes: "Social conditions that facilitated the drug sales in the target area were identified. Grass was cut, trash was removed. Street lights were installed, repaired, or replaced. Buildings were inspected for code violations, and the owners were notified to correct the problems. Low lying areas were filled with dirt to prevent water from standing, and abandoned properties frequented by drug users were boarded up and secured."

Operation Broken Window was a success. The drug dealers left, and crime rates went down. An important side benefit also occurred, as Yonce noted (p. 69):

> An important by-product of the operation was a fundamental change in the attitudes of officers within the department concerning the target area. As a result of the long hours that many invested in the area, their attitude is now one of partnership and ownership, and a resolve not to allow the dealers back in. Additionally, the attitudes of the residents, business people and citizens, improved toward the police as a result of their efforts in this critical area.

> However the yardstick by which we measure the success of this type of operation is how the people in the area feel. In a local newspaper article praising the actions of the city in returning the streets to the people, residents reported that they were able to walk the streets again and sit on their front porches. Four businesses known to be associated with the illegal drug trade closed during the operation—and, importantly, two new legitimate businesses moved into the area.

In another approach dealing with the drug problem, the FBI has reassigned approximately 300 agents formerly assigned to duty in areas within the Communist regimes in Eastern Europe to help in the "war against drugs and gangs." According to an Associated Press release (1992, p. A7), the FBI has some important tools to contribute, including "broader powers to use wiretaps and seize drug dealers' property, an ability to prosecute under federal laws on extortion, racketeering and interstate crime, and longer prison terms for some crimes."

Another effort that has received national attention is the Justice Department's **Weed and Seed** program. This program is a community-based, multiagency approach to fighting drug use, violent crime and gang activity in high crime neighborhoods. The goal is to "weed out" crime and then "seed" the neighborhoods with a variety of crime and drug prevention programs.

The National Crime Prevention Council provides three additional examples of community efforts to combat the drug problem:

### HELPING PARENTS GET DRUG TREATMENT IN OHIO

A congregation was the focus for efforts to reach addicted parents and their children. Tutoring for children, courtesy of the local college, courses on black history taught by church members, and recreational activities helped the spirits and self-esteem of the children rise. The addicted parents were counseled and supported by church members both during and after treatment. The majority of the parents are now holding steady jobs and reaching out to help others.

### ENFORCING LOCAL CODES TO REDUCE DRUGS IN OAKLAND, CALIFORNIA

Residents allied themselves with police, utility workers, housing and other code inspectors, and sanitation crews to help rid the neighborhood of drug activity.

They worked to aggressively enforce a variety of laws and codes against drugs, ranging from noise abatement to building codes to health standards.

## DISCOURAGING DRUG DEALERS IN CLEVELAND, OHIO

A community-based organization helped police remove drug pushers operating on a vacant lot. City officials then pitched in to help the nonprofit group build affordable, owner-occupied homes on the site. Meanwhile, the group used a series of strategies including vigils and rallies to help discourage drug dealers from operating on the neighborhood's main thoroughfare. They also enlisted the support of businesses and residents to tidy up the area and keep it clean.

## Dealing with Drug Problems in Public Housing

Dealing with the drug problem in public housing requires the collaborative efforts of the police, public housing authorities, other agencies and, most importantly, the residents themselves. Initiatives to deal with the problem have been identified by Weisel (1990, pp. 99–112).

◆

Strategies to deal with the drug problem include improving the physical environment, removing offenders, reducing the demand for drugs, improving intelligence and empowering residents.

◆

Although aimed specifically at public housing, with modification the same strategies would also work in many inner-city neighborhoods.

**Improving the Physical Environment.** Improving indoor and exterior lighting has been successfully used in some projects. Clean-up efforts in trash-strewn lots which provide easy hiding places for drugs have also been successful. As noted by Weisel (1990, p. 100): "In many cities, including Chicago, police have worked with housing officials to develop access control for buildings. By limiting entrances and exits to one per building, non-residents can be kept outside." Some housing projects have developed identification cards for their residents so that outsiders can be readily observed.

**Removing Offenders.** Increased efforts at *enforcing laws* against dealing drugs and *increasing prosecution* are also deterrents to drug dealers. Sometimes the housing authority makes an apartment available to the local police department in which to set up an office. This visible police presence can be a strong deterrent. It can also provide residents with a feeling of security as well as concrete evidence that the city is working on the problem.

Some housing agencies, residents and police departments have worked to create drug-free zones (*DFZs*) similar to those used around schools. Patrol efforts

*Students at a Minneapolis high school examine a 1988 high-performance Calloway Corvette valued at $65,000. The police confiscated the car from a drug dealer and converted it into a police car.*

are concentrated in DFZs and being arrested for drug dealing carries increased penalties. Other cities, such as Fort Lauderdale, Tampa and Louisville, have targeted small geographic areas known as *Oases*. As noted by Weisel (p. 102): "The Oasis Program . . . is an approach that includes analyzing slum areas, building a coalition with community groups and police, and developing drug-free oases as an initial step toward a safer community. The oases are intended to have a domino effect over time until the larger community becomes revitalized."

*Asset seizures* of drug dealers is another strategy frequently used by police. Police departments use federal or state forfeiture laws that allow them to seize property and assets of drug dealers, including drugs, cars, boats, airplanes, mobile homes, land and cash—a type of financial death sentence. Asset seizures not only punish the offenders, but also send a strong message to the youth of the community who may be quite impressed with the material possessions that drug dealers flaunt.

According to Martin (1993, p. 46): "Assets seizure is big business. As of early 1993, law enforcement officials had seized more than $2.6 billion worth of houses, cash, cars and assets since 1985. Another $1.5 billion in seized assets are currently 'in process.'"

According to Ison (1991, p. A12): "The Justice Department's goal is twofold. One is to punish drug traffickers and other criminals by hitting them in the pocketbook. The second goal is to pour proceeds from the seized assets back into law enforcement. In effect, the government is using the crooks' own booty to finance the war against other crooks."

Police may also use *lease enforcement.* Beginning in April 1989, the Department of Housing and Urban Development (HUD) has required that leases include an explicit provision permitting eviction if any member of a household engages in drug-related criminal activity.

Finally police have found that, simply *making drug dealing inconvenient* may be an effective deterrent. San Diego police, for example, discovered that drug dealers were using public telephones on certain street corners. The police worked with the telephone company to fix the telephones so that they could be used only for outgoing calls, thereby stopping outsiders from calling in orders for drugs.

**Reducing the Demand.** Another approach to the drug problem is to focus on those who use drugs. Some police departments have used *sting operations* during which undercover police agents sell drugs and then arrest those who buy them. These operations have sometimes been criticized as unethical or even an illegal form of entrapment. Police must exercise extreme care if they use such operations as a strategy to reduce the drug problem.

*Educating users* may be a more fruitful and perhaps more ethical approach to the drug problem. School programs such as DARE seek to help youth resist peer pressure to experiment with drugs. *Providing diversion or alternatives* to finding acceptance or excitement through drug use may also help. Providing community recreational programs, improving ballfields and parks, installing a basketball court or sponsoring athletic contests are all important additions to a community in its fight against drugs.

*Providing treatment and rehabilitation* for drug users is sometimes also an effective strategy. Often residents are not aware of the existence of such treatment facilities. In many communities, however, such facilities do not exist.

**Improving Intelligence.** If police can enlist citizens to provide information about drug dealing to the police, much can be accomplished. Most residents in public housing know where drug deals are made. Many also believe, however, that the police either do not care or are actually corrupt because they arrest few dealers. When dealers are arrested, they are often back on the street within hours. Residents should be educated about the difficulties of prosecuting drug dealers and the need for evidence.

Some departments conduct *community surveys* in low income neighborhoods to learn about how residents view the drug problem. Some departments have established *tip lines* where residents can provide information anonymously.

*Improved reporting* can be accomplished in a number of ways, as described by Weisel (1990, p. 110):

In Philadelphia, police developed a radio bypass of police communication so that beat officers could be telephoned directly by citizens for calls that would have been assigned a low priority by police dispatch.

Police can also improve the information they receive about problems in other ways. Intelligence can be increased by unusual procedures. Police have been known to interview arrestees to obtain inside information on how certain criminal activities are conducted. In other agencies, arrestees have been interviewed in jail with a jail debriefing form. This kind of data is useful as police continue to document the link between drugs and criminal activity.

Housing personnel are often the closest to drug problems in public housing. These housing personnel can be trained to identify drugs or drug dealing behaviors, and cooperate with police in following up on complaints.

Intelligence information can also be improved by facilitating the communication between narcotics investigators and patrol officers. For example, in Atlanta, a narcotics supervisor recognized that patrol and narcotics had historically used a different radio frequency and were unable to communicate. The problem was quickly corrected.

**Empowering Residents.** Many police agencies have focused on the broader needs of residents of low-income housing. In Tulsa, for example, officers believed that limited job opportunities were a problem for youth living in public housing. The officers now steer youths into Job Corps, a training and job service program that is an alternative to the traditional high school. Weisel (p. 98) cautions:

> Police should always remember that the problems in many of these poor neighborhoods have been there for many years and are deeply rooted in poverty and other enduring social problems. There are real limits to what the police can actually accomplish. . . .
>
> Thus, it is important to set modest objectives and take pride in even very small successes in troubled areas. Because drug problems are particularly complex and enduring problems in poor neighborhoods, modest successes are very important. These small successes are instrumental in improving the quality of life for the people who reside in the drug-ravaged areas. If police try to reduce the harms caused by drug dealing in a specific area, great strides can be made in terms of improving the lives of the law-abiding citizens who call the community home.

## COMPREHENSIVE, COORDINATED COMMUNITY APPROACHES

The Des Moines Police Department has a *Community Involvement Handbook,* developed jointly by the police department, the United Way and over thirty-five neighborhood groups. The handbook serves as a resource of information as well as a guide for action. It is intended to help neighborhood groups become active and start making a difference. Called the "municipal approach," the program has four "prongs": community involvement, enforcement, prevention/education and treatment. Portions of the handbook have been translated into Spanish, Vietnamese, Cambodian and Laotian. The handbook covers such topics as:

- When to call the police.
- "Dear John" letters.
- Street lighting and residential security lighting.
- Trash and litter.
- Working with good landlords.
- Working with businesses in your area.
- Boarding up abandoned houses.
- Forming neighborhood associations.
- Neighborhood block walks.
- Red ribbons (symbolizing drug-free environments).
- Cutting down shrubbery.
- Rallies and marches.
- Occupying parks and streets.
- Newsletters.

This practical guide might serve as a model for other police departments that wish to involve the community in not only the fight against drugs but also against crime and violence.

Groups that can benefit from a partnership with law enforcement include home/school organizations such as parent-teacher associations; neighborhood associations; tenants' groups; fraternal, social and veteran's groups; community service clubs (such as Lions, Kiwanis, JayCees, Rotary); religiously affiliated groups; and associations of homeowners, merchants or taxpayers.

Schmitt (1995, pp. 52–56) describes the Resident Officer Program of Elgin, Illinois (ROPE). ROPE officers live and work in a specific neighborhood, dealing only with problems affecting their neighborhood and residents. According to Schmitt (p. 56): "The most important thing an officer can do in their neighborhood, however, seems merely to be a reliable presence in the area."

Whiteside (1997, p. 3) suggests an eight-step process for initiating community action to solve problems of crime, disorder and fear of crime:

1. Information gathering.
2. Community analysis—history, past conflicts, current politics and problems.
3. Relevant group identification—police, citizens, elected civic officials, the business community, other agencies, the media.

4. Identification of leaders.
5. Bring leaders of relevant groups together.
6. Identify areas of agreement and disagreement and discuss them.
7. Implementation.
8. Quality control and continuous development and updating. Requires meaningful feedback from the relevant groups, testing of new ideas, evaluation and individual and group introspection.

The National Crime Prevention Council (*Working as Partners:* 1994, pp. 3–6) recommends the following:

- Acknowledge the reality of fear of crime.
- Agree on a strategy (or strategies) to address the problems.
- Secure broad-based participation.
- Train members of the partnership.
- Secure resources.
- Implement the strategies in a sound environment.
- Evaluate the results.
- Celebrate successes.

The National Crime Prevention Council concludes (p. 6): "Crime prevention that is problem-focused, based in communities and neighborhoods, fueled by the energies of the people who live and work there, helped by outside resources and can be supported by all levels of government is a model that has consistently produced positive results."

Wilson (1995, p. 128) stresses: "Always remember that relationships are built with people, not organizations."

## SUMMARY

Synergism occurs when individuals channel their energies toward a common purpose and accomplish what they could not accomplish alone. Among the most commonly implemented crime prevention programs have been street lighting projects, property marking projects, security survey projects, citizen patrol projects and crime reporting, neighborhood watch or block projects.

The Guardian Angels are private citizen patrols who seek to deter crime and to provide a positive role model for young children. Specialized crime watch programs include mobile crime watch, youth crime watch, business crime watch, Realtor watch and carrier alert.

Model crime prevention programs have been developed by a hospital auxiliary, churches, foundations, businesses and civic groups. Volunteers may serve as reserve officers, auxiliary patrol, community service officers or on an as-needed basis. The four Rs of volunteer management are research, recruitment, retention and recognition.

Among the most visible organizations focused on crime are citizen crime prevention associations, Crime Stoppers and MADD. The two main messages of anti-car theft programs are (1) do not leave the keys in the ignition and (2) lock the car. The Combat Auto Theft program allows the police to stop any car marked with a special decal between 1 A.M. and 5 A.M.

Strategies to deal with the drug problem include improving the physical environment, removing offenders, reducing the demand for drugs, improving intelligence and empowering residents.

## Discussion Questions

1.  What examples of synergy have you been a part of or witnessed?
2.  What crime prevention programs are in your community? Have you participated in any of them?
3.  Which of the programs discussed in this chapter seem most exemplary to you? Why?
4.  Do you have an Operation Identification program in your community? If so, have you participated? If not, why not?
5.  Do you feel the Guardian Angels and similar volunteer citizen patrol groups serve a valuable function?
6.  Do you favor the use of volunteers within the police department? If so, in what capacities?
7.  Does your police department use volunteers? If so, how?
8.  How effective do you think the FBI agents are as they join local efforts to combat the drug and gang problem? What factors are important?
9.  Do you have any "broken windows" in your community? If so, how would you characterize them?
10. What steps might be taken to repair a community's "broken windows" and protect against having them broken again?

## References

Associated Press. "FBI Brings Spy Catching Skills Into War Against Gangs." (Minneapolis/ St. Paul) *Star Tribune.* (January 16, 1992): A7.

Brann, Joseph E. "Programs through Partnerships." *Community Links.* (January 1997, Vol. 1, No. 1): 1.

Clark, Jacob R. "New Look for Military Model: Homeless Vets Patrolling NYC." *Law Enforcement News.* (September 30, 1991): 8–9.

Clede, Bill. "Guardian Angels: Bane or Blessing?" *Law and Order.* (December 1990): 37–39.

Crowe, Timothy D. "The Secure Store: A Clean, Well-Lighted Place." *Security Management.* (March 1992): 22A–24A.

Federal Bureau of Investigation. *Uniform Crime Reports.* Washington: U.S. Department of Justice, September 1975.

Freeman, Ted. "New Jersey Seniors Don't Sit Still for Crime." *Community Policing Exchange.* (November/December 1995): 8.

Gendler, Neal. "Signs Give Extra Power to Police in Inner City." (Minneapolis/St. Paul) *Star Tribune.* (September 28, 1991): B1, B5.

Greenberg, Martin Alan. "Volunteer Police: The People's Choice for Safer Communities." *The Police Chief.* (May 1991): 42–44.

Grow, Doug. "Drug Warriors Try to Take Portland Ave. Back from Crack Dealers." (Minneapolis/St. Paul) *Star Tribune.* (February 17, 1992): A1, A16.

Hildreth, Reed. "The CAT Program." *Law and Order.* (May 1990): 92–93.

Horne, Peter. "Not Just Old Wine in New Bottles." *The Police Chief.* (May 1991): 24–29.

Ison, Chris. "Tables Turned: U.S. Government Uses Criminals' Assets to Finance War Against Drugs." (Minneapolis/St. Paul) *Star Tribune.* (July 29, 1991): A1, A12.

Leavy, James G. "Community Resources: Volunteers and Special Officers." *Law and Order.* (February 1992): 69.

Lonetree, Anthony. "St. Paul Police, Residents Forge Alliance to Fight Drug Dealers." (Minneapolis/St. Paul) *Star Tribune.* (July 16, 1992): B5.

Martin, Deirdre. "Assets Seizure: Poetic Justice or Taking Justice Into One's Own Hands?" *Law Enforcement Technology.* (October 1993): 46–50.

McLean, Herbert E. "Watching Out for Honolulu." *Law and Order.* (June 1991): 58–62.

Pace, Denny F. *Community Relations Concepts.* Incline Village, Nev.: Copperhouse Publishing Company, 1991.

Schmitt, Sheila. "ROPE: The Resident Officer Program of Elgin." *Law and Order.* (May 1995): 52–58.

Shilaos, Aleck K. "Substance Abuse Awareness Sabbath." *Law and Order.* (December 1990): 43.

Sulton, Anne Thomas. *Inner-City Crime Control: Can Community Institutions Contribute?* Washington: The Police Foundation, 1990.

Tempe Community Relations Office. "No Mere Paper-Pushers, Tempe Police Volunteers Are Making a Difference." *Law Enforcement News.* (November 30, 1991): 9, 15.

Weinblatt, Richard B. "The Birth of a Volunteer Officer Program." *Law and Order.* (December 1991): 19–20.

Weisel, Deborah Lamm. *Tackling Drug Problems in Public Housing: A Guide for Police.* Washington: Police Executive Research Forum, 1990.

Whiteside, William B. "Initiating Action." *Community Links.* (January 1997): 4.

Wilson, Laurie J. "Placing Community-Oriented Policing in the Broader Realm of Community Cooperation." *The Police Chief.* (April 1995): 127–28.

*Working as Partners with Community Groups.* Washington: BJA Community Partnerships Bulletin, September 1994.

Yonce, Thomas C. " 'Broken Window' Stops Drug Sales." *Law and Order.* (April 1992): 67–70.

### Resources

Many organizations offer expertise in building partnerships and provide a variety of publications, training and services that can strengthen local efforts. A sampling follows.*

Bureau of Justice Assistance Clearinghouse, Box 6000, Rockville, MD 20850; (800) 688-4252.

Center for Community Change, 1000 Wisconsin Ave. NW, Washington, DC 20007; (202) 342-0519.

## BJA has a range of publications related to law enforcement-community partnerships, including:

- ***Problem-Oriented Drug Enforcement: A Community-Based Approach for Effective Policing, NCJ 143710.***

- ***The Systems Approach to Crime and Drug Prevention: A Path to Community Policing, NCJ 143712.***

- ***Understanding Community Policing: A Framework for Action, NCJ 148457***

- ***Neighborhood-Oriented Policing in Rural Communities: A Planning Guide, NCJ 143709.***

- ***A Police Guide to Surveying Citizens and Their Environment, NCJ 143711.***

- ***National Service and Public Safety: Partnerships for Safer Communities, NCJ 146842.***

- ***Partnerships to Prevent Youth Violence, NCJ 148459.***

- ***An Introduction to DARE: Drug Abuse Resistance Education, NCJ 129862.***

- ***An Introduction to the National DARE Parent Program, NCJ 142422.***

### Call the BJA Clearinghouse at 800–688–4252 to order these publications.

*Every interested organization has a web page on the Internet, including several federal agencies. A search using the words *community policing* or *crime prevention* will yield a tremendous amount of current information.

Citizens Committee for New York City, 305 7th Ave., 15th Floor, New York, NY 10001; (212) 989-0909.

Community Policing Consortium, 1726 M St. NW, Suite 801, Washington, DC 20006; (202) 833-3305 or (800) 833-3085.

National Center for Community Policing, School of Criminal Justice, Michigan State University, East Lansing, MI 48824; (517) 355-2322.

National Crime Prevention Council, 1700 K St. NW, 2d Floor, Washington, DC 20006-3817; (202) 466-6272.

National Training and Information Center, 810 North Milwaukee Ave., Chicago, IL 60622-4103; (312) 243-3035.

Police Executive Research Forum, 2300 M St. NW, Suite 910, Washington, DC 20006; (202) 466-7820.

# *Epilog*

As noted throughout this text, the role of the police is changing and will continue to do so. Tyre (1995, p. 108) reviews recent changes within the criminal justice system:

> As we move into the mid-1990s, we continue to see the criminal justice system evolve. We are still learning lessons from the private sector, still trying to clarify our role in our communities and still trying to figure out how to make the most of our limited resources.
>
> We have gone from just putting people in jail to attempting to identify problems and develop solutions. We have gone from employing marginally qualified law enforcement officers to recruiting highly trained personnel who see law enforcement as just one of their many roles. We have evolved in our philosophies from encumbrance to empowerment. We have experienced a change in the police culture from a closed, top-down organization steeped in bureaucracy to one open to the community and to the employees who are really doing the job.

Another view of the evolving role of law enforcement is presented by Sharp (1995, p. 68):

> Hollywood has portrayed the 21st-century cop as a cross between a human and a robot with a penchant for violence to resolve societal problems. Law enforcement administrators, on the other hand, envision a highly-trained, more sensitive police officer who will rely on psychology and logic to settle disputes and reduce crime.

The paradigm shift that is occurring in many departments across the country also requires significant change. As noted by Berg (1996, p. 148): "Changing the policing paradigm requires more than laudable goals and good intentions. It requires a major shift in the thinking and attitudes of line officers, substantial support from other city departments and the active participation of a significant percentage of every neighborhood's residents. Achieving all three tasks takes money as well as skilled planning and implementation and, perhaps most important, it takes considerable time."

Horne (1991, p. 29) summarizes the change taking place in police departments across the country: "The greatest potential for improved crime control may not be in the continued enhancement of response times, patrol tactics and investigative techniques. Rather, improved crime control can be achieved by (1) diagnosing and managing problems in the community that produce serious crimes; (2) fostering close relations with the community to facilitate crime solving; and (3) building self-defense capabilities within the community itself." He concludes: "Crime prevention in conjunction with community policing can help diminish crime and enhance security in the neighborhoods of our nation."

# FUTURE OF COMMUNITY POLICING

In the future, community policing principles will be transferred to most local government operations. As police departments transition from traditional service delivery to a community orientation, cities and counties will gain a glimpse of forthcoming changes that will occur in other departments. Two major factors underlie this transition:

- Subtle, yet powerful, macro-trends have shifted the way we live and interact, causing a fundamental shift in public needs and expectations.
- Changes in police service delivery are affecting how other governmental agencies interact with their communities.

# MEGA-TRENDS

Traditionally, the driving forces of change in police work have been legislative and judicial mandates. Though no Miranda-like decisions are coercing change today, a fundamental shift in the way officers do their jobs is taking place in departments across our country. Why is this happening? Profound changes in our world have occurred and are forcing police departments to adapt. These changes are forever shifting the way American institutions respond to the external environment. Those most profound trends are:

- **Public expectations.** We have more educated Americans than at any time in our history. As a result, they know how governmental systems work and that the "squeaky wheel gets the grease." Consequently, there is an ever-increasing demand by Americans to have a say in the way all levels of government operate.
- **Worker expectations.** Pyramidal-shaped organizations cannot rely on traditional order-giving tactics to enhance worker productivity and effectiveness. In public and private sectors, today's workers are demanding to have a say in the decisions that will affect them.
- **Technology.** Technological advances give line personnel an array of information previously unavailable to line workers. Consequently, they are capable of making some work decisions once restricted to supervisors and managers. Hence, technological advances have increased the importance of line workers.
- **Strategic alliances/partnerships.** From NAFTA to the Saturn automobile, government and private industry are increasingly reliant on developing synergies created by strategic partnerships. Likewise, the partnership

component of community policing is emulating this trend which is occurring on a much broader scale.

- **Commitment to the value of diversity.** The most effective partnerships will be those that capitalize on the diversity within the community and within the police department.

The role of diversity in community policing and the importance of the two core components of community policing—community partnerships and problem solving—are described in the following sections by Commander Michael J. Nila, Aurora (Illinois) Police Department.

## DIVERSITY—AN INTEGRAL PART OF COMMUNITY POLICING

by Michael J. Nila

As policing in America changes from "traditional" to "community policing," the critical challenge is to change the relationship between the police and the community. Namely, communities at risk—our poor, our youth, our elderly and our minority communities. The "us v. them" mentality which exists between the police and the community often prevents officers from willingly engaging citizens in the neighborhoods we spend the greatest amount of our time policing.

In any typical urban setting, the police very often have an adversarial relationship with citizens whose background, culture, economic condition and race is very different from their own. Too often, the police see citizens in at-risk neighborhoods as "the enemy" while the community views the police as an "invading army." Rarely, until the community policing movement took root, did the police proactively and sincerely cultivate positive relationships and truly commit to resolving problems in at-risk neighborhoods.

Progressive police agencies today recognize that embracing a community policing philosophy means making a commitment to improving police/community relationships and changing the police culture, often the greatest barrier to true police-community partnerships. The growing commitment to diversity is exemplified by the increasing number of police agencies who include "diversity" in their official organizational values such as in Aurora, Illinois:

> We value diversity, and commit to nurturing a welcoming environment of inclusion, in which we recognize the unique skills, knowledge, abilities and backgrounds of all people as our strength.

*Diversity* is a term often misunderstood by police officers who consider diversity initiatives intrusive, unnecessary, often accusatory and an opportunity for "finger pointing." Through aggressive diversity discussions and training, coupled with a strong diversity/harassment policy, and most importantly, a commitment from top management to a "managing diversity" concept—police departments are changing the internal culture and their external relationships.

In the past, inclusion of diversity in the workforce reflected legal requirements, moral imperatives or social responsibility. Today, community policing makes managing diversity critical to success and, simply, is good management!

*Workforce 2000,* a report by the Hudson Institute, projected that between 1985 and 2000, minorities, women and immigrants would comprise 85 percent of the net growth in the workforce (William B. Johnston and Arnold H. Paker, *Workforce 2000: Work and Workers for the 21st Century.* Indianapolis: Hudson Institute, 1987). As is clearly evident, today all organizations are in the throes of the explosion of a diverse workforce; and it is the police in any community who have the most contacts with a wider range of diverse people than any other profession.

"Managing diversity" is a management philosophy developed by Dr. Roosevelt Thomas who established the American Institute for Managing Diversity at Moorehouse College in Atlanta, Georgia. Recognizing that the changing face of America, driven by rapidly growing minority and immigrant populations, would lead to increasingly diverse organizations, Dr. Thomas moved beyond affirmative action and quota systems. He developed a philosophy of diversity that focuses not only on understanding and respecting differences, but goes further by creating an environment where *all people* can contribute to their maximum potential. As described by one diversity student, "Managing diversity is about getting 100 percent out of 100 percent of our people."

All organizations must realize that diversity does not stop at ethnicity and gender. Instead, diversity must include developing understanding, acceptance and respect of all differences including lifestyle, sexual preference, geographic origin, style of dress, hobbies, habits, interests, physical differences, etc. Diversity is about developing an environment of inclusion where those who are different from the mainstream are made valuable contributors to any organization's success.

While managing diversity is critical to organizational success and maximizing productivity, the concept holds true for communities as well. Only when the police and the community both understand and respect each other can true collaboration take place. Maximizing any community's "human capital" requires everyone's involvement and commitment.

Changing the police culture, changing the police perception of the community and the community's feelings toward the police is a difficult, challenging undertaking. If the culture does not support the desired behavior change, the culture must be addressed. While difficult, this can be achieved if the commitment is made.

One success story in diversity initiatives is the Reno (Nevada) Police Department which began community policing in 1987 under Chief of Police Robert

Bradshaw. Chief Bradshaw boldly reorganized the department under a community policing philosophy. He also recognized that community policing and cultural diversity could not be separated. With equal emphasis, Bradshaw directed massive community policing and cultural diversity training for all personnel. The result—in Reno today, police officers view diversity as a way of life that's critical to community policing as exemplified by one Reno sergeant who stated: "The driving motivation to diversity is community policing—developing all community resources as partnerships through understanding."

While focusing on the internal culture is important to changing police officers' behaviors, so too is developing proactive initiatives that change citizen's perceptions of the police and one another. In Aurora, Illinois, community policing officers have developed a number of outreach strategies to overcome barriers with the minority community such as:

- A Spanish Citizens Police Academy that targets Hispanic community members and teaches police topics while providing information that facilitates community involvement and assimilation.
- Diversity training conducted for citizen groups that patrol and take proactive steps to address crime and disorder problems in the neighborhoods. This prevents the tendency to "pick on" the minority element in the community simply because they are the neighborhood "newcomers."
- Police-sponsored neighborhood festivals and community events which bring minority neighborhoods together with mainstream neighborhoods in celebrating the community's diversity.

Effectively managing diversity programs that work to change the culture and behaviors of all those within the organization must include the following components:

- An internal audit to assess organizational health as related to diversity issues such as employee relations, perceptions of employees to minorities, inappropriate jokes and cartoons, etc.
- A strict harassment/diversity policy which is adhered to.
- Non-confrontational introductory training (4–8 hours) which should be a soft sell to diversity, emphasizing the need for agency-wide commitment.
- Advanced training (ongoing training in four-hour blocks) that addresses specific racial issues in the community, historical issues, gay/lesbian issues and sexual harassment concerns.
- Specialized needs training which focuses on the needs of specialized units such as Field Training Officers, Gang Officers, Community Policing and Recruiting. Each of these specialized areas has a unique role to fill that heavily impacts on minority relations and internal cultural issues.

- Establishing an organizational commitment to diversity through developing a core set of organizational values that reflect a diversity commitment (see example in Appendix C) and living that commitment through every decision and action.

Organizational change begins with a vision articulated throughout the organization and which, over time, begins to change an organization's very heart, soul and culture. In developing a foundation for organizational success and a vision for the next century, progressive police leaders will include effective diversity programs that target internal behaviors and attitudes and external relationships with all segments of the community. The key to community policing lies in the strength of our diversity commitment and our ability to successfully engage our communities.

## COMMUNITY POLICING AND COMMUNITY ENGAGEMENT*

By Michael J. Nila

The two core components of community policing are community partnerships and problem solving. A community policing philosophy demands that the police develop partnerships with all components of our communities to facilitate community problem solving. Police officers do not generally resist problem solving—however, it is difficult to overcome the unwillingness of officers to engage the community. Community partnerships demand that the police actively engage the community if problem-solving efforts are to be effective.

If we were to analyze why community engagement is difficult, we would focus on barriers which prevent police/community partnerships. These barriers include:

1. The police culture is one that promotes an "us v. them" mentality which by its very nature inhibits building trust and positive relationships with our citizens.

2. The police have accepted the responsibility for crime in our communities and have become the crime "experts" and openly resist efforts by the citizens to assist with the crime issues.

3. The police rarely make any efforts to understand the very people with which we spend the majority of our time policing. The profile of the average police officer is very different than the profile of the citizens

*Presented at the 1995 IACP Conference by Commander Michael J. Nila, Aurora (Illinois) Police Department.

who make up the neighborhoods demanding continuous police ser-vices. The two profiles illustrate a clash of cultures, values, expectations and accepted behaviors which result in an unwillingness and inability to partner with our citizens. It is human nature to resist what we are unfamiliar with: the unknown makes us uncomfortable, and what makes us uncomfortable we tend to avoid.

4. Our citizens often perceive the police negatively, and the police have an equally negative perception of the citizens whose problems we are ask-ing them to solve through partnerships.

5. Community organizations and mobilization attempts by the police often lead to frustration due to citizens' apparent unwillingness to get involved and to work with the police. Police view the reluctance to "get involved" as apathy and quickly lose interest. The common refrain becomes, "If they don't care, why should we?" Police officers must have patience and be persistent during the building of trust and confidence in our citizens.

6. Police often fail to realize how much the police need the community, and the community has a narrow view of the police role in their communities.

7. The reality of policing is that the police cannot resolve crime and com-munity issues alone. The police simply do not have enough presence, resources or skills to address the challenges our communities are facing today. Partnering with the community and enhancing citizen involve-ment ultimately increases our numbers, resources and skills, making policing safer and easier.

We often hear police chiefs state that the police are "empowering the com-munity," when in fact, it is the reverse. Sir Robert Peel, in his Nine Principles of Modern Policing, addresses that fact stating that the police receive their author-ity from the public; and he succinctly addresses the partnership issue with this principle:

> To maintain at all times a relationship with the public that gives reality to the historic tradition that the police are the public and the public are the police; the police being the only members of the public that are paid to give full time attention to the duties which are incumbent on every citizen in the interest of the community welfare and existence.

Most of Peel's Principles of Modern Policing actually address the importance of community support and participation if the police are to be effective.

Community engagement means that the police must begin:

- Talking to, listening to and collaborating with citizens;
- Valuing sharing information with citizens;

- Valuing all people and all groups in the community;
- Replacing an "us v. them" mentality with "we";
- Replacing "we do it for" with "we do it together";
- Reorganizing policing as a service, and citizens and the community as our customers;
- Allowing the community to identify problems and solutions;
- Bringing the community into the department to help define mission, vision, values and priorities; and
- Developing and working with civilian advisory councils.

When we think of "community," we must think of all the community stakeholders and the many communities and neighborhoods within the larger community. Community policing has a strong neighborhood focus where beat officers work to instill a strong sense of shared "community" and responsibility for one another. It means providing customized policing services to all neighborhoods.

The goal is to recapture a sense of "community" which appears to be lost in today's communities. Neighborhoods are no longer caretakers for their fellow neighbors. In fact, we are becoming a "nation of strangers" where neighbors don't know or interact with neighbors and the community as a whole.

If we are to regain a sense of "community," then we must instill a sense of "community" in our neighborhoods—we accomplish this by developing a sense that citizens can affect what is occurring in their lives and neighborhoods.

The community partnership process involves the police, government and the community collaborating, not when a problem arises, but as a way of conducting daily business. In community policing communities, the collaboration is continuous, ongoing and leads to constant communication and an environment of trust. The greater the extent of collaboration, the more effective partnerships will become. The goal of community policing is to enlarge the area of community collaboration. If community collaboration is to be successful, the following conditions must exist:

1. A common need, purpose and/or vision;
2. Recognized leadership to guide the process;
3. A perception that personal involvement can make a difference; and
4. Information available about how to realistically change the existing conditions.

Citizens in community policing communities are more likely to willingly, enthusiastically support the police and engage in active partnerships activities such as:

- Participate in Neighborhood Watch Groups;
- Participate in Business Watch Groups;

- Attend Citizen Police Academies;
- Serve in citizen patrols coordinated by the police;
- Serve on citizen advisory councils at the neighborhood and community-wide level;
- Work with the police to identify and resolve community or neighborhood problems;
- Help to develop policing philosophies and strategies including mission, vision, values and priorities; and
- Organize and work with teen and youth organizations.

For community policing to be successful, the police must overcome barriers to partnerships. We must work to actively engage all aspects of our communities and aggressively pursue a sense of "community" in our neighborhoods. Only by policing "with" the community can we effectively solve community problems.

## COMMUNITY POLICING TRAINING TO REACH ALL FIFTY STATES

May, 1997, the Department of Justice announced that thirty-five sites in twenty-nine states will be provided more than $33 million to develop community policing institutes for law enforcement agencies across the nation. According to Acting Associate Attorney General John Dwyer: "Community policing and the administration's 100,000 COPS program have been widely credited with the recent decline in crime nationally. These Regional Community Policing Institutes will take community policing in America to a new level by providing training in speciality areas, such as problem-solving, community-based partnerships, technology, and community policing in rural, urban and suburban settings. . . . These Regional Institutes will be the vanguard for not only perpetuating community policing, but in developing it to meet the law enforcement needs of the new millennium." (U.S. Dept. of Justice Press Release, May 30, 1997.)

### References

Berg, Gregory R. "Promises vs. Reality in Community Policing." *Law and Order.* (September 1996): 147–48.

Horne, Peter. "Not Just Old Wine in New Bottles." *The Police Chief.* (May 1991): 24–29.

Sharp, Arthur G. "The 21st Century Cop: Administrators Predict Law Enforcement's Evolving Role in the Future." *Law and Order.* (February 1995): 68–75.

Tyre, Mitchell L. "Criminal Justice Crossroads." *The Police Chief.* (October 1995): 108–14.

# Appendix A

## Solution to the Nine-Dot Exercise

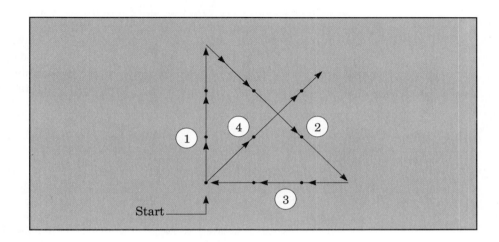

# Police-Media Relations

## Model Policy

| Effective Date<br>October 31, 1991 | | Number |
|---|---|---|
| Subject<br>Police-Media Relations | | |
| Reference | | Special Instructions |
| Distribution | Reevaluation Date<br>November 1, 1992 | No. Pages<br>3 |

I. PURPOSE

It is the purpose of this policy to establish guidelines for release and dissemination of public information to print and broadcast news media.

II. POLICY

It is the policy of this law enforcement agency to cooperate fully and impartially with authorized news media representatives in their efforts to gather factual, public information pertaining to activities of the department, as long as these activities do not unduly interfere with departmental operation, infringe upon individual rights or violate the law.

III. DEFINITIONS

A. *Public Information:* Information that may be of interest to the general public regarding policy, procedures or events involving the department or other newsworthy information that is not legally protected, does not unduly interfere with the mission of the department, infringe upon the rights of a defendant or compromise the legitimate safety and privacy interests of officers, victims, witnesses or others.

B. *News Media Representatives:* Those individuals who are directly employed by agencies of the electronic or print media such as radio, television, and newspapers. Freelance workers in this field are to be regarded as other members of the general public unless otherwise designated by the departmental chief executive.

C. *Public Information Officer (PIO):* The department's PIO serves as a central source of information for release by the department and responds to requests for information by the news media and the community.

IV. PROCEDURES

A. Duties of the PIO

The department's PIO is available to

1. assist news personnel in covering routine news stories, and at the scenes of incidents;
2. assist the news media on an on-call basis;
3. prepare and distribute news releases;
4. arrange for, and assist at, news conferences;
5. coordinate and authorize the release of information about victims, witnesses and suspects;

582

6. assist in crisis situations within the agency; and

7. coordinate the release of authorized information concerning confidential agency investigations and operations.

B. Cooperation with the Media

1. Authorized news media representatives shall have reasonable access to the PIO, the agency's chief executive or his designee and operations of the department as governed by this policy. When information must be denied to a media representative, the basis for that denial shall be fully and courteously explained.

2. This department recognizes authorized identification from all local, national and international news organizations. Failure of media personnel to present authorized identification may provide grounds for restricting access to requested information or to incident scenes.

3. Public information shall be released to the media as promptly as circumstances allow, without partiality and in as objective a manner as possible.

4. Public information may be provided to media representatives by telephone if the identity of the representative is known or can be authenticated.

5. Ranking officers at crime or incident scenes may release information of a factual nature to the media as governed by this policy or refer the inquiry to the PIO. Where the officer is unsure of the facts or the propriety of releasing information, he shall refer the inquiry to the PIO.

6. Written press statements shall be released only following approval of the department's chief executive or his designee.

7. The department's communications center shall inform the watch commander as soon as possible upon receipt of information about events or activities that may have media interest.

8. The watch commander shall be responsible for ensuring that the agency's PIO or chief executive is informed of events that may have media interest.

C. Investigative Information

From the initial stage of a criminal investigation until the completion of trial or disposition without trial, police personnel shall refer all requests for information to the department chief executive or his designee.

1. Information that may be released in connection with an investigation of an event or crime includes

a. the type or nature of an event or crime;

b. the location, date and time, injuries sustained, damages and a general description of how the incident occurred;

c. type and quantity of property taken;

d. the identity and approximate address of a victim with the exception of sex crime victims, and in other cases where reprisals or intimidation may be employed;

e. requests for aid in locating evidence, a complainant or a suspect;

f. numbers of officers or people involved in an event or investigation, and the length of the investigation; and

g. name of the officer in charge of a case, his supervisor and division or unit assignment (exception: the name of any undercover officer will not be released).

2. Information that *may not be released* in connection with an investigation of an event or crime, unless authorized by the department chief executive or his designee, include

a. the identity of a suspect prior to arrest unless such information would aid in apprehending the suspect or serve to warn the public of potential danger;

b. the identity of any victim of a sex crime or any related information which, if divulged, could lead to the victim's identity;

c. the identity of victims or witnesses if such disclosure would prejudice an investigation to any significant degree, or if it would place the victim in personal danger;

d. the identity of any juvenile who is a suspect or defendant in a case subject to the jurisdiction of the juvenile court;

e. the identity of any critically injured or deceased person prior to notification of next of kin;

f. the results of any investigative procedure such as lineups, polygraph tests, fingerprint comparison, ballistics test or other procedures (the fact that these tests have been performed may be revealed without further comment);

g. information which, if prematurely released, may interfere with the investigation or apprehension such as the nature of leads, specifics of an "MO," details of the crime known only to the perpetrator and the police, or information that may cause the suspect to flee or more effectively avoid apprehension;

h. information that may be of evidentiary value in criminal proceedings;

i. specific cause of death unless officially determined by the medical examiner; and

j. the home address or telephone number of any member of the department.

D. Arrest Information

1. Following arrest, issuance of an arrest warrant or filing of an information or indictment, it is permissible to release

   a. the accused's name, age, residence, occupation and family status;

   b. the time and place of arrest, whether pursuit or resistance was encountered, whether weapons were used, charges placed against the suspect and description of contraband seized;

   c. the identity of the arresting officers and the duration of the investigation unless the officers are engaged in undercover operations; and

   d. the amount of bond, scheduled court dates and place of the suspect's detention.

2. Following arrest and formal charging of a suspect, but prior to adjudication, the following types of information should not be released without express permission of the department's chief executive:

   a. Prior criminal conviction record, character or reputation of a defendant

   b. Existence or contents of any confession, admission or statement of a defendant, or his failure or unwillingness to make a statement

   c. Performance or results of any tests, or a defendant's refusal or failure to submit to tests such as a polygraph

   d. Identity, statement or expected testimony of any witness or victim

   e. Any opinion about the guilt or innocence of a defendant or the merits of the case

   f. Any opinion or knowledge of the potential for a plea bargain or other pretrial action

E. Special Considerations—Criminal Matters

1. Departmental personnel shall extend every reasonable courtesy to news media representatives at crime scenes. This may include closer access of personnel and equipment than available to the general public to the degree that it does not interfere with the police mission or the movement of traffic.

2. The news media shall not be allowed access to any area or scene of an incident or crime where there is a possibility that evidence may be damaged, altered, destroyed or otherwise prejudiced by its existence being published or portrayed. Once evidence has been processed, removed and secured by the department, the media may be allowed to enter by permission of the commanding officer at the scene.

   a. On private property, photography, film or videotape recording requires the permission of the owner or the owner's representative.

   b. Suspects or accused persons in custody shall not be posed or arrangements made for photographs, telecasts or interviews, nor shall departmental personnel pose with suspects or accused persons in custody.

   c. When an individual is charged with a criminal offense and is sought by law enforcement authorities, photographs or mug shots may be released to the media to help locate the individual. No departmental photographs, mug shots, videotape, film or composites of subjects in custody shall otherwise be released to the media unless authorized by the department chief executive or authorized designee.

3. At the scene of major crimes, such as hostage and barricade situations, the officer in charge

shall designate a preliminary press area as early as possible and as close to the scene as safety and operational requirements allow.

4. The fact that a suicide or suspected suicide has occurred may be reported to the media, along with factual information describing how it happened. The name, age, address, sex and occupation of the victim may also be released following notification of next of kin. The fact that a suicide note exists may also be acknowledged without further comment. The content of such notes is personal and confidential and shall not be released except as provided by law.

F. Special Considerations—Noncriminal Matters

1. At the scene of significant accidents, man-made or natural catastrophes, the principles of media cooperation shall be maintained to the degree that they do not interfere with the mission of the police, fire, medical or other emergency relief workers.

2. Media access to and movement within fire lines shall be controlled by the fire officer in charge. In consultation with the fire officer in charge, the ranking police officer at the scene shall establish an observation point from which the media may observe and photograph the incident.

   a. At the discretion of the officer in charge, an inner perimeter may be established for the media from which to record the event.

3. News media representatives should not be prevented from access to any area solely because of the possibility of their injury or death. If this is the only consideration, the media representative should be advised of the danger and allowed to make the decision to enter on his own volition.

4. Sensitive information relating to internal investigation of police officers shall not be released without the express permission of the department chief executive.

5. Daily administrative reports of criminal activity will be made available on a routine basis to media representatives. Statistical reports of criminal activity will also be made available to the media.

6. Media representatives shall be denied access to the contents of investigative or incident reports and records where release of the information would

   a. interfere with law enforcement proceedings, including pending investigations;

   b. deprive a person of the right to a fair trial or an impartial adjudication, or give one party to a controversy an undue advantage by exclusive access to such information;

   c. constitute an unwarranted invasion of the personal privacy rights of another person;

   d. reveal the identity of an individual who has furnished information to the department under confidential circumstances;

   e. disclose investigative techniques and procedures, thereby impairing future effectiveness of the department; or

   f. endanger the life or physical safety of any person.

This project was supported by Grant No. *87-SN-CX-K077* awarded by the Bureau of Justice Assistance, Office of Justice Programs, U.S. Department of Justice. The Assistant Attorney General, Office of Justice Programs, coordinates the activities of the following program offices and bureaus: the Bureau of Justice Assistance, the Bureau of Justice Statistics, National Institute of Justice, Office of Juvenile Justice and Delinquency Prevention, and the Office of Victims of Crime. Points of view or opinions in this document are those of the author and do not represent the official position or policies of the United States Department of Justice.

Every effort has been made by the IACP National Law Enforcement Policy Center staff and advisory board to ensure that this model policy incorporates the most current information and contemporary professional judgement on this issue. However, law enforcement administrators should be cautioned that no "model" policy can meet all the needs of any given law enforcement agency. Each law enforcement agency operates in a unique environment of federal court rulings, state laws, local ordinances, regulations, judicial and administrative decisions and collective bargaining agreements that must be considered. In addition, the formulation of specific agency policies must take into account local political and community perspectives and customs, prerogatives and demands; often divergent law enforcement strategies and philosophies, and the impact of varied agency resource capabilities among other factors.

# IACP National Law Enforcement

# Policy Center
# Police-Media Relations
### Concepts and Issues Paper
### February 1992

## I. INTRODUCTION
### A. Purpose of the Document
This paper is designed to accompany the model policy on police-media relations developed by the IACP National Law Enforcement Policy Center. This paper provides essential background information and supporting documentation to provide greater understanding of the developmental philosophy and implementation requirements for the model policy. This material will be of value to law enforcement executives in their efforts to tailor the model to the requirements and circumstances of their community and their law enforcement agency.

### B. Background
To be successful and effective, the relationship between police departments and the news media must be both cooperative and communicative. The public obtains most of its information about police activities from the news media—television, radio and newspapers. The public has a right to know about certain police actions and police departments should want them to have this information. Unfortunately, many police officers and administrators harbor a basic mistrust of the media and tend to avoid interaction with media representatives whenever possible. These fears are often based on some prior unpleasant experience. Media personnel are routinely in a rush to meet deadlines and are typically in competition with other media sources and representatives to "corner" a story or be the first source for its release. These and other pressures can lead to incomplete or inaccurate reporting or, in a worst case situation, to a glamorized or embellished story based on fragments of information or unreliable sources. Police officers who have been caught up in these situations or who feel they have been misrepresented in the press may have an understandable concern about dealing with the media.

Yet, in spite of some recognized problems with "fair" reporting practices, the media is generally a highly professional industry that attempts to do its best under often immense logistical and operational constraints. Moreover, police officers who come to view the media in an adversarial relationship do more to perpetuate the perceived problem of fair reporting by unnecessarily guarding or withholding information or coloring the facts to meet their own interests. The issue of honesty and fairness works both ways between the media and its sources of information. The media is under an obligation to serve the public and it will provide the news or, if necessary, informed speculation with or without the assistance of those who are in a position to know. Therefore, if police administrators and personnel deal with the media in a fair and professional manner they are more likely to get their message across to the public rather than one that is based on someone else's perceptions or viewpoints. To this end, there are techniques and procedures that can assist law enforcement officers in bolstering and maintaining a mutually productive relationship with the media in their community.

### C. Legal and Historical Perspective
During the 1960s, the U.S. Supreme Court reversed several lower court decisions based, in part, on the influence news coverage had on jurors. The news source in a number of these cases was a police person. One of the most celebrated of these cases was *Sheppard* v. *Maxwell*. Sheppard was convicted in 1954 of bludgeoning his wife to death in the bedroom of their home. This case, reversed by the Supreme Court in 1966, was a landmark decision because it made specific recommendations for avoiding the effects of prejudicial publicity, one of which was to control the release of information by police officers. This and other Supreme Court cases prompted a 1967 presidential commission, studying the nation's

administration of the justice system, to suggest that police departments throughout the country identify the types of information that should not be disclosed to the press before or during a trial.

Also during the 1960s, police officers were often portrayed in the media as overly aggressive as they confronted race riots and demonstrations over civil rights issues and the Vietnam War. Particularly harsh was the television coverage of the Chicago police as they confronted large numbers of demonstrators during the National Democratic Convention in 1968. Certain postconvention studies of this portrayal indicated an imbalance in the news reports. That is, they adequately covered the police response but inadequately covered what provoked these actions. A special subcommittee report of the U.S. House of Representatives in 1969 indicated that the television networks provided little information on the "nature and motives of the demonstrators."

The combination of Supreme Court decisions that admonished police for furnishing what the Court termed inappropriate information to the news media, and the harsh media portrayal of police during the riots and demonstrations, had a chilling effect on the willingness of police to cooperate with the media. This understandable caution, etched in the 1960s, still affects many police departments today.

The Supreme Court decisions also prompted a study by the American Bar Association's Legal Advisory Committee on Fair Trial and Free Press. As a result of the study, a manual was published in 1969 entitled "The Rights of Fair Trial and Free Press." This publication served as the initial guide for police departments developing standards for their relationship with the news media, and much of today's police/media policy is derived from the standards it suggested.

In 1973, the National Advisory Commission on Criminal Justice Standards and Goals urged police agencies to develop policy and guidelines for working with the media and encouraged them to maintain a cooperative and communicative relationship. This report stressed the importance of the police chief in setting a professional and positive tone for police/press relations and in communicating that tone to all members of the department. Also mentioned in the report was the need to create an office of public information to handle the relationship on a daily basis.

The efforts of police departments over the years to develop policy and maintain a professional relationship with the media has been somewhat erratic but progress is being made.

## II. DEVELOPING MEDIA POLICIES
### A. The Police-Media Relationship

The police-media relationship is governed primarily by two separate guarantees of the U.S. Constitution. The First Amendment states that "Congress shall make no law . . . abridging the freedom of speech or freedom of the press," and the Sixth Amendment declares, "In all criminal prosecutions, the accused shall enjoy the right to a speedy and public trial, by an impartial jury of the state and district wherein the crime shall have been committed . . ."

These are two very diverse, and at first glance, contradictory statements. The former guarantees freedom of the press while the latter guarantees the rights of the individual to a fair and unbiased trial. Both must be served, and striking a balance between the two can be both difficult and sensitive.

Police departments that are successful in maintaining this balance have well-defined policy and guidelines which serve in the best interests of the department, the accused and the news media.

Police departments should have written policy and guidelines for an effective relationship with the news media. In order to be mutually beneficial, this policy must be specific, stressing the importance of informing the public by providing appropriate information to the news media and thus maintaining public support.

The following factors are essential to any department's police-media policy and guidelines:

• The policy must set a positive tone for the police-media relationship by stressing the importance of establishing and maintaining a professional, working relationship.

• The policy should identify the department's public information function; that is, who is in charge, who speaks for the department and when is it appropriate to speak.

• The types of information that should be released to the news media and information that should not be released concerning criminal matters should be identified.

• The department's position on various matters such as crime scenes, crisis situations, press credentials and photographs should be specified.

## B. The Public Information Officer

Unless the department is so small that the chief handles all media relations, he should designate a person to handle the routine matters associated with the public information function. In smaller departments that person may also have other responsibilities, whereas larger departments will normally have a full-time public information officer (PIO) and possibly additional staff personnel. Whatever the arrangement, the chief should remain the principal spokesperson for the department on issues and concerns that warrant his attention. In order to facilitate an equitable and cooperative relationship with the news media (if available) the PIO should coordinate all public information activities and serve as a liaison between the department and the media.

The PIO should be authorized to speak for the chief and the department and is responsible for

- gathering information for the news media;
- releasing information to the news media;
- arranging media interviews and news conferences;
- responding to major incidents to support department and assist news media;
- assisting departmental personnel in interpreting media policy and guidelines and handling any media concerns or problems; and
- handling other assignments as determined by the chief of police.

The PIO must also be professionally familiar with legitimate news organizations, their reporters and their deadlines, and must be available on a 24-hour basis. Police officers should understand that their department has an obligation to report on its activities to the public it serves. In doing so, it maintains the public's trust, cooperation and support. The most effective means to meet this obligation is to develop and maintain a satisfactory relationship with the news media by providing them with timely and appropriate information and access to the department's activities.

On occasion, however, the news media should be denied certain types of information on criminal matters in the interest of protecting the rights of both the accused and the prosecution from possible prejudicial publicity.

## C. Release of Information

Although the chief, his designee or the PIO are the principal spokespersons, all police officers in the department should be authorized, whenever feasible or warranted, to furnish information to the media upon request.

For the purpose of coordination, these requests should be processed through the PIO. However, in the absence of a supervisor or PIO, officers directly involved at the scene of a major crime, incident or disaster should provide basic factual information to the press until a supervisor or PIO arrives on the scene. If an officer is prohibited from speaking to the media where he is the only representative from the department, it could be demeaning, frustrating and awkward for him. If the officer is trained and instructed to provide brief and basic facts until a supervisor or PIO arrives and, if it does not interfere with his law enforcement responsibilities, the media most likely will credit the department and the officer for being responsive. If the officer does not speak to the media, the reporter will probably seek someone else to speak with and their comments might not be based on fact or in the best interests of the department. Restrictions on lower-ranking officers from making appropriate remarks to the media in the course of their duties may also inadvertently encourage inappropriate remarks from anonymous officers. However, news media inquiries concerning administrative and policy matters of the department should be responded to by the PIO, the chief or his designee. All departmental personnel who provide information to the news media should be guided by the law, departmental policy and guidelines as well as discretion and common sense.

## D. News Release Guidelines in Criminal Cases

The following information *should be released* to the news media in criminal matters:

- The arrested person's name, age, sex, residence, employment, marital status and any similar biographical information.
- The substance or text of the charge, complaint, indictment or information.
- The amount of bail.
- The identity of the investigating and arresting agency and the length of the investigation.
- The circumstances immediately surrounding the arrest, including the time and place of arrest, resistance, pursuit, possession and use of weapons, and a description of items seized at the time of the arrest.
- The type of force used against the victim and extent of injuries to the victim or the assailant.
- When rape or sex offenses are involved, the age and sex of a victim (no name) and general location of crime (no address).

• Information that may assist in an investigation, such as lookouts for persons or vehicles.

The following information *should not be released* to the news media in criminal matters:

• Observations about a defendant's prior criminal record, character or reputation.

• Statements, admissions, confessions or alibis attributable to a defendant, or the refusal or failure of the accused to make a statement.

• The results of any examinations or tests, or the refusal or failure of the accused to submit to an examination or test.

• Statements concerning the identity, anticipated testimony or credibility of prospective witnesses.

• Any opinions regarding the guilt or innocence of the accused, or the possibility of a plea of guilty or to a lesser charge.

• Any opinions regarding the merits of the case or quality of the evidence.

• Information received from other law enforcement agencies without their prior concurrence to release that information.

• Names and addresses of victims of rape or sexual assault, child abuse, juvenile defendants, witnesses and informants.

• Personnel records of members of the department. In cases of death, officers must first notify the next of kin and obtain an identification of a deceased or seriously injured victim of a criminal act or accident prior to releasing the victim's name and address to the news media. However, if the next of kin has not been located after a reasonable length of time, this information may be released.

## III.  MANAGING NEWS MEDIA ACCESS
### A.  Major Crimes, Incidents or Disasters

In the event of a major crime, incident or disaster, police lines are established to preserve evidence as well as to control crowds and preserve public safety. Although media persons cannot arbitrarily cross these lines, legitimate news media representatives may be permitted in the area of a crime scene, incident or disaster by or with the consent of the officer in charge or the PIO. Special areas for the media can also be arranged at major crime scenes and at hostage and barricade situations. Normally either a PIO or another officer should be with the media on these occasions.

Police personnel have no authority to invite the news media onto private premises. Only the owner, legal occupant or their agent may grant permission.

In the interest of their health and safety, police can prohibit media persons from entering hazardous areas. However, there are occasions when members of the media will enter dangerous areas at their own risk such as during riots, earthquakes or hurricanes. On such occasions, the department is not responsible for the safety of media persons and their activities must not interfere with the police function or jeopardize the life of a police officer or others.

### B.  Press Identification

The issuance of press identification passes to members of the news media to cover police activities is a matter of departmental choice. Small police jurisdictions do not always need to identify their news media persons, while other jurisdictions, for a variety of reasons, simply decline to do so. Nevertheless, the issuance of press passes has mutual benefits. It facilitates news media access to the department's activities while also making the news person more accountable, since his pass can be revoked for violations of rules or regulations.

### C.  Press Photography

Police officers should not prevent the news media from taking photographs or videotapes if they have a lawful right to be in a given location. Officers should also not encourage or discourage the media from photographing persons in the custody of departmental personnel. Photographs of a defendant may be released provided the photograph will not jeopardize an investigation or violate the defendant's rights. In addition, the department may provide photographs and other information to the media when enlisting support in apprehending fugitives.

A newsperson's major responsibility is to gather information and pictures at newsworthy events—an opportunity that is often short-lived. Therefore, members of the department must not unnecessarily obstruct news representatives from carrying out their assignments as long as they are acting in a lawful capacity.

Similarly, news from the department should be made available to all media organizations, and no media representative should receive preferential treatment. The one exception to this rule is an "exclusive" news story in which a reporter has information that was not released by the department and that other news agencies do not have. The department, in most situations, should not provide that information to other news organizations.

In instances where more than one public service agency (such as police, fire or coroner's office) is involved, the agency having primary jurisdiction should be responsible for releasing, or coordinating the release of, information. Department spokespersons should take into consideration the deadlines of the respective news representatives so that reporters may conveniently and adequately cover the story in their news reports.

When there is information to be released to the news media and time permits, the department should prepare a news release and submit it to all news organizations at the same time without favoritism. This can be accomplished by reading the news release over the telephone or, if available, using a fax machine. In addition, news organizations can receive the release through the wire services. Most media organizations subscribe to a wire service such as United Press International or the Associated Press.

These wire services distribute news releases twice a day—in the morning and late in the afternoon. Once the department's information has been provided to the wire services, telephone calls from the media should be expected.

The news conference is another method of providing information to the news media. The chief or PIO typically invites the media or agrees to meet with news media representatives at a given location and time in order to provide newsworthy information or photo opportunities. If a major story is breaking, the news conference may be the most appropriate method of handling media inquiries. When the department is involved in a critical incident such as a major crime, hostage or barricade situation or natural disaster, it may be best to hold a news conference at the scene.

A brief statement followed by a question and answer period is the standard format for a news conference. Additionally, it should be understood that only the topic for which the news conference was called will be discussed.

#### D. Talking with the Media
In the best interest of the department, officers should use the following fundamentals and techniques when talking with the media:

- Be prepared. It is impossible to be overly prepared. Know the subject, know the interviewer, know the audience and know the points that are to be made.
- Be pleasant and professional. The audience will be impressed or unimpressed based largely on how a spokesperson appears and sounds. Maintain a positive demeanor and use candid and knowledgeable responses.
- Be enthusiastic. Do not exaggerate enthusiasm but sell the mission and the efforts of the department.

- Be in charge. This is the most important consideration during a media appearance. As much as possible, control the interview and if it goes astray, guide it back on course.
- Concentrate on the question and wait until it is finished before responding. If the question is unclear, ask that it be repeated or rephrased.
- Use bridging. Move the conversation from where someone else wants it to be to where *you* want it to be.
- Turn negatives into positives. Turn the inevitable negative statement by moving into a positive point you would like to make.
- Use concise responses. Stick with the facts and state them succinctly. The longer the response, the more likely it will be edited in a news situation—also the more information that is provided can prompt questions better left unasked. Occasionally, however, longer responses may be appropriate, such as when providing illustrations or examples for clarification and enhancing audience interest.
- Remember the audience. The viewing and listening audience generally functions at a 10th grade level of comprehension, so big words and police jargon should be avoided.
- Never bluff or lie—such actions can destroy credibility.
- Do not be afraid to say "I don't know." The spokesperson is under no obligation to know everything there is to know. Be honest, say "I don't know, but I'll try to find out."
- Do not get emotional or angry. A lost temper is news all by itself.

#### E. Public Service Time
In addition to providing information to the media regarding newsworthy events, law enforcement agencies should also consider the opportunity to present information to the public via public service announcements (PSAs). These announcements generally pertain to public safety in such areas as drugs, alcohol and driving, fireworks, and neighborhood and home protection. Public service time for PSAs is that portion of the program schedule donated by radio and television to nonprofit organizations for the presentation of information considered to be of public interest. This donated air time is a requirement of the Federal Communication Commission and must be provided by a station before it can be granted a broadcast license. However, individual stations have the freedom to decide how much of their total

schedule will be devoted to public service programs, what material will be broadcast during this time and when these programs will be scheduled. To solicit public service time, a station's director of public affairs or community services is generally a police department's best contact.

### F. Freedom of Information

Most police departments are governed by state laws protecting individual rights to information and privacy that are patterned after the federal Freedom of Information Act (FOIA) and privacy acts. The FOIA is the chief federal law on openness in government and is frequently brought into play by investigative reporters researching a news story. In general, it provides any U.S. citizen or legal alien with the right to request any record maintained by and under the control of a police agency. The FOIA also provides the agency with the option to withhold specific types of information when responding to such requests.

FOIA exemptions for most police departments preclude the release of information from investigatory records that would

- interfere with law enforcement proceedings, including pending investigations;
- deprive a person of the right to a fair trial or an impartial adjudication, or give one party to a controversy an undue advantage by exclusive access to such information;
- constitute an unwarranted invasion of the personal privacy of another person;
- reveal the identity of an individual who has furnished information to the department under confidential circumstances;
- disclose investigate techniques and procedures, thereby impairing future effectiveness; or
- endanger the life or physical safety of department personnel.

The following rules and regulations apply to most police departments under the FOIA:

- Law enforcement agencies must give individuals access to their records, unless the department has exempted the entire system of records from the access provisions.

- The department will normally withhold records from an exempt system of records if release would impair the department's ability to perform its authorized functions.
- With certain exceptions, the act prohibits a department from disclosing information about an individual to anyone outside the department without prior consent of the subject of the record.

### G. Resolving Police-Media Difficulties

The success of the department's relationship with the news media will depend on its ability to handle media requests and maintain a communicative relationship.

No matter how good the relationship, problems will occur, but it is generally possible and advisable to talk it over and attempt to get the problems resolved. For instance, a department that has been portrayed unfairly or inaccurately by a news organization should bring such treatment to the organization's attention. The complaint probably will not result in a retraction; however, if the problem is professionally debated and the department has a good media relationship, the chances of the same problem recurring are held to a minimum.

The department should work toward resolving media problems when they occur by first calling or writing the reporter in question and asking for a meeting. If a meeting does not resolve the problem, then a meeting with the organization's manager and the involved reporter should be requested. If the problem involves interference by members of the press in a public safety matter, the news manager should be contacted immediately.

Although problems will arise under the best of circumstances, they most likely will be in direct proportion to the type of relationship the department has with the press. A large part of that relationship depends upon the way in which law enforcement personnel present themselves and deal with media representatives in their daily encounters. Respect and courtesy for media personnel and maintenance of a professional demeanor are essential ingredients to a good relationship. They also leave media personnel with the very important image of a law enforcement agency that subscribes to a high standard of performance and service.

*This project was supported by Grant No. 87-SN-CX-K077 awarded by the Bureau of Justice Assistance, Office of Justice Programs, U.S. Department of Justice. The assistant attorney general, Office of Justice Programs, coordinates the activities of the following program offices and bureaus: the Bureau of Justice Assistance, the Bureau of Justice Statistics, National Institute of Justice, Office of Juvenile Justice and Delinquency Prevention and the Office of Victims of Crime. Points of view or opinions in this document are those of the author and do not represent the official position or policies of the U.S. Department of Justice.*

*Every effort has been made by the IACP National Law Enforcement Policy Center staff and advisory board to ensure that this model policy incorporates the most current information and contemporary professional judgment on this issue. However, law enforcement administrators should be cautioned that no "model" policy can meet all the needs of any given law enforcement agency. Each law enforcement agency operates in a unique environment of federal court rulings, state laws, local ordinances, regulations, judicial and administrative decisions and collective bargaining agreements that must be considered. In addition, the formulation of specific agency policies must take into account local political and community perspectives and customs, prerogatives and demands; often divergent law enforcement strategies and philosophies; and the impact of various agency's resource capabilities, among other factors.*

A publication of the IACP National Law Enforcement Policy Center
1110 N. Glebe Rd., Suite 200, Arlington, VA 22201
This document is the result of work performed by the IACP National Law Enforcement Policy Center. The views and opinions expressed in this document are sanctioned by the center's advisory board and do not necessarily represent the official position or policies of the International Association of Chiefs of Police.

# Cultural Diversity Value Statement

As professional police officers, we commit to:

- The fair and impartial treatment of all individuals, placing the highest emphasis on respect for fundamental human rights.
- Nurturing and protecting the individual dignity and worth of all persons with whom we come into contact.
- Understanding the differences of all peoples.
- Zero tolerance for racially, sexual, gender or religious biased behavior.
- Maintaining a welcoming environment of inclusion through which communication is open to all peoples whose problems become our priorities to resolve.

SOURCE: Aurora (Illinois) Police Department. Reprinted by permission.

# Glossary

Number in parentheses indicates the chapter in which the term is introduced.

**AARP**   American Association of Retired Persons. (9)

**acculturation**   A society takes in or assimilates another culture. Also called *assimilation*. (7)

**AD**   Alzheimer's disease. (9)

**ADA**   Refers to the Americans with Disabilities Act. (8)

**allocution**   Speaking before a judge or a court. (12)

**Alzheimer's disease**   A progressive, irreversible brain disease affecting four million elderly Americans. The classic symptom is loss of memory. (9)

**American Dream**   Anyone can become rich and powerful if they work hard enough. (7)

**Ameslam**   Stands for American Sign Language, the preferred communication mode for the majority of deaf individuals. (8)

**assimilation**   A society takes in or assimilates another culture. Also called *acculturation*. (7)

**attention deficit hyperactivity disorder**   A common disruptive behavior disorder of children characterized by heightened motor activity (fidgeting and squirming), short attention span, distractibility, impulsiveness and lack of self-control. (10)

**bias**   A prejudice that inhibits objectivity. Bias can evolve into hate. (6)

**bias crime**   Any act or attempted act to cause physical injury, emotional suffering or property damage through intimidation, harassment, racial or ethnic slurs and bigoted epithets, vandalism, force or the threat of force. Motivated all or in part by hostility to the victim's real or perceived race, ethnicity, religion or sexual orientation. Also called *hate crime*. (7)

**Big D's of juvenile justice**   Refers to diversion, decriminalization, deinstitutionalization and due process. (10)

**body language**   Messages conveyed by how a person looks, moves and gestures. (6)

**broken window phenomenon**   Suggests that if it appears no one cares about the community as indicated by broken windows not being repaired, disorder and crime will thrive. (2)

**CAT**   Combat Auto Theft, a program that gives the police the authority to stop any car marked with a special decal between 1 A.M. and 5 A.M. (17)

**catastrophic reactions**   Occur when a situation overloads an individual's mental ability to act rationally and he or she reverts to impulsive behavior. Associated with Alzheimer's disease. (9)

**cognitive restructuring**   A coping mechanism in which victims reinterpret their experience to ameliorate the adverse effects of the incident. (12)

**communication**   The transfer of information and understanding from one person to another. (6)

**communication process**   Involves a sender, a message, a channel, a receiver and sometimes feedback. (6)

**community**   Refers to the specific geographic area served by a police department or law enforcement agency and the individuals, organizations and agencies within that area. (2)

**community policing**   A philosophy or orientation that emphasizes working with citizens to solve crime-related problems and prevent crime. (1)

**community relations**   Efforts to interact and communicate with the community—team policing, community resource officers, school liaison officers. See *public relations*. (1)

**community wellness** Emphasizes a proactive police-community partnership to prevent crime. (1)

**CPTED** Crime prevention through environmental design—-altering the physical environment to enhance safety. (14)

**crack children** Children who were exposed to cocaine while in the womb. (10)

**creativity** A process of breaking old connections and making useful new connections. Often synonymous with innovation. (4)

**crime-specific planning** Uses the principles of problem-solving policing to focus on identified crime problems. (4)

**crisis behavior** Results when a person has a temporary breakdown in coping skills. (8)

**cross-sectional analysis** A research method whereby data is analyzed by area rather than by individuals responding. (14)

**culpability** Any action of the victim that in some measure may contribute to the victimization. (12)

**cultural conflict** A theory that suggests that diverse cultures sharing the same territory will compete with and attempt to exploit one another. (7)

**cultural pluralism** A theory that suggests there are many melting pots. Some groups fuse into one pot, other groups into another. (7)

**cultural window** A person's world-view through which he or she interprets events. (7)

**culturally literate** Possessing the basic information needed to thrive in one's society. (7)

**culture** A collection of artifacts, tools, ways of living and a language common to a fairly large group of people, all passed on to the next generation with few changes. (7)

**DARE** Drug Abuse Resistance Education program aimed at elementary age school children, seeking to teach them to "say no to drugs." (16)

**deaf** Persons having hearing loss to such a degree they cannot understand spoken words. (8)

**decision** A judgment or conclusion. (4)

**decriminalization** Refers to the efforts to make status offenses noncriminal actions. Has also been used in attempts to legalize marijuana. (10)

**deinstitutionalization** Refers to the release of thousands of mentally ill individuals into society to be cared for by family or a special network of support services. (8) Also refers to efforts to release incarcerated youth through parole and community programs. (10)

**delusional (paranoid) disorder** Illness characterized by nonbizarre delusions focused on a single theme or a series of connected themes. Common themes include persecution, jealousy and grandiosity. (8)

**demographics** The characteristics of a human population or community. (2)

**directed imbalance** Those imbalances within an organization that are created in anticipation of a proposed change in orientation. (15)

**disability** A physical or mental impairment that substantially limits one or more of an individual's major life activities. (8)

**discretion** Freedom to make choices among possible courses of action or inaction—to arrest or not arrest, for example. (3)

**discrimination** Showing a preference or prejudice in treating individuals or groups. Discrimination is a behavior based on an attitude or prejudice. (6)

**diversion** Turning a youth away from the criminal justice system, rerouting him or her to another agency or program. (2) Finding alternatives to placing juveniles into detention facilities. (10)

**due process** The rights guaranteed by the Fifth Amendment: notice of a hearing, full information regarding the charges made, the opportunity to present evidence in self-defense before an impartial judge or jury and to be presumed innocent until proven guilty by legally obtained evidence. (10)

**EBD**   Emotionally/behaviorally disturbed. (10)

**effectiveness**   Producing the desired result or goal. Doing the right things. (4)

**efficiency**   Minimizing waste, expense or unnecessary effort. Results in a high ratio of output to input. Doing things right. (4)

**elder abuse**   Includes physical and emotional abuse, financial exploitation and general neglect. (9)

**empathy**   Truly understanding another person. (6)

**empirical study**   Research based on observation or practical experience. (14)

**ephebiphobia**   A fear and loathing of adolescents. (10)

**epilepsy**   A disease of the central nervous system which results in seizures. (8)

**ethnocentrism**   The opinion that one's own way of life is better than all others. (7)

**experimental imbalance**   An atmosphere of trial and error or risk taking. (15)

**extensional world**   The world that comes to us through experience. (6)

**fetal alcohol syndrome (FAS)**   Children who suffer from the effects of their mother consuming alcohol while pregnant. Effects include impulsivity, poor communication skills and inability to predict consequences or to use appropriate judgment in daily life. Small children may be very active and easily distracted. Adolescents may be frustrated and depressed. (10)

**formal power structure**   Includes those with wealth and political influence: federal, state and local agencies and governments, commissions, regulatory agencies and power groups. (2)

**four-minute barrier**   The point in an initial meeting at which most people have formed a positive or negative opinion about someone. (6)

**frankpledge system**   The Norman system requiring all freemen to swear loyalty to the king's law and to take responsibility for maintaining the local peace. (1)

**gang**   A somewhat organized group of some duration with a special interest in violence for status-providing purposes. See also *street gang* and *youth gang*. (11)

**ghetto**   An area of a city usually inhabited by individuals of the same race or ethnic background who live in poverty and social disorganization. (2)

**ghetto syndrome**   A vicious circle of failure: poverty, poor education, joblessness, low motivation to work, welfare and poverty. (7)

**graffiti**   Writing on buildings and walls. Used by gangs to mark their turf. (11)

**granny bashing**   Physically abusing the elderly. (9)

**granny dumping**   Abandoning the elderly. (9)

**graying of America**   A metaphor reflecting the fact that our population is aging. (9)

**Guardian Angels**   Private citizen patrols who seek to deter crime and to provide a positive role model for young children. (17)

**hate crime**   Any act or attempted act to cause physical injury, emotional suffering or property damage through intimidation, harassment, racial or ethnic slurs and bigoted epithets, vandalism, force or the threat of force. Motivated all or in part by hostility to the victim's real or perceived race, ethnicity, religion or sexual orientation. Also called *bias crime*. (7)

**hearing impaired**   Refers to individuals who have some residual hearing, that is, sounds may be audible, but not clear. Words are not just softer, they are garbled. Also called *hard of hearing*. (8)

**heterogeneous**   Involving things (including people) that are unlike, dissimilar, different. The opposite of homogeneous. (2)

**homogeneous**   Involving things (including people) that are basically similar, alike. The opposite of heterogeneous. (2)

**hue and cry**   The ancient practice of citizens calling out if they saw a wrongdoing, summoning all citizens within earshot to join in pursuing and capturing the wrong-doer. (1)

**human relations**   Efforts to relate to and understand other individuals or groups of individuals. (1)

**hyphenated American**   Tendency to include ethnic background in a person's nationality—for example, Italian-American, Polish-American—illustrating America's tendency to pluralism or a multicultural approach. (7)

*in loco parentis*   Acting "in place of parents"; gives the schools the authority to act as a parent might in situations requiring discipline or need. (16)

**incident**   An event calling for some sort of police assistance. (1)

**informal power structure**   Includes religious groups, wealthy subgroups, ethnic groups, political groups and public interest groups. (2)

**innovation**   A new way of doing something, often synonymous with creativity. (4)

**jargon**   The technical language of a profession. (6)

**justice model**   Views lawbreakers as responsible for their own actions. Sometimes called the punishment model. In comparison to the medical or welfare model. (2) (10)

**killer phrases**   Judgmental, critical statements that serve as put-downs. They stifle creativity. (4)

**kinesics**   The study of body movement. (6)

**learning disability**   One or more significant deficits in the essential learning processes. (10)

**magnet address**   An address that is easy for people to give and consequently is often mistakenly associated with reported crimes. (4)

**magnet phenomenon**   Occurs when a phone number or address is associated with a crime simply because it was a convenient number or address to use. (4)

**magnet telephone**   One that is available when no other telephones are and consequently it is often mistakenly associated with reported crimes. (4)

**medical model**   Sees those who break the law as victims of society, not responsible for their own actions. Sometimes called the welfare model. In comparison to the justice or punishment model. (2)

**mental health**   The ability to integrate one's self with one's environment. (8)

**mental illness**   A severe disturbance in thinking, feeling and relating that results in substantially diminished capacity to cope with life's ordinary demands. (8)

**mental locks**   Ways of thinking that prevent creativity. (4)

**mental retardation**   Normal intellectual development fails to occur. Significant subaverage general intellectual functioning resulting in, or associated with, defects or impairments in adaptive behavior, such as personal independence and social responsibility, with onset by age 18. (8)

**mission statement**   A written declaration of purpose. (5)

**mood disorders**   Severe depression, mania or cycles of depression and mania. (8)

**multi-culturalism trap**   Occurs when people get so involved with their own cultural concerns they ignore the rest of the society in which they live. (7)

**negative contacts**   Unpleasant interactions between the police and the public. They may or may not deal with criminal activity. (3)

**neighborhood-oriented policing (NOP)**   A philosophy of policing stressing a responsive style of policing dependent on quality day-to-day interactions between the police and the public. (1)

**networking**   Building and keeping professional relationships for mutual interest and mutual help. (6)

**networks**   The complex pathways of human interaction that guide and direct an individual's perception, motivation and behavior. (6)

**NIMBY syndrome**    "Not in *my* backyard." It is fine to have a half-way house—across town, not in my backyard. (2)

**nonverbal communication**    Includes everything other than the actual words in a message: tone, pitch and pacing. (6)

**"Norman Rockwell" family**    A working father, a housewife mother and two children of school age—only 6 percent of U.S. households today. (10)

**one-pot jurisdictional approach**    Treating children who are abused or neglected, those who are status offenders and those who are truly criminal all the same. (10)

**Pager Information Network (PIN)**    A system to simultaneously notify all the media. (13)

**PAL**    Police Athletic League, developed to provide opportunities for youth to interact with police officers in gyms or ballparks instead of in juvenile detention hall. (16)

**panel analysis**    A research method where data is analyzed by individuals responding rather than by area. (14)

**paradigm**    A model or a way of viewing a specific aspect of life such as politics, medicine, education and the criminal justice system. (1)

**paradigm shift**    A new way of thinking about a specific subject. (1)

**paradox**    A seemingly contradictory statement that may, nonetheless, be true; for example, the less one has, the less one has to lose. (3)

**parens patriae**    Refers to the government's responsibility to take care of minors and others who cannot legally take care of themselves. (10)

**participatory leadership**    A management style in which each individual has a voice in decisions, but top management still has the ultimate decision-making authority. (5)

**patronage system**    Politicians rewarded those who voted for them with jobs or special privileges. Also called the *spoils system.* (1)

**perception**    What is seen; the process of giving meaning or organization to experience. (6)

**personality disorders**    Inflexible and maladaptive personality traits and significant impairment in social and occupational functioning. (8)

**phenomenological point of view**    Stresses the fact that reality is different for each individual. (6)

**plea bargaining**    A practice in which prosecutors will charge a less serious crime in exchange for a guilty plea, thus eliminating the time and expense of a trial. (2)

**police-community relations (PCR)**    The relationship existing between the police and the citizens organizations and agencies they serve and protect. (1)

**police-school liaison program**    Places an officer, uniformed or not, into a school to work with school authorities, parents and students, to prevent crime and antisocial behavior and to improve police-youth relationships. (16)

**post traumatic stress disorder (PTSD)**    A persistent reexperiencing of a traumatic event through intrusive memories, dreams and a variety of anxiety-related symptoms. (12)

**poverty syndrome**    Includes inadequate housing, inadequate education, inadequate jobs and a resentment of those who control the social system. (7)

**preference**    Selecting someone or something over another. (6)

**prejudice**    A negative judgment not based on fact; an irrational, preconceived negative opinion. An attitude that may result in discriminatory behavior. (6)

**press information officers (PIOs)**    Officers assigned to disseminate all information to the press, thereby providing accurate information in a consistent manner while controlling leaks of confidential or inaccurate information. (13)

**primacy effect**    The tendency to form impressions of people quickly. (6)

**primary victim**    A person actually harmed by an incident. (12)

**privatization**    Using private security officers or agencies to provide services typically considered to be law enforcement functions. (2)

**proactive**   Anticipating problems and seeking solutions to those problems. The opposite of *reactive*. (1)

**problem**   A deviation from what is desired; a difficulty. (4)

**problem-oriented policing (POP)**   Focuses on grouping incidents to identify problems and then determine possible underlying causes. (1) A department-wide strategy aimed at solving persistent community problems. (4)

**professional model**   Emphasized crime control by preventive automobile patrol coupled with rapid response to calls. The predominant policing model of the 1970s and 1980s. (1)

**Progressive Era**   Also called the *Reform Era*. Emphasized preventive automobile patrol and rapid response to calls for service. (1)

**PSAs**   Public service announcements. (14)

**psychotic symptoms**   Demonstrate a significant loss of contact with reality and include illogical thought, incoherent speech, disorientation, extreme mood fluctuation, social withdrawal, hallucinations and delusions and neglect of family and occupational obligations. (8)

**public relations**   Efforts geared at raising the image of the police and the police organization. (1)

**qualitative evaluations**   Such evaluations are more descriptive and less statistical. The opposite of quantitative evaluation. (14)

**reactive**   Responding after the fact, for example, responding to calls for service. The opposite of *proactive*. (1)

**recidivism**   A tendency to relapse into a former pattern of behavior, especially criminal habits. (2)

**reciprocity**   A cooperative interchange. Each party in the effort has something to offer and also something to gain from the relationship. (14)

**representing**   A means to show allegiance or opposition through clothing. Uses an imaginary line drawn vertically through the body. (11)

**restorative justice**   Seeks to use a balanced approach involving offenders, victims, local communities and government to alleviate crime and violence and obtain peaceful communities. (2) (12)

**schizophrenia**   A deterioration in one's personality to the point where feelings, thoughts and behavior are not coherent. (8)

**second injury**   Occurs to victims when they are treated badly by professionals who should be helping them, including police officers and the entire criminal justice system. (12)

**secondary victim**   A person indirectly affected by a trauma. (12)

**seizure**   A sudden, uncontrolled event or episode of excessive electrical activity in the brain. It may alter behavior, consciousness, movement, perception and/or sensation. Does not always involve a stiffening or jerking of the body. (8)

**selective enforcement**   The use of police discretion, deciding to concentrate on specific crimes such as drug dealing and to downplay other crimes such as white-collar crime. (3)

**self-fulfilling prophecy**   Believing self-talk or what others say about you and causing it to come true. (6)

**semantic environment**   The way words are used and the way they are interpreted shape beliefs, prejudices, ideals and aspirations. They constitute the moral and intellectual atmosphere in which a person lives. (6)

**semantics**   The study of meaning. (6)

**sensorium**   That part of the brain that interprets what the eye takes in. (6)

**social contract**   A theory in law which suggests that for everyone to receive justice, each person must give up some individual freedom. (2)

**spoils system**   Politicians rewarded those who voted for them with jobs or special privileges. Also called the *patronage system*. (1)

**station adjustment**   When police release minor offenders, with or without a warning, and without making an official record or taking further action. (10)

**statistically significant**   A predetermined level at which the results would not occur by chance. The most common level is .05 meaning the results would occur by chance no more than five times in one hundred. (14)

**status offenses**   Actions by a juvenile that would not be a crime if committed by an adult, for example, truancy or smoking cigarettes. (10)

**stereotyping**   Assuming all people within a specific group are the same, lacking individuality. (6)

**street gang**   A group of people who form an allegiance based on various social needs and engage in acts injurious to public health and public morals. The preferred term of most local law enforcement agencies. (11)

**street justice**   Occurs when police officers use their discretionary powers to simply talk to youth who are status offenders rather than taking them into custody. (10)

**symbiotic**   A relationship in which those involved depend upon each other for existence. (13)

**symbolic process**   The process by which people can arbitrarily make certain things stand for other things. (6)

**syndrome of crime**   A group of signs, causes and symptoms that occur together to foster specific crimes. (2)

**synergism**   Occurs when individuals channel their energies toward a common purpose and accomplish what none of them alone could accomplish. (17)

**TAB**   Temporarily able-bodied. (8)

**TDD**   Telecommunication device for the deaf. (8)

**"thin blue line"**   The distancing of the police from the public served. (1)

**tithing**   A group of ten families. (1)

**tithing system**   The Anglo-Saxon principle establishing collective responsibility for maintaining law and order. (1)

**turf**   Territory occupied by a gang, often marked by graffiti. (11)

**verbal world**   The world that comes to us through words. (6)

**victim impact statement (VIS)**   A written report describing in detail the full effect of a crime on the victim. May influence the sentence passed by the judge. (12)

**victim service programs**   Provide crisis counseling, shelter and other specialized treatment. (12)

**victim statement of opinion (VSO)**   Victim's opinion of what an offender's sentence should be. (12)

**victimization**   Being harmed or made to suffer. (12)

**victimology**   The study of crime victims; includes the concepts of vulnerability and culpability. (12)

**victim/witness assistance programs**   Seek to provide assistance to victims and witnesses as they move through the judicial process. (12)

**vulnerability**   Suggests that certain groups of people are more susceptible to being victimized because of demographics rather than anything they control as individuals. (12)

**weed and seed**   A community-based, multi-agency approach to fighting drug use, violent crime and gang activity in high-crime neighborhoods. The goal is to "weed out" crime and then "seed" the neighborhoods with a variety of crime and drug prevention programs. (17)

**welfare model**   View that children are basically good and in need of help. (10)

**youth gang**   A self-formed association of peers, bound together by mutual interests, with identifiable leadership, well-developed lines of authority and other organizational features, who act in concert to achieve a specific purpose or purposes which generally include the conduct of illegal activity and control over a particular territory, facility or type of enterprise. (11)

# *Subject Index*

# $\mathcal{P}hoto\ \mathcal{C}redits$